Abstracts

of the Standard Edition of
the Complete Psychological Works of

Sigmund Freud

Edited by
Carrie Lee Rothgeb

Chief, Technical Information Section,
National Clearinghouse for Mental Health Information

with an introduction

On Reading Freud

By Robert R. Holt, Ph.D.

𝒜

JASON ARONSON INC.
Northvale, New Jersey
London

ACKNOWLEDGMENT

Preparation of this paper was supported by a United States Public Health Service Research Career Award, Grant No. 5-K06-MH-12455, from the National Institute of Mental Health.

THE MASTER WORK SERIES

Copyright © 1973 by Jason Aronson Inc.

First softcover edition 1993

Library of Congress Cataloging-in-Publication Data

Library of Congress Catalog Number: 73-17649
ISBN: 1-56821-140-6

Manufactured in the United States of America. Jason Aronson Inc. offers books and cassettes. For information and catalog write to Jason Aronson Inc., 230 Livingston Street, Northvale, New Jersey 07647.

Contents

On Reading Freud

By Robert R. Holt, Ph.D. [1]

RESEARCH CENTER FOR MENTAL HEALTH, NEW YORK UNIVERSITY

On Reading Freud

ERICH FROMM once remarked, in a seminar I attended at the Washington School of Psychiatry approximately 30 years ago, that Freud and Marx had this in common: both were the indispensable starting points for students of their respective subject matters, although practically everything they said was wrong. Fresh from my own psychoanalysis and fired with enthusiasm as I was for Freud's work, I greeted this judgment with incredulity, even scorn; but as the decades have taken me deeper into the repeated study of Freud's writings, I have begun to feel that Fromm's statement was indeed worth remembering. In its dramatic hyperbole, it was itself a very Freudian proposition, as I shall try to demonstrate below, making a point the validity of which could be appreciated if one saw its vehicle as rhetoric rather than as scientific weighing of evidence.

Yes, much of what Freud had to say is more or less false unless read sympathetically—that is, not, with the desire to find him right at all costs, but to learn from him. He is vulnerable to almost any diligent critic who wants to find him in error, and he has never lacked for that kind of antagonist though many of them have been so heavy-handed and obviously biased as to defeat their own destructive purpose. Major figures in other sciences who were Freud's contemporaries are comparably vulnerable, of course. It would be no trick for a pathologist to find many statements in the writings of Rudolf Virchow that are false by contemporary standards, or for a physiologist to do a hatchet job on Claude Bernard; but in other sciences that kind of hostile evaluation of the great historical figures is not common, because it is taken for granted that scientific truth is always partial, relative to and limited by its historical context, and inevitably subject to correction even when not wholly superseded. It would be difficult indeed to find another scientist born in the middle decade of the nineteenth century whose work has not been left behind just as much as Freud's.

And yet Freud is much more than a historical figure. Again Fromm was right: he is surely the indispensable starting point for any serious student of psychoanalysis or psychotherapy and for (at the least) *many* serious students of psychology, psychiatry, and the other behavioral sciences; not as a source of infallible wisdom, for there is none such to be found anywhere; not as an intellectual father to be swallowed whole in a fantasied act of magical identification; and not as a generator of propositions that can be carried directly to the laboratory for rigorous verification or falsification. But read sympathetically and with appropriate caution, Freud still has an enormous amount to teach us about myriad aspects of human beings, their ways of growing up and of failing to thrive, their peculiarities, kinks, and quirks, and above all about their secret lives.

This collection of indexed abstracts, now easily available to a wide audience, will prove particularly valuable as a sample of and guide to the formidable bulk of the *Standard Edition of the Complete Psychological Works of Sigmund Freud*. Any reader who picks it up in the hope of finding a quick and easy summary, a Freud boiled down to one delicious and supernutritious drop, is bound to be disappointed. It is no *Reader's Digest* job, not a "classic condensed for everyman" in the American commercial tradition that reduces any work of substance to a few easily digested clichés. I see it, rather, as much more like the psychologist's indispensable bibliographic aid, the *Psychological Abstracts*: an entry into a large literature through an index by which articles relevant to a topic of interest can be located and then sampled with the aid of expertly condensed summaries. It will not substitute for, but will facilitate, a reading of Freud in his own words.

The remainder of these introductory remarks has the same objective. In a different way, they are intended to orient, forearm, alert, prime, or precondition the reader, so that he or she may enjoy Freud more, be less confused by him, misinterpret him less often, and grasp better what he has to offer, than would be the case by approaching his writings unprepared. For the modern reader of Freud must expect a mixture of delights and difficulties. On the positive side, Freud remains enjoyably and absorbingly readable, even in translation plainly a master of prose. On the negative, however, anyone who is not thoroughly versed in his works and acquainted with certain other literatures, repeatedly encounters baffling difficulties in grasping his meaning in any but a general sense.

Historical Background for a Reading of Freud

To some degree, the problems are those to be expected in reading European works of almost any kind that are from 35 to more than 80 years old. Some terminology is bound to be outdated, some references to scientific or literary works or to then–current events that Freud could assume his contemporary readers were familiar with convey nothing any longer or even give misleading impressions; and an American reader who does not know the continental literary classics is especially handicapped. To a large extent but not completely, the devoted editorship of Strachey anticipates such problems and his footnotes provide helpful explanations.

Other problems arise from Freud's habit of occasionally assuming that the reader knew his previous works, even his unpublished ones. Thus, a great deal that was baffling about Chapter 7 of *The Interpretation of Dreams* (Freud, 1900)—e.g., his reference to the undefined and unexplained -systems—became intelligible only after the belated publication of the "Project" (Freud, 1895). But in any event, many students of Freud have pointed out the necessity of reading him sequentially. His thought cannot be understood if his developing ideas are taken out of their own context. Fortunately, the chronological ordering of the *Standard Edition* and of these abstracts encourages such a reading.

On Reading Freud

THE DEVELOPMENT OF FREUD'S IDEAS

There were four major and overlapping phases of Freud's scientific work:

1. His prepsychoanalytic work, which lasted about 20 years, may be subdivided into an initial 10 years of primarily histological–anatomical research and a partly overlapping 14 years of clinical neurology, with increasing attention to psychopathology, beginning in 1886 when he returned from Paris.

2. The first theory of neurosis dates from the decade of the 1890's, when Freud used hypnosis and Breuer's cathartic method of psychotherapy, gradually developing the psychoanalytic methods of free association, dream interpretation, and the analysis of transference. The first dozen truly psychoanalytic papers appeared during this time, expounding the view that neurosis is a defense against intolerable memories of a traumatic experience—infantile seduction at the hands of a close relative. With the discovery of his own Oedipus complex, however, Freud came to see that such reports by his patients were fantasies, which led him to turn his interest away from traumatic events in external reality and toward subjective psychic reality. A notable but only recently discovered event in the development of Freud's thought occurred in 1895 after the publication of the book he wrote with Breuer. He wrote but did not publish a "Psychology for Neurologists" (or "Project for a Scientific Psychology," hereafter called merely "the Project"), presenting a comprehensive anatomical–physiological model of the nervous system and its functioning in normal behavior, thought, and dreams, as well as in hysteria. He sent it to his friend Fliess in high excitement, then quickly became discouraged by the difficulties of creating a thoroughgoing mechanistic and reductionistic psychology. He tinkered with the model for a couple of years in letters to Fliess, and finally gave it up.

6

The turn of the century marked many basic changes in Freud's life and work: he severed his close and dependent friendships with colleagues (first Breuer, then Fliess) and his contacts with the Viennese medical society; his father died; his last child was born; he psychoanalyzed himself; he gave up neurological practice, research, and conceptual models; and he created his own new profession, research method, and theory, in terms of which he worked thereafter.

3. Freud's topographic model of the "psychic apparatus" was the foundation of two decades of work during which he published his major clinical discoveries: notably, *The Interpretation of Dreams* (1900) and *Three Essays on the Theory of Sexuality* (1905b); his papers on the technique used in psychoanalytic treatment; his five major case histories; the central works of metapsychology; and a series of important surveys and popularizations of his ideas, in addition to his principal applications of his theories to jokes, literature and art, biography, and anthropology. A complete or metapsychological explanation, Freud wrote in 1915, requires "describing a psychical process in its dynamic, topographical and economic aspects"—that is, in terms of a theoretical model in which the central concepts are psychological forces, structures, and quantities of energy (Rapaport & Gill, 1959). Hence, we speak of three metapsychological points of view. The topographic model, which was first set forth in Chapter 7 of *The Interpretation of Dreams* and was further elaborated in the metapsychological papers of 1915, conceptualizes thought and behavior in terms of processes in three psychological systems: the Conscious, Preconscious, and Unconscious (none of which has an explicit locus in the brain).

4. In the final period, between the two world wars, Freud made four main types of contribution: the final form of his theory of instinctual drives (*Beyond the Pleasure Principle*, 1920); a group of major modifications of both general and clinical theory—most notably, the structural model of the psychic apparatus (*The Ego and the Id*, 1923) and the theory of anxiety and

defense (*Inhibitions, Symptoms and Anxiety,* 1926a); applications of psychoanalysis to larger social problems; and a group of books reviewing and reformulating his theories.

To grasp the structure of Freud's work, it is useful not only to adopt such a developmental approach but also to view his theories from the perspective of the following threefold classification.

First and best known is the clinical theory of psychoanalysis, with its psychopathology, its accounts of psychosexual development and character formation, and the like. The subject matter of this type of theorizing consists of major events (both real and fantasied) in the life histories of persons, events occurring over spans of time ranging from days to decades. This theory is the stock in trade of the clinician—not just the psychoanalyst, but the vast majority of psychiatrists, clinical psychologists, and psychiatric social workers. Loosely referred to as "psychodynamics," it has even penetrated into general academic psychology via textbooks on personality.

Second, there is what Rapaport (1959) has called the general theory of psychoanalysis, also called metapsychology. Its subject matter—processes in a hypothetical psychic apparatus or, at times, in the brain—is more abstract and impersonal; and the periods of time involved are much shorter —from fractions of a second up to a few hours. The processes dealt with are mostly those occurring in dreams, thinking, affect, and defense. Freud's reasoning in working out this theory is much closer, and he made more use of theoretical models of the psychic apparatus. The main works are the "Project for a Scientific Psychology," Chapter 7 of *The Interpretation of Dreams,* and the metapsychological papers.

Third is what might be called Freud's phylogenetic theory. The subject matter is man as a species or in groups, and the periods of time involved range from generations to eons. Here are Freud's grand speculations, largely evolutionary and teleological in character. They contain no explicit models of a psychic apparatus, employing instead many literary, metaphorical concepts. The principal works of this type are *Totem and Taboo* (1913), *Beyond the Pleasure Principle* (1920), *Group Psychology and the Analysis of the Ego* (1921), *The Future of an Illusion* (1927), *Civilization and Its Discontents* (1930), and *Moses and Monotheism* (1934–1938).

His clinical contributions are among the earliest of Freud's papers that are still being read, and he continued to write in this vein all his life. As for the other two types of theory, the major metapsychological works came early, the main phylogenetic ones late. As Freud's concepts became more metaphorical and dealt with such remote issues as man's ultimate origins and the meaning of life and death, he became less concerned with describing or systematically accounting for the course and fate of an impulse or thought.

Even when Freud's works are read in the order in which he wrote them, much remains obscure if one has no conception of the contemporary status of the scientific and professional issues he was discussing. Fortunately for us, modern scholars are supplying a good deal of this needed background (e.g., Amacher, 1965; Andersson, 1962; Bernfeld, 1944; Ellenberger, 1970; Jackson, 1969; Spehlmann, 1953; see also Holt, 1965a, 1968). The relevant chapters of Ellenberger's masterly history are especially recommended for the scholarly but absorbingly readable way in which they give the social and political as well as scientific, medical, and general intellectual contexts in which Freud was writing. Here, I can do no more than touch lightly on a number of the most important and relevant intellectual currents of the nineteenth century.

NATURPHILOSOPHIE AND ITS REJECTION

The way for the romantic revolt that broadly characterized all aspects of intellectual life in the early 1800's had been prepared by *Naturphilosophie*, a mystical and often rhapsodic view of Nature as perfused with spirit and with conflicting unconscious forces and as evolving according to an inner, purposive design. Not a tightly knit school, its constituent thinkers included (in chronological order) Kant, Lamarck, Goethe, Hegel, Schelling (perhaps the central figure), Oken, and Fechner. With the exception of Fechner, who lived from 1801 to 1887, they all lived athwart the eighteenth and nineteenth centuries. *Naturphilosophie* encouraged the recrudescence of vitalism in biology, championed by the great physiologist Johannes Müller, and stimulated a humanistic school of romantic medicine (Galdston, 1956). In psychiatry, the early part of the century was dominated by the reforms of Pinel, Esquirol, and their followers, who introduced an era of "moral treatment": firm kindness in place of restraints, therapeutic optimism based on etiological theories of a more psychological than organic cast, and an attempt to involve inmates of asylums in constructive activities.

The tough–minded reaction to this tender–minded era was greatly aided by the strides being made in physics and chemistry. Three of Müller's students, Brücke, du Bois–Reymond, and Helmholtz, met Carl Ludwig in 1847 and formed a club (which became the Berlin Physical Society) to "constitute physiology on a chemico–physical foundation, and give it equal scientific rank with Physics" (Ludwig, quoted by Cranefield, 1957, p. 407). They did not succeed in their frankly reductionist aim but did attain their other objectives: to promote the use of scientific observation and experiment in physiology, and to combat vitalism. Among themselves, they held to the following program:

> No other forces than the common physical–chemical ones are active within the organism. In those cases which cannot at the time be explained by these forces one has either to find the specific way or form of their action by means of the physical–mathematical method, or to assume new forces equal in dignity to the chemical–physical forces inherent in matter, reducible to the force of attraction and repulsion. (du Bois–Reymond, quoted by Bernfeld, 1944, p. 348)

In Germany especially, this materialistic ferment of physicalistic physiology, mechanism, and reductionism became the mode, gradually putting romantic medicine, vitalism, and other aspects of *Naturphilosophie* to rout. Where earlier there had been Psychic, Psycho–somatic, and Somatic schools in German psychiatry (see Earle, 1854, in Hunter & Macalpine, 1963, pp. 1015–1018), the Somatic gradually won out; Meynert (Freud's teacher of psychiatry), for example, conceived mental disorders to be diseases of the forebrain. Despite its therapeutic successes, moral treatment was banished along with its psychogenic (often sexual) theories as "old wives' psychiatry," in favor of strictly organic–hereditarian views and very little by way of therapy (Bry & Rifkin, 1962).

The University of Vienna medical school was an outpost of the new hyperscientific biology, with one of its promulgators, Brücke, holding a major chair and directing the Physiological Institute (Bernfeld, 1944). Ironically, Freud tells us that his decision to enter medical school was determined by hearing the "Fragment on Nature" attributed to Goethe read aloud at a public lecture. This short prose poem is an epitome of *Naturphilosophie*, and it must have swayed Freud because of his longstanding admiration for Goethe and perhaps because of a "longing for philosophical knowledge," which had dominated his early years, as he said later in a letter to Fliess. Evolution had been a major tenet of *Naturphilosophie;* so it is not surprising that this 1780 dithyramb could be part of a lecture on comparative anatomy, the discipline that furnished much of the crucial evidence for Darwin's *Origin of Species* (1859).

ENERGY AND EVOLUTION.

Perhaps the two most exciting concepts of the nineteenth century were energy and evolution. Both of these strongly influenced Freud's teachers at the medical school. Helmholtz had read to the 1847 group his fundamental paper on the conservation of energy—presented as a contribution to physiology. Thirty years later, Brücke's lectures were full of the closely related (and still poorly differentiated) concepts of energy and force. To use these dynamic concepts was the very hallmark of the scientific approach; Brücke taught that the "real causes are symbolized in science by the word 'force' "(Bernfeld, 1944, p. 349). It seems obvious that the first of Freud's three metapsychological points of view, the dynamic (explanation in terms of psychological forces), had its origins in this exciting attempt to raise the scientific level of physiology by the diligent application of mechanics and especially of dynamics, that branch of mechanics dealing with forces and the laws of motion. The heavily quantitative emphasis of the school of Helmholtz and its stress on energy are clearly the main determinants of metapsychology seen from the economic point of view (explanation in terms of quantities of energy). The fact that, among authors Freud respected most, such disparate figures as Fechner and Hughlings Jackson held to dynamic and economic viewpoints no doubt strengthened Freud's unquestioning conviction that these viewpoints are absolutely necessary elements of an explanatory theory.

Despite its physicalistic program, the actual work of Brücke's institute was largely classical physiology and histology. Freud had had his Darwinian scientific baptism under Claus in a microscopic search for the missing testes of the eel, and his several attempts at physiological and chemical experiments under other auspices were fruitless. He was happy, therefore, to stay at the microscope where Brücke assigned him neurohistological studies, inspired by and contributing to evolutionary theory. When he worked with Meynert, it was again in a structural discipline with a genetic method—the study of brain anatomy using a series of fetal brains to trace the medullar pathways by following their development. His subsequent clinical practice was in neurology, a discipline which, as Bernfeld (1951) has noted, was "merely a diagnostic application of anatomy." Moreover, Freud's first full–scale theoretical model, the "Project" of 1895, is foremost a theory about the structural organization of the brain, both gross and fine. His early training thus demonstrably convinced him that a scientific theory has to have a structural (or topographic) base.

It was Bernfeld (1944) who first pointed out the strikingly antithetical content of these two coexisting intellectual traditions—*Naturphilosophie* and physicalistic physiology—both of which profoundly influenced Freud, and in that order. In his published works, to be sure, hardly anything of *Naturphilosophie* can be seen in the papers and books of his first two periods, and it emerged almost entirely in what I have cited above as his phylogenetic, speculative works. Many properties of his concept of psychic energy can nevertheless be traced to the vitalism that was a prominent feature of *Naturphilosophie* (Holt, 1967). Moreover, these two schools of thought may also be seen as particular manifestations of even broader, more inclusive bodies of ideas, which I call (following Chein, 1972) *images of man*.

Freud's Two Images of Man

I believe that there is a pervasive, unresolved conflict within all of Freud's writings between two antithetical images; a conflict that is responsible for a good many of the contradictions in his entire output but that his cognitive make-up allowed him to tolerate (as we shall shortly see). On the one hand, the main thrust of Freud's theoretical effort was to construct what he himself called a metapsychology, modeled on a mid-nineteenth-century grasp of physics and chemistry. Partly embodied in this and partly lying behind it is what I call his *mechanistic image* of man. The opposing view, so much less prominent that many students are not aware that Freud held it, I like to call a *humanistic image* of man. It may be seen in his clinical works

13

and in the broad, speculative, quasi-philosophical writings of his later years, but it is clearest in Freud's own life and interactions with others, best verbalized for us perhaps in his letters. Unlike the mechanistic image, the humanistic conception of man was never differentiated and stated explicitly enough to be called a model; yet it comprises a fairly rich and cohesive body of assumptions about the nature of human beings, which functioned in Freud's mind as a corrective antagonist of his mechanistic leanings.

There is little evidence after 1900 that Freud was conscious of harboring incompatible images of man, neither of which he could give up. Nevertheless, many otherwise puzzling aspects of psychoanalysis become intelligible if we assume that both images were there, functioning in many ways like conflicting motive systems.

Let me emphasize that what I am going to present is not an epitome of various theories specifically proposed by Freud. Rather, the two images are inferred complexes of ideas, extracted from Freud's life and writings and reconstructed in much the same way he taught us to use in understanding neurotic people: by studying a patient's dreams, symptoms, and "associations," we infer unconscious fantasies, complexes, or early memories that never become fully conscious, but which enable us to make sense out of his productions, which seem on the surface so bewilderingly diverse. This endeavor is fraught with a certain amount of risk. Even the mechanistic image was made explicit as a theoretical model only in the "Project," the unpublished attempt at a neuropsychology that Freud wrote in 1895. Thereafter, this model seems to have been largely forgotten or suppressed along with its antithesis, the humanistic image.

FREUD'S HUMANISTIC IMAGE OF MAN

Neither of Freud's images was especially original with him; each was his personal synthesis of a body of ideas with a long cultural history, expressed and transmitted to him in considerable part through books we know he read. Long before and long after Freud decided to become a scientist, he was an avid reader of the belletristic classics that are often considered the core of western man's humanistic heritage. He had an excellent liberal and classical education, which gave him a thorough grounding in the great works of Greek, Latin, German, and English authors, as well as the Bible, Cervantes, Molière, and other major writers in other languages, which he read in translation. He was a man of deep culture, with a lifelong passion for reading poetry, novels, essays, and the like and for learning about classical antiquity in particular but the arts generally, through travel, collecting, and personal communication with artists, writers, and close friends who had similar tastes and education.[2] And despite his later, negative comments about philosophy, he attended no less than five courses and seminars with the distinguished philosopher-psychologist Brentano during his years at the University of Vienna.

Very few of the many nonphysicians who were drawn to psychoanalysis and who became part of Freud's circle were trained in the "harder" or natural sciences. Mainly, they came from the arts and humanities. For every Waelder (a physicist) there were a few like Sachs and Kris (students primarily of literature and art). Surely this tells us something not only about influences on Freud but the kind of man he was, the conception of man by which he lived and which was conveyed by subtle means to his co–workers.

In various ways, then, Freud came under the influence of the prevailing image of man conveyed by the important sector of western culture we call the humanities. Let me now outline some of the major components of this image of man, which can be discerned in Freud's writings.

1. Man is both an animal and something more, a creature with aspirations to divinity. Thus, he has a *dual nature*. He possesses carnal passions, vegetative functions, greed and lust for power, destructiveness, selfish concern with maximizing pleasure and minimizing pain; but he also has a

capacity to develop art, literature, religion, science, and philosophy—the abstract realms of theoretical and esthetic values—and to be unselfish, altruistic, and nurturant. This is a complex view of man from the outset, as a creature who cares deeply about higher as well as lower matters.

2. Each human being is unique, yet all men are alike, one species, each one as human as any other. This assumption carries a strong value commitment as well, to the proposition that each person is worthy to be respected and to be helped, if in trouble, to live up to the extent of his capacities, however limited they may be. Freud was one of the main contributors of an important extension of this assumption through his discovery that there was indeed method in madness (as Shakespeare knew intuitively), that the insane or mentally ill could be understood and in fact were actuated by the same basic desires as other men. Thus, in the tradition of such psychiatrists as Pinel, Freud did a great deal to reassert the humanity of the mentally and emotionally abnormal and their continuity with the normal.

3. Man is a creature of longings, a striver after goals and values, after fantasies and images of gratification and of danger. That is, he is capable of imagining possible future states of pleasure, sensual joy or spiritual fulfillment, and of pain, humiliation, guilt, destruction, etc.; and his behavior is guided and impelled by wishes to obtain the positive goals and to avoid or nullify the negative ones, principally anxiety.

4. Man is a producer and processor of subjective meanings, by which he defines himself, and one of his strongest needs is to find his life meaningful. It is implicit in the humanistic image that meanings are primary, irreducible, causally efficacious, and of complete dignity as a subject of systematic interest. Psychopathology, accordingly, is conceived of in terms of maladaptive complexes or configurations of ideas, wishes, concepts, percepts, etc.

5. There is much more to man than he knows or would usually want us to think, more than is present in his consciousness, more than is presented to

the social world in public. This secret side is extraordinarily important. The meanings that concern a person most, including fantasies and wishes, are constantly active without awareness, and it is difficult for people to become aware of many of them. To understand a person truly, it is therefore necessary to know his subjective, inner life—his dreams, fantasies, longings, preoccupations, anxieties, and the special coloring with which he sees the outer world. By comparison, his easily observed, overt behavior is much less interesting and less important.

6. Inner conflict is inevitable because of man's dualities—his higher and lower natures, conscious and unconscious sides; moreover, many of his wishes are mutually incompatible or bring him into conflict with demands and pressures from other people.

7. Perhaps the most important of these wishes comprises the complex instinct of love, of which sexual lust is a major (and itself complicated) part. Man's urge for sexual pleasure is almost always strong, persistent, and polymorphous, even when it seems thoroughly inhibited or blocked, and may be detached from love. At the same time, Freud was always sensitive to the many forms of anger, hate, and destructiveness, long before he formally acknowledged them with his theory of the death instinct.

8. Man is an intensely social creature, whose life is distorted and abnormal if not enmeshed in a web of relationships to other people—some of these relationships formal and institutionalized, some informal but conscious and deliberate, and many of them having important unconscious components. Most human motive systems are interpersonal in character, too: we love and hate other people. Thus, the important reality for man is social and cultural. These Sullivanian–sounding propositions are clearly implicit in Freud's case histories.

9. A central feature of this image of man is that he is not static but is always changing—developing and declining, evolving and devolving. His most important unconscious motives derive from experiences in

childhood—the child is father to the man. Man is part of an evolutionary universe, thus in principle almost infinitely perfectible though in practice always subject to setbacks, fixations, and regressions.

10. Man is both the active master of his own fate and the plaything of his passions. He is capable of choosing among alternatives, of resisting temptations and of governing his own urges, even though at times he is a passive pawn of external pressures and inner impulses. It therefore makes sense to try to deal with him in a rational way, to hope to influence his behavior by discussing things and even urging him to exert his will. Thus, man has both an id and an autonomous ego.

Extracted from a body of work in which it has no systematic place, this humanistic image, as presented, is somewhat vague and poorly organized. Nevertheless, I see no intrinsic reason why it could not be explicated and developed in a more systematic way.

FREUD'S MECHANISTIC IMAGE OF MAN

This humanistically educated and philosophically inclined young man, fired by a romantic and vitalistic conception of the biology he wanted to study, went to the University of Vienna medical school, where he found himself surrounded by men of great prestige and intellectual substance teaching exciting scientific doctrines of a very different kind. He underwent a hasty conversion first to a radical materialism, and then to physicalistic physiology, a principal heir of the mechanistic tradition that started with Galileo and sought to explain everything in the universe in terms of Newtonian physics.

Freud was for years under the spell of Brücke, whom he once called the greatest authority he ever met. Several of his other teachers and colleagues were also enthusiastic members of the mechanistic school of Helmholtz, notably Meynert, Breuer, Exner, and Fliess. The outlook of this narrow but rigorous doctrine was forever after to shape Freud's scientific ideals, lingering behind the scenes of his theorizing, almost in the role of a scientific superego. In this sense, I believe that the mechanistic image of man underlies and may be discerned in Freud's metapsychological writings, even when certain aspects of that image seem to be contradicted.

In many details, the mechanistic image is sharply antithetical to the humanistic one. I have attempted to bring out this contrast in the following catalogue of assumptions.

1. Man is a proper subject of natural science, and as such is no different from any other object in the universe. All of his behavior is completely determined, including reports of dreams and fantasies. That is, all human phenomena are lawful and in principle possible to explain by natural-scientific, quantitative laws. From this vantage, there is no meaning to subdividing his behavior or to considering his nature to be dual—he is simply an animal, best understood as a machine or *apparatus*, composed of ingenious *mechanisms*, operating according to Newton's laws of motion, and understandable without residue in terms of physics and chemistry. One need not postulate a soul or vital principle to make the apparatus run, though *energy* is an essential concept. All the cultural achievements of which man is so proud, all his spiritual values and the like, are merely sublimations of basic instinctual drives, to which they may be reduced.

2. The differences among men are scientifically negligible; from the mechanistic standpoint, all human beings are basically the same, being subject to the same universal laws. The emphasis is put upon discovering these laws, not on understanding particular individuals. Accordingly, metapsychology takes no note of individual differences and does not seem to be a theory of personality.

3. Man is fundamentally motivated by the automatic tendency of his nervous system to keep itself in an unstimulated state, or at least to keep its

tensions at a constant level. The basic model is the *reflex arc:* external or internal stimulus leads to activity of the CNS which leads to response. All needs and longings must, for scientific purposes, be conceptualized as forces, tensions that must be reduced, or energies seeking discharge.

4. There is no place for meanings or value in science. It deals with quantities, not qualities, and must be thoroughly objective. Phenomena such as thoughts, wishes, or fears are epiphenomenal; they exist and must be explained, but have no explanatory power themselves. Energies largely take their place in the mechanical model.

5. There is no clear antithesis to the fifth humanistic assumption, the one dealing with the importance of the unconscious and the secret, inner side of man. A corresponding reformulation of the same point in mechanistic terms might be: consciousness too is an epiphenomenon,[3] and what happens in a person's awareness is of trivial interest compared to the busy activities of the nervous system, most of which go on without any corresponding consciousness.

6. The many forces operating in the apparatus that is man often collide, giving rise to the subjective report of *conflict.*

7. The processes sentimentally known as love are nothing more than disguises and transformations of the sexual instinct, or, more precisely, its energy *(libido).* Even platonic affection is merely aim–inhibited libido. Sex, not love, is therefore the prime motive. And since the fundamental tendency of the nervous system is to restore a state of unstimulated equilibrium, the total passivity of death is its ultimate objective. Rage and destructiveness are merely disguises and transformations of the death instinct.

8. *Objects* (that is to say, other people) are important only insofar as they provide stimuli that set the psychic apparatus in motion and provide necessary conditions for the reduction of internal tensions that brings it to rest again. Relationships as such are not real; a psychology can be complete without considering more than the individual apparatus and events within it,

plus the general class of external stimuli. Reality contains "only masses in motion and nothing else" (Freud, 1895, p. 308).

9. The genetic emphasis is not very different for Freud as mechanist and as humanist, so let us go to the last point:

10. Since man's behavior is strictly determined by his past history and by the contemporary arrangement of forces, free will is a fallacious illusion. To allow the idea of *autonomy* or freedom of choice would imply spontaneity instead of passivity in the nervous system, and would undermine the assumption—considered scientifically necessary—that behavior is determined strictly by the biological drives and by external stimuli.

IMPLICATIONS OF THE TWO IMAGES

Psychoanalytic theory as we know it is a tissue of compromises between these two opposing images. The influence of the mechanistic image is clearest in the metapsychology, where the general structure of the major propositions as well as a good deal of the terminology can be seen to derive directly from the explicitly mechanistic and reductionistic model of the "Project." The most striking change was Freud's abandoning an anatomical-neurological framework for the abstract ambiguity of the "psychic apparatus," in which the structures and energies are psychic, not physical. Unwittingly, Freud took a plunge into Cartesian metaphysical dualism, but staved off what he felt was the antiscientific threat of the humanistic image by continuing to claim ultimate explanatory power for metapsychology as opposed to the theoretically less ambitious formulation of clinical observations in language that was closer to that of everyday life. And in the metapsychology, by using the trick of translating subjective longings into the terminology of forces and energies, Freud did not have to take the behavioristic tack of rejecting the inner world; by replacing the subjective, willing self with the ego defined as a psychic structure, he was able to allow enough autonomy to achieve a fair fit with clinical observation.

Without realizing it, therefore, Freud did not give up the passive reflex model of the organism and the closely related physicalistic concept of reality even when he put aside deliberate neuropsychologizing. Although he explicitly postponed any attempt to relate the terms of metapsychology to processes and places in the body, he substituted psychological theories that carry the same burden of outmoded assumptions.

The relation between the humanistic image and *Naturphilosophie* remains to be clarified. In one sense, the latter can be considered a part of the former; yet in a number of respects it has a special status. I think of it as a peculiarly European intellectual anomaly, naturally related to its matrix of early nineteenth-century ideas and already anachronistic by Freud's time. Where the modern temper (even in history and the other social sciences) looks for detailed, prosaic chains and networks of demonstrable causes, the intellectuals of that era saw nothing wrong with postulating a conceptual shortcut, an *ad hoc* "force" or "essence" or another theoretical *deus ex machina* to which an observed outcome was directly attributed. Loose analogies were readily accepted as adequate means of forming hypotheses (usually genetic), and hardly anyone grasped the distinction between generating a plausible bright idea and reaching a defensible conclusion. To this temper, audacity was more to be admired than caution. A brilliantly unexpected linkage of events or phenomena was a better achievement than a laboriously nailed-down conclusion. Thus, the grand sweep of Darwin's ideas caught the public fancy, preconditioned as it was by a legacy of *Naturphilosophie*, much more than his extraordinary assemblage of detailed empirical evidence. Darwin did not introduce the idea of evolution; his contribution was to work out in convincing detail a nonteleological mechanism by which the gradual origin of species could be accounted for. It was an irony indeed that his great book seemed in the popular mind a *confirmation* of the teleological, even animistic, notions of *Naturphilosophie*, though there have been many such events in the history of science. Perhaps the majority of people approach new ideas "assimilatively" (to use Piaget's term), reducing them to their nearest equivalent in the stock of already existing concepts, so that a revolutionary proposal may end up reinforcing a reactionary idea.

One might even argue that in the world of today, the main function of grand, integrative speculations—philosophical or pseudoscientific "theories of the universe"—is to help adolescents gain a temporary intellectual mastery of the confusion they experience upon the sudden widening of their horizons, both emotional and ideational. In a sense, Freud the medical student was quite justified in feeling that his Nature–philosophical leanings were among the childish things that a man had to put away. Jones (1953, p. 29) writes that when he once asked Freud how much philosophy he had read, the answer came: "Very little. As a young man I felt a strong attraction towards speculation and ruthlessly checked it."

On the basis of this and many relevant remarks and passages, I have summarized (see table) the aspects of Freud's thought that seem traceable to *Naturphilosophie* and to his philosophical studies with Brentano, along with their counterparts, drawn from the tradition of mechanistic science and in particular from Freud's own apprenticeship in physicalistic physiology. To an unknown extent, some items on the left may have derived from other humanistic sources, but this one seems most plausible. (Evidence that the various elements were associated in the manner indicated is presented in Holt, 1963.) Freud usually spoke slightingly about all of the methods and procedures of the formal disciplines, as in the quotation above, where it is noteworthy (and characteristic) that he equated philosophy and speculation. Deduction, comprehensiveness of a theory's coverage, and rigorous definition were associated in his mind with the sterile, formalistic aspects of philosophy. And yet (perhaps because of the bridge–concept of evolution),

TABLE: *Latent Structure of Freud's Methodological Conceptions.*

	Derived largely from philosophy, especially *Naturphilosophie:*	Derived largely from physicalistic physiology:
Associated disciplines	Philosophy; academic philosophical psychology	Physiology; neuropsychology; metapsychology
Nature of theorizing	Complete, comprehensive theories, with precise definitions of concepts	Partial, ad hoc theories with groping imprecisely defined concepts
Procedures and methods:	Deductive procedure, use of mathematics; speculation; synthesis	Inductive procedure (nonformalistic); observation; dissection; analysis

Naturphilosophie and the rest of this complex of ideas were linked in Freud's mind with Darwinian biology and to the similarly genetic discipline of archaeology. These respectable sciences which, unlike philosophy and mathematics, were concretely empirical, reconstructed the remote past of man by a genetic method. Perhaps the thought that he was following their method enabled Freud, finally, to indulge his long–suppressed yearning for broad, speculative theorizing. In his autobiography (Freud, 1925, p. 57), he wrote: "In the works of my later years (*Beyond the Pleasure Principle, Group Psychology and the Analysis of the Ego,* and *The Ego and the Id*), I have given free rein to the inclination, which I kept down for so long, to speculation. . . ."

In a sense, of course, it is only an extension of the method of genetic reconstruction to go back beyond the beginnings of an individual life and attempt to trace the development of socially shared customs in the larger life history of a people, as Freud did in *Totem and Taboo*. The conceptions of Haeckel (that ontogeny recapitulates phylogeny) and of Lamarck (that acquired characteristics may be passed on genetically) were generally known during Freud's scientifically formative years and enjoyed a far more widespread acceptance by the scientific world than they did during Freud's later years. This acceptance made it difficult for him to give them up. If the functional anthropologists had appeared a generation sooner and if the evolutionary approach had not been so popularized by Sir James Frazer, Freud might have been able to understand how pervasive and unconscious the patterning of a culture can be. This intricate interconnection makes it possible for culture to be transmitted via subtle and almost imperceptible kinds of learning, a fact that obviates what Freud (1934–38) declared was the necessity that a social psychology should postulate the inheritance of acquired characteristics.

Freud's Cognitive Style

Let us turn now to the last major source of difficulty the modern reader encounters in understanding Freud: his cognitive style. Anyone who has read Freud at all may react to that proposition with astonishment, for Freud's style is much admired for its limpid clarity. Even in translation, Freud is vivid, personal, and charmingly direct in a way that makes him highly readable; he uses imaginative and original figures of speech, and often leads the reader along by a kind of stepwise development that enables him to penetrate into difficult or touchy areas with a minimum of effort. Anyone who has read much of his writing can easily understand why he received the Goethe prize for literature.

25

Nevertheless, there are stylistic difficulties in understanding him; but they relate to his *cognitive,* not his literary style. A couple of decades ago George Klein (1951, 1970) coined the term cognitive style to mean the patterning of a person's ways of taking in, processing, and communicating information about his world. Freud has an idiosyncratic way not just of writing but of thinking, which makes it surprisingly easy for the modern reader to misinterpret his meaning, to miss or distort many subtleties of his thought. To some degree, I myself may be subtly distorting Klein's concept, for he operationalized it in the laboratory, not the library. He presented subjects with hidden figures to be extracted from camouflage, series of squares to be judged for size, and other unusual tasks, some of his own and some of others' devising. By contrast, the methods I have used are more like those of the literary critic. I have collected notes on what struck me as characteristic ways in which Freud observed, processed data, obtained ideas by means other than direct observation, thought about them, and put his personal stamp on them. In doing so, however, I have been guided by my long association with Klein and his own way of approaching cognitive processes and products; so I trust that I have been true to the spirit of his contribution, which is now so widely used as to be virtually a part of psychology's common property.

CHARACTER STYLE

Perhaps as good a place to start as any is with Ernest Jones's well–known biography. Much of the little that he has to say on this topic can be organized in the form of antitheses or paradoxes. First of all, there was a great deal about Freud that was *compulsively orderly and hard-working.* He led a stable, regular life in which his work was a basic necessity. As he wrote to Pfister: ''I could not contemplate with any sort of comfort a life without work. Creative imagination and work go together with me; I take no delight in anything else." Yet he went on, "That would be a prescription for happiness were it not for the terrible thought that one's productivity depends entirely on sensitive moods" (Jones, 1955, p. 396f.). As Jones brings out, he did indeed work by fits and starts, not quite so steadily and regularly as, say, Virgil, but when the mood was on him.

Again, Jones remarks on "Freud's close attention to verbal detail, the striking patience with which he would unravel the meaning of phrases and utterances" (ibid., p. 398). On the other hand:

> His translators will bear me out when I remark that minor obscurities and ambiguities, of a kind that more scrupulous circumspection could have readily avoided, are not the least of their trials. He was of course aware of this. I remember once asking him why he used a certain phrase, the meaning of which was not clear, and with a grimace he answered: *"Pure Schlamperei"* (sloppiness) (1953, p. 33f.).

He was himself not a meticulous translator, though a highly gifted one. "Instead of laboriously transcribing from the foreign language, idioms and all, he would read a passage, close the book, and consider how a German writer would have clothed the same thoughts . . . His translating work was both brilliant and rapid" (Jones, 1953, p. 55). Similarly, Jones remarks on Freud's "quickness of thought and observation" generally, and the fact that "His type of mind was such as to penetrate through the material to something really essential beyond rather than to dally or play with it" (1955, p. 399). In short, he was intuitive rather than ploddingly systematic.

This particular paradox can be resolved, I believe, by the recognition that Freud was, basically, an obsessive-compulsive personality, in which this type of ambivalence is familiar. He had a good measure of the fundamental anal traits of orderliness and compulsive attention to detail; yet when it came to his mode of working with such details as the slightest turn of phrase in the telling of a dream (which only a compulsive would have noticed in the first place), he showed a gift for intuition. After all, as Jones never tires of reminding us, he *was* a genius, a man of extraordinary intelligence.

NATURE OF FREUD'S INTELLECT

What *kind* of intelligence was it, then? If we adopt the frame of reference of the Wechsler intelligence tests, it was first of all predominantly a verbal rather than a performance sort of ability. I have seen no evidence that Freud was specially gifted with his hands. He failed as a chemical experimenter (Jones, 1953, p. 54), and though he was a good microscopist and invented a new tissue stain during his years of scientific apprenticeship in Brücke's physiological laboratory, there is no evidence that he was skilled at the mechanical end of it. He was never what we call "an apparatus man," an ingenious tinkerer.[4] Incidentally, the usual implication of a markedly higher verbal over performance IQ would be borne out in Freud's case: he was surely never given to acting out, but was always an intellectualizer and internalizer. Moreover, "That there was a pronounced passive side to Freud's nature is a conclusion for which there is ample evidence." Jones (1953, p. 53) notes; "He once remarked that there were three things to which he felt unequal: governing, curing, and educating." He gave up hypnosis as "a coarsely interfering method" and soon abjured the laying on of hands despite the fact that he treated several of the ladies in *Studies in Hysteria* by physical massage. Sitting quietly and listening to free associations, responding only verbally (largely by interpretations), is the method par excellence of a man with verbal gifts and a disinclination to manipulate.

Within the realm of verbal intelligence, we can make some more specific statements as well. "He had an enormously rich vocabulary,"

Jones (1955, p. 402) attests, "but he was the reverse of a pedant in words." He knew eight languages, having enough mastery of English and French to write scientific papers in those tongues. There is a fair amount of evidence between the lines of Freud's writings that the modality of his thought was largely verbal, as opposed to imageless, visual, auditory, or kinesthetic. He gives evidence that he had been a virtual *Eidetiker* until well into his schooling, however:

> . . . for a short period of my youth some unusual feats of memory were not beyond me. When I was a schoolboy I took it as a matter of course that I could repeat by heart the page I had been reading; and shortly before I entered the University I could write down almost verbatim popular lectures on scientific subjects directly after hearing them. (1901, p. 135)

His auditory imagery could be extraordinarily vivid, too, at least up until a few years later, when he was studying with Charcot in Paris. During these days, he reports, "I quite often heard my name suddenly called by an unmistakable and beloved voice," which he goes on to refer to unblinkingly as a "hallucination" (1901, p. 261). Yet he writes about these experiences in such a way as to indicate that, like most other eidetic imagers, he gradually lost the ability as he grew older. True, his dreams remained vividly visual, and he occasionally was able to get a sharp visual image in waking life, but he emphasized that such occasions were exceptional. On the other hand, I have never found any indication that Freud was even aware that such a phenomenon as imageless thought exists; though investigators from Galton to Anne Roe have found that it characterizes many leading figures in such disciplines as mathematics and theoretical physics—disciplines that Jones specifically says (1953, p. 33) Freud could never have excelled in.

Perhaps there is a hint here that Freud's mind was not at the very forefront as far as highly abstract thinking is concerned. Surely he was not much of a mathematician. He once characterized himself as follows:

I have very restricted capacities or talents. None at all for the natural sciences; nothing for mathematics; nothing for anything quantitative. But what I have, of a very restricted nature, was probably very intensive. (Quoted in Jones, 1955, p. 397)

As we shall see a little later, this relative weakness in the quantitative factor had a number of noticeable effects on Freud's manner of thinking.

To summarize so far, in terms of abilities, Freud had a predominantly verbal intelligence and mode of thinking. He was extraordinarily gifted at memory, concentration, passive (or as he put it, "evenly–suspended") attention, and creative concept–formation. His gift was more analytic than synthetic, just as his preference was for the former over the latter aspect of thinking. He had no notable gifts along sensorimotor, manipulative, or quantitative lines, nor in the most abstract types of thought. Above all, it may not be superfluous to add, he was productive, original, and creative.

SELF-CRITICAL DOUBTS VERSUS
SELF-CONFIDENT DETERMINATION

In moving on to some more stylistic aspects of his thought, I shall continue to pursue antitheses. One such is the cognitive side of a prominent theme in Freud's personality: a self–critical, even retiring and self–doubting modesty versus a largely covert and negated thirst for fame coupled with great self–confidence. A number of the quotations both from Freud and from Jones have touched on his self–critical side, and the evidence for his deep–seated longing to see his name carved on a rock for the ages is omnipresent in Jones's three volumes, though the disciple outdid the master in protesting that it wasn't so. Both of these facets of Freud's mind come out in relation to the ideas he set forth in *Beyond the Pleasure Principle*. He wrote:

What follows is speculation, often far–fetched speculation, which the reader will consider or dismiss according to his individual predilection. (1920, p. 24)

And:

It may be asked whether and how far I am myself convinced of the truth of the hypotheses that have been set out in these pages. My answer would be that I am not convinced myself and that I do not seek to persuade other people to believe in them. Or, more precisely, that I do not know how far I believe in them. . . . Since we have such good grounds for being distrustful, our attitude towards the results of our own deliberations cannot well be other than one of cool benevolence. (1920, p. 59)

He was speaking, of course, about his most controversial speculations, those concerning the death instinct. Yet only a few years later, he wrote this:

To begin with it was only tentatively that I put forward the views I have developed here, but in the course of time they have gained such a hold upon me that I can no longer think in any other way. To my mind, they are far more serviceable from a theoretical standpoint than any other possible ones; they provide that simplification, without either ignoring or doing violence to the facts, for which we strive in scientific work. (1930, p. 119)

In short, he had a tendency to become so "accustomed to the face" of his own ideas as to consider them indispensable and, finally, as established, even though they were originally presented with great modesty. Indeed, he looked back on the shaky speculations of *Beyond the Pleasure Principle* as a basis for supporting his fundamental assumption that there had to be two classes of instinctual drives:

Over and over again we find, when we are able to trace instinctual impulses back, that they reveal themselves as derivatives of Eros. If it were not for the considerations put forward in *Beyond the Pleasure Principle*, and ultimately for the sadistic constituents which have attached themselves to Eros, we should have difficulty in holding to our fundamental dualistic point of view [in instinct theory]. (1923, p. 46)

Here we have the first hint of one of the basic problems with which Freud struggled, and which helped shape the nature of his thought. Working as he did in a new field, with no conventional criteria for establishing valid knowledge, he had to be sustained against the inevitable self-doubts, even the despair that what he was doing could lead anywhere, by an irrational confidence in himself, a faith that his intuitions and hypotheses would be vindicated, and even a certain degree of self–deception that he had established points more firmly than he in fact had been able to do.

His determination to persist in the face of his recognition that progress was difficult is well expressed in the following quotation:

It is almost humiliating that, after working so long, we should still be having difficulty in understanding the most fundamental facts. But we have made up our minds to simplify nothing and to hide nothing. If we cannot see things clearly we will at least see clearly what the obscurities are. (1926a, p. 124)

One of the positive aspects of Freud's ability to be self-critical was his willingness to change his ideas:

We must be patient and await fresh methods and occasions of research. We must be ready, too, to abandon a path that we have followed for a time, if it seems to be leading to no good end. Only believers, who demand that science shall be a substitute for the catechism they have given up, will blame an investigator for developing or even transforming his views. (1920, p. 64)

If he was not always able to live up to this brave program, if he failed to recognize that many of his unquestioned assumptions were not as axiomatically true as he thought, these are the necessary consequences of being human. Freud was surely sustained in his long quest by a passionate interest in penetrating the mysteries of nature and a capacity to care deeply about his ideas. All the more natural, therefore, that he should have tended at times to lose scientific detachment and confuse his concepts with realities. Thus, he would refer to "the 'super–ego,' one of the later *findings* of psycho-analysis" (1900, p. 558 n. 1), or to "the *discovery* that the ego itself is cathected with libido" (1930, p. 118; emphasis added in both quotations). When I spoke above about his unquestioned assumptions, I had principally in mind the passive reflex model of the organism, which is today demonstrably false (Holt, 1965). Yet to Freud it seemed so self–evidently true that he referred to it as a fact on which he could found one of his most questionable constructs:

> The dominating tendency of mental life, and perhaps of nervous life in general, is the effort to reduce, to keep constant or to remove internal tension due to stimuli . . .—a tendency which finds expression in the pleasure principle; and our recognition of that *fact* is one of our strongest reasons for believing in the existence of death instincts. (1920, p. 55f.; emphasis added)

Another aspect of this same antithesis was Freud's conviction that the essence of what he was setting forth was *truth,* which would be fully appreciated only by future generations, versus his expectation that much of what he taught would be quickly overthrown, as in the following 1909 letter to Jung in response to the latter's expressed fear that Freud's writings would be treated as gospel:

> Your surmise that after my departure my errors might be adored as holy relics amused me enormously, but I don't believe it. On the contrary, I think my followers will hasten to demolish as swiftly as possible everything that is not safe and sound in what I leave behind. (Quoted in Jones, 1955, p. 446)

On Reading Freud

Freud showed here the strength of his faith that there were kernels of eternal truth as well as chaff in the harvest of his labors.

ANALYSIS VERSUS SYNTHESIS

Another familiar antithesis in the realm of thinking is analysis versus synthesis. Here, the preference of the inventor and namer of psychoanalysis was clear and marked. In 1915 he wrote to Lou Andreas-Salomé:

> I so rarely feel the need for synthesis. The unity of this world seems to me something self–understood, something unworthy of emphasis. What interests me is the separation and breaking up into its component parts what would otherwise flow together into a primeval pulp. . . .In short, I am evidently an analyst and believe that synthesis offers no obstacles once analysis has been achieved. (1960, p. 310)

Yet in spite of the fact that the concept of the synthetic function of the ego is associated less with Freud than with Nunberg, the latter's paper by this name (Nunberg, 1931) is in large part simply a drawing together of points Freud made in passing in many contexts. Freud could perform remarkable feats of synthesizing many disconnected facts—see for example his masterly review of the scientific literature on dreams (1900, Ch. 1)—and he taught us a great deal about synthetic functioning; nevertheless, his ability and his predilection ran predominantly along the lines of analysis.

DIALECTIC DUALISM.

One reason I have adopted the antithetical method in this exposition is that a preference for opposed binary concepts was itself highly characteristic of Freud's thinking. Even in the realm of art, he strongly preferred the balance of classical antiquity; a letter to Romain Rolland in 1930 speaks of his "Hellenic love of proportion" (1960, p. 392). And in his own theory, it is surely a striking and well–known fact that his major concepts come in matched opposing pairs. Perhaps the most notable is his motivational theory in its various guises. Fairly early, he pitted unconscious wish against preconscious cathexis, then the libidinal versus the ego–instincts, going on to narcissistic versus object–libido, to Eros versus the death instincts (or love against hate); but it was always a dual drive theory. Or recall *"the three great polarities that dominate mental life"*: activity—passivity, ego —external world, and pleasure—unpleasure (1915a, p. 140; emphasis Freud's), to which might be added that of masculine—feminine. Many other such oppositions come to mind: quantity versus quality, autoplastic versus alloplastic, ego–syntonic versus ego–alien, pleasure principle versus reality principle, free versus bound cathexis, and the primary process versus the secondary process. It is not difficult to show that Freud conceived of a continuous series of actual thought processes between the theoretical extremes of the primary and the secondary process, but he typically used them in a dichotomous fashion. Even when he proposed triads of concepts *(Cs., Pcs.,* and *Ucs.;* ego, superego, and id), he had a strong tendency to reduce them to binary form. The 1923 work is, after all, entitled merely *The Ego and the Id;* and the distinction between conscious and unconscious always impressed Freud as "our one beacon–light in the darkness of depth–psychology" (1923, p. 18). Terms like ambivalence and conflict conceptualize this trait as fundamental facts of psychology. Indeed, one might argue that many of the antithetical dynamic concepts are a direct consequence of Freud's recognizing how important conflict was in both normal and pathological development.

On Reading Freud

TOLERATED CONTRADICTION (SYNTHESIS DEFERRED)

Further, Freud's thinking is characterized by an unusual tolerance for inconsistency. If you went through the works of any author as prolific as Freud, you would doubtless find many mutually contradictory statements, and many propositions that are actually incompatible with his basic assumptions. But it is not difficult to find other reasons for the presence of inconsistencies in Freud's work besides its sheer bulk, which is enormous: his preference for what I shall expound shortly as seriatim theorizing and piecemeal empiricism, both of which are clearly to be expected from a man with an orientation away from synthesis, and a confessed sloppiness with concepts. As Jones puts it,

> He wrote easily, fluently, and spontaneously, and would have found much rewriting irksome. . . .one of his main characteristics [was] his dislike of being hampered or fettered. He loved to give himself up to his thoughts freely, to see where they would take him, leaving aside for the moment any question of precise delineation; that could be left for further consideration. (1953, p. 33f.)

True, he did rewrite and revise several of his books many times. Fortunately, the *Standard Edition* provides a variorum text and scrupulously informs us of every change, edition by edition. It is not difficult, therefore, to characterize Freud's style of revision by studying *The Interpretation of Dreams, The Psychopathology of Everyday Life,* and *Three Essays on the Theory of Sexuality.* These books, first published from 1900 to 1905, went through eight, ten, and six editions respectively, all of them containing additions from at least as late as 1925. Thus, they span at least two major periods in the development of Freud's thought, including a far–reaching change in models. Yet one statement covers the vast majority of the revisions: he added things. There was never any fundamental reconsideration and precious little synthesis. Perhaps if Freud had not had such a superb

36

command of written communication so that he rarely had even to polish his first drafts, he would have reworked his books more thoroughly as they went through new editions. At most, he added an occasional footnote pointing out the incompatibility of a statement with later doctrines. Even Chapter 7 of *The Interpretation of Dreams,* Freud's most ambitious and important theoretical work, was left virtually untouched except for interpolations, after the tinkerings of 1915 and 1917 that undid the possibility of topographical regression, even after the jettisoning of the whole topographic model in 1923 and its replacement by the structural model, which makes no provision for the conceptualization of *any* complete cognitive process. Indeed, to the end, Chapter 7 contained anachronistic carry–overs from the neurological model of the unpublished "Project," which had preceded it by four years. Throughout all the revisions, Freud never eliminated the lapses into references to "neurones," "pathways," and "quantity."

Freud built theory, then, much as Franklin D. Roosevelt constructed the Executive branch of the government: when something wasn't working very well, he seldom reorganized; he just supplied another agency—or concept—to do the job. To tolerate this much inconsistency surely took an unusual capacity to delay the time when the gratification of an orderly, internally consistent, logically coherent theory might be attained. Compare his self-characterization in the following letter to Andreas-Salomé in 1917; he had been contrasting himself with "the system–builders" Jung and Adler.

> . . . you have observed how I work, step by step, without the inner need for completion, continually under the pressure of the problems immediately on hand and taking infinite pains not to be diverted from the path. (1960, p. 319)

Seven years earlier, he had written to Jung:

I notice that you have the same way of working as I have: to be on the look out in whatever direction you feel drawn and not take the obvious straightfor-ward path. I think that is the best way too, since one is astonished later to find how directly those circuitous routes led to the right goal. (Quoted in Jones, 1955, p. 449)

To follow one's nose empirically, adding to the theory whatever bits and pieces might accrue along the way—this was the procedure with which Freud felt at home, with his faith that ultimately the truth would prevail.

CONCEPTION OF SCIENTIFIC METHOD AND CONCEPTS.

This attitude was of a piece with Freud's basic conception of scientific work. Science was first and foremost a matter of empirical observation, which he usually contrasted with speculation to the latter's discredit. As Freud conceived it, a speculative, or philosophical, system started with "clear and sharply defined basic concepts," (1915a, p. 117) and built on this "smooth, logically unassailable foundation" (1914, p. 77) a "complete and ready–made theoretical structure," (1923, p. 36) which could "easily spring into existence complete, and thereafter remain unchangeable" (1906, p. 271). But "no science, not even the most exact," operates this way:

The true beginning of scientific activity consists rather in describing phenomena and then in proceeding to group, classify and correlate them. Even at the stage of description it is not possible to avoid applying certain abstract ideas to the material in hand, ideas derived from somewhere or other but certainly not from the new observations alone. . . .They must at first necessar-ily possess some degree of indefiniteness; . . .we come to an understanding about their meaning by making repeated references to the material of observa-tion from which they appear to have been derived, but upon which, in fact, they have been imposed. . . . It is only after more thorough investigation of the field of observation that we are able to formulate its basic scientific concepts with increased precision, and progressively so to modify them that they become serviceable and consistent over a wide area. Then, indeed, the time may have come to confine them in definitions. The advance of knowledge, however, does not tolerate any rigidity even in definitions. (1915a, p. 117)

When tackling a new topic, therefore:

Instead of starting from a definition, it seems more useful to begin with some indication of the range of the phenomena under review, and to select from among them a few specially striking and characteristic facts to which our enquiry can be attached. (1921, p. 72)

Thereafter, any psychoanalytic inquiry must

. . .find its way step by step along the path towards understanding the intricacies of the mind by making an analytic dissection of both normal and abnormal phenomena. (1923, p. 36)

But because of the complexity of its subject matter, psychoanalysis cannot hope for quick successes:

The extraordinary intricacy of all the factors to be taken into consideration leaves only one way of presenting them open to us. We must select first one and then another point of view, and follow it up through the material as long as the application of it seems to yield results. Each separate treatment of the subject will be incomplete in itself, and there cannot fail to be obscurities where it touches upon material that has not yet been treated; but we may hope that a final synthesis will lead to a proper understanding. (1915b, p. 157f.)

The truth, when attained, will be simpler:

. . . we have no other aim but that of translating into theory the results of observation, and we deny that there is any obligation on us to achieve at our first attempt a well–rounded theory which will commend itself by its simplicity. We shall defend the complications of our theory so long as we find that they meet the results of observation, and we shall not abandon our expectations of being led in the end by those very complications to the discovery of a state of affairs which, while simple in itself, can account for all the complications of reality. (1915c, p. 190)

Freud thus demonstrated a capacity to tolerate, in addition to inconsistency and delay, considerable conceptual indefiniteness or, in the terminology of today, ambiguity. "It is true," he was ready to admit, "that notions such as that of an ego–libido, an energy of the ego–instincts, and so on, are neither particularly easy to grasp, nor sufficiently rich in content." Nevertheless, psychoanalysis would "gladly content itself with nebulous, scarcely imaginable basic concepts, which it hopes to apprehend more clearly in the course of its development, or which it is even prepared to replace by others" (1914, p. 77). Note the obligation stated here, which follows clearly enough from his position regarding definition, for a periodic conceptual stocktaking; if consistent and useful definitions never precipitate out, the concept should be abandoned. As we have seen, however, such a process of regular review was quite incompatible with Freud's style of working and thinking, and he rarely discarded concepts when he added new ones. It is a little sad, but not surprising, to find that instincts, which in 1915 (1915a, p. 117f.) were "at the moment . . . still somewhat obscure," were characterized 18 years later as "mythical entities, magnificent in their indefiniteness" (1933, p. 95).

A few years ago, I decided to try my hand at this winnowing process, taking one of Freud's central but tantalizingly ill–defined concepts (the binding of cathexis; see Holt, 1962) and following it through his writings to see what kind of definition emerged. The labor of finding and collating the contexts in which it occurred, and educing the 14 different meanings that I was able to discern—I have found still others since then!—was great enough to make me realize that if Freud had undertaken to work his own theories over continuously in this way, after a few years he would not have had time to analyze any more patients, much less write anything new. It is true, I was able to sift out a core meaning to my own satisfaction, but it remains to be seen whether many psychoanalysts will be convinced that they should abandon the other dozen or so types of usage. With Freud's free–and–easy example for precedent, some find it easy to justify putting off the evil day when terms will start to have definite, restrictive meanings.

So far, I have emphasized the knowingly provisional, tentative nature of Freud's theorizing, his deliberate abjuring of any attempt to build a complete and internally coherent system, in favor of piecemeal empiricism instead—quite a contrast to the view of Freud as the dogmatic systematist who would brook no deviation from a rigid "party line" of theory! Yet this popular conception has its roots in fact also. For one thing, Freud seems to have had a fluctuating, never explicit set of standards about what parts of psychoanalysis had been proved, which only he might change with impunity, and what parts were modifiable by others. True to his agglutinative principle of revision, he welcomed additions so long as they did not explicitly call for reconsideration of concepts and propositions that had come to seem basic and necessary. Thus, Adler's ideas about organ inferiority and the will to power were acceptable until the disciple started insisting that they clashed with the libido theory and demanded the latter's drastic revision.

STYLE OF THEORIZING

Quite aside from Freud's relation to the contributions of others (a matter that is obviously a great deal more complicated than the above brief discussion might seem to imply), there are bases for the conception of Freud as a doctrinaire dogmatist in certain stylistic peculiarities of his own theorizing. Let me summarize first and then expand, with examples. Freud was fond of stating things "as it were, dogmatically—in the most concise form and in the most unequivocal terms" (1940, p. 144); indeed, hyperbole was one of his favorite rhetorical devices. When he thought that he glimpsed a law of nature, he stated it with sweeping universalism and generality. He was likewise fond of extending concepts to the limit of their possible applicability, as if stretching the realm of phenomena spanned by a concept was a way to make it more abstract and useful. His device for escaping the dangers of oversimplification to which this pattern exposed him was to follow one flat statement with another that qualified it by partial contradiction. Therefore, the inconsistency in many of Freud's propositions is only apparent. He was perfectly well aware that one statement undid another, and used such sequences as a way of letting a richly complicated conception grow in the reader's mind as considerations were introduced one at a time.

Here, then, is one reason why Freud is at once so delightfully easy to read, and so easy to misunderstand, particularly when statements are taken out of context. His view of human behavior was unusually subtle, complex, and many–layered; if he had tried to set it forth in sentences of parallel complexity and hierarchical structure, he would have made Dr. Johnson look like Hemingway. Instead, he writes simply, directly, forcefully; he dramatizes by grand overstatement, setting out in hard black outlines what he considers the basic truth about a matter as the reader's initial orientation. Then he fills in shadows; or, by another boldly simple stroke, suddenly shows that forms are disposed on different planes. Gradually, a three-dimensional reality takes shape before the eyes of the one who knows how to read Freud.

Here is an example of an initial flat statement, followed by qualifications:

The way in which dreams treat the category of contraries and contradictories is highly remarkable. It is simply disregarded. 'No' seems not to exist so far as dreams are concerned. (1900, p. 318)
I have asserted above that dreams have no means of expressing the relation of a contradiction, a contrary or a 'no.' I shall now proceed to give a first denial of this assertion. [The idea of 'just the reverse' is plastically represented as something turned around from its usual orientation.] (p. 326)
. . . the ''not being able to do something'' in this dream was a way of expressing a contradiction—a 'no'—; so that my earlier statement that dreams cannot express a ''no'' requires correction. (p. 337)
(A third ''denial'' appears on p. 434.)

Perhaps an even more familiar sweeping generalization is the following:

Psycho-analysis is justly suspicious. One of its rules is that *whatever interrupts the progress of analytic work is a resistance.* (1900, p. 517)

Less often quoted is Freud's footnote, in which he makes this statement—so infuriating to many an analyzand!—more palatable; it is

. . . easily open to misunderstanding. It is of course only to be taken as a technical rule, as a warning to analysts. It cannot be disputed that in the course of an analysis various events may occur the responsibility for which cannot be laid upon the patient's intentions. His father may die without his having murdered him; or a war may break out which brings the analysis to an end. But behind *its obvious exaggeration* the proposition is asserting something both true and new. Even if the interrupting event is a real one and independent of the patient, it often depends on him how great an interruption it causes; and resistance shows itself unmistakably in the readiness with which he accepts an occurrence of this kind or the exaggerated use which he makes of it. (emphasis added)

All too often (and unfortunately difficult to illustrate by quotation), the

43

softening statement following the initial overgeneralization is not explicitly pointed out, may not follow very soon, or is not obviously related. For Freud, however, this was a conscious strategy of scientific advance; the transformations of scientific opinion are developments, not revolutions. A law which was held at first to be universally valid proves to be a special case of a more comprehensive uniformity, or is limited by another law, not discovered till later; a rough approximation to the truth is replaced by a more carefully adapted one, which in turn awaits further perfecting (cf. 1927, p. 55).

Many examples of statements formulated with arresting exaggeration can easily be cited.

> On the basis of our analysis of the ego it cannot be doubted that in cases of mania the ego and the ego ideal have fused together. (1921, p. 132)
> . . . hysteria . . . is concerned only with the patient's repressed sexuality. (1906, p. 278)
> . . . no one can doubt that the hypnotist has stepped into the place of the ego ideal. (1921, p. 114)
> It is certain that much of the ego is itself unconscious, and notably what we may describe as its nucleus; only a small part of it is covered by the term "preconscious." (1920, p. 19)

Strachey appends the following rather amusing footnote to the above passage:

> In its present form this sentence dates from 1921. In the first edition (1920) it ran: "It may be that much of the ego is itself unconscious; only a part of it, probably, is covered by the term 'preconscious'."

In this case, it took only a year for a cautious probability to become a certainty.

44

In other instances, hyperbole takes the form of the assertion of an underlying unity where only a correlation is observed:

> All these three kinds of regression [topographical, temporal, and formal] are, however, one at bottom and occur together as a rule; for what is older in time is more primitive in form and in psychical topography lies nearer to the perceptual end. (1900, p. 548)

All too often, the sweeping formulation takes the form of a declaration that something like the Oedipus complex is *universal*. I believe that Freud was less interested in making an empirical generalization from his limited data than in groping in this way for a basic law of nature. As Jones summarizes the letter of October 15, 1897, to Fliess,

> He had discovered in himself the passion for his mother and jealousy of his father; he felt sure that this was a general human characteristic and that from it one could understand the powerful effect of the Oedipus legend. (Jones, 1953, p. 326)

Again, four years later, he generalized universally from his own case:

> There thus runs through my thoughts a continuous current of 'personal reference,' of which I generally have no inkling, but which betrays itself by such instances of my forgetting names. It is as if I were obliged to compare everything I hear about other people with myself; as if my personal complexes were put on the alert whenever another person is brought to my notice. This cannot possibly be an individual peculiarity of my own: it must rather contain an indication of the way in which we understand "something other than ourself" in general. I have reasons for supposing that other people are in this respect very similar to me. (1901, p. 24)

To the contemporary psychologist, trained to be cautious in generalizing from small samples, it seems audacious to the point of foolhardiness to jump from self–observation to a general law. But Freud was emboldened by the very fact that he was dealing with vital issues:

> I feel a fundamental aversion towards your suggestion that my conclusions [about the sexual etiology of neurosis] are correct, but only for certain cases . . . That is not very well possible. Entirely or not at all. They are concerned with such fundamental matters that they could not be valid for one set of cases only. . . . There is only our kind or else nothing at all is known. *Au fond* you must be of the same opinion. So now I have confessed all my fanaticism! (Letter to Jung, April 19, 1909; in Jones, 1955, p. 439)

Remember, also, the fact that Freud's initial scientific efforts considerably antedated the invention of statistics, sampling theory, or experimental design. In his early days, when he was most secure in his role as scientist, Freud was studying neuroanatomy at the microscope, and like his respected teachers and colleagues, generalizing freely and automatically from samples of one!

Then too, recall that Freud was the promulgator of the principle of exceptionless determinism in psychology: all aspects of behavior were lawful, he believed, which made it easy for him to confuse (a) the universal applicability of abstract laws and concepts with (b) the universal occurrence of empirically observable behavioral sequences.

Finally, we are so used to considering Freud a "personality theorist" that we forget how little interested he was in individual differences as against general principles. He once wrote to Abraham:

> "Personality" . . . is a rather indefinite expression taken from surface psychology, and it doesn't contribute much to our understanding of the real processes, i.e. metapsychologically. (Quoted in Jones, 1955, p. 438)

Despite the fact that he wrote great case histories, he used them to illustrate his abstract formulations, and had no conviction about the scientific value or interest of the single case except as a possible source of new ideas.

The inclination to generalize sweepingly may be seen also in Freud's tendency to stretch the bounds of his concepts. The best–known, not to say most notorious example, is that of sexuality. In his earliest papers, the "sexual etiology of neurosis" meant literal seduction, always involving the stimulation of the genitals. Rather quickly, in the *Three Essays,* the concept was expanded, first to include all of the "partial drives," based on the oral, anal, and phallic–urethral erogenous zones, plus the eye (for voyeurism and exhibitionism). But as he found cases in which other parts of the body seemed to serve the function of sexual organs, Freud extended the concept of erogenous zone to include the proposition that all parts of the skin, plus all the sensitive internal organs, might give rise to sexual excitation. Further, "all comparatively intense affective processes, including even terrifying ones, trench upon sexuality" (1905b, p. 203); and finally:

> It may well be that nothing of considerable importance can occur in the organism without contributing some component to the excitation of the sexual instinct. (p. 205)

A similar process seems to have gone on in Freud's blurring of the distinctions among the various ego instincts, and that between ego instincts and narcissistic libido, which was resolved by his finally putting everything together in the notion of Eros, the life instinct.

METHOD OF WORK.

Having so far surveyed some of the general features of Freud's thinking and his style of scientific theorizing, let us now ask how he worked with his data. So far, we have seen only that he stressed *observation* as the primary tool of scientific empiricism. His most important patient, let us remember, was himself. In his self–analysis (particularly during the late 1890's), he made his fundamental discoveries: the meaning of dreams, the Oedipus complex, childhood sexuality, and so forth. This fact should remind us of his gift for self–observation. It was of course the age of trained introspection as a scientific method of the academic psychologists; but that was something else again. Freud's self–observation was of that kind we call psychologically-minded; he was no phenomenologist, curious about the raw givens of experience or interested in analyzing the data of consciousness in their "presentational immediacy" (Whitehead). Even when looking inward, he tried to penetrate the surface of what he found there, to look for causes in terms of wishes. affects, hopes, fantasies, and the residues of childhood emotional experiences. Consider how little one ever heard of such matters from Wundt or Titchener, and it becomes apparent that Freud's cognitive style played a role in his unique use of a common instrument.

Observation, when applied to his other patients, meant first of all the use of free association. The patient was encouraged to report everything about himself without censorship, so that the analyst might observe directly the struggle to comply with this seemingly simple request, and observe indirectly the broadest range of important life experiences as reported. But these therapeutically significant facts, and the even more important manifestations of the transference that developed in the actual interpersonal situation of treatment, were typically buried in a haystack of trivial details. Freud accordingly had to develop himself into a highly selective instrument which at the same time was as much as possible free of bias. The solution he adopted, that of an "evenly-suspended attention" (1912a, p. 111), matched in its seeming unselectiveness the attitude urged on the freely associating patient; in both, the theory affirmed that the process of suspending conventional standards of conscious judgment would let unconscious forces guide the production and the reception of the data. Only a man with a basic trust in the depths of his own being would have been willing to let his conscious intelligence partially abdicate in this manner.

The principal activity of the analyst, Freud indicated, was offering *interpretations* of the patient's productions. In a way, these constitute a first level of conceptualization (that is, a first processing of data) as well as an intervention that was calculated to produce further and altered material from the patient. In the later processing of the accumulated data on a case, and indeed of other types of data, interpretation plays a crucial role; in some respects, it is what gives psychoanalysis its unique character as a mode of inquiry into human behavior. Whether Freud offered the interpretation to the patient or merely used it in his formulation of the essential features of the case, it often took the *genetic* form of a historical reconstruction of sequences of critical events in the patient's past. Here we see a characteristic feature of Freud's thinking: the use of historical (rather than ahistorical) causality. Since Kurt Lewin, the fashion in psychology has been strongly in favor of ahistorical causality, though the historical form has recently been vigorously argued in a highly sophisticated way (Culbertson, 1963).

As Freud used interpretation in the narrower sense, it was essentially a process of translation, in which meanings in the patient's behavior and words were replaced by a smaller set of other meanings according to more or less specifiable rules (Holt, 1961). But these rules were loose and peculiar, for they incorporated the assumption that the patient's communications had been subjected to a set of (largely defensive) distortions according to the irrational primary process. The analyst's job, therefore, was to reverse the distortions in decoding the patient's productions in order to discern the nature of his unconscious conflicts and his modes of struggling with them. It is thus a method of discovery. With the minor exception of a number of recurrent symbols, the rules for such decoding can be stated in only general terms, and a great deal is left to the analyst's creative use of his own primary process.

Interpretation is therefore obviously difficult to use and easy to abuse, as Freud knew full well. One of his favorite criticisms of dissident former followers was that *their* interpretations were arbitrary or farfetched.

What, then, were his criteria for distinguishing deep and insightful from merely strained and remote interpretations? The most detailed discussions that I have found of this question date back to the middle 1890's, when Freud was defending his theory that neurosis was caused by the repressed trauma of actual sexual seduction in infancy. He gave a number of criteria, like the kind and amount of affect and resistance shown, by which he satisfied himself that the interpretations (or historical constructions) that he offered his patients along these lines were valid, and for believing the reports by some of them that initially stimulated him to essay this approach. Yet as we know, none of those presumed safeguards was sufficient; Freud finally decided to reject the "recollections" as fantasies. To this day, providing criteria for evaluating interpretations remains one of the major unsolved methodological problems in all schools of psychoanalysis.

METHOD OF PROVING POINTS (VERIFICATION)

Once he had made his interpretations and genetic explanations of his various types of data to his own satisfaction, Freud had formed his principal hypotheses. Now he set about proving them. Let us examine the ways he attempted to establish his points by marshalling his evidence and his arguments.

Surprisingly, he often used what is essentially statistical reasoning to make his points. True, it generally takes the simple form of assuring the reader that he has seen the phenomenon in question repeatedly:

> If it were a question of *one* case only like that of my patient, one would shrug it aside. No one would dream of erecting upon a single observation a belief which implies taking such a decisive line. But you must believe me when I assure you that this is not the only case in my experience. (1933, p. 42)

Many psychologists seem to have the impression that Freud frequently based major propositions on single cases; but I have carefully searched all his major case histories for instances, and have found none.[5] He wrote as early as the case of Dora, ''A single case can never be capable of proving a theorem so general as this one'' (1905c, p. 115). In his earliest psychoanalytic papers, Freud again and again quoted such statistics as the following:

> . . . my assertion . . . is supported by the fact that in some eighteen cases of hysteria I have been able to discover this connection in every single symptom, and, where the circumstances allowed, to confirm it by therapeutic success. No doubt you may raise the objection that the nineteenth or the twentieth analysis will perhaps show that hysterical symptoms are derived from other sources as well, and thus reduce the universal validity of the sexual aetiology to one of eighty per cent. By all means let us wait and see; but, since these eighteen cases are at the same time *all* the cases on which I have been able to carry out the work of analysis and since they were not picked out by anyone for my convenience, you will find it understandable that I do not share such an expectation but am prepared to let my belief run ahead of the evidential force of the observations I have so far made. (1896, p. 199f.)

Boring (1954) has pointed out that in such a use of statistical reasoning as this, Freud did not advance beyond Mill's method of agreement, which is his most elementary and least trustworthy canon of induction. In the paper I have just quoted, Freud considered the possibility of using the essence of Mill's recommended joint method of agreement and disagreement. It will be objected, he says, that many children are seduced but do not become hysterical, which he allows to be true without undermining his argument; for he compares seduction to the ubiquitous tubercle bacillus, which is ''inhaled by far more people than are found to fall ill of tuberculosis'' (p. 209), yet the bacillus is the specific determinant of the disease—its necessary but not sufficient cause. He considered the possibility that there may be hysterical patients who have not undergone seduction but quickly dismissed it; such supposed instances had not been psychoanalyzed, so the allegation had not been proved. In the end, therefore, Freud simply argued his way out of the necessity to consider any but his own positive cases, and was thus unable to use statistical reasoning in any cogent or coercive way.

In point of fact, references in his papers to numbers of cases treated dropped out almost entirely after 1900; instead, one finds confident quasi–quantitative claims of this kind: ''This discovery, which was easy to make and could be confirmed as often as one liked . . .'' (1906, p. 272), or such severe admonitions as this:

> The teachings of psychoanalysis are based on an incalculable number of observations and experiences, and only someone who has repeated these observations on himself and on others is in a position to arrive at a judgment of his own upon it. (1940, p. 144)

In the long quotation from 1896 just above, note the entry of another characteristic mode of argument often used by Freud: the theory is proved by its therapeutic successes. Sometimes it is stated with what we have seen to be characteristic hyperbole:

> The fact that in the technique of psycho-analysis a means has been found by which the opposing force [of anticathexis in repression] can be removed and the ideas in question made conscious renders this theory irrefutable. (1923, p. 14)

I could quote many passages in which the same general type of argument is made: Freud cites as ''proof'' or as ''confirmation'' a set of circumstances that does serve to enhance the probability that the statement made is true, but does not nail it down in a rigorous way. The ultimate means of proof, for Freud, was the simple ostensive one:

> We are told that the town of Constance lies on the Bodensee. A student song adds: "if you don't believe it, go and see." I happen to have been there and can confirm the fact ... (1927, p. 25)

In many places, Freud applied this basic principle of reality testing to psychoanalysis—if you don't believe, go and see for yourself; and until you have been analyzed and, preferably, also have been trained to carry out psychoanalyses of others yourself, you have no basis to be skeptical.

Freud did not see that the promulgator of an assertion takes on himself the burden of proving it. It is doubtful that he ever heard of the null hypothesis; surely he had no conception of the sophisticated methodology that this strange term connotes. In several places, he, as it were, quite innocently reveals his unawareness that for empirical propositions to be taken seriously, they should be in principle refutable. For example, after asserting that *"a wish which is represented in a dream must be an infantile one,"* (1900, p. 553; emphasis is Freud's), he remarks:

> I am aware that this assertion cannot be proved to hold universally; but it can be proved to hold frequently, even in unsuspected cases, and it cannot be *contradicted* as a general proposition. (1900, p. 554)

At least, in this passage he showed the realization that a universal proposition cannot be proved; yet later he was to refer to another such

> rule laid down in *The Interpretation of Dreams* . . . [as] since confirmed beyond all doubt, that words and speeches in the dream–content are not freshly formed . . . (1917, p. 228)

On Reading Freud

True, every fresh instance of a claimed universal proposition does strengthen its credibility and the probability that it is trustworthy. If we keep in mind that nothing more is meant in psychoanalytic writing by claims of proof, we shall be on relatively safe ground.

Freud did not usually write as if he were familiar with the distinction between forming hypotheses and testing them. Yet he was aware of it, and at times was modest enough about the exploratory nature of his work:

> Thus this view has been arrived at by inference; and if from an inference of this kind one is led, not to a familiar region, but on the contrary, to one that is alien and new to one's thought, one calls the inference a "hypothesis" and rightly refuses to regard the relation of the hypothesis to the material from which it was inferred as a "proof" of it. It can only be regarded as "proved" if it is reached by another path as well [N.B.: cross–validation!] and if it can be shown to be the nodal point of still other connections. (1905a, p. 177f.)

I have examined Freud's methods of arraying his data and reasoning about them in the attempt to prove his points in two ways: by making a general collection whenever I came across instances where he drew conclusions explicitly, and by a careful scrutiny of all his arguments for the concept of a psychic unconscious in two of his major papers, "A Note on the Unconscious in Psychoanalysis" (1912b) and "The Unconscious" (1915c). It would be tedious and time–consuming to document my analyses of his modes of argument; I shall merely give my conclusion.

It is, quite simply, that Freud seldom *proved* anything in a rigorous sense of the word. He rarely subjected hypotheses to the kind of cross–validational check that he advocated in the last passage quoted. He is often convincing, almost never coercively so. He was quite ready to use devices he spoke of slightingly in his sharp critiques of the reasoning used by his opponents: the authoritative dictum, begging the question, arguments by analogy, and retreats to the discussion of "matters which are so remote from the problems of our observation, and of which we have so little cognizance, that it is as idle to dispute . . . as to affirm" them (1914, p. 79).

Actually, what Freud does is to make use of all the resources of rhetoric. He backs up a general statement by a telling example in which it is clearly operative; he constructs plausible chains of cause and effect (after the principle of *post hoc ergo propter hoc*); he argues a fortiori; and he uses enthymemes to draw reasoned conclusions. An enthymeme corresponds in rhetoric to the syllogism in logic.[6] In it, one premise is often but not necessarily suppressed, and, unlike the syllogism, it is a method of establishing probable rather than exact or absolute truth.

Further, he seeks to win our agreement by a disarming directness of personal address, and by stepping into the role of the opponent to raise difficult arguments against himself, after which his points in refutation seem all the more telling. His writing is vivid with metaphor and personification, with flashes of wit, poetical flights into extended analogies or similes, and many other such devices to avoid a consistently abstract level of discourse. When the line of reasoning in a number of his enthymemes in "The Unconscious" is carefully explicated, it is surprisingly weak and involves several *non sequiturs*. In his attempts to refute others, he frequently made use of the rhetorical device of making the other's argument appear improbable by appealing to its implausibility to common sense and everyday observation.

> In the first place, he [Rank] assumes that the infant has received certain sensory impressions, in particular of a visual kind, at the time of birth, the renewal of which can recall to its memory the trauma of birth and thus evoke a reaction of anxiety. This assumption is quite unfounded and extremely improbable. It is not credible that a child should retain any but tactile and general sensations relating to the process of birth. (1926a, p. 135)

55

On Reading Freud

USE OF FIGURES OF SPEECH

Because I have a special interest in figures of speech, I paid particular attention to the way Freud used this rhetorical device. The editors of the *Standard Edition* have made the task relatively easy by index entries, for each volume, under the heading "Analogies." Picking two volumes more or less at random (XII and XIV), I looked up the 31 analogies so indexed and attempted to see in what way Freud employed them.

As one professor of rhetoric (Genung, 1900) has said, "The value both of example and of analogy is after all rather illustrative than argumentative; they are in reality instruments of exposition, employed to make the subject so clear . . . that men can see the truth or error of it for themselves." For the most part, in these two volumes Freud used analogies as "instruments of exposition," included *after* an argument had been completely stated in its own terms, to add lively, visualizable concreteness; some of them are little jokes, adding a touch of comic relief to lighten the reader's burden. At times, however, the analogy moves into the mainstream of the argument and serves a more direct rhetorical purpose; this is true, surprisingly enough, a good deal more often in Vol. XIV, which contains the austere meta-psychological papers, than in Vol. XII, largely devoted to the case of Schreber and the papers on technique. It turns out, however, that the argumentative use of analogy occurs largely in the polemical passages where Freud is attempting to refute the principal arguments with which Jung and Adler severed their ties to classical psychoanalysis; mostly, it takes the form of ridicule, a form of discrediting an opponent by making his argument appear ludicrous rather than meeting it on its own grounds. It is not difficult to understand how angry Freud must have felt at the apostasies in rapid succession of two of his most gifted and promising adherents, so that strong affect had its usual effect of degrading the level of argument.

Freud used analogies in two other kinds of ways in the metapsychological papers, however. In a few instances, the analogy seems to have played the role of a model. That is, when he wrote that "The complex of melancholia behaves like an open wound, drawing to itself . . . 'anticathexes' . . . from all directions, and emptying the ego until it is totally impoverished'' (1917, p. 253), he revived an image that he had used in an unpublished draft, written and sent to Fliess 20 years earlier (1887-1902, p. 107f.); moreover, he was to use it again five years later in the theory of traumatic neurosis (1920, p. 30). Interestingly enough, in none of these versions did Freud say explicitly what there is about a wound that makes it a useful analogue. Obviously, however, he had in mind the way that leuco-cytes gather around the margins of a physical lesion, a medical mechanism of defense that may well be a principal ancestor of the concept of psychic defense mechanisms. Surely it formed an important pattern of Freud's thought, one that directly influenced the kinds of psychological constructs he invoked and some of what he did with them.

The other use of an extended figure of speech does not employ an analogy in the strict sense and so is not indexed. (Indeed, the vast majority of Freud's analogies are not indexed; only the protracted ones that resemble epic similes. But the text is so dense with tropes of one kind or another that a complete index would be impractically enormous.) I am referring to an example of a characteristic Freudian device, the "scientific myth," as he called the best–known example, the legend of the primal horde. Near the beginning of "Instincts and their Vicissitudes" (1915a), after considering the drive concept quite abstractly from the standpoint of physiology, and in relation to the concept of "stimulus," he suddenly says:

> Let us imagine ourselves in the situation of an almost entirely helpless living organism, as yet unorientated in the world, which is receiving stimuli in its nervous substance. (p. 119)

What an arresting image! And note that this is no mere conventional figure of speech, in which man is compared point by point to a hypothetical primitive organism. Instead, here we are given an invitation to *identification*. Freud encourages us to anthropomorphize, to picture how it would be if we, as adult and thinking people, were in the helpless and exposed position he goes on to sketch so graphically. It seems natural, therefore, when he easily attributes to the little animalcule not only consciousness but self-awareness—an attribute we realize, on sober reflection, to be a uniquely human and rather sophisticated achievement. His introductory phrase, however, invites us at once to suspend disbelief and waive the usual rules of scientific thinking. It's like a child's "let's pretend"; it leads us to expect that this is not so much a way of pushing his argument forward as a temporary illustrative digression; like his usual analogies, a pictorial holiday from hard theoretical thinking. We soon discover that he uses this suspension of the rules as a way of allowing himself a freedom and fluidity of . reasoning that would not otherwise be acceptable. And yet he proceeds thereafter as if the point had been proved in a rigorous way.

The conception of a completely vulnerable organism swimming in a sea of dangerous energies was another recurrent image that seems to have made a profound impression on Freud. It plays an even more critical role in the development of his argument in *Beyond the Pleasure Principle*, though it is introduced in a somewhat soberer fashion ("Let us picture a living organism in its most simplified possible form as an undifferentiated vesicle of a substance that is susceptible to stimulation"; 1920, p. 26). Yet he does not explicitly present it as a hypothesis about the nature of the first living organism; in fact, it never becomes quite clear just what kind of existential status this "vesicle" has. Freud proceeds with some digressions to suppose that the organism would be killed by the "most powerful energies" surrounding it if it remained unprotected, and that the cooking of its outer layer formed a crust that protected what lay underneath. Suddenly, Freud takes a mighty leap from this original, partly damaged living cell: "In highly developed organisms the receptive cortical layer of the former vesicle has long been withdrawn into the depths of the interior of the body, though portions of it have been left behind on the surface immediately beneath the general shield against stimuli'' (p. 27f.). Implicitly, he has assumed that his unicellular Adam has been fruitful and has populated the earth, always passing along its original scabs by the inheritance of acquired characters.

Just when you think that Freud is presenting a highly fanciful, Lamarckian theory about the origin of the skin, he switches the metaphor. First, however, he hypothesizes that ''The specific unpleasure of physical pain is probably the result of the protective shield having been broken through . . . Cathectic energy is summoned from all sides to provide sufficiently high cathexes of energy in the environs of the breach. An 'anticathexis' on a grand scale is set up, for whose benefit all the other psychical systems are impoverished'' (p. 30). Along about here, the sharp-eyed reader will do a double take: it sounded as if Freud was talking about a physical wound in the skin, but what gets summoned to its margins is not the white blood cells but quanta of psychic energy! Then on the next page, we learn that ''preparedness for anxiety and the hypercathexis of the receptive systems constitute the last line of defense of the shield against stimuli'' (p. 31). This shield, which seemed so concrete and physical, turns out to be a metaphor wrapped in a myth.

It is true that this whole fourth chapter was introduced by the following disarmingly candid paragraph:

> What follows is speculation, often far–fetched speculation, which the reader will consider or dismiss according to his individual predilection. It is further an attempt to follow out an idea consistently, out of curiosity to see where it will lead. (1920, p. 24)

In light of the later development of Freud's theories, in which as we have seen he came to lean on this curious tissue of speculations as if it were a stoutly supportive fabric, it seems that this modest disclaimer is another "let's pretend," so that Freud, like Brittania, may waive the rules.

FREUD'S RHETORIC.

The upshot of this survey of the means Freud used in his search after truth is that he relied heavily on all the classical devices of rhetoric. The effect is not to prove, in any rigorous sense, but to persuade, using to some extent the devices of an essayist but even more those of an orator or advocate, who writes his brief and then argues the case with all the eloquence at his disposal. Notice that I have based this conclusion primarily on a survey of Freud's most technical, theoretical papers and books. In such masterly works for the general reader as his various series of introductory lectures (1916-17; 1933) or *The Question of Lay Analysis* (1926b), the rhetorical form is even more explicit; the last named work is actually cast in the form of an extended dialogue, harking directly back to the classic Greek texts of which Freud was so fond.

There is a tendency today to take "rhetoric" as a slightly pejorative term. Except in the minds of the Platonists, it had no such connotation in classical times. As Kennedy (1963) points out,

> One of the principal interests of the Greeks was rhetoric . . . . In its origin and intention rhetoric was natural and good: it produced clarity, vigor and beauty, and it rose logically from the conditions and qualities of the classical mind. Greek society relied on oral expression . . . . Political agitation was usually accomplished or defeated by word of mouth. The judicial system was similarly oral . . . All literature was written to be heard, and even when reading to himself a Greek read aloud (p. 3f.)

Rhetoric, as the theory of persuasive communication, was necessarily a good deal more than that; it was the only form of *criticism* in Greek thought. In one of Aristotle's definitions, rhetoric is "a process of criticism wherein lies the path to the principles of all inquiries" *(Topics I;* quoted in McBurney, 1936, p. 54).

Since science was not as sharply differentiated from other methods of seeking truth then as it later became, rhetoric was the closest thing to scientific methodology that the Greeks had. In Artistotle's presentation, there were two kinds of truth: exact or certain, and probable. The former was the concern of science, which operated by means of syllogistic logic or complete enumeration. All other kinds of merely probabilistic knowledge were the realms of argumentative inquiry, which operated by means of dialectic and rhetoric. But the only discipline to which Aristotle's criterion of "unqualified scientific knowledge" applies is mathematics (today construed to include symbolic logic); only in such a purely formal science can strict deductive procedure be used and certainty attained.

I go into this much detail about Greek rhetoric because it suggests to me a possibly illuminating hypothesis. About all I can do to make it plausible is to point out that Freud did know Greek well and read the classics in the original; and among the five courses or seminars he took with Brentano was one on Logic and at least one on "The philosophy of Aristotle" (Bernfeld, 1951). If Freud received any formal training in methodology, the critical philosophy of science, it was with the Aristotelian philosopher–psychologist Brentano. I have not found anywhere in Freud's works any reference to Aristotle's *Rhetoric* or any direct evidence that he knew it; the best I can do is to offer these bits of circumstantial evidence (or, as Aristotle would have put it, to make an argument from signs). It is, then, possible that Freud was in this way introduced to the devices of rhetoric and enthymemetic or probabilistic reasoning as the legitimate instruments of inquiry into empirical matters. His rejection of speculative, deductively exact system–building may indicate that he was accepting the Aristotelian dichotomy between exact (or mathematical) and probable truth and choosing to work in the real and approximate world where rhetoric was the appropriate means of approaching an only relative truth.

The way I have put this point of view deliberately blurs a fine but important distinction between two kinds of probabilism: that of rhetoric, in which the technical means of plausible reasoning are used to enhance in the mind of the listener the subjective probability that the speaker's thesis is true; and that of modern skeptical science, which uses the most exact and rigorous methods possible to measure the probability of a thesis—that is, the amount of confidence we can have that it is a good approximation to a reality that can be approached only asymptotically. For the former, proof is the establishment of belief; for the latter, verification is the rejection of a surely false null hypothesis and the temporary acceptance of an alternative as the best one available at the moment. I do not believe that Freud saw this distinction clearly; at any rate, he did not write as if he thought in these terms.

Surely he was a superb rhetorician, whether he was a conscious one or not. He was a master of all its five parts, of which we have discussed so far primarily aspects of the first, invention, which includes the modes of proof: direct evidence, argumentation from the evidence, and indirect means of persuasion by the force of personal impression or presence *(ethos)* or by "the emotion he is able to awaken by his verbal appeals, his gestures," etc. *(pathos)* (Kennedy, 1963, p. 10). Freud's excellence at ethos and pathos, and at the last two of the parts, memory and delivery, is described by Jones:

> He was a fascinating lecturer. The lectures were always enlightened by his peculiar ironic humor . . . He always used a low voice, perhaps because it could become rather harsh if strained, but spoke with the utmost distinctness. He never used any notes, and seldom made much preparation for a lecture . . .

The adoring biographer goes on to state that "He never used oratory," but he seems to be using the term in the modern sense as synonymous with bombast, which was surely not what the ancient Greeks meant. What Jones's description conveys is a very effective kind of personal presence. Freud

> talked intimately and conversationally . . . One felt he was addressing himself to us personally . . . There was no flicker of condescension in it, not even a hint of a teacher. The audience was assumed to consist of highly intelligent people to whom he wished to communicate some of his recent experiences . . . (Jones, 1953, p. 341f.)

With respect to the remaining two parts in the Aristotelian five-part division of rhetoric, arrangement and style, much could be written, but it would trench on literary criticism. The Greeks analyzed style evaluatively in terms of the four virtues of correctness, clarity, ornamentation, and propriety; I will merely record my impression that Freud would earn top grades on all of these counts.

Freud prided himself on having held aloof from the brawling controversy of polemics. Only once, he says with some pride in his *Autobiography* (1925), did he directly answer a critic, in 1894. Yet it is obvious that he wrote in a polemical mood much of the rest of his life, always with a consciousness that the reader might be hostile. He was explicit about it in many letters to his followers. For example, to Jung in 1909:

> We cannot avoid the resistances, so why not rather challenge them at once? In my opinion attack is the best defense. Perhaps you underestimate the intensity of these resistances when you hope to counter them with small concessions. (Quoted in Jones, 1955, p. 436)

And to Pfister two years later:

> It is scarcely possible to have a public debate on psychoanalysis; one has no common ground and there is nothing to be done against the lurking emotions.

63

On Reading Freud

> The movement is concerned with the depths, and debates about it must remain as unsuccessful as the theological disputations at the time of the Reformation. (Jones, 1955, p. 450f.)

Feeling this strongly, Freud could not have done other than to approach the task of exposition as one of argument. The amazing thing is that the skilled verbal swordsman let the scientist in Freud have the floor as much as he did.[7]

SUMMARY

And now let me return to cognitive style in its contemporary technical sense. As Klein uses it, a cognitive style characterizes a person and his unique way of processing information. There are, of course, similarities among people in these respects, and the dimensions into which cognitive styles may be analyzed are called *cognitive control principles*. (The most nearly definitive statement of the principles discovered by Klein and his collaborators is contained in the monograph by Gardner, Holzman, Klein, Linton, & Spence, 1959.)

We have seen that Freud had, to an unusual degree, a tolerance for ambiguity and inconsistency. He needed it. As I argued in earlier sections, above, his thinking always took place in the context of pervasive conflicts. In the first of these, tender-minded, speculative, wide-ranging and fantasylike thinking deriving from *Naturphilosophie* was pitted against the disciplined physicalistic physiology of his revered teachers. The second conflict involved sets of propositions about reality and human beings and, more generally, two opposing world views, a humanistic and a mechanistic image of man—one artistic, literary, and philosophical, the other grounded in a reductionistic ideal of Science and its promise of progress through objectivity and rigor. Moreover, Freud's metapsychological model clashes at many crucial points with reality; so a further conflict took place between one set of Freud's basic orienting assumptions and his growing knowlege of the facts about behavior.

Because of all these conflicts, I believe that he had to operate in his characteristically loose–jointed way. If he had had a compulsive need for clarity and consistency, he would probably have had to make choices and resolve his intellectual conflicts. If he had followed the way of hard-nosed science, he would have been the prisoner of the methods and assumptions he learned in his medical school and its laboratories—another, more gifted Exner, who might have written a series of excellent neurological books like the one on aphasia, but who would probably have emulated his cautious contemporaries in steering clear of hysterical patients. And if he had turned his back on the effort at scientific discipline and had opened the floodgates to his speculative inventiveness, we might have had a spate of Nature-philosophical essays but nothing like psychoanalysis; or if the humanist in him had decisively won over the mechanist, he might have written brilliant novels but would never have made his great discoveries.

But because Freud was able to keep one foot in art and one in science, because he could comfortably retain the security of a model inherited from respected authorities without its wholly blinding him to the aspects of reality for which it had no place, he was able to be extraordinarily creative. Productive originality in science involves a dialectic of freedom and control, flexibility and rigor, speculation and self–critical checking. Without some loosening of the chains of conventional, safe, secondary–process thinking, there can be little originality; Pegasus must have a chance to take wing. But liberation alone is not enough. If flexibility is not accompanied by disci-pline, it becomes fluidity, and then we have a visionary, a *Phantast* (as Freud once called himself and Fliess) instead of a scientist. It was just this that Freud feared in himself. The daring but fruitful ideas must be sorted from the merely daring or positively harebrained ones; insights must be painstakingly checked; new concepts must be worked into a structure of laws so that they fit smoothly, buttress and extend the edifice. All of this takes an attitude that is antithetical to the earlier, more strictly creative one. It is asking a great deal of a man, therefore, that he be adept in both types of thinking and able to shift appropriately from the role of dreamer to that of critic. Perhaps that is one reason that we have so few truly great scientists.

This first major characteristic of Freud's cognitive style is strikingly reminiscent of the principle of cognitive control called by Klein and his associates *tolerance for instability* or for unrealistic experiences. "'Tolerant' subjects [as compared to intolerant ones] seemed in equally adequate contact with external reality, but were much more relaxed in their acceptance of both ideas and perceptual organizations that required deviation from the conventional'' (Gardner et al., 1959, p. 93). It is a relaxed and imaginative kind of mind, opposed to the kind that rigidly clings to a literally interpreted reality. And Freud (1933) was unusually willing to entertain parapsychological hypotheses that go well beyond scientifically conventional concepts of reality. Telepathy is quite literally an "unrealistic experience."

If Freud was tolerant of ambiguity, inconsistency, instability, and unrealistic experiences, there was one similar-sounding state that he could *not* tolerate: meaninglessness, the assumption that a process was stochastic or that a phenomenon occurred because of random error. No doubt this attitude led him at times into overinterpreting data and reading meaning —especially dynamic or motivational meaning—into behavior unwarrantedly. But it also spurred his basic discoveries, such as that of the primary process and the interpretability of dreams, neurotic and psychotic symptoms.

Let us see whether the remaining five dimensions described by Gardner, Holzman, Klein, Linton, and Spence do not form a useful framework for summarizing Freud's manner of thinking. It surely seems probable that Freud was strongly field–independent. Inner–directed he surely was, and Graham (1955) has shown an empirical connection between Riesman's (1950) and Witkin's (1949) concepts. Here is the Gardner et al. description of the kind of person who is field–independent—not markedly dependent on the visual field for orientation to the upright: he is characterized by "(a) activity in dealing with the environment; (b) . . .'inner life' and effective control of impulses, with low anxiety; and (c) high self-esteem, including confidence in the body and a relatively adult body–image." It sounds a good deal like Freud, except possibly for his ambivalent and rather hypochondriacal attitude towards his body—"poor Konrad," as he wryly called it. Linton (1955) has further shown that field–independent people are little susceptible to group influence, surely true of Freud.

In his preference for a small number of extremely broadly defined motivational concepts, Freud seems to have had a broad *equivalence range*. And on Klein's dimension of *flexible versus constricted control*, Freud would assuredly have scored well over at the flexible end. Was he not "relatively comfortable in situations that involved contradictory or intrusive cues . . . not overimpressed with a dominant stimulus organization if . . . another part of the field [was] more appropriate"? And surely he "did not tend to suppress feeling and other internal cues." This is the description of the flexibly–controlled subject (Gardner et al., 1959, p. 53f.).

The other two dimensions of cognitive control seem less relevant. *Scanning* (as against *focusing*) as a way of using attention might seem to suggest the way Freud attended to his patients, but it is qualitatively different. Scanning is accompanied by the ability to concentrate on what is important, but at the cost of isolation of affect and overintellectualization; it is not so much passively relaxed attending as a restlessly roaming search for everything that might be useful. And so far as I can determine, Freud was not either a *leveler* or a *sharpener*; he neither habitually blurred distinctions and oversimplified nor was he specially alert to fine differences and always on the lookout for slight changes in situations.

It is fair to conclude, I think, that some of these principles of cognitive control seem quite apt and useful, though a good deal of the flavor of Freud's uniqueness as a thinker is lost when we apply them to him. In addition, a couple of other aspects of cognitive style have been suggested as characterizing Freud. Kaplan (1964) begins a general discussion of the cognitive style of behavioral scientists thus: '' . . .thought and its expression are surely not wholly unrelated to one another, and how scientific findings are formulated for incorporation into the body of knowledge often reflects stylistic traits of the thinking behind them'' (p. 259). He goes on to describe six principal styles, and mentions Freud in connection with the first two of them: the literary and the academic styles. The literary style is often concerned with individuals, interpreted ''largely in terms of the specific purposes and perspectives of the actors, rather than in terms of the abstract and general categories of the scientist's own explanatory scheme . . . Freud's studies of Moses and Leonardo . . . exhibit something of this style.'' The academic style, by contrast, is ''much more abstract and general . . . There is some attempt to be precise, but it is verbal rather than operational. Ordinary words are used in special senses, to constitute a technical vocabulary. . . . [Treatment of the data] tends to be highly theoretical, if not, indeed, purely speculative. System is introduced by way of great 'principles,' applied over and over to specific cases, which illustrate the generalization rather than serve as proofs for it.'' Kaplan cites ''essays in psychoanalytic theory'' generally as examples, but I trust it will be apparent how well these descriptions characterize and summarize much of what I have brought out about Freud.

A Decalogue for the Reader of Freud

To conclude, let me come back to my original statement that a better understanding of Freud's intellectual background and cognitive style would help the contemporary reader to read him with insight rather than confusion, and try to give it substance in the form of ten admonitions. Like another decalogue, they can be reduced to one golden rule: be empathic rather than projective—learn what are the man's own terms and take him on them.

1. Beware of lifting statements out of context. This practice is particularly tempting to textbook writers, polemical critics, and research–minded clinical psychologists who are more eager to get right to the testing of propositions than to undertake the slow study of a large corpus of theory. There is no substitute for reading enough of Freud to get his full meaning, which is almost never fully expressed in a single paragraph on no matter how specific a point.

2. Don't take Freud's extreme formulations literally. Treat them as his way of calling your attention to a point. When he says "never," "invariably," "conclusively," and the like, read on for the qualifying and softening statements. Remember the change that has taken place in the general atmosphere since Freud wrote his major works; social acceptance and respectability have replaced shock and hostility, which made Freud feel that his was a small and lonely voice in a cold wilderness, so that he had to shout in order to be heard at all.

3. Look out for inconsistencies; don't either trip over them or seize on them with malicious glee, but take them as incomplete dialectic formulations awaiting the synthesis that Freud's cognitive style made him consistently draw back from.

4. Be on the watch for figurative language, personification in particular (reified formulations of concepts as homunculi). Remember that it is there

primarily for color even though it did at times lead Freud astray himself, and that it is fairest to him to rely primarily on those of his statements of issues that are least poetic and dramatic.

5. Don't expect rigorous definitions; look rather for the meanings of his terms in the ways they are used over a period of time. And don't be dismayed if you find a word being used at one place in its ordinary, literary meaning, at another in a special technical sense which changes with the developmental status of the theory. An enterprise like the *Dictionary of Psychoanalysis*, put together by a couple of industrious but misguided analysts who lifted definition-like sentences from many of Freud's works, is completely mistaken in conception and betrays a total misunderstanding of Freud's style of thinking and working.

6. Be benignly skeptical about Freud's assertions of proof that something has been established beyond doubt. Remember that he had different standards of proof than we do today, that he rejected experiment partly from a too-narrow conception of it and partly because he had found it stylistically incompatible long before even the first works of R. A. Fisher, and tended to confuse a replicated observation with a verified theory of the phenomenon in question.

7. Remember that Freud was overfond of dichotomies, even when his data were better conceptualized as continuous variables; in general, don't assume that the theory is invalidated by its being stated much of the time in methodologically indefensible form.

8. Be wary of Freud's persuasiveness. Keep in mind that he was a powerful rhetorician in areas where his scientific footing was uncertain. Though he was often right, it was not always for the reasons he gave, which are almost never truly sufficient to prove his case, and not always to the extent that he hoped.

Finally, be particularly cautious not to gravitate toward either of two extreme and equally untenable positions: that is,

9. Don't take Freud's every sentence as a profound truth which may present difficulties but only because of our own inadequacies, our pedestrian difficulty in keeping up with the soaring mind of a genius who did not always bother to explicate steps that were obvious to him, but which we must supply by laborious exegetical scholarship. This is the temptation of the scholars working from within the psychoanalytic institutes, those earnest Freudians who, to Freud's annoyance, had already begun to emerge during his lifetime. For most of us in the universities, the corresponding temptation is the more dangerous one:

10. Don't let yourself get so offended by Freud's lapses from methodological purity that you dismiss him altogether. Almost any reader can learn an enormous lot from Freud if he will listen carefully and sympathetically and not take his pronouncements too seriously.

Notes

1. Parts of the text have been adapted, with permission of the publishers, from previously published papers (Holt, 1963, 1965b, 1968, 1972). I am grateful to Aldine Publishing Co., the American Image, and the Macmillan Co. for their kind cooperation.

2. Ellenberger (1970, p. 460) tells us that Freud showed the playwright Lenormand "the works of Shakespeare and of the Greek tragedians on his [office] shelves and said: 'Here are my masters.' He maintained that the essential themes of his theories were based on the intuition of the poets."

3. True (as M. M. Gill has kindly pointed out to me), in the "Project" Freud did explicitly deny that consciousness is an epiphenomenon. Yet the whole trend of the "Project" demands the view he was unwilling to espouse: it is an attempt to account for behavior and neurosis in purely mechanistic terms, without the intervention of any mental entities in the causal process. Indeed, I believe that it was largely because he could not succeed in his aim without postulating a conscious ego as an agent in the process of defense, and because he could not attain a satisfactory mechanistic explanation of consciousness, that Freud abandoned the "Project."

4. "As a young doctor I worked for a long time at the Chemical Institute without ever becoming proficient in the skills which that science demands; and for that reason in my waking life I have never liked thinking of this barren and indeed humiliating episode in my apprenticeship. On the other hand I have a regularly recurring dream of working in the laboratory, of carrying out analyses and of having various experiences there. These dreams are disagreeable in the same way as examination dreams and they are never very distinct. While I was interpreting one of them, my attention was eventually attracted by the word *'analysis'*, which gave me a key to their understanding. Since those days I have become an 'analyst', and I now carry out analyses which are very highly spoken of . . ." (1900, p. 475)

5. See above, however, for examples of his generalizing freely from self-observation. Apparently, the inherently compelling nature of introspective data overrode his general caution.

6. For examples, see the passages quoted from Freud (1901, on p. 45 above, and the next passage quoted, on p. 46), above.

7. As a brief ecological aside, I would like to suggest that Freud might have been less of a fighter in his writing if he had worked from the protective security of an academic position. His precious Professorship did not carry tenure nor a salary; Freud operated always from the exposed and lonely situation of private practice.

References

Amacher, P. 1965. Freud's neurological education and its influence on psychoanalytic theory. *Psychological Issues*, 4: Monograph No. 16.

Andersson, O. 1962. *Studies in the prehistory of psychoanalysis: the etiology of psychoneuroses and some related themes in Sigmund Freud's scientific writings and letters, 1886–1896*. Stockholm: Svenska Bokförlaget Norstedts.

Bernfeld, S. 1944. Freud's earliest theories and the school of Helmholtz. *Psychoanalytic Quarterly*, 13: 342–362.

———— 1951. Sigmund Freud, M.D., 1882–1885. *International Journal of Psychoanalysis*, 32: 204–217.

Boring, E. G. 1954. Review of "The life and work of Sigmund Freud," Vol. I, by Ernest Jones. *Psychological Bulletin*, 51: 433–437.

Breuer, J., and Freud, S. 1955. Studies on hysteria. *Standard Edition*, Vol. 2. London: Hogarth.

Bry, Ilse, and Rifkin, A.H. 1962. Freud and the history of ideas: primary sources, 1886–1910. In *Science and Psychoanalysis*, Vol. V., ed. J.H. Masserman. New York: Grune & Stratton.

Chein, I. 1972. *The science of behavior and the image of man*. New York: Basic Books.

Cranefield, P.F. 1957. The organic physics of 1847 and the biophysics of today. *Journal of the History of Medicine*, 12: 407–423.

Culbertson, J.T. 1963. *The minds of robots*. Urbana: University of Illinois Press.

Darwin, C. (1859) *On the origin of species*. Cambridge: Harvard University Press, 1964.

Ellenberger, H. F. 1956. Fechner and Freud. *Bulletin of the Menninger Clinic*, 20: 201–214.

———— 1970. *The discovery of the unconscious; the history and evolution of dynamic psychiatry*. New York: Basic Books.

Freud, S. (1895) Project for a scientific psychology. *Standard Edition*, Vol. 1. london: Hogarth Press, 1966.

———— (1896) The aetiology of hysteria. *Standard Edition*, Vol. 3. London: Hogarth, 1962.

———— (1887–1902) *The origins of psychoanalysis*. New York: Basic Books, 1954.

———— (1900) The interpretation of dreams. *Standard Edition*, Vols. 4 & 5. London: Hogarth, 1953.

———— (1901) The psychopathology of everyday life. *Standard Edition*, Vol. 6. London: Hogarth, 1960.

———— (1905a) Jokes and their relation to the unconscious. *Standard Edition*, Vol. 8. London: Hogarth, 1960.

———— (1905b) Three essays on the theory of sexuality. *Standard Edition*, Vol. 7. London: Hogarth, 1953.

———— (1905c) Fragment of an analysis of a case of hysteria. *Standard Edition*, Vol. 7. London: Hogarth, 1953.

———— (1906) My views on the part played by sexuality in the aetiology of the neuroses. *Standard Edition*, Vol. 7. London: Hogarth, 1953.

———— (1912a) Recommendations to physicians practising psycho-analysis. *Standard Edition*, Vol. 12. London: Hogarth, 1958.

———— (1912b) A note on the unconscious in psycho-analysis. *Standard Edition*, Vol. 12. London: Hogarth, 1958.

———— (1913) Totem and taboo. *Standard Edition*, Vol. 13. London: Hogarth, 1955.

———— (1914) On narcissism: An introduction. *Standard Edition*, Vol. 14. London: Hogarth, 1957.

———— (1915a) Instincts and their vicissitudes. *Standard Edition*, Vol. 14. London: Hogarth, 1957.

———— (1915b) Repression. *Standard Edition*, Vol. 14. London: Hogarth, 1957.

———— (1915c) The unconscious. *Standard Edition*, Vol. 14. London: Hogarth, 1957.

———— (1916–17) Introductory lectures on psycho-analysis. *Standard Edition*, Vols. 15 & 16. London: Hogarth, 1963.

———— (1917) Mourning and melancholia. *Standard Edition*, Vol. 14. London: Hogarth, 1957.

———— (1920) Beyond the pleasure principle. *Standard Edition*, Vol. 18. London: Hogarth, 1955.

———— (1921) Group psychology and the analysis of the ego. *Standard Edition*, Vol. 18. London: Hogarth, 1955.

———— (1923) The ego and the id. *Standard Edition*, Vol. 19. London: Hogarth, 1961.

———— (1925) An autobiographical study. *Standard Edition*, Vol. 20. London: Hogarth, 1959.

———— (1926a) Inhibitions, symptoms and anxiety. *Standard Edition*, Vol. 20. London: Hogarth, 1959.

———— (1926b) The question of lay analysis. *Standard Edition*, Vol. 20. London: Hogarth, 1959.

References —On Reading Freud

——— (1927) The future of an illusion. *Standard Edition*, Vol. 21. London: Hogarth, 1961.

——— (1930) Civilization and its discontents. *Standard Edition*, Vol. 21. London: Hogarth, 1961.

——— (1933) New introductory lectures on psycho-analysis. *Standard Edition*, Vol. 22. London: Hogarth, 1964.

——— (1934–38) Moses and monotheism: three essays. *Standard Edition*, Vol. 23. London: Hogarth, 1964.

——— (1940) An outline of psycho-analysis. *Standard Edition*, Vol. 23. London: Hogarth, 1964.

——— 1960) *Letters of Sigmund Freud*. E. L. Freud. New York: Basic Books.

Galdston, I. 1956. Freud and romantic medicine. *Bulletin of the History of Medicine*, 30: 489–507.

Gardner, R. W., Holzman, P. S., Klein, G. S. , Linton, Harriet B., and Spence, D. P. 1959. Cognitive control, a study of individual consistencies in cognitive behavior. *Psychological Issues*, 1, Monograph No. 4.

Genung, J. F. 1900. *The working principles of rhetoric*. Boston: Ginn.

Graham, Elaine. 1955. Inner-directed and other-directed attitudes. Unpublished doctoral dissertation, Yale University

Holt, R. R. 1961. Clinical judgment as a disciplined inquiry. *Journal of Nervous and Mental Disease*, 133: 369–382.

——— 1962. A critical examination of Freud's concept of bound vs. free cathexis. *Journal of the American Psychoanalytic Association*, 10: 475–525.

——— 1963. Two influences on Freud's scientific thought: a fragment of intellectual biography. In *The study of lives*, ed. R. W. White. New York: Atherton Press.

——— 1964. Imagery: the return of the ostracized. *American Psychologist*, 194: 254–264.

——— 1965a. A review of some of Freud's biological assumptions and their influence on his theories. In *Psychoanalysis and current biological thought*, ed. N. Greenfield and W. Lewis. Madison: University of Wisconsin Press.

——— 1965b. Freud's cognitive style. *American Imago*, 22: 167–179.

——— 1967. Beyond vitalism and mechanism: Freud's concept of psychic energy. In *Science and Psychoanalysis*, ed. J. H. Masserman. Vol. XI, New York: Grune & Stratton.

References— On Reading Freud

———— 1968. Freud, Sigmund. *International Encyclopedia of the Social Sciences*, Vol. 6. New York: Macmillan, The Free Press.

———— 1972a. Freud's mechanistic and humanistic images of man. In *Psychoanalysis and contemporary science*, ed. R.R. Holt and E. Peterfreund. Vol. I. New York: Macmillan

———— 1972b. On the nature and generality of mental imagery. In *The function and nature of imagery*, ed. P. W. Sheehan. New York: Academic Press.

Hunter, R. A., and Macalpine, I., eds. 1963. *Three hundred years of psychiatry, 1535–1860: a history presented in selected English texts*. London: Oxford University Press.

Jackson, S. W. 1969. The history of Freud's concepts of regression. *Journal of the American Psychoanalytic Association*, 17: 743–784.

Jones, E. 1953, 1955, 1957. *The life and work of Sigmund Freud*, Vols. I, II, & III. New York: Basic Books.

Kaplan, A. 1964. *The conduct of inquiry*. San Francisco: Chandler.

Kennedy, G. 1963. *The art of persuasion in Greece*. Princeton: Princeton University Press.

Klein, G. S. 1951. The personal world through perception. In *Perception: An approach to personality*, ed. R. R. Blake and G. V. Ramsey. New York: Ronald Press.

———— 1970. *Perception, motives, and personality*. New York: Knopf.

Linton, Harriet B. 1955. Dependence on external influence: correlates in perception, attitudes, and judgment. *Journal of Abnormal and Social Psychology*, 51: 502–507.

McBurney, J. H. 1936. The place of the enthymeme in rhetorical theory. *Speech Monographs*, 3: 49–74.

Nunberg, H. (1931) The synthetic function of the ego. *In Practice and theory of psychoanalysis*. New York: Nervous & Mental Diseases Publishing Co., 1948, pp. 120–136.

Rapaport, D. 1959. The structure of psychoanalytic theory: A systematizing attempt. In *Psychology: A study of a science*, Vol. 3, ed. S. Koch. New York: McGraw-Hill.

———— and Gill, M. M. 1959. The points of view and assumptions of metapsychology. *International Journal of Psycho–Analysis*, 40: 153–162.

Riesman, D. 1950. *The lonely crowd*. New Haven: Yale University Press.

References — On Reading Freud

Spehlmann, R. 1953. *Sigmund Freuds neurologische Schriften: Eine Unter-suchung zur Vorgeschichte der Psychoanalyse.* Berlin: Springer Verlag. (English summary by H. Kleinschmidt in *Annual Survey of Psychoanalysis, 1953,* 4: 693–706).

Witkin, H. A. 1949. Perception of body position and of the position of the visual field. *Psychological Monographs,*63, (7, Whole No. 302).

Abstracts

of the Standard Edition of
the Complete Psychological Works of

Sigmund Freud

Edited by
Carrie Lee Rothgeb

Foreword
to the Abstracts of the Standard Edition

The mental health needs of our Nation are being met in a variety of ways—one of them the important area of dissemination and integration of existing knowledge.

We at the National Institute of Mental Health are convinced that those responsible for research and training in mental health, regardless of their theoretical persuasions, stand to benefit from the infusion of new knowledge—to stimulate their critical processes and to contribute to the growing body of scientific knowledge through their fresh appraisals.

Such benefits and contributions are enhanced and facilitated when interpreted and acted upon in the light of existing knowledge. An important aim of the Institute, through its National Clearinghouse for Mental Health Information, is to make that knowledge available widely and in a form to encourage its use.

In this spirit, the Clearinghouse collaborated with the American Psychoanalytic Association in a pioneer effort to abstract the *Standard Edition of Freud.*

While we recognize that Freud's theoretical concepts are representative of but one school of thought in psychiatry, we are certain they are unique in the dialogues they have stimulated, in the research they have fostered, and in the contribution they have made to major therapeutic efforts. This, then, is one step toward our ultimate aim of providing access to knowledge that will promote far ranging investigation of a host of philosophies and approaches.

Abstracts of the Standard Edition of Freud is a comprehensive compilation of abstracts, keyed to all the psychoanalytic concepts found in the *Standard Edition of Freud* edited by James Stachey. The index is designed as a guide for both the professional and the lay person. We feel the abstracts will spur further inquiry to lead to more efficient investigation. This volume is symbolic of the NIMH effort, through the National Clearinghouse for Mental Health Information to aid the communication process.

In this, the twenty-fifth anniversary year of the National Mental Health Act, it is fitting not only that we look to future advances in the mental health sciences but also that we gain a greater perspective of past contributions. This work serves as a model of what can be done and what will be done with increasing frequency by the Institute and, just as importantly, by others.

BERTRAM S. BROWN, M.D.
Director

Editor's Preface
to the Abstracts of the Standard Edition

Work was begun on the abstracting of the *Standard Edition of the Complete Psychological Works of Sigmund Freud* (James Strachey, ed., Hogarth Press, London) in order to make these abstracts available through the computer search system of the National Clearinghouse for Mental Health Information. It soon became evident that their utility could be greatly enhanced by providing a printed volume of all abstracts and a subject index. This publication was, therefore, prepared to fill a pressing need regarding secondary reference to Freud's work.

The accession number assigned to each abstract relates the Tyson and Strachey "Chronological Hand-list of Freud's Works" (*International Journal of Psycho-analysis*, 1956) to the volume and page number of the *Standard Edition*. Thus, in the number 1886F 1/21 1886F refers to the Tyson and Strachey number and 1/21 refers to Vol. 1 page 21 of the *Standard Edition*. A few of the page numbers have been adjusted (moved forward or backward) by one or two pages due to editor's notes or introductions. This numbering system is also used in the KWOC (Key-Word-Out-of-Context) subject index. Sequence of the abstracts in this publication follows the *Standard Edition*.

The National Clearinghouse for Mental Health Information is grateful to Dr. Bernard D. Fine, Chairman, Committee on Indexing, American Psychoanalytic Association for preparing the list of units for abstracting and for assisting with the review of the abstracts; and to Dr. George H. Klumpner, Coordinator, Chicago Psychoanalytic Indexing Research Group for preparing the cross-references from the Tyson-Strachey numbers to the *Standard Edition* and assisting in the preparation of the KWOC Index.

CARRIE LEE ROTHGEB, *Chief*
Technical Information Section
National Clearinghouse for
Mental Health Information

Preface to the Abstracts of the Standard Edition

The publication during the past 18 years of the definitive English language edition of the psychological writings of Sigmund Freud has been a milestone achievement for psychoanalysis, for the behavioral sciences, and for the advancement of scientific thought and intellectual progress in general.

These 23 volumes of the *Standard Edition* (it is expected that a final 24th Index volume will be published shortly) with their careful and fluent translation and the thoughtful and extensive synthesizing editorial notes by the late James Strachey and his co-workers have become a unique educational and research source for the graduate psychoanalyst, for the advanced psychological practitioner and research worker, as well as for students and workers in the broad area of the behavioral sciences.

The present volume consisting of abstracts of each paper and editor's notes comprising the complete *Standard Edition* is an outgrowth of the combined persistent interests and efforts of the Committee on Indexing of the American Psychoanalytic Association and the National Clearinghouse for Mental Health Information (NIMH).

The work of the Committee on Indexing in the preparation and quality control of these abstracts has been strongly supported and encouraged consistently by the presiding officers, the Executive Council, and the entire membership of the American Psychoanalytic Association.

It must be understood and appreciated that any attempt to abstract the uniquely literate, closely reasoned writings of Sigmund Freud with their clear, relevant (at times, vivid) clinical examples is an extremely difficult and challenging task. The revised translations of Freud's works in the *Standard Edition* posed major problems (see *Standard Edition* vol. I, General Preface, pp. xviii - xx) in terms of accuracy and meaning; the difficulties in abstracting from these translations are equally monumental. The fact that the abstracting has been attempted at all is an achievement, and a tribute to those who accepted the challenge, especially the National Clearinghouse for Mental Health Information and the professional abstracting service with which it worked.

To the experienced and serious student of Freud's writings and concepts, there will certainly be seen gaps and areas of incompleteness in some of the abstracts, partly due to the intrinsic difficulties mentioned above, and partly to the requirements and rigors of an important and complex computerization project seeking to index and abstract the current behavioral science literature (with the limitation of each abstract to a maximum of 350 words).

During the course of the abstracting project, various additions and revisions were suggested by the Committee on Indexing (aided by several advanced psychoanalytic candidates from the Division of Psychoanalytic Education, Downstate Medical Center, State University of New York, and of the New York Psychoanalytic Institute). As many as possible of these corrections have been incorporated into the final text.

Despite these limitations, the abstracts in their present form should be of inestimable value to those individuals who are interested in an initial understanding of the major concepts of psychoanalysis seen in a historical context as developed by Sigmund Freud. While they will be of considerable assistance in terms of general reference and survey to the graduate psychoanalyst, they will offer tremendous advantages and scope to all workers in the behavioral sciences. Here we may certainly include psychiatrists, psychiatric residents, psychologists and psychiatric social workers, as well as college, graduate, and medical students who are developing or continuing a further and deeper interest and understanding of classical psychoanalysis. Among other incidental yet important uses of these abstracts will be their contribution to the development and publication of an additional index to the *Standard Edition.*

The publication of these abstracts on the occasion of the 25th anniversary of the National Mental Health Act seems an unusually felicitous and appropriate way of honoring Sigmund Freud, psychoanalysis, and the spirit of the legislative act that ushered in a national recognition of the significance of the solution of mental health problems affecting the people of the United States.

BERNARD D. FINE, M.D., F.A.P.A.
Chairman, Committee on Indexing
American Psychoanalytic Association

Abstracts
of the Standard Edition of
the Complete Psychological Works of
Sigmund Freud

Edited by
Carrie Lee Rothgeb

Abstracts of the Standard Edition of the Complete Psychological Works of Sigmund Freud

VOL. I   Pre-Psycho-Analytic Publications and Unpublished Drafts (1886–1899)

1/xxi

General preface (1966).

The aim of this work is to include the whole of Freud's published psychological writings in *The Complete Psychological Works of Sigmund Freud* (the *Standard Edition*). The *Standard Edition* does not include Freud's correspondence. Nor, again, does the *Standard Edition* contain any reports or abstracts, published in contemporary periodicals, of the many lectures and papers given by Freud in his early days at meetings of various medical societies in Vienna. The whole contents of the *Gesammelte Werke* appear in the *Standard Edition*. In general, each volume contains all the works belonging to a specified span of years. The translations are based on the last German editions published in Freud's lifetime. This edition was framed with the serious student in mind. The commentaries in the *Standard Edition* are of various kinds. First, there are the purely textual notes. Next come elucidations of Freud's very numerous historical and local allusions and literary quotations. Another class of annotations is constituted by the cross references. Lastly, and more rarely, there are notes explanatory of Freud's remarks. Each separate work is provided with an introductory note. The rule of uniform translation is used and is extended to phrases and to whole passages. Some technical terms, whose translation call for comment, are presented.

1956   1/3

Report on Freud's studies in Paris and Berlin (1886).

A report by Freud on some activities in Paris and Berlin is presented. The Salpetriere, in Paris, was converted into a home for aged women and provided a refuge for 5000 persons. Chronic nervous diseases appeared with particular frequency. A clinical section was opened in which both male and female patients were admitted for treatment. In his study of hysteria, Charcot, holder of a Chair of Neuropathology at the Salpetriere, started out from the most fully developed cases. He began by reducing the connection of the neurosis with the genital system to its correct proportions by demonstrating the unsuspected frequency of cases of male hysteria and especially of traumatic hysteria. In these typical cases, he next found a number of somatic signs which enabled him to establish the diagnosis of hysteria with certainty on the basis of positive indications. By making a scientific study of hypnotism, a region of neuropathology which had to be wrung on the one side of scepticism and on the other from fraud, he himself arrived at a kind of theory of hysterical symptomatology. By his efforts, hysteria was lifted out of the chaos of the neuroses and was differentiated from other conditions with a similar appearance. In Berlin, there was ample opportunity for examining children suffering from nervous diseases in the outpatient clinics.

1886F   1/19

Preface to the translation of Charcot's lectures on the diseases of the nervous system (1886).

By the winter of 1885, Professor Charcot was no longer studying nervous diseases that were based on organic changes and was devoting himself exclusively to research into the neuroses, and particularly hysteria. Charcot gave his permission to have a German translation made of his lectures by Freud. The core of his book of translated lectures lies in the masterly and fundamental lectures on hysteria, which, along with their author, were expected to open a new epoch in the estimation of this little known and, instead, much maligned neurosis.

1886D   1/23

Observation of a severe case of hemianaesthesia in a hysterical male (1886).

The observation by Freud of a severe case of hemianaesthesia in a hysterical male is presented. The patient is a 29-year-old engraver; an intelligent man, who readily offered himself for examination in the hope of an early recovery. The patient developed normally in his childhood. At the age of 8, he was run over in the street. This resulted in a slight hearing loss. His present illness dated back for some 3 years. At that time he fell into a dispute with his dissolute brother, who refused to pay him back a sum of money. His brother threatened to stab him and ran at him with a knife. This threw the patient into indescribable fear. He ran home and remained unconscious for about 2 hours. The feeling in the left half of his body seemed altered, and his eyes got easily tired at his work. With a few oscillations, his condition remained like this for 3 years, until 7 weeks ago, a fresh agitation brought on a change for the worse. The patient was accused by a woman of a theft, had violent palpitations, was so depressed for about a fortnight that he thought of suicide, and at the same time a fairly severe tremor set in his left extremities. The only sense that was not diminished on the left side was hearing. The anaesthesia was also present in the left arm, trunk, and leg. His reflexes were brisker than normal, and showed little consistency with one another. In accordance with a hysterical hemianaesthesia, the patient exhibited both spontaneously and on pressure, painful areas on what was otherwise the insensitive side of his body, what are known as hysterogenic zones, though in this case their connection with the provoking of attacks was not marked. The right side of the body was not free from anaesthesia, though this was not of a high degree and seemed to affect only the skin.

1887B 1/35
Two short reviews. Averbeck's Acute Neurasthenia and Weir Mitchell's Neurasthenia and Hysteria (1887).

A review by Freud of Averbeck's *Die Akute Neurasthenia* is presented. Neurasthenia may be described as the commonest of all the diseases in the society: it complicates and aggravates most other clinical pictures in patients of the better classes and it is either still quite unknown to the many scientifically educated physicians or is regarded by them as no more than a modern name with an arbitrarily compounded content. Neurasthenia is not a clinical picture in the sense of textbooks based too exclusively on pathological anatomy: it should rather be described as a mode of reaction of the nervous system. A review of Weir Mitchell's *Die Behandlung Gewisser Formen von Neurasthenie und Hysterie* is presented. The therapeutic procedure proposed by Weir Mitchell was first recommended in Germany by Burkart and has been given full recognition during the last year in a lecture by Leyden. This procedure, by a combination of rest in bed, isolation, feeding up, massage and electricity in a strictly regulated manner, overcomes severe and long established states of nervous exhaustion.

1888B 1/39
Hysteria (1888).

The name hysteria originates from the earliest times of medicine and is a precipitate of the prejudice which links neuroses with diseases of the female sexual apparatus. Hysteria is a neurosis in the strictest sense of the word. Hysteria is fundamentally different from neurasthenia and is contrary to it. The symptomatology of major hysteria is composed of a series of symptoms which include the following: convulsive attacks, hysterogenic zones, disturbances of sensibility, disturbances of sensory activity, paralyses, and contractures. The symptomatology of hysteria has a number of general characteristics. Hysterical manifestations have the characteristic of being excessive. At the same time, any particular symptom can occur in isolation: anesthesia and paralysis are not accompanied by the general phenomena which, in the case of organic lesions, give evidence of a cerebral affection and which as a rule by their importance put the localizing symptoms in the shade. It is especially characteristic of hysteria for a

disorder to be at the same time most highly developed and most sharply limited. Furthermore, hysterical symptoms shift in a manner which from the outset excludes any suspicion of a material lesion. In addition to the physical symptoms of hysteria, a number of psychical disturbances are observed. These are changes in the passage and in the association of ideas, inhibitions of the activity of the will, magnification and suppression of feelings, etc. Hysteria represents a constitutional anomaly rather than a circumscribed illness. First signs of it are probably exhibited in early youth. Hysteria may be combined with many other neurotic and organic nervous diseases, and such cases offer great difficulties to analysis. From the standpoint of treatment, 3 tasks must be separated: the treatment of the hysterical disposition, of hysterical outbreaks, and of individual hysterical symptoms.

1/61
Papers on hypnotism and suggestion (Editor's Introduction) (1966).

After Freud's return to Vienna from Paris in 1886, he devoted much of his attention for some years to a study of hypnotism and suggestion. Freud had extensive clinical experience with hypnotism. While he was still a student he attended a public exhibition given by Hansen the magnetist and was convinced of the genuineness of the phenomena of hypnosis. After settling in Vienna as a nerve specialist, he made attempts at using various procedures, such as electrotherapy, hydrotherapy, and rest cures, for treating the neuroses, but fell back in the end on hypnotism. He soon stopped using hypnotism; however, his interest in the theory of hypnotism and suggestion lasted longer than his use of hypnotism. In spite of his early abandonment of hypnosis as a therapeutic procedure, Freud never hesitated throughout his life to express his sense of gratitude to it.

1888X 1/73
Preface to the translation of Bernheim's suggestion (1888).

The work of Dr. Bernheim of Nancy provides an admirable introduction to the study of hypnotism. The achievement of Bernheim consists in stripping the manifestations of hypnotism of their strangeness by linking them up with familiar phenomena of normal psychological life and of sleep. The subject of hypnotism has had a most unfavorable reception among the leaders of German medical science. The prevalent view doubted the reality of hypnotic phenomena and sought to explain the accounts given of them as due to a combination of credulity on the part of the observers and of simulation on the part of the subjects of the experiments. Another line of argument hostile to hypnosis rejects it as being dangerous to the mental health of the subject and labels it as an experimentally produced psychosis. Bernheim's book, *Hypnotism and Suggestion* discusses another question, which divides the supporters of hypnotism into 2 opposing camps. One party, whose opinions are voiced by Dr. Bernheim, maintains that all the phenomena of hypnotism have the same origin; they arise, that is, from a suggestion, a conscious idea, which has been introduced into the brain of the hypnotized person by an external influence and has been accepted by him as though it has arisen spontaneously. On this view all hypnotic manifestations would be psychical phenomena, effects of suggestions. The other party, on the contrary, stand by the view that the mechanism of some at least of the manifestations of hypnotism is based upon physiological changes occurring without the participation of those parts of it which operate with consciousness; they speak, therefore, of the physical or physiological phenomena of hypnosis. Hypnosis, whether it is produced in the one way or in the other, is always the same and shows the same appearances.

1889A   1/89
Review of August Forel's hypnotism (1889).

Forel's *Hypnotism, Its Significance, and Its Management* is concise, expressed with great clarity and decisiveness, and covers the whole field of phenomena and problems which are comprised under the heading of the theory of hypnotism. In the opening sections of his book Forel endeavors so far as possible to distinguish among facts, theories, concepts, and terminology. The main fact of hypnotism lies in the possibility of putting a person into a particular condition of mind which resembles sleep. This condition is known as hypnosis. A second set of facts lies in the manner in which this condition is brought about (and ended). A third set of facts concerns the performances of the hypnotized person. Further unquestionable facts are the dependence of the hypnotized subject's mental activity on that of the hypnotist and the production of what are known as posthypnotic effects in the former. Three fundamentally different theories have been set up to explain the phenomena of hypnosis. The oldest of these supposes that, in the act of hypnotizing, an imponderable material passes over from the hypnotist into the hypnotized organism (magnetism). A second, somatic, theory explains hypnotic phenomena on the pattern of spinal reflexes; it regards hypnosis as a physiologically altered condition of the nervous system brought about by external stimuli. Forel takes his stand on a third theory. According to this, all the phenomena of hypnosis are psychical effects, effects of ideas which are provoked in the hypnotized subject either intentionally or not. The second section of the book deals with suggestion and covers the whole field of the psychical phenomena that have been observed in subjects under hypnosis. A section

on the forensic significance of suggestion concludes the volume.

1891D   1/103
Hypnosis (1891).

The technique of hypnotizing is just as difficult a medical procedure as any other. Hypnotic treatment should not be applied to symptoms which have an organic basis and should be reserved only for purely functional, nervous disorders, for ailments of psychical origin, and for toxic as well as other addictions. It is valuable for the patient who is to be hypnotized to see other people under hypnosis, to learn by imitation how he is to behave, and to learn from others the nature of the sensations during the hypnotic state. What is of decisive importance is only whether the patient has become somnambulistic or not; that is, whether the state of consciousness brought about in the hypnosis is cut off from the ordinary one sufficiently sharply for the memory of what occurred during hypnosis to be absent after waking. The true therapeutic value of hypnosis lies in the suggestions made during it. Through suggestion, either an immediate effect is called for, particularly in treating paralyses, contractures, and so on, or a post-hypnotic effect is called for; that is, one which is stipulated for a particular time after awakening. The duration of a hypnosis is arranged according to practical requirements; a comparatively long continuance under hypnosis, up to several hours, is certainly not unfavorable to success. The depth of hypnosis is not invariably in direct proportion to its success. The field of hypnotic treatment is far more extensive than that of other methods of treating nervous illnesses. If hypnosis has had success, the stability of the cure depends on the same factors as the stability of every cure achieved in another way.

1892B   1/115
A case of successful treatment by hypnotism (1892–3).

A case of successful treatment by hypnotism is presented. The subject was a young woman between 20 and 30 years old. She had had difficulty in feeding her first child and the baby was finally given out to a wet nurse. Three years later, her second child was born, and she again had difficulty in feeding the child. She had no milk, retained no food, and was quite distressed with her inability to feed the baby. After two hypnotic sessions, she was able to feed the baby and nursed it until the baby was 8 months old. The next year, a third child made the same demands on the mother and she was as unable to meet them as on the previous occasions. Once again, after the second hypnosis the symptoms were so completely cut short that a third was not required. This child too, was fed without any trouble and the mother has enjoyed uninterrupted good health. There are certain ideas which have an affect of expectancy attached to them. They are of two kinds: intentions and expectations. The affect attached to these ideas is dependent on two factors: first on the degree of importance associated with the outcome, and secondly on the degree of uncertainty inherent in the expectation of that outcome. The subjective uncertainty (the counter expectation) is itself represented by a collection of ideas which are called distressing antithetic ideas. In neuroses, where primary presence of a tendency toward depression and low self-confidence exists, great attention is paid by the patient to antithetic ideas against his intentions. When this intensification of antithetic ideas relates to expectations, if the case is one of a simple nervous state, the effect is shown in a generally pessimistic frame of mind; if the case is one of neurasthenia, associations with the most accidental sensations occasion the numerous phobias of neurasthenics.

1892A   1/131
Preface and footnotes to the translation of Charcot's Tuesday Lectures (1892—4).

Charcot's *Tuesday Lectures* contain so much that is novel that there is nobody, not even among experts, who will read them without a substantial increase of his knowledge. These lectures owe a peculiar charm to the fact that they are entirely, or for the most part, improvisations. The Professor does not know the patient who is brought before him, or knows him only superficially. He questions the patient, examines one symptom or another, and in that way determines the diagnosis of the case and restricts it or confirms it by further examination. Interest in a lecture was often properly aroused only when the diagnosis had been made and the case had been dealt with in accordance with its peculiarities. After this, Charcot would take advantage of the freedom afforded by this method of instruction in order to make remarks on similar cases in his recollection and for introducing the most important discussions on the genuinely clinical topics of their etiology, heredity and connection with other illnesses. Extracts from the footnotes to the translation of Charcot's *Tuesday Lectures* are presented.

1941A   1/147
Sketches for the "preliminary communication" of 1893. On the theory of hysterical attacks.

In a letter from Freud to Josef Breuer, the following theories of hysteria are offered: the theorem concerning the constancy of the sum of excitation; the theory of memory; and the theorem which lays it down that the contents of different states of consciousness are not associated with one another. The recollections lying behind hysterical phenomena are absent from the patient's accessible memory, whereas under hypnosis

they can be awakened with hallucinatory vividness. Therapy consists in removing the results of the ideas that have not been abreacted, either by reviving the trauma in a state of sommambulism, and then abreacting and correcting it, or by bringing it into normal consciousness under comparatively light hypnosis. The opinions on hysterical attacks have been reached by treating hysterical subjects by means of hypnotic suggestion and by questioning them under hypnosis and thus investigating their psychical processes during the attack. The constant and essential content of a (recurrent) hysterical attack is the return of a psychical state which the patient has already experienced earlier. The memory which forms the content of a hysterical attack is not any chance one; it is the return of the event which caused the outbreak of hysteria: the psychical trauma. The memory which forms the content of a hysterical attack is an unconscious one; that is, it is part of the second state of consciousness which is present in every hysteria. If a hysterical subject seeks intentionally to forget an experience or forcibly repudiates, inhibits and suppresses an intention or an idea, these psychical acts enter the second state of consciousness; from there they produce their permanent effects and the memory of them returns as a hysterical attack.

1893C   1/157
Some points for a comparative study of organic and hysterical motor paralyses (1893).

Clinical neurology recognizes two kinds of motor paralyses: peripherospinal (or bulbar) paralysis and cerebral paralysis. The type of the former is the facial paralysis in Bell's Palsy, the paralysis in acute infantile poliomyelitis, etc. Cerebral paralysis, on the contrary, is always a disorder that attacks a large portion of the periphery, a limb, a segment of an extremity or a complicated motor apparatus. Hysteria has fairly often been credited with a faculty for simulating various organic nervous disorders. Only flaccid hysterical paralyses never affect single muscles (except where the muscle concerned is the sole instrument of a function). They are always paralyses en masse and in this respect they correspond to organic cerebral paralyses. Hysterical paralysis can be more dissociated, more systematized, than cerebral paralysis. Hysteria is a disease of excessive manifestations; it tends to produce its symptoms with the greatest possible intensity. This characteristic is shown not only in its paralyses but also in its contractures and anesthesia. Hysterical paralysis is characterized by precise limitation and excessive intensity. It possesses both these qualities at once, whereas in organic cerebral paralysis, these two characteristics are not associated with each other. Hysterical paralyses are much more frequently accompanied by disorders of sensibility than are organic paralyses. The lesion in hysterical paralyses consists in nothing other than the inaccessibility of the organ or function concerned to the associations of the conscious ego. This purely functional alteration is caused by the fixation of this conception in a subconscious association with the memory of the trauma; and this conception does not become liberated and accessible so long as the quota of affect of the psychical trauma has not been eliminated by an adequate motor reaction or by conscious psychical activity.

1950A 1/173
Extracts from the Fliess papers (1892–1899).

Wilhelm Fliess, a man 2 years younger than Freud, was a nose and throat specialist living in Berlin with whom Freud carried on a voluminous and intimate correspondence between 1887 and 1902. Fliess was a man of great ability, with very wide interests in general biology; but he pursued theories in that field which are regarded today as eccentric and quite untenable. Freud communicated his thoughts to him with the utmost freedom and did so not only in his letters but in a series of papers which presented organized accounts of his developing views. These papers were totally unknown until the time of the Second World War. The material in these drafts and letters was not intended by their author as the considered expression of his opinions, and it is often framed in a highly condensed form.

1950A 1/177
Draft A. Aetiology of actual neuroses (1892).

Some of the problems in the study of hysteria are presented. They include: Is the anxiety of anxiety neuroses derived from the inhibition of the sexual function or from the anxiety linked with their etiology? To what extent does a healthy person respond to later sexual traumas differently from an unhealthy one? Is there an innate neurasthenia with innate sexual weakness or is it always acquired in youth? What plays a part in the etiology of periodic depression? Is sexual anesthesia in women anything other than a result of impotence? The theses include: 1) no neurasthenia or analogous neurosis exists without a disturbance of the sexual function; 2) this either has an immediate causal effect or acts as a disposition for other factors; 3) neurasthenia in men is accompanied by relative impotence; 4) neurasthenia in women is a direct consequence of neurasthenia in men; 5) periodic depression is a form of anxiety neurosis; 6) anxiety neurosis is in part a consequence of inhibition of the sexual function; 7) hysteria in neurasthenic neuroses indicates suppression of the accompanying affects. The following groups were proposed for observation: men and women who have

remained healthy, sterile women, women infected with gonorrhoea, loose living men who are gonorrhoeal, members of severely tainted families who have remained healthy, and observations from countries in which particular sexual abnormalities are endemic. The etiological factors include: exhaustion owing to abnormal satisfaction, inhibition of the sexual function, affects accompanying these practices, and sexual traumas before the age of understanding.

1950A 1/179
Draft B. The Aetiology of the neuroses (1893).

The etiology of the neuroses is discussed. Neurasthenia is a frequent consequence of an abnormal sexual life. Neurasthenia in males is acquired at puberty and becomes manifest in the patient's twenties. Its source is masturbation, the frequency of which runs completely parallel with the frequency of male neurasthenia. Girls are sound and not neurasthenic; and this is true as well of young married women, in spite of all the sexual traumas of this period of life. In comparatively rare cases neurasthenia appears in married women and in older unmarried ones in its pure form; it is then to be regarded as having arisen spontaneously. The mixed neurosis of women is derived from neurasthenia in men in all those not infrequent cases in which the man, being a sexual neurasthenic, suffers from impaired potency. The admixture of hysteria results directly from the holding back of the excitation of the act. Every case of neurasthenia is marked by a certain lowering of self confidence, by pessimistic expectation and an inclination to distressing antithetic ideas. Anxiety neurosis appears in two forms: as a chronic state and as an attack of anxiety. The chronic symptoms are: 1) anxiety relating to the body (hypochondria); 2) anxiety relating to the functioning of the body (agoraphobia, claustrophobia, giddiness on heights); and 3) anxiety relating to decisions and memory. Periodic depression, an attack of anxiety lasting for weeks or months, is another form of anxiety neurosis. It is concluded that the neuroses are entirely preventable as well as entirely incurable. The physician's task is wholly shifted on to prophylaxis.

1950A 1/184
Letter 14. Coitus interruptus as an aetiological factor (1893).

Four new cases are discussed whose etiology, as shown by the chronological data, was given as coitus interruptus. The first case is a 41-year-old woman. She was very intelligent and had no fear of having children.

Her diagnosis was that of simple anxiety neurosis. The second case is a 24-year-old woman. She was described as a nice, stupid young woman in whom the anxiety was highly developed. After a short while she had hysteria for the first time. The third case is a 42-year-old man with anxiety neurosis and heart symptoms. He was a very potent man who was a great smoker. The fourth case is a 34-year-old man who was (without having masturbated) only moderately potent.

1950A   1/186
Draft D.   On the aetiology and theory of the major neuroses (1894).

The etiology and theory of the major neuroses are presented. Included in the morphology of the neuroses are the following categories: neurasthenia and the pseudoneurasthenias, anxiety neurosis, obsessional neurosis, hysteria, melancholia and mania, the mixed neuroses, and the ramifications of the neuroses and transitions to the normal. The etiology of the neuroses covers the following neuroses: neurasthenia, anxiety neurosis, obsessional neurosis and hysteria, melancholia, and the mixed neuroses. It also covers: the basic etiological formula, the sexual factors in their etiological significance, an examination of the patients, objections and proofs, and the behavior of asexual people. A discussion of the relationship between etiology and heredity was planned. The following points were to be included in a discussion of theory: the points of contact with the theory of constancy, the sexual process in the light of the theory of constancy, the mechanism of the neuroses, the parallel between the neuroses of sexuality and neuroses.

1950A   1/188
Letter 18.   Effect of sexual noxae (1894).

Three mechanisms of the neuroses are presented: transformation of affect (conversion hysteria), displacement of affect (obsessions), and exchange of affect (anxiety neurosis and melancholia). In every case what seems to undergo these alterations is sexual excitation, but the impetus to them is not, in every case, something sexual. In every case in which neuroses are acquired, they are acquired owing to disturbances of sexual life; but there are people in whom the behavior of their sexual affects is disturbed hereditarily, and they develop the corresponding forms of hereditary neuroses. The most general aspects from which the neuroses can be classified are the following: degeneracy, senility, conflict, and conflagration.

1950A   1/189
Draft E.   How anxiety originates (1894)

The anxiety of the neurotic patient has a great deal to do with sexuality; and in particular, with coitus interruptus. Anxiety neurosis affects women who are anesthetic in coitus just as much as sensitive ones. Several cases in which anxiety arose from a sexual cause are presented: anxiety in virginal people; anxiety in intentionally abstinent people; anxiety of necessarily abstinent people; anxiety of women living in coitus interruptus; anxiety of men practicing coitus interruptus; anxiety of men who go beyond their desire or strength; and anxiety of men who abstain on occasion. Anxiety neurosis is a neurosis of damming up, like hysteria. In anxiety neurosis there must be a deficit to be noted in sexual affect, in psychical libido. If this connection is put before women patients, they are always indignant and declare that on the contrary they now have no desire whatever. Men patients often confirm it as an observation that since suffering from anxiety they have felt no sexual desire. When there is an abundant development of physical sexual tension, but this cannot be turned into affect by psychical working over, the sexual tension is transformed into anxiety. A part is played in this by the accumulation of physical tension and the prevention of discharge in the psychical direction. There is a kind of conversion in anxiety neurosis just as there is in hysteria; but in hysteria it is psychical excitation that takes a wrong path exclusively into the somatic field, whereas here it is a physical tension, which cannot enter the psychical field and therefore remains on the physical path.

1950A   1/195
Draft F.   Collection III   Two case histories (1894).

Two cases are presented with a discussion of each one. In the first case, that of a 27-year-old man, there was a hereditary disposition: his father suffered from melancholia and his sister had a typical anxiety neurosis. The subject's libido had been diminishing for some time; the preparations for using a condom were enough to make him feel that the whole act was something forced on him and his enjoyment of it something he was persuaded into. The fear of infection and the decision to use a condom laid the foundation for what has been described as the factor of alienation between the somatic and the psychical. The effect would be the same as in the case of coitus interruptus with men. The subject brought psychical sexual weakness on himself because he spoiled coitus for himself, and his physical health and production of sexual stimuli being unimpaired, the situation gave rise to the generation of anxiety. The second case involves a healthy 44-year-old man. He complained that he was losing his liveliness and zest, in a way that was not natural in a man of his age. This was described as a mild but very characteristic case of periodic depression, melancholia. The symptoms, apathy, inhibition, intracranial pressure, dyspepsia, and insomnia complete the picture.

1950A   1/199
Letter 21.   Two case histories (1894).

Two cases are presented and discussed. The first, a 34-year-old physician, suffered for many years from organic sensitivity of the eyes: phospheum (flashes), dazzle, scotomas, etc. This increased enormously, to the point of preventing him from working. This was diagnosed as a typical case of hypochondria in a particular organ in a masturbater at periods of sexual excitation. The second case is that of a 28-year-old boy from a highly neurotic family. He suffered for some weeks from lassitude, intracranial pressure, shaky knees, reduced potency, premature ejaculation, and the beginnings of perversion. He alleged that his potency has been capricious from the first; admitted masturbation, but not too prolonged; and had a period of abstinence behind him now. Before that, he had anxiety states in the evening. There was some doubt as to his honesty.

1950A   1/200
Draft G. Melancholia (1895).

There are striking connections between melancholia and anesthesia. Melancholia is generated as an intensification of neurasthenia through masturbation. Melancholia appears in typical combination with severe anxiety. The type and extreme form of melancholia seems to be the periodic or cyclical hereditary form. The affect corresponding to melancholia is that of mourning. The nutritional neurosis parallel to melancholia is anorexia. Potent individuals easily acquire anxiety neuroses; impotent ones incline to melancholia. A description of the effects of melancholia includes: psychical inhibition with instinctual impoverishment and pain concerning it. Anesthesia seems to encourage melancholia; however, anesthesia is not the cause of melancholia but a sign of disposition to it.

1950A   1/206
Draft H. Paranoia (1895).

In psychiatry, delusional ideas stand alongside of obsessional ideas as purely intellectual disorders, and paranoia stands alongside of obsessional insanity as an intellectual psychosis. Paranoia, in its classical form, is a pathological mode of defense, like hysteria, obsessional neurosis and hallucinatory confusion. People become paranoiac over things that they cannot put up with, provided that they possess the peculiar psychical disposition for it. The purpose of paranoia is to fend off an idea that is incompatible with the ego, by projecting its substance into the external world. The transposition is effected very simply. It is a question of an abuse of a psychical mechanism which is very commonly employed in normal life: transposition or projection. Paranoia is the abuse of the mechanism of projection for purposes of defense. Something quite analogous takes place with obsessional ideas. The mechanism of substitution is a normal one. This normally operating mechanism of substitution is abused in obsessional ideas for purposes of defense. The delusional idea is maintained with the same energy with which another, intolerably distressing, idea is fended off from the ego. They love their delusions as they love themselves. Paranoia and hallucinatory confusion are the two psychoses of defense or contrariness.

1950A   1/213
Letter 22. Dream as analogy to D's dream psychosis (1895).

A small analogy to D's dream psychosis is reported. Rudi Kaufmann, a very intelligent nephew of Breuer's, and a medical student too, is a late riser. He gets himself called by a servant, but is very reluctant about obeying her. One morning she woke him up a second time and, as he would not respond, called him by his name: 'Herr Rudi!' Thereupon the sleeper had a hallucination of a notice board over a hospital bed with the name 'Rudolf Kaufmann' on it, and said to himself: 'R.K.'s in the hospital in any case, then; so I needn't go there!' and went on sleeping.

1950A   1/214
Draft I. Migraine: Established points (1895).

The established points concerning migraine are presented. There is an interval of hours or days between the instigation and the outbreak of the symptoms. Even without an instigation there is an impression that there must be an accumulating stimulus which is present in the smallest quantity at the beginning of the interval and in the largest quantity towards its end. Migraine appears to be a matter of summation, in which susceptibility to etiological factors lies in the height of the level of the stimulus already present. Migraine has a complicated etiology, perhaps on the pattern of a chain etiology, where approximate cause can be produced by a number of factors directly and indirectly, or on the pattern of a summation etiology, where, alongside of a specific cause, stock causes can act as quantitative substitutes. Migraines appear rarest in healthy males; are restricted to the sexual time of life; and appear frequently in people with disturbed sexual discharge. Migraine can be produced by chemical stimuli too, such as: human toxic emanations, scirocco, fatigue, and smells. There is a cessation of migraine during pregnancy. The pain of a neuralgia usually finds its discharge in tonic tension. Therefore, it is not impossible that migraine may include a spastic innervation of the muscles of blood vessels in the reflex sphere of the dural region.

1950A   1/215
Draft J. Frau P.J. (aged 27) (1895).

The subject of this study is a 27-year-old woman. She had been married for 3 months. Her husband, a commercial traveller, had had to leave her a few weeks after their marriage. She missed him very much and longed for him. To pass the time, she was sitting at the piano singing, when suddenly she felt ill in her abdomen and stomach, her head swam, she had feelings of oppression and anxiety and cardiac paraesthesia; she thought she was going mad. Next day, the servant told her that a woman living in the same house had gone mad. From that time on she was never free of an obsession, accompanied by anxiety, that she was going to go mad too. It was assumed that her condition then had been an anxiety attack: a release of sexual feeling which was transformed into anxiety. With probing, it was discovered that she had had another attack 4 years earlier, also while she was singing. An effort was made to determine the other ideas present in order to account for the release of sexual feeling and the fright. However, instead of revealing these intermediate links, she discussed her motives.

1/219
Note. By Strachey (1966).

During the whole of the latter part of the year 1895 Freud was largely occupied with the fundamental theoretical problem of the relation between neurology and psychology. His reflections finally led to the uncompleted work which was named a *Project for a Scientific Psychology*. This was written in September and October, 1895, and should appear, chronologically, at this point in the Fliess papers. It stands so much

apart, however, from the rest of them, and constitutes such a formidable and self contained entity, that it was printed in a detached shape at the end of the first volume of the *Standard Edition*. One letter, Number 39, written on January 1, 1896, is so closely connected with the Project that it too has been removed from its proper place in the correspondence and printed as an appendix to the Project. That Freud had also during all this period been concerned with clinical matters as well, is conclusively shown by the fact that on the very same day on which he dispatched this letter, he also sent Fliess Draft K.

1950A   1/220
Draft K. The neuroses of defence: A Christmas fairy tale (1896).

The neuroses of defense are discussed. There are 4 types of neuroses of defense. A comparison is made between 3 different emotional states: hysteria, obsessional neurosis, and one form of paranoia. They have various things in common. They are all pathological aberrations of normal psychical affective states: of conflict (hysteria), of self-reproach (obsessional neurosis), of mortification (paranoia), of mourning (acute hallucinatory amentia). They differ from these affects in that they do not lead to anything being settled but to permanent damage to the ego. Heredity is a precondition, in that it facilitates and increases the pathological affect. It is this precondition which mainly makes possible the gradations between the normal and extreme case. There is a normal trend toward defense; however, the trend toward defense becomes detrimental if it is directed against ideas which are also able, in the form of memories, to release fresh unpleasure, as is the case with sexual ideas. The course taken by the illness in neuroses of repression is almost always the same: 1) there is a sexual experience which is traumatic and premature and becomes repressed. 2) its repression on some later occasion arouses a memory of it; at the same time, there is the formation of a primary symptom. 3) there is a stage of successful defense, which is equivalent to health except for the existence of the primary symptom. 4) the last stage is that in which the repressed ideas return, and in which during the struggle between them and the ego, new symptoms are formed which are those of the illness proper; that is, a stage of adjustment, of being overwhelmed, or of recovery with a malformation. In obsessional neuroses, the primary experience has been accompanied by pleasure. In paranoia, the primary experience seems to be of a similar nature to that in obsessional neurosis; repression occurs after the memory of it has released unpleasure. Hysteria presupposes a primary experience of unpleasure of a passive nature.

1950A 1/229
Letter 46. Four periods of life and aetiology (1896).

The following solution to the etiology of the psychoneuroses are presented. Four periods of life are distinguished: up to 4 years, preconscious; up to 8 years, infantile; up to 14 years, prepubertal; and up to infinity, maturity. The periods between 8 to 10 and 13 to 17 are the transitional periods during which repression occurs. The scenes for hysteria occur in the first period of childhood (up to 4 years), in which the mnemic residues are not translated into verbal images. Hysteria always results, and in the form of conversion. The scenes for obsessional neuroses belong to the infantile period. The scenes for paranoia fall in the prepubertal period and are aroused in maturity. In that case, defense is manifested in disbelief. Hysteria is the only neurosis in which symptoms are possible even without defense. Consciousness, as regards memories, consists of the verbal consciousness pertaining to them; that is, in access to the associated word presentations. Consciousness is not attached exclusively and inseparably either to the so-called unconscious or to the so-called conscious realm, so that these names seem to call for rejection. Consciousness is determined by a compromise between the different psychical powers which come into conflict with one another when repressions occur. These powers include: the inherent quantitative strength of a presentation and a freely displaceable attention which is attracted according to certain rules and repelled in accordance with the rule of defense. It is in the conflict between uninhibited and thought-inhibited psychical processes that symptoms arise. One species of psychical disturbance arises if the power of the uninhibited processes increases; another if the force of the thought inhibition relaxes.

1950A 1/233
Letter 50. Funeral dream (1896).

Freud presented a report of a dream: I was in some public place and read a notice there: You are asked to close the eyes. I recognized the place as the barber's to which I go every day. On the day of the funeral I was kept waiting there and therefore reached the house of mourning rather late. At that time my family was displeased with me because I had arranged for the funeral to be quiet and simple, which they later agreed was quite right. They also took my being late in somewhat bad part. The sentence on the notice board has a double sense, and means in both of them: 'one should do one's duty to the dead'. (An apology, as though I had not done it and my conduct needed overlooking, and the duty taken literally.) Thus the dream is an outlet for the inclination to self-reproach which is regularly present among survivors.

1950A 1/234
Letter 52. Stratification of memory traces (1896).

A thesis is presented that memory is present not once but several times over, that it is laid down in various species of indications. There are at least 3 registrations, probably more. The different registrations are also separated (not necessarily topographically) according to the neurones which are their vehicles. The perceptions are neurones in which perceptions originate, to which consciousness attaches, but which in themselves retain no trace of what has happened. Consciousness and memory are mutually exclusive. The indication of perception is the first registration of the perceptions; it is quite incapable of consciousness, and is arranged according to associations by simultaneity. Unconsciousness is the second registration, arranged according to other (perhaps causal) relations. The unconsciousness traces correspond to conceptual memories; equally inaccessible to consciousness. Preconsciousness is the third transcription, attached to word presentations and corresponding to the official ego. The cathexes proceeding from preconsciousness become conscious according to certain rules; and this secondary thought consciousness is subsequent in time, and is probably linked to the hallucinatory activation of word presentations, so that the neurones of consciousness would once again be perceptual neurones and in themselves without memory. The successive registrations represent the psychical achievement of successive epochs of life. At the frontier between 2 such epochs a translation of the psychical material must take place. A failure of translation is known as repression. There are 3 groups of sexual psychoneuroses: hysteria, obsessional neurosis, and paranoia. Repressed memories relate to what was current in the case of hysteria between the ages of 1½ and 4, of obsessional neurosis between 4 and 8, and of paranoia between 8 and 14.

1950A 1/240
Letter 55. Determinants of psychosis (1897).

Two ideas, based on analytic findings, are presented. The determinant of a psychosis (amentia or a confusional psychosis), instead of a neurosis seems to be sexual abuse that occurs before the end of the first intellectual stage (before 15 to 18 months). It is possible that the abuse may date back so far that these experiences lie concealed behind the later ones. Epilepsy goes back to the same period. The perversions regularly lead into zoophilia, and have an animal character. They are explained not by the functioning of erotogenic zones which have later been abandoned, but by the operation of erotogenic sensations which lose this force later. The principal sense in animals is that of smell, which has lost that position in human beings. So long ãs smell (or taste) is dominant, hair, faces, and the whole surface of the body have a sexually exciting effect. The increase in the sense of smell in hysteria is no doubt connected with this.

1950A   1/242
Letter 56. Hysteria and witches (1897).

The medieval theory of possession, held by the ecclesiastical courts, is said to be identical with the theory of a foreign body and a splitting of consciousness. The cruelties made it possible to understand some symptoms of hysteria which have hitherto been obscure. The inquisitors pricked with needles, to discover the Devil's stigmata, and in a similar situation the victims invented the same old cruel story (helped by the seducer's disguises). Thus, not only the victims but the executioners recalled in this their earliest youth.

1950A   1/243
Letter 57. Witches and symbolism (1897).

The idea of bringing in the witches is gaining strength. Details are beginning to crowd in. Their flying is explained; the broomstick they ride on is probably the great Lord Penis. Their secret gatherings, with dancing and other amusements, can be seen any day in the streets where children play. Alongside of flying and floating on the air can be put the gymnastic feats of boys in hysterical attacks. Perverse actions are always the same. They are made with a meaning and a pattern which one day will be understood. The dream is of a primeval Devil religion, whose rites are carried on secretly. There is a class of people, paranoiacs, who tell stories like those of the witches. These paranoiacs complain that people put feces in their food, illtreat them at night in the most abominable way, sexually, etc. There is a distinction between delusion of memory and interpretative delusions. The latter are connected with the characteristic indefiniteness concerning the evildoers, who are concealed by the defense. In hysterical patients, their fathers are seen behind their high standards in love, their humility towards their lover, or their being unable to marry because their ideals are unfulfilled.

1950A   1/244
Letter 59. Age of hysterical fantasies (1897).

The point that escaped me in the solution of hysteria lies in the discovery of a new source from which a new element of unconscious production arises. What I have in mind are hysterical phantasies, which regularly, as it seems to me, go back to things heard by children at an early age and only understood later. The age at which they take in information of this kind is very remarkable, from the age of 6 to 7 months onwards!

1950A   1/245
Letter 60. Dream about Fliess (1897).

A dream is presented and discussed. The provoking cause of the dream was the events from the previous day. The dream was a telegraph message. It said Via, Casa Secerno, Villa. The interpretation of the dream was that it collected together all the annoyance that was unconsciously present in the dreamer. The complete interpretation occurred only after a lucky chance brought a fresh confirmation of paternal etiology. That case was an ordinary case of hysteria with the usual symptoms.

1950A   1/247
Letter 61. Structure of hysteria (1897).

The structure of hysteria is presented. Everything goes back to the reproduction of scenes, some of which can be arrived at directly, but others always by way of phantasies set up in front of them. The phantasies are derived from things that have been heard but understood subsequently and all their material is genuine. They are protective structures, sublimations of the facts, embellishments of them, and at the same time exonerations. Their precipitating origin is perhaps from masturbation phantasies. A second important piece of insight is that the psychical structures which, in hysteria, are affected by repression are not in reality memories, but impulses which arise from the primal scenes. All 3 neuroses (hysteria, obsessional neurosis, and paranoia) exhibit the same elements (along with the same etiology); that is, mnemic fragments, impulses (derived from the memory) and protective fictions. The breakthrough into consciousness and the formation of compromises (that is, of symptoms) occurs in them at different points. In hysteria, the memories; in obsessional neurosis, the perverse impulses; in paranoia, the protective fictions (phantasies), are what penetrate into normal life distorted by compromise.

1950A   1/248
Draft L.   Architecture of hysteria (1897).

The architecture of hysteria is presented. The aim of hysteria seems to be to arrive back at the primal scenes. In a few cases this is achieved directly, but in others only by a roundabout path. Phantasies are psychical facades constructed in order to bar the way to these memories. Phantasies at the same time serve the trend towards refining the things that are heard, and made use of subsequently; thus they combine things that have been experienced and things that have been perceived. An immense load of guilt, with self-reproaches, is made possible by identification with people of low morals, who are so often remembered as worthless women connected sexually with a father or a brother. There was a girl who was afraid to pick a flower or even to pull up a mushroom, because it was against the command of God, who did not wish living seeds to be destroyed. In hysteria, the following events and topics have been seen: the part played by servant girls, mushrooms, pains, multiplicity of psychical personalities, wrapping up, multiple editions of phantasies, and wishful dreams.

1950A   1/250
Draft M. Repression in hysteria (1897).

The architecture of hysteria is presented. Some of the scenes are accessible directly, but others only by way of phantasies set up in front of them. The scenes are arranged in the order of increasing resistance: the more slightly repressed ones come to light first, but only incompletely on account of their association with the severely repressed ones. It is to be suspected that the essentially repressed element is always what is feminine. Phantasies arise from an unconscious combination, in accordance with certain trends, of things experienced and heard. These trends are toward making inaccessible the memory from which the symptoms have emerged or might emerge. Phantasies are constructed by a process of amalgamation and distortion analogous to the decomposition of a chemical body which is compounded with another one. All anxiety symptoms (phobias) are derived from phantasies. The kinds of compromise displacement are: displacement by association, hysteria; displacement by (conceptual) similarity, obsessional neurosis (characteristic of the place at which the defense occurs, and perhaps also of the time); and causal displacement, paranoia. Repression proceeds backwards from what is recent, and affects the latest events first. The phantasies in paranoia are systematic, all of them in harmony with

each other. The phantasies in hysteria are independent of one another and contradictory.

1950A   1/253
Letter 64. Two dreams (1897).

Freud reported and discussed two dreams. The first dream was of having over-affectionate feelings towards Mathilde, only she was called Hella and afterwards the word Hella was printed in heavy type. The solution was that Hella is the name of an American niece. Mathilde could be called Hella because she has recently wept so much over the Greek defeats. She is enthusiastic about the mythology of ancient Hellas and naturally regards all Hellenes as heroes. The dream shows the fulfillment of the wish to catch a father as the originator of neurosis, and so to put an end to the doubts which still persist. The second dream concerned going up a staircase with very few clothes on. The dreamer was moving with great agility. Suddenly, a woman was coming and thereupon the experience set in of being glued to the spot. The accompanying feeling was not anxiety but an erotic excitation.

1950A   1/254
Draft N. Impulses, fantasies and symptoms (1897).

Hostile impulses against parents are an integral constituent of neuroses. They come to light consciously as obsessional ideas. In paranoia, delusions of persecution correspond to these impulses. They are repressed at times when compassion for the parents is active. On such occasions, it is a manifestation of mourning to reproach oneself for their death or to punish oneself in a hysterical fashion with the same states that they have had. It seems as though this death wish is directed in sons against their fathers and in daughters against their mothers. Memories appear to bifurcate: part of them is put aside and replaced by phantasies; another, more accessible, part seems to lead directly to impulses. Belief (and doubt) is a phenomenon that belongs wholly to the system of the ego and has no counterpart in the unconscious. In the neuroses, belief is displaced; it is refused to the repressed material if it forces its way to reproduction and, as a punishment, transposed onto the defending material. The mechanism of poetry is the same as that of hysterical phantasies. Remembering is never a motive but only a way, a method. The first motive for the construction of symptoms is, chronologically, libido. Thus symptoms, like dreams, are the fulfillment of a wish. The repression of impulses seems to produce not anxiety but perhaps depression, melancholia. In this way the melancholias are related to obsessional neurosis. Holiness is something based on the fact that human beings, for the benefit of the larger community, have sacrificed a portion of their sexual liberty and their liberty to indulge in perversions.

1950A   1/257
Letter 66. Defense against memories (1897).

Defense against the memories does not prevent their giving rise to higher psychical structures, which persist for a while and are then themselves subjected to defense. This, however, is of a most highly specific kind, precisely as in dreams, which contain, in a nutshell, the psychology of the neuroses quite generally. The most assured thing seems to be the explanation of dreams, but it is surrounded by a vast number of obstinate riddles. The organological questions await a solution. There is an interesting dream of wandering about among strangers, totally or half undressed and with feelings of shame and anxiety. The people do not notice it. This dream material, which goes back to exhibiting in childhood, has been misunderstood and worked over didactically in a well-known fairy tale.

1950A   1/259
Letter 67. Doubts about theory of neuroses (1897).

A letter reflected various personal feelings of Freud. Things were fermenting but nothing had been finished. The psychology was satisfactory, but there were grave doubts about the theory of the neuroses. The mind was sluggish. After having been very cheerful, there was a period of ill temper. The mild hysteria, very much aggravated by work, however, had been resolved but the rest was still at a standstill.

1950A   1/260
Letter 69. Doubts about theory of neuroses (1897).

The author's original traumatic theory of the neuroses is no longer held. There are 4 reasons given for its abandonment: 1) the continual disappointments in the attempts at bringing analysis to a real conclusion, the running away of people who had for a time seemed most in the grasp, the absence of the complete successes and the possibility of explaining the partial successes in other ways. 2) In every case the father had to be blamed as a

pervert. 3) The discovery that there are no indications of reality in the unconscious, so that one cannot distinguish between the truth and fiction that is cathected with affect. 4) The reflection that in the most deep-going psychosis the unconscious memory does not break through, so that the secret of the childhood experience is not betrayed even in the most confused delirium. These doubts were the results of honest and forcible intellectual work.

1950A   1/261
Letter 70. Freud's early memories from self-analysis (1897).

Freud's self-analysis, which he considered to be indispensable for throwing light upon a problem, proceeded in dreams and presented several valuable inferences and clues. In summary, it seemed that the father played no active part in the case, but an inference was drawn by analogy on to him. The prime originator was a woman, ugly, elderly, but clever, who told a great deal about God Almighty and Hell and who instilled in him a high opinion of his capacities. Later, between 2 and 2½ years of age the libido was stirred up towards the mother. A dream is reported concerning his teacher in sexual matters who scolds him for being clumsy, washes him in reddish water and makes him give her silver coins. This is summed up as 'bad treatment', and alludes to his powerlessness as a therapist since he gets money from his bad treatment of patients.

1950A   1/263
Letter 71. Universality of Oedipus complex (1897).

Self-analysis appeared to be the most essential task for Freud. An interpretation of a dream was confirmed by a discussion with his mother. It was concluded that to be completely honest with oneself is good practice. Falling in love with the mother and jealousy of the father was regarded as a universal event of early childhood. Because of this, the riveting power of *Oedipus Rex* can be understood. It was speculated that Hamlet had the same kinds of feelings to his father and mother.

1950A   1/266
Letter 72. Resistances reflect childhood (1897).

Resistance, which finally brings work to a halt, is nothing other than the child's past degenerate character, which (as a result of those experiences which one finds present consciously in what are called degenerate cases) has developed or might have developed, but which is overlaid here by the emergence of repression. This infantile character develops during the period of longing, after the child has been withdrawn from the sexual experiences. Longing is the main character trait of hysteria, just as anesthesia is its main symptom. During this period of longing, the phantasies are constructed and masturbation is practiced, which afterwards yields to repression. If it does not give way, then there is no hysteria; the discharge of sexual excitation removes for the most part, the possibility of hysteria.

1950A   1/267

Letter 73. Children's speech during sleep (1897).

His analysis proceeds and remains Freud's chief interest. Everything is still obscure, even the problems; but there is a comfortable feeling that one has only to rummage in one's own storeroom to find, sooner or later, what one needs. The most disagreeable things are the moods, which often completely hide reality. For someone like him, too, sexual excitation is no longer of use. The speech of a 1½-year-old child was reported and interpreted as wish fulfillment. Little Anna had to starve one day because she was sick in the morning, which was put down to a meal of strawberries. During the following night she called out a whole menu in her sleep: 'Stwawbewwies, wild stwawbewwies, omblet, pudden!'

1950A   1/268

Letter 75. Erotogenic zones (1897).

Something organic plays a part in repression. This notion was linked to the changed part played by the sensations of smell: the upright carriage that is adopted. The nose raised from the ground, at the same time a number of formerly interesting sensations attached to the earth becoming repulsive, by a unknown process. The zones, which no longer produce a release of sexuality in normal and mature human beings, must be the regions of the anus and of the mouth and throat. The appearance and idea of these zones no longer produce an exciting effect, and the internal sensations arising from them furnish no contribution to the libido, in the way in which the sexual organs do. In animals these sexual zones continue in force in both respects: if this persists in human beings too, perversion results. As we turn away

our sense organs (the head and nose) in disgust, so do our preconsciousness and our conscious sense turn away from the memory. This is repression. Experiences in childhood which merely affect the genitals never produce neurosis in males (or masculine females) but only compulsive masturbation and libido. The choice of neurosis (hysteria, obsessional neurosis, or paranoia) depends on the nature of the wave of development (that is to say, its chronological placing) which enables repression to occur.

1950A   1/272

Letter 79. Masturbation, addiction and obsessional neurosis (1897).

Masturbation is the one major habit, the 'primal addiction' and it is only as a substitute and replacement for it that the other addictions for alcohol, morphine, tobacco, etc. come into existence. The part played by this addiction in hysteria is quite enormous; and it is perhaps there that the outstanding obstacle is to be found. As regards obsessional neurosis, the fact is confirmed that the locality at which the repressed breaks through is the word presentation and not the concept attached to it. Hence the most disparate things are readily united as an obsessional idea under a single word with more than one meaning. Obsessional ideas are often clothed in a remarkable verbal vagueness in order to permit multiple employment.

1950A   1/274

Letter 84. Dreams and phylogenesis (1898).

In a letter, Freud wrote that the dream book has come to a halt again and the problem has deepened and widened. The theory of wish fulfillment has brought about only the psychological solution and not the biological, or, rather, metaphysical one. Biologically, dream life seems to derive entirely from the residues of the prehistoric period of life, the same period which is the source of the unconscious and alone contains the etiology of all the psychoneuroses, the period normally characterized by an amnesia analogous to hysterical amnesia. The following formula was suggested: what is seen in the prehistoric period produces dreams; what is heard in it produces phantasies; and what is experienced sexually in it produces the psychoneuroses. The repetition of what was experienced in that period is in itself the fulfillment of a wish; a recent wish only leads to a dream if it can put itself in connection with material from this prehistoric period, if the recent wish is a derivative of a prehistoric one or can get itself adopted by one.

1950A   1/275
Letter 97.   Childhood enuresis (1898).

The subject of a new case is a young man of 25, who can scarcely walk owing to stiffness of the legs, spasms, tremors, etc. A safeguard against any wrong diagnosis is provided by the accompanying anxiety, which makes him cling to his mother's apron strings. The death of his brother and the death of his father in a psychosis precipitated the onset of his condition, which has been present since he was 14. He feels ashamed in front of anyone who sees him walking in this way and he regards that as natural. His model is a tabetic uncle, with whom he identified himself at the age of 13 on account of the accepted etiology (leading a dissolute life). The shame is merely appended to the symptoms and must relate to the other precipitating factor. His uncle was not the least ashamed of his gait. The connection between his shame and his gait was rational many years ago when he had gonorrhoea which was naturally noticeable in his gait, and even some years earlier, too, when constant (aimless) erections interfered with his walking. The whole story of his youth, on the one hand, has its climax in the leg symptoms and, on the other hand, releases the affect belonging to it, and the 2 are soldered together only for his internal perception.

1950A   1/276
Letter 101.   Retrospective fantasies (1899).

In a letter, Freud wrote that a small bit of self-analysis has forced its way through, and confirmed that phantasies are products of later periods and are projected back from the then present on to the earliest childhood, and the manner in which this occurs has also emerged, once more a verbal link. Another psychical element has been found which is regarded as of general significance and as being a preliminary stage of symptoms. The dream pattern is capable of the most general application, and the key to hysteria, as well, really lies in dreams.

1950A   1/277
Letter 102.   Hysteria and fantasies (1899).

Hysterical headaches rest on an analogy in phantasy which equates the top with the bottom end of the body, so that an attack of migraine can be used to represent a forcible defloration, while, nevertheless, the whole ailment also represents a situation of wish fulfillment. In a woman patient there were constant states of despair with a melancholic conviction that she was of no use, was incapable of anything, etc. When she was a girl of 14 she discovered that she had an imperforate hymen and was in despair that she would be no use as a wife. The diagnosis was melancholia, that is, fear of impotence. With another woman patient, there was a conviction that there really was such a thing as hysterical melancholia.

1950A   1/278
Letter 105.   Importance of wish fulfillment (1899).

It is not only dreams that are wish fulfillments but hysterical attacks as well. This is true of hysterical symptoms and probably, of every neurotic event too. A symptom is the wish fulfillment of the repressing thought when, for instance, it is a punishment, a self-punishment, the final replacement of self-gratification, of masturbation. One woman suffers from hysterical vomiting because in phantasy she is pregnant, because she is so insatiable that she cannot put up with not having a baby by her last phantasy lover as well. But she must vomit too, because in that case she will be starved and emaciated, and will lose her beauty and no longer be attractive to anyone. Thus the sense of the symptom is a contradictory pair of wish fulfillments. A man turns red and sweats as soon as he sees one of a particular category of acquaintances. He is ashamed of a phantasy in which he figures as the deflowerer of every person he meets.

1950A   1/279
Letter 125.   Choice of neurosis (1899).

The problem of 'choice of neurosis' is discussed. The lowest sexual stratum is autoeroticism, which does without any psychosexual aim and demands only local feelings of satisfaction. It is succeeded by alloerotism (homo and heteroerotism); but it certainly also continues to exist as a separate current. Hysteria (and its variant, obsessional neurosis) is alloerotic: its main path is identification with the person loved. Paranoia dissolves the identification once more; it reestablishes all the figures loved in childhood which have been abandoned and it dissolves the ego itself into extraneous figures. Paranoia is regarded as a forward surge of the autoerotic current, as a return to the standpoint prevailing then.

The perversion corresponding to it would be what is known as 'idiopathic insanity'. The special relations of autoeroticism to the original ego would throw a clear light on the nature of this neurosis.

1950A   1/283

Project for a scientific psychology: Editor's introduction and key to abbreviations in the project (1966).

The present translation of *Project for a Scientific Psychology* is a completely revised one, edited in accordance with the original manuscript. The ideas contained in the *Project* persisted, and eventually blossomed into the theories of psychoanalysis. Freud was not a meticulously careful writer, and a certain number of obvious slips occur. These were corrected in this version, except where the mistake is a doubtful one or of special importance. Freud's punctuation is unsystematic and in any case often differs from English usage. The main problem raised by Freud's manuscript is his use of abbreviations. The *Project* was written in 2 or 3 weeks, left unfinished, and criticized severely at the time of its writing. There is very little in these pages to anticipate the technical procedures of psychoanalysis. Free association, the interpretation of unconscious material, and transference are barely hinted at. Only in the passages on dreams is there any anticipation of later clinical developments. All the emphasis in the *Project* is upon the environment's impact upon the organism and the organism's reaction to it. The *Project* is a pre-id description of the mind. The abbreviations used in the *Project* are: Q = Quantity (of the intercellular order of magnitude); phi = system of permeable neurones; psi = system of impermeable neurones; omega = system of perceptual neurones; W = perception; V = idea; and M = motor image.

1950A   1/295

Project for a scientific psychology. General scheme—Part I: Introduction and sections 1-8 (1895).

The intention is to furnish a psychology that is a natural science: that is, to represent psychical processes as quantitatively determinate states of specifiable material particles. The first principal theorem is the quantitative conception (Qn). This is derived directly from pathological clinical observation especially where excessively intense ideas were concerned. The second principal theorem is the neurone theory. The nervous system consists of distinct and similarly constructed neurones, which have contact with one another through the mediums of a foreign substance, which terminate upon one another as they do upon portions of foreign tissue, in which certain lines of conduction are laid down in so far as the neurones receive excitations through cell processes (dendrites) and give them off through an axis cyclinder (axon). The hypothesis of there being 2 systems of neurones, phi and psi, of which phi consists of permeable elements and psi of impermeable, seems to provide an explanation of one of the peculiarities of the nervous system, that of retaining and yet of remaining capable of receiving. The intercellular stimuli are of a comparatively small order of magnitude and of the same order as the resistances of the contact barriers. The nervous system has an inclination to a flight from pain. The transmission of quality is not durable; it leaves no traces behind and cannot be reproduced. There is a coincidence between the characteristics of consciousness and processes in the omega neurones which vary in parallel with them.

1950A   1/312

Project for a scientific psychology. General scheme—Part I: Sections 9-13 (1895).

The amounts of excitation penetrate from outside to the endings of the phi system of permeable neurones. The qualitative characteristic of the stimuli now proceeds unhindered through phi (the system of permeable neurones to psi) the system of impermeable neurones to omega (the system of perceptual neurones) where it generates sensation; it is represented by a particular period of neuronal motion, which is certainly not the same as that of the stimulus, but has a certain relation to it in accordance with a reduction formula. The nucleus of psi is connected with the paths by which endogenous quantities of excitation ascend. It is assumed that the endogenous stimuli are of an intercellular nature. The filling of the nuclear neurones in psi will have as its result an effort to discharge, an urgency which is released along the motor pathway. Pain has a peculiar quality, which makes itself felt along with the unpleasure. If the mnemic image of the hostile object is freshly cathected in some way, a state arises which is not pain but which nevertheless has a resemblance to it. The residues of the 2 kinds of experiences of pain and of satisfaction are affects and wishful states.

1950A   1/322

Project for a scientific psychology. General scheme—Part I: Sections 14-18 (1895).

With the hypotheses of wishful attraction and of the inclination to repression, the state of the system of permeable neurones (phi) has been touched. These 2 processes indicate than an organization has been formed in the system of impermeable neurones (psi) whose presence interferes with passages of quantity which on the first occasion occurred in a particular way; *i.e.*, accompanied by satisfaction or pain. The ego in psi, which can be treated like the nervous system as a whole, will, when the processes in psi are uninfluenced, be made helpless and suffer injury. This will happen if, while it is in a wishful state, it newly cathects the memory of an object and then sets discharge in action. Both wishful cathexis and release for unpleasure, where the memory in question is cathected anew, can be biologically detrimental. During the process of wishing, inhibition by the ego brings about a moderated cathexis of the wished for object, which allows it to be cognized as not real. Simultaneously with the wishful cathexis of the mnemic image, the perception of it is present. Judging is a psi process which is only made possible by inhibition by the ego and which is evoked by the dissimilarity between the wishful cathexis of a memory and a perceptual cathexis that is similar to it. Reproductive thought has a practical aim and a biologically established end. The aim and end of all thought processes is to bring about a state cf identity. Cognitive or judging thought seeks an identity with a bodily cathexis, reproductive thought seeks it with a psychical cathexis of an experience of one's own.

1950A   1/335

Project for a scientific psychology. General scheme—Part I: Sections 19-21 and Appendix A (1895).

The primary processes of the system of impermeable neurones (psi) are presented daily during sleep. The essential precondition of sleep is a lowering of the endogenous load in the psi nucleus. Dreams exhibit transitions to the waking state and to a mixture with normal psi processes; yet it is easy to sift out what is genuine and what is not in the nature of a dream. Dreams are devoid of motor discharge and, for the most part, of motor elements. The connections in dreams are partly nonsensical, partly feeble minded, or even meaningless or strangely crazy. Dream ideas are of a hallucinatory kind; they awaken consciousness and meet with belief. The aim and sense of dreams can be established with certainty. Dreams are poorly remembered. Consciousness in dreams furnishes quality with as little trouble as in waking life. Consciousness of dream ideas is discontinuous.

1950A   1/347

Project for a scientific psychology. Psychopathology— Part II: Sections 1-2 (1895).

Every observer of hysteria is struck by the fact that hysterical patients are subject to a compulsion which is exercised by excessively intense ideas. Hysterical compulsion is unintelligible, incapable of being resolved by the activity of thought, and incongruous in its structure. There is a defensive process emanating from the cathected ego which results in hysterical repression and, along with it, in hysterical compulsion. To that extent the process seems to be differentiated from the primary process of the system of impermeable neurones.

1950A   1/351

Project for a scientific psychology. Psychopathology— Part II: Sections 3-6 (1895).

The outcome of hysterical repression differs very widely from that of normal defense. It is quite generally the case that we avoid thinking of what arouses only unpleasure, and we do this by directing our thoughts to something else. Hysterical repression takes place with the help of symbol formation, of displacement on to other neurones. Hysterical compulsion originates from a peculiar kind of symbol formation which is probably a primary process. Although it does not usually happen in psychical life that a memory arouses an affect which it did not give rise to as an experience, this is nevertheless something quite usual in the case of a sexual idea, precisely because the retardation of puberty is a general characteristic of the organization. The disturbance of the normal psychical process had 2 determinants: 1) that the sexual release was attached to a memory instead of to an experience; and 2) that the sexual release took place prematurely. It is the business of the ego not to permit any release of affect, because this at the same time permits a primary process.

1950A   1/360

Project for a scientific psychology. Attempt to represent normal psi processes—Part III (1895).

Attention consists in establishing the psychical state of expectation even for those perceptions which do not coincide in part with wishful cathexes. Attention is biologically justified; it is only a question of guiding the ego as to which expectant cathexis it is to establish and this purpose is served by the indications of quality. Speech association makes cognition possible. The indications of speech discharge put thought processes on a level with perceptual processes, lend them reality, and make memory of them possible. It is characteristic of the process of cognitive thought that during it, attention is, from the first, directed to the indications of thought discharge, to the indications of speech. A bound state, which combines high cathexis with small current, mechanically characterizes the processes of thought. For the ego, the biological rule of attention runs: If an indication of reality appears, then the perceptual cathexis which is simultaneously present is to be hypercathected. Thought accompanied by a cathexis of the indications of thought reality or the indications of speech is the highest, securest form of cognitive thought process. Memory consists in facilitations that are not altered by a rise in the level of cathexis; but there are facilitations that come into effect only at a particular level. Alongside of cognitive and practical thought, there is a reproductive, remembering thought, which in part enters into practical thought, but does not exhaust it. Thought may lead to unpleasure or to contradiction.

1950A   1/388

Project for a scientific psychology. Attempt to represent normal psi processes—Part III: Appendices B and C (1895).

There are 3 ways in which the neurones affect one another: 1) they transfer quantity to one another; 2) they transfer quality to one another; and 3) they have an exciting effect on one another. The perceptual processes involve consciousness and would only produce their further psychical effects after becoming conscious. The nature of quantity (Q) is discussed. Q appears in 2 distinguishable forms. The first of these is Q in flow, passing through a neurone or from one neurone to another. The second, more static, form is shown by a cathected neurone filled with Q. Q would appear to be measurable in 2 ways: by the height of the level of cathexis within a neurone and by the amount of flow between cathexes. Whatever may be the precise details of the mechanism responsible for bringing about the transformation of free into bound Q, it is evident that Freud attached the greatest importance to the distinction itself.

VOL. II   Studies on Hysteria (1893–1895)

2/ix
Studies on Hysteria (1955). Editor's introduction and prefaces to the first and second editions.

The present translation by James and Alix Strachey of *Studies on Hysteria* includes Breuer's contributions, but is otherwise based on the German edition of 1925, containing Freud's extra footnotes. Some historical notes on the *Studies on Hysteria* are presented including Breuer's treatment of Fraulein Anna O., on which the whole work is founded, and the case of Frau Emma von N. which was the first one treated by the cathartic method. It was through the study of the case of Frau Cacilie M. that led directly to publication of "Preliminary Communication". The bearing of these studies of hysteria on psychoanalyses is discussed. It is thought that the most important of Freud's achievements is his invention of the first instrument for the scientific examination of the human mind. In the years immediately following the Studies, Freud abandoned more and more of the machinery of deliberate suggestion and came to rely more and more on the patient's flow of free associations. Freud originated the technical developments, together with the vital theoretical concepts of resistance, defense, and repression which arose from them. Breuer originated the notion of hypnoid states, and it seems possible that he was responsible for the terms catharsis and abreaction. The second edition of *Studies on Hysteria* appears without any alterations, though the opinions and methods which were put forward in the first edition have since undergone far reaching and profound developments. The initial views are not regarded as errors but as valuable first approximations to knowledge which could only be fully acquired after long and continuous efforts.

1893A   2/1
Studies on Hysteria (1893–1895). Chapter I. On the psychical mechanism of hysterical phenomena: Preliminary communication (1893) (Breuer and Freud).

A great variety of different forms and symptoms of hysteria which have been traced to precipitating factors include neuralgias and anesthesias of various kinds, contractures and paralyses, hysterical attacks and epileptoid convulsions, chronic vomiting and anorexia, etc. The connection between the precipitating event and the development of hysteria is often quite clear while at other times the connection is 'symbolic.' Observation of these latter cases establishes an analogy between the pathogenesis of common hysteria and that of traumatic neurosis and justify an extension of the concept of traumatic hysteria. It was found that each individual hysterical symptom immediately and permanently disappeared when the event by which it was provoked was clearly brought to light and when the patient described the event in great detail and had put the affect into words. The fading of a memory or the losing of its affect depends on various factors, the most important of these is whether there has been an energetic reaction to the event that provokes an affect. The memories correspond to traumas that have not been sufficiently abreacted. The splitting of consciousness which is so striking in the well known classical cases under the form of double conscience is present to a rudimentary degree in every hysteria. The basis of hysteria is the existence of hypnoid states. Charcot gave a schematic description of the major hysterical attack, according to which 4 phases can be distinguished in a complete attack: 1) the epileptoid phase, 2) the phase of large movements, 3) the phase of attitudes passionelles (the hallucinatory phase), and 4) the phase of terminal delirium. The psychotherapeutic procedure has a curative effect on hysteria: It brings to an end the operative force of the idea which was not abreacted in the first instance, by allowing its strangulated affect to find a way out through speech, and it subjects it to associative correction by introducing it into normal consciousness or by removing it through the physician's suggestion.

1895D   2/21
Studies on Hysteria (1893–1895). Chapter II. Case histories: 1 Fraulein Anna O. (Breuer).

The case history of Anna O. is presented. Illness started at 21 years of age and the course of illness fell into several clearly separable phase: latent incubation; the manifest illness; a period of persisting somnambulism, subsequently alternating with more normal states; and gradual cessation of the pathological states and symptoms. Throughout her illness, Fraulein Anna O. fell into a somnolent state every afternoon and after sunset this period passed into a deeper sleep or hypnosis called "clouds". During the 'other' states of consciousness (called absences) she would complain of lost time and of a gap in her train of conscious thought. If she was able to narrate the hallucinations she had had in the course of the day, she would wake up with a clear mind, calm and cheerful. The essential features of this phenomenon, the mounting up and intensification of her absences into her autohypnosis in the evening, the effect of the products of her imagination as psychical stimuli, and the easing and removal of her state of stimulation when she gave utterance to them in her hypnosis, remained constant throughout the whole 18 months during which she was under observation. The psychical characteristics, present in Fraulein Anna O. while she was still completely healthly, acted as predisposing causes for her subsequent hysterical illness. One was her monotonous family life and the absence of adequate intellectual occupation which left her with an unemployed surplus of

mental liveliness and energy, and this found an outlet in the constant activity of her imagination. The second characteristic was her habit of daydreaming which laid the foundation for a dissociation of her mental personality.

1895D   2/48
Studies on Hysteria (1893–1895). Chapter II. Case histories: 2. Frau Emmy von N. (Freud).

The case history of Emmy von N. is discussed. On May 1, 1889, Freud took on the case of a woman whose symptoms and personality interested him so greatly that he devoted a large part of his time to her and determined to do all he could for her recovery. She was a hysteric and could be put into a state of somnambulism with the greatest ease. Delirium was the last considerable disturbance in Frau Emmy von N's condition. Hypnosis was used primarily for the purpose of giving her maxims which were to remain constantly present in her mind and to protect her from relapsing into similar conditions when she got home. The mildness of her deliria and hallucinations, the change in her personality and store of memories when she was in a state of artificial somnambulism, the anesthesia in her painful leg, certain data revealed in her anamnesis, her ovarian neuralgia, etc., admit of no doubt as to the hysterical nature of the illness or of the patient. The psychical symptoms in this case of hysteria with very little conversion can be divided into alterations of mood, phobias, and abulias. These phobias and abulias were, for the most part, of traumatic origin. The distressing effects attached to her traumatic experiences had remained unresolved. Her memory exhibited a lively activity which brought her traumas with their accompanying affects bit by bit into her present day consciousness.

1895D   2/106
Studies on Hysteria (1893–1895). Chapter II. Case histories: 3. Miss Lucy R. (Freud).

At the end of the year 1892, Miss Lucy R. was referred to Freud by an acquaintance who was treating her for chronically recurrent suppurative rhinitis. She was suffering from depression and fatigue and was tormented by subjective sensations of smell. Freud concluded that experiences which have played an important pathogenic part, and all their subsidiary concomitants, were accurately retained in the patient's memory even when they seemed to be forgotten, when he is unable to call them to mind. Before hysteria can be acquired for the first time, one essential condition must be fulfilled: an idea must be intentionally repressed from consciousness and excluded from associative modification. This intentional repression is also the basis for the conversion, whether total or partial, of the sum of excitation. The sum of excitation, being cut off from psychical association, finds its way all the more easily along the wrong path to a somatic innervation. The basis for repression itself can only be a feeling of unpleasure, the incompatibility between the single idea that is to be repressed and the dominant mass of ideas constituting the ego. It was found that as one symptom was removed, another developed to take its place. The case history of Miss Lucy R. was regarded as a model instance of one particular type of hysteria, namely the form of this illness which can be acquired even by a person of sound heredity, as a result of appropriate experiences. The actual traumatic moment is the one at which the incompatibility forces itself upon the ego and at which the latter decides on the repudiation of the incompatible idea. When this process occurs for the first time there comes into being a nucleus and center of crystallization for the formation of a psychical group divorced from the ego, a group around which everything which would imply an acceptance of the incompatible idea subsequently collects. The splitting of consciousness in these cases of acquired hysteria is accordingly a deliberate and intentional one. It was concluded that the therapeutic process in this case consisted in compelling the psychical group that had been split off to unite once more with the ego-consciousness.

1895D   2/125
Studies on Hysteria. (1893–1895). Chapter II. Case histories: 4. Katharina (Freud).

The case history of Katharina, an employee at a mountain retreat that Freud visited, is presented. The girl approached him with a problem of an anxiety attack that had first appeared 2 years previously. Katharina realized that her uncle had been making advances to her and that he had also been involved with her cousin. It was hoped that she, Katharina, whose sexual sensibility had been injured at an early age, derived some benefit from the conversation with Freud. Katharina agreed that what Freud interpolated into her story was probably true; but she was not in a position to recognize it as something she had experienced. The case was fitted into the schematic picture of an acquired hysteria. In every analysis of a case of hysteria based on sexual traumas, the impressions from the presexual period which produce no effect on the child attain traumatic power at a later date as memories, when the girl or married women acquires an understanding of sexual life. The anxiety which Katharina suffered in her attacks was a hysterical one; that is, it was a reproduction of the anxiety which had appeared in connection with each of the sexual traumas.

1895D   2/135
Studies on Hysteria (1893–1895). Chapter II. Case histories: 5. Fraulein Elisabeth von R. (Freud).

The case of Fraulein Elisabeth von R., a young patient of 24, who walked with the upper part of her body bent forward, but without making use of any support, is studied. The diagnosis of hysteria was proposed for the following reasons: 1) The descriptions and character of her pains were indefinite. 2) If the hyperalgesic skin and muscles of her legs were touched, her face assumed a peculiar expression, which was one of pleasure rather than pain. For a long time, Freud was unable to grasp the connection between the events in her illness and her actual symptoms, the obscurity due to the fact that analysis pointed to the occurrence of a conversion of psychical excitation into physical pain. It was thought that the conversion did not take place in connection with her impressions when they were fresh, but in connection with her memories of them. Such a course of events is not unusual in hysteria and plays a regular part in the genesis of hysterical symptoms. This assertion is substantiated by the following instances. Fraulein Rosalia H., 23 years old, had for some years been undergoing training as a singer, had a good voice, but complained that in certain parts of its compass it was not under her control. A connection was established between her singing and her hysterical paraesthesia, a connection for which the way was prepared by the organic sensations set up by singing. To rid her of this retention hysteria Freud tried to get her to reproduce all her agitating experiences and to abreact them after the event. Frau Cacilie M. suffered from an extremely violent facial neuralgia which appeared suddenly 2 or 3 times a year, and lasted from 5 to 10 days, resisted any kind of treatment and then ceases abruptly. Her case involved conflict and defense. The neuralgia had come to be indicative of a particular psychical excitation by the usual method of conversion, but afterwards, it could be set going through associative reverberations from her mental life, or symbolic conversion, in fact the same behavior found in the case of Elisabeth von R.

1895D   2/186
Studies on Hysteria (1893–1895). Chapter III. Theoretical Section (Breuer): 1. Are all hysterical phenomena ideogenic?

It is not believed that all the phenomena of hysteria are all ideogenic, that is, determined by ideas. This theory differs from Moebius who defined as hysterical all pathological phenomena that are caused by ideas. Hysteria is regarded as a clinical picture which has been empirically discovered and is based on observation. Hysteria must remain a clinical unity even if it turns out that its phenomena are determined by various causes, and that some of them are brought about by a psychical mechanism and others without it. It seems certain that many phenomena described as hysterical are not caused by ideas alone. Even though some of the phenomena of hysteria are ideogenic, nevertheless it is precisely they that must be described as the specifically hysterical ones, and it is the investigation of them, the discovery of their psychical origins, which constitutes the most important recent step forward in the theory of the disorder. The concept of excitations which flow away or have to be abreacted, is fundamentally important in hysteria and for the theory of neurosis in general.

1895D   2/192
Studies on Hysteria (1893—1895). Chapter III. Theoretical Section (Breuer): 2. Intracerebral tonic excitations—affects.

The 2 extreme conditions of the central nervous system are a clear waking state and dreamless sleep. A transition between these is afforded by conditions of varying degrees of decreasing clarity. When the brain is performing actual work, a greater consumption of energy is no doubt required than when it is merely prepared to perform work. Spontaneous awakening can take place in complete quiet and darkness without any external stimulus, thus demonstrating that the development of energy is based on the vital process of the cerebral elements themselves. Speech, the outcome of the experience of many generations, distinguishes with admirable delicacy between those forms and degrees of heightening of excitation which are still useful for mental activity because they raise the free energy of all cerebral functions uniformly, and those forms and degrees which restrict that activity because they partly increase and partly inhibit these psychical functions in a manner that is not uniform. The first are given the name of incitement, and the second excitment. While incitement only arouses the urge to employ the increased excitation functionally, excitement seeks to discharge itself in more or less violent ways which are almost or even actually pathological. A disturbance of the dynamic equilibrium of the nervous system is what makes up the psychical side of affects. All the disturbances of mental equilibrium which are called acute affects go along with an increase of excitation. Affects that are active, level out the increased excitation by motor discharge. If, however, the affect can find no discharge of excitation of any kind, then the intracerebral excitation is powerfully increased, but is employed neither in associative nor in motor activity.

1895   2/203
Studies on Hysteria (1893—1895). Chapter III. Theoretical Section (Breuer): 3. Hysterical conversion.

Resistances in normal people against the passage of cerebral excitation to the vegetative organs correspond to the insulation of electrical conducting lines. At points at which they are abnormally weak they are broken through when the tension of cerebral excitation is high, and this, the affective excitation, passes over to the peripheral organs. There ensues an abnormal expression of emotion with 2 factors responsible for this. The first is a high degree of intracerebral excitation which has failed to be leveled down either by ideational activities or by motor discharge, or which is too great to be dealt with in this way. The second is an abnormal weakness of the resistances in particular paths of conduction. Intracerebral excitation and the excitatory process in peripheral paths are of reciprocal magnitudes: the former increases if and so long as no reflex is released; it diminishes and disappears when it has been transformed into peripheral nervous excitation. Thus it seems understandable that no observable affect is generated if the idea that should have given rise to it immediately releases an abnormal reflex into which the excitation flows away as soon as it is generated. The 'hysterical conversion' is then complete. Hysterical phenomena (abnormal reflexes) do not seem to be ideogenic even to intelligent patients who are good observers, because the idea that gave rise to them is no longer colored with affect and no longer marked out among other ideas and memories. The discharge of affect follows the principle of least resistance and takes place along those paths whose resistances have already been weakened by concurrent circumstances. The genesis of hysterical phenomena that are determined by traumas finds a perfect analogy in the hysterical conversion of the psychical excitation which originates, not from external stimuli nor from the inhibition of normal psychical reflexes, but from the inhibition of the course of association. In all cases there must be convergence of several factors before a hysterical symptom can be generated in anyone who has hitherto been normal. Two ways in which affective ideas can be excluded from association were observed: through defense and in situations where the idea cannot be remembered such as in hypnosis or states similar to hypnosis. The latter seem to be of extreme importance for the theory of hysteria.

1895D   2/215
Studies on Hysteria (1893—1895). Chapter III. Theoretical Section (Breuer): 4. Hypnoid states.

The basis of hysteria is the existence of hypnoid states. The importance of these states which resemble hypnosis, lies in the amnesia that accompanies them and in their power to bring about the splitting of the mind. It must also be pointed out that conversion (the ideogenic production of somatic phenomena) can also come about apart from hypnoid states. True autohypnoses (originating spontaneously) are found in a number of fully developed hysterias, occurring with varying frequency and duration, and often alternating rapidly with normal waking states. What happens during auto-hypnotic states is subject to more or less total amnesia in waking life. The hysterical conversion takes place more easily in autohypnosis than in the waking state, just as suggested ideas are realized physically as hallucinations and movements so much more easily in artificial (non-spontaneous) hypnosis. Neither absence of mind (hypnoid state) during energetic work nor unemotional twilight states are pathogenic; on the other hand, reveries that are filled with emotion and states of fatigue arising from protracted affects are pathogenic. The method by which pathogenic autohypnosis would seem to develop is by affect being introduced into a habitual reverie. It is not known whether reveries may not themselves be able to produce the same pathological effect as auto-hypnosis, and whether the same may not also be true of a protracted affect of anxiety. The term hypnoid points to auto-hypnosis itself, the importance of which in the genesis of hysterical phenomena rests on the fact that it makes conversion easier and protects (by amnesia) the converted ideas from wearing away, a protection which ultimately leads to an increase in the psychical splitting.

1895D   2/222
Studies on Hysteria (1893–1895). Chapter III. Theoretical Section (Breuer): 5. Unconscious ideas and ideas inadmissible to consciousness—Splitting of the mind.

Ideas that we are aware of are called conscious. A great deal of what is described as mood comes from ideas that exist and operate beneath the threshold of consciousness. The whole conduct of our life is constantly influenced by subconscious ideas. All intuitive activity is directed by ideas which are to a large extent subconscious. Only the clearest and most intense ideas are perceived by self-consciousness, while the great mass of current but weaker ideas remains unconscious. There seems to be no theoretical difficulty in recognizing unconscious ideas as causes of pathological phenomena. The existence of ideas that are inadmissible to consciousness is pathological. Janet regards a particular form of congenital mental weakness as the disposition to hysteria. Freud and Breuer say that it is not the case that the splitting of consciousness occurs because the patients are weak minded; they appear to be weakminded because their mental activity is divided and only a part of its capacity is at the disposal of their conscious thought. What underlies dissociation is an excess of efficiency, the habitual coexistence of 2 heterogeneous trains of ideas. In their initial stages, hysterias of a severe degree usually exhibit a syndrome that may be described as acute hysteria. The weakness of mind caused by a splitting of the psyche seems to be a basis of the suggestibility of some hysterical patients. The uncon-

scious split of mind in hysteria is preeminently suggestible on account of the poverty and incompleteness of its ideational content.

1895D   2/240
Studies on Hysteria (1893–1895). Chapter III. Theoretical Section (Breuer): 6. Innate disposition—Development of hysteria.

Most of the hysteria phenomena that Freud and Breuer have been endeavoring to understand can be based on an innate idiosyncracy. The capacity to acquire hysteria is undoubtedly linked with an idiosyncracy of the person concerned. The reflex theory of symptoms (nervous symptoms) should not be completely rejected. The idiosyncracy of the nervous system and of the mind seems to explain some familiar properties of many hysterical patients. The surplus of excitation which is liberated by their nervous system when in a state of rest determines their incapacity to tolerate a monotonous life and boredom and their craving for sensations which drive them to interrupt this monotony with incidents of which the most prominent are pathological phenomena. They are often supported in this by autosuggestion. A surplus of excitation also gives rise to pathological phenomena in the motor sphere, often tic-like movements. Like the stigmata, a number of other nervous symptoms, some pains and vasomotor phenomena and perhaps purely motor convulsive attacks, are not caused by ideas but are direct results of the fundamental abnormality of the nervous system. Closest to them are the ideogenic phenomena, simply conversations of affective excitation. These phenomena are, by repetition, a purely somatic hysterical symptom while the idea that gave rise to it is fended off and therefore repressed. The most numerous and important of the fended-off and converted ideas have a sexual content. The tendency towards fending off what is sexual is intensified by the fact that in young unmarried women sensual excitation has an admixture of anxiety, of fear of what is coming, what is unknown and half-suspected, whereas in normal and healthy young men it is unmixed aggressive instinct. Besides sexual hysteria, there are also hysterias due to fright, traumatic hysteria proper, which constitutes one of the best known and recognized forms of hysteria. Another constitutent of the hysterical disposition is the hypnoid state, the tendency to autohypnosis. The hypnoid element is most clearly manifested in hysterical attacks and in those states which can be described as acute hysteria. The essential change that occurs in hysteria is that the mental state becomes temporarily or permanently similar to that of a hypnotized subject.

1895D 2/253

Studies on Hysteria (1893–1895). Chapter IV. The psychotherapy of hysteria (Freud).

The psychotherapy of hysteria is discussed. Each individual hysterical symptom immediately and permanently disappears when the memory of the event by which it was provoked was brought to light along with its accompanying affect and when the patient had described that event in the greatest possible detail and had put the affect into words. The etiology of the acquisition of neuroses is to be looked for in sexual factors. Different sexual factors produce different pictures of neurotic disorders. The neuroses which commonly occur are mostly to be described as mixed. Pure forms of hysteria and obsessional neurosis are rare; as a rule these 2 neuroses are combined with anxiety neurosis. Not all hysterical symptoms are psychogenic and they all cannot be alleviated by a psychotherapeutic procedure. A number of patients could not be hypnotized, although their diagnosis was one of hysteria and it seemed probable that the psychical mechanism described by Freud and Breuer operated in them. For these patients, Freud by means of psychical work had to overcome a psychical force in the patients which was opposed to the pathogenic ideas becoming conscious. The pathogenic idea is always close at hand and can be reached by associations that are easily accessible, just a question of removing the subjects will. Once a picture has emerged from the patients's memory, it becomes fragmentary and obscure in proportion as he proceeds with his description of it. The patient appears to be getting rid of it by turning it into words. It is found from cases in which guessing the way in which things are connected and telling the patient before uncovering it that therapists are not in a position to force anything on the patient about things of which he is ostensibly ignorant or to influence the products of the analysis by arousing an expectation. An external obstacle to successful psychotherapy happens when the patient's relation to the therapist is disturbed such as if there is personal estrangement, if the patient is seized by a dread of becoming accustomed to the therapist personally or of losing independence in relation to him, or if the patient is frightened at finding she is transferred her distressing ideas onto the therapist.

1895D 2/307

Studies on Hysteria (1893–1895). Appendix A: The chronology of the case of Frau Emmy von N. Appendix B: List of writings by Freud dealing principally with conversion hysteria.

The chronology of the case of Frau Emmy von N. is presented. There are serious inconsistencies in the dating of the case history. There is reason to believe that Freud altered the place of Frau Emmy's residence. It is possible

that he also altered the time as an extra precaution against betraying his patient's identity. A list of writings by Freud dealing principally with conversion hysteria is also presented. They are dated from 1886 to 1910 and include: The Observation of Pronounced Hemi—Anesthesia in a Hysterical Male; Hysteria in Villaret's *Handworterbuch*; A Letter to Josef Breuer; On the Theory of Hysterical Attacks; A Case of Successful Treatment by Hypnotism; On the Psychical Mechanism of Hysterical Phenomena; The Neuro-Psychoses of Defense; Studies on Hysteria; Project for a Scientific Psychology; and the Aetiology of Hysteria.

VOL. III Early Psycho-Analytic Publications (1893-1899)

1906B 3/3

Preface to Freud's shorter writings (1893–1906)

Volume Three of the *Standard Edition* includes the majority of the contents of the first of Freud's 5 collected volumes of shorter papers. The volume contains 2 papers which Freud omitted from his collection: the discussion on forgetting, which was afterwards developed into the first chapter of *The Psychopathology of Everyday Life* and the paper on *Screen Memories*. It also includes the list of abstracts of Freud's earlier works, which he himself drew up with an eye to his application for a professorship. The preface to Freud's collection of shorter writings on the theory of the neuroses from the years 1893 to 1906 is presented. The collection serves as an introduction and supplement to the larger publications dealing with the same topics. The Obituary of J.-M. Charcot is first of the collection of short papers.

1893F 3/9

Charcot (1893)

From October, 1885, to February, 1886, Freud worked at the Salpetriere in Paris under Charcot. This was the turning point in Freud's career, for during this period his interest shifted from neuropathology to psychopathology, from physical science to psychology. The obituary, written only a few days after Charcot's death, is some evidence of the greatness of Freud's admiration for him. Charcot treated hysteria as just another topic in neuropathology. He gave a complete description of its phenomena, demonstrated that they had their own laws and uniformities, and showed how to recognize the symptoms which enable a diagnosis of hysteria to be made. Heredity was to be regarded as the sole cause of hysteria. Charcot's concern with hypnotic phenomena in hysterical patients led to very great advances in this important field of hitherto neglected and despised facts, for the weight of his name put an end to any doubt about the reality of hypnotic manifestations.

1893H 3/25
On the psychical mechanism of hysterical phenomena: A lecture (1893).

The English translation, "On the Psychical Mechanism of Hysterical Phenomena," is a shorthand report of a lecture delivered and revised by Freud. It is pointed out that all the modern advances made in the understanding and knowledge of hysteria are derived from the work of Charcot. There is an affectively colored experience behind most phenomena of hysteria. If this experience is equated with the major traumatic experience underlying traumatic hysteria the following thesis is derived: there is a complete analogy between traumatic paralysis and common, nontraumatic hysteria. The memories in hysterical patients, which have become pathogenic, occupy an exceptional position as regards the wearing away process; and observation shows that, in the case of all the events which have become determinants of hysterical phenomena, the psychical traumas have not been completely abreacted. There are 2 groups of conditions under which memories become pathogenic. In the first group, the memories to which the hysterical phenomena can be traced back have for their content ideas which involve a trauma so great that the nervous system has not sufficient power to deal with it in any way. In a second group of cases the reason for the absence of a reaction lies not in the content of the psychical trauma but in other circumstances.

1894A 3/43
The neuro-psychoses of defence (1894).

The problems of the neuroses, which Freud investigated during the years 1893 to 1894, fell into 2 fairly distinct groups, concerned respectively with what were later to become known as the actual neuroses and the psychoneuroses. After making a detailed study of a number of nervous patients suffering from phobias and obsessions, Freud was led to attempt an explanation of these symptoms, thus arriving successfully at the origin of the pathological ideas in new and different cases. The syndrome of hysteria justifies the assumption of a splitting of consciousness, accompanied by the formation of separate psychical groups. The characteristic factor in hysteria is not the splitting of consciousness but the capacity for conversion. If someone with a disposition to neurosis lacks the aptitude for conversion, but if, in order to fend off an incompatible idea, he sets about separating it from its affect, then that affect is

obliged to remain in the psychical sphere. In all cases that Freud analyzed, it was the subject's sexual life that had given rise to a distressing affect of precisely the same quality as that attaching to his obsession. In 2 instances considered, defense against the incompatible idea was effected by separating it from its affect; the idea itself remained in consciousness, even though weakened and isolated. In another type of defense the ego rejects the incompatible idea together with its affect and behaves as if the idea had never occurred to the ego at all. But from the moment at which this has been successfully done the subject is in a psychosis, which can only be classified as hallucinatory confusion. The content of a hallucinatory psychosis of this sort consists precisely in the accentuation of the idea which was threatened by the precipitating cause of the onset of illness. The ego has fended off the incompatible idea through escape into psychosis. In summary, a working hypothesis for the neuroses of defense is as follows: In mental functions something is to be distinguished (a quota of affect or sum of excitation) which possess all the characteristics of a quantity which is capable of increase, diminution, displacement and discharge, and which is spread over the memory traces of ideas.

3/62
The neuro-psychoses of defence (1894). Appendix: The emergence of Freud's fundamental hypotheses.

With the first paper on the neuropsychoses of defense, Freud gives public expression, to many of the most fundamental of the theoretical notions on which all his later work rests. At the time of writing this paper, Freud was deeply involved in the first series of psychological investigations. In his "History of the Psycho-Analytic Movement", Freud declared that the theory of repression, or defense, to give it its alternative name, is the cornerstone on which the whole structure of psychoanalysis rests. The clinical hypothesis of defense, however, is itself necessarily based on the theory of cathexis. Throughout this period, Freud appeared to regard the cathectic processes as material events. The pleasure principle, no less fundamental than the constancy principle, was equally present, though once more only by implication. Freud regarded the 2 principles as intimately connected and perhaps identical. It is probably correct to suppose that Freud was regarding the quota of affect as a particular manifestation of the sum of excitation. Affect is what is usually involved in the cases of hysteria and obsessional neurosis with which Freud was chiefly concerned in early days. For that reason he tended at that time to describe the displaceable quantity as a quota of affect rather than in more general terms as an excitation; and this habit seems to have persisted even in the metaphysical papers where a more precise differentiation might have contributed to the clarity of his argument.

1895C 3/71

Obsessions and phobias: Their psychical mechanism and their aetiology (1895).

Obsessions and phobias cannot be included under neurasthenia proper. Since the patients afflicted with these symptoms are no more often neurasthenics than not. Obsessions and phobias are separate neuroses, with a special mechanism and etiology. Traumatic obsessions and phobias are allied to the symptoms of hysteria. Two constituents are found in every obsession: 1) an idea that forces itself upon the patient; and 2) an associated emotional state. In many true obsessions it is plain that the emotional state is the principal thing, since that state persists unchanged while the idea associated with it varies. It is the false connection between the emotional state and the associated idea that accounts for the absurdity so characteristic of obsessions. The great difference between phobias is that in the latter the emotion is always one of anxiety, fear. Among the phobias, 2 groups may be differentiated according to the nature of the object feared: 1) common phobias, an exaggerated fear of things that everyone detests or fears to some extent; and 2) contingent phobias, the fear of special conditions that inspire no fear in the normal man. The mechanism of phobias is entirely different from that of obsessions - nothing is ever found but the emotional state of anxiety which brings up all the ideas adapted to become the subject of a phobia. Phobias then are a part of the anxiety neurosis, which has a sexual origin.

3/83

Obsessions and phobias: Their psychical mechanism and their aetiology (1895). Appendix: Freud's views on phobias.

Freud's earliest approach to the problem of phobias was in his first paper on the neuropsychoses of defense. In the earliest of his papers, he attributed the same mechanism to the great majority of phobias and obsessions, while excepting the purely hysterical phobias and the group of typical phobias of which agoraphobia is a model. This latter distinction is the crucial one, for it implies a distinction between phobias having a psychical basis and those without. This distinction links with what were later to be known as the psychoneuroses and the actual neuroses. In the paper on obsessions and phobias, the distinction seems to be made not between 2 different groups of phobias but between the obsessions and the phobias, the latter being declared to be a part of the anxiety neurosis. In the paper on anxiety neurosis, the main distinction was not between obsessions and phobias but between phobias belonging to obsessional

neurosis and those belonging to anxiety neurosis. There remain undetermined links between phobias, hysteria, obsessions, and anxiety neurosis.

1895B 3/90

On the grounds for detaching a particular syndrome from neurasthenia under the description "anxiety neurosis" (1895). Editors' note, introduction and Part I. The clinical symptomatology of anxiety neurosis.

The paper, "On the Grounds for Detaching a Particular Syndrome from Neurasthenia under the Description Anxiety Neurosis" may be regarded as the first part of a trail that leads through the whole of Freud's writings. According to Freud, it is difficult to make any statement of general validity about neurasthenia, so long as it is used to cover all the things which Beard has included under it. It was proposed that the anxiety neurosis syndrome be detached from neurasthenia. The symptoms of this syndrome are clinically much more closely related to one another than to those of genuine neurasthenia; and both the etiology and the mechanism of this neurosis are fundamentally different from the etiology and mechanism of genuine neurasthenia. What Freud calls anxiety neurosis may be observed in a completely developed form or in a rudimentary one, in isolation or combined with other neuroses. The clinical picture of anxiety neurosis comprises some of the following symptoms: general irritability; anxious expectation; sudden onslaughts of anxiety; waking up at night in a fright, vertigo, disturbances in digestive activities and attacks of paraesthesias. Several of the symptoms that are mentioned, which accompany or take the place of an anxiety attack, also appear in a chronic form.

1895B 3/99

On the grounds for detaching a particular syndrome from neurasthenia under the description "anxiety neurosis" (1895). Part II. Incidence and aetiology of anxiety neurosis.

In some cases of anxiety neurosis no etiology at all is discovered. But where there are grounds for regarding the neurosis as an acquired one, careful inquiry directed to that end reveals that a set of noxae and influences from sexual life are the operative etiological factors. In females, disregarding their innate disposition, anxiety neurosis occurs in the following cases: as virginal anxiety or anxiety in adolescents; as anxiety in the newly married; as anxiety in women whose husbands suffer from ejaculatio praecox or from markedly impaired potency; and whose husbands practice coitus interruptus or reservatus; anxiety neurosis also occurs as anxiety in widows and intentionally abstinent women; and as anxiety in the climacteric during the last major increase of sexual need. The sexual determinants of anxiety neurosis in men include: anxiety of intentionally abstinent men, which is frequently combined with symptoms of defense; anxiety in men in a state of unconsummated excitation, or in those who content themselves with touching or looking at women; anxiety in men who practice coitus interruptus; and anxiety in senescent men. There are 2 other cases which apply to both sexes. 1) People who, as a result of practicing masturbation, have been neurasthenics, fall victim to anxiety neurosis as soon as they give up their form of sexual satisfaction. 2) Anxiety neurosis arises as a result of the factor of overwork or exhausting exertion.

1895B   3/106

On the grounds for detaching a particular syndrome from neurasthenia under the description "anxiety neurosis" (1895). Part III. First steps towards a theory of anxiety neurosis.

According to Freud, the mechanism of anxiety neurosis is to be looked for in a deflection of somatic sexual excitation from the psychical sphere, and in a consequent abnormal employment of that excitation. This concept of the mechanism of anxiety neurosis can be made clearer if the following view of the sexual process, which applies to men, is accepted. In the sexually mature male organism, somatic sexual excitation is produced and periodically becomes a stimulus to the psyche. The group of sexual ideas which is present in the psyche becomes supplied with energy and there comes into being the physical state of libidinal tension which brings with it an urge to remove that tension. A psychical unloading of this kind is possible only by means of what is called specific or adequate action. Anything other than the adequate action would be fruitless, for once the somatic sexual excitation has reached threshold value, it is turned continuously into psychical excitation and something must positively take place which will free the nerve endings from the pressure on them. Neurasthenia develops whenever the adequate unloading is replaced by a less adquate one. This view depicts the symptoms of anxiety neurosis as being in a sense surrogates of the omitted specific action following on sexual excitation. In the neurosis, the nervous system is reacting against a source of excitation which is internal, whereas in the corresponding affect it is reacting against an analogous source of excitation which is external.

1895B   3/112

On the grounds for detaching a particular syndrome from neurasthenia under the description "anxiety neurosis" (1895). Part IV. Relation to other neuroses.

The purest cases of anxiety neurosis, usually the most marked, are found in sexually potent youthful individuals, with an undivided etiology, and an illness that is not too long standing. More often, however, symptoms of anxiety occur at the same time as, and in combination with symptoms of neurasthenia, hysteria, obsessions, or melancholia. Wherever a mixed neurosis is present, it will be possible to discover an intermixture of several specific etiologies. The etiological conditions must be distinguished for the onset of the neuroses from their specific etiological factors. The former are still ambiguous, and each of them can produce different neuroses. Only the etiological factors which can be picked out in them, such as inadequate disburdening, psychical insufficiency or defense accompanied by substitution, have an unambiguous and specific relation to the etiology of the individual major neuroses. Anxiety neurosis presents the most interesting agreement with, and differences from, the other major neuroses, in particular neurasthenia and hysteria. It shares with neurasthenia one main characteristic, namely, that the source of excitation lies in the somatic field instead of the psychical one as is the case in hysteria and obsessional neurosis. The symptomatology of hysteria and anxiety neurosis shows many points in common. The appearance of the following symptoms either in a chronic form or in attacks, the paraesthesias, the hyperaesthesias and pressure points are found in both hysterias and anxiety attacks.

3/116

On the grounds for detaching a particular syndrome from neurasthenia under the description "anxiety neurosis" (1895). Appendix: The term "Angst" and its English translation.

There are at least 3 instances in which Freud discusses the various shades of meaning expressed by the German word Angst and the cognate Furcht and Schreck. Though he stresses the anticipatory element and absence of an object in Angst, the distinctions he draws are not entirely convincing, and his actual usage is far from invariably obeying them. Angst may be translated to many similarly common English words: fear, fright, alarm, etc. Angst often appears as a psychiatric term: The word universally adopted for the purpose has been anxiety. The English translator is driven to compromise: he must use anxiety in technical or semitechnical connections, and must elsewhere choose whatever everyday English word seems most appropriate.

1895F   3/121

A reply to criticisms of my paper on anxiety neurosis (1895).

A reply to Lowenfeld's criticisms of Freud's paper (January 1895) on anxiety neurosis is presented. It is Freud's view that the anxiety appearing in anxiety neurosis does not admit of a psychical derivation and he maintains that fright must result in hysteria or a traumatic neurosis, but not in an anxiety neurosis. Lowenfeld insists that in a number of cases 'states of anxiety' appear immediately or shortly after a psychical shock. Freud states that in the etiology of the neuroses, sexual factors play a predominant part. Lowenfeld relates experiences where he has seen anxiety states appear and disappear when a change in the subject's sexual life had not taken place but where other factors were in play. The following concepts are postulated in order to understand the complicated etiological situation which prevails in the pathology of the neuroses: precondition, specific cause, concurrent causes, and precipitating or releasing cause. Whether a neurotic illness occurs at all depends upon a quantitative factor, upon the total load on the nervous system as compared with the latter's capacity for resistance. What dimensions the neurosis attains depends in the first instance on the amount of the hereditary taint. What form the neurosis assumes is solely determined by the specific etiological factor arising from sexual life.

1896A 3/141
Heredity and the aetiology of the neuroses (1896).

The paper, "Heredity and the Etiology of the Neuroses" is a summary of Freud's contemporary view on the etiology of all 4 of what he then regarded as the main types of neurosis: the 2 psychoneuroses, hysteria and obsessional neurosis; and the 2 actual neuroses, neurasthenia and anxiety neurosis. Opinion of the etiological role of heredity in nervous illness ought to be based on an impartial statistical examination. Certain nervous disorders can develop in people who are perfectly healthy and whose family is above reproach. In nervous pathology, there is similar heredity and also dissimilar heredity. Without the existence of a special etiological factor, heredity could do nothing. The etiological influences, differing among themselves in their importance and in the manner in which they are related to the effect they produce, can be grouped into 3 classes: preconditions, concurrent causes, and specific causes. In the pathogenesis of the major neuroses, heredity fulfills the role of a precondition. Some of the concurrent causes of neuroses are: emotional disturbance, physical exhaustion, acute illness, intoxications, traumatic accidents, etc. The neuroses have as their common source the subject's sexual life, whether they lie in a disorder of his contemporary sexual life or in important events in his past life.

1896B 3/162
Further remarks on the neuro-psychoses of defence (1896). Part I. The "specific" aetiology of hysteria.

"Further Remarks on the Neuropsychoses of Defense" takes up the discussion at a point that Freud

reached in his first paper, (1894). The ultimate case of hysteria is always the seduction of a child by an adult. The actual traumatic event always occurs before the age of puberty, though the outbreak of the neurosis occurs after puberty. This whole position is later abandoned by Freud, and its abandonment signalizes a turning point in his views. In a short paper published in 1894, Freud grouped together hysteria, obsessions, and certain cases of acute hallucinatory confusion under the name of neuropsychoses of defense because those affections turned out to have one aspect in common. This was that their symptoms arose through the psychical mechanism of defense, that is, in an attempt to repress an incompatible idea which had come into distressing opposition to the patient's ego. The symptoms of hysteria can only be understood if they are traced back to experiences which have a traumatic effect. These psychical traumas refer to the patient's sexual life. These sexual traumas must have occurred in early childhood and their content must consist of an actual irritation of the genitals. All the experiences and excitations which, in the period of life after puberty, prepare the way for, or precipitate, the outbreak of hysteria, demonstrably have their effect only because they arouse the memory trace of these traumas in childhood, which do not thereupon become conscious but lead to a release of affect and to repression. Obsessions also presuppose a sexual experience in childhood.

1896B 3/168
Further remarks on the neuro-psychosis of defence (1896). Part II. The nature and mechanism of obsessional neurosis.

Sexual experiences of early childhood have the same significance in the etiology of obsessional neurosis as they have in that of hysteria. In all the cases of obsessional neurosis, Freud found a substratum of hysterical symptoms which could be traced back to a scene of sexual passivity that preceded the pleasurable action. Obsessional ideas are transformed self-reproaches which have reemerged from repression and which relate to some sexual act that was performed with pleasure in childhood. In the first period, childhood immorality, events occur which contain the germ of the later neurosis. This period is brought to a close by the advent of sexual maturation. Self-reproach now becomes attached to the memory of these pleasurable actions. The second period, illness, is characterized by the return of the repressed memories. There are 2 forms of obsessional neurosis, according to whether what forces an entrance into consciousness is solely the mnemic content of the act involving self-reproach, or whether the self-reproachful affect connected with the act does so as well. The first form includes the typical obsessional ideas, in which the content engages the patient's attention and, he merely feels an indefinite unpleasure, whereas the only affect which would be suitable to the obsessional idea would be one of self-reproach. A second form of obsessional neurosis comes about if what has forced its way to representation in conscious psychical life is not the repressed mnemic content but the repressed self-reproach.

1896B   3/174
Further remarks on the neuro-psychosis of defense (1896). Part III. Analysis of a case of chronic paranoia.

Freud postulates that paranoia, like hysteria and obsessions, proceeds from the repression of distressing memories and that its symptoms are determined in their form by the content of what has been repressed. The analysis of a case of chronic paranoia is presented. Frau P., 32 years of age, has been married for 3 years and is the mother of a 2-year-old child. Six months after the birth of her child, she became uncommunicative and distrustful, showed aversion to meeting her husband's brothers and sisters and complained that the neighbors in the small town in which she lived were rude and inconsiderate to her. The patient's depression began at the time of a quarrel between her husband and her brother. Her hallucinations were part of the content of repressed childhood experiences, symptoms of the return of the repressed while the voices originated in the repression of thoughts which were self-reproaches about experiences that were analogous to her childhood trauma. The voices were symptoms of the return of the repressed. Part of the symptoms arose from primary defense, namely, all the delusional ideas which were characterized by distrust and suspicion and which were concerned with ideas of being persecuted by others. Other symptoms are described as symptoms of the return of the repressed. The delusional ideas which have arrived in consciousness by means of a compromise make demands on the thought activity of the ego until they can be accepted without contradiction.

1896C   3/189
The aetiology of hysteria (1896).

"The Etiology of Hysteria" may be regarded as an amplified repetition of the first section of its predecessor, the second paper on the neuropsychoses of defense. No hysterical symptom can arise from a real experience alone, but in every case, the memory of earlier experiences plays a part in causing the symptoms. Whatever case and symptom are taken as out point of departure leads to the field of sexual experience. After the chains of memories have converged, we come to the field of sexuality and to a small number of experiences which occur for the most part at the same period of life, namely, at puberty. If we press on with the analysis into early childhood, we bring the patient to reproduce experiences which are regarded as the etiology of his

neurosis. Freud put forward the thesis that for every case of hysteria there are one or more occurrences of premature sexual experience, occurrences which belong to the earliest years of childhood but which can be reproduced through the work of psychoanalysis in spite of the intervening decades. Sexual experiences in childhood consisting in stimulation of the genitals must be recognized as being the traumas which lead to a hysterical reaction to events at puberty and to the development of hysterical symptoms. Sensations and paraesthesias are the phenomena which correspond to the sensory content of the infantile scenes, reproduced in a hallucinatory fashion and often painfully intensified.

1897B   3/225
Abstracts of the scientific writings of Dr. Sigm. Freud, 1877–1897 (1897).

Freud was appointed a Privatdozent at the Vienna University in 1885. Twelve years later, Freud's name was put forward to the Council of the Faculty as Professor Extraordinarius. The necessary preliminaries included a Curriculum Vitae and a bibliographical abstract of publications. Thirteen abstracts of the scientific writings of Dr. Sigmund Freud written before, and 26 abstracts written after his appointment as Privatdozent are presented.

1898A   3/261
Sexuality in the aetiology of the neuroses (1896).

In every case of neurosis there is a sexual etiology; but in neurasthenia it is an etiology of a present day kind, whereas in the psychoneuroses the factors are of an infantile nature. The sexual causes are the ones which most readily offer the physician a foothold for his therapeutic influence. When heredity is present, it enables a strong pathological effect to come about where otherwise only a very slight one would have resulted. Neurasthenia is one of those affections which anyone might easily acquire without having any hereditary taint. It is only the sexual etiology which makes it possible for us to understand all the details of the clinical history of neurasthenics, the mysterious improvements in the middle of the course of the illness and the equally incomprehensible deteriorations, both of which are usually related by doctors and patients to whatever treatment has been adopted. Since the manifestations of the psychoneuroses arise from the deferred action of unconscious psychical traces, they are accessible to psychotherapy. The main difficulties which stand in the way of the psychoanalytic method of cure are due to the lack of understanding among doctors and laymen of the nature of the psychoneuroses.

1898B 3/287
The psychical mechanism of forgetfulness (1898).

The phenomenon of forgetfulness, which has been universally experienced, usually affects proper names. Two accompanying features of forgetfulness are an energetic deliberate concentration of attention which proves powerless, to find the lost name and in place of the name we are looking for, another name promptly appears, which we recognize as incorrect and reject, but which persists in coming back. The best procedure of getting hold of the missing name is not to think of it and after a while, the missing name shoots into one's mind. While Freud was vacationing, he went to Herzegovina. Conversation centered around the condition of the 2 countries (Bosnia and Herzegovina), and the character of their inhabitants. The discussion turned to Italy and of pictures. Freud recommended that his companions visit Orvieto some time, in order to see the frescoes there of the End of the World and the Last Judgement. Freud was unable to think of the artist's name. He could only think of Botticelli and Boltraffio. He had to put up with this lapse of memory for several days until he met someone who told him that the artist's name was Luca Signorelli. Freud interpreted the forgetting as follows: Botticelli contains the same final syllables as Signorelli; the name Bosnia showed itself by directing the substitution to 2 artists' names which began with the same syllable "Bo". The place where a piece of news about death and sexuality reached Freud was called "Trafoi" similar to the second half of the name Boltraffio. This example may serve as a model for the pathological processes to which the psychical symptoms of the psychoneuroses, hysteria, obsessions and paranoia, owe their origin. A repressed train of thought takes possession in neuroses of an innocent recent impression and draws it down with itself into repression.

1899A 3/301
Screen memories (1899).

The age to which the content of the earliest memories of childhood is usually referred back is the period between the ages of 2 and 4. The most frequent content of the first memories of childhood are occasions of fear, shame, physical pain, etc., and important events such as illnesses, deaths, fires, births of brothers and sisters, etc. A case is presented of a man of university education, aged 38, who moved at the age of 3. His memories of his first place of residence fall into 3 groups. The first group consists of scenes of which his parents have repeatedly since described to him. The second group comprises scenes which have not been described and some of which could not have been described to him. The pictures and scenes of the first 2 groups are probably displaced memories from which the essential element has for the

most part been omitted. In the third group, there is material, which cannot be understood. Two sets of phantasies were projected onto one another and a childhood memory was made of them. A screen memory is a recollection whose value lies in that it represents in the memory impressions and thoughts of a later date whose content is connected with its own by symbolic or similar links. The concept of screen memory owes its value as a memory not to its own content but to the relation existing between that content and some other, that has been suppressed. Different classes of screen memories can be distinguished according to the nature of that relation. A screen memory may be described as retrogressive. Whenever in a memory the subject himself appears as an object among other objects, the contrast between the acting and the recollecting ego may be taken as evidence that the original impression has been worked over.

1901C 3/323
Autobiographical note (1901).

Freud's autobiographical note, written in the autumn of 1899 is presented. He regarded himself as a pupil of Brucke and of Charcot. His appointment as Privatdozent was in 1885 and he worked as physician and Dozent at Vienna University after 1886. Freud produced earlier writings on histology and cerebral anatomy, and subsequently, clinical works on neuropathology; he translated writings by Charcot and Bernheim. Since 1895, Freud turned to the study of the psychoneuroses and especially hysteria, and in a series of shorter works he stressed the etiological significance of sexual life for the neuroses. He has also developed a new psychotherapy of hysteria, on which very little has been published.

VOL. IV   The Interpretation of Dreams (I) (1900)

4/xi
The Interpretation of Dreams (1953). Editor's introduction.

The Interpretation of Dreams is regarded by Freud as his most important work. This translation is based on the eighth (1930) German edition, the last published during Freud's life. Students of Freud's theoretical writings have been aware that even in his profoundest psychological speculations little or no discussion is to be found upon some of the most fundamental of the concepts of which he makes use: such concepts, for instance, as mental energy, sums of excitation, cathexis, quantity, quality, intensity, etc. A principal part was played in Freud's scheme by a hypothetical division of the neurons into 3 classes or systems, differentiated according to their modes of functioning. Of these the first 2 were concerned respectively with external stimuli and internal excitations. Both of these operated on a purely quantitative basis; with their actions wholly determined by the magnitude of the nervous excitations impinging on them. The third system was correlated with the qualitative differences which distinguish conscious sensations and feelings. Freud asserted that *The Interpretation of Dreams* was finished in all essentials at the beginning of 1896. Through the Fliess correspondence the progress of composition can be followed in detail.

1900A 4/xxi

The Interpretation of Dreams (1900). Preface to the first, second, third, fourth, fifth, sixth, eighth editions and third (revised) English edition (1900–1931).

The prefaces to the editions 1 through 6, 8 and the third revised English edition are presented. The second edition was called for 10 years after the publication of the book. The third edition was published 1 year later. The theory of dream interpretation has been developed further in a direction in which insufficient stress has been laid in the first edition of this book. The importance of symbolism in dreams was increasingly stressed. Dr. Brill's first translation of *The Interpretation of Dreams* appeared in 1913. This third revised English edition with the new contribution to psychology which surprised the world when it was published (1900), remains essentially unaltered. It contains, even according to Freud's judgment, the most valuable of all his discoveries.

1900A 4/1

The Interpretation of Dreams (1900). Chapter I: The scientific literature dealing with the problems of dreams. (A) The relation of dreams to waking life.

The scientific literature dealing with the problems of dreams is discussed. The prescientific view of dreams adopted by the peoples of antiquity was in complete harmony with their view of the universe in general, which led them to project into the external world as though they were realities, things which in fact enjoyed reality only within their own minds. The unsophisticated waking judgment of someone who has just awakened from sleep assumes that his dreams, even if they did not themselves come from another world, had carried him off into another world. Two views of the relation of dreams to waking life are discussed: 1) that the mind is cut off in dreams, almost without memory, from the ordinary content and affairs of waking life or 2) that dreams carry on waking life and attach themselves to the ideas previously residing in consciousness. Due to the contradiction between these 2 views, a discussion of the

subject is presented by Hildebrandt who believes that it is impossible to describe the characteristics of dreams at all except by means of a series of (3) contrasts which seem to sharpen into contradictions. It is concluded that the dream experience appears as something alien inserted between 2 sections of life which are perfectly continuous and consistent with each other.

1900A 4/11

The Interpretation of Dreams (1900). Chapter I: The scientific literature dealing with the problems of dreams. (B) The material of dreams—Memory in dreams.

All the material making up the content of a dream is in some way derived from experience. Dreams have at their command memories which are inaccessible in waking life. It is a very common event for a dream to give evidence of knowledge and memories which the waking subject is unaware of possessing. One of the sources from which dreams derive materials for reproduction, material which is in part neither remembered nor used in the activities of waking thought, is childhood experience. A number of writers assert that elements are to be found in most dreams, which are derived from the last very few days before they were dreamt. The most striking and least comprehensible characteristic of memory in dreams is shown in the choice of material reproduced: what is found worth remembering is not, as in waking life, only what is most important, but what is most indifferent and insignificant. This preference for indifferent, and consequently unnoticed, elements in waking experience is bound to lead people to overlook the dependence of dreams upon waking life and to make it difficult in any particular instance to prove that dependence. The way memory behaves in dreams is of the greatest importance for any theory of memory in general.

1900A 4/22

The Interpretation of Dreams (1900). Chapter I: The scientific literature dealing with the problems of dreams. (C) The stimuli and sources of dreams.

There are 4 kinds of sources of dreams: external (objective) sensory excitations; internal (subjective) sensory excitations; internal (organic) somatic stimuli; and purely psychical sources of stimulation. There are a great number of sensory stimuli that reach us during sleep, ranging from unavoidable ones which the state of sleep itself necessarily involves or must tolerate, to the accidental, rousing stimuli which may or do put an end to sleep. As sources of dream images, subjective sensory excitations have the advantage of not being dependent, like objective ones, upon external chance. The body, when in a diseased state, becomes a source of stimuli for dreams. In most dreams, somatic stimuli and the psychical instigators work in cooperation.

1900A 4/43

The Interpretation of Dreams (1900). Chapter I: The scientific literature dealing with the problems of dreams. (D) Why dreams are forgotten after waking.

It is a proverbial fact that dreams melt away in the morning. All the causes that lead to forgetting in waking life are operative for dreams as well. Many dream images are forgotten because they are too weak, while stronger images adjacent to them are remembered. It is in general as difficult and unusual to retain what is nonsensical as it is to retain what is confused and disordered. Dreams, in most cases, are lacking in intelligibility and orderliness. The compositions which constitute dreams are barren of the qualities (strength intensity, nonunique experience, orderly groupings) which would make it possible to remember them, and they are forgotten because as a rule they fall to pieces a moment after awakening, and because most people take very little interest in their dreams.

1900A 4/48

The Interpretation of Dreams (1900). Chapter I: The scientific literature dealing with the problems of dreams. (E) The distinguishing psychological characteristics of dreams.

It is assumed that dreams are products of our own mental activity. One of the principal peculiarities of dream life makes its appearance during the very process of falling asleep and may be described as a phenomenon heralding sleep. Dreams think predominantly in visual images, but make use of auditory images as well. In dreams, the subjective activity of our minds appears in an objective form, for our perceptive faculties regard the products of our imagination as though they were sense impressions. Sleep signifies an end of the authority of the self, hence, falling asleep brings a certain degree of passivity along with it. The literature that involves the psychological characteristics of dreams shows a very wide range of variation in the value which it assigns to dreams as psychical products. This range extends from the deepest disparagement through hints at a yet undisclosed worth, to an overvaluation which ranks dreams far higher than any of the functions of waking life.

1900A 4/63

The Interpretation of Dreams (1900). Chapter I: The scientific literature dealing with the problems of dreams. (F) The moral sense in dreams.

The moral sense in dreams is discussed. Some assert that the dictates of morality have no place in dreams,

while others maintain that the moral character of man persists in his dream life. Those who maintain that the moral personality of man ceases to operate in dreams should, in strict logic, lose all interest in immoral dreams. Those who believe that morality extends to dreams are careful to avoid assuming complete responsibility for their dreams. The emergence of impulses which are foreign to our moral consciousness is merely analogous to the fact that dreams have access to ideational material which is absent in our waking state or plays but a small part in it. Affects in dreams cannot be judged in the same way as the remainder of their content; and we are faced by the problem of what part of the psychical processes occurring in dreams is to be regarded as real (has a claim to be classed among the psychical processes of waking life).

1900A 4/75

The Interpretation of Dreams (1900). Chapter I: The scientific literature in dealing with the problems of dreams. (G) Theories of dreaming and its function.

Theories of dreaming and its function are discussed. Some theories (*i.e.* Delboeuf) states that the whole of psychical activity continues in dream. The mind does not sleep and its apparatus remains intact; but, since it falls under the conditions of the state of sleep, its normal functioning necessarily produces different results during sleep. There are other theories which presuppose that dreams imply a lowering of psychical activity, a loosening of connections, and an impoverishment of the material accessible. These theories must imply the attribution to sleep of characteristics quite different from those suggested by Delboeuf. A third group of theories ascribe to the dreaming mind a capacity and inclination for carrying out special psychical activities of which it is largely or totally incapable in waking life. The putting of these faculties into force usually provides dreaming with a utilitarian function. The explanation of dreaming by Scherner as a special activity of the mind, capable of free expansion only during the state of sleep is presented. He states that the material with which dream imagination accomplishes its artistic work is principally provided by the organic somatic stimuli which are obscure during the daytime.

1900A 4/88

The Interpretation of Dreams (1900). Chapter I: The scientific literature dealing with the problems of dreams. (H) The relations between dreams and mental diseases.

When we speak of the relation of dreams to mental disorders we may have 3 things in mind: 1) etiological and clinical connections, as when a dream represents a psychotic state, or introduces it, or is left over from it; 2) modifications to which dream life is subject in cases of mental disease; and 3) intrinsic connections between dreams and psychoses, analogies pointing to their being essentially akin. In addition to the psychology of dreams physicians will some day turn their attention to psychopathology of dreams. In cases of recovery from mental diseases it can often be observed that while functioning is normal during the day, dream life is still under the influence of the psychosis. The indisputable analogy between dreams and insanity is one of the most powerful factors of the medical theory of dream life which regards dreaming as a useless and disturbing process and as the expression of a reduced activity of the mind.

1900A 4/96

The Interpretation of Dreams (1900). Chapter II: The method of interpreting dreams: An analysis of a specimen dream.

The method of interpreting dreams is presented. The aim that Freud sets is to show that dreams are capable of being interpreted. The lay world has hitherto made use of 2 essentially different methods: 1) It considers the content of the dream as a whole and seeks to replace it by another content which is intelligible and in certain respects analogous to the original one, this is (symbolic dream interpreting). 2) The decoding method, which treats dreams as a kind of cryptography in which each sign can be translated into another sign having a known meaning, in accordance with a fixed key. Neither of the 2 popular procedures for interpreting dreams can be employed for a scientific treatment of the subject. The object of the attention is not the dream as a whole but the separate portions of its content.

1900A 4/106

The Interpretation of Dreams (1900). Chapter II: The method of interpreting dreams: An analysis of a specimen dream (preamble and dream).

An analysis of one of Freud's dreams, the dream of July twenty-third to the twenty-fourth, 1895, is presented. During the summer of 1895, Freud had been giving psychoanalytic treatment to a woman who was on very friendly terms with him and his family. This woman was involved in the dream as a central figure (Irma). The dream was analyzed, one line or thought at a time. The dream fulfilled certain wishes which were initiated by the events of the previous evening. The conclusion of the dream was that Freud was not responsible for the persistence of Irma's pains, but that Otto (a junior colleague) was. Otto had annoyed Freud by his remarks about Irma's incomplete cure, and the dream gave Freud his revenge by throwing the reproach back. Certain other themes played a part in the dream, which were not so

obviously connected with his exculpation from Irma's illness: his daughter's illness and that of his patient who bore the same name, the injurious effect of cocaine, the disorder of his patient who was traveling in Egypt, his concern about his wife's health and about that of his brother and of Dr. M., his own physical ailments, and his anxiety about his absent friend who suffered from suppurative rhinitis. Freud concluded that when the work of interpretation is completed, it is perceived that a dream is the fulfillment of a wish.

1900A 4/122

The Interpretation of Dreams (1900). Chapter III: A dream is the fulfillment of a wish.

It is easy to prove that dreams often reveal themselves as fulfillments of wishes. In a dream of convenience, dreaming has taken the place of action, as it often does elsewhere in life. Dreams which can only be understood as fulfillments of wishes and which bear their meaning upon their faces without disguise are found under the most frequent and various conditions. They are mostly short and simple dreams, which afford a pleasant contrast to the confused and exuberant compositions that have in the main attracted the attention of the authorities. The dreams of young children are frequently pure wish fulfillments and are subsequently quite uninteresting compared with the dreams of adults. A number of cases of dreams of children are presented and interpreted.

1900A 4/134

The Interpretation of Dreams (1900). Chapter IV: Distortion in dreams.

The fact that the phenomena of censorship and of dream distortion correspond to their smallest details justifies assumption that they are similarly determined, therefore, it is supposed that dreams are given their shape in individual human beings by the operation of 2 psychical forces; and that one of these forces constructs the wish which is expressed by the dream, while the other exercises a censorship upon this dream wish and, by the use of that censorship, forcibly brings about a distortion in the expression of the wish. The very frequent dreams, which appear to stand in contradiction to Freud's theory because their subject matter is the frustration of a wish or the occurrence of something clearly unwished for, may be brought together under the heading of counter wish dreams. If these dreams are considered as a whole, it seems possible to trace them back to 2 principles. One of the 2 motive forces is the wish that Freud may be wrong, the second motive involves the masochistic component in the sexual constitution of many people. Those who find their pleasure, not in having physical pain inflicted on them, but in humiliation and mental torture, may be described as mental masochists. People of this kind can have counter wish dreams and unpleasurable dreams, which are none the less wish fulfillments since they satisfy their masochistic inclinations. Anxiety dreams (a special subspecies of dreams with a distressing content) do not present a new aspect of the dream problem but present the question of neurotic anxiety. The anxiety that is felt in a dream is only apparently explained by the dream's content. In cases of both phobias and anxiety dreams the anxiety is only superficially attached to the idea that accompanies it; it originates from another source. Since neurotic anxiety is derived from sexual life and corresponds to libido which has been diverted from its purpose and has found no employment, it can be inferred that anxiety dreams are dreams with a sexual content, the libido belonging to that which has been transformed into anxiety.

1900A   4/163

The Interpretation of Dreams (1900). Chapter V: The material and sources of dreams. (A) Recent and indifferent material in dreams.

Recent and indifferent material and sources of dreams are discussed. Dreams show a clear preference for the impressions of the immediately preceding days and make their selection upon different principles from our waking memory, since they do not recall what is essential and important but what is subsidiary and unnoticed. Dreams have at their disposal the earliest impressions of childhood and details from that period of life which is trivial and which in the waking state are believed to have been long forgotten. In each of Freud's dreams, it is possible to find a point of contact with the experiences of the previous day. The instigating agent of every dream is to be found among the experiences which one has not yet slept on. Dreams can select their material from any part of the dreamer's life, provided that there is a train of thought linking the experience of the dream day with the earlier ones. The analysis of a dream will regularly reveal its true, psychically significant source in waking life, though the emphasis has been displaced from the recollection of that source on to that of an indifferent one. The source of a dream may be either: 1) a recent and psychically significant experience, 2) several recent and significant experiences combined into 1 unit by the dream, 3) 1 or more recent and significant experiences represented in the dream content by a mention of a contemporary but indifferent experience or 4) an internal significant experience which is invariably represented in the dream by mention of a contemporary but indifferent impression. Considering these 4 cases, a psychical element which is significant but not recent can be replaced by an element which is recent but indifferent provided 1) the dream content is connected with a recent experience, and 2) the dream instigator remains a psychically significant process.

Freud concludes that there are no indifferent dream instigators, therefore, no innocent dreams.

1900A   4/189

The Interpretation of Dreams (1900). Chapter V: The material and sources of dreams. (B) Infantile material as a source of dreams.

Infantile material is discussed as a source of dreams. Experiences from childhood play a part in dreams whose content would never have led one to suppose it. In the case of another group of dreams, analysis shows that the actual wish which instigated the dream, and the fulfillment of which is represented by the dream, is derived from childhood, so that we find the child and the child's impulses still living on in the dream. The deeper one carries the analysis of a dream, the more often one comes upon the track of experiences in childhood which have played a part among the sources of that dream's latent content. Trains of thought reaching back to earliest childhood lead off even from dreams which seem at first sight to have been completely interpreted, since their sources and instigating wish have been discovered without difficulty. Dreams frequently seem to have more than one meaning. Not only may they include several wish fulfillments, one alongside the other, but a succession of meanings or wish fulfillments may be superimposed on one another, the bottom one being the fulfillment of a wish dating from earliest childhood.

1900A   4/221

The Interpretation of Dreams (1900). Chapter V: The material and sources of dreams. (C) The somatic sources of dreams.

The somatic sources of dreams are discussed. There are 3 different kinds of somatic sources of stimulation: objective sensory stimuli arising from external objects, internal states of excitation of the sense organs having only a subjective basis, and somatic stimuli derived from the interior of the body. The significance of objective excitations of the sense organs is established from numerous observations and has been experimentally confirmed. The part played by subjective sensory excitations is demonstrated by the recurrence in dreams of hypnagogic sensory images. Though it is impossible to prove that the images and ideas occurring in dreams can be traced to internal somatic stimuli, this origin finds support in the universally recognized influence exercised upon dreams by states of excitation in digestive, urinary, and sexual organs. When external nervous stimuli and internal somatic stimuli are intense enough to force psychical attention to themselves, they then serve as a fixed point for the formation of a dream, a nucleus in its material; a wish fulfillment is then desired that shall correspond to this nucleus. Somatic sources of stimulation during sleep, unless they are of unusual intensity, play a similar part in the formation of dreams to that played by recent but indifferent impressions remaining from the previous day.

1900A 4/242

The Interpretation of Dreams (1900). Chapter V: The material and sources of dreams. (D) Typical dreams: (a) Embarassing dreams of being naked.

There are a certain number of typical dreams which almost everyone has dreamt and which we assume must have the same meaning for everyone. Dreams of being naked or insufficiently dressed in the presence of strangers sometimes occur with the additional feature of their being a complete absence of any such feeling of shame on the dreamer's part. Freud is concerned only with those dreams of being naked in which one does feel shame and embarassment and tries to escape or hide, and is then overcome by a strange inhibition which prevents one from moving and makes one feel incapable of altering the distressing situation. The nature of the undress involved is customarily far from clear. The people in whose presence one feels ashamed are almost always strangers, with their features left indeterminate. The core of a dream of exhibiting lies in the figure of the dreamer himself (not as he was as a child but as he appears at the present time) and his inadequate clothing (which emerges indistinctly, whether owing to superimposed layers of innumerable later memories of being in undress or as a result of the censorship). Repression plays a part in dreams of exhibiting; for the distress felt in such dreams is a reaction against the content of the scene of exhibiting having found expression in spite of the ban upon it.

1900A 4/248

The Interpretation of Dreams (1900). Chapter V: The material and sources of dreams. (D) Typical dreams: (b) Dreams of the death of persons of whom the dreamer is fond.

There is a group of dreams which contains the death of some loved relative; for instance, of a parent, of a brother or sister, or of a child. Two classes of such dreams are distinguished: those in which the dreamer is unaffected by grief, so that on awakening he is astonished at his lack of feeling, and those in which the dreamer feels deeply pained by the death and may even weep bitterly in his sleep. Analyses of the dreams of class 1 show that they have some meaning other than the apparent one, and that they are intended to conceal some other wish. The meaning of the second class of dreams, as their content indicates, is a wish that the person in question may die. A child's death wishes against his brothers and sisters are explained by the childish egoism which makes him regard them as his

rivals. Dreams of the death of parents apply with preponderant frequency to the parent who is of the same sex as the dreamer. It is as though a sexual preference were making itself felt at an early age: as though boys regarded their fathers and girls their mothers as their rivals in love, whose elimination could not fail to be to their advantage.

1900A 4/271

The Interpretation of Dreams (1900). Chapter V: The material and sources of dreams. (D) Typical dreams: (c) Other typical dreams.

Since Freud has no experience of his own regarding other typical dreams in which the dreamer finds himself flying through the air to the accompaniment of agreeable feelings or falling with feelings of anxiety, he uses information provided by psychoanalysis to conclude that these dreams reproduce impressions of childhood and they relate to games involving movement, which are extraordinarily attractive to children. What provokes dreams of flying and falling is not the state of the tactile feelings during sleep or sensations of the movement of lungs: These sensations are themselves reproduced as part of the memory to which the dream goes back: rather, they are part of the content of the dream and not its source. All the tactile and motor sensations which occur in these typical dreams are called up immediately when there is any psychical reason for making use of them and they can be disregarded when no such need arises. The relation of these dreams to infantile experiences has been established due to indications from the analyses of psychoneurotics.

1900A 4/273

The Interpretation of Dreams (1900). Chapter V: The material and sources of dreams. (D) Typical dreams: (d) Examination dreams.

Everyone who has passed the matriculation examination at the end of his school studies complains of the obstinacy with which he is pursued by anxiety dreams of having failed, or of being obliged to take the examination again, etc. In the case of those who have obtained a University degree this typical dream is replaced by another one which represents them as having failed in the University finals; and it is in vain that they object, even while still asleep, that for a year they have been practicing medicine or working as University lecturers or heads of offices. The examination anxiety of neurotics owes its intensification to childhood fears. Anxious examination dreams search for some occasion in the past in which great anxiety has turned out to be unjustified and has been contradicted by the event. This situation would be a striking instance of the content of a dream being misunderstood by the waking agency (the dreamer).

1900A 4/279

The Interpretation of Dreams (1900). Chapter VI: The dream-work: (A) The work of condensation.

Every attempt that has hitherto been made to solve the problem of dreams has dealt directly with their manifest content as it is presented in memory. The dream thoughts and the dream content are presented like 2 versions of the same subject matter in 2 different languages. The dream content seems like a transcript of dream thoughts into another mode of expression, whose characters are syntactic laws are discovered by comparing the original and the translation. The dream thoughts are immediately comprehensible, as soon as we have learned them. The dream content is expressed as it were in a pictographic script, the characters of which have to be transposed individually into the language of the dream thoughts. The first thing that becomes clear to anyone who compares the dream content with the dream thoughts is that a work of condensation on a large scale has been carried out. Dreams are brief, meager, and laconic in comparison with the range and wealth of the dream thoughts. The work of condensation in dreams is seen at its clearest when it handles words and names. The verbal malformations in dreams greatly resemble those which are familiar in paranoia but which are also present in hysteria and obsessions. When spoken sentences occur in dreams and are expressly distinguished as such from thoughts, it is an invariable rule that the words spoken in the dream are derived from spoken words remembered in the dream material.

1900A 4/305

The Interpretation of Dreams (1900). Chapter VI: The dream-work. (B) The work of displacement.

The dream is differently centered from the dream thoughts; its content has different elements as its central point. It seems plausible to suppose that in dream work a psychical force is operating which strips the elements which have a high psychical value of their intensity and, by means of overdetermination, creates from elements of low psychical value new values, which afterwards find their way into the dream content. If that is so, a transference and displacement of psychical intensities occurs in the process of dream formation, and it is as a result of these that the difference between the test of the dream content and that of the dream thoughts come about. We may assume that dream displacement comes about through the influence of the censorship of endopsychic defense. Those elements of the dream thoughts which make their way into the dream must escape the censorship imposed by resistance.

1900A 4/310

The Interpretation of Dreams (1900). Chapter VI: The dream-work. (C) The means of representation in dreams.

The means of representation in dreams are discussed. In the process of transforming the latent thoughts into the manifest content of a dream, 2 factors are at work: dream condensation and dream displacement. The logical relation between the dream thoughts are not given any separate representation in dreams. If a contradiction occurs in a dream, it is either a contradiction of the dream itself or a contradiction derived from the subject matter of one of the dream thoughts. Dreams take into account the connection which undeniably exists between all the portions of the dream thoughts by combining the whole material into a single situation or event. Similarity, consonance, and the possession of common attributes are all represented in dreams by unification which may either by already present in the material of the dream thoughts or may be freshly constructed. Identification or the construction of composite figures serves various purposes in dreams: firstly to represent an element common to 2 persons, secondly to represent a displaced common element, and thirdly, to express a merely wishful common element. The content of all dreams that occur during the same night forms part of the same whole; the fact of their being divided into several sections, as well as the groupings and number of those sections has a meaning and may be regarded as a piece of information arising from the latent dream thoughts.

VOL. V The Interpretation of Dreams (II) and On Dreams (1900–1901)

1900A 5/339

The Interpretation of Dreams (1900). Chapter VI: The dream-work. (D) Considerations of representability.

The material of the dream thoughts, stripped to a large extent of its interrelations, is submitted to a process of compression, while at the same time displacements of intensity between its elements necessarily bring about a psychical transvaluation of the material. There are 2 sorts of displacements. One consists in the replacing of a particular idea by another in some way closely associated with it, and they are used to facilitate condensation in so far as, instead of 2 elements, a single common element intermediate between them finds its way into the dream. Another displacement exists and reveals itself in a change in verbal expression of the thoughts concerned. The direction taken by the displacement usually results in the exchange of a colorless and abstract expression in dream thought for a pictorial and concrete one. Of the various subsidiary thoughts attached to the essential dream thoughts, those which admit of visual representations will be preferred. The dream work does not shrink from the effort of recasting unadaptable thoughts into a new verbal form, provided that that process facilitates representation and so relieves the psychological pressure caused by constricted thinking.

1900A 5/350

The Interpretation of Dreams (1900). Chapter VI: The dream-work. (E) Representation by symbols in dreams— Some further typical dreams.

Since symbolism is used for representing sexual material in dreams, the question arises whether many of these symbols do not occur with a permanently fixed meaning. This symbolism is not peculiar to dreams, but is characteristic of unconscious ideation, in particular among the people (laymen). It is to be found in folklore, in popular myths, legends, linguistic idioms, proverbial wisdom and current jokes, to a more complete extent than in dreams. The following ideas or objects show dream representation by symbols: a hat as a symbol of a man or of male genitals; a little hat as the genital organ; being run over as a symbol of sexual intercourse; the genitals represented by buildings, stairs, and shafts; the male organ represented by persons and the female organ by a landscape. The more one is concerned with the solution of dreams, the more one is driven to recognize that the majority of the dreams of adults deal with sexual material and give expression to erotic wishes. Many dreams, if they are carefully interpreted, are bisexual, since they unquestionably admit of an over interpretation in which the dreamer's homosexual impulses are realized, impulses which are contrary to his normal sexual activities. A large number of dreams, often accompanied by anxiety and having as their content such subjects as passing through narrow spaces or being in water, are based upon phantasies of intrauterine life, of existence in the womb, and of the act of birth.

1900A 5/405

The Interpretation of Dreams (1900). Chapter VI: The dream-work. (F) Some examples. Calculations and speeches in dreams.

A few instances of peculiar or unusual modes of representation in dreams are presented. For the purpose of representation in dreams, the spelling of words is far less important than their sound. The dream work makes use, for the purpose of giving a visual representation of the dream thoughts, of any methods within its reach, whether waking criticism regards them as legitimate or illegitimate. The dream work can often succeed in representing very refractory material, such as proper names, by a farfetched use of out-of-the-way associations. The dream work does not in fact carry out any calculations at all, whether correctly or incorrectly; it merely throws into the form of a calculation numbers which are present in the dream thoughts and can serve as allusions to matter that cannot be represented in any other way. The dream work treats numbers as a medium for the expression of its purpose in precisely the same way as it treats any other idea, including proper names and speeches that occur recognizably as verbal presentations. The dream work cannot actually create speeches. However much speeches and conversations, whether reasonable or unreasonable in themselves, may figure in dreams, analysis invariably proves that all that the dream has done is to extract from the dream thoughts fragments of speeches which have really been made or heard.

1900A 5/426

The Interpretation of Dreams (1900). Chapter VI: The dream-work. (G) Absurd dreams—Intellectual activity in dreams.

Absurdity in dreams is discussed. The frequency with which dead people appear in dreams and act and associate with us as though they were alive has produced some remarkable explanations which emphasize our lack of understanding of dreams. Often we think, what would that particular person do, think or say if he were alive. Dreams are unable to express an if of any kind except by representing the person concerned as present in some particular situation. Dreams of dead people whom the dreamer has loved raise problems in dream interpretation and these cannot always be satisfactorily solved due to the strongly marked emotional ambivalence which dominates the dreamer's relation to the dead person. A dream is made absurd if a judgment that something is absurd is among the elements included in the dream thoughts. Absurdity is accordingly one of the methods by which the dream work represents a contradiction, besides such other methods as the reversal in the dream content of some material relation in the dream thoughts, or the exploitation of the sensation of motor inhibition. Everything that appears in dreams as the ostensible activity of the function of judgment is to be regarded, not as an intellectual achievement of the dream work, but as belonging to the material of the dream thought and as having been lifted from them into the manifest content of the dream as a readymade structure. Even the judgments, made after waking, upon a dream that has been remembered, and the feelings called up by the reproduction of such a dream form part of the latent content of the dream and are to be included in its interpretation. An act of judgment in a dream is only a repetition of some prototype in the dream thoughts.

1900A   5/460

The Interpretation of Dreams (1900). Chapter VI: The dream-work. (H) Affects in dreams.

In dreams, the ideational content is not accompanied by the affective consequences that should be regarded as inevitable in waking thought. In the case of a psychical complex which has come under the influence of the censorship imposed by resistance, the affects are least influenced and can indicate how we should derive the missing thoughts. In some dreams the affect remains in contact with the ideational material which has replaced that to which the affect was originally attached, in others, the dissolution of the complex has proceeded further. The affect makes its appearance completely detached from the idea which belongs to it and is introduced at some other point in the dream, where it fits in with the new arrangement of the dream elements. If an important conclusion is drawn in the dream thoughts, the dream also contains a conclusion, but this latter conclusion may be displaced on to quite different material. Such a displacement not infrequently follows the principle of antithesis. The dream work can also turn the affects in the dream thoughts into their opposite. A dominating element in a sleeper's mind may be constituted by a tendency to some affect and this may then have a determining influence upon his dreams. A mood of this kind may arise from his experiences or thoughts during the preceding day, or its sources may be somatic. In either case it will be accompanied by trains of thought appropriate to it.

1900A   5/488

The Interpretation of Dreams (1900). Chapter VI: The dream-work. (1) Secondary revision.

A majority of the critical feelings in dreams are not in fact directed against the content of the dream, but are portions of the dream thoughts which have been taken over and used to an appropriate end. The censoring agency is responsible for interpolations and additions (secondary revisions) in the dream content. The interpolations are less easily retained in the memory than genuine derivatives of the material of the dream thoughts; if the dream is to be forgotten they are the first part of it to disappear. Daytime phantasies share a large number of their properties with night dreams. Like dreams, they are wish fulfillments; like dreams, they are based to a great extent on impressions of infantile experiences; like dreams, they benefit by a certain degree of relaxation of censorship. Dream work makes use of a ready made phantasy instead of putting one together out of the material of the dream thoughts. The psychical function which carries out what is described as the secondary revision of the content of dreams is identified with the activity of our waking thought. Our waking (preconscious) thinking behaves towards any perceptual material with which it meets in just the same way as

secondary revision behaves towards the content of dreams. Secondary revision is the one significant factor in the dream work which has been observed by the majority of writers on the subject.

1900A   5/509

The Interpretation of Dreams (1900). Chapter VII: The psychology of the dream-processes. (A) The forgetting of dreams.

The psychology of forgetting dreams is discussed. What we remember of a dream and what we exercise our interpretative arts upon has been mutilated by the untrustworthiness of our memory, which seems incapable of retaining a dream and may well have lost precisely the most important parts of its content. Our memory of dreams is not only fragmentary but positively inaccurate and falsified. The most trivial elements of a dream are indispensable to its interpretation and the work in hand is held up if attention is not paid to these elements until too late. The forgetting of dreams remains inexplicable unless the power of the psychical censorship is taken into account. The forgetting of dreams is tendentious and serves the purpose of resistance. Waking life shows an unmistakable inclination to forget any dream that has been formed in the course of the night, whether as a whole, directly after waking, or bit by bit in the course of the day. The agent chiefly responsible for this forgetting is the mental resistance to the dream which has already done what it could against it during the night. We need not suppose that every association that occurs during the work of interpretation has a place in the dream work during the night.

1900A   5/533

The Interpretation of Dreams (1900). Chapter VII: The psychology of the dream processes. (B) Regression.

The path leading through the preconscious to consciousness is barred to the dream thoughts during the daytime by the censorship imposed by resistance, but during the night they are able to obtain access to consciousness. In hallucinatory dreams, the excitation moves in a backward direction, instead of being transmitted towards the motor system it moves towards the sensory system and finally reaches the perceptual system. If we describe as 'progressive' the direction taken by psychical processes arising from the unconscious during waking life, then dreams are spoken of as having a regressive character. We call it regression when in a dream an idea is turned back into the sensory image from which it was originally derived. Regression is an effect of a resistance opposing the progress of a thought into consciousness along the normal path, and of a simultaneous attraction exercised upon the thought by the presence of memories possessing great sensory force. In the case of dreams, regression may perhaps be further facilitated by the cessation of the progressive current which streams in during the daytime from the sense organs; in other forms of regression, the absence of this accessory factor must be made up for by a greater intensity of other motives for regression. There are 3 kinds of regression: topographical regression, temporal regression, and formal regression.

1900A 5/550

The Interpretation of Dreams (1900). Chapter VII: The psychology of the dream processes. (C) Wish-fulfillment.

Dreams are fulfillments of wishes. There are some dreams which appear openly as wish fulfillments, and others in which the wish fulfillment is unrecognizable and often disguised. Undistorted wishful dreams are found principally in children; however, short, frankly wishful dreams seem to occur in adults as well. There are 3 possible origins for the wish. 1) It may have been aroused during the day and for external reasons may not have been satisfied. 2) It may have arisen during the day but been repudiated. 3) It may have no connection with daytime life and be one of those wishes which only emerge from the suppressed part of the mind and become active at night. Children's dreams show that a wish that has not been dealt with during the day can act as a dream instigator. A conscious wish can only become a dream instigator if it succeeds in awakening an unconscious wish with the same tenor and in obtaining reinforcement from it. Dreaming is a piece of infantile mental life that has been superseded. Wishful impulses left over from conscious waking life must be relegated to a secondary position in respect to the formation of dreams. The unconscious wishful impulses try to make themselves effective in daytime as well, and the fact of transference, as well as the psychoses, show us that they endeavor to force their way by way of the preconscious system into consciousness and to obtain control of the power of movement. It can be asserted that a hysterical symptom develops only where the fulfilments of 2 opposing wishes, arising each from a different psychical system, are able to converge in a single expression.

1900A 5/573

The Interpretation of Dreams (1900). Chapter VII: The psychology of the dream processes. (D) Arousal by dreams—The function of dreams—Anxiety-dreams.

The function of dreams is discussed. The state of sleep makes the sensory surface of consciousness which is directed toward the preconscious far more insusceptible to excitation than the surface directed towards the perceptual systems. Interest on the thought processes during sleep is abandoned while unconscious wishes always remain active. There are 2 possible outcomes for any particular unconscious excitatory process: Either it

may be left to itself, in which case it eventually forces its way through consciousness and finds discharge for its excitation in movement; or it may come under the influence of the preconscious, and its excitation, instead of being discharged, may be bound by the preconscious. This second alternative occurs in the process of dreaming. The cathexis from the preconscious which goes halfway to meet the dream after it has become perceptual binds the dream's unconscious excitation and makes it powerless to act as a disturbance. The theory of anxiety dreams forms part of the psychology of the neuroses. Since neurotic anxiety arises from sexual sources Freud analyses a number of anxiety dreams in order to indicate the sexual material present in their dream thoughts.

1900A 5/588

The Interpretation of Dreams (1900). Chapter VII: The psychology of the dream processes. (E) The primary and secondary processes—Repression.

The view that dreams carry on the occupations and interest of waking life has been confirmed by the discovery of concealed dream thoughts. The theory of dreams regards wishes originating in infancy as the indispensable motive force for the formation of dreams. A dream takes the place of a number of thoughts which are derived from our daily life and which form a completely logical sequence. Two fundamentally different kinds of psychical processes are concerned in the formation of dreams: One of these produces perfectly rational dream thoughts, of no less validity than normal thinking; while the other treats these thoughts in a manner which is bewildering and irrational. A normal train of thought is only submitted to abnormal psychical treatment if an unconscious wish, derived from infancy and in a state of repression, has been transferred on to it. As a result of the unpleasure principle, the first psychical system is totally incapable of bringing anything disagreeable into the context of its thoughts. It is unable to do anything but wish. The second system can only cathect an idea if it is in a position to inhibit any development of unpleasure that may proceed from it. Anything that could evade that inhibition would be inaccessible to the second system as well as to the first; for it would promptly be dropped in obedience to the unpleasure principle. Described is the psychical process of which the first system alone admits as the primary process, and the process which results from the inhibition imposed by the second system as the secondary process. The second system is obliged to correct the primary process. Among the wishful impulses derived from infancy there are some whose fulfillment would be a contradiction of the purposive ideas of secondary thinking. The fulfillment of these wishes would no longer generate an affect of pleasure but of unpleasure; and it is this transformation of affect which constitutes the essence of 'repression.' It is concluded that what is suppressed continues to exist in normal people as well as abnormal, and remains capable of psychical functioning.

1900A   5/610

The Interpretation of Dreams (1900). Chapter VII: The psychology of the dream processes. (F) The unconscious and consciousness—Reality.

The unconscious is the true psychical reality; in its innermost nature it is as much unknown to us as the reality of the external world, and it is as incompletely presented by the data of consciousness as is the external world by the communications of our sense organs. A dream is recognized as a form of expression of impulses which are under the pressure of resistance during the day but which have been able to find reinforcement during the night from deep-lying sources of excitation. The theoretical value of the study of dreams is looked for in the contributions it makes to psychological knowledge and in the light it throws on the problems of psychoneuroses.

1941C   5/623

The Interpretation of Dreams (1900). Appendix A: A premonitory dream fulfilled. Appendix B: List of writings by Freud dealing predominantly or largely with dreams.

A case of a premonitory dream fulfilled is discussed. Frau B. told Freud that she dreamt that she had met Dr. K., a friend and former family doctor of hers, in front of Hiess's shop. The next morning, while she was walking along the same street, she in fact met the person in question at the very spot she had dreamt of. There was no evidence of her having had any recollection at all of the dream on the morning after she dreamt it, until after her walk. The dream was interpreted in terms of Frau B.'s previous life. It was concluded that she did not actually dream this dream the preceding night but that the dream was created after the event. The creation of a dream after the event, which alone makes prophetic dreams possible, is nothing other than a form of censoring, thanks to which the dream is able to make its way through into consciousness. An appendix is included which lists (in chronological order) the writings by Freud dealing predominantly with dreams.

1901A   5/631

On Dreams (1901). Parts I and II.

During the prescientific epoch, men had no difficulty in finding an explanation of dreams. When they remembered a dream after waking up, they regarded it as either a favorable or a hostile manifestation by higher powers, demonic and divine. Since the rejection of the mythological hypothesis, however, dreams have needed explanation. The majority of medical writers adopt a view according to which dreams scarcely reach the level of being psychical phenomena at all, stating that the sole instigators of dreams are the sensory and somatic stimuli which either impinge upon the sleeper from outside or become accidentally active in his internal organs. Freud believes that we obtain material that enables us to resolve any pathological idea if we turn our attention to those associations which are involuntary, which interfere with our reflection, and which are normally dismissed by our critical faculty as worthless rubbish. If we make use of this procedure upon ourselves, we can best assist the investigation of the dream by at once writing down what are at first unintelligible associations. The dream is regarded as a sort of substitute for the thought processes, full of meaning and emotion. The content of the dream is very much shorter than the thoughts for which it is regarded as a substitute.

1901A   5/642

On Dreams (1901). Parts III and IV.

The transformation of the latent dream thoughts into the manifest dream content is the first instance of psychical material being changed from a mode of expression which is immediately intelligible to another which we can only come to understand with the help of guidance and effort, though it must be recognized as a function of our mental activity. Dreams can be divided into 3 categories in respect to the relation between their latent and manifest content. We may distinguish those dreams which make sense, are intelligible, and can be inserted without further difficulty into the context of our mental life. A second group is formed by those dreams which, though connected in themselves have a bewildering effect because we cannot see how to fit that sense into our mental life. Group 3 contains those dreams which are without either sense or intelligibility, which seem disconnected, confused, and meaningless. There is an intimate and regular relation between the unintelligible and confused nature of dreams and the difficulty of reporting the thoughts behind them. It is supposed that a transformation of some kind occurs even in confused dreams. The material in the dream thoughts which is packed together for the purpose of constructing a dream situation must in itself be adaptable for the purpose of condensation. There must be one or more common elements in all the components. It is thought that condensation, together with the transformation of thoughts into situations, is the most important and peculiar characteristic of the dream work. A formula is given for condensation in dreams.

1901A 5/654
On Dreams (1901). Parts V and VI.

In the case of the complicated and confused dreams, condensation and dramatization are not enough to account for the dissimilarity between the content of the dream and the dream thoughts. Through analysis, we have arrived at a knowledge of the dream thoughts, thus observing that the manifest dream content deals with quite different material from the latent thoughts. In the course of the dream work, the psychical intensity passes over from the thoughts and ideas to which it properly belongs on to others which have no claim to any such emphasis. If what make their way into the content of dreams are impressions and material which are indifferent and trivial rather than justifiably stirring and interesting, that is only the effect of the process of displacement. Keeping in mind insights gained from replacing the manifest by the latent content of dreams it can be concluded that dreams are never concerned with things which we should not think it worth while to be concerned with during the day, and trivialities which do not affect us during the day are unable to pursue us in our sleep. The process of displacement is chiefly responsible for our being unable to discover or recognize the dream thoughts in the dream content, unless we understand the reason for their distortion. The manifest content of dreams consists mostly in pictorial situations; and the dream thoughts must accordingly be submitted to a treatment which will make them suitable for a representation of this kind. The psychical material of the dream thoughts habitually includes recollections of impressive experiences which are thus themselves perceived as situations having a visual subject matter. Dream content, however, does not consist entirely of situations, but also includes disconnected fragments of visual images, speeches and even bits of unmodified thoughts. Dreams take into account the connection which exists between all the portions of the dream thoughts by combining the whole material into a single situation. They reproduce logical connection by approximation in time and space.

1901A 5/666
On Dreams (1901). Parts VII, VIII, IX and X.

Considerations of intelligibility lead to the final revision of a dream and this reveals the origin of the activity. It behaves towards the dream content lying before it just as our normal psychical activity behaves in general towards any perceptual content that may be presented to it. Dreams which have undergone a revision at the hands of a psychical activity completely analogous to waking thought may be described as well constructed.

Dream work is not creative. It develops no phantasies of its own; it makes no judgments and dreams no conclusions. A conclusion drawn in a dream is nothing other than the repetition of a conclusion in the dream thoughts. If the conclusion is taken over into the dream unmodified, it will appear impeccable; if the dream work has displaced it on to some other material, it will appear nonsensical. Displacement is the most striking of the special achievements of the dream work. The essential determining condition of displacement is a purely psychological one: something in the nature of a motive. Dreams which are intelligible and have a meaning are undisguised wish fulfillments. In the case of obscure and confused dreams, the dream situation represents a wish as fulfilled; however, the wish in such cases is either itself a repressed one and alien to consciousness, or it is intimately connected with repressed thoughts and is based upon them. The fundamental pattern for the generation of dreams is: repression, relaxation of the censorship, and the formation of a compromise.

1901A 5/678
On Dreams (1901). Parts XI, XII and XIII.

Dreams are regarded as the guardians of sleep. A psychical agency exists which exercises a dominating and inhibiting influence upon mental impulses and maintains that influence with severity, and which, owing to its relation to consciousness and to voluntary movement, contains the strongest instruments of psychical power. A portion of the impulses of childhood has been suppressed by this agency as being useless to life, and any thought material derived from those impulses is in a state of repression. While this agency, in which we recognize our normal ego, is concentrated on the wish to sleep, it it compelled by the psychophysiological conditions of sleep to relax the energy which it uses to repress material during the day. The dream provides a kind of psychical consummation for the wish that has been suppressed by representing it as fulfilled; while it also allows sleep to continue. The function of the dream as a guardian of sleep becomes particularly evident when an external stimulus impinges upon the senses of a sleeper. Most dreams of adults are traced back by analysis to erotic wishes. The majority of dream symbols serve to represent persons, parts of the body and activities invested with erotic interest; in particular the genitals are represented by a number of often very surprising symbols and the greatest variety of objects are employed to denote them symbolically. It is the task of dream interpretation to replace the dream by the latent dream thoughts, thus to unravel what the dream work has woven.

VOL. VI The Psychopathology of Everyday Life (1901)

1901B 6/ix

The Psychopathology of Everyday Life (1901). Editor's introduction (1960).

Only one other of Freud's works, the *Introductory Lectures* (1916 to 1917) rivals *The Psychopathology of Everyday Life* in the number of German editions it has passed through and the number of foreign languages into which it has been translated. In *The Psychopathology of Everyday Life* almost the whole of the basic explanations and theories were already present in the earliest editions; the great mass of what was added later consisted merely in extra examples and illustrations to amplify what he had already discussed. Freud first mentioned parapraxis in a letter to Fliess of August 26, 1898. The special affection with which Freud regarded parapraxes was no doubt due to the fact that they, along with dreams, were what enabled him to extend to normal mental life the discoveries he had first made in connection with neuroses.

1901B 6/1

The Psychopathology of Everyday Life (1901). Chapter 1: The forgetting of proper names.

There are certain characteristics of the forgetting of proper names which can be recognized clearly in individual cases. These are cases in which a name is in fact not only forgotten, but wrongly remembered. In the course of our efforts to recover the name that has dropped out, substitute names enter our consciousness; we recognize them at once as incorrect, but they keep on returning and force themselves upon us with great persistence. The process that should lead to the reproduction of the missing name has been displaced and therefore has led to an incorrect substitute. Freud's hypothesis is that this displacement is not left to arbitrary psychical choice but follows paths which can be predicted and which conform to laws. The name or names which are substituted are connected in a discoverable way with the missing name. The conditions necessary for forgetting a name, when forgetting it is accompanied by paramnesia, may be summarized as follows: 1) a certain disposition for forgetting the name, 2) a process of suppression carried out shortly before, and 3) the possibility of establishing an external association between the name in question and the element previously suppressed.

1901B 6/8

The Psychopathology of Everyday Life (1901). Chapter 11: The forgetting of foreign words.

The current vocabulary of our own language, when it is confined to the range of normal usage, seems to be protected against being forgotten. With the vocabulary of a foreign language it is notoriously otherwise and the disposition to forget it extends to all parts of speech. An early stage in functional disturbance is revealed by the fluctuations in the control we have over our stock of foreign words, according to the general condition of our health and to the degree of our tiredness. The forgetting of a nonsubstantial word in a Latin quotation is presented. The appearance or nonappearance in the memory of incorrect substitutes cannot be made the basis for any radical distinction. The disturbance in reproduction in the example presented occurred from the very nature of the topic in the quotation, since opposition unconsciously arose to the wishful idea expressed in it.

1901B 6/15

The Psychopathology of Everyday Life (1901). Chapter III: The forgetting of names and sets of words.

The forgetting of names and sets of words is discussed. The forgotten or distorted matter is brought by some associative path into connection with an unconscious thought content, a thought content which is the source of the effect manifested in the form of forgetting. There are various reasons why names and sets of words are forgotten. Some of them are: professional complex, family complex, personal reference, sublimated grudge against the bearer of it, guilty conscience, and personal complex. In a large number of cases, a name is forgotten not because the name itself arouses such motives, but because, owing to similarity in sound and to assonance, it touches upon another name against which these motives do operate. The mechanism of names being forgotten consists in the interference with the intended reproduction of the name by an alien train of thought which is not at the time conscious. Between the name interfered with and the interfering complex either a connection exists from the outset, or else such a connection has established itself, often in ways that appear artificial. Among the interfering complexes, those of personal reference prove to have the greatest effect. In general, 2 main types of name forgetting may be distinguished: those cases where the name itself touches on something unplasant, and those where it is brought into connection with another name which has that effect.

1901B   6/43

The Psychopathology of Everyday Life (1901). Chapter IV: Childhood memories and screen memories.

A person's earliest childhood memories seem frequently to have preserved what is indifferent and unimportant, whereas no trace is found in an adult's memory of impressions dating from that time which are important, impressive and rich in affect. There is a similarity between the forgetting of proper names accompanied by paramnesia, and the formation of screen memories. Of the childhood memories that have been retained a few strike us as perfectly understandable, while others seem odd or unintelligible. It is not difficult to correct certain errors regarding both sorts. If the memories that a person has retained are subjected to an analytic enquiry, it is easy to establish that there is no guarantee of their accuracy. Some of the mnemic images are falsified, incomplete, or displaced in time and place. Remembering in adults makes use of a variety of psychical material but all dreams are predominantly of visual images only. This development is reversed in childhood memories; they are plastically visual even in people whose later function of memory has to do without any visual element. Thus visual memory preserves the type of infantile memory. It is suspected that in the so called earliest childhood memories we possess not the genuine memory trace but a later revision of it, a revision which may have been subjected to the influences of a variety of later psychical forces. Thus the childhood memories of individuals acquire the significance of screen memories.

1901B   6/53

The Psychopathology of Everyday Life (1901). Chapter V: Slips of the tongue.

The slips of the tongue that are observed in normal people give an impression of being the preliminary stages of the so-called paraphasias that appear under pathological conditions. Among the slips of the tongue that Freud collected only a very few can be solely attributed to the contact effects of sounds. He almost invariably discovers a disturbing influence which comes from something outside the intended utterance; and the disturbing element is either a single thought that has remained unconscious, which manifests itself in the slip of the tongue and which often can be brought to consciousness only by means of searching analysis, or it is a more general psychical motive force which is directed against the entire utterance. Slips of the tongue are contagious. A slip of the tongue has a cheering effect during psychoanalytic work, when it serves as a means of providing the therapist with a confirmation that may be very welcome to him if he is engaged in a dispute with the patient. People give slips of the tongue and other parapraxes the same interpretation that Freud advocates even if they do not theoretically endorse his view and

even if they are disinclined, so far as it applies to themselves, to renounce the convenience that goes along with tolerating parapraxes.

1901B   6/106

The Psychopathology of Everyday Life (1901). Chapter VI: Misreadings and slips of the pen. (A). Misreadings.

Misreadings and slips of the pen are discussed. When we come to mistakes in reading and writing, we find that our general approach and our observations in regard to mistakes in speaking hold here also. Some examples of misreadings are presented, carefully analyzed and the misreadings found to be due to some of the following causes: questions of priority; long standing habits; the reader's preparedness; the reader's profession or present situation; something which rouses the reader's defenses; and personal motives.

1901B   6/116

The Psychopathology of Everyday Life (1901). Chapter VI: Misreadings and slips of the pen (B). Slips of the pen.

Slips of the pen are made more readily than slips of the tongue for the following reason: In the course of normal speaking the inhibitory function of the will is continuously directed to bringing the course of ideas and the articulatory movements into harmony with each other. If the expressive movement which follows the ideas is retarded (as in writing) such anticipations make their appearance easily. Twenty-one examples of slips of the pen are presented, analyzed and thought due to some of the following causes: the expression of a wish; unconscious hostility; similar subject matter; making a joke; and secondary revision. These examples have not justified assumption that there is a quantitative lessening of attention, but rather, a disturbance of attention by an alien thought which claims consideration. Between slips of the pen and forgetting may be inserted the situation where someone forgets to append a signature. An unsigned check has the same significance as a forgotten check.

1901B   6/134

The Psychopathology of Everyday Life (1901). Chapter VII: The forgetting of impressions and intentions. (A). The forgetting of impressions and knowledge.

The forgetting of impressions is discussed. No psychological theory can give a connected account of the fundamental phenomenon of remembering and forgetting. We assume that forgetting is a spontaneous process which may be regarded as requiring a certain length of time. Some examples of forgetting, most of which Freud observed in himself, are presented. Freud distinguishes the forgetting of impressions and experiences from the forgetting of intentions. He states the invariable result of the entire series of observations: in every case the forgetting turned out to be based on a motive of unpleasure. Mislaying something is really the same as forgetting where it has been put. There are abundant signs to be found in healthy nonneurotic people that the recollection of distressing impressions and the occurrence of distressing thoughts are opposed by a resistance. The architectonic principle of the mental apparatus lies in a stratification, a building up of superimposed agencies. It is quite possible that this defensive endeavor belongs to a lower psychical agency and is inhibited by higher agencies. In a very similar way to the forgetting of names, the forgetting of impressions can be accompanied by faulty recollection; and this, where it finds credence, is described as paramnesia.

1901B   6/151

The Psychopathology of Everyday Life (1901). Chapter VII: The forgetting of impressions and intentions. (B). The forgetting of intentions.

No group of phenomena is better qualified than the forgetting of intentions for demonstrating the thesis that, in itself, lack of attention does not suffice to explain parapraxes. An intention is an impulse to perform an action: an impulse which has already found approval but whose execution is postponed to a suitable occasion. There are 2 situations in life in which even the layman is aware that forgetting cannot in any way claim to be considered as an elementary phenomenon not further reducible, but entitles him to conclude that there are such things as unavowed motives: love relationships are military disciplines. But the service of women and military service demand that everything connected with them should be immune to forgetting. Freud made a collection of the cases of omitting to do something as a result of forgetting which he observed in himself. He found that they could be traced to interference by unknown and unavowed motives; or, to a counter-will. Where intentions of some importance are concerned we have found in general that they are forgotten when obscure motives rise against them. In the case of rather less important intentions we can recognize a second mechanism of forgetting: a counter-will is transferred to the intention from some other topic, after an external association has been formed between the other topic and the content of the intention.

190113   6/162

The Psychopathology of Everyday Life (1901). Chapter VIII: Bungled actions.

The term 'bungled actions' is used to describe all the cases in which a wrong result, *i.e.*, a deviation from what

was intended, seems to be the essential element. The others, in which it is rather the whole action that seems to be inappropriate, Freud calls symptomatic and chance actions. No sharp line can be drawn between them, and we are forced to conclude that all the divisions made in this study have no significance other than a descriptive one and run counter to the inner unity in this field of phenomena. Included in the category of bungled actions are also those actions which result in breakage or self-injury.

1901B   6/191

The Psychopathology of Everyday Life (1901). Chapter IX: Symptomatic and chance actions.

Chance actions differ from 'bungled' actions because they do not have the support of a conscious intention, are in no need of a pretext and appear on their own account. We perform them without thinking there is anything in them, quite accidentally, just to have something to do; and such information will put an end to any enquiry into the significance of the action. These actions, which cannot be excused on grounds of clumsiness have to fulfill certain conditions: they must be unobtrusive and their effects must be slight. Symptomatic acts is a better name for these actions than chance actions. They give expression to something which the agent himself does not suspect in them, and which he does not as a rule intend to impart to other people but to keep to himself. The richest supply of such chance or symptomatic acts is obtained during psychoanalytic treatment of neurotics. An example is given of how there can be a close connection between a symbolic action performed through force of habit and the most intimate and important aspects of a healthy person's life. Chance actions and symptomatic acts occurring in matrimonial matters (often of serious significance) are discussed along with the human habit of 'losing things,' with examples given of each. Following these is a brief and varied collection of symptomatic acts found in healthy and neurotic people. The images and turns of phrase to which a person is particularly given are rarely without significance when one is forming a judgment of him; and others often turn out to be allusions to a theme which is being kept in the background at the time, but which has powerfully affected the speaker.

1901B   6/217

The Psychopathology of Everyday Life (1901). Chapter X: Errors.

Errors of memory are distinguished from forgetting accompanied by paramnesia by the single feature that in the former the error (the paramnesia) is not recognized as such but finds credence. Of all parapraxes errors seem to have the least rigid mechanism. The occurrence of an error is a quite general indication that the mental activity in question has had to struggle with a disturbing influence; but the particular form that the error takes is not determined by the quality of the concealed disturbing idea. Every time we make a skip in talking or writing we may infer that there has been a disturbance due to mental processes lying outside our intention; but it must be admitted that slips of the tongue and of the pen often obey the laws of resemblance, of indolence or of the tendency to haste, without the disturbing element succeeding in imposing any part of its own character on the resulting mistake in speech or writing. Seventeen examples of errors are reported.

1901B   6/230

The Psychopathology of Everyday Life (1901). Chapter XI: Combined parapraxes.

Combined parapraxes are discussed and examples given. Mislaying, breaking, and forgetting were interpreted as an expression of a counterwill that has been pushed back. Repeated forgetfulness resulted in an eventually bungled performance. A change in the form taken by the parapraxis while outcome remains the same gives a vivid impression of a will striving for a definite aim, and contradicts the notion that a parapraxis is a matter of chance and needs no interpretation. It was found that a conscious intention completely failed to prevent the success of the parapraxis.

1901B   6/239

The Psychopathology of Everyday Life (1901). Chapter XII: Determinism, belief in chance and superstition — Some points of view. (A) and (B).

Certain shortcomings in our psychical functioning and certain seemingly unintentional performances are proven by analysis to have valid motives and to be determined by motives unknown to consciousness. In order to be included in a class of phenomena explicable in this way, a psychical parapraxis must fulfill the following conditions: 1) it must not exceed certain dimensions fixed by our judgment, 2) it must be in the nature of a momentary and temporary disturbance; and 3) if we perceive the parapraxis at all, we must not be aware in ourselves of any motive for it. If we agree that a part of our psychical functioning cannot be explained by purposive ideas, we are failing to appreciate the extent of determination in mental life. A number of examples indicate that one cannot make a number occur to one at one's own free arbitrary choice any more than a name,

rather, that it is strictly determined by certain circumstances, memories, etc. Many people contest the assumption of complete psychical determinism by appealing to a special feeling of conviction that there is a free will. It is not necessary to dispute the right to the feeling of conviction of having a free will. If the distinction between conscious and unconscious motivation is taken into account, our feeling of conviction informs us that conscious motivation does not extend to all our motor decisions.

1901B   6/254

The Psychopathology of Everyday Life (1901). Chapter XII: Determinism, belief in chance and superstition — Some points of view. (C) and (D).

There are 2 spheres in which it is possible to demonstrate phenomena that appear to correspond to an unconscious, and therefore displaced, knowledge of that motivation. A striking and generally observed feature of the behavior of paranoics is that they attach the greatest significance to the minor details of other people's behavior which we ordinarily neglect, interpret them and make them the basis of far reaching conclusions. Another indication that we possess unconscious and displaced knowledge of the motivation in chance actions and parapraxes is to be found in the phenomenon of superstition. Superstition is in large part the expectation of trouble. We must also include in the category of the miraculous and the uncanny the peculiar feelings we have, in certain moments and situations, of having once before been in the same place, though our efforts never succeed in clearly remembering the previous occasion.

1901B   6/269

The Psychopathology of Everyday Life (1901). Chapter XII: Determinism, belief in chance and superstition — Some points of view. (E), (F) and (G).

Every time Freud analyzed forgetting, a connection was clearly shown to exist between the forgetting of a name and a reason for the forgetting. It is not possible to interpret every dream but a dream which proves refractory during an attempt to solve it the next day will be more vulnerable to analysis a week or a month later, after a change has come about and has reduced the contending psychical values. The same applies to the solving of parapraxes and symptomatic acts. Parapraxes have a hidden motivation. The basic determinants of the normal process of forgetting are unknown while the motive for forgetting (in cases that require a special explanation) is invariably an unwillingness to remember something which can evoke distressing feelings. In the forgetting of intentions another factor emerges. The conflict, which could only be surmised in the repression of what was distressing to remember, here becomes tangible, and in the analysis of the examples a counter will can regularly be recognized which opposes the intention without putting an end to it. Consequently, 2 types of psychical process are recognized: either the counter-will is turned directly against the intention or it is unrelated in its nature to the intention itself and establishes its connection with it by means of an external association. The same conflict governs 'bungled' actions while in chance or symptomatic actions and internal conflict becomes less and less important. The mechanism of parapraxes and chance actions correspond in its most essential points with the mechanism of dream formation. In both cases we find condensations and compromise formations. It is concluded that both severe and mild psychopathology (and also in parapraxes and chance actions) have 1 factor in common: the phenomena can be traced back to incompletely suppressed psychical material, which, although pushed away by consciousness, has nevertheless not been robbed of all capacity for expressing itself.

6/291

The Psychopathology of Everyday Life (1901). Index of parapraxes.

An index of parapraxes is presented. The parapraxes are grouped as follows: bungled actions; errors; forgetting impressions and intentions; forgetting names and words; lost and mislaid objects; misreadings; slips of the pen and misprints; slips of the tongue; and symptomatic and chance actions. The list does not entirely follow Freud's grouping of parapraxes according to the titles of the various chapters. Items have been classified under the most appropriate headings, regardless of where they appear in the book. The source of each parapraxis is given where it is other than Freud himself.

VOL. VII A Case of Hysteria, Three Essays on Sexuality and Other Works (1901–1905)

1905E 7/3
Fragment of an analysis of a case of hysteria: (1953) Editor's note.

The *Fragment of an Analysis of a Case of Hysteria* was published in October and November, 1905; however, the greater part of it was written in January 1901. On October 14, 1900, Freud told Fliess that he had recently begun work with a new patient, an 18-year-old

girl. Her treatment came to an end some 3 months later. The analysis was grouped around 2 dreams and contained solutions of hysterial symptoms and considerations on the sexual organic basis of the whole condition. Three times in his later writings, Freud assigned his treatment of Dora to the wrong year, to 1899 instead of 1900. Dora was born in 1882, her father was ill in 1888, bed wetting appeared in 1889 and dyspnea in 1890. Her father's detached retina occurred in 1892 and in 1894, her father had his confusional attack and visited Freud. April 1902 was Dora's last visit to Freud.

1905E 7/7
Fragment of an analysis of a case of hysteria (1905). Prefatory remarks.

Prefatory remarks to a *Fragment of an Analysis of a Case of Hysteria* are presented. If it is true that the causes of hysterical disorders are to be found in the intimacies of the patients' psychosexual life, and that hysterical symptoms are the expression of their most secret and repressed wishes, then the complete elucidation of a case of hysteria involves the revelation of those intimacies and the betrayal of those secrets. Freud believes it is the physician's duty to publish what he believes he knows of the causes and structure of hysteria, and it becomes cowardice to neglect doing so, as long as he can avoid causing direct personal injury to the patient concerned. Some ways in which Freud overcame some of the technical difficulties in drawing up the report of this case history are presented. The material which elucidated the case was grouped around 2 dreams and the treatment covered only 3 months and was not carried through to its appointed end, but was broken off at the patient's request when it reached a certain point.

1905E 7/15
Fragment of an analysis of a case of hysteria (1905). Chapter I: The clinical picture.

The family of the 18-year-old girl (Dora), who is the patient, included her parents and a brother who was 1½ years her senior. Her father was the dominating figure in the family, owing to his intelligence and character as much as to the circumstances of his life. His daughter was very tenderly attached to him, and for that reason her critical powers, which developed early, took all the more offense at many of his actions and peculiarities. Her affection for him was further increased by the many severe illnesses which he had since her sixth year. The patient had begun to develop neurotic symptoms at the age of 8 and became subject at that time to chronic dyspnea with occasional episodes in which the symptom was very much aggravated. Freud first saw her when she was 16 at which time she was suffering from a cough and from hoarseness. The experience with Herr K., his making love to her and the insult to her honor which was involved seem to provide the psychical trauma which Breuer and Freud declared to be the indispensable prerequisite for the production of a hysterical disorder. Thus there are 3 symptoms, disgust, sensation of pressure on the upper part of the body, and the avoidance of men engaged in affectionate conversation, all derived from this single experience. Next considered were her motives for being ill. The relation between Dora and her father, Herr K. and Frau K. and the relation between Dora's father and Frau K. were the primary contributors to Dora's hysteria. It was concluded that no one can undertake the treatment of a case of hysteria until he is convinced of the impossibility of avoiding the mention of sexual subjects, or unless he is prepared to allow himself to be convinced by experience.

1905E 7/64

Fragment of an analysis of a case of hysteria (1905). Chapter II: The first dream.

Dora's first dream which keeps recurring is presented: "A house was on fire." My father was standing beside my bed and woke me up. I dressed quickly. Mother wanted to stop and save her jewel case; but Father said, 'I refuse to let myself and 2 children be burnt for the sake of your jewel case.' We hurried downstairs, and as soon as I was outside I woke up." Freud's task was to establish the relation between the events at L. (the place where the scene with Herr K. had taken place) and the recurrent dreams which she had had there. Jewel case was interpreted as a means of expressing the female genitals. The dream interpreted as an intention which Dora carried with her into her sleep was repeated each night until the intention had been carried out; and it reappeared years later when an occasion arose for forming an analogous intention. The intention might have been consciously expressed in words as these: "I must fly from this house, for I see that my virginity is threatened here; I shall go away with my father, and I shall take precautions not to be surprised while I am dressing in the morning." The dream was a reaction to a fresh experience of an exciting nature; and this experience must have revived the memory of the only previous experience which was at all analogous to it. The latter was the scene of the kiss in Herr K.'s place of business, when she had been seized with disgust.

1905E 7/94

Fragment of an analysis of a case of hysteria (1905). Chapter III: The second dream.

A few weeks after the first dream, a second dream occurred. Dora was wandering about alone in a strange town, and saw streets and squares. The wandering about

was overdetermined and led back to one of the exciting causes from the day before. Dora returned to her own house and found a note from her mother saying that since she had left home without her parents' knowledge, the mother had not wanted to write and say her father was ill. Now he was dead, and Dora could come if she liked. This was interpreted as revenge against her father. The fact that she asked a certain question, "Where is the station?" nearly a hundred times in her dream led to another cause of the dream which was related to the previous evening. The thick wood near the station in her dream was interpreted as a symbolic geography of sex. There lay concealed behind the first situation in the dream a phantasy of defloration, the phantasy of a man seeking to force an entrance into the female genitals. It was concluded that incapacity for meeting a real erotic demand is one of the most essential features of a neurosis and that neurotics are dominated by the opposition between reality and phantasy. If what they long for most intensely in their phantasies is presented to them in reality, they flee from it; and they abandon themselves to their phantasies most readily where they need no longer fear to see them realized.

1905E 7/112

Fragment of an analysis of a case of hysteria (1905). Chapter IV: Postscript.

The theory of hysteria does not by any means fail to point out that neuroses have an organic basis, though it does not look for that basis in any pathological anatomical changes, and provisionally substitutes the conception of organic functions for the chemical changes which we should expect to find but which we are at present unable to apprehend. Sexuality does not simply intervene on one single occasion, at some point in the working of the processes which characterize hysteria, but it provides the motive power for every single symptom, and for every single manifestation of a symptom. The symptoms of the disease are nothing else than the patient's sexual activity. During psychoanalytic treatment, the formation of new symptoms is invariably stopped. But the productive powers of the neurosis are by no means extinguished; they are occupied in the creation of a special class of mental structures, for the most part unconscious, to which the name of transference may be given. Transferences are new editions or facsimiles of the impulses and phantasies which are aroused and made conscious during the progress of the analysis; however, they replace some earlier person by the person of the physician.

1905D 7/125

Three essays on the theory of sexuality: Editor's note (1953) and prefaces (1909–1920).

Freud's *Three Essays on the Theory of Sexuality* stand beside his *Interpretation of Dreams* as his most momentous and original contributions to psychoanalytic knowledge. The history of Freud's concern with the subject can be followed in detail. Clinical observations of the importance of sexual factors in the causation, first, of anxiety neurosis and neurasthenia, and later, of the psychoneuroses, were what first led Freud into a general investigation of the subject of sexuality. His first approaches, during the early nineties, were from the physiological and chemical standpoints. In the preface to the third edition, Freud makes a few remarks intended to prevent misunderstandings and expectations that cannot be fulfilled. It must be emphasized that the exposition is based entirely upon everyday medical observation, to which the findings of psychoanalytic research should lend additional depth and scientific significance. Throughout the entire work the various factors are placed in a particular order of precedence: preference is given to the accidental factors, while disposition is left in the background, and more weight is attached to ontogenesis than to phylogenesis. In the preface to the fourth edition, Freud states that some of the contents of the book, its insistence on the importance of sexuality in all human achievements and the attempt it makes at enlarging the concept of sexuality, have from the first provided the strongest motives for the resistance against psychoanalysis.

1905D 7/136

Three essays on the theory of sexuality (1905). Chapter I: The sexual aberrations: (1). Deviations in respect of the sexual object. a.) Inversion b.) Sexually immature persons and animals as sexual objects.

Sexual aberrations are discussed. The person from whom sexual attraction proceeds is called the sexual object and the act towards which the instinct tends is called the sexual aim. Some deviations in respect of the sexual object are presented. The behavior of inverts (people with 'contrary sexual feelings,' such as homosexuals) varies greatly in several respects: 1) They may be absolute inverts; 2) they may be amphigenic inverts, that is psychosexual hermaphrodites, or: 3) they may be contingent inverts. The earliest assessments regarded inversion as an innate indication of nervous degeneracy. The attribution of degeneracy in this connection is open to the objections which can be raised against the indiscriminate use of the word in general. Innateness is only attributed to the first class of inverts. The existence of the 2 other classes is difficult to reconcile with the hypothesis of the innateness of inversion. The nature of inversion is explained neither by the hypothesis that it is innate nor by the alternative hypothesis that it is acquired. The facts of anatomy lead us to suppose that an originally bisexual physical disposition has, in the course of evolution, become modified into a unisexual one,

leaving behind only a few traces of the sex that has become atrophied. The theory of psychical hermaphroditism presupposes that the sexual object of an invert is the opposite of that of a normal person. No one single aim can apply in cases of inversion. Sexual instinct and the sexual object are merely close together: sexual instinct is independent of its object and its origin is not likely due to its object's attractions. Cases in which sexually immature persons (children) are chosen as sexual objects and cases of sexual intercourse with animals are judged as sporadic aberrations. It is concluded that under a great number of conditions and in surprisingly numerous individuals, the nature and importance of the sexual object recedes into the background. What is essential and constant in the sexual instinct is something else.

1905D 7/149

Three Essays on the theory of sexuality (1905). Chapter I: The sexual aberrations. (2). Deviations in respect of the sexual aim. a). Anatomical extensions. b). Fixation of preliminary sexual aims.

Some deviations of the sexual aim are presented. Perversions are sexual activities which either extend, in an anatomical sense, beyond the regions of the body that are designed for sexual union, or linger over the intermediate relations to the sexual object which should normally be traversed rapidly on the path towards the final sexual aim. The use of the mouth as a sexual organ is regarded as a perversion if the lips (or tongue) of one person are brought into contact with the genitals of another, but not if the mucous membranes of the lips of both of them come together. Where the anus is concerned it becomes still clearer that it is disgust which stamps that sexual aim as a perversion. Unsuitable substitutes, called fetishes, (such as hair, piece of clothing, etc.) for the sexual object are discussed. Every external or internal factor that hinders or postpones the attainment of the normal sexual aim will evidently lend support to the tendency to linger over the preparatory activities and to turn them into new sexual aims that can take the place of the normal one. Pleasure in looking (scopophilia) becomes a perversion if it is restricted exclusively to the genitals, or if it is concerned with the overriding of disgust, or if, instead of being preparatory to the normal sexual aim, it supplants it. The most common and the most significant of all the perversions is the desire to inflict pain (sadism) upon the sexual object, and its reverse (masochism). The roles of passivity and activity in sadism and masochism are discussed in view of the fact that in this perversion both forms are habitually found in the same individual.

1905D 7/160

Three essays on the theory of sexuality (1905). Chapter I: The sexual aberrations. (3). The perversions in general.

The perversions in general are discussed. In the majority of instances, the pathological character in a perversion is found to lie not in the content of the new sexual aim but in its relation to the normal. If a perversion, instead of appearing merely alongside the normal sexual aim and object, supplants it completely and takes its place in all circumstances, so that the perversion has the characteristics of exclusiveness and fixation, then we shall be justified in regarding it as a pathological symptom. The sexual instinct has to struggle against certain mental forces which act as resistances, of which shame and disgust are the most prominent. Some perversions are only made intelligible if we assume the convergence of several motive forces.

1905D 7/163

Three essays on the theory of sexuality (1905). Chapter I: The sexual aberrations. (4). The sexual instinct in neurotics.

The sexual instinct in neurotics is discussed. The only means of obtaining information about the sexual life of persons known as psychoneurotics is through psychoanalytic investigation. Experience shows that these psychoneuroses, hysteria, obsessional neuroses, neurasthenia, schizophrenia, and paranoia, are based on sexual instinctual forces. The removal of the symptoms of hysterial patients by psychoanalysis proceeds on the supposition that those symptoms are substitutes for a number of emotionally cathected mental processes, wishes and desires, which, by the operation of a special psychical procedure (repression), have been prevented from obtaining discharge in psychical activity that is admissible to consciousness. The findings of psychoanalysis show that symptoms represent a substitute for impulses the sources of whose strength is derived from the sexual instinct. In the case of anyone who is predisposed to hysteria, the onset of his illness is precipitated when he finds himself faced by the demands of a real sexual situation. Between the pressure of the instinct and his antagonism to sexuality, illness offers excape. The sexual instinct of psychoneurotics exhibits all the aberrations and manifestations of abnormal sexual life. The unconscious mental life of all neurotics shows inverted impulses, fixation of their libido upon persons of their own sex. In any fairly marked case of psychoneurosis it is unusual for only a single one of the perverse instincts to be developed.

1905D 7/167

Three essays on the theory of sexuality (1905). Chapter I: The sexual aberrations. (5). Component instincts and erotogenic zones.

The component instincts and erotogenic zones are discussed. An instinct is provisionally understood to be the psychical representative of an endosomatic, continuously flowing source of stimulation, as contrasted with a stimulus, which is set up by single excitations coming from without. Excitations of 2 kinds arise from the somatic organs, based upon differences of a chemical nature. One of these kinds of excitation is specifically sexual, and the organ concerned is the erotogenic zone of the sexual component instinct arising from it. The part played by the erotogenic zones is immediately obvious in the case of those perversions which assign a sexual significance to the oral and anal orifices. In hysteria these parts of the body and the neighboring tracts of mucous membrane become the seat of new sensations and of changes in innervation in just the same way as do the actual genitalia under the excitations of the normal sexual processes. In obsessional neurosis, what is striking is the significance of those impulses which create new sexual aims and seem independent of erotogenic zones. In scopophilia and exhibitionism the eye corresponds to an erotogenic zone, while in the case of those components of the sexual instinct which involve pain and cruelty the same role is assumed by the skin.

1905D 7/170

Three essays on the theory of sexuality (1905). Chapter I: The sexual aberrations. (6). Reasons for the apparent preponderance of perverse sexuality in the psychoneuroses. (7). Intimation of the infantile character of sexuality.

Most psychoneurotics fall ill only after the age of puberty as a result of the demands made upon them by normal sexual life, or illnesses of this kind set in later when the libido fails to obtain satisfaction along normal lines. In both cases the libido behaves like a stream whose main bed has become blocked and it proceeds to fill up collateral channels which may hitherto have been empty. Thus what appears to be the strong tendency of psychoneurotics to perversion may be collaterally determined and must be collaterally intensified. Different cases of neurosis may behave differently: in one case the preponderating factor may be the innate strength of the tendency to perversion, in another it may be the collateral increase of that tendency owing to the libido being forced away from a normal sexual aim and sexual object. Neurosis will always produce its greatest effects when constitution and experience work together in the same direction. The disposition to perversions is itself of no great rarity but must form a part of what passes as the normal constitution. It is debatable whether the perversions go back to innate determinants or arise owing to chance experiences. There is something innate lying behind the perversions but it is something innate in everyone, though as a disposition it may vary in its intensity and may be increased by the influences of actual life. The postulated constitution, containing the germs of all the perversions, will only be demonstrable in children, even though in them it is only with modest degrees of intensity that any of the instincts can emerge. Thus a formula emerges which states that the sexuality of neurotics has remained in, or has been brought back to, an infantile state.

1905D 7/173

Three essays on the theory of sexuality (1905). Chapter II: Infantile sexuality: (1). The period of sexual latency in childhood and its interruptions.

Infantile amnesia, which turns everyone's childhood into something like a prehistoric epoch and conceals from him the beginnings of his own sexual life, is responsible for the fact that no importance is attached to childhood in the development of sexual life. The period of sexual latency in childhood and its interruptions are discussed. The germs of sexual impulses are already present in the newborn child and these continue to develop for a time, but are then overtaken by a progressive process of suppression; this in turn is itself interrupted by periodical advances in sexual development or may be held up by individual peculiarities. The sexual life of children usually emerges in a form accessible to observation around the third or fourth year of life. It is during the period of total or only partial latency that the mental forces which later impede the course of the sexual instinct are built up. Powerful components are acquired for every kind of cultural achievement by the diversion of sexual instinctual forces from sexual aims and their direction to new ones, a process called sublimation. The same process plays a part in the development of the individual and its beginning is in the period of sexual latency of childhood. Interruptions of the latency period are discussed.

1905D 7/179

Three essays on the theory of sexuality (1905). Chapter II: Infantile sexuality. (2). The manifestations of infantile sexuality.

The manifestations of infantile sexuality are discussed. Thumbsucking (or sensual sucking) is regarded as an example of the sexual manifestations of childhood. Thumbsucking appears in early infancy and may continue into maturity, or even persist all through life. A grasping instinct may appear and may manifest itself as a simultaneous rhythmic tugging at the lobes of the ears or

a catching hold of some part of another person for the same purpose. Sensual sucking involves a complete absorption of the attention and leads either to sleep or even to a motor reaction in the nature of an orgasm. The behavior of a child who indulges in thumbsucking is determined by a search for some pleasure which has already been experienced and is now remembered. To begin with, sexual activity attaches itself to functions serving the purpose of self-preservation and does not become independent of them until later. The 3 essential characteristics of an infantile sexual manifestation are: 1) at its origin it attaches itself to one of the vital somatic functions; 2) it has as yet no sexual object, and is thus autoerotic; and 3) its sexual aim is dominated by an erotogenic zone.

1905D 7/183

Three essays on the theory of sexuality (1905). Chapter II: Infantile sexuality. (3). The sexual aim of infantile sexuality.

The sexual aim of infantile sexuality is discussed. An erotogenic zone is a part of the skin or mucous membrane in which stimuli of a certain sort evoke a feeling of pleasure possessing a particular quality. A rhythmic character must play a part among the special conditions which produce the pleasure. There are predestined erotogenic zones; however, any other part of the skin or mucous membrane can take over the functions in that direction. Thus the quality of the stimulus has more to do with producing the pleasurable feeling than has the nature of the part of the body concerned. A child who indulges in sensual sucking searches about his body and chooses some part of it to suck, a part which is afterwards preferred by him by force of habit. A precisely analogous tendency to displacement is also found in the symptomatology of hysteria; here repression affects most of all the actual genital zones and these transmit their susceptibility to stimulation to other erotogenic zones which then behave exactly like genitals. The sexual aim of the infantile instinct consists in obtaining satisfaction by means of an appropriate stimulation of the erotogenic zone which has been selected in one way or another. This satisfaction must have been previously experienced in order to have left behind a need for its repetition. A sexual aim consists in replacing the projected sensation of stimulation in the erotogenic zone by an external stimulus which removes that sensation by producing a feeling of satisfaction.

1905D 7/185

Three essays on the theory of sexuality (1905). Chapter II: Infantile sexuality. (4). Masturbatory sexual manifestations.

Masturbatory sexual manifestations are discussed. The anal zone is well suited by its position to act as a medium through which sexuality may attach itself to other somatic functions. The intestinal disturbances which are so common in childhood see to it that this zone does not lack intense excitations. The masturbation of early infancy seems to disappear after a short time, but at some point of childhood (usually before the fourth year) the sexual instinct belonging to the genital zone usually revives and persists for a time until it is once more surpressed, or it may continue without interruption. The sexual excitation returns, either as a centrally determined tickling stimulus which seeks satisfaction in masturbation, or as a process in the nature of nocturnal emission which, like the nocturnal emissions of adult years, achieves satisfaction without the help of any action by the subject. The reappearance of sexual activity is determined by internal causes and external contingencies, both of which can be guessed at in cases of neurotic illness from the form taken by their symptoms. Under the influence of seduction, children can become polymorphously perverse, and can be led into all possible kinds of sexual irregularities. This shows that an aptitude for them is innately present in their disposition. Infantile sexual life, in spite of the preponderating dominance of erotogenic zones, exhibits components which involve other people as sexual objects. Such are the instincts of scopophilia, exhibitionism and cruelty. The cruel component of the sexual instinct develops in childhood even more independently of the sexual activities that are attached to erotogenic zones. The impulse of cruelty arises from the instinct for mastery and appears at a period of sexual life at which the genitals have not yet taken over their later role. It then dominates a phase of sexual life which is described as a pregenital organization.

1905D 7/194

Three essays on the theory of sexuality (1905). Chapter II: Infantile sexuality. (5). The sexual researches of childhood.

At about the same time as the sexual life of children reaches its first peak, between the ages of 3 and 5, the children begin to show signs of the activity which may be ascribed to the instinct for knowledge or research. Its activity corresponds to a sublimated manner of obtaining mastery, while it also makes use of the energy of scopophilia. A male child believes that a genital like his own is to be attributed to everyone he knows, and he cannot make its absence tally with his picture of these other people. This conviction is energetically maintained by boys; is obstinately defended against the contradictions which soon result from observation; and is only abandoned after severe internal struggles (the castration complex). The substitutes for the penis which they feel is missing in women play a great part in determining the form taken by many perversions. When girls see that

boys' genitals are formed differently from their own, they are ready to recognize them immediately and are overcome by envy for the penis. Children's theories of birth are discussed as is their sadistic view of sexual intercourse. The sexual theories of children are, in general, reflections of their own sexual constitution. In spite of their grotesque errors, the theories show more understanding of sexual processes than children are given credit for.

1905D 7/197

Three essays on the theory of sexuality (1905). Chapter II: Infantile sexuality. (6). The phases of development of the sexual organization.

Infantile sexual life is essentially autoerotic and its individual component instincts are disconnected and independent of one another in their search for pleasure. The study of the inhibitions and disturbances of the process of development of the sexual organization enables us to recognize abortive beginnings and preliminary stages of a firm organization of the component instincts. The name pregenital is given to organizations of sexual life in which the genital zones have not yet taken over their predominant part. The first of these is the oral organization. A second pregenital phase is that of the sadistic anal organization. In this stage sexual polarity and an extraneous object are observable but organization and subordination to the reproductive function are still absent. This form of sexual organization can persist throughout life and can permanently attract a large portion of sexual activity. The opposing pairs of instincts (activity and passivity) are developed to an equal extent and are described by the term ambivalence. It is concluded that the whole of the sexual currents have become directed towards a single person in relation to whom they seek to achieve their aims, this then being the closest approximation possible in childhood to the final form taken by sexual life after puberty. It may be regarded as typical of the choice of an object that the process is diphasic, that is, that it occurs in 2 waves. The first of these begins between the ages of 2 and 5, and is brought to a halt or to a retreat by the latency period. The second wave starts with puberty and determines the final outcome of sexual life.

1905D 7/200

Three essays on the theory of sexuality (1905). Chapter II: Infantile sexuality. (7). The sources of infantile sexuality.

Sexual excitation arises: 1) as a reproduction of a satisfaction experienced in connection with other organic processes; 2) through appropriate peripheral stimulation of erotogenic zones; and 3) as an expression of certain instincts. Sexual excitation can also be produced by rhythmic mechanical agitation of the body. Stimuli of this kind operate in 3 different ways: on the sensory apparatus of the vestibular nerves, on the skin, and on the deeper parts. Children feel a need for a large amount of active muscular exercise and derive extraordinary pleasure from satisfying it. In many people, the infantile connection between romping and sexual excitation is among the determinants of the direction subsequently taken by their sexual instinct. All comparatively intense affective processes, including even terrifying ones, infringe upon sexuality, a fact which may incidentally help to explain the pathogenic effect of emotions of that kind. Concentration of the attention upon an intellectual task and intellectual strain in general produce a concomitant sexual excitation in many young people as well as adults. The same pathways along which sexual disturbances infringe upon the other somatic functions also perform another important function in normal health; they serve for the attraction of sexual instinctual forces to aims that are other than sexual, that is to say, for the sublimation of sexuality.

1905D 7/207

Three essays on the theory of sexuality (1905). Chapter III: The transformations of puberty. (1). The primacy of the genital zones and the fore-pleasure.

With the arrival of puberty, changes set in which are destined to give infantile sexual life its final, normal shape. A normal sexual life is only assured by an exact convergence of the affectionate current and the sensual current both being directed towards the sexual object and sexual aim. The new sexual aim in men consists in the discharge of the sexual products. The most striking of the processes at puberty has been picked upon as constituting its essence: the manifest growth of the external genitalia. Stimuli can impinge on it from 3 directions: from the external world by means of the excitation of the erotogenic zones, from the organic interior, and from mental life, which is a storehouse for external impressions and a receiver for internal excitations. All three types of stimuli produce sexual excitement. The erotogenic zones are used to provide a certain amount of pleasure by being stimulated in the way appropriate to them. This pleasure then leads to an increase in tension which in its turn is responsible for producing the necessary motor energy for the conclusion of the sexual act. The penultimate stage of that act is once again the appropriate stimulation of an erotogenic zone by the appropriate object; and from the pleasure yielded by this excitation the motor energy is obtained, this time by a reflex path, which brings about the discharge of the sexual substances.

1905D 7/212

Three essays on the theory of sexuality (1905). Chapter III: The transformations of puberty. (2). The problem of sexual excitation.

The problem of sexual excitation is discussed. We remain in complete ignorance both of the origin and of the nature of the sexual tension which arises simultaneously with the pleasure when erotogenic zones are satisfied. A certain degree of sexual tension is required for the excitability of the erotogenic zones. The accumulation of the sexual substances creates and maintains sexual tension; the pressure of these products upon the walls of the vesicles containing them might be supposed to act as a stimulus upon a spinal center, the condition of which would be perceived by higher centers and would then give consciousness to the familiar sensation of tension. Observations on castrated males seem to show that sexual excitation can occur to a considerable degree independently of the production of the sexual substances. It seems probable that special chemical substances are produced in the interstitial portion of the sex glands; these are then taken up in the blood stream and cause particular parts of the central nervous system to be charged with sexual tension. It is concluded that substances of a peculiar kind arise from sexual metabolism.

1905D 7/217

Three essays on the theory of sexuality (1905). Chapter III: The transformations of puberty. (3). The libido theory.

The libido theory is discussed. Libido is defined as a quantitatively variable force which could serve as a measure of processes and transformations occurring in the field of sexual excitation. The idea of a quantity of libido is presented and the mental representation of it is given the name of ego libido. The production, increase or diminution, distribution and displacement of it should afford us possibilities for explaining the psychosexual phenomena observed. This ego libido is, however, only conveniently accessible to analytic study when it has been put to the use of cathecting sexual objects, that is, when it has become object libido. It should be the task of a libido theory of neurotic and psychotic disorders to express all the observed phenomena and inferred processes in terms of the economics of the libido. In contrast to object libido, ego libido is described as narcissistic libido. Narcissistic or ego libido seems to be the great reservoir from which the object cathexes are sent out and into which they are withdrawn once more; the narcissistic libidinal cathexis of the ego is the original state of things, realized in earliest childhood, and is merely covered by the later extrusions of libido, but in essentials persists behind them.

1905D 7/219

Three essays on the theory of sexuality (1905). Chapter III: The transformations of puberty (4). The differentiation between men and women.

The differentiation between men and women is discussed. It is not until puberty that the sharp distinction is established between the masculine and feminine characters. From that time on, this contrast has a more decisive influence than any other upon the shaping of human life. The development of the inhibitions of sexuality takes place in little girls earlier and in the face of less resistance than in boys. The autoerotic activity of the erotogenic zones is, however, the same in both sexes. The leading erotogenic zone in female children is located at the clitoris, and is thus homologous to the masculine genital zone of the glans penis. Puberty, which brings about so great an accession of libido in boys, is marked in girls by a fresh wave of expression, in which it is precisely clitoral sexuality that is affected. When erotogenic susceptibility to stimulation has been successfully transferred by a woman from the clitoris to the vaginal orifice, it implies that she has adopted a new leading zone for the purpose of her later sexual activity. A man retains his leading zone unchanged from childhood.

1905D 7/222

Three essays on the theory of sexuality (1905). Chapter III: The transformations of puberty. (5). The finding of an object.

The processes at puberty establish the primacy of the genital zones; and in a man, the penis, which has now become capable of erection, presses forward insistently towards the new sexual aim, penetration into a cavity in the body which excites his genital zone. Simultaneously on the psychical side the process of finding an object, for which preparations have been made from earliest childhood, is completed. All through the period of latency children learn to feel for other people who help them in their helplessness and satisfy their needs. Their love is modeled after and a continuation of, their relation as sucklings to their mother. Children behave as though their dependence on the people looking after them were in the nature of sexual love. Anxiety in children is originally an expression of the fact that they are feeling the loss of the person they love. The barrier against incest is maintained by the postponing of sexual maturation until the child can respect the cultural taboo upheld by society. The sexual life of maturing youth is almost entirely restricted to indulging in phantasies. When incestuous fantasies are overcome, detachment from parental authority is completed. The closer one comes to the deeper disturbances of psychosexual development, the more unmistakably the importance of incestuous object choice emerges. In psychoneurotics, a large portion or the whole of their psychosexual activity in finding an object remains in the unconscious as a result of their repudiation of sexuality. Even a person who has avoided an incestuous fixation of his libido does not entirely escape its influence. One of the tasks implicit in object choice is that it should find its way to the opposite sex.

1905D 7/231

Three essays on the theory of sexuality (1905). Summary.

The onset of sexual development in human beings occurs in 2 phases. This appears to be one of the necessary conditions of the aptitude of men for developing a higher civilization, but also of their tendency to neurosis. It is not rare to find perversions and psychoneuroses occurring in the same family, and distributed between the 2 sexes in such a way that the male members of the family are positive perverts, while the females, are negative perverts, that is, hysterics. This is good evidence of the essential conditions which exist between the 2 disorders. If an abnormal relationship between all the different dispositions persists and grows stronger at maturity, the result can only be a perverse sexual life. If the genital zone is weak, the combination, which is required to take place at puberty, is bound to fail, and the strongest of the other components of sexuality will continue its activity as a perversion. If in the course of development some of the components which are of excessive strength in the disposition are submitted to the process of repression, the excitations concerned continue to be generated as before; but they are prevented by psychical obstruction from attaining their aim and are diverted into numerous other channels until they find their way to expression as symptoms. Sublimation enables excessively strong excitations arising from particular sources of sexuality to find an outlet and use in other fields, so that an increase in psychical efficiency results from a disposition which in itself is perilous.

7/244

Three essays on the theory of sexuality (1905). Appendix: List of writings by Freud dealing predominantly or largely with sexuality.

A list of writings by Freud dealing predominantly or largely with sexuality is presented. References to sexuality are to be found in a large majority of Freud's writings. This list of 33 writings comprises those which are more directly concerned with the subject. They date from 1898 to 1940 and include: Sexuality in the Etiology of the Neuroses; The Sexual Enlightenment of Children; Character and Anal Erotism; Contributions to a Discussion on Masturbation; The Disposition to Obsessional Neurosis; On Narcissism: an Introduction;

On the Transformation of Instincts, with Special Reference to Anal Erotism; The Taboo of Virginity; The Infantile Genital Organization; The Economic Problem of Masturbation; The Dissolution of the Oedipus Complex; Fetishism; Libidinal Types; and Splitting of the Ego in the Process of Defense.

1904A   7/249
Freud's psycho-analytic procedure (1904).

Freud's psychotherapeutic procedure, described as psychoanalysis, is an outgrowth of the cathartic method. The cathartic method presupposed that the patient could be hypnotized, and was based on the widening of consciousness that occurs under hypnosis. Its aim was the removal of the pathological symptoms. The cathartic method renounced suggestion; Freud gave up hypnosis as well and found a substitute for hypnosis in the associations of his patients. Freud insisted that the patients include everything that comes into their heads when they discuss their case history. Freud noticed that gaps (amnesias) appeared in the patient's memory thus making up the determining factor of his entire theory. If the patient is urged to fill the gaps discomfort occurs when the memory really returns. From this Freud concludes that the amnesias are the result of a process which he calls repression and the motive for which he finds in feelings of unpleasure. The psychical forces which have brought about this repression can be detected in the resistance which operates against the recovery of the lost memories. The factor of resistance has become a cornerstone of his theory. The greater the resistance, the greater the distortion of the repressed psychical phenomena. Freud developed the art of interpretation which takes on the task of extracting repressed thoughts from unintentional ideas. The work of interpretation is applied not only to the patient's ideas but also to his dreams. The therapeutic procedure remains the same for all the various clinical pictures that may be presented in hysteria and all forms of obsessional neurosis. The qualifications that are required for anyone who is to be beneficially affected by psychoanalysis include: periods of psychically normal condition, natural intelligence, and ethical development.

1905A   7/257
On psychotherapy (1905).

On Psychotherapy was delivered as a lecture before the Wiener medizinisches Doktorenkollegium on December 12, 1904. Psychotherapy is not a modern method of treatment. The majority of primitive and ancient medical methods must be classed under the head of psychotherapy. Certain diseases, in particular, the psychoneuroses, are far more readily accessible to mental influences than to any other form of medication. The many

ways and means of practicing psychotherapy that lead to recovery are good. Several thoughts are presented concerning psychotherapy. 1) This method is often confused with hypnotic treatment by suggestion. There is the greatest possible degree of antithesis between these 2 techniques. Suggestion is not concerned with the origin, strength and meaning of morbid states but superimposes a suggestion hopefully capable of restraining the pathogenic idea. Analysis concerns itself with the genesis of the morbid symptoms and its function is to bring out factors during analysis. 2) The technique of searching for the origins of an illness and removing its manifestations is not easy and can not be practiced without training. 3) The analytic investigation and probing do not indicate speedy results and resistance can result in unpleasantness; however, all the effort of psychoanalytic therapy seems worthwhile when we consider that it has made a large number of patients who were permanently unfit for existence, fit for existence. 4) The indications or contraindications for psychoanalysis are that a patient should have a reasonable degree of education and a fairly reliable character, a normal mental condition, and be less than 50 yrs. old. Psychoanalysis should not be attempted when speedy removal of dangerous symptoms is required. 5) No injury to the patient is to be feared when the treatment is conducted with comprehension. 6) It is concluded that this therapy is based on the recognition that unconscious ideas, or the unconsciousness of certain mental processes, are the direct cause of the morbid symptoms. Psychoanalytic treatment may, in general, be conceived of as a re-education in overcoming internal resistances. Freud's last comment is to advise against recommending sexual activity in psychoneuroses.

1906A   7/271
My views on the part played by sexuality in the aetiology of the neuroses (1906).

The part played by sexuality in the etiology of the neuroses is discussed. Originally, Freud's theory related only to the clinical pictures comprised under the term neurasthenia including neurasthenia proper and anxiety neurosis. With more experiences, it was discovered that the cause of lifelong hysterical neuroses lies in what are in themselves the trivial sexual experiences of early childhood. A number of phantasies of seduction are explained as attempts at fending off memories of the subject's own sexual activity (infantile masturbation). The importance of sexuality and of infantilism are stressed. The patient's symptoms constitute his sexual activity, which arise from the sources of the normal or perverse component instincts of sexuality. The etiology of the neuroses comprises everything which can act in a detrimental manner upon the processes serving the sexual function. The most important are the noxae which affect the sexual function itself; next are every other type of noxa and trauma which, by causing general damage to the organism, may lead secondarily to injury to its sexual processes. The onset of illness is the product of a summation of etiological factors and the necessary total of these factors can be completed from any direction.

1905B 7/283
Psychical (or mental) treatment (1905).

Psychical treatment denotes treatment taking its start in the mind, treatment (whether of mental or physical disorders) by measures which operate upon the human mind. Foremost among such measures is the use of words, and words are the essential tool of mental treatment. There is a large number of patients, suffering from disorders of greater or less severity, whose disorders and complaints make great demands on the skill of their physicians, but in whom no visible or observable signs of a pathological process can be discovered. One group of these patients are distinguished by the copiousness and variety of their symptoms (which are influenced by excitement). In this case, the illness is of the nervous system, as a whole and is called "nervousness" (neurasthenia or hysteria). The affects are often sufficient in themselves to bring about both diseases of the nervous system accompanied by manifest anatomical changes and also diseases of other organs. States of illness that are already present can be considerably influenced by violent affects. The processes of volition and attention are also capable of exercising a profound effect on somatic processes and of playing a large part in promoting or preventing physical illnesses. The mental state of expectation puts in motion a number of mental forces that have the greatest influence on the onset and cure (such as faith or miracle cure) of physical diseases. The use of hypnosis and the knowledge gained from it are discussed. By means of hypnosis the mind can increase its control over the body and the physician can cause changes in the patient's waking state by posthypnotic suggestion. Disadvantages of hypnosis include the damage it can cause and the patient's dependence on the physician.

1942A 7/305
Psychopathic characters on the stage (1942).

Psychopathic characters on the stage are discussed. The purpose of drama is to reveal sources of pleasure or enjoyment in our emotional life. In this respect the prime factor is the process of getting rid of one's own emotions; the consequent enjoyment corresponds to the relief produced by a thorough discharge and to an accompanying sexual excitation. The spectator's enjoyment is based on illusion; it is someone other than himself who is acting and suffering on the stage, and it is

only a game, which can not damage his personal security. Drama seeks to explore emotional possibilities and give an enjoyable shape even to forebodings of misfortune. Suffering of every kind is the subject matter of drama, and from this suffering it promises to give the audience pleasure. The other precondition of this art form is that it should not cause suffering to the audience but should compensate for the sympathetic suffering which is aroused. People are acquainted with mental suffering principally in connection with the circumstances in which it is acquired; accordingly, dramas dealing with it require some event out of which the illness shall arise and they open with an exposition of this event. The event must involve conflict and must include an effort of will together with resistance. Religious drama, social drama, and drama of character differ essentially in the terrain on which the action that leads to the suffering is fought out. Psychological and psychopathological drama are discussed next. *Hamlet* is distinguished with reference to 3 characteristics. 1) The hero is not psychopathic, but only becomes psychopathic in the course of the play. 2) The repressed impulse is one of those which are similarly repressed in all of us; this repression is shaken up by the situation in the play. 3) The impulse that is struggling into consciousness is never given a definite name so that in the spectator the process is carried through with his attention averted, and he is in the grip of his emotions instead of taking stock of what is happening. A certain amount of resistance is saved in this way. It is concluded that the neurotic instability of the public and the dramatist's skill in avoiding resistances and offering forepleasures can alone determine the limits set upon the use of abnormal characters on the stage.

VOL. VIII   Jokes and their Relation to the Unconscious (1905)

1905C 8/3
Jokes and their relation to the unconscious (1960). Editor's preface.

In the course of discussing the relation between jokes and dreams, Freud mentions his own subjective reason for taking up the problem of jokes: the fact that when Wilhelm Fliess was reading the proofs of *The Interpretation of Dreams* in the autumn of 1899, he complained that the dreams were too full of jokes. The episode acted as a precipitating factor, and led to Freud's giving closer attention to the subject; but it cannot possibly have been the origin of his interest in it. Quite apart from dreams, there is evidence of Freud's early theoretical interest in jokes. There is a serious difficulty in translating this particular work, a terminological difficulty which runs through the whole of it. The German and English terms covering the phenomena discussed seem never to coincide.

1905C 8/9

Jokes and their relation to the unconscious (1905). A. Analytic part. I. Introduction.

Anyone who has had occasion to enquire from the literature of esthetics and psychology the nature of jokes and the position they occupy will probably have to admit that jokes have not received nearly as much philosophical consideration as they deserve in view of the part they play in mental life. The first impression one derives from the literature is that it is quite impracticable to deal with jokes otherwise than in connection with the comic. A favorite definition of joking has long been the ability to find similarity between dissimilar things, that is, hidden similarities. The criteria and characteristics of jokes include: activity, relation to the content of our thoughts, the characteristic of playful judgment, the coupling of dissimilar things, contrasting ideas, sense in nonsense, the succession of bewilderment and enlightenment, the bringing forward of what is hidden, and the peculiar brevity of wit. We are entirely without insight into the connection that presumably exists between the separate determinants (*i.e.* what the brevity of a joke can have to do with its characteristic of being a playful judgment).

1905C 8/16

Jokes and their relation to the unconscious (1905). A. Analytic part. II. The technique of jokes (1) & (2). Jokes are similar to dreams.

The character of a joke does not reside in the thought but in the technique. Examples are given of jokes in which the thought is condensed by introducing, as a substitute, a striking composite word (e.g. anecdotage for anecdote and dotage) which is unintelligible in itself but is immediately understood in its context. In related cases the substitute is not a composite word but a slight modification (e.g. tete-a-bete for tete-a-tete). In general, the slighter the modification, the better the joke. Condensation and modification involved in these types of jokes are compared to condensation and modification which occurs in dream-work.

1905C 8/29

Jokes and their relation to the unconscious (1905). A. Analytic part. II. The technique of jokes. (3). Condensations and substitutive formations in dreams.

The first thing that we want to learn is whether the process of condensation with substitute formation is to be discovered in every joke, and can therefore be regarded as a universal characteristic of the technique of jokes. Three examples are presented in which substitute

formation does not occur. In each of them, a name is used twice, once as a whole and again divided up into its separate syllables, which, when they are thus separated, give another sense. The multiple use of the same word, once as a whole and again in the syllables into which it falls, is the first instance we have come across of a technique differing from that of condensation. The cases of multiple use, which can also be brought together under the title of double meaning, can easily be divided into subclasses: 1) cases of the double meaning of a name and of a thing denoted by it; 2) double meaning arising from the literal and metaphorical meanings of a word; and 3) double meaning proper, or play upon words.

1905C 8/45

Jokes and their relation to the unconscious (1905). A. Analytic part. II. The technique of jokes. (4) & (5). Summary and puns.

The different joke techniques are summarized as follows: condensation, with formation of composite word or with modification; the multiple use of the same material as a whole and in parts, in a different order, with slight modification, and of the same words full and empty; and double meaning as a name and as a thing, metaphorical and literal meanings, double meaning proper (play upon words), double entendre, and double meaning with an allusion. The multiple use of the same material is only a special case of condensation; play upon words is nothing other than a condensation without substitute formation. All these techniques are dominated by a tendency to compression; or rather to saving (economy). The most numerous group of jokes is influenced by the contempt with which they are regarded. This kind is generally known as puns and passes as the lowest form of verbal joke, probably because it can be made with the least trouble. Puns make the least demand on the technique of expression, just as the play upon words proper makes the highest. Puns merely form a subspecies of the group which reaches its peak in the play upon words proper.

1905C 8/47

Jokes and their relation to the unconscious (1905). A. Analytic part. II. The technique of jokes. (6) & (7). Puns; absurdity as a joke technique.

There are jokes whose technique resists almost any attempt to connect it with the groups (those derived from condensation, multiple use of the same material or double meaning) that have been considered. In the case of a displacement joke, the joke itself contains a train of thought in which a displacement has been accomplished. The displacement is part of the work which has created the joke; it is not part of the work necessary for understanding it. The technique of the nonsensical or absurd jokes consists in presenting something that is stupid and nonsensical, the sense of which lies in the revelation and demonstration of something else that is stupid and nonsensical. A number of displacement and nonsensical jokes are presented and analyzed.

1905C 8/60

Jokes and their relation to the unconscious (1905). A. Analytic part. II. The technique of jokes. (8) & (9). Relation of jokes to the comic; unification as a joke technique.

The uncovering of psychical automatism is one of the techniques of the comic, just as is any kind of revelation or self-betrayal. The technique of this group of jokes lies in bringing forward faulty reasoning. Unification lies at the bottom of jokes that can be described as ready repartees. Repartee consists in the defense going to meet the aggression, in turning the tables on someone, or paying someone back in his own coin, that is, in establishing an unexpected unity between attack and counterattack. Unification has another, quite specially interesting technical instrument at its disposal: stringing things together with the conjunction 'and'. If things are strung together in this way, it implies that they are connected: understanding it as so cannot be helped.

1905C 8/70

Jokes and their relation to the unconscious (1905). A. Analytic part. II. The technique of jokes. (10) & (11). Representation by opposite; conceptual jokes.

Examples are presented of jokes in which the technique employed is "representation by the opposite", e.g. representation of ugliness through resemblances to what is most beautiful. In some cases this technique can be combined with displacement. A related technique is the use of overstatement. Representation by the opposite is not confined to jokes but may be used in irony. Representation by something similar or akin forms the basis for another category of jokes. This technique is often complicated by allusion. The replacing element may be merely a resemblance in sound but, in contrast to puns, the resemblance in sound involves whole sentences or phrases rather than just 2 words. Another kind of allusion consists in omission; this type of joke often cannot be distinguished from condensation without formation of a substitute. Allusion, which is probably the commonest and most easily used method of joking and which forms a basis for most short-lived jokes found in conversations, can be described as indirect representation. Categories of jokes discussed so far which would fall into this category include faulty reasoning, unification, and representation by the opposite.

1905C 8/81

Jokes and their relation to the unconscious (1905). A. Analytic part. II. The technique of jokes. (12). Analogy as a joke technique.

Analogy is a kind of indirect representation used by jokes. There are remarkably fine and effective examples of analogies that do not strike us as being jokes. There are also analogies which contain a striking juxtaposition, often a combination that sounds absurd, or which are replaced by something of the sort as the outcome of the analogy. A strange juxtaposition or the attribution of an absurd epithet can stand by itself as the outcome of an analogy. An analogy can in itself possess the characteristics of being a joke, without this impression being accounted for by a complication with one of the familiar joke techniques. Analogy is included among the species of indirect representation used by the joke technique.

1905C 8/91

Jokes and their relation to the unconscious (1905). A. Analytic part. III. The purposes of jokes. (1) & (2). Innocent jokes; smut and the purpose of jokes.

The purpose of jokes is discussed. Innocent or abstract jokes (both are nontendentious) do not have the same meaning as jokes that are trivial or lacking in substance; they merely connote the opposite of the tendentious jokes. An innocent joke may be of great substance, it may assert something of value. We receive from joking remarks a total impression in which we are unable to separate the share taken by the thought content from the share taken by the joke work. Where a joke is not an aim in itself (where it is not innocent), it is either a hostile joke (serving the purpose of aggressiveness, satire, or defense) or an obscene joke (serving the purpose of exposure). The technical species of the joke, whether it is a verbal or a conceptual joke, bears no relation to these 2 purposes. A tendentious joke calls for 3 people: in addition to the one who makes the joke, there must be a second who is taken as the object of the hostile or sexual aggressiveness, and a third in whom the joke's aim of producing pleasure is fulfilled. When the first person finds his libidinal impulse inhibited by a woman, he develops a hostile trend against that second person and calls on the originally interfering third person as his ally. Through the first person's smutty speech the woman is exposed before the third, who, as a listener, has now been bribed by the effortless satisfaction of his own libido. Thus jokes make possible the satisfaction of instinct (whether lustful or hostile) in the face of an obstacle which stands in the way. The obstacle in the way is woman's incapacity to tolerate undisguised sexuality. This power which makes it difficult or impossible for women, and to a lesser degree for men as well, to enjoy undisguised obscenity is termed repression. Tendentious jokes have sources of pleasure at their disposal besides those open to innocent jokes, in which all the pleasure is in some way linked to their technique.

1905C 8/102
Jokes and their relation to the unconscious (1905). A. Analytic part. III. The purpose of jokes. (3), (4), (5). Hostile, cynical and skeptical jokes.

Hostile impulses against our fellow men have always been subject to the same restrictions, the same progressive repression, as our sexual urges. A joke will allow us to exploit something ridiculous in our enemy which we could not, on account of obstacles in the way, bring forward openly or consciously; here again the joke will evade restrictions and open sources of pleasure that have become inaccessible. Tendentious jokes are highly suitable for attacks on the great, the dignified and the mighty, who are protected by internal inhibition and external circumstances from direct disparagement. Among the institutions which cynical jokes are in the habit of attacking none is more important or more strictly guarded by oral regulations than the institution of marriage, at which the majority of cynical jokes are aimed. There is no more personal claim than that for sexual freedom and at no point has civilization tried to exercise more severe suppression than in the sphere of sexuality. A particularly favorable occasion for tendentious jokes is presented when the intended rebellious criticism is directed against the subject himself, or against someone in whom the subject has a share, a collective person, (the subject's own nation, for instance). Jokes that attack not a person or an institution but the certainty of our knowledge itself are called skeptical jokes.

1905C 8/117
Jokes and their relation to the unconscious (1905). B. Synthetic part. IV. The mechanism of pleasure and the psychogenesis of jokes. (1).

The mechanism of pleasure and the psychogenesis of jokes is discussed. The pleasure in the case of a tendentious joke arises from a purpose being satisfied whose satisfaction would otherwise not have taken place. The techniques of jokes are themselves sources of pleasure. In one group of jokes, the technique consists in focusing our psychical attitude upon the sound of the word instead of upon its meaning. A second group of technical methods used in jokes (unification, similarity of sound, multiple use, modification of familiar phrases, allusions to quotations) has as the common characteristic the fact that in each of them something familiar is rediscovered. This is the basis for the use of another technical resource in jokes, topicality. The third group of joke techniques for the most part conceptual jokes, which comprises faulty thinking, displacements, absurdity, representation by the opposite, etc., may at first

glance seem to bear a special impress and to have no kinship with the techniques of rediscovery of what is familiar or the replacement of object associations by word associations. Nevertheless the theory of economy or relief in psychical expenditure applies here. The first and third of these groups, the replacement of thing associations by word associations and the use of absurdity, can be brought together as reestablishing old liberties and getting rid of the burden of intellectual upbringing; they are psychical reliefs, which can be contrasted with the economizing which constitutes the technique of the second group. From these 2 principles all the techniques of jokes, and accordingly all pleasure from these techniques, are derived: relief from psychical expenditure that is already there and economizing in psychical expenditure that is only about to be called for.

1905C 8/128
Jokes and their relation to the unconscious (1905). B. Synthetic part. IV. The mechanism of pleasure and the psychogenesis of jokes. (2). The purpose and functions of jokes.

Before there is such a thing as a joke, there is something that we may describe as play or as a jest. Play with words and thoughts, motivated by certain pleasurable effects of economy, are the first stages of jokes. This play is brought to an end by the strengthening of a factor described as the critical faculty or reasonableness. Next a second preliminary stage of jokes sets in, the jest. It is now a question of prolonging the yield of pleasure from play, but at the same time silencing the objections raised by criticism which would not allow the pleasurable feeling to emerge. The psychogenesis of jokes reveals that the pleasure in a joke is derived from play with words or from the liberation of nonsense, and that the meaning of the joke is merely intended to protect that pleasure from being done away with by criticism. If what a jest says possesses substance and value, it turns into a joke. The tendentious jokes use the pleasure from jokes as a fore-pleasure to produce new pleasure by lifting suppressions and repressions.

1905C 8/140
Jokes and their relation to the unconscious (1905). B. Synthetic part. V. The motives of jokes—Jokes as a social process.

Jokes are discussed as a social process. Although the joke work is an excellent method of getting pleasure out of psychical processes, it is nevertheless evident that not everyone is equally capable of making use of that method. The impression is given that the subjective determinants of the joke work are often not far removed from those of neurotic illness. The great majority of jokes, and especially those that are constantly being newly produced in connection with the events of the day, are circulated anonymously. The motive force for the production of innocent jokes is not infrequently an ambitious urge to show one's cleverness, to display oneself. In laughter, the conditions are present under which a sum of psychical energy which has hitherto been used for cathexis is allowed free discharge. Since laughter is an indication of pleasure, we shall be inclined to relate this pleasure to the lifting of the cathexis which has previously been present. If a quota of cathectic energy capable of discharge is to be liberated, there are several conditions which must be fulfilled or which are desirable in order to act as encouragement: 1) it must be ensured that the person is really making this cathectic expenditure; 2) it is necessary to guard against the cathectic expenditure, when it is liberated, finding some other psychical use instead of offering itself for motor discharge; and 3) it is an advantage if the cathexis which is to be liberated in the third person is intensified beforehand.

1905C   8/159

Jokes and their relation to the unconscious (1905). C. Theoretic part. VI. The relation of jokes to dreams and to the unconscious.

The relation of jokes to dreams and to the unconscious is discussed. Thought transformation with a view to the possibility of representation, condensation and displacement are the 3 major achievements that may be ascribed to the dream work. The characteristics and effects of jokes are linked with certain forms of expression or technical methods, among which the most striking are condensation, displacement, and indirect representation. Processes, however, which lead to the same results have become known to us as peculiarities of the dream work. Jokes are formed as a preconscious thought is given over for a moment to unconscious revision and the outcome of this is at once grasped by conscious perception. The characteristics of jokes which can be referred to their formation in the unconscious are presented: 1) the peculiar brevity of jokes; 2) displacements; 3) representation by the opposite; and 4) the use of nonsense. Dreams serve predominantly for the avoidance of unpleasure, jokes for the attainment of pleasure; but all our mental activities converge in these 2 aims.

1905C   8/181

Jokes and their relation to the unconscious (1905). C. Theoretic part. VII. Jokes and the species of the comic. (1).

Jokes are a subspecies of the comic. The comic, which behaves differently socially from jokes; is concerned with 2 persons, (the first who finds what is comic and a second in whom it is found) while a third person intensifies, but doesn't add to the comic process. A joke is made, the comic is found. The type of the comic

which stands nearest to jokes is the naive. The comic arises as an unintended discovery derived from human social relations. It is found in people, in their movements, forms, actions and traits of character, originally in all probability only in their physical characteristics but later in their mental ones as well or in the expression of those characteristics. Nonsense and stupidity, which so often produce a comic effect, are nevertheless not felt as comic in every case. The comic that is found in someone else's intellectual and mental characteristics is the outcome of a comparison between him and self, though a comparison which has produced the opposite result to that in the case of a comic movement or action. A person appears comic to us if, in comparison with ourselves, he makes too great an expenditure on his bodily functions and too little on his mental ones. It can not be denied that in both these cases our laughter expresses a pleasurable sense of the superiority which we feel in relation to him.

1905C   8/199

Jokes and their relation to the unconscious (1905). C. Theoretic part. VII. Jokes and the species of the comic. (2). Psychical location distinguishes jokes from the comic.

It is possible to produce the comic in relation to oneself in order to amuse other people. To make other people comic, the principal means is to put them in situations in which a person becomes comic as a result of human dependence on external events, particularly on social factors, without regard to the personal characteristics of the individual concerned. This putting of someone in a real comic situation is called a practical joke. Other means of making things comic which deserve special consideration and also indicate fresh sources of comic pleasure include mimicry, caricature, parody, and travesty. Contact with the comic is not to be found in all jokes or even in the majority of them and, in most cases, a clear distinction is to be made between jokes and the comic. The pleasure in jokes is located in the unconscious while there is no justification for making the same localization in the case of the comic. Jokes and the comic are distinguished in their psychical localization: the joke is the contribution made to the comic from the realm of the unconscious.

1905C   8/208

Jokes and their relation to the unconscious (1905). C. Theoretic part. VII. Jokes and the species of the comic. (3) & (4). Differences between jokes and comic.

The comic of mimicry is permeated with caricature, the exaggeration of traits that are not otherwise striking, and also involves the characteristic of degradation. Jokes present a double face to their hearer, force him to adopt 2 different views of them. In a nonsense joke, the one view regards it as nonsense; the other view passes through the hearer's unconscious and finds an excellent sense in it. Every theory of the comic is objected to by its critics on the score that its definition overlooks what is essential to the comic: The comic is based on a contrast between ideas. The most favorable condition for the production of comic pleasure is a generally cheerful mood in which one is inclined to laugh. A similarly favorable effect is produced by an expectation of the comic, by being attuned to comic pleasure. Unfavorable conditions for the comic arise from the kind of mental activity with which a particular person is occupied at the moment. The opportunity for the release of comic pleasure disappears, too, if the attention is focused precisely on the comparison from which the comic may emerge. The comic is greatly interfered with if the situation from which it ought to develop gives rise at the same time to a release of strong affect. The generating of comic pleasure can be encouraged by any other pleasurable accompanying circumstance as though by some sort of contagious effect.

1905C   8/221

Jokes and their relation to the unconscious (1905). C. Theoretic part. VII. Jokes and the species of the comic. (5), (6), (7), (8). Comic things are not proper in jokes; relation of humour to jokes.

The comic of sexuality and obscenity are discussed using the starting point of exposure. A chance exposure has a comic effect on us because we compare the ease with which we have enjoyed the sight with the great expenditure which would otherwise be required for reaching this end. Every exposure of which we are made the spectator by a third person is equivalent to the exposed person being made comic. The comic difference is found either by a comparison between another person and oneself, or by a comparison entirely within the other person, or by a comparison entirely within oneself. The first case includes the comic of movement and form, of mental functioning and of character. The second case includes the most numerous possibilities, the comic of situation, of exaggeration, of mimicry, of degradation, and of unmasking. The comic of expectation, the third case is the remotest in children. The release of distressing affects is the greatest obstacle to the emergence of the comic. Humor is the most easily satisfied among the species of comic. It completes its course within a single person. An economy of pity is one of the most frequent sources of humourous pleasure. The pleasure in jokes arises from an economy in expenditure upon inhibition, the pleasure in the comic from an economy in expenditure upon ideation (upon cathexis) and the pleasure in humor from an economy in expenditure upon feeling.

1905C   8/237

Jokes and their relation to the unconscious (1905). Appendix: Franz Brentano's riddles.

In 1879 Franz Brentano published a booklet of some 200 pages with the title *New Riddles*. This book included specimens of various different types of riddles, the last of which was described as fill-up riddles. According to him, this type of riddle was a favorite pastime in the Main region of Germany, but had only recently reached Vienna. The booklet includes 30 examples of the fill-up riddles, among them 2 that are quoted by Freud. These 2 examples are presented along with the following English specimen: Burglars had broken into a large furrier's store. But they were disturbed and went off without taking anything, though leaving the show room in the greatest confusion. When the manager arrived in the morning, he gave instructions to his assistants: "Never mind the cheaper goods. The urgent thing is to get the -----." Answer: 'first rate furs straight.'

VOL. IX   Jensen's 'Gradiva' and Other Works (1906–1908)

1907A   9/3

Delusions and dreams in Jensen's *Gradiva* (1959). Editor's note.

Delusions and Dreams in Jensen's Gradiva is Freud's first published analysis of a work of literature, apart from his comments on *Oedipus Rex* and *Hamlet* in *The Interpretation of Dreams*. It was Jung who brought Jensen's book to Freud's notice, and Freud is reported to have written the present work especially to please Jung. This was in the summer of 1906, several months before the 2 men had met each other, and the episode was thus the herald of their 5 or 6 years of cordial relations. Apart from the deeper significance which Freud saw in Jensen's work, there is no doubt that he must have been specially attracted by the scene in which it was laid. His interest in Pompeii was an old established one. In reading Freud's study, it is worth bearing in mind its chronological place in his writings as one of his earliest psychoanalytic works.

1907A   9/7

Delusions and dreams in Jensen's *Gradiva* (1907). Part I. Synopsis of Jensen's *Gradiva*.

The story of Gradiva is summarized by Freud. A young archaeologist, Norbert Hanold, had discovered in a museum of antiquities in Rome a relief which attracted him. He obtained a plaster cast of it. The sculpture represented a fully grown girl stepping along, with her flowing dress a little pulled up so as to reveal her sandaled feet. The interest taken by the hero of the story in this relief is the basic psychological fact in the narrative. As an outcome of studies, he was forced to the conclusion that Gradiva's gait was not discoverable in reality; and this filled him with regret and vexation. Soon afterwards he had a terrifying dream, in which he found himself in ancient Pompeii on the day of the eruption of Vesuvius and witnessed the city's destruction. Gradiva disappeared and the hero searched for her. She appeared to come to life in someone else's body. Hanold met her, Zeo Bertgang, and they went away together. With the triumph of love, what was beautiful and precious in the delusion found recognition as well. In his last simile, however, of the childhood friend who had been dug out of the ruins, Jensen presented the key to the symbolism of which the hero's delusion made use in disguising his repressed memory.

1907A   9/41

Delusions and dreams in Jensen's *Gradiva* (1907). Part II. *Gradiva* and the psychology of the unconscious.

In *Gradiva* Jensen presented a perfectly correct psychiatric study, upon which we may measure our understanding of the workings of the mind, a case history and the history of a cure which might have been designed to emphasize certain fundamental theories of medical psychology. Norbert Hanold's condition is often spoken of as a delusion, and we have no reason to reject that designation. The state of permanently turning away from women produces a susceptibility or a predisposition to the formation of a delusion. The development of the mental disorder sets in at the moment when a chance impression arouses the childhood experiences which have been forgotten and which have traces, at least, of an erotic coloring. Norbert Hanold's memories of his childhood relations with the girl with the graceful gait were repressed. The first manifestations of the process that had been set going in Hanold by the relief that he saw were phantasies, which played around the figure represented in it. Norbert Hanold's delusion was carried a step further by a dream which occurred in the middle of his efforts to discover a gait like Gradiva's in the streets of the town where he lived. Hanold's dream was an anxiety dream; its content was frightening; the dreamer felt anxiety while he slept and he was left with painful feelings afterwards.

1907A   9/64

Delusions and Dreams in Jensen's *Gradiva* (1907). Part III. Relations between dreams and delusions.

The construction of the fresh delusion about Gradiva's death during the destruction of Pompeii in the year 79 was not the only result of the first dream in Jensen's *Gradiva*. Immediately after it, Hanold decided on his journey to Italy. The journey was undertaken for reasons which its subject did not recognize at first and only admitted to himself later, reasons described as unconscious. The view of Hanold's journey as a flight from his awakening erotic longing for the girl whom he loved and who was so close to him is the only one which will fit in with the description of his emotional states during his stay in Italy. The appearance of Zoe Bertgang marks the climax of tension in the story. This unusually clever girl was determined to win her childhood friend for her husband, after she had recognized that the young man's love for her was the motive force behind the delusion. If a patient believes in his delusion so firmly, it is not because his faculty of judgment has been overturned and does not arise from what is false in the delusion. On the contrary, there is a grain of truth concealed in every delusion, there is something in it that really deserves belief, and this is the source of the patient's conviction, which is to that extent justified. Hanold's second dream concerns the replacement of an elderly gentlemen by Gradiva and the introduction of an enigmatic female colleague.

1907A   9/87

Delusions and dreams in Jensen's *Gradiva* (1907). Part IV. Treatment of the delusions in *Gradiva*. Postscript to the second edition (1912).

Jensen has arbitrarily tacked a love story on to his archaeological phantasy. The beginnings of a change in Hanold were not shown only in his abandoning his delusion. Simultaneously, and before his delusion was cleared up, an unmistakable craving for love awakened in him, which found its outcome in his courting the girl who had freed him from his delusion. The procedure which Zoe adopts for curing her childhood friend's delusion agrees with the therapeutic method, introduced by Breuer and Freud, called cathartic by Breuer and analytic by Freud. The similarity between Gradiva's procedure and the analytic method of psychotherapy includes: the making conscious of what has been repressed, the coinciding of explanation with cure, and the awakening of feelings. The latent dream thoughts in *Gradiva* are day's residues. But in order for a dream to develop out of them, the cooperation of a wish (usually an unconscious one) is required; this contributes the motive force for constructing the dream, while the day's residues provide the material. The first was a wish to have been present as an eyewitness at the catastrophe in the year 79. The other wish was to be there when the girl he loved lay down to sleep. Two other stories by Jensen (*The Red Parasol* and *In the Gothic House*) were discussed in the postscript to the second edition. All 3 stories treat the same theme: the development of a love as an aftereffect of an intimate association in childhood of a brother and sister kind.

1906C   9/99
Psycho-analysis and the establishment of the facts in legal proceedings (1959). Editor's note.

Psychoanalysis and the Establishment of the Facts in Legal Proceedings was originally delivered in June 1906 as a lecture. The lecture is of some historical interest, since it contains Freud's first published mention of the name of Jung. Its whole purpose seemed to be to introduce the Zurich association experiments and the theory of complexes to Vienna students. Association experiments were first systematically made by Wundt, and later introduced into psychiatry by Krapelin and, more especially, Aschaffenburg. The Zurich findings were chiefly of interest for the stress they laid on the importance of one particular factor in influencing the reactions. This factor was described as an emotionally colored ideational complex. This is explained as meaning the totality of ideas relating to a particular emotionally colored event.

1906C   9/103
Psycho-analysis and the establishment of the facts in legal proceedings (1906).

There is a growing recognition of the untrustworthiness of statements made by witnesses, on which many convictions are based in court cases. A new method of investigation, the aim of which is to compel the accused person himself to establish his own guilt or innocence by objective signs, is presented. The method consists of a psychological experiment and is based on psychological research. A word is called out to the subject and he replies as quickly as possible with some other word that occurs to him, his choice of this reaction not being restricted by anything. The points to be observed are the time required for the reaction and the relation between the stimulus word and the reaction word. It has become customary to speak of an ideational content which is able to influence the reaction to the stimulus word, as a complex. This influence works either by the stimulus word touching the complex directly or by the complex succeeding in making a connection with the word through intermediate links. The following reactions to the stimulus word can be observed. The content of the reaction may be unusual. The reaction time may be prolonged. There may be a mistake in reproducing the reaction. The phenomenon of perseveration may occur. It was suggested that the legal profession adopt the experimental method presented by Freud in an effort to establish guilt or innocence by objective signs.

1907B   9/115
Obsessive actions and religious practices (1907).

Obsessive Actions and Religious Practices was written in February 1907. This was Freud's introductory incursion into the psychology of religion. Freud was struck by the resemblance between obsessive actions in sufferers from nervous disorders and the observances by means of which believers give expression to their piety. People who carry out obsessive actions or ceremonials belong to the same class as those who suffer from obsessive thinking, obsessive ideas, obsessive impulses, and the like. Neurotic ceremonials consist in making small adjustments to particular everyday actions, small additions or restrictions or arrangements which have always to be carried out in the same, or in a methodically varied manner. Any activities may become obsessive actions if they are elaborated by small additions or given a rhythmic character. In obsessive actions everything has its meaning and can be interpreted. The same is true of ceremonials in the strict sense. A ceremonial starts as an action for defense or insurance, a protective measure. The sense of guilt of obsessional neurotics finds its counterpart in the protestations of pious people that they know at heart they are miserable sinners; and the pious observances with which such people preface every daily act, seem to have the value of defensive or protective measures. Obsessional neurosis is regarded as a pathological counterpart of the formation of a religion. That neurosis is described as an individual religiosity and religion is described as a universal obsession.

1907C   9/129
The sexual enlightenment of children (1907)

The *Sexual Enlightenment of Children* was written at the request of a Hamburg doctor, Dr. M. Furst, for publication in a periodical devoted to social medicine and hygiene of which he was the editor. It is commonly believed that the sexual instinct is absent in children and only begins to emerge in them at puberty when the sexual organs mature. This is a gross error, equally serious in its effects both on knowledge and on practice. The newborn baby brings sexuality with it into the world, certain sexual sensations accompany its development as a suckling and during early childhood, and only very few children would seem to escape sexual activities and sensations before puberty. A child's intellectual interest in the riddles of sex, his desire for sexual knowledge, shows itself at an unexpectedly early age. The question of the origin of babies also exercises a child's mind. This is usually started by the unwelcome arrival of a small brother or sister. Freud does not think that there is a single good reason for denying children the enlightenment which their thirst for knowledge demands. The child's curiosity will never reach a very high degree of intensity unless it finds appropriate satisfaction at each stage of his learning. Enlightenment about the specific facts of human sexuality and an indication of its social significance should, therefore, be given to the child at the end of his elementary school years and before he enters his intermediate school, *i.e.,* before he is 10 years old.

1908E   9/141
Creative writers and day-dreaming (1908).

Creative Writers and Day Dreaming was originally delivered as a lecture on December 6, 1907. Every child at play behaves like a creative writer in that he creates a world of his own or rearranges the things of his world in a new way which pleases him. The opposite of play is not what is serious but what is real. The creative writer does the same thing as the child at play: he creates a world of phantasy which he takes very seriously. As people grow up, they cease to play, and they seem to give up the yield of pleasure which they gained from playing. The growing child, when he stops playing, gives up nothing but the link with real objects; instead of playing, he now phantasizes. People's phantasies are less easy to observe than the play of children. The adult is ashamed of his phantasies and hides them from other people. A child's play is determined by wishes: by a single wish, one that helps in his upbringing, the wish to be big and grow up. The motive forces of phantasies are unsatisfied wishes, and every phantasy is the fulfillment of a wish, a correction of unsatisfying reality. A strong experience in the present awakens in the creative writer a memory of an earlier experience from which there proceeds a wish which finds its fulfillment in the creative work. The work itself exhibits elements of the recent provoking occasion as well as of the old memory.

1908A   9/157
Hysterical phantasies and their relation to bisexuality (1908).

Hysterical Phantasies and Their Relation to Bisexuality consists of a discussion of the relation between phantasies and symptoms. A common source and normal prototype of all the creations of phantasy is found in the day dreams of youth. They occur with equal frequency in both sexes. In girls and women, they are of an erotic nature; in men they may be either erotic or ambitious. A closer investigation of a man's day dreams shows that all his heroic exploits are carried out and all his successes achieved in order to please a woman and to be preferred by her to other men. These phantasies are satisfactions of wishes proceeding from deprivation and longing. The day dreams are cathected with a large amount of interest. Unconscious phantasies have either been unconscious all along and have been formed in the uncon-

scious, or they were once conscious phantasies, day dreams, and have since been purposely forgotten and have become unconscious through repression. Unconscious phantasies are the immediate psychical precursors of a number of hysterical symptoms. The following characteristics of hysterical symptoms are presented: mnemic symbols, substitutes, an expression of the fulfillment of a wish, the realization of an unconscious phantasy. They serve the purpose of sexual satisfaction; correspond to a return of a mode of sexual satisfaction, arise as a compromise between 2 opposite affective and instinctual impulses, are never without a sexual significance, and are the expression of a masculine unconscious sexual phantasy and also a feminine one. The bisexual nature of hysterical symptoms is a confirmation of the view that the postulated existence of an innate bisexual disposition in man is clearly visible in the analysis of psychoneurotics.

1908B   9/167
Character and anal erotism (1908).

The relationship between character and anal eroticism is discussed. The people that Freud describes are noteworthy for a regular combination of the 3 following characteristics. They are especially orderly, parsimonious, and obstinate. These people took a comparatively long time to overcome their infantile fecal incontinence, and even in later childhood they suffered from isolated failures of this function. Anal erotism is one of the components of the sexual instinct which, in the course of development and in accordance with the education demanded by our present civilization, has become unserviceable for sexual aims. It is therefore plausible to suppose that these character traits of orderliness, parsimony, and obstinacy, which are so often prominent in people who were formerly anal erotics, are to be regarded as the first and most constant results of the sublimation of anal erotism. Freud theorizes that the permanent character traits are either unchanged prolongations of the original instincts, or sublimations of those instincts, or reaction formations against them.

1908D   9/177
'Civilized' sexual morality and modern nervous illness (1908).

Civilized Sexual Morality and Modern Nervous Illness was the earliest of Freud's full length discussions of the antagonism between civilization and instinctual life. It is not difficult to suppose that under the domination of a civilized sexual morality the health and efficiency of single individuals may be liable to impairment and that ultimately this injury, caused by the sacrifices imposed on them, may reach such a pitch that, by this indirect path, the cultural aim in view will be endangered as well.

The injurious influence of civilization reduces itself to the harmful suppression of the sexual life of civilized peoples through the 'civilized' sexual morality prevalent in them. Careful clinical observation allows us to distinguish 2 groups of nervous disorders: the neuroses and the psychoneuroses. In the former, the disturbances, whether they show their effects in somatic or mental functioning, appear to be of a toxic nature. The sexual factor is essential in the causation of the neurosis. With the psychoneuroses, the influence of heredity is more marked and the causation less transparent. Here the psychogenic symptoms of the psychoneuroses show a sexual content in their unconscious complexes. Generally speaking, our civilization is built upon the suppression of instincts. In man, the sexual instinct does not originally serve the purposes of reproduction at all, but has as its aim the gaining of particular kinds of pleasure. Bearing in mind the evolution of the sexual instinct, 3 stages of civilization can be distinguished: 1) one in which the sexual instinct may be freely exercised without regard to the aims of reproduction; 2) one in which all of the sexual instinct is suppressed except what serves the aims of reproduction; (this includes discussion of perversions which do not serve this aim) and 3) one in which only legitimate reproduction (within marriage) is allowed as a sexual aim. This third stage is reflected in our present civilized sexual morality. The sexual behavior of a human often lays down the pattern for all his other modes of reaction to life. The question is raised whether our civilized sexual morality is worth the sacrifice (neuroses) it imposes upon us.

1908C 9/205
On the sexual theories of children.

On the Sexual Theories of Children presents the notions of fertilization through the mouth, of birth through the anus, of parental intercourse as something sadistic, and of the possession of a penis by members of both sexes. The material is derived from several sources: the direct observation of what children say and do; what adult neurotics consciously remember from their childhood and relate during psychoanalytic treatment; and the inferences and constructions and the unconscious memories translated into conscious material, which result from the psychoanalysis of neurotics. The false sexual theories all contain a fragment of truth. Childhood opinions about the nature or marriage, which are not seldom retained by conscious memory, have great significance for the symptomatology of later neurotic illness.

1909A 9/227
Some general remarks on hysterical attacks (1909).

When one carries out the psychoanalysis of a hysterical woman whose complaint is manifested in attacks, one soon becomes convinced that these attacks are nothing else but phantasies translated into the motor sphere, projected on to motility and protrayed in pantomime. A hysterical attack needs to be subjected to the same interpretive revision as that employed for night dreams. The attack becomes unintelligible since it represents several phantasies in the same material simultaneously. The attack becomes obscured because the patient attempts to carry out the activities of both the figures who appear in the phantasy through multiple identification. The onset of hysterical attacks follows certain laws. Since the repressed complex consists of a libidinal cathexis and an ideational content, the attack can be evoked associatively, organically, in the service of the primary purpose, or in the service of the secondary purposes. Investigation of the childhood history of hysterical patients shows that the hysterical attack is designed to take the place of an autoerotic satisfaction previously practiced and since given up. What points the way for the motor discharge of the repressed libido in a hysterical attack is the reflex mechanism of the act of coition, a mechanism which is ready to hand in everybody, including women, and which we see coming into manifest operation when an unrestrained surrender is made to sexual activity.

1909C 9/235
Family romance (1909).

The psychology of the neuroses teaches us that, among other factors, the most intense impulses of sexual rivalry contribute to the feeling of being slighted. As a child grows up and tries to break away from the authority of his parents he regards this authority as hostility and responds by feeling that his own affection is not reciprocated fully. A boy has more hostile impulses towards his father than his mother. The next of later stages in the development of the neurotic's estrangement from his parents is described as 'the neurotic's family romance.' When the child comes to know the difference in the parts played by fathers and mothers in their sexual relations, the family romance undergoes a curious curtailment: it contents itself with exalting the child's father, but no longer casts any doubt on his maternal origin. This second (sexual) stage of the family romance is actuated by another motive as well, which is absent in the first (asexual) stage. The child, having learned about sexual processes, tends to picture to himself erotic situations and relations, the motive force behind this being his desire to bring his mother into situations of secret infidelity and into secret love affairs. In this way the child's phantasies, which started by being asexual, are brought up to the level of his later knowledge. The overvaluation that characterizes a child's earliest years is evident in these phantasies.

1907D   9/245
Contribution to a questionnaire on reading (1907).

Freud is asked to name 10 good books. The books that he names are: Multatuli, *Letters and Works;* Kipling, *Jungle Book*; Anatole France, *Sur la pierre blanche*; Zola, *Fecondite*; Merezhkovsky, *Leonardo da Vinci*; G. Keller, *Leute von Seldwyla*; C. F. Meyer, *Huttens letzte Tage*; Macaulay, *Essays*; Gomperz, *Griechische Denker*; and Mark Twain, *Sketches*.

1907E   9/248
Prospectus for *Schriften zur angewandten Seelenkunde* (1907).

The *Schriften zur angewandten Seelenkunde* (Papers on Applied Mental Science) are aimed at that wider circle of educated people who, without actually being philosophers or medical men, are nevertheless able to appreciate the science of the human mind for its significance in the understanding and deepening of our lives. Each paper deals with a single subject. Collectively they will attempt to apply psychological knowledge to subjects in art and literature, in the history of civilizations and religions, and in analogous fields. The series is open to the exponents of divergent opinions and hopes to be able to give expression to the variety of points of view and principles in contemporary science.

1908F   9/250
Preface to Wilhelm Stekel's 'Nervous anxiety-states and their treatment' (1908).

Freud's investigations into the etiology and psychical mechanism of neurotic illnesses, which he pursued since 1893, attracted little notice in the beginning among his fellow specialists. At length, however, those investigations have met with recognition from a number of medical research workers and have also drawn attention to the psychoanalytic methods of examination and treatment. Dr. Wilhelm Stekel, who was one of the first of the colleagues to whom Freud was able to impart a knowledge of psychoanalysis, and who has himself become familiar with its technique through many years of paractice, has now undertaken the task of working over one topic in the clinical aspects of these neuroses on the basis of Freud's views and of presenting medical readers with the experiences he has obtained through the psychoanalytic method. Dr. Stekel's work is founded upon rich experience and is calculated to stimulate other physicians into confirming by their own efforts the views on the etiology of these conditions.

1910B   9/252
Preface to Sandor Ferenczi's 'Psycho-analysis: essays in the field of psycho-analysis' (1910).

Psychoanalytic research into the neuroses (the various forms of nervous illness with a mental causation) has

endeavored to trace their connection with instinctual life and the restriction imposed on it by the claims of civilization, with the activities of the normal individual in phantasies and dreams, with the creations of the popular mind in religion, myths, and fairy tales. Sandor Ferenczi is familiar with all the difficulties of psychoanalytic problems and is the first Hungarian to undertake the task of creating an interest in psychoanalysis among doctors and men of education in his own country through writings composed in their mother tongue.

1903A   9/253
1904B
1904E
Contributions to the 'Neue Freie Presse' (1903-1904).

Three contributions to the *Neue Freie Presse* are presented. In the review of George Biedenkapp's *Im Kampfe Gegen Hirnbacillen*, Freud states that concealed behind this somewhat unpromising title is the book of a brave man who succeeds in presenting much that is worthly of consideration. Biedenkapp is fighting against those, "little words and arrangements of words which exclude or include too much," and which reveal, in people who have the habit of using them for preference, a tendency towards, "exclusive or superlative judgments." The exhortation to moderation in judgment and expression serves the author only as a point of departure for further discussions on other errors of thought of human beings, on the central delusion, faith, on atheistic morality, etc. In a review of John Bigelow's *The Mystery of Sleep*, Freud states that solving the mystery of sleep might well have been reserved to science; the author, however, operates with biblical arguments and teleological causes. Bigelow states that the important processes of unconscious mental and even intellectual activity continue even during profound sleep. The obituary of Professor S. Hammerschlag (a Jewish religious teacher) reveals him as one of those personalities who possess the gift of leaving ineradicable impressions on the development of their pupils.

VOL. X   The Cases of 'Little Hans' and the 'Rat Man' (1909)

1909B   10/3
Analysis of a phobia in a five-year-old boy. Editor's note (1955). Part I. Introduction (1909).

The Analysis of a Phobia in a 5-Year-Old Boy describes the course of the illness and recovery of a very youthful patient. The first reports of Hans date from a period when he was not quite 3 years old. At that time he was showing a quite peculiar lively interest in that portion of his body which he used to describe as his 'widdler.' Around the age of 3½ he realized an essential characteristic for differentiating between animate and inaminate objects: the presence or absence of a widdler. His thirst for knowledge seemed to be inseparable from sexual curiosity and his curiosity was particularly directed towards his parents through his interest in the presence of his mother's and father's widdlers. At 3½, Hans' mother threatened him with castration because he was masturbating. The great event of Hans' life was the birth of his little sister Hanna when he was exactly 3½, He noticed and remarked on the smallness of her widdler. At 3¾ he showed his first, but not his last trace of homosexuality. When he was 4¼, he made it clear that having his knickers unbuttoned and his penis taken out was pleasurable. When Hans was 4½, he finally acknowledged the distinction between male and female genitals.

1909B   10/22

Analysis of a phobia in a five-year-old boy (1909). Part II. Case history and analysis of little Hans.

The case history and analysis of Little Hans is presented. Hans, almost 5 years old, woke up one morning in tears. Asked why he was crying, he said to his mother that he thought she was gone. This is interpreted as an anxiety dream. The fundamental phenomenon in his condition was that his affection for his mother became enormously intensified. Hans relates a phantasy concerning a big giraffe and a crumpled giraffe. This is interpreted as the big giraffe (long neck) being his father's penis and the crumpled one as his mother's genital organ. Hans comes to his mother's bed in the morning and is caressed by her, thus defying his father. Hans was afraid of big animals (especially horses) because big animals have big widdlers. His anxiety, which corresponded to a repressed erotic longing was, like every infantile anxiety, without an object to begin with. After an attack of influenza, his phobia of horses increased so much that he could not be induced to go out. The immediate precipitating cause of his phobia was the fall of a big heavy horse; one of the interpretations of this impression seems to be that emphasized by his father, namely, that Hans at that moment perceived a wish that his father might fall down in the same way and be dead. Hans wished that his father would die and then he, Hans, would take his father's place with his mother. The theme of Han's sister Hanna is discussed in relation to his viewing her as being in a box (womb).

Analysis of a phobia in a five-year-old boy (1909). Part III. Discussion: I.

The observation of the development and resolution of a phobia in a boy under 5 years of age is examined. It is possible that Hans was not normal, but a neurotic degenerate; however, Freud discounts this. Little Hans was described by his parents as a cheerful, straightforward child. The first trait in Hans which can be regarded as part of his sexual life was a peculiar interest in his 'widdler,' This interest aroused in him the spirit of inquiry, and he thus discovered that the presence or absence of a widdler made it possible to differentiate between animate and inanimate objects. He assumed that all animate objects were like himself and possessed this important bodily organ; he observed that it was present in the larger animals, suspected that this was so too in both his parents, and was not deterred by the evidence of his own eyes from authenticating the fact in his newborn sister. In little Hans' sexual constitution, the genital zone was from the outset the one among his erotogenic zones which afforded him the most intense pleasure. The most important influence upon the course of Hans' psychosexual development was the birth of a baby sister when he was 3½ years old. That event accentuated his relations to his parents and gave him some insoluble problems to think about. In his triumphant final phantasy, he summed up all his erotic wishes, both those derived from his autoerotic phase and those connected with his object love. Hans really was a little Oedipus who wanted to have his father out of the way so that he could sleep with his mother. In that phantasy he was married to his beautiful mother and had innumerable children whom he could look after in his own way.

Analysis of a phobia in a five-year-old-boy (1909). Part III. Discussion: 11. Little Hans case sheds light on phobias.

The observation of the development and resolution of a phobia in a boy under 5 years of age is examined. One day while Hans was in the street he was seized with an attack of anxiety. Hans's phobia soon ceased having any relation to the question of locomotion and became more and more clearly concentrated upon horses. In the early days of his illness, when the anxiety was at its highest pitch, he expressed a fear that a horse would come into his room. The outbreak of the anxiety state was not as sudden as it appeared. A few days earlier the child had awakened from an anxiety dream to the effect that his mother had gone away. His parents represented to him that his anxiety was the result of masturbation, and encouraged him to break himself of the habit. Hans was not only afraid of horses biting him but also of carts, of furniture vans, and of buses, of horses that started moving, of horses that looked big and heavy, and of horses that drove quickly. The meaning of these specifications was explained by Hans himself: he was afraid of horses falling down, and consequently incorporated in his phobia everything that seemed likely to facilitate their falling down. The falling horse represented not only his dying father but also his mother in childbirth. The birth of his sister aroused in Hans the question of birth and the idea that his father had something to do with it. The anxiety in this phobia is explained as being due to the repression of Hans's aggressive propensities.

1909B 10/141

Analysis of a phobia in a five-year-old boy (1909). Part III. Discussion: III. Little Hans case and childhood education. Postscript (1922).

The observation of the development and resolution of a phobia in a boy under 5 years of age is examined. Hans was not a degenerate child. On the contrary, he was well formed physically, and was a cheerful, amiable, active-minded young fellow who might give pleasure to more people than his own father. He was not the only child who has been overtaken by phobia at some time or other in his childhood. The only results of the analysis were that Hans recovered, that he ceased to be afraid of horses, and that he got on to rather familiar terms with his father. Analysis replaced the process of repression, which was an automatic and excessive one, by a temperate and purposeful control on the part of the highest agencies of the mind. Freud claims that he would have ventured to give the child one remaining piece of enlightenment which his parents withheld from him. He would have confirmed his instinctive premonitions, by telling him of the existence of the vagina and of copulation, thus diminishing further his unsolved residue, and putting an end to his stream of questions. Freud was tempted to claim for this neurosis of childhood the significance of being a type and a model, and to suppose that the multiplicity of the phenomena of repression exhibited by neuroses and the abundance of their pathogenic material do not prevent their being derived from a very limited number of processes concerned with identical ideational complexes.

1909D 10/153

Notes upon a case of obsessional neurosis. Editor's note (1955) and Introduction (1909).

Notes upon a Case of Obsessional Neurosis concerns a case, the treatment of which began on October 1, 1907. This case judged by its length, the injuriousness of its effects, and the patient's own view of it, deserves to be classed as a moderately severe one. The treatment, which

lasted for about a year, led to the complete restoration of the patient's personality, and to the removal of his inhibitions. Persons suffering from a severe degree of obsessional neurosis present themselves far less frequently for analytic treatment than hysterical patients. Obsessional neurosis is not an easy thing to understand. Because we are less familiar with obsessional neurosis, we are less able to have expectations about it.

1909D 10/158

Notes upon a case of obsessional neurosis (1909). Part I. Extracts from the case history: (A) The beginning of the treatment. (B) Infantile sexuality.

Extracts from a case history of obsessional neurosis are presented. A youngish man of university education introduced himself with the statement that he had suffered from obsessions ever since his childhood, but with particular intensity for the last 4 years. The chief features of his disorder were fears that something might happen to 2 people of whom he was very fond, his father and a lady whom he admired. Besides this he was aware of compulsive impulses, such as an impulse to cut his throat with a razor; and further he produced prohibitions, sometimes in connection with quite unimportant things. The beginning of the treatment involved a pledge on the part of the patient to say everything that came into his head, even if it was unpleasant to him, or seemed unimportant or irrelevant, or senseless. As a result of his statements, Freud discovered that the patient was under the domination of a component of the sexual instinct, the desire to look (scopophilia), as a result of which there was a constant recurrence in him of a very intense wish connected with persons of the female sex who pleased him, the wish to see them naked. This wish corresponded to the later obsessional or compulsive idea. Side by side with the obsessive wish, and intimately associated with it, was an obsessive fear: every time he had a wish of this kind he could not help fearing that something dreadful would happen. Obsessional neuroses make it much more obvious than hysterias that the factors which go to form a psychoneurosis are to be found in the patient's infantile sexual life and not in his present one.

1909D 10/165

Notes upon a case of obsessional neurosis (1909). Part I. Extracts from the case history. (C) The great obsessive fear.

Extracts from a case history of obsessional neurosis are presented. The patient revealed his great obsessive fear that some rats would bore their way into the anus of a lady whom he admired and also into the anus of his father. As his father had died many years previously, this obsessive fear was much more nonsensical even than the first, and accordingly the fear concerning his father was not confessed to for a little while longer. He had ordered a replacement pince nez which was sent to him through the mails. He felt that unless he paid the charge back directly to a particular person, (Lieutenant A) the rat would actually act upon the lady. He vowed to pay the money directly to that particular person. He stated this vow in such a way that the actual payment was made very difficult. In reality, he owed the money to no one but the official at the post office. The captain who had told him he owed Lieutenant A the money made a mistake which the patient must have known was a mistake. In spite of this the patient made his vow of payment founded upon the mistake. In so doing he suppressed the episode of the other Captain (B) and the trusting young lady at the post office. He was determined to see a doctor and thought that a doctor would give him a certificate to the effect that it was necessary for him, in order to recover his health, to perform his particular obsessional actions.

1909D   10/173

Notes upon a case of obsessional neurosis (1909). Part I. Extracts from the case history. (D) Initiation into the nature of the treatment.

Extracts from a case history of obsessional neurosis are presented. Nine years previously the patient's father had died one evening, when the patient was not there, and the son had felt guilty ever since. Freud helped him to conclude that he actually wished for the death of his father. The patient confessed that from the age of 7, he had had a fear that his parents guessed his thoughts, and this fear had persisted all his life. When he was 12 he felt that if his father died his death might make him rich enough to marry a girl he loved. During the seventh session, he said that he could not believe that he had ever entertained such a wish against his father. He went on to state that his illness had become so enormously intensified since his father's death; and Freud said that he agreed with him in so far as he regarded his sorrow at his father's death as the chief source of the intensity of his illness. His sorrow had found a pathological expression in his illness. Whereas a normal period of mourning would last from 1 to 2 years, a pathological one like this would last indefinitely.

1909D   10/186

Notes upon a case of obsessional neurosis (1909). Part I. Extracts from the case history. (E) Some obsessional ideas and their explanation.

Extracts from a case history of obsessional neurosis are presented. Obsessional ideas have an appearance of being either without motive or without meaning, just as dreams have. The wildest and most eccentric obsessional ideas can be cleared up if they are investigated deeply enough. The solution is effected by bringing the obses-

sional ideas into temporal relationship with the patient's experiences, that is to say, by enquiring when a particular obsessional idea made its first appearance and in what external circumstances it is apt to recur. One of the suicidal impulses which appeared frequently in the patient was explained. It was related to the absence of his lady because she was taking care of her mother. He wanted to kill her mother for depriving him of his lady, and suicide was the way to punish himself for these thoughts. His obsession for protecting can only have been a reaction, as an expression of remorse and penitence, to a contrary, that is a hostile, impulse which he must have felt towards his lady. His obsession for counting during the thunderstorm can be interpreted as having been a defensive measure against fears that someone was in danger of death.

1909D   10/195

Notes upon a case of obsessional neurosis (1909). Part I. Extracts from the case history. (F) The precipitating cause of the illness.

Extracts from a case history of obsessional neurosis are presented and the precipitating cause of the illness discussed. The infantile precondition of obsessional neurosis may be overtaken by amnesia, though this is often an incomplete one; but the immediate occasions of the illness are, on the contrary, retained in the memory. Repression makes use of another, and in reality a simpler, mechanism. The trauma, instead of being forgotten, is deprived of its affective cathexis so that what remains in consciousness is nothing but its ideational content, which is perfectly colorless and is judged to be unimportant. The distinction between what occurs in hysteria and in an obsessional neurosis lies in the psychological processes which we can reconstruct behind the phenomenon. The chief result of his illness was an obstinate incapacity for work, which allowed him to postpone the completion of his education for years. A conflict was stirred in him as to whether he should remain faithful to the lady he loved in spite of her poverty, or whether he should follow in his father's footsteps and marry the lovely, rich, and well-connected girl who had been assigned to him. By falling ill he avoided the task of resolving the conflict in real life.

1909D   10/200

Notes upon a case of obsessional neurosis (1909). Part I. Extracts from the case history. (G) The father complex and the solution of the rat idea.

Extracts from a case history of obsessional neurosis about rats are presented. The patient found himself in a situation similar to that in which, as he knew or suspected, his father had been before his marriage; and the patient was thus able to identify himself with his father. The conflict at the root of his illness was a struggle between the persisting influence of his father's wishes and his own amatory predilections. Freud put forward a construction that, when the patient was a child of under 6 he had been guilty of some sexual misdemeanor connected with masturbation and had been soundly castigated for it by his father. This punishment put an end to his masturbating, but left behind it a grudge against his father and had established him in his role of an interferer with the patient's sexual enjoyment. The patient's mother said that he was punished because he had bitten someone. The story of the rat punishment (a rat boring its way into the anus of his lady and his father), provoked all his suppressed cruel, egoistic and sexual impulses. The rat punishment evoked anal eroticism, which played an important part in his childhood and had been kept in activity for many years by a constant irritation due to worms. In this way rats came to have the meaning of money (Rattus is the genus for rat and Rate is German for installment). The relation of some sexual theories of children to this obsession is presented.

1909D   10/221

Notes upon a case of obsessional neurosis (1909). Part II. Theoretical section. (A) Some general characteristics of obsessional structures.

Some general characteristics of obsessional structures are discussed. Obsessional structures can be classed as wishes, temptations, impulses, reflections, doubts, commands, or prohibitions. During the secondary defensive struggle, which the patient carries on against the obsessional ideas that have forced their way into his consciousness, psychical structures make their appearance which deserve to be given a special name. They are not purely reasonable considerations arising in opposition to the obsessional thoughts, but, as it were, hybrids between the 2 species of thinking. They accept certain of the premises of the obsession they are combating, and thus, while using the weapons of reason, are established upon a basis of pathological thought. The patients themselves do not know the wording of their own obsessional ideas. Obsessional thoughts have undergone a distortion similar to that undergone by dream thoughts before they become the manifest content of a dream. The technique of distortion by ellipsis seems to be typical of obsessional neuroses.

1909D   10/229

Notes upon a case of obsessional neurosis (1909). Part II. Theoretical section. (B) Some psychological peculiarities of obsessional neurotics: Their attitude towards reality, superstition and death.

Some psychological peculiarities of obsessional neurotics are discussed, especially their attitude towards reality, superstition, and death. The patient was highly superstitious, although he was a well educated and enlightened man of considerable acumen, and although he was able at times to assure Freud that he did not believe a word of all this rubbish. His superstition was that of an educated man, and he avoided such prejudices as being afraid of Friday or of the number 13, and so on. But he believed in premonitions and in prophetic dreams. He would constantly meet the very person of whom, for some inexplicable reason, he had just been thinking. Another mental need which is shared by obsessional neurotics is the need for uncertainty, or for doubt in their life. The creation of uncertainty which is among the objects of every psychoneurotic disorder, is one of the methods employed by the neurosis for drawing the patient away from reality and isolating him from the world. In obsessional neuroses, the uncertainty of memory is used to the fullest extent as a help in the formation of symptoms. The patient had a quite peculiar attitude towards the question of death. He showed the deepest sympathy whenever anyone died. In his imagination he was constantly making away with people so as to show his heartfelt sympathy for their bereaved relatives. In every conflict which enters their lives they are on the lookout for the death of someone who is of importance to them.

1909D   10/237

Notes upon a case of obsessional neurosis (1909). Part II. Theoretical section. (C) The instinctual life of obsessional neurotics, and the origins of compulsion and doubt.

The instinctual life of obsessional neurotics and the origins of compulsion and doubt are discussed. The patient fell ill when he was in his twenties, on being faced with a temptation to marry another woman instead of the one whom he had loved so long, and he avoided a decision of this conflict by postponing all the necessary preliminary actions. The means for doing this was given him by his neurosis. If we consider a number of analyses of obsessional neurotics, we shall find it impossible to escape the impression that a relation between love and hatred such as we have found in our present patient is among the most frequent, the most marked, and probably, therefore, the most important characteristic of obsessional neurosis. It is doubt that leads the patient to uncertainty about his protective measures and to his continual repetition of them in order to banish that uncertainty. It is this doubt, too, that eventually brings it about that the patient's protective acts themselves become as impossible to carry out as his original inhibited decision in connection with his love. The compulsion is an attempt at a compensation for the doubt and at a correction of the intolerable conditions of inhibition to which the doubt bears witness. By a sort of regression, preparatory acts become substituted for the final decision, thinking replaces acting, and, instead of the substitutive act, some thought preliminary to it asserts itself with all the force of compulsion. An obsessive or compulsive thought is one whose function it is to represent an act regressively.

1955A   10/251

Notes upon a case of obsessional neurosis (1909). Part II. Theoretical section. Addendum: Original record of the case: Editor's note (1955).

It was Freud's practice throughout his life, after one of his works had appeared in print, to destroy all the material on which the publication was based. It is accordingly true that extremely few of the original manuscripts of his works have survived, still less the preliminary notes and records from which they were derived. The present record, *A Case of Obsessional Neurosis*, provides an unexplained exception to this rule, having been found among Freud's papers in London after his death. Approximately the first third of the original record was reproduced by Freud almost verbatim in the published version. This covers the preliminary interview on October 1, 1907, and the first 7 sessions. The second two-thirds of Freud's record are translated in full. It contains some material taken up by Freud into the published case history, but a large proportion is new material.

1955A   10/259

Notes upon a case of obsessional neurosis (1909). Part II. Theoretical section. Original record of the case.

The original record of the case of the 'Rat Man' is produced. On October 10, the patient announced that he wanted to talk about the beginning of his obsessional ideas. An account of the visits proceeds through January 20, when the manuscript ends. The patient's resistances are discussed and his many dreams are interpreted to and for him. His masturbation and his lack of masturbation are discussed and the role that his father had in this situation is discussed. The connection between rats, worms, and penis is explained. The patient had had a great deal of annoyance over money matters with his friends and did not like it if analysis was diverted toward money matters. Rats have a special connection with money.

VOL. XI   Five Lectures on Psycho-Analysis, Leonardo and Other Works (1910)

1910A   11/3

Five lectures on psycho-analysis. Editor's note (1957).

In 1909, Clark University, Worcester, Massachusetts, celebrated the twentieth year of its foundation and its President, Dr. G. Stanley Hall, invited Freud and some of his principal followers to take part in the occasion and to be awarded honorary degrees. Freud's 5 lectures were delivered on Monday, September 6, 1909, and the 4 following days. The lectures were, according to Freud's almost universal practice, delivered extempore without notes, and after very little preparation. It was only after his return to Vienna that he was induced unwillingly to write them out. All through his career Freud was constantly ready to give exposition of his discoveries. In spite of all the additions that were to be made to the structure of psychoanalysis during the following quarter of a century, these lectures provide an admirable preliminary picture which calls for very little correction. They give an excellent idea of the ease and clarity of style and the unconstrained sense of form which made Freud such a remarkable expository lecturer.

1910A   11/9

Five lectures on psycho-analysis (1910). First lecture. Symptoms have psychological meaning.

Dr. Josef Breuer first used the procedure of psychoanalysis on a 21-year-old girl who was suffering from hysteria. Her illness lasted for over 2 years, and in the course of it she developed a series of physical and psychological disturbances which deserved to be taken seriously. She suffered from a rigid paralysis, accompanied by loss of sensation of both extremities on the right side of her body; and the same trouble from time to time affected her on the left side. It was observed that, while the patient was in her states of absence (altered personality accompanied by confusion), she was in the habit of muttering words to herself. Breuer put her into a type of hypnosis and repeated the muttered words to her so as to induce her to use them as a starting point. Her mental creations during the absences were melancholy phantasies. It was possible to bring about the disappearance of the painful symptoms of her illness, if she could remember, with an accompanying expression of affect, on what occasion and in what connection the symptoms had first appeared. Hysterical patients suffer from reminiscences and their symptoms are residues and mnemic symbols of particular (traumatic) experiences. Breuer's patient, in almost all her pathogenic situations, was obliged to suppress a powerful emotion instead of allowing its discharge in the appropriate signs of emotion, words or actions. She exhibited a number of mental peculiarities: Conditions of absence, confusion, and alterations of character.

1910A 11/21

Five lectures on psycho-analysis (1910). Second lecture. Repression and symptom formation.

At about the same time at which Breuer was carrying on the 'talking cure' with his patient, Charcot in Paris had begun the researches into hysterical patients at the Salpetriere. Pierre Janet first attempted a deeper approach to the peculiar psychical processes present in hysteria. According to him, hysteria is a form of degenerate modification of the nervous system, which shows itself in an innate weakness in the power of psychical synthesis. Without using hypnosis, Freud succeeded in obtaining from the patients whatever was required for establishing the connection between the pathogenic scenes they had forgotten and the symptoms left over from those scenes. The memories were in the patient's possession and were ready to emerge in association to what was still known by him; but there was some force that prevented them from becoming conscious and compelled them to remain unconscious. The force which was maintaining the pathological condition became apparent in the form of resistance on the part of the patient. It was on this idea of resistance that Freud based his view of the course of psychical events in hysteria. The investigation of hysterical patients and of other neurotics leads to the conclusion that their repression of the idea to which the intolerable wish is attached has been a failure. It is true that they have driven it out of consciousness and out of memory and have apparently saved themselves a large amount of unpleasure. But the repressed wishful impulse continues to exist in the unconscious.

1910A 11/29

Five lectures on psycho-analysis (1910). Third lecture. Psychic determinism, dreams, and parapraxes.

Freud cherished a high opinion of the strictness with which mental processes are determined, and found it impossible to believe that an idea produced by a partient while his attention was focused could be an arbitrary one and unrelated to the idea being sought. The fact that the 2 ideas were not identical could be satisfactorily explained from the postulated psychological state of affairs. In the patient under treatment, 2 forces were in operation against each other: on the one hand, his conscious endeavor to bring into consciousness the forgotten idea in his unconscious; and, on the other hand, the resistance which was striving to prevent what was repressed or its derivatives from becoming conscious. It is highly convenient to follow the Zurich school (Bleuler, Jung, etc.) in describing a group of interdependent ideational elements cathected with affect as a complex. If, in the search for a repressed complex in one of the patients, we start from the last thing he remembers, we have every prospect of discovering the complex, provided that the patient puts a sufficient number of his free associations at our disposal. Working over the ideas that occur to patients when they submit to the main rule of psychoanalysis is not the only technical method of discovering the unconscious. The same purpose is served by 2 other procedures: the interpretation of patients' dreams and the exploitation of their faulty and haphazard actions. Psychoanalysis is seeking to bring to conscious recognition the things in mental life which are repressed.

1910A 11/40

Five lectures on psycho-analysis (1910). Fourth lecture. Infantile sexuality and neurosis.

Psychoanalytic research, which consistently traces back the symptoms of patients' illnesses to impressions from their erotic life, shows that the pathogenic wishful impulses are in the nature of erotic instinctual components. It forces us to suppose that among the influences leading to the illness, the predominant significance must be assigned to erotic disturbances; this is the case in both sexes. It is the experiences in childhood that explain susceptibility to later traumas and it is only by uncovering these forgotten memory traces and by making them conscious that we acquire the power to get rid of the symptoms. These powerful wishful impulses of childhood are described as sexual. The chief source of infantile sexual pleasure is the appropriate excitation of certain parts of the body that are especially susceptible to stimulus: apart from the genitals, these are the oral, anal and urethral orifices, as well as the skin and other sensory surfaces. Satisfaction, termed autoeroticism, is obtained from the subject's own body. Thumsucking (or sensual sucking) is a good example of autoerotic satisfaction from an erotogenic zone. Direct inhibitions in the development of the sexual function comprise the perversions and general infantilism in sexual life. An instinct which remains independent leads to a perversion, and may substitute its own sexual aim for the normal one. The predisposition to neurosis is also traceable to impaired sexual development.

1910A 11/49

Five lectures on psycho-analysis (1910). Fifth lecture. Transference and resistance.

Human beings fall ill when, as a result of external obstacles or of an internal lack of adaptation, the satisfaction of their erotic needs in reality is frustrated. They take flight into illness in order that they may find a satisfaction to take the place of what has been frustrated. The pathological symptoms constitute a portion of the subject's sexual activity or even the whole of his sexual life; the withdrawal from reality is the main purpose of the illness but also the main damage caused by it. Resistance to recovery is compounded of several motives. The flight from unsatisfactory reality into illness takes place along the path of involution, of regression, of a return to earlier phases of sexual life. In every psychoanalytic treatment of a neurotic patient the strange phenomenon that is known as transference makes its appearance. The patient directs towards the physician a degree of affectionate feeling which is based on no real relation between them and which can only be traced back to old wishful phantasies of the patient's which have become unconscious. What becomes of the unconscious wishes which have been set free by psychoanalysis can take several paths. First, the wishes can be destroyed by the rational mental activity of the better impulses that are opposed to them. A second outcome is that it then becomes possible for the unconscious instincts revealed by it to be employed for the useful purposes which they would have found earlier if the development had not been interrupted. A third possible outcome is the individual's own happiness.

1910C 11/59
Leonardo da Vinci and a memory of his childhood. Editor's note (1957).

Freud's interest in Leonardo da Vinci is of long standing. The immediate stimulus to writing *Leonardo da Vinci and a Memory of his Childhood* appears to have come in the autumn of 1909 from one of his patients who, as he remarked in a letter to Jung, seemed to have the same constitution as Leonardo without his genius. This work of Freud's was not the first application of the methods of clinical psychoanalysis to the lives of historical figures in the past. The main body of Freud's study consists of the detailed construction of Leonardo's emotional life from his earliest years, the account of the conflict between his artistic and his scientific impulses, the deep analysis of his psychosexual history. In addition to this main topic, the study presents us with a number of not less important side themes: a more general discussion of the nature and workings of the mind of the creative artist, an outline of the genesis of one particular type of homosexuality, and the first full emergence of the concept of narcissism.

1910C 11/63
Leonardo da Vinci and a memory of his childhood (1910). Part I. Biographical material.

Leonardo da Vinci (1452 to 1519) was admired even by his contemporaries as one of the greatest men of the Italian renaissance. It is possible that the idea of a radiantly happy and pleasure-loving Leonardo is only

applicable to the first and longer period of the artist's life. Afterwards, when he was forced to leave Milan, until he found his last asylum in France, the sparkle of his temperament may have grown dim and some strange sides of his nature may have been thrown into prominence. The slowness with which Leonardo worked was proverbial. The slowness which had all along been conspicuous in Leonardo's work is seen to be a symptom of his inhibition and to be the forerunner of his subsequent withdrawal from painting. Leonardo was notable for his quiet peaceableness and his avoidance of all antagonism and controversy. In an age which saw a struggle between sensuality without restraint and gloomy asceticism, Leonardo represented the cool repudiation of sexuality, a thing that would scarcely be expected of an artist and a portrayer of feminine beauty. When he became a Master, he surrounded himself with handsome boys and youths whom he took as pupils. The core of his nature, and the secret of it, would appear to be that after his curiosity had been activated in infancy in the service of sexual interest he succeeded in sublimating the greater part of his libido into an urge for research.

1910C 11/82
Leonardo da Vinci and a memory of his childhood (1910). Part II. Leonardo's childhood memory.

One of Leonardo's childhood memories concerns a vulture that came down while Leonardo was in his cradle, opened his mouth with its tail, and struck him many times with its tail against his lips. This scene with the vulture is not a memory of Leonardo's but a phantasy, which he formed at a later date and transposed to his childhood. This is often the way in which childhood memories originate. What the phantasy conceals is merely a reminiscence of suckling, or being suckled, at his mother's breast, a scene of human beauty that he, like so many artists, undertook to depict with his brush in the guise of the mother of god and her child. The reminiscence has been transformed by the man Leonardo into a passive homosexual phantasy. The replacement of his mother by the vulture indicates that the child was aware of his father's absence and found himself alone with his mother. The fact of Leonardo's illegitimate birth is in harmony with his vulture phantasy; it was only on this account that he could compare himself to a vulture child.

1910C 11/93
Leonardo da Vinci and a memory of his childhood (1910). Part III. Sexual interpretation of Leonardo's childhood memory.

There is a strong presumption that Leonardo da Vinci, who had phantasies of a vulture was a homosexual. In this phantasy a mother who suckles her child is turned into a vulture and her breast into a vulture's tail which signifies a penis. He appears as a man whose sexual need and activity were exceptionally reduced, as if a higher aspiration had raised him above the common animal need of mankind. It has always been emphasized that he took only strikingly handsome boys and youths as pupils, treated them with kindness and consideration, looked after them and, when they were ill, nursed them himself. Leonardo's mother came to Milan in 1493 to visit her son; she fell ill there, was taken to the hospital by Leonardo, and when she died was honored by him with a costly funeral. A comparison with what happens in obsessional neurosis can explain Leonard's account of the expenses of his mother's funeral. In his unconscious he was still tied to her by erotically colored feeling, as he had been in childhood. Before a child comes under the dominance of a castration complex, at a time when he still holds women at full value, he begins to display an intense desire to look, as an erotic instinctual activity. It was through Leonardo's erotic relation with his mother that he became a homosexual. The opposition that came from the subsequent repression of this childhood love did not allow him to set up a different and worthier memorial to her in his diary. But what emerged as a compromise from this neurotic conflict had to be carried out; and thus it was that the financial account was entered in the diary, and has come to the knowledge of posterity as something unintelligible.

1910C   11/107

Leonardo da Vinci and a memory of his childhood (1910). Part IV. The blissful smiles in Leonardo's paintings.

Leonardo's vulture phantasy is compounded from the memory of being suckled and being kissed by his mother. The idea that 2 distinct elements are combined in Mona Lisa's smile is one that has struck several crities. They accordingly find in the beautiful Florentine's expression the most perfect representation of the contrasts which dominate the erotic life of women; the contrast between reserve and seduction, and between the most devoted tenderness and a sensuality that is ruthlessly demanding. Leonardo da Vinci spent 4 years painting at this picture which contains the synthesis of the history of his childhood: its details are to be explained by reference to the most personal impressions in Leonardo's life. In his father's house he found not only his kind stepmother, Donna Albiera, but also his grandmother, his father's mother, Monna Lucia, who was no less tender to him than grandmothers usually are. If Leonardo was successful in reproducing on Mona Lisa's face the double meaning which this smile contained, the promise of unbounded tenderness and at the same time sinister menace, then here too he had

remained true to the content of his earliest memory. For this mother's tenderness was fateful for him; it determined his destiny and the privations that were in store for him. The violence of the caresses, to which his phantasy of the vulture points, was only too natural.

1910C   11/119

Leonardo da Vinci and a memory of his childhood (1910). Part V. Effects of father-loss on Leonardo.

Among the entries in Leonardo's notebooks there is one which catches the reader's attention owing to the importance of what it contains and to a minute formal error. The note refers to the death of Leonardo's father. The small error consists of the repetition of the time of day (at 7 o'clock), which is given twice, as if Leonardo had forgotten at the end of the sentence that he had already written it at the beginning. This type of repetition is called perseveration and indicates affective color. The note is a case in which Leonardo was unsuccessful in suppressing his affect. The effect which Leonardo's identification with his father had on his paintings was a fateful one. He created them and then cared no more about them. Psychoanalysis has shown that there is a connection between the father complex and belief in God. Leonardo was charged with unbelief or with apostasy from Christianity during his lifetime. The great Leonardo remained like a child for the whole of his life. Even as an adult he continued to play, and this was one of the reasons why he often appeared uncanny and incomprehensible to his contemporaries. Whenever children feel their sexual urges, they dream of fulfilling their wishes through flying. Leonardo admits that he has always felt bound to the problem of flight. It is probable that Leonard's play instinct vanished in his mature years; but its long duration can teach us how slowly anyone tears himself from his childhood if in his childhood days he has enjoyed the highest erotic bliss, which is never again attained.

1910C   11/130

Leonardo da Vinci and a memory of his childhood (1910). Part VI. Justification of pathobiography.

Freud insists that he never reckoned Leonardo da Vinci as a neurotic. The aim of the work has been to explain the inhibitions in Leonardo's sexual life and in his artistic activity. His illegitimate birth deprived him of his father's influence until perhaps his fifth year, and left him open to the tender seductions of a mother whose only solace he was. A powerful wave of repression brought his childhood excess to an end and established the dispositions which were to become manifest in the years of puberty. The most obvious result of the transformation was the avoidance of every crudely sensual activity; Leonardo was enabled to live in abstinence and to give the impression of being an asexual human being. Leonardo emerges from the obscurity of his boyhood as an artist, a painter and a sculptor. It seems as if only a man who had had Leonardo's childhood experiences could have painted the Mona Lisa and the St. Anne.

1910D   11/139
The future prospects of psycho-analytic therapy (1910).

The Future Prospects of Psychoanalytic Therapy was delivered as an address at the opening of the Second Psychoanalytical Congress, held at Nuremberg on March 30 and 31, 1910. We have not come to the end of our resources for combating the neuroses but can soon expect a substantial improvement in therapeutic prospects. This reinforcement will come from 3 directions: 1) from internal progress including advances in analytic knowledge and in technique; 2) from increased authority; and 3) from the general effect of psycho-analytic work. Every advance in knowledge means an increase in therapeutic power. The treatment is made up of 2 parts: what the physician infers and tells the patient, and the patient's working over of what he has heard. New things are to be learned in the field of symbolism in dreams and in the unconscious. Technique has changed from the cathartic treatment to uncovering the complexes. Authority is necessary since only very few civilized people are capable of existing without reliance on others or are even capable of coming to an independent opinion. The general effect of the work will hopefully result in a Utopian-like community. All the energies which are consumed in the production of neurotic symptoms serving the purposes of a world of phantasy isolated from reality will help to strengthen the clamor for the changes in our civilization through which we can look for the well-being of future generations.

1910E   11/153
The antithetical meaning of primal words (1910).

The Antithetical Meaning of Primal Words is a review of the pamphlet by Karl Abel, bearing the same title. The dream interpreters of antiquity have made use of the notion that a thing in a dream can mean its opposite. The dream work disregards negation and employs the same means of representation for expressing contraries. The behavior of the dream work is identical with a peculiarity in the oldest languages known to us. In the Egyptian language, there are a number of words with 2 meanings, one of which is the exact opposite of the other. Of all the eccentricities of the Egyptian vocabulary, perhaps the most extraordinary feature is that, quite apart from the words that combine antithetical meanings, it possesses other compound words in which 2 vocables of antithetical meanings are united so as to form a compound which bears the meaning of only 1 of its 2 constituents. According to Abel, it is in the oldest

roots that antithetical double meanings are found to occur. In the subsequent course of the language's development this ambiguity disappeared and, in Ancient Egyptian at any rate, all the intermediate stages can be followed, down to the unambiguousness of modern vocabularies. The concepts which could only be arrived at by means of an antithesis became, in course of time, sufficiently familiar to men's minds to make an independent existence possible for each of their 2 parts and accordingly to enable a separate phonetic representative to be formed for each part.

1910H   11/163
A special type of choice of object made by men. (Contributions to the psychology of love I) (1910).

In the course of psychoanalytic treatment there are opportunities for collecting impressions of the way in which neurotics behave in love. A number of necessary preconditions for loving a particular object choice are presented. The first of the preconditions for loving is termed the precondition that there should be an injured third party; it stipulates that the person in question shall never choose as his love object a woman who is disengaged but only one to whom another man can claim right of possession. The second precondition is that a woman who is chaste and whose reputation is irreproachable never exercises an attraction that might raise her to the status of a love object but only a woman who is in some way or other, of bad repute sexually. This is connected with the experiencing of jealousy. The lover's behavior towards the object he has chosen is also presented. In normal love the woman's value is measured by her sexual integrity and is reduced by any approach to the characteristic of being like a prostitute. Hence the fact that women with this characteristic are considered by neurotic men to be love objects of the highest value seems to be a striking departure from the normal. A fourth precondition is where the relationship is a compulsive one with the man showing an urge to rescue the woman he loves. The psychical origins of neurotic love are derived from the infantile fixation of tender feelings on the mother and represent one of the consequences of that fixation. The love objects are mother surrogates. There is a connection between the rescue motif and the parental complex which results in an urge to rescue the loved one.

1912D   11/177
On the universal tendency to debasement in the sphere of love. (Contributions to the psychology of love II) (1912).

Psychical impotence affects men of strongly libidinous natures and manifests itself in a refusal to carry out the sexual act. A failure of this kind arises when the attempt is made with certain individuals. The foundation of the disorder is provided by an inhibition in the developmental history of the libido before it assumes the form of its normal termination. Two factors whose union is necessary to ensure a completely normal attitude in love have failed to combine: the affectionate and the sensual. The affectionate current springs from the earliest years of childhood; it is formed on the basis of the self-preservative instinct and is directed to the close members of the family. These affectionate fixations persist throughout childhood, and continually carry along with them eroticism, which is consequently diverted from its sexual aims. Then at the age of puberty they are joined by the powerful sensual current which no longer mistakes its aims. Two factors decide whether the advance in the developmental path of the libido is to fail: 1) the amount of frustration in reality and 2) the amount of attraction which the relinquished infantile objects are able to exercise. The behavior in love of men in the civilized world bears the stamp of psychical impotence. The curb put upon love by civilization involves a universal tendency to debase sexual objects. The irreconcilable difference between the demands of the sexual and egoistic instincts has made men capable of ever higher achievements, though subject to a constant danger of neurosis to which the weaker succumb.

1918A   11/191

The taboo of virginity. (Contributions to the psychology of love III) (1918).

For primitive peoples, defloration is a significant act; but it has become the subject of a religious taboo. Instead of reserving it for the girl's bridegroom and future partner in marriage, custom demands that he shall shun the performance of it. The first attempt at explanation is based on the horror of blood among primitive races who consider blood as the seat of love. A second explanation suggests that primitive man is prey to a perpetual lurking apprehensiveness, just as the psychoanalytic theory of the neuroses claims it to be the case with people suffering from anxiety neurosis. A third explanation draws attention to the fact that the taboo of virginity is part of a large totality which embraces the whole of sexual life. Wherever primitive man has set up a taboo he fears some danger and it cannot be disputed that a generalized dread of women is expressed. The intention underlying the taboo of defloration is that of denying or sparing the future husband something which cannot be dissociated from the first sexual act. The first act of intercourse mobilizes a number of impulses which are out of place in the desired feminine attitude. Defloration has not only the one, civilized consequence of binding the woman lastingly to the man; it also unleashes an archaic reaction of hostility towards him, which is expressed in the appearance of inhibitions in

the erotic side of married life, and to which we may ascribe the fact that second marriages so often turn out better than the first.

1910I   11/209

The psycho-analytic view of psychogenic disturbance of vision (1910).

The psychoanalytic view of psychogenic disturbance of vision is presented. Hysterical blindness is taken as the type of a psychogenic visual disturbance. In a hysteric, the idea of being blind arises spontaneously. In patients predisposed to hysteria there is an inherent tendency to dissociation, to a falling apart of the connections in their mental field, as a consequence of which some unconscious processes do not continue as far as into the conscious. The hysterical patient is blind, not as the result of an autosuggestive idea that he cannot see, but as the result of a dissociation between unconscious and conscious processes in the act of seeing. The eyes perceive not only alterations in the external world, which are important for the preservation of life, but also characteristics of objects which lead to their being chosen as objects of love, their charms. The closer the relation into which an organ with a dual function enters with one of the major instincts, the more it withholds itself from the other. This principle is bound to lead to pathological consequences if the 2 fundamental instincts are disunited and if the ego maintains a repression of the sexual component instinct concerned. If an organ which serves the 2 sorts of instinct increases its erotogenic role, it is to be expected that this will not occur without the excitability and innervation of the organ undergoing changes which will manifest themselves as disturbances of its function in the service of the ego.

1910K   11/219

'Wild' Psycho-analysis (1910).

A middle aged lady called upon Freud for a consultation complaining of anxiety states. The precipitating cause of her anxiety states had been a divorce from her last husband but these states became worse after she consulted a young physician and he had informed her that the cause of her anxiety was her lack of sexual satisfaction. The doctor's advice to the lady shows in what sense he understands the expression sexual life, namely, in which by sexual needs nothing is meant but the need for coitus or analogous acts producing orgasms and emission of the sexual substances. In contrast, in psychoanalysis, the concept of what is sexual comprises all the activities of the tender feelings which have primitive sexual impulses as their source. For this reason we prefer to speak of psychosexuality, thus laying stress on the point that the mental factor in sexual life should not be overlooked or underestimated. The doctor's suggesting she solve this need for sexual satisfaction by going back to her husband, taking a lover, or masturbating leaves no room for psychoanalysis. It is a long superseded idea that the patient suffers from a sort of ignorance, and that if one removes this ignorance by giving him information he is bound to recover. The pathological factor is not his ignorance in itself, but the root of this ignorance in his inner resistances. The task of the treatment lies in combating these resistances. Psychoanalytic intervention requires a fairly long period of contact with the patient. First, the patient must reach the area of what he has repressed, and secondly, he must have formed a sufficient attachment (transference) to the physician for his emotional relationship to him to make a fresh flight into neurosis impossible. It is concluded that 'wild' analysts do more harm to the cause of psychoanalysis than to the individual patients.

1910G   11/231
Contributions to a discussion on suicide (1910).

If it is the case that youthful suicide occurs not only among pupils in secondary schools but also among apprentices and others, this fact does not acquit the secondary schools of their guilt in precipitating causes but it must perhaps be interpreted as meaning that (as regards its pupils) the secondary school takes the place of the traumas with which other adolescents meet in other walks of life. A secondary school should offer its students support and backing at a time of life at which the conditions of their development compel them to relax their ties with their parental home and their family. Schools fail in this, and in many respects fall short of their duty of providing a substitute for the family and of arousing interest in life in the world outside. The school must never forget that it has to deal with immature individuals who cannot be denied a right to linger at certain stages of development and even at certain disagreable ones.

1910F   11/233
Letter to Dr. Friedrich S. Krauss on 'Anthropophyteia' (1910).

In a letter to Dr. Friedrich S. Krauss, Freud discusses *Anthropophyteia*. The erotic quips and comic anecdotes that have been collected and published in *Anthropophyteia* have been produced and repeated because they gave pleasure both to their narrators and their hearers. These tales give us direct information as to which of the component instincts of sexuality are retained in a given group of people as particularly efficient in producing pleasure; and in this way they give the neatest confirmation of the findings reached by the psychoanalytic examination of neurotics. Psychoanalysis has led us to assert that the anal region is the site of an erotogenic sensitivity. *Anthropophyteia* shows how

universally people dwell with pleasure upon this part of the body, its performances and indeed the product of its function. In psychoanalysis today we describe a congeries of ideas and its associated affect as a complex; and we are prepared to assert that many of the most admired jokes are complexive jokes and that they owe their exhilarating and cheerful effect to the ingenious uncovering of what are as a rule repressed complexes. It is safe to hope that the psychological importance of folklore will be more and more clearly recognized, and that the relations between that branch of study and psychoanalysis will soon become more intimate.

1910J   11/236
Two instances of pathogenic phantasies revealed by the patients themselves (1910).

Two instances of pathogenic phantasies revealed by the patients themselves are presented. A 20-year-old patient gave an unmistakable picture of a schizophreinic (dementia praecox, hebephrenia). During the initial stages of his illness he had exhibited periodic changes of mood and had made a considerable improvement. His relapse followed upon a week of festivities. When he was brought back to the institution, he said that the consulting physician had advised him to flirt with his mother a little. There can be no doubt that in his delusory paramnesia he was giving expression to the excitement which had been provoked in him by being in his mother's company and which had been the immediate provocation of his relapse. More than 10 years ago, at a time when the findings and hypotheses of psychoanalysis were known to only a few people, the following events were reported. A girl, who was the daughter of a medical man, fell ill of hysteria with local symptoms. One day a friend of the patient's asked her if she ever thought of consulting Dr. Freud. The patient replied that he would ask if she ever had the idea of having sexual intercourse with her father. It is not Freud's practice to ask such questions; however, it is worth remarking that much of what patients report of the words and actions of their physicians may be understood as revelations of their own pathogenic phantasies.

1910M   11/238
Review of Wilhelm Neutra's 'letters to neurotic women' (1910).

A review of Wilhelm Neutra's *Letters to Neurotic Women* is presented. The book cannot be hailed as an encouraging phenomenon. The author, who is an assistant physician in the Gainfarn hydropathic institute near Vienna, has borrowed the form of Oppenheim's *Psychotherapeutische Briefe* and has given that form a psychoanalytic content. The author fails to attain the merits of his model, tact and moral seriousness, and in his presentation of psychoanalytic theory he often drops into empty rhetoric and is also guilty of some misstatements. Nevertheless, much of what he writes is neatly and aptly expressed; and the book may pass muster as a work for popular consumption.

VOL. XII Case History of Schreber, Papers on Technique and Other Works (1911–1913)

1911C 12/3
Psycho-analytic notes on an autobiographical account of a case of paranoia (dementia paranoides): Editor's note (1958) and Introduction (1911).

Psychoanalytic Notes upon an Autobiographical Account of a Case of Paranoia (Dementia Paranoides) is a reissue, with a number of corrections and additional notes, of the one published in 1925. Schreber's *Memoirs* were published in 1903; but, though they had been widely discussed in psychiatric circles, they seem not to have attracted Freud's attention till the summer of 1910. Freud had attacked the problem of paranoia at a very early stage of his researches in psychopathology. The importance of the Schreber analysis, however, is not restricted to the light it throws on the problems of paranoia. A number of subjects are touched upon which were to be discussed afterwards at greater length. Thus, the remarks on narcissism were preliminary to the paper devoted to that subject, the account of the mechanism of repression was to be taken up again in the course of a few years, and the discussion of the instincts was feeling its way towards the more elaborate one in "Instincts and their Vicissitudes". The case history makes use of only a single fact (Schreber's age at the time he fell ill) that was not contained in the *Memoirs*. The psychoanalytic investigation of paranoia would be altogether impossible if the patients themselves did not possess the peculiarity of betraying (in a distorted form, it is true) precisely those things which other neurotics keep hidden as a secret.

1911C 12/12
Psycho-analytic notes on an autobiographical account of a case of paranoia (dementia paranoides) (1911). Part I. Case history of Schreber.

A case history of paranoia is discussed. Dr. Schreber's first illness began in the autumn of 1884, and by the end of 1885 he had completely recovered. The second illness set in at the end of October 1893 and grew rapidly worse. The patient was very preoccupied with his pathological experiences. He was inaccessible to any other impression and would sit perfectly rigid and motionless for hours. His delusional ideas gradually assumed a mystical and religious character. There were certain people (especially his physician, Flechsig) by whom he thought he was being persecuted and injured, and upon whom he poured abuse. By 1899, the patient's condition had undergone a great change, and he now considered himself capable of carrying on an independent existence. The court judgment that gave Dr. Schreber back his liberty summarizes the content of his delusional system in a few sentences: He believed that he had a mission to redeem the world and to restore it to its lost state of bliss. This, however, he could only bring about if he were first transformed from a man into a woman. The emasculation phantasy was of a primary nature and originally independent of the Redeemer motif. The idea of being transformed into a woman was the salient feature and the earliest germ of his delusional system. He thought there was a conspiracy against him that once his illness was recognized as incurable he would be handed over to a certain person who would take his soul and then to another person who would transform him into a female and sexually abuse him. Schreber's mixture of reverence and rebelliousness in his attitudes towards God are discussed at length. One of the delusions the patient felt was that through God's misunderstanding of living men, He was the instigator of the plot against him. In Schreber's system, the 2 principal elements of his delusions (his transformation into a woman and his favored relation to God) are linked in his assumption of a feminine attitude towards God. It will be shown that there is a genetic relationship between these 2 elements.

1911C 12/35
Psychoanalytic notes on an autobiographical account of a case of paranoia (dementia paranoides) (1911). Part II. Attempts at interpretation.

Attempts at interpretation of the case history of paranoia are presented. Schreber's case, at first took the form of delusions of persecution, and did not begin to lose it until the turning point of his illness. During the incubation period of his illness, between June 1893, and the following October, Schreber repeatedly dreamt that his old nervous disorder had returned. Schreber dreamed that Flechsig committed, or attempted to commit, soul murder upon him. This act was thought to be comparable to the efforts made by the devil or by demons to gain possession of a soul. The exciting cause of the illness was the appearance in him of a feminine (that is, a passive homosexual) wishful phantasy, which took as its object the figure of his doctor. An intense resistance to this phantasy arose on the part of Schreber's personality, and the ensuing defensive struggle, took on that of a delusion of persecution. The person he longed for now became his persecutor, and the content of his wishful phantasy became the content of his persecution. The patient's struggle with Flechsig became revealed to him as a conflict with God. This is construed as an infantile conflict with the father whom he loved; the details of that conflict were what determined the content of his delusions. In the final stage of Schreber's delusion a magnificent victory was scored by the infantile sexual urge; for voluptuousness became God-fearing, and God Himself (his father) never tired of demanding it from him. His father's most dreaded threat, castration, actually provided the material for his wishful phantasy of being transformed into a woman.

1911C 12/59
Psycho-analytic notes on an autobiographical account of a case of paranoia (dementia paranoides) (1911). Part III. On the mechanism of paranoia.

The distinctive character of paranoia is found in the form assumed by the symptoms. Paranoia is a disorder in which a sexual etiology is by no means obvious; rather, the strikingly prominent features in the causation of paranoia, especially among males, are social humiliations and slights. The really operative factor in these social injuries lies in the part played in them by the homosexual components of emotional life. What lies at the core of the conflict in cases of paranoia among males is a homosexual wishful phantasy of loving a man. The familiar principal forms of paranoia can all be represented as contradictions of the single proposition: "I (a man) love him (a man)," and that they exhaust all the possible ways in which such contradictions could be formulated. The proposition is contradicted by: 1) delusions of persecution; 2) erotomania; and 3) jealousy, alcoholic delusions of jealousy and delusions of jealousy in women. We can detect an element of megalomania in most other forms of paranoiac disorder. The most striking characteristic of symptom formation in paranoia is the process which deserves the name of projection. Repression is also connected with paranoia in the following 3 phases: fixation, repression proper, and irruption. Freud concluded that the neuroses arise from a conflict between the ego and the sexual instinct, and that the forms which the neuroses assume, retain the imprint of the course of development followed by the libido, and by the ego.

1912A 12/80
Psycho-analytic notes on an autobiographical account of a case of paranoia (dementia paranoides) (1911). Postscript.

In dealing with the case history of Schreber, Freud purposely restricted himself to a minimum of interpretation. Since he published his work upon Schreber, a chance acquisition of knowledge has put him in a position to appreciate one of his delusional beliefs more adequately, and to recognize the wealth of its bearing upon mythology: the patient's peculiar relation to the sun, explained as a sublimated father symbol. When

Schreber boasts that he can look into the sun unscathed and undazzled, he has rediscovered the mythological method of expressing his filial relation to the sun, and has confirmed Freud once again in his view that the sun is a symbol of the father.

12/85
Papers on technique (1911–1915). Editor's introduction (1958).

In his contribution to *Studies on Hysteria,* Freud gave a very full account of the psychotherapeutic procedure which he had evolved on the basis of Breuer's discoveries. This may be described as the pressure technique and it still included considerable elements of suggestion, though it was advancing rapidly towards what he was soon to call the psychoanalytic method. Six papers, *On the Technique of Psychoanalysis,* cover a great number of important subjects. The relative paucity of Freud's writings on technique, as well as his hesitations and delays over their production, suggests that there was some feeling of reluctance on his part to publishing this kind of material. Behind all his discussion of technique, however, Freud never ceased to insist that a proper mastery of the subject could only be acquired from clinical experience and not from books: clinical experience with patients, no doubt, but, above all clinical experience from the analyst's own analysis. This, as Freud became more and more convinced, was the fundamental necessity for every practicing psychoanalyst.

1911E 12/89
Papers on technique. The handling of dream-interpretation in psycho-analysis (1911).

The handling of dream interpretation in psychoanalysis is presented. Anyone coming from dream interpretation to analytic practice will retain his interest in the content of dreams, and his inclination will be to interpret as fully as possible every dream related by the patient. The amount of interpretation which can be achieved in one session should be taken as sufficient and it is not to be regarded as a loss if the content of the dream is not fully discovered. On the following day, the interpretation of the dream is not to be taken up again as a matter of course, until it has become evident that nothing else has meanwhile forced its way into the foreground of the patient's thoughts. Dream interpretation should not be pursued in analytic treatment as an art for its own sake, but its handling should be subject to those technical rules that govern the conduct of the treatment as a whole. The great majority of dreams forge ahead of the analysis; so that, after subtraction of everything in them which is already known and understood, there still remains a more or less clear hint at something which has hitherto been hidden.

1912B   12/97

Papers on technique. The dynamics of transference (1912).

The dynamics of transference are discussed. Each individual, through the combined operation of his innate disposition and the influences brought to bear on him during his early years, has acquired a specific method of his own in his conduct of his erotic life. This produces what might be described as a stereotype plate, which is constantly repeated in the course of the person's life. If someone's need for love is not entirely satisfied by reality, he is bound to approach every new person whom he meets with libidinal anticipatory ideas. Thus it is a perfectly normal and intelligible thing that the libidinal cathexis of someone who is partly unsatisfied, a cathexis which is held ready in anticipation, should be directed as well to the figure of the doctor. The cathexis will introduce the doctor into one of the psychical series which the patient has already formed. When anything in the complexive material (in the subject matter of the complex) is suitable for being transferred on to the figure of the doctor, that transference is carried out. It is inferred that the transference idea has penetrated into consciousness in front of any other possible associations because it satisfies the resistance. Transference in the analytic treatment invariably appears in the first instance as the strongest weapon of the resistance, and we may conclude that the intensity and persistence of the transference are an effect and an expression of the resistance. Transference to the doctor is suitable for resistance to the treatment only in so far as it is a negative transference or a positive transference of repressed erotic impulses.

1912E   12/109

Papers on technique. Recommendations to physicians practising psycho-analysis (1912).

Recommendations are presented to physicians practicing psychoanalysis. The first problem is the task of keeping in mind all the innumerable names, dates, detailed memories and pathological products which each patient communicates, and of not confusing them with similar material produced by other patients under treatment simultaneously or previously. The physician should maintain the rule of giving equal notice to everything. This is the necessary counterpart to the demand made on the patient that he should communicate everything that occurs to him without criticism or selection. Freud cannot advise the taking of full notes, the keeping of a shorthand record, etc., during analytic sessions. The notes focus attention, tie up mental activity, and make an unfavorable impression. It is not a good thing to work on a case scientifically while treatment is still proceeding. The most successful cases are those in which one

proceeds without any purpose in view. Under present day conditions the feeling that is most dangerous to a psychoanalyst is the therapeutic ambition to achieve, by this novel and much disputed method, something that will produce a convincing effect upon other people. The doctor should be opaque to his patients and, like a mirror, should show them nothing but what is shown to him. He should not bring his own feelings into play. Efforts to make use of the analytic treatment to bring about sublimation of instinct are, far from advisable in every case. The patient's intellectual capacities should not be taxed. Mental activities such as thinking something over or concentrating the attention solve none of the riddles of a neurosis. This can be done only by obeying the psychoanalytic rule.

1913C   12/121

Papers on technique. On beginning the treatment. (Further recommendations on the technique of psychoanalysis I) (1913).

Recommendations on the technique of psychoanalysis concerning beginning the treatment are presented. Lengthy preliminary discussions before the beginning of the analytic treatment, previous treatment by another method and also previous acquaintance between the doctor and the patient who is to be analyzed, have special disadvantageous consequences for which one must be prepared. They result in the patient's meeting the doctor with a transference attitude which is already established and which the doctor must first slowly uncover instead of having the opportunity to observe the growth and development of the transference from the outset. One must mistrust all prospective patients who want to make a delay before beginning their treatment. Points of importance at the beginning of the analysis are arrangement about time and money. What the material is with which one starts the treatment is a matter of indifference. But in any case the patient must be left to do the talking and must be free to choose at what point he shall begin. So long as the patient's communications and ideas run on without any obstruction, the theme of transference should be left untouched. In each case we must wait until the disturbance of the transference by the successive emergency of transference resistances has been removed.

1914G   12/145

Papers on technique. Remembering, repeating and working-through. (Further recommendations on the technique of psycho-analysis II) (1914).

Remembering, repeating, and working through are discussed. Forgetting impressions, scenes or experiences nearly always reduces itself to shutting them off. There is one special class of experiences for which no memory can as a rule be recovered. These are experiences which occurred in very early childhood and were not understood at the time but which were subsequently understood and interpreted. The patient does not remember anything of what he has forgotten and repressed, but acts it out. He reproduces it not as a memory but as an action; he repeats it, without knowing that he is repeating it. Transference is itself only a piece of repetition; the repetition is a transference of the forgotten past not only on to the doctor but also on to all the other aspects of the current situation. The patient yields to the compulsion to repeat, which now replaces the impulsion to remember, not only in his personal attitude to his doctor but also in every other activity and relationship which may occupy his life at the time. The main instrument for curbing the patient's compulsion to repeat and for turning it into a motive for remembering, lies in the handling of the transference. We render the compulsion harmless, and indeed useful, by giving it the right to assert itself in a definite field. The first step in overcoming the resistances is made by the analyst's uncovering the resistance, which is never recognized by the patient, and acquainting him with it. One must allow the patient time to become more conversant with the resistance with which he has now become acquainted, to work through it, to overcome it, by continuing, in defiance of it, the analytic work. Only when the resistance is at its height can the analyst discover the repressed instinctual impulses which are feeding the resistance. The working through of the resistances may in practice turn out to be an arduous task for the subject of the analysis and a trial of patience for the analyst. Theoretically, working through may correlate with the abreacting of the quotas of affect strangulated by repression.

1915A 12/157

Papers on technique. Observations on transference-love. (Further recommendations on the technique of psychoanalysis III) (1915).

Observations on transference love (when a woman patient declares her love for the doctor) are presented. For the doctor, the phenomenon signifies a valuable piece of enlightenment and a useful warning against any tendency to a counter transference. He must recognize that the patient's falling in love is induced by the analytic situation. The patient has 2 alternatives; she must relinquish psychoanalytic treatment, or she must accept falling in love with her doctor as an inescapable fate. After falling in love, the patient loses all understanding of the treatment and all interest in it. This transference love is interpreted as a form of resistance. The analytic technique requires that the physician should deny to the patient, who is craving for love, the satisfaction she demands. The treatment must be carried out in abstinence. The analyst must keep firm hold of the transfer-

ence love, but treat it as something unreal, as a situation which has to be gone through in the treatment and traced back to its unconscious origins and which must assist in bringing all that is most deeply hidden in the patient's erotic life into her consciousness and therefore under her control. For the doctor, ethical motives unite with the technical ones to restrain him from giving the patient his love. However highly he may prize love he must prize even more highly the opportunity for helping his patient over a decisive stage in her life.

1957A 12/175

Dreams in folklore (Freud and Oppenheim) (1957) (1911).

Dreams in Folklore was written jointly by Freud and Professor D. E. Oppenheim of Vienna. The symbolism employed in the dreams in folklore coincides completely with that accepted by psychoanalysis. A number of these dreams are understood by the common people in the same way as they would be interpreted by psychoanalysis, that is, not as premonitions about a still unrevealed future, but as the fulfillment of wishes, the satisfaction of needs which arise during the state of sleep. Penis symbolism appears in dreams occurring in folklore. The penis appears as: a sceptre, fat earthworm, a dagger and other sharp weapons. Feces symbolism and related dream actions also appear. In the very earliest period of childhood, feces is a highly prized substance, in relation to which coprophilic instincts find satisfaction. The most important residue of this former esteem is, however, that all the interest which the child has had in feces is transferred in the adult on to another material which is set above almost everything else, gold. In dreams in folklore, gold is seen in the most unambiguous way to be a symbol of feces. Occasionally, the Devil appears as a bestower of treasure and a seducer. The defecation dreams in which the victim is a woman, deal with impotence. If the sleeper feels a need to defecate, he dreams of gold, of treasure. A few other dreams are analyzed including one about a lottery taken to symbolize a marriage contract.

1913M 12/205

On psycho-analysis (1913).

Psychoanalysis is discussed. Psychoanalysis is a remarkable combination for it comprises not only a method of research into the neuroses but also a method of treatment based on the etiology thus discovered. Psychoanalysis started with researches into hysteria, but in the course of years it has extended far beyond that field of work. It was conclusively proved that hysterical symptoms are residues (reminiscences) of profoundly moving experiences, which have been withdrawn from everyday consciousness, and that their form is determined (in a manner that excludes deliberate action) by details of the traumatic effects of the experiences. The first psychoanalytic examinations and attempts at treatment were made with the help of hypnotism. Afterwards, this was abandoned and the work was carried out by the method of free association with the patient remaining in his normal state. In all neuroses the pathological symptoms are really the end products of conflicts, which have led to repression and splitting of the mind. The symptoms are generated by different mechanisms: either as formations in substitution for the repressed forces, or as compromises between the repressing and repressed forces, or as reaction formations and safeguards against the repressed forces.

1911B 12/213
Formulations on the two principles of mental functioning (1911).

Formulations on the Two Principles of Mental Functioning has as its main theme the distinction between the regulating principles (the pleasure principle and the reality principle) which respectively dominate the primary and secondary mental processes. Every neurosis has as its result a forcing of the patient out of real life. Neurotics turn away from reality because they find it unbearable. The most extreme type of this turning away from reality is shown by certain cases of hallucinatory psychosis which seek to deny the particular event that occasioned the outbreak of their insanity. In the psychology which is founded on psychoanalysis, we have become accustomed to taking as our starting point the unconscious mental processes. We consider these to be the older, primary processes. The governing purpose obeyed by these primary processes is described as the pleasure principle. The setting up of the reality principle was a momentous step. The increased significance of external reality heightened the importance of the sense organs that are directed towards the external world. With the introduction of the reality principle, phantasizing and daydreaming were split off. The supersession of the pleasure principle by the reality principle is not accomplished all at once; nor does it take place simultaneously all along the line. Just as the pleasure ego can do nothing but wish, work for a yield of pleasure, and avoid unpleasure, so the reality ego need do nothing but strive for what is useful and guard itself against damage. Education is described as an incitement to the conquest of the pleasure principle. Art brings about a reconciliation between the 2 principles. While the ego goes through its transformation from a pleasure ego into a reality ego, the sexual instincts undergo the changes that lead them from the autoeroticism through various intermediate phases to object love in the service of procreation.

1912C 12/227
Types of onset of neurosis (1912).

Types of onset of neurosis are described. The first type may be described in general terms as frustration. In the second type, the subject does not fall ill as a result of a change in the external world which has replaced satisfaction by frustration, but as a result of an internal effort. He falls ill of his attempt to adapt himself to reality and to fulfill the demands of reality, an attempt in the course of which he comes up against insurmountable internal difficulties. The third type concerns those people who fall ill as soon as they get beyond the irresponsible age of childhood. The essential feature of the dispositional processes is that their libido has never left its infantile fixations; the demands of reality are not suddenly made upon a wholly or partly mature person, but arise from the very fact of growing older. The fourth type involves people who fall ill who have hitherto been healthy, who have met with no fresh experience and whose relation to the external world has undergone no change. As a result of their having reached a particular period of life, and in conformity with regular biological processes, the quantity of libido in their mental economy has experienced an increase which is in itself enough to upset the equilibrium of their health and to set up the necessary conditions for a neurosis.

1912F 12/239
Contributions to a discussion on masturbation (1912).

Contributions to a discussion on masturbation are presented. The discussion on masturbation in the Vienna Psychoanalytical Society lasted for several months and was conducted on the plan of each speaker in turn reading a paper, which was followed by an exhaustive debate. All of the members agreed on the following points: 1) the importance of the phantasies which accompany or represent the act of masturbation; 2) the importance of the sense of guilt which is attached to masturbation; and 3) the impossibility of assigning a qualitative determinant for the injurious effects of masturbation. The following unresolved differences of opinion appeared: 1) a denial of a somatic factor in the effects of masturbation; 2) a general denial of the injurious effects of masturbation; 3) the origin of the sense of guilt; and 4) the ubiquity of masturbation in childhood. Significant uncertainties exist: 1) the mechanism of the injurious effects of masturbation, and 2) the etiological relation of masturbation to the actual neuroses. We are confronted, in the neuroses, with cases in which masturbation has done damage. This damage seems to occur in 3 different ways: 1) organic injury may occur by some unknown mechanism; 2) the injury may occur through the laying down of a psychical pattern according to which there is no necessity for trying to alter the external world in order to satisfy a great need; or 3) a fixation of infantile sexual aims may be made possible, and a persistence of psychical infantilism.

1912G 12/255
A note on the unconscious in psycho-analysis (1912).

The unconscious in psychoanalysis is discussed. A conception, or any other psychical element, which is now present to the consciousness may become absent the next moment, and may become present again, after an interval, unchanged, and from memory, not as a result of a fresh perception by our senses. It is this fact which we are accustomed to account for by the supposition that during the interval the conception has been present in our mind, although latent in consciousness. The conception which is present to our consciousness and of which we are aware is the meaning of the term conscious. As for latent conceptions, they are denoted by the meaning of the term conscious. We learn by the analysis of neurotic phenomena that a latent or unconscious idea is not necessarily a weak one, and that the presence of such an idea in the mind admits of indirect proofs of the most cogent kind, which are equivalent to the direct proof furnished by consciousness. A foreconscious activity passes into consciousness with no difficulty; an unconscious activity remains so and seems to be cut off from consciousness. The latent thoughts of the dream differ in no respect from the products of our regular conscious activity; they deserve the name of foreconscious (preconscious) thoughts, and may indeed have been conscious at some moment of waking life.

1913A 12/267
An evidential dream (1913).

An evidential dream is discussed. A lady suffering from doubting mania and obsessive ceremonials, insisted that her nurses should never let her out of their sight for a single moment: otherwise she would begin to brood about forbidden actions that she might have committed while she was not being watched. One evening, while she was resting on the sofa, she thought she saw that the nurse on duty had fallen asleep. When questioned, the nurse started up and replied that she saw the patient. This gave the patient grounds for a fresh doubt, and after a time she repeated her question, which the nurse met with renewed protestations; just at that moment another attendant came in bringing the patient's supper. This incident occurred one Friday evening. The next morning, the nurse recounted a dream which had the effect of dispelling the patient's doubts. The essential factor in the construction of dreams is an unconscious wish, as a rule a now repressed infantile wish, which can come to expression in this somatic or psychical material (in the day's residues too, therefore) and can thus supply

these with a force which enables them to press their way through to consciousness even during the suspension of thought at night. The dream is in every case a fulfillment of this unconscious wish, whatever else it may contain: warning, reflection, admission, or any other part of the rich content of preconscious waking life that has persisted undealt with into the night.

1913D 12/279
The occurrence in dreams of material from fairy tales (1913).

The occurrence in dreams of material from fairy tales is discussed. Psychoanalysis confirms our recognition of the important place which folk fairytales have acquired in the mental life of our children. In a few people, a recollection of their favorite fairytales takes the place of memories of their own childhood; they have made the fairytales into screen memories. Elements and situations derived from fairytales are also frequently to be found in dreams. A dream of a young married woman who had had a visit from her husband a few days before was presented. In the dream a manikin entered the same room as the woman and proceeded to dance and carry on. The description of the manikin's personal appearance fitted the dreamer's father-in-law without any alteration being necessary. Immediately afterwards, however, she thought of the story of Rumpelstiltskin. The brown room she saw reminded her of her parents' dining room, panelled in brown wood. Then she began to speak of beds too uncomfortable for two to sleep in. The brown wood room became in the first place a bed, and through the connection with a dining room, it was a marriage bed. The situation was a representation of intercourse. A young man told Freud about a dream that concerned night time and he was lying in his bed. Suddenly the window opened of its own accord and there were 6 or 7 wolves sitting on the big walnut tree in front of the window. He thought that the picture of a wolf standing upright must have been an illustration to the story of Little Red Riding Hood. It is the earliest anxiety dream that the dreamer remembered from his childhood. It was interpreted that the wolf was merely a first father surrogate.

1913F 12/289
The theme of the three caskets (1913).

The theme of the 3 caskets from *The Merchant of Venice* is discussed. Portia is bound to take as her husband that one who chooses the right casket from among the 3 before him. The 3 caskets are of gold, silver, and lead. Two suitors have already departed unsuccessful: they have chosen gold and silver. Bassanio, the third, decides in favor of lead; thereby he wins the bride, whose affection was already his before the trial of fortune. Shakespeare did not invent this oracle of the choice of a casket; he took it from a tale in the *Gesta Romanorum,* in which a girl has to make the same choice to win the Emperor's son. Here too, the third metal, lead, is the bringer of fortune. The theme is a human one, a man's choice between 3 women. This same content is found in *King Lear* when the King resolves to divide his kingdom while he is still alive, among his 3 daughters. He disowns Cordelia and divides the kingdom between the other 2, to his own and the general ruin. The shepherd Paris has to choose between 3 goddesses, of whom he declares the third to be the most beautiful. Cinderella is a youngest daughter, who is preferred by the prince to her 2 elder sisters. Psyche, in Apuleius's story, is the youngest and fairest of 3 sisters. Gold and silver are considered "loud"; while lead is considered dumb. In all the stories, there are 3 women of whom the youngest is the best. The *Twelve Brothers,* a Grimm Fairy Tale, involves a woman who remains dumb for 7 years in order to save her brothers. The earliest Greek mythology only knew a single Moera. She later developed into 3 sister goddesses. It is argued that what is represented are the 3 forms taken by the figure of the mother in the course of a man's life: the mother, the wife, and Mother Earth who receives him after death.

1913G 12/303
Two lies told by children (1913).

Two lies told by children are discussed. A number of lies told by well reared children have a particular significance and should cause those in charge of them to reflect rather than be angry. These lies occur under the influence of excessive feelings of love, and become momentous when they lead to a misunderstanding between the child and the person it loves. Taking money from anyone had come to mean to one of Freud's patients a physical surrender, an erotic relation. Taking money from her father was equivalent to a declaration of love. She could not admit, however, that she had appropriated the money; she was obliged to disavow it, because her motive for the deed, which was unconscious to herself, could not be admitted. Her father's punishment was thus a rejection of the tenderness she was offering him, and so it broke her spirit. A woman who was seriously ill in consequence of a frustration in life was in her earlier years a particularly capable, truth-loving, serious and virtuous girl, and became an affectionate wife. As the eldest of 5 children, the little girl early developed an unusually strong attachment to her father, which was destined, when she was grown up to wreck her happiness in life. The sense of guilt that was attached to her excessive fondness for her father found its expression in connection with her attempted deception; an admission was impossible because it would inevitably have been an admission of her hidden incestuous love.

1913I 12/311
The disposition to obsessional neurosis. A contribution to the problem of choice of neurosis (1913).

The Disposition to Obsessional Neurosis was read by Freud before the Fourth International Psychoanalytical Congress. The grounds for determining the choice of neurosis are in the nature of dispositions and are independent of experiences which operate pathogenically. The dispositions are inhibitions in development. The order in which the main forms of psychoneurosis are usually enumerated: Hysteria, Obsessional Neurosis, Paranoia, and Schizophrenia (Dementia Praecox), corresponds (even though not exactly) to the order of the ages at which the onset of these disorders occurs. Hysterical forms of illness can be observed even in earliest childhood; obsessional neurosis usually shows its first symptoms in the second period of childhood (between the ages of 6 and 8); while the 2 other psychoneuroses do not appear until after puberty and during adult life. Once the sexual organization which contains the disposition to obsessional neurosis is established it is never afterwards completely surmounted. The impulses of hatred and anal eroticism play a strong part in the symptomatology of obsessional neurosis. Psychoanalysis stands or falls with the recognition of the sexual component instincts, of the erotogenic zones and of the extension thus made possible of the concept of a sexual function in contrast to the narrower genital function. The antithesis between male and female is not present at the stage of pregenital object choice. The processes of the formation of character are more obscure and less accessible to analysis than neurotic ones. The developmental disposition to a neurosis is only complete if the phase of the development of the ego at which fixation occurs is taken into account as well as that of the libido. There remains for hysteria an intimate relation to the final phase of libidinal development, which is characterized by the primacy of the genitals and the introduction of the reproductive function.

1913B 12/327
Introduction to Pfister's 'The psycho-analytic method' (1913).

The Introduction to Pfister's *The Psychoanalytic Method* is presented. Psychoanalysis had its origin on medical soil, as a therapeutic procedure for the treatment of certain nervous illnesses which were termed functional and which were considered with increasing certainty to be consequences of disturbances in emotional life. It attains its end by assuming that the symptoms are not the only possible and final outcome of particular psychical processes. It uncovers the history of the development of the symptoms in the patient's memory, it revivifies the processes underlying them, and then conducts them, under the doctor's guidance, to a more favorable outlet. Education and therapeutics stand in an assignable relation to each other. Education seeks to ensure that certain of a child's innate dispositions and inclinations shall not cause any damage either to the individual or to society. Therapeutics come into action if these same dispositions have already led to the unwished for result of pathological symptoms. Let us hope that the application of psychoanalysis to the service of education will quickly fulfill the hopes which educators and doctors may rightly attach to it.

1913K   12/333
Preface to Bourke's 'Scatalogic rites of all nations' (1913).

The Preface to Bourke's *Scatalogic Rites of All Nations,* is presented. The lesson that bodily cleanliness is far more readily associated with vice than with virtue often occurred to Freud, when psychoanalytic work made him acquainted with the way in which civilized men deal with the problem of their physical nature. They are clearly embarrassed by anything that reminds them too much of their animal origin. The chief finding from psychoanalytic research has been the fact that the human infant is obliged to recapitulate during the early part of his development the changes in the attitude of the human race towards excremental matters which probably had their start when *homo sapiens* first raised himself off Mother Earth. In the earliest years of infancy there is no trace of shame about the excretory functions or of disgust at excreta. Psychoanalysis shows that, to begin with, excremental and sexual instincts are not distinct from each other in children. Folklore shows us how incompletely the repression of coprophilic inclinations has been carried out among various peoples at various times and how closely at other cultural levels the treatment of excretory substances approximates to that practiced by children.

1911D   12/341
The significance of sequences of vowels (1911).

The significance of sequences of vowels is discussed. In dreams and associations, names which have to be concealed seem to be replaced by others that resemble them only in containing the same sequence of vowels. A striking analogy is, however, provided from the history of religion. Among the ancient Hebrews the name of God was taboo; it might neither be spoken aloud nor written down. This prohibition was so implicitly obeyed that to this very day the vocalization of the 4 consonants in God's name (YHVH) remains unknown. It was, however, pronounced Jehovah, being supplied with the vowels of the word Adnoai, against which there was no such prohibition.

1911F   12/342
'Great is Diana of the Ephesians' (1911).

The ancient Greek city of Ephesus in Asia Minor was especially celebrated in antiquity for its splendid temples dedicated to Artemis (Diana). The evidence of excavations shows that in the course of centuries several temples were erected on the same site in honor of the goddess. In about A.D. 54, the apostle Paul spent several years at Ephesus. He preached, performed miracles, and found a large following among the people. He was persecuted and accused by the Jews; and he separated from them and founded an independent Christian community. The church founded by Paul at Ephesus did not long remain faithful to him. It came under the influence of a man named John. The city was conquered by Islam and finally was ruined and abandoned, because the river on which it stood became choked with sand. But even then the great goddess of Ephesus had not abandoned her claims. In our own days she appeared as a saintly virgin to a pious German girl, Katharina Emmerich, at Dulmen. She described to her, her journey to Ephesus, the furnishings of the house in which she had lived there and in which she had died, the shape of her bed, and so on. And both the house and the bed were in fact found, exactly as the virgin had described them, and they are once more the goal of the pilgrimages of the faithful.

1913E   12/345
Preface to Maxim Steiner's 'The psychical disorders of male potency' (1913).

"The preface to Maxim Steiner's *The Psychical Disorders of Male Potency*" is presented. Steiner is one of the small band of physicians who recognized the importance of psychoanalysis for the special branch of medicine and who have never since ceased to perfect themselves in its theory and technique. Only a small part of neurotic ailments are dealt with in neuropathology itself. The greater number of them find a place among the disorders of the particular organ which is the victim of a neurotic disturbance. It is therefore expedient and proper that the treatment of these symptoms or syndromes should also be the business of the specialist, who is alone capable of making a differential diagnosis between a neurotic and an organic illness, who can draw the line, in the case of mixed forms, between their organic and neurotic elements, and who can in general give us information on the way in which the 2 factors in the disease mutually reinforce each other. We may hope that the time is not far distant when it will be generally recognized that no sort of nervous disturbance can be understood and treated without the help of the line of approach and often of the technique of psychoanalysis.

VOL. XIII   Totem and Taboo and Other Works (1913–1914)

1912X   13/ix
Totem and taboo (1913). Editor's note (1955) and prefaces (1913, 1930).

In his Preface to *Totem and Taboo*, Freud tells us that his first stimulus for writing these essays came from the works of Wundt and Jung. Actually, his interest in social anthropology went back much further. The major elements of Freud's contribution to social anthropology made their first appearance in this work, and more especially in the fourth essay, which contains his hypothesis of the primal horde and the killing of the primal father and elaborates his theory tracing from them the origins of almost the whole of later social and cultural institutions. Freud had begun his preparations for the work, and in particular his reading of a large amount of literature on the subject, as early as in 1910. *Totem and Taboo* was translated into several languages besides English during Freud's lifetime: into Hungarian, Spanish, Portuguese, French, Japanese, and Hebrew. The 4 essays were originally published in the first 2 volumes of *Imago*. They represent a first attempt on Freud's part to apply the point of view and the findings of psychoanalysis to some unsolved problems of social psychology. The analysis of taboo is put forward as an assured and exhaustive attempt at the solution of the problem. The investigation of totemism does no more than declare that here is what psychoanalysis can at the moment contribute towards elucidating the problem of the totem.

1912X   13/1
Totem and taboo (1913). Part I. The horror of incest.

The horror of incest is discussed. The Australian aborigines, set before themselves with the most scrupulous care and the most painful severity the aim of avoiding incestuous sexual relations. Their whole social organization seems to serve that purpose or to have been brought into relation with its attainment. Among the Australians the place of all the religious and social institutions which they lack is taken by the system of totemism. A totem is, as a rule, an animal and more rarely a plant or a natural phenomenon, which stands in a peculiar relation to the whole clan. In almost every place where there are totems there is also a law against persons of the same totem having sexual relations with one another and consequently against their marrying. The violation of the prohibition is avenged in the most energetic fashion by the whole clan. Exogamy linked with the totem effects more than the prevention of incest with a man's mothers and sisters. It makes sexual intercourse impossible for a man with all the women of

his own clan by treating them all as blood relatives. Totemic exogamy appears to have been the means for preventing group incest. In an Australian tribe, 12 totem clans are divided into 4 subphratries and 2 phratries. All the divisions are exogamous. Various customary prohibitions (avoidances) are discussed such as those in Melanesia where intercourse between a boy and his mother and sisters is avoided by the boy moving out of the house. He subsequently does not meet them in public or speak of them. Similar customs prevail in New Caledonia, New Britain, New Mecklenburg, Fiji and Sumatra. The most widespread and strictest avoidance is that which restricts a man's intercourse with his mother-in-law. Incestuous wishes (childhood incestuous wishes that have been repressed) later become unconscious, and are regarded by savage peoples as immediate perils against which the most severe measures of defense must be enforced.

1912X   13/18
Totem and taboo (1913). Part II. Taboo and emotional ambivalence. (1).

Taboo has about it a sense of something unapproachable, and it is principally expressed in prohibitions and restrictions. Taboo restrictions are distinct from religious or moral prohibitions. Wundt described taboo as the oldest human unwritten code of laws. The source of taboo is attributed to a peculiar magical power which is inherent in persons and spirits and can be conveyed by them through the medium of inanimate objects. Taboos may be permanent or temporary. Behind all the prohibitions there seems to be something in the nature of a theory that they are necessary because certain persons and things are charged with a dangerous power, which can be transformed through contact with them, almost like an infection. The quantity of this dangerous attribute also plays a part. Some people or things have more of it than others and the danger is actually proportional to the difference of potential of the charges. Anyone who has transgressed one of these prohibitions himself acquires the characteristic of being prohibited. The word taboo denotes everything, whether a person or a place or a thing or a transitory condition, which is the vehicle or source of the mysterious attribute. According to Wundt, the true sources of taboo lie deeper than in the interests of the privileged classes: they have their origin in the source of the most primitive and at the same time most lasting of human instincts, in fear of 'demonic' powers. The original characteristic of taboo (that a demonic power lies hidden in an object and if the object is touched it takes its vengeance by casting a spell over the wrong-doer) is still 'objectified fear.' That fear has not yet split into the 2 forms into which it later develops: veneration and horror. Also according to Wundt, the distinction between sacred and unclean did not exist in the primitive beginnings of taboo; therefore taboo applies both to what is sacred and what is unclean through dread of contact with it.

1912X   13/26

Totem and taboo (1913). Part II. Taboo and emotional ambivalence. (2). Parallel between taboo and obsessional neurosis.

Anyone approaching the problem of taboo from the angle of psychoanalysis, will recognize that the phenomena of taboo are far from unfamiliar. The most obvious and striking point of agreement between the obsessional prohibitions of neurotics and taboos is that these prohibitions are equally lacking in motive and equally puzzling in their origin. As in the case of taboo, the principal prohibition, the nucleus of the neurosis, is against touching; thus sometimes known as touching phobia. Obsessional prohibitions are extremely liable to displacement. Obsessional prohibitions involve just as extensive renunciations and restrictions in the lives of those who are subject to them as do taboo prohibitions; but some of them can be lifted if certain actions are performed. Thereafter, these actions must be performed: they become compulsive or obsessive acts, and there can be no doubt that they are in the nature of expiation, penance, defensive measures, and purification. A continuing conflict between the prohibition and the instinct to do something is called a psychical fixation. The principal characteristic of this psychological constellation is described as the subject's ambivalent attitude towards a single object or an act connected with that object. The transmissibility of taboo is a reflection of the tendency for the unconscious instinct in the neurosis to shift constantly along associative paths on to new objects. If the violation of a taboo can be made good by atonement or expiation, which involve the renunciation of some possession or some freedom, this proves that obedience to the taboo injunction meant in itself the renunciation of something desirable. It is concluded that taboo is a primaeval prohibition forcibly imposed from outside, and directed against the most powerful longings to which human beings are subject. The desire to violate it persists in their unconscious; those who obey the taboo have an ambivalent attitude to what the taboo prohibits.

1912X   13/35

Totem and taboo (1913). Part II. Taboo and emotional ambivalence. (3). The treatment of enemies.

The taboos connected with the treatment of enemies are discussed. The killing of a man is governed by a number of observances which are included among the usages of taboo. These observances fall into the following 4 groups: 1) the appeasement of the slain enemy; 2)

restrictions upon the slayer; 3) acts of expiation and purification by him; and 4) certain ceremonial observances. The conclusion that is drawn from all these observances is that the impulses which they express towards an enemy are not solely hostile ones. They are also manifestations of remorse, of admiration for the enemy, and of a bad conscience for having killed him. In the accepted explanation of all the observances of appeasement, restriction, expiation, and purification, 2 principles are combined: the extension of the taboo from the slain man on to everything that has come in contact with him, and the fear of the slain man's ghost. In Freud's explanation, stress is put on the unity of the view, which derives all of these observances from emotional ambivalence towards the enemy.

1912X   13/41

Totem and taboo (1913). Part II. Taboo and emotional ambivalence. (3). (b). The taboo upon rulers.

The taboos connected with the treatment of rulers are discussed. The attitude of primitive peoples to their chiefs, kings, and priests is governed by 2 basic principles. A ruler must not only be guarded, he must also be guarded against. Rulers must be guarded against because they are vehicles of the mysterious and dangerous magical power which is transmitted by contact like an electric charge and which brings death and ruin to anyone who is not protected by a similar charge. The need to protect the king from every possible form of danger follows from his immense importance to his subjects. The ceremonial taboo of kings is ostensibly the highest honor and protection for them, while actually it is a punishment for their exaltation, a revenge taken on them by their subjects. An element of distrust may be traced among the reasons for the taboo observances that surround the king. One of the most glaring instances of a sacred ruler being fettered and paralysed by taboo ceremonials was found in the mode of life of the Japanese Mikado in earlier centuries. Some of the taboos laid upon barbarian kings are similar to the restrictions imposed upon murderers. The taboos not only pick out the king and exalt him above all common mortals, but also make his existence a torment and an intolerable burden, and reduce him to a bondage worse than that of his subjects.

1912X   13/51

Totem and taboo (1913). Part II. Taboo and emotional ambivalence. (3). (c). The taboo upon the dead. (4). Taboo and conscience.

The taboo upon the dead is especially virulent among most primitive peoples. It is manifested in the consequences that follow contact with the dead and in the treatment of mourners. The taboo observances after bodily contact with the dead are the same for Polynesia, Melanesia and a part of Africa. Their most regular feature is the prohibition against those who have had such contact to the touching of food themselves, and the consequent necessity for their being fed by other people. Essentially the same prohibitions apply to those who have been in contact with the dead only in a metaphorical sense. One of the most puzzling, but at the same time instructive, usages in connection with mourning is the prohibition against uttering the name of the dead person, since the name is regarded as an essential part of a man's personality and as an important possession. Obsessional neurotics behave exactly like savages in relation to names. Those who employ this taboo are afraid of the presence or of the return of the dead person's ghost. It is supposed that a dearly loved relative turns into a demon at the moment of his death and his survivors can expect nothing but hostility. Here we see the ambivalence of human emotions where a mourner reproaches himself for the death of a loved one, knowning that unconsciously he wished for the death. Unconscious hostility is projected on to demons in the case of taboo of the dead. The explanation of taboo also throws light on the nature and origin of conscience: that conscience arose also on the basis of emotional ambivalence and under the same conditions, (that one of the opposing feelings involved shall be unconscious and kept under repression by the compulsive domination of the other one). Violation of taboo among primitive peoples results in punishment of whoever was responsible for violating the taboo while in obsessional neuroses performance of the forbidden act causes punishment of a person other than the one committing the act. What actually happens in the latter case is that the original wish that the loved person may die is replaced by the fear that he may die, thus giving a neurosis that is compensating for an underlying contrary attitude of brutal egoism. The neuroses are asocial structures; they endeavour to achieve by private means what is effected in society by collective effort. Taboo observances, like neurotic symptoms, have this double sense.

1912X   13/75
Totem and taboo (1913). Part III. Animism, magic and the omnipotence of thoughts. (1). Animism. (2). Magic.

The psychoanalytic approach states that it is not to be supposed that men were inspired to create their first system of the universe by pure speculative curiosity. The practical need for controlling the world around them must have played its part. Sorcery is essentially the art of influencing spirits by treating them in the same way as one would treat men in like circumstances: appeasing them, making amends to them, propitiating them, intimidating them, robbing them of their power, subduing them to one's will, etc. Magic, on the other hand, is something different: fundamentally, it disregards

spirits and makes use of special procedures and not of everyday psychological methods. Magic has to serve the most varied purposes: it must subject natural phenomena to the will of man, it must protect the individual from his enemies and from dangers, and it must give him power to injure his enemies. One of the most widespread magical procedures for injuring an enemy is by making an effigy of him from any convenient material. Whatever is then done to the effigy is believed to happen to the detested original. There is another procedure by which an enemy can be injured. One gets possession of some of his hair or nails or other waste products or even a piece of his clothing, and treats them in some hostile way. The principle governing magic, the technique of the animistic mode of thinking, is the principle of the omnipotence of thought.

1912X   13/85
Totem and taboo (1913). Part III. Animism, magic, omnipotence of thoughts. (3). Omnipotence of thoughts. (4). Totemism is a system.

In obsessional neuroses the survival of the omnipotence of thoughts (strange and uncanny events which pursue) is most clearly visible. The primary obsessive acts of neurotics are of an entirely magical character. In primitive man, the process of thinking is sexualized; this attitude may plausibly be brought into relation with narcissism and be regarded as an essential component of it. In only a single field of our civilization, art, has the omnipotence of thoughts being retained. The first picture which man formed of the world, animism, was a psychological one. The technique of animism, magic, reveals in the clearest and most unmistakable way an intention to impose the laws governing mental life upon real things; in this, spirits need not as yet play any part, though spirits may be taken as objects of magical treatment. Spirits and demons are only projections of man's own emotional impulses. He turns his emotional cathexes into persons, he peoples the world with them and meets his internal mental processes again outside himself. Thus man's first theoretical achievement, the creation of spirits, seems to have arisen from the observances of taboo. With primitive man, superstition need not be the only or the real reason for some particular custom or observance and does not excuse us from the duty of searching for its hidden motives. Under the domination of an animistic system it is inevitable that every observance and every activity shall have a systematic basis, which we now describe as superstitious.

1912X   13/100
Totem and taboo (1913). Part IV. The return of totemism in childhood: (1). The nature of totemism.

The return of totemism in childhood is discussed. A totem is a class of material objects which a savage regards with superstitious respect, believing that there exists between him and every member of the class an intimate and special relation. There are at least 3 kinds of totems: 1) the clan totem, common to a whole clan, and passing by inheritance from generation to generation; 2) the sex totem, common either to all the males or to all the females of a tribe, to the exclusion in either case of the other sex; and 3) the individual totem, belonging to a single individual and not passing to his descendants. The clan expects to receive protection and care from its totem. The appearance of the totem in or about a house is often regarded as an omen of death. In particularly important circumstances the clansman seeks to emphasize his kinship with the totem by making himself resemble it externally by dressing in the skin of an animal, by incising a picture of the totem upon his own body, etc. The social aspect of totemism is principally expressed in a severely enforced injunction and a sweeping restriction. The members of a totem clan are brothers and sisters and are bound to help and protect one another. The corresponding taboo restriction prohibits members of the same clan from marrying or having sexual intercourse with each other. If we seek to penetrate to the original nature of totemism, we find that its essential characteristics are these: originally, all totems were animals, and were regarded as the ancestors of the different clans. Totems were inherited only through the female line. There was a prohibition against killing the totem. Members of a totem clan were forbidden to practice sexual intercourse with one another.

1912X   13/108

Taboo and totem (1913). Part IV. The return of totemism in children. (2). The origin of totemism; the origin of exogamy and its relation to totemism.

The published theories on the origin of totemism are divided into 3 groups: the nominalist, the sociological, and the psychological. Some of the explanations of totemism exclude any connection with exogamy, so that the 2 institutions fall completely apart. There are 2 opposing views: one which seeks to maintain the original presumption that exogamy forms an inherent part of the totemic system, and the other which denies that there is any such connection and holds that the convergence between these 2 features of the oldest cultures is a chance one. Most of the authorities agree that totemism is older than exogamy. The view which explains horror of incest as an innate instinct must be abandoned. Not only must the prohibition against incest be older than any domestication of animals which might have enabled men to observe the effects of inbreeding upon racial characters, but even today the detrimental results of inbreeding are not established with certainty and cannot easily be demonstrated in man.

1912X   13/126

Totem and taboo (1913). Part IV. The return of totemism in childhood. (3). Animal phobias. (4). Sacrificial feasts.

There is a great deal of resemblance between the relations of children and of primitive men towards animals. Not infrequently, a strange rift occurs in the excellent relations between children and animals. A child will suddenly begin to be frightened of some particular species of animal and to avoid touching or seeing any individual of that species. This is due to a displacement of affect. Analysis is able to trace the associative paths along which the displacement passes, both the fortuitous paths and those with a significant content. Analysis also enables us to discover the motives for the displacement. It may be said that in these children's phobias some of the features of totemism reappear, but reversed into their negative. If the totem animal is the father, then the 2 principal ordinances of totemism, the 2 taboo prohibitions which constitute its core, not to kill the totem and not to have sexual relations with a woman of the same totem, coincide in their content with the 2 crimes of Oedipus, who killed his father and married his mother, as well as with the 2 primal wishes of children, the insufficient repression or the reawakening of which forms the nucleus of perhaps every psychoneurosis. The sacramental killing and communal eating of the totem animal, whose consumption is forbidden on all other occasions, is an important feature of totemic religion.

1912X   13/140

Totem and taboo (1913). Part IV. The return of totemism in childhood. (5), (6). Relation of totem meals to father and God.

A festival is a permitted, or rather an obligatory, excess, a solemn breach of a prohibition. It is not that men commit the excess because it is of the essence of a festival; the festive feeling is produced by the liberty to do what is as a rule prohibited. The clansmen acquire sanctity by consuming the totem. Psychoanalysis has revealed that the totem animal is in reality a substitute for the father; and this tallies with the contradictory fact that, though the killing of the animal is as a rule forbidden, yet its killing is a festive occasion, with the fact that it is killed and yet mourned. Psychoanalysis requires us to assume that totemism and exogamy were intimately connected and had a simultaneous origin. The ancient totem meal recurs in the original form of sacrifice. It is supposed that the god himself was the totem animal, and that he developed out of it at a later state of religious feeling. As time went on, the animal lost its sacred character and the sacrifice lost its connection with the totem feast; it became a simple offering to the deity, an act of renunciation in favor of the god. We can trace through the ages the identity of the totem meal with animal sacrifice, with the anthropic human sacrifice and with the Christian Eucharist, and we can recognize in all these rituals the effect of the crime by which men were so deeply weighted down but of which they must none the less have felt so proud. The Christian communion, however, is essentially a fresh elimination of the father, a repetition of the guilty deed.

1912X 13/155
Totem and Taboo (1913). Part IV. Return of totemism in childhood. (7). Oedipus complex and society.

An event such as the elimination of the primal father by the company of his sons must inevitably have left ineradicable traces in the history of humanity; and the less it itself was recollected, the more numerous must have been the substitutes to which it gave rise. The beginnings of religion, morals, society, and art converge in the Oedipus complex. This is in complete agreement with the psychoanalytic findings that the same complex constitutes the nucleus of all neuroses, so far as our present knowledge goes. It seems that the problems of social psychology should prove soluble on the basis of one single concrete point: man's relation to his father. No one can have failed to observe that the existence of a collective mind is taken as the basis of the position. It is supposed that the sense of guilt for an action has persisted for many thousands of years and has remained operative in generations which can have had no knowledge of that action. Without the assumption of a collective mind, social psychology in general cannot exist. Another difficulty might actually be brought forward from psychoanalytic quarters. The earliest moral precepts and restrictions in a primitive society have been explained as reactions to a deed which gave those who performed it the concept of crime. They felt remorse for the deed and decided that it should never be repeated. This creative sense of guilt still persists among us.

1913J 13/165
The claims of psycho-analysis to scientific interest (1913). Part I. The psychological interest of psycho-analysis.

Psychoanalysis is a medical procedure which aims at the cure of certain forms of nervous disease (the neuroses) by a psychological technique. There are a large number of phenomena related to facial and other expressive movements and to speech, as well as many processes of thought, which have hitherto escaped the notice of psychology. What Freud means are parapraxes, haphazard actions and dreams in normal people, and convulsive attacks, deliria, visions, and obsessive ideas or acts in neurotic subjects. The commonest motive for suppressing an intention is the avoidance of unpleasure. The explanation of parapraxes owes its theoretical value to the ease with which they can be solved and their frequency in normal people. The interpretation of dreams brought psychoanalysis into conflict with official science. Medical research explains dreams as purely somatic phenomena. Psychoanalysis has demonstrated that all dreams have a meaning. Psychoanalysis raises the status of dreams into that of psychical acts possessing meaning and purpose, and having a place in the subject's mental life, and thus disregards their strangeness, incoherence, and absurdity. Dream work brings about the distortion which makes the dream thoughts unrecognizable in the content of the dream. All dreams involve wish fulfillment. The dream work compels us to assume the existence of an unconscious psychical activity which is more comprehensive and more important than the familiar activity that is linked with consciousness. Psychoanalysis ascribes the primacy in mental life to affective processes, and it reveals an unexpected amount of affective disturbance and blinding of the intellect, in normal, no less than in sick people.

1913J 13/176
The claims of psycho-analysis to scientific interest (1913). Part II. The claims of psycho-analysis to the interest of the non-psychological sciences. (A), (B), (C). The philological, philosophical and biological interest of psychoanalysis.

The interpretation of dreams is analogous to the decipherment of an ancient pictographic script. In both cases there are certain elements which are not intended to be interpreted but are only designed to serve as determinatives, that is to establish the meaning of some other element. The language of dreams may be looked upon as the method by which unconscious mental activity expresses itself. Philosophy will be unable to avoid taking the psychoanalytic contributions to psychology fully into account and reacting to this new enrichment in our knowledge. Psychoanalysis can indicate the subjective and individual motives behind philosophical theories which have ostensibly sprung from impartial logical work, and can draw a critic's attention to the weak spots in the system. Psychoanalysis has done justice to the sexual function in man by making a detailed examination of its importance in mental and practical life. Sexual interests and activities are present in the human child at almost every age and from the first. The normal sexuality of adults emerges from infantile sexuality by a series of developments, combinations, divisions and suppressions, which are scarcely ever achieved with ideal perfection and consequently leave behind predispositions to a retrogression of the function in the form of illness.

1913J   13/182
The claims of psycho-analysis to scientific interest (1913). Part II. The claims of psycho-analysis to the interest of the non-psychological sciences. (D). The interest of psycho-analysis from a developmental point of view. (E), (F), (G), (H).

Psychoanalysis has been obliged to derive the mental life of adults from that of children, and has had to take seriously the old saying that the child is father to the man. Some notable discoveries have been made in the course of the investigation of the infantile mind including the extraordinarily important influence exerted by the impressions of childhood on the whole course of later development. In spite of all the later development that occurs in the adult, none of the infantile mental formations perish. It seems quite possible to apply the psychoanalytic views derived from dreams to products of ethnic imagination such as myths and fairy tales. Psychoanalysis has established an intimate connection between psychical achievements of individuals and societies by postulating one and the same dynamic source for both of them. The principal function of the mental mechanism is to relieve the individual from the tensions created in him by his needs. An investigation of primitive peoples shows mankind in a childish belief in its own omnipotence. Art constitutes a region halfway between a reality which frustrates wishes and the wish fulfilling world of the imagination, a region in which, as it were, primitive man's strivings for omnipotence are still in full force. Social feelings (the emotional basis of the relation of the individual to society) invariably contain an erotic element. In general, the neuroses are asocial in their nature. They always aim at driving the individual out of society and at replacing the safe monastic seclusion of earlier days by the isolation of illness. Psychoanalysis fully demonstrates the part played by social conditions and requirements in the causation of neurosis. Psychoanalysis has brought to light the wishes, the thought structures, and the developmental processes of childhood, thus allowing better insight into educational methods. When educators become familiar with the findings of psychoanalysis they will not overestimate the importance of the socially unserviceable or perverse instinctual impulses which emerge in children but will refrain from forcibly suppressing such impulses (knowing that suppression often results in worse results). To forcibly suppress these impulses results in repression, which establishes a predisposition to later nervous illness.

1913H   13/193
Observations and examples from analytic practice (1913).

Observations and examples from analytic practice are presented. Twenty-two different dreams are presented.

They include: a dream with an unrecognized precipitating cause; the time of day in dreams which stands for the age of the dreamer at some particular period in his childhood; the representation of ages in dreams; the position when waking from a dream; 2 rooms (the female genitals) being made into 1 room; an overcoat as a symbol for a man; disgraced feet (shoes); considerations of representability; dreams about dead people; fragmentary dreams; self-criticism by neurotics; and the appearance in the dream of the symptoms of the illness.

1914A   13/201
Fausse reconnaissance ('deja raconte') in psycho-analytic treatment (1914).

It not infrequently happens in the course of an analytic treatment that the patient, after reporting some fact that he has remembered, will go on to say that he has already said that, while the analyst himself feels sure that this is the first time he has heard the story. The explanation of this frequent occurrence appears to be that the patient really had an intention of giving this information, that once or even several times he actually made some remark leading up to it, but that he was then prevented by resistance from carrying out his purpose, and afterwards confused a recollection of his intention with a recollection of its performance. The phenomenon presented by the patient in cases like this deserves to be called a *fausse reconnaissance*, and is completely analogous to what occurs in certain other cases and has been described as a *deja vu*. There is another kind of *fausse reconnaissance* which not infrequently makes its appearance at the close of a treatment. After he has succeeded in forcing the repressed event upon the patient's acceptance in the teeth of all resistances, and has succeeded, as it were, in rehabilitating it, the patient may say that he now feels as though he had known it all the time. With this, the work of the analysis has been completed.

1914B   13/209
The Moses of Michelangelo (1914). Part I. Description of critics.

Descriptions by various critics of the Moses of Michelangelo, a fragment of the gigantic tomb which the artist was to have erected for the powerful Pope Julius the Second, is presented. There is not the slightest doubt that it represents Moses holding the Tables of the Ten Commandments. Moses is represented as seated; his body faces forward, his head with its mighty beard looks to the left, his right foot rests on the ground and his left leg is raised so that only the toes touch the ground. The facial expression of Moses is characterized as showing a mixture of wrath, pain, and contempt. A majority of critics describe the statue as the descent from Mount Sinai, where Moses has received the Tables from God, and it is the moment when he perceives that the people are rejoicing around the Golden Calf. The figure of Moses cannot be supposed to be springing to his feet; but is in sublime repose like the other figures and like the proposed statue of the Pope. Without the display of the emotions of anger, contempt and pain it would not have been possible to portray the nature of a superman of this kind. Michelangelo has created, not a historical figure, but a character type, embodying an inexhaustible inner force which tames the recalcitrant world; and he has given a form not only to the Biblical narrative of Moses, but to his own inner experiences, and to his impressions both of the individuality of Julius himself, and also, of the underlying springs of Savonarola's perpetual conflicts.

1914B   13/222
The Moses of Michelangelo (1914). Part II. Freud's description.

In 2 places in the figure of Moses there are certain details which have hitherto not only escaped notice but have not even been properly described. These are the attitude of his right hand and the position of the 2 Tables of the Law. The thumb of the hand is concealed and the index finger alone is in effective contact with the beard. It is pressed so deeply against the soft masses of hair that they bulge out beyond it both above and below. We have assumed that the right hand was, to begin with, away from the beard; that then it reached across to the left of the figure in a moment of great emotional tension and seized the beard; that it was finally drawn back again, taking a part of the beard with it. There are some difficulties involved in this interpretation since the right hand is responsible for the tables which are upside down. The Tables are stood on their heads and practically balanced on one corner. The upper edge is straight, the lower one has a protuberance like a horn on the part nearest the viewer, and the Tables touch the stone seat precisely with this protuberance. It is to prevent the Tables from hitting the ground that the right hand retreated, let go the beard, a part of which was drawn back with it unintentionally, came against the upper edge of the Tables in time and held them near the hind corner, which had now come uppermost. Thus the singularly constrained air of the whole, beard, hand, and tilted Tables, can be traced to that one passionate movement of the hand and its natural consequences.

1914B   13/229
1927B
The Moses of Michelangelo (1914). Part III, IV, and postscript.

In his first transport of fury, Moses desired to act, to spring up and take vengeance and forget the Tables; but he has overcome the temptation, and he will not remain seated and still, in his frozen wrath and in his pain mingled with contempt. Nor will he throw away the Tables so that they will break on the stones, for it is on their especial account that he has controlled his anger; it was to preserve them that he kept his passion in check. As our eyes travel down it, the figure exhibits 3 distinct emotional strata. The lines of the face reflect the feelings which have won the ascendancy; the middle of the figure shows the traces of suppressed movement; and the foot still retains the attitude of the projected action. The Moses of legend and tradition had a hasty temper and was subject to fits of passion. But Michelangelo placed a different Moses on the tomb of the Pope, one superior to the historical or traditional Moses. In his creations Michelangelo has often enough gone to the utmost limit of what is expressible in art; and perhaps in his statue of Moses he has not completely succeeded, if his purpose was to make the passage of a violent gust of passion visible in the signs left behind it in the ensuing calm.

1914F   13/241
Some reflections on schoolboy psychology (1914).

Some reflections on schoolboy psychology are presented. Psychoanalysis has taught that the individual's emotional attitudes to other people, which are of such extreme importance to his later behavior, are already established at an unexpectedly early age. The nature and quality of the human child's relations to people of his own and the opposite sex have already been laid down in the first 6 years of his life. Of all the images of a childhood which, as a rule, is no longer remembered, none is more important for a youth or a man than that of his father. In the second half of childhood, a change sets in in the boy's relation to his father. He finds that his father is no longer the mightiest, wisest, and richest of beings. It is in this pahse of a youth's development that he comes into contact with his teachers. These men, not all of whom were in fact fathers themselves, become the substitute fathers. That was why, even though they were still quite young, they struck us as so mature and so unattainably adult.

VOL. XIV A History of the Psycho-Analytic Movement, Papers on Metapsychology and Other Works (1914–1916)

1914D   14/3
On the history of the psycho-analytic movement (1914). Editor's note (1957).

The History of the Psychoanalytic Movement was written in 1914. The aim of the paper was to state clearly the fundamental postulates and hypotheses of psychoanalysis, to show that the theories of Adler and

Jung were totally incompatible with them, and to draw the inference that it would lead to nothing but general confusion if these contradictory sets of views were all given the same name. In order to make the essential principles of psychoanalysis perfectly plain, Freud traced the history of their development from their preanalytic beginnings.

1914D 14/7

On the history of the psycho-analytic movement (1914). Part I. Early history. Freud working alone.

Psychoanalysis is Freud's creation; for 10 years he was the only person who concerned himself with it, and all the dissatisfaction which the new phenomenon aroused in his contemporaries has been poured out in the form of criticisms on his head. In 1909, in the lecture room of an American University, Freud had his first opportunity of speaking in public about psychoanalysis. The theory of repression is the corner stone on which the whole structure of psychoanalysis rests. It is the most essential part of it; and yet it is nothing but a theoretical formulation of a phenomenon which may be observed as often as one pleases if one undertakes an analysis of a neurotic without resorting to hypnosis. In such cases, one comes across a resistance which opposes the work of analysis and in order to frustrate it pleads a failure of memory. The history of psychoanalysis proper, therefore, only begins with the new technique that dispenses with hypnosis. The theoretical consideration of the fact that this resistance coincides with an amnesia leads inevitably to the view of unconscious mental activity which is peculiar to psychoanalysis and which, too, distinguishes it quite clearly from philosophical speculation about the unconscious. It may be said that the theory of psychoanalysis is an attempt to account for 2 striking and unexpected facts of observation which emerge whenever an attempt is made to trace the symptoms of a neurotic back to their sources in his past life: the facts of transference and of resistance. Another product of psychoanalytic work is the hypothesis of infantile sexuality, a theoretical inference legitimately drawn from innumberable observations. At first, Freud felt that patients' descriptions of infantile sexual traumas were based on reality, only later finding that such traumatic scenes were usually created in phantasy (becoming part of psychic reality).

1914D 14/25

On the history of the psycho-analytic movement (1914). Part II. The early psychoanalytic movement.

From the year 1902 onwards, a number of young doctors gathered round Freud with the express intention of learning, practicing and spreading the knowledge of psychoanalysis. The small circle soon expanded, and in

the course of the next few years often changed its composition. In 1907, it appeared that psychoanalysis had unobtrusively awakened interest and gained friends, and that there were even some scientific workers who were ready to acknowledge it. Freud repeatedly acknowledged with gratitude the great services rendered by the Zurich School of Psychiatry in the spread of psychoanalysis, particularly by Bleuler and Jung. In Jung's work on occult phenomena, published in 1902, there was already an allusion to Freud's book on dream interpretation. In the years following 1907, when the schools of Vienna and Zurich were united, psychoanalysis made the extraordinary surge forward of which the momentum is felt even today; this is shown by the spread of psychoanalytic literature and by the constant increase in the number of doctors who are practicing or studying it, as well as by the frequency of the attacks made on it at Congresses and in learned societies. Hand in hand with the expansion of psychoanalysis in space went an expansion in content; it extended from the field of the neuroses and psychiatry to other fields of knowledge. Another path led from the investigation of dreams to the analysis of works of imagination and ultimately to the analysis of their creators.

1914D 14/42

On the history of the psycho-analytic movement (1914). Part III. Departures of Jung and Adler.

Two years after the first private Congress of psychoanalysis, the second took place at Nuremberg in March, 1910. Freud considered it necessary to form an official association because he feared the abuses to which psychoanalysis would be subjected as soon as it became popular. At this Congress, 3 local groups were constituted: one in Berlin, under the chairmanship of Abraham; one in Zurich, whose head had become the President of the whole Association; and one in Vienna, the direction of which Freud made over to Adler. Two secessions took place which caused Freud unhappiness: Adler and Jung. The Adlerian theory was a system which emphasized the egoistic constituent in libidinal instinctual impulses. Adler's secession took place before the Weimar Congress in 1911. In 1912, Jung boasted that his modifications of psychoanalysis had overcome the resistances of many people. Jung's arguments rest on the optimistic assumption that the progress of the human race has always pursued an unbroken line. The development of the periodicals devoted to psychoanalysis was traced. The first was a series of monographs entitled *Papers on Applied Mental Science;* the second was the *Yearbook for Psychoanalytic and Psychopathological Researches;* the third was the *International Journal for Medical Psychoanalysis* and the fourth was *Imago.* The first task confronting psychoanalysis was to explain the neuroses; it used the 2 facts of resistance and transference as starting points, and, taking into consideration the third fact of amnesia, accounted for them with its theories of repression, sexual motive forces in neurosis, and the unconscious.

1914C 14/67

On narcissism: an introduction (1914). Editor's note. (1957).

On Narcissism: an Introduction is among the most important of Freud's writings and may be regarded as one of the pivots in the evolution of his views. It sums up his earlier discussions on the subject of narcissism and considers the place taken by narcissism in sexual development; but it goes far beyond this. For it enters into the deeper problems of the relations between the ego and external objects, and it draws the new distinction between ego libido and object libido. Furthermore, most important of all, perhaps, it introduces the concepts of the ego ideal and of the self-observing agency related to it, which were the basis of what was ultimately to be described as the super ego. In addition to all this, at 2 points in the paper it touches upon the controversies with Adler and Jung. One of Freud's motives in writing this paper was, no doubt, to show that the concept of narcissism offers an alternative to Jung's nonsexual libido and to Adler's masculine protest.

1914C 14/73

On narcissism: an introduction (1914). Part I. Discussion of narcissism in various conditions.

The term narcissism is derived from clinical description and was chosen by Paul Nacke in 1899 to denote the attitude of a person who treats his own body in the same way in which the body of a sexual object is ordinarily treated. Psychoanalytic observers were subsequently struck by the fact that individual features of the narcissistic attitude are found in many people who suffer from other disorders; it seemed probable that an allocation of the libido such as described as narcissism might be present far more extensively, and that it might claim a place in the regular course of human sexual development. A pressing motive for occupying ourselves with the conception of a primary and normal narcissism arose when the attempt was made to subsume what we know of dementia parecox or schizophrenia under the hypotheses of the libido theory. The extension of the libido theory receives reinforcement from our observations and views on the mental life of children and primitive peoples. A unity comparable to the ego cannot exist in the individual from the start; the ego has to be developed. The autoerotic instincts, however, are there from the first; so there must be something added to autoeroticism, a new psychical action, in order to bring about narcissism. Freud concluded that we may repudiate Jung's assertion that the libido theory has come to grief in the attempt to explain dementia praecox, and that it is therefore disposed of for the other neuroses as well.

1914C 14/82

On narcissism: an introduction (1914). Part II. Narcissism in organic disease, hypochondria, and erotic life.

Certain special difficulties seem to lie in the way of a direct study of narcissism. The chief means of access to it will probably remain in the analysis of the paraphrenias. Hypochondria, like organic disease, manifests itself in distressing and painful bodily sensations, and it has the same effect as organic disease on the distribution of libido. The hypochondriac withdraws both interest and libido from the objects of the external world and concentrates both of them upon the organ that is engaging his attention. The difference between paraphrenic affections, and the transference neuroses appears to lie the circumstance that, in the former, the libido that is liberated by frustration does not remain attached to objects in phantasy, but withdraws on to the ego. Megalomania would accordingly correspond to the psychical mastering of this latter amount of libido, and would thus be the counterpart of the introversion on to phantasies that is found in the transference neuroses; a failure of this psychical function gives rise to the hypochondria of paraphrenia and this is homologous to the anxiety of the transference neuroses. Since paraphrenia frequently, if not usually, brings about only a partial detachment of the libido from objects, we can distinguish 3 groups of phenomena in the clinical picture: 1) those representing what remains of a normal state of neurosis; 2) those representing the morbid process; and 3) those representing restoration, in which the libido is once more attached to objects, after the manner of a hysteria, or of an obsessional neurosis.

1914C 14/92

On narcissism: an introduction (1914). Part III. Ego-ideal, inheritor of narcissism.

Psychoanalytic research has recognized the existence and importance of the masculine protest, but it has regarded it, in opposition to Adler, as narcissistic in nature and derived from the castration complex. We have learned that libidinal instinctual impulses undergo the vicissitude of pathogenic repression if they come into conflict with the subject's cultural and ethical ideas. For the ego, the formation of an ideal is the conditioning factor of repression. This ideal ego is the target of the self-love which was enjoyed in childhood by the actual ego. Sublimation is a process that concerns object libido and consists in the instinct's directing itself towards an other than sexual satisfaction. Idealization is a process that concerns the object; by it that object is aggrandized and exalted in the subject's mind. There is a special psychical agency which performs the task of seeing that narcissistic satisfaction from the ego ideal is ensured and constantly watches the actual ego and measures it by that ideal. Delusions of being watched present this power (watching, discovering, criticizing) in a regressive form, revealing the origin of the ego-ideal. Self-regard appears to be an expression of the size of the ego. The self-regarding attitude is discussed for normal and neurotic people. The relations of self-regard to erotism (libidinal object-cathexes) may be expressed after 2 cases are distinguished: whether the erotic cathexes are ego-syntonic or have suffered repression. The development of the ego consists in a departure from primary narcissism and gives rise to a vigorous attempt to recover that stage. This departure is brought about by means of the displacement of libido on to an ego ideal imposed from without; and satisfaction is brought about from fulfilling this ideal. The auxiliary relation of the sexual ideal to the ego ideal is discussed. The ego ideal binds not only a person's narcissistic libido, but also a considerable amount of his homosexual libido, which is in this way turned back into the ego.

14/105

Papers on metapsychology (1915). Editor's introduction (1957).

Freud published his first extended account of his views on psychological theory in the seventh chapter of *The Interpretation of Dreams*. The *5 Papers on Metapsychology* form an interconnected series. They were all written in a period of some 7 weeks between March 15 and May 4, 1915. He wrote 7 other papers, too, but they were never published and it seems probable that Freud destroyed them. The subjects with which 5 of the last 7 papers dealt were: consciousness, anxiety, conversion hysteria, obsessional neurosis, and the transference neuroses in general. The collection of 12 papers would have been a comprehensive one, dealing with the underlying processes in most of the principal neuroses and psychoses as well as in dreams, with the mental mechanisms of repression, sublimation, introjection, and projection, and with the 2 mental systems of consciousness and the unconscious.

1915C 14/111

Papers on metapsychology (1915). Instincts and their vicissitudes (1915). Editor's note (1957).

In *Instincts and their Vicissitudes*, Freud describes an instinct as a concept on the frontier between the mental

and the somatic, the psychical representative of the stimuli originating from within the organism and reaching the mind. In a number of passages, Freud expressed his dissatisfaction with the state of psychological knowledge about the instincts. The instincts make their appearance at a comparatively late point in the sequence of his writings. But the instincts were there under other names. Their place was taken, to a great extent, by such things as excitations, affective ideas, wishful impulses, endogenous stimuli, and so on.

1915C 14/117

Papers on metapsychology (1915). Instincts and their vicissitudes (1915).

The vicissitudes of instincts are discussed. By the pressure of an instinct, we understand its motor factor, the amount of force or the measure of the demand for work which it represents. The aim of an instinct is in every instance satisfaction, which can only be obtained by removing the state of stimulation at the source of the instinct. The object of an instinct is the thing in regard to which or through which the instinct is able to achieve its aim. By the source of an instinct is meant the somatic process which occurs in an organ or part of the body and whose stimulus is represented in mental life by an instinct. The essential feature in the vicissitudes undergone by instincts lies in the subjection of the instinctual impulses to the influence of the 3 great polarities that dominate mental life. Of these 3 polarities, we might describe that of activity-passivity as the biological; that of ego-external world as real; and finally that of pleasure-unpleasure as the economic polarity.

1915D 14/141

Papers on metapsychology (1915). Repression (1915). Editor's note (1957).

In his *History of the Psychoanalytic Movement* Freud declared that the theory of repression is the cornerstone on which the whole structure of psychoanalysis rests. The concept of repression goes back historically to the very beginning of psychoanalysis. In the account given in the *Studies on Hysteria,* the term actually used to describe the process is not repression, but defense. The form of repression which Freud had chiefly in mind here was that which occurs in hysteria. The special problem of the nature of the motive force which puts repression into operation was one which was a constant source of concern to Freud, though it is scarcely touched on in the present paper. In particular, there was the question of the relation between repression and sex, and to this, Freud in his early days gave fluctuating replies. Subsequently, however, he firmly rejected any attempt at sexualizing repression.

1915D 14/146
Papers on metapsychology (1915). Repression (1915).

One of the vicissitudes an instinctual impulse may undergo is to meet with resistances which seek to make it inoperative. Under certain conditions, the impulse then passes into the state of repression. Repression is a preliminary stage of condemnation, something between flight and condemnation; it is a concept which could not have been formulated before the time of psychoanalytic studies. Repression does not arise in cases where the tension produced by lack of satisfaction of an instinctual impulse is raised to an unbearable degree. It has become a condition for repression that the motive force of unpleasure shall have acquired more strength than the pleasure obtained from satisfaction. Repression is not a defensive mechanism which is present from the beginning. The essence of repression lies simply in turning something away, and keeping it at a distance, from the conscious. We have reason to assume that there is a primal repression, a first phase of repression, which consists in the psychical representative of the instinct being denied entrance into the conscious. The second stage of repression, repression proper, affects conscious mental derivatives of the repressed representative, or such conscious trains of thought as, originating elsewhere, have come into associative connection with it. The motive and purpose of repression is nothing else than the avoidance of unpleasure. The mechanism of repression does not coincide with the mechanisms of forming substitutes. The mechanisms of repression have at least this one thing in common: a withdrawal of the cathexis of energy.

1915E 14/159
Papers on metapsychology (1915). The unconscious (1915). Editor's note (1957).

The concept of the existence of unconscious mental processes is one that is fundamental to psychoanalytic theory. Freud was never tired of insisting upon the arguments in support of it and combating the objections to it. Freud's interest in the assumption was never a philosophical one; his interest was a practical one. He found that without making that assumption, he was unable to explain or even to describe a large variety of phenomena which he came across. By making that assumption, he found the way open to an immensely fertile region of fresh knowledge. In *The Interpretation of Dreams*, the unconscious was established once and for all.

1915E 14/166
Papers on metapsychology (1915). The unconscious (1915). Chapter I. Justification for the concept of the unconscious.

We have learned from psychoanalysis that the essence of the process of repression lies, not in putting an end to the idea which represents an instinct, but in preventing it from becoming conscious. When this happens we say of the idea that it is in a state of being unconscious. The assumption of the existence of something mental that is unconscious is necessary and legitimate. It is necessary because the data of consciousness have a very large number of gaps in them; both in healthy and in sick people, psychical acts often occur which can be explained only by presupposing other acts, of which nevertheless, consciousness affords no evidence. At any given moment consciousness includes only a small content, so that the greater part of what we call conscious knowledge must be, for very considerable periods of time, in a state of latency, that is to say, of being psychically unconscious. The assumption of an unconscious is, moreover, a perfectly legitimate one, inasmuch as in postulating it, we are not departing a single step from our customary and generally accepted mode of thinking. In psychoanalysis there is no choice for us but to assert that mental processes are in themselves unconscious, and to liken the perception of them by means of consciousness to the perception of the external world by means of the sense organs.

1915E 14/172
Papers on metapsychology (1915). The unconscious (1915). Chapter II. Various meanings of 'The Unconscious'–The topographical point of view.

The attribute of being unconscious (Ucs) is only one feature that is found in the psychical and is by no means sufficient to characterize it fully. The unconscious comprises acts which are merely latent, temporarily unconscious, but which differ in no other respect from conscious ones. A psychical act goes through 2 phases as regards its state, between which is interposed a kind of testing (censorship). In the first place the psychical act is unconscious and belongs to the system Ucs; if, on testing, it is rejected by the censorship, it is not allowed to pass into the second phase; it is then said to be repressed and must remain unconscious. If, however, it passes this testing, it enters the second phase and henceforth belongs to the second system, the conscious (Cs) system. It is not yet conscious, but it is capable of becoming conscious. In consideration of this capacity for becoming conscious we also call the system Pcs the preconscious.

1915E 14/177

Papers on metapsychology (1915). The unconscious (1915). Chapter III. Unconscious emotions.

The antithesis of conscious and unconscious is not applicable to instincts. An instinct can never become an object of consciousness, only the idea that represents the instinct can. Even in the unconscious, moreover, an instinct cannot be represented otherwise than by an idea. If the instinct did not attach itself to an idea or manifest itself as an affective state we could know nothing about it. The use of the terms "unconscious affect" and "unconscious emotion" has reference to the vicissitudes undergone, in consequence of repression, by the quantitative factor in the instinctual impulse. We know that 3 such vicissitudes are possible: either the affect remains, wholly or in part, as it is; or it is transformed into a qualitatively different quota of affect, above all into anxiety; or it is suppressed, *i.e.*, it is prevented from developing at all. In every instance where repression has succeeded in inhibiting the development of affects, we term those affects (which we restore when we undo the work of repression) unconscious. It is possible for the development of affect to proceed directly from the unconscious system; in that case the affect always has the character of anxiety, for which all repressed affects are exchanged. Often, however, the instinctual impulse has to wait until it has found a substitutive idea in the conscious system. The development of affect can then proceed from this conscious substitute, and the nature of that substitute determines the qualitative character of the affect.

1915E 14/180

Papers on metapsychology (1915). The unconscious (1915). Chapter IV. Topography and dynamics of repression.

Repression is essentially a process affecting ideas on the border between the unconscious (Ucs) system and the preconscious (Pcs) or conscious (Cs). The idea either remains uncathected, or receives cathexis from the Ucs, or retains the Ucs cathexis which it already had. Freud proposed that when we have succeeded in describing a psychical process in its dynamic, topographical, and economic aspects, we should speak of it as a metapsychological presentation. In anxiety hysteria a first phase of the process is frequently overlooked, and may perhaps be in fact missed; on careful observation, however, it can be clearly discerned. It consists in anxieties appearing without the subject knowing what he is afraid of. In the second phase of anxiety hysteria, the anticathexis from the system Cs has led to substitute formation. The third phase repeats the work of the second on an ampler scale. The system Cs now protects itself against the activation of the substitutive idea by an anticathexis of its environment, just as previously it had

secured itself against the emergence of the repressed idea by a cathexis of the substitutive idea. A great deal of what we have found in anxiety hysteria also holds good for the other 2 neuroses. In conversion hysteria, the instinctual cathexis of the repressed idea is changed into the innervation of the symptom. As regards obsessional neurosis, the anticathexis from the system Cs comes most noticeably into the foreground.

1915E 14/186

Papers on metapsychology (1915). The unconscious (1915). Chapter V. The special characteristics of the system Ucs.

The nucleus of the unconscious (Ucs) system consists of instinctual representatives which seek to discharge their cathexis, the wishful impulses. There is, in this system no negation, no doubt, no degree of certainty: all this is only introduced by the work of the censorship between the Ucs and the preconscious (Pcs) system. Negation is a substitute, at a higher level, for repression. In the Ucs there are only contents, cathected with greater or lesser strength. The characteristics which we may expect to find in processes belonging to the system Ucs are: exemption from mutual contradiction, primary process (mobility of cathexes), timelessness, and replacement of external by psychical cathexes. Unconscious processes only become cognizable by us under the conditions of dreaming and of neurosis, when processes of the Pcs system are set back to an earlier stage by regression. The processes of the system Pcs display an inhibition of the tendency of cathected ideas towards discharge. It devolves upon the system Pcs to make communication possible between the different ideational contents so that they can influence one another, to give them an order in time, and to set up a censorship or serveral censorships.

1915E 14/190

Papers on metapsychology (1915). The unconscious (1915). Chapter VI. Communication between the two systems.

The unconscious (Ucs) system is continued into what are known as derivatives; it is accessible to the impressions of life, it constantly influences the preconscious (Pcs) system, and is even, for its part, subjected to influences from the Pcs. Among the derivatives of the Ucs instinctual impulses, there are some which unite in themselves characters of an opposite kind. On the one hand, they are highly organized, free from self-contradition, have made use of every acquisition of the conscious (Cs) system and would hardly be distinguished in our judgement from the formation of that system. On the other hand, they are unconscious and are incapable of becoming conscious. A very great part of this preconscious originates in the unconscious, has the character of its derivatives, and is subjected to a censorship before it can become conscious. The Ucs is turned back on the frontier of the Pcs, by censorship, but derivatives of the Ucs can circumvent this censorship, achieve a high degree of organization and reach a certain intensity of cathexis in the Pcs. When, however, this intensity is exceeded and they try to force themselves into consciousness, they are recognized as derivatives of the Ucs and are repressed afresh at the new frontier of censorship, between the Pcs and the Cs. Thus the first of these censorships is exercised against the Ucs itself, and the second against its Pcs derivatives.

1915E 14/196

Papers on metapsychology (1915). The unconscious (1915). Chapter VII. Assessment of the unconscious.

An assessment of the unconscious is presented. In schizophrenia, we observe a number of changes in speech. The patient often devotes peculiar care to his way of expressing himself. Some reference to bodily organs or innervation is often given prominence in the content of these remarks. In such symptoms of schizophrenia, as are comparable with the substitutive formations of hysteria or obsessional neurosis, the relation between the substitute and the repressed material nevertheless displays peculiarities which would surprise us in these 2 forms of neurosis. In schizophrenia, words are subjected to the same process as that which makes the dream images out of latent dream thoughts; to what we have called the primary psychical process. They undergo condensation, and by means of displacement transfer their cathexes to one another in their entirety. The character of strangeness of the substitutive formation in schizophrenia is the predominance of what has to do with words over what has to do with things. The conscious presentation comprises the presentation of the thing plus the presentation of the word belonging to it, while the unconscious presentation is the presentation of the thing alone.

1891B 14/205
1926G

Papers on metapsychology (1915). The unconscious (1915). Appendix A: Freud and Ewald Hering. Appendix B: Psycho-physical parallelism. Appendix C: Words and things.

Among Freud's seniors in Vienna was the physiologist Ewald Hering who offered the young man a post as his assistant at Prague in 1884. Hering's influence may have contributed to Freud's views on the unconscious. Freud's earlier views on the relation between the mind and the nervous system were greatly influenced by Hughlings Jackson. The chain of physiological events in the nervous system does not stand in a causal connection with the psychical events. The physiological events do not cease as soon as the psychical ones begin; on the contrary, the physiological chain continues. The final section of Freud's paper on the *The Unconscious* seems to have roots in his early monograph on aphasia (1891). We learn to speak by associating a sound image of a word with a sense of the innervation of a word. We learn to speak the language of other people by endeavoring to make the sound image produced by ourselves as like as possible to the one which gave rise to our speech innervation. We learn to spell by linking the visual images of the letters with new sound images, which for their part, must remind us of verbal sounds which we already know. We learn to read by linking up in accordance with certain rules the succession of innervatory and motor word presentations which we receive when we speak separate letters, so that new motor word presentations arise. There corresponds to the word a complicated associative process into which the elements of visual, acoustic, and kinesthetic origin enter together. A word, however, acquires its meaning by being linked to an object presentation.

1917D 14/219

Papers on metapsychology (1915). A metapsychological supplement to the theory of dreams (1917).

A *Metapsychological Supplement to the Theory of Dreams* resolves itself largely into a discussion of the effects produced by the state of sleep on the different systems of the mind. It is the study of dreams which has taught us what we know of the psychical characteristics of the state of sleep. Dreams only show us the dreamer in so far as he is not sleeping; nevertheless they are bound to reveal, at the same time, characteristics of sleep itself. A dream tells us that something was going on which tended to interrupt sleep, and it enables us to understand in what way it has been possible to fend off this interruption. A dream is, therefore, among other things, a projection: an externalization of an internal process. The narcissism of the state of sleep implies a withdrawal of cathexis from all ideas of objects, from both the unconscious and the preconscious portions of those ideas. The completion of the dream process consists in the thought content, regressively transformed and worded over into a wishful phantasy, becoming conscious as a sense perception; while this is happening it undergoes secondary revision, to which every perceptual concept is subject. The dream wish is hallucinated, and, as a hallucination, meets with belief in the reality of its fulfillment. Dreams are a residue of mental activity, made possible by the fact that the narcissistic stage of sleep has not been able to be completely established. In dreams, the withdrawal of cathexis affects all systems equally.

1917E 14/237

Papers on metapsychology (1915). Mourning and melancholia (1917). Editor's note. (1957).

Mourning and Melancholia may be regarded as an extension of the paper on narcissism which Freud had written a year earlier, in 1914. Just as that paper had described the workings of the critical agency in cases of paranoia, so this one sees the same agency in operation in melancholia. The implications of this paper were destined to be more important than the explanation of the mechanism of one particular pathological state, though those implications did not become immediately obvious. The material contained here led on to the further consideration of the critical agency; and this in turn led to the hypothesis of the superego and to a fresh assessment of the sense of guilt. Along another line, this paper called for an examination of the whole question of the nature of identification. Freud seems to have been inclined at first to regard it as closely associated with, and perhaps dependent on, the oral or cannibalistic phase of libidinal development. In *Mourning and Melancholia*, he speaks of identification as a preliminary stage of object choice, the first way in which the ego picks out an object and adds that the ego wants to incorporate this object into itself, and, in accordance with the oral or cannibalistic phase of libidinal development at which it is, it wants to do so by devouring it. What Freud seems later to have regarded as the most significant feature of this paper was, however, its account of the process by which in melancholia an object cathexis is replaced by an identification.

1917E 14/243

Papers on Metapsychology (1915). Mourning and melancholia (1917).

Melancholia, whose definition fluctuates even in descriptive psychiatry, takes on various clinical forms, the grouping together of which into a single unity does not seem to be established with certainty; and some of these forms suggest somatic rather than psychogenic affections. The correlation of melancholia and mourning seems justified by the general picture of the 2 conditions. Mourning is regularly the reaction to the loss of a loved person. In some people the same influences produce melancholia instead of mourning and we consequently suspect them of a pathological disposition. The distinguishing mental features of melancholia are a profoundly painful dejection, cessation of interest in the outside world, loss of the capacity to love, inhibition to all activity, and a lowering of the self-regarding feelings to a degree that finds utterance in self-reproaches and self-reviling, and culminates in a delusional expectation of punishment. The disturbance of self-regard is absent in mourning; but otherwise the features are the same. Melancholia borrows some of its features from

mourning, and the others from the process of regression from narcissistic object choice to narcissism. The most remarkable characteristic of melancholia is its tendency to change into mania. In mania the ego has recovered from loss of the object. This makes available all of the anticathexis which the painful suffering of melancholia has drawn to itself from the ego and bound. The accumulation of cathexis which is at first bound and then, after the work of melancholia is finished, becomes free and makes mania possible must be linked with regression of the libido to narcissism.

1915F 14/261

A case of paranoia running counter to the psycho-analytic theory of the disease (1915).

A case of paranoia running counter to the psychoanalytic theory of the disease is presented. A lawyer consulted Freud about a case which had raised some doubts in his mind. A young woman had asked him to protect her from the molestations of a man who had drawn her into a love affair. She declared that this man had abused her confidence by getting unseen witnesses to photograph them while they were making love, and that by exhibiting these pictures it was now in his power to bring disgrace on her and force her to resign the post she occupied. The view had already been put forward in psychoanalytic literature that patients suffering from paranoia are struggling against an intensification of their homosexual trends, a fact pointing back to a narcissistic object choice. And a further interpretation had been made: that the persecutor is at bottom someone whom the patient loves or has loved in the past. The girl seemed to be defending herself against love for a man by directly transforming the lover into a persecutor: there was no sign of the influence of a woman, no trace of a struggle against a homosexual attachment. She later revealed that her department in the business was under the direction of an elderly lady whom she described as like her mother. The white-haired elderly superior was a substitute for her mother. In spite of his youth, her lover had been put in the place of her father. It was the strength of her mother complex which had driven the patient to suspect a love relationship between these ill-matched partners, however unlikely such a relationship might be.

1915B 14/275

Thoughts for the times on war and death (1915). Chapter I. The disillusionment of the war.

In the confusion of wartime in which we are caught up, relying as we must on one-sided information, standing too close to the great changes that have already taken place or are beginning to, and without a glimmering of the future that is being shaped, we ourselves are at a loss as to the significance of the impressions which press in upon us and as to the value of the judgments which we form. We cannot but feel that no event has ever destroyed so much that is precious in the common possessions of humanity, confused so many of the clearest intelligences, or so thoroughly debased what is highest. The individual who is not himself a combatant feels bewildered in his orientation, and inhibited in his powers and activities. Two things in this war have aroused our sense of disillusionment: the low morality shown externally by states which in their internal relations pose as the guardians of moral standards, and the brutality shown by individuals whom, as participants in the highest human civilization, one would not have thought capable of such behavior.

1915B 14/289
1915G
Thoughts for the times on war and death (1915). Chapter II. Our attitude towards death. Appendix: Letter to Dr. Frederik Van Eeden.

Our attitude towards death is discussed. To anyone who listened to us, we were prepared to maintain that death was the necessary outcome of life, that everyone owes nature a death and must expect to pay the debt. In reality, however, we were accustomed to behave as if it were otherwise. We showed an unmistakable tendency to put death on one side, to eliminate it from life. The civilized adult can hardly entertain the thought of another person's death without seeming to himself hardhearted or wicked. This attitude of ours towards death has a powerful effect on our lives. Life is impoverished, it loses in interest, when the highest stake in the game of living, life itself, may not be risked. It is evident that war is bound to sweep away this conventional treatment of death. Death will no longer be denied; we are forced to believe in it. People really die; and no longer one by one, but many, often tens of thousands, in a single day. Death is no longer a chance event. Our unconscious is just as inaccessible to the idea of our own death, just as murderously inclined towards strangers, just as divided (that is, ambivalent) towards those we love, as was primeval man. But how far we have moved from this primal state in our conventional and cultural attitude towards death. War strips us of the latter accretions of civilization, and lays bare the primal man in each of us.

1916A 14/303
On transience (1916).

Transience is discussed. The proneness to decay of all that is beautiful and perfect can give rise to 2 different impulses in the mind. The one leads to the aching despondency felt by the young poet, while the other leads to rebellion against the fact asserted. Transience value is scarcity value in time. Limitation in the

possibility of an enjoyment raises the value of the enjoyment. Mourning over the loss of something that we have loved or admired seems so natural to the layman that he regards it as self-evident. But to psychologists, mourning is a great riddle, one of those phenomena which cannot themselves be explained but to which other obscurities can be traced back. Mourning comes to a spontaneous end. When it has renounced everything that has been lost, then it has consumed itself, and our libido is once more free to replace the lost objects by fresh ones equally or still more precious.

1916D 14/311
Some character-types met with in psycho-analytic work (1916). Chapter I. The 'exceptions'.

Some character types met with in psychoanalytic work are discussed. Psychoanalytic work is continually confronted with the task of inducing the patient to renounce an immediate and directly attainable yield of pleasure. The patient is not asked to renounce all pleasure, only such satisfactions as will inevitably have detrimental consequences. There are individuals who resist such an appeal on a special ground. They say that they have renounced enough and suffered enough, and have a claim to be spared any further demands; they will submit no longer to any disagreeable necessity, for they are exceptions and, moreover, intend to remain so. There is a common peculiarity in the earlier experiences of these patients' lives. Their neuroses were connected with some experience or suffering to which they had been subjected in their earliest childhood, one in which they could look upon as an unjust disadvantage imposed upon them. The privileges that they claimed as a result of this injustice, and the rebelliousness it engendered, had contributed not a little to intensifying the conflicts leading to the outbreak of their neurosis.

1916D 14/316
Some character-types met with in psycho-analytic work (1916). Chapter II. Those wrecked by success.

Psychoanalytic work has furnished us with the thesis that people fall ill of a neurosis as a result of frustration. What is meant is the frustration of the satisfaction of their libidinal wishes. For a neurosis to be generated there must be a conflict between a person's libidinal wishes and his ego, which is the expression of his instinct of self-preservation and which also includes his ideals of his personality. Privation, frustration of a real satisfaction, is the first condition for the generation of a neurosis. There are some people who collapse on reaching success: One such person is Shakespeare's Lady Macbeth. An extensive analysis of Lady Macbeth is presented. The practicing psychoanalyst knows how frequently, or how invarably, a girl who enters a household as servant, companion or governess, will consciously or unconsciously weave a daydream, which derives from the Oedipus complex, of the mistress of the house disappearing and the master taking the newcomer as his wife in her place. Psychoanalytic work teaches that the forces of conscience which induce illness in consequence of success, instead of, as normally, in consequence of frustration, are closely connected with the Oedipus complex, the relation of father and mother, as perhaps is our sense of guilt in general.

1916D 14/332
Some character-types met with in psycho-analytic work (1916). Chapter III. Criminals from a sense of guilt.

In telling Freud about their early youth, particularly before puberty, people who have afterwards often become very respectable have informed him of forbidden actions which they committed at that time. Analytic work brought the surprising discovery that such deeds were done principally because they were forbidden, and because their execution was accompanied by mental relief for their doer. He was suffering from an oppressive feeling of guilt, of which he did not know the origin, and after he had committed a misdeed this oppression was mitigated. His sense of guilt was at least attached to something. These people might be described as criminals from a sense of guilt. The preexistence of the guilty feeling had been demonstrated by a whole set of other manifestations and effects. This obscure sense of guilt was derived from the Oedipus complex and was a reaction to the 2 great criminal intentions of killing the father and having sexual relations with the mother.

1916B 14/337
A mythological parallel to a visual obsession (1916).

A mythological parallel to a visual obsession is presented. In a patient of about 21 years, the products of unconscious mental activity became conscious not only in obsessive thoughts but also in obsessive images. The 2 could accompany each other or appear independently. At one particular time, whenever he saw his father entering the room, there came into his mind, in close connection, an obsessive word and an obsessive image. The word was father arse; the accompanying image represented his father as the naked lower part of a body, provided with arms and legs, but without the head or upper part. The genitals were not indicated, and the facial features were painted on the abdomen. Father arse was soon explained as a jocular Teutonizing of the honorific title of patriarch. The obsessive image is an obvious caricature. It recalls other representations which, with a derogatory end in view, replace a whole person by one of his organs; it reminds us, too, of unconscious phantasies which lead to the identification of the genitals with the whole person, and also of joking figures of speech, such as "I am all ears." According to a

Greek legend, Demeter came to Eleusis in search of her daughter after she had been abducted, and was given lodging by Dysaules and his wife Baubo; but in her great sorrow she refused to touch food or drink. Thereupon her hostess Baubo made her laugh by suddenly lifting up her dress and exposing her body. In the excavations at Priene in Asia Minor some terracottas were found which represented Baubo. They show the body of a woman without a head or chest and with a face drawn on the abdomen: the lifted dress frames the face like a crown of hair.

1916C 14/339
A connection between a symbol and a symptom (1916).

A connection between a symbol and a symptom is proposed. Experience in the analysis of dreams has sufficiently well established the hat as a symbol of the genital organ, most frequently of the male organ. In phantasies and in numerous symptoms the head too appears as a symbol of the male genitals. Patients suffering from obsessions express an amount of abhorrence of and indignation against punishment by beheading far greater than they do in the case of any other form of death; and in such cases the analyst may be led to explain to them that they are treating being beheaded as a substitute for being castrated. It may be that the symbolic meaning of the hat is derived from that of the head, in so far as a hat can be regarded as a prolonged, though detachable head. This leads to a symptom of obsessional neurotics: when they are in the street they are on the look-out to see whether some acquaintance will greet them first by taking off his hat (a meaning of abasement before the person saluted) or whether he seems to be waiting for their salutation. The neurotics' own sensitiveness on the subject of greeting therefore means that they are unwilling to show themselves less important than the other person thinks he is. The resistance of their sensitiveness to explanations suggests that a motive related to the castration complex is present.

1919J 14/341
Letter to Dr. Hermine Von Hug-Hellmuth (1919).

A letter to Dr. Hermine von Hug-Hellmuth is presented. The diary of a little girl shows clear and truthful views of the mental impulses that characterize the development of a girl in our social and cultural stratum during the years before puberty. We are shown how her feelings grow up out of a childish egoism till they reach social maturity; we learn what form is first assumed by her relations with her parents and with her brothers and sisters and how they gradually gain in seriousness and inward feeling; how friendships are made and broken; and how the secret of sexual life begins to dawn on her.

VOL. XV Introductory Lectures on Psycho-Analysis (Parts I and II) (1915–1916)

1916X 15/3
Introductory lectures on psycho-analysis (1916-17). Editor's introduction (1963) & prefaces (1917, 1930).

The *Introductory Lectures on Psychoanalysis* had a wider circulation than any of Freud's works except *The Psychopathology of Everyday Life*. Among Freud's works, it is predominantly the expository works that appear as lectures. The *Introductory Lectures* may be regarded as stock taking of Freud's views and the position of psychoanalysis at the time of the first World War. The secessions of Adler and Jung were already past history, the concept of narcissism was some years old, the epoch making case history of the Wolf Man had been written a year before the lectures began. In his preface to these lectures Freud speaks a little depreciatively of the lack of novelty in their contents. But no one, however well read in psychoanalytic literature, need feel afraid of being bored by them or could fail to find plenty in them that is not to be found elsewhere. The *Introductory Lectures* have thoroughly deserved their popularity. The *Introduction to Psychoanalysis* is not designed to compete in any way with such general accounts of this field of knowledge as are already in existence. The lectures were delivered in 1916 and 1917.

1916X 15/15
Introductory lectures on psycho-analysis (1916-17). Part I. Parapraxes (1916). Lecture I: Introduction.

Psychoanalysis is a procedure for the medical treatment of neurotic patients. In psychoanalysis, nothing takes place in treatment but an interchange of words between the patient and the analyst. The patient talks, tells of his past experiences and present impressions, complains, confesses to his wishes and his emotional impulses. The doctor listens, tries to direct the patient's processes of thought, exhorts, forces his attention in certain directions, gives him explanations and observes the reactions of understanding or rejection which he in this way provokes in him. It is true that psychoanalysis cannot easily be learned and there are not many people who have learned it properly. One learns psychoanalysis on oneself, by studying one's own personality. Psychoanalysis tries to give psychiatry its missing psychological foundation. It hopes to discover the common ground on the basis of which the convergence of physical and mental disorder will become intelligible. One of the unpopular assertions made by psychoanalysis is that mental processes are in themselves unconscious and that of all mental life, it is only certain individual acts and portions that are conscious. The second thesis which psychoanalysis puts forward as one of its findings, is an assertion that instinctual impulses which can only be described as sexual, both in the narrower and wider sense of the word, play an extremely large and never hitherto appreciated part in the causation of nervous and mental diseases.

1916X 15/25
Introductory lectures on psycho-analysis (1916-17). Part I. Parapraxes (1916). Lecture II: Parapraxes.

Everyone is liable to parapraxes. It may happen, for instance, that a person who intends to say something may use another word instead (a slip of the tongue), or he may do the same thing in writing, and may or may not notice what he has done. Another group of these phenomena has, as its basis, forgetting, not, however, a permanent forgetting but only a temporary one. In a third group the temporary character is absent, for instance in the case of mislaying. In addition to all this there are particular sorts of errors, in which the temporary character is present once more; for in their instance we believe for a time that something is the case which both before and afterwards we know is not so. A man who can usually speak correctly may make a slip of the tongue 1) if he is slightly indisposed and tired, 2) if he is excited, and 3) if he is too much occupied with other things. The most usual, and at the same time the most striking kinds of slips of the tongue, however, are those in which one says the precise opposite of what one intended to say. Included among the causes of parapraxes are relations between sounds, verbal similarity, and the influence of word associations. It has repeatedly happened that a creative writer has made use of a slip of the tongue or some other parapraxis as an instrument for producing an imaginative effect.

1916X 15/40
Introductory lectures on psycho-analysis (1916-17). Part I. Parapraxes (1916). Lecture III. Parapraxes (continued).

There are categories of cases of slips of the tongue in which the intention, the sense, of the slip is plainly visible. There are those in which what was intended is replaced by its contrary. In other cases, where the slip does not express the precise contrary, an opposite sense can be brought out by it. In other cases, the slip of the tongue merely adds a second sense to the one intended. Parapraxes are not chance events but serious mental acts; they have a sense; they arise from the concurrent action, or perhaps the mutually opposing action of 2 different intentions. Freud is inclined to think that this is the explanation of all cases of slips of the tongue. The forgetting of intentions can in general be traced to an opposing current of thought, which is unwilling to carry out the intention. A particularly ambiguous and obscure kind of parapraxis is losing and mislaying. We ourselves play an intentional part in what is so often the painful accident of losing something. Accumulated and combined parapraxes are the finest flower of their kind. An accumulation of these phenomena betrays an obstinacy that is scarcely ever a characteristic of chance events but fits in well with something intentional. The mutual interchangeability between different species of parapraxes demonstrates the important and characteristic meaning in parapraxes: the purpose which they serve and which can be achieved in the most various ways.

1916X 15/60

Introductory lectures on psycho-analysis (1916-17). Part I. Parapraxes (1916). Lecture IV: Parapraxes (concluded).

It is probably the case that every single parapraxis that occurs has a sense. Parapraxes are the product of mutual interference between 2 different intentions, of which one may be called the disturbing intention and the other the disturbed one. In a slip of the tongue the disturbing intention may be related in its content to the disturbed one, in which case it will contradict it or correct it or supplement it. Or, the content of the disturbing intention may have nothing to do with that of the disturbed one. Parapraxes are mental acts, in which we can detect sense and intention. They come about through mutual interference between 2 different intentions. One of these intentions must have been in some way forced back from being put into effect before it can manifest itself as a disturbance of the other intention. Slips of the pen are closely akin to slips of the tongue. Misreading is a psychical situation which differs from that in slips of the tongue or pen. The forgetting of intentions is unambiguous. Its interpretation is not disputed. The purpose which disturbs the intention is in every instance a counter intention, an unwillingness. The forgetting of proper names and foreign names, as well as of foreign words, can be traced back to a counter intention, which is aimed either directly or indirectly against the name concerned. The forgetting of impressions and experiences demonstrates the operation of the purpose of keeping disagreeable things out of memory. Losing and mislaying have in common the fact that there is a wish to lose something; they differ in the basis of that wish. Bungled actions, like other errors, are often committed to fulfill wishes which one ought to deny oneself.

1916X 15/83

Introductory lectures on psycho-analysis (1916-17). Part II. Dreams (1916). Lecture V: Difficulties and first approaches.

Dreams have become a subject of psychoanalytic research. One thing common to all dreams would seem to be that we are asleep during them. Dreaming is evidently mental life during sleep, something which has certain resemblances to waking mental life but which, on the other hand, is distinguished from it by large differences. A dream is the manner in which the mind reacts to stimuli that impinge upon it in the state of sleep. The stimuli can be either internal or external. Dreams do not simply reproduce the stimulus; they work it over, they make allusions to it, they include it in some context, they replace it by something else. Dreams are often senseless, confused, and absurd; but there are also sensible, matter of fact, and reasonable dreams. Daydreams are phantasies; they are very general phenomena, observable, in healthy as well as in sick people and are easily accessible to study in our own mind.

1916X 15/100

Introductory lectures on psycho-analysis (1916-17). Part II. Dreams (1916). Lecture VI: The premises and technique of interpretation.

Let us take as a premise that dreams are not somatic but psychical phenomena. It is quite possible, and highly probable indeed, that the dreamer does know what his dream means: only he does not know that he knows it and for that reason thinks he does not know it. A dream differs from a slip of the tongue, among other things in the multiplicity of its elements. The dream has to be divided into its elements and a separate enquiry has to be made into each element. The occurrence of ideas with links has been the subject of very instructive experimental researches, which have played a notable part in the history of psychoanalysis. The school of Wundt had introduced what are known as association experiments, in which a stimulus word is called out to the subject and he has the task of replying to it as quickly as possible with any reaction that occurs to him. It is then possible to study the interval that passes between the stimulus and the reaction, the nature of the answer given as a reaction, possible errors when the same experiment is repeated later, and so on. The associations to the dream element will be determined both by the dream element and also by the unconscious genuine thing behind it.

1916X 15/113

Introductory lectures on psycho-therapy (1916-17). Part II. Dreams (1916). Lecture VII: The manifest content of dreams and the latent dream-thoughts.

The manifest content of dreams and the latent dream thoughts are discussed. A dream as a whole is a distorted substitute for something else, something unconscious, and the task of interpreting a dream is to discover the unconscious material. We must not concern ourselves with what the dream appears to tell us, whether it is intelligible or absurd, clear or confused, since it cannot possibly be the unconscious material we are in search of. The work of interpreting can be performed on one's own dreams just as on other people's. The work of interpreting dreams is carried out in the face of a resistance, which opposes it and of which the critical objections are manifestations. This resistance is independent of the dreamer's theoretical conviction. If the resistance is small, the substitute cannot be far distant from the unconscious material; but a greater resistance means that the unconscious material will be greatly distorted and that the path will be a long one from the substitute back to the unconscious material. What the dream actually tells us is the manifest dream content, and the concealed material, which we hope to reach by pursuing the ideas that occur to the dreamer as the latent dream thoughts.

1916X 15/126

Introductory lectures on psycho-analysis (1916-17). Part II. Dreams (1916). Lecture VIII: Children's dreams.

Children's dreams are discussed. They are short, clear, coherent, easy to understand and unambiguous. From the dreams of 4- and 5-year-old children, we can draw conclusions on the essential nature of dreams in general. Dreams are not senseless; they are intelligible, completely valid mental acts. The dreams of children are without any dream distortion, and therefore call for no interpretive activity. The manifest and the latent dream coincide. A child's dream is a reaction to an experience of the previous day, which has left behind it a regret, a longing, a wish that has not been dealt with. The dream produces a direct, undisguised fulfillment of that wish. Dreams are not disturbers of sleep, but guardians of sleep which get rid of disturbances of sleep. What instigates a dream is a wish, and the fulfillment of that wish is the content of the dream. A dream does not simply give expression to a thought, but represents the wish fulfilled as a hallucinatory experience. There is another class of dreams which are undistorted and, like children's dreams, can easily be recognized as wish fulfillments. These are the dreams which all through life are called up by imperative bodily needs, such as hunger, thirst, and sexual need. They are wish fulfillments as reactions to internal somatic stimuli. There are also dreams of impatience and dreams of convenience.

1916X 15/136

Introductory lectures on psycho-analysis (1916-17). Part II. Dreams (1916). Lecture IX: The censorship of dreams.

The censorship of dreams is discussed. Dreams are things which get rid of psychical stimuli disturbing to sleep, by the method of hallucinatory satisfaction. Dream distortion is what makes a dream seem strange and unintelligible to us. Dream distortion is carried out

by dream work. Wherever there are gaps in the manifest dream, the dream censorship is responsible for them. Another manifestation of the censorship occurs whenever a dream element is remembered especially faintly, indefinitely, and doubtfully among other elements that are more clearly constructed. Censorship takes effect more frequently by producing softenings, approximations, and allusions instead of the genuine thing. The distortion of accent is one of the chief instruments of dream distortion. It gives the dream the strangeness which the dreamer himself does not recognize as his own production. Omission, modification, and fresh grouping of the material are the activities of the dream censorship and the instruments of dream distortion. The dream censorship itself is the originator, or one of the originators, of the dream distortion. The purposes which exercise the censorship are those which are acknowledged by the dreamer's waking judgment. The wishes which are censored and given a distorted expression in dreams are first and foremost manifestations of an unbridled and ruthless egoism. The dreamer's own ego appears in every dream and plays the chief part in it.

1916X 15/149

Introductory lectures on psycho-analysis (1916-17). Part II. Dreams (1916). Lecture X: Symbolism in dreams.

Symbolism in dreams is discussed. Symbols realize to some extent the ideal of the ancient as well as of the popular interpretation of dreams. The essence of the symbolic relation is that it is a comparison, though not a comparison of any sort. Special limitations seem to be attached to the comparison. Not everything with which we can compare an object or a process appears in dreams as a symbol for it. A dream does not symbolize every possible element of the latent dream thought but only certain definite ones. The range of things which are given symbolic representation in dreams is not wide: the human body as a whole, parents, children, brothers and sisters, birth, death, nakedness, and sexual life. The one typical representation of the human figure as a whole is a house. One's parents appear as the Emperor and Empress, the King and Queen, etc. Children and brothers and sisters are symbolized as small animals or vermin. Birth is almost invariably represented by something which has a connection with water. Dying is replaced in dreams by departure, being dead by various obscure timid hints and nakedness by clothes and uniforms. Sexual life is represented by rich symbolism. The male organ finds symbolic substitutes in things that are long and upstanding. The female genitals are symbolically represented by objects that share their characteristic of enclosing a hollow space which can take something into itself.

1916X   15/170

Introductory lectures on psycho-analysis (1916-17). Part II. Dreams (1916). Lecture XI: The dream-work.

The work which transforms the latent dream into the manifest one is called the dream work. The work which proceeds in the contrary direction, is the work of interpretation. The first achievement of the dream work is condensation. The manifest dream has a smaller content than the latent one. Condensation is brought about by: 1) the total omission of certain latent elements, 2) only a fragment of some complexes in the latent dream passing over into the manifest one, and 3) latent elements which have something in common being combined and fused into a single unity in the manifest dream. The second achievement of the dream work is displacement. It manifests itself in 2 ways: in the first, a latent element is replaced not by a component part of itself but by something more remote, that is, by an allusion; and in the second, the psychical accent is shifted from an important element on to another which is unimportant. The third achievement of the dream work consists in the regressive transformation of thoughts into visual images. Nonsense and absurdity in dreams have their meaning. Conformities in the latent material are replaced by condensations in the manifest dream. Contraries are treated in the same way as conformities. Speeches in dreams are copies and combinations of speeches which one has heard or spoken oneself on the day before the dream. The dream work is equally unable to carry out calculations.

1916X   15/184

Introductory lectures on psycho-analysis (1916-17). Part II. Dreams (1916). Lecture XII: Some analyses of sample dreams.

Some analyses of sample dreams are presented. The first dream that is presented consists only of 2 short pictures: His uncle was smoking a cigarette although it was a Saturday. A woman was caressing and fondling him as though he were her child. This dream means that cuddling with his mother was something impermissible, like smoking on a Saturday to a pious Jew. When anyone has lost someone near and dear to him, he produces dreams of a special sort for some time afterwards, in which knowledge of the death arrives at the strangest compromises with the need to bring the dead person to life again. In some of these dreams the person who has died is dead and at the same time still alive, because he does not know he is dead; only if he did know would he die completely. In others, he is half dead and half alive, and each of these states is indicated in a particular way. The sexual life is represented by rich symbolism in the dreams: Pursuit and the breathless climbing upstairs represent the sexual act; drawers, chests, and cases, stand

for the female genitals; a pit with a tree torn out refers to a piece of infantile sexual theory, to the belief that girls originally had the same genitals as boys and that their later shape was the result of castration; a triad of figures represent the male genitals; a landscape represents the female ones; and trunks are symbols of women.

1916X   15/199

Introductory lectures on psycho-analysis (1916-17). Part II. Dreams (1916). Lecture XIII: The archaic features and infantilism of dreams.

The archaic features and infantilism of dreams are discussed. The mode of the dream work is described as archaic or regressive. The death wish against someone they love, which is later so mysterious, originates from the earliest days of their relationship to that person. Whenever anyone in the course of one's life gets in one's way, a dream is promptly ready to kill that person, even if it be father or mother, brother or sister, husband or wife. It is an untenable error to deny that children have a sexual life and to suppose that sexuality only begins at puberty with the maturation of the genitals. From the very first, children have a copious sexual life, which differs at many points from what is later regarded as normal. Children may be described as polymorphously perverse, and if these impulses only show traces of activity, that is because they are of less intensity compared with those in later life and because all a child's sexual manifestations are energetically suppressed by education. Among the forbidden wishes, special emphasis deserves to be laid on the incestuous ones, that is, on those aiming at sexual intercourse with parents and brothers and sisters. The material of the forgotten experiences of childhood is accessible to dreams, but the mental life of children, with all its characteristics, its egoism, its incestuous choice of love objects, still persist in dreams, that is, in the unconscious and dreams carry us back to this infantile level.

1916X   15/213

Introductory lectures on psycho-analysis (1916-17). Part II. Dreams (1916). Lecture XIV: Wish-fulfillment.

Wish fulfillment is discussed. The dream work consists essentially in the transformation of thoughts into a hallucinatory experience. It is the intention of the dream work to get rid of a mental stimulus, which is disturbing sleep, by means of the filfillment of a wish. If dreams are the fulfillment of wishes, distressing feelings should be impossible in them. But 3 kinds of complications must be taken into account. First, it may be that the dream work has not completely succeeded in creating a wish fulfillment; so that a portion of the distressing effect in the dream thoughts has been left over in the manifest dream. Second, an anxiety dream is often the undisguised fulfillment of a wish, not, of course, of an acceptable wish, but of a repudiated one. The generation of anxiety has taken the place of the censorship. Third, there is a possibility that the fulfillment of a wish may bring about something very far from pleasant, namely, a punishment. The only essential thing about dreams is the dream work that has influenced the thought material. The latent dream thoughts are unconscious to the dreamer and consist partly in residues of the previous day's mental impulses and intellectual operations and partly in powerful, repressed, wishful impulses, stemming from an earlier period of life, which provide the psychical energy for the construction of the dream.

1916X   15/228

Introductory lectures on psycho-analysis (1916-17). Part II. Dreams (1916). Lecture XV: Uncertainties and criticisms.

Uncertainties and criticisms of the theory of dreams are presented. The dream work makes a translation of the dream thoughts into a primitive mode of expression similar to picture writing. All such primitive systems of expressions are characterized by indefiniteness and ambiguity. The coalescence of contraries in the dream work is analogous to the so-called antithetical meaning of primal words in the most ancient languages. The points of uncertainty which people have tried to use as objections to the soundness of Freud's dream interpretations are regular characteristics of all primitive systems of expression. A second group of doubts is closely connected with the impression that a number of the solutions to which we find ourselves driven in interpreting dreams seem to be forced, artificial, arbitrary, or even comic, and facetious. With the help of displacement, the dream censorship creates substitutive structures which are described as allusions. But they are allusions which are not easily recognizable as such. Another objection, made by psychoanalysts, is that dreams are concerned with attempts at adaptation to present conditions and with attempts at solving future problems, that they have a prospective purpose. This assertion is based on a confusion between the dream and the latent dream thoughts and is based on disregarding the dream work. It is often possible to influence dreamers as to what they shall dream about, but never as to what they shall dream. The mechanism of the dream work and the unconscious dream wish are exempt from any outside influence.

VOL. XVI   Introductory Lectures on Psycho-Analysis (Part III) (1916–1917)

1916X   16/243

Introductory lectures on psycho-analysis (1916-17). Part III. General theory of the neuroses (1917). Lecture XVI: Psycho-analysis and psychiatry.

The psychoanalytic view of the phenomena of neurosis is presented. Some patients do not close the doors between the waiting room and the office. This happens only when the waiting room is empty, not full. This action is not a matter of chance but has a motive, a sense and an intention. It has a place in an assignable mental context. A case history is presented of a woman suffering from delusions of jealousy. The patient actually was in love with her son-in-law. This love was not conscious; but it remained in existence and, even though it was unconscious, it exercised a severe pressure. Some relief had to be looked for. The easiest mitigation was offered by the mechanism of displacement which plays a part so regularly in the generating of delusional jealousy. The phantasy of her husband's unfaithfulness acted as a cooling compress on her burning wound. Psychoanalysis showed that the delusion ceased to be absurd or unintelligible, it had a sense, it had good motives and it fitted into the context of an emotional experience of the patient's. The delusion was necessary, as a reaction to an unconscious mental process, and it was to this connection that it owed its delusional character and its resistance to every logical and realistic attack. The fact that the delusion turned out to be a jealous one and not one of another kind was unambiguously determined by the experience that lay behind the illness.

1916X   16/257

Introductory lectures on psycho-analysis (1916-17). Part III. General theory of the neurosis (1917). Lecture XVII: The sense of symptoms.

The sense of neurotic symptoms was first discovered by Josef Breuer. Obsessional neurosis is shown in the patient's being occupied with thoughts in which he is in fact not interested, in his being aware of impulses in himself which appear very strange to him and in his being led to actions, the performance of which, give him no enjoyment, but which it is quite impossible for him to omit. Two examples of the analysis of an obsessional symptom are presented. The first patient is a lady, nearly 30 years of age, who suffered from the most severe obsessional manifestations. She ran from her room into another neighboring one, took up a particular position there beside a table that stood in the middle, rang the bell for her housemaid, sent her on some indifferent errand or let her go without one, and then ran back into her own one. The obsessional action appeared to have been a representation, a repetition, of a significant scene; that of her wedding night. The second patient was a 19-year-old girl. She developed a sleep ceremonial as follows: the big clock in her room was stopped, all the other clocks or watches in the room were removed, and her tiny wrist watch was not allowed inside her bedside table. The patient gradually came to learn that it was a symbol of the female genitals that clocks were banished from her equipment for the night.

1916X   16/273

Introductory lectures on psycho-analysis (1916-17). Part III. General theory of the neuroses (1917). Lecture XVIII: Fixation to traumas—The unconscious.

The closest analogy to the behavior of neurotics is afforded by illnesses which are produced by war, traumatic neuroses. The traumatic neuroses give a clear indication that a fixation at the moment of the traumatic accident lies at their root. These patients regularly repeat the traumatic situation in their dreams. The existence of unconscious mental processes is revealed in the obsessional behavior of neurotics. These patients are not aware of the link between their obsessional behavior and the precipitating circumstance. The sense of the symptoms is regularly unconscious. There is an inseparable relation between this fact of the symptoms being unconscious and the possibility of their existing. Symptoms are never constructed from conscious processes; as soon as the unconscious processes concerned have become conscious, the symptom must disappear. The task of psychoanalysis is to make conscious everything that is pathogenically unconscious. Its task is to fill up all the gaps in the patient's memory, to remove his amnesias.

1916X   16/286

Introductory lectures on psychoanalysis (1916-17). Part III. General theory of the neuroses (1917). Lecture XIX: Resistance and repression.

When we undertake to restore a patient to health, to relieve him of the symptoms of his illness, he meets us with a violent and tenacious resistance, which persists throughout the whole length of the treatment. In psychoanalytic therapy, we instruct the patient to put himself into a state of quiet, unreflecting self-observation, and to report whatever internal perceptions he is able to make in the order to which they occur to him. One hardly comes across a single patient who does not make an attempt at reserving some region or other for himself so as to prevent the treatment from having access to it. Some patients put up intellectual resist-

ances. The patient also knows how to put up resistances, without going outside the framework of the analysis, the overcoming of which is among the most difficult of technical problems. Instead of remembering, he repeats attitudes and emotional impulses from his early life which can be used as a resistance against the doctor and the treatment by means of what is known as transference. If the patient is a man, he usually extracts this material from his relation to his father, into whose place he fits the doctor. The pathogenic process which is demonstrated by resistance is called repression. It is the precondition for the construction of symptoms. Symptoms are a substitute for something that is held back by repression. Neurotic symptoms are substitutes for sexual satisfactions.

1916X   16/303

Introductory lectures on psycho-analysis (1916-17). Part III. General theory of the neuroses (1917). Lecture XX: The sexual life of human beings.

The sexual life of human beings is discussed. By means of careful investigations we have come to know groups of individuals whose sexual life deviates from the usual picture of the average. Only members of their own sex can rouse their sexual wishes. They are called homosexuals or inverts. This class of perverts behave to their sexual object in approximately the same way as normal people do to theirs. There is a long series of abnormal people whose sexual activity diverges more and more widely from what seems desirable to a sensible person. They are divided into those in whom, like the homosexuals, the sexual object has been changed, and others in whom the sexual aim is what has primarily been altered. Neurotic symptoms are substitutes for sexual satisfaction. Of the many symptomatic pictures in which obsessional neurosis appears, the most important turn out to be those provoked by the pressure of excessively strong sadistic sexual impulses. Psychoanalytic research has had to concern itself with the sexual life of children. This is because the memories and associations arising during the analysis of symptoms in adults regularly led back to the early years of childhood. The first area of sexual interest in a baby is the mouth. The next erotogenic zone is the anus. A sign of maturity is the passing of sexual interest to the genitals.

1916X   16/320

Introductory lectures on psycho-analysis (1916-17). Part III. General theory of the neuroses (1917). Lecture XXI: The development of the libido and the sexual organizations.

The development of the libido and of the sexual organizations are discussed. The sexual life of children cannot be doubted from the third year of life onwards: at about that time the genitals already begin to stir; a period of infantile masturbation, of genital satisfaction, sets in. From about the sixth to the eighth year of life onwards, we can observe a halt and retrogression in sexual development, which, in cases where it is most propitious culturally, deserves to be called a period of latency. The majority of experiences and mental impulses before the start of the latency period fall victim to infantile amnesia. The task for psychoanalysis is to bring this forgotten period back into memory. From the third year of life, a child's sexual life shows much agreement with an adult's. A kind of loose organization which might be called pregenital exists before that. During this earlier phase, what stands in the forefront are not the genital component instincts but the sadistic and anal ones. The sadistic anal organization is the immediate forerunner of the phase of genital primacy. The turning point of the sexual development is the subordination of all the component sexual instincts under the primacy of the genitals. Erotic desires become focused upon the parent of the opposite sex, in association with the murderous wish to do away with all rivals, in the Oedipus complex.

1916X 16/339

Introductory lectures on psycho-analysis (1916-17). Part III. General theory of the neurosis (1917). Lecture XXII: Some thoughts on development and regression— Aetiology.

The libidinal function goes through a lengthy development before it can be enlisted in the service of reproduction. A development of this kind involves 2 dangers: inhibition and regression. There are 2 kinds of regressions: a return to the objects first cathected by the libido which are of an incestuous nature; and a return of the sexual organization as a whole to earlier stages. Repression is the process by which an act which is admissible to consciousness, one which belongs to the preconscious system, is made unconscious. In hysteria, there is a regression to an earlier stage of the sexual organization. The chief part in the mechanism of hysteria is played by repression. In obsessional neurosis, it is the regression of the libido to the preliminary stage of the sadistic anal organization that is the most striking fact and the one which is decisive for what is manifested in symptoms. The meaning of psychical conflict can be adequately expressed by saying that for an external frustration to become pathogenic an internal frustration must be added to it. Another factor in the etiology of the neuroses, the tendency to conflict, is as much dependent on the development of the ego as on that of the libido. The transition from the pleasure principle to the reality principle is one of the most important steps foward in the ego's development.

1916X 16/358

Introductory lectures on psycho-analysis (1916-17). Part III. General theory of the neuroses (1917). Lecture XXIII: The paths to the formation of symptoms.

Psychical (or psychogenic) symptoms and psychical illness are acts that are detrimental, or at least useless, to the subject's life as a whole, often complained of by him as unwelcome and bringing unpleasure or suffering to him. The main damage they do resides in the mental expenditure which they themselves involve and in the further expenditure that becomes necessary for fighting against them. Neurotic symptoms are the outcome of a conflict which arises over a new method of satisfying the libido. The path to perversion branches off sharply from that to neurosis. The libido's escape under conditions of conflict is made possible by the presence of fixations. The regressive cathexis of these fixations leads to the circumvention of the repression and to a discharge of the libido, subject to the conditions of a compromise being observed. The libido finds the fixations which it requires in order to break through the repressions in the activities and experiences of infantile sexuality, in the abandoned component trends, in the objects of childhood which have been given up. The symptoms create a substitute for the frustrated satisfaction by means of a regression of the libido to earlier times. Among the occurrences which recur again and again in the youthful history of neurotics are: observation of parental intercourse, seduction by an adult, and threat of being castrated. The libido's retreat to phantasy is an intermediate stage on the path to the formation of symptoms and it seems to call for a special name. Jung called it introversion.

1916X 16/378

Introductory lectures on psycho-analysis (1916-17). Part III. General theory of the neuroses (1917). Lecture XXIV: The common neurotic state.

One of the ways in which the ego is related to its neurosis is most clearly recognizable in traumatic neurosis. In traumatic neuroses, and particularly in those brought about by the horrors of war, we are unmistakably presented with a self-interested motive on the part of the ego, seeking for protection and advantage, a motive which cannot create the illness by itself but which assents to it and maintains it when once it has come about. The ego takes a similar interest in the development and maintenance of the neurosis in every other case. In average circumstances, we recognize that by escaping into a neurosis the ego obtains a certain internal gain from illness. The symptoms of the actual neuroses, intracranial pressure, sensations of pain, a state of irritation in an organ, and weakening or inhibition of a function have no sense, no psychical meaning. They are not only manifested predominantly in the body but they are also themselves entirely somatic processes, in the generating of which all the complicated mental mechanisms are absent. There are 3 pure forms of actual neuroses: neurasthenia, anxiety neurosis, and hypochondria.

1916X 16/392
Introductory lectures on psycho-analysis (1916-17). Part III. General theory of the neuroses (1917). Lecture XXV: Anxiety.

The problem of anxiety is discussed. Realistic anxiety is rational and expedient. It calls for drastic revision. The first thing about it is preparedness for the danger, which manifests itself in increased sensory attention and motor tension. The preparedness for anxiety seems to be the expedient element in anxiety, and the generation of anxiety the inexpedient one. In the anxiety manifested by neurotics, there is a general apprehensiveness, a kind of freely floating anxiety which is ready to attach itself to any idea that is in any way suitable, which influences judgment, selects what is to be expected, and lies in wait for any opportunity that will allow it to justify itself. This is called expectant anxiety or anxious expectation. A second form of anxiety is bound psychically and attached to particular objects or situations. This is the anxiety of phobias. In the third of the forms of neurotic anxiety, the connection between anxiety and a threatening danger is completely lost to view. Anxiety may appear in hysteria as an accompaniment to hysterical symptoms, or in some chance condition of excitement; or it may make its appearance, divorced from any determinants and equally incomprehensible to us and to the patient, as an unrelated attack of anxiety. There is a connection between sexual restraint and anxiety states. The deflection of the libido from its normal employment, which causes the development of anxiety, takes place in the region of somatic processes.

1916X 16/412
Introductory lectures on psycho-analysis (1916-17). Part III. General theory of the neuroses (1917). Lecture XXVI: The libido theory and narcissism.

The libido theory and narcissism are discussed. Sexuality is the single function of the living organism which extends beyond the individual and is concerned with his relation to the species. The cathexes of energy which the ego directs towards the objects of its sexual desires are termed libido; all the others, which are sent out by the self-preservative instincts, are called interest. In 1908, Karl Abraham pronounced the main characteristic of schizophrenia to be that in it the libidinal cathexis of objects was lacking. In a sleeper, the primal state of distribution of the libido is restored, total narcissism, in which libido and ego interest, still united and indistinguishable, dwell in the self-sufficing ego. Narcissism is the libidinal complement to egoism. When we speak of egoism, we have in view only the individual's advantage; when we talk of narcissism we are also taking his libidinal satisfaction into account. Object choice, the step forward in the development of the libido which is made after the narcissistic stage, can take place according to 2 different types: either according to the narcissistic type, where the subject's own ego is replaced by another one that is as similar as possible, or according to the attachment type, where people who have become precious through satisfying the other vital needs are chosen as objects by the libido as well.

1916X 16/431
Introductory lectures on psycho-analysis (1916-17). Part III. General theory of the neuroses (1917). Lecture XXVII: Transference.

Transference is discussed. By carrying what is unconscious on into the conscious, we lift the repression, we remove the preconditions for the formation of symptoms. The repression must be gotten rid of, after which the substitution of the conscious material for the unconscious can proceed smoothly. The resistance is removed by discovering it and showing it to the patient. The anticathexis or the resistance does not form part of the unconscious but of the ego. The patient, who ought to want nothing else but to find a way out of his distressing conflicts, develops a special interest in the person of the doctor. For a time, relations with him become very agreeable. But then, difficulties arise in the treatment. The patient behaves as though he were outside the treatment and as though he had not made an agreement with the doctor. The cause of the disturbance is that the patient has transferred on to the doctor intense feelings of affection which are justified neither by the doctor's behavior nor by the situation that has developed during the treatment. Transference can appear as a passionate demand for love or in more moderate forms; the libidinal desire can be toned down into a proposal for an inseparable, but ideally nonsensual, friendship. With his male patients, the doctor comes across a form of expression of the transference which is hostile or negative. The transference is necessary in order for a cure.

1916X 16/448
Introductory lectures on psychoanalysis (1916-17). Part III. General theory of the neuroses (1917). Lecture XXVIII: Analytic therapy.

Analytic theory is discussed. Direct suggestion is suggestion aimed against the manifestation of the symptoms; it is a struggle between your authority and the motives for the illness. Experience shows that in renouncing direct suggestion we are not giving up anything of irreplaceable value. Hypnotic treatment seeks to expose and get rid of something. An analytic treatment demands from both doctor and patient the accomplishment of serious work, which is employed in lifting internal resistances. Through the overcoming of these resistances the patient's mental life is permanently changed, is raised to a high level of development, and remains protected against fresh possibilities of falling ill. A neurotic is incapable of enjoyment and of efficiency, the former because his libido is not directed toward any real object and the latter because he is obliged to employ a great deal of his available energy on keeping his libido under repression and on warding off its assaults. He would become healthy if the conflict between his ego and his libido came to an end and if his ego had his libido again at its disposal. The therapeutic task consists, in freeing the libido from its present attachments, which are withdrawn from the ego, and in making it once more serviceable to the ego. The therapeutic work falls into 2 phases: 1) all the libido is forced from the symptoms into the transference and concentrated there; and 2) the struggle is waged around this new object and the libido is liberated from it.

1916X 16/478
Introductory lectures on psycho-analysis (1916-17). Index of parapraxes.

An index of parapraxes is presented. The source of each parapraxis is given where it is other than Freud himself. The 6 parapraxes include: bungled and symptomatic actions, errors; forgetting intentions, lost objects; forgetting names; misreadings; slips of the pen and misprints; and slips of the tongue. In addition to Freud, the sources include: Brill, Maeder, Bernard Shaw, Jones, Dattner, Jung, Lichtenberg, Crown Prince, Stekel, Reitler, Meringer and Mayer, Rank, Constable, Lattman, Schiller and Graf.

1916X 16/480
Introductory lectures on psycho-analysis (1916-17). Index of dreams.

An index of dreams is presented. The subject matter of the dreams includes a trip across Lake Aussee, a black-edged visiting card, 2 rows of boys, a brother in a box, a brown dachshund, a shop in Cairo, the English Channel, a basket of cherries, church and landscape, church bells, a clock man, broken crockery, a customs officer, a dead daughter, an exhumed father, an extensive view, God in a paper cocked hat, a kiss in an automobile, love services, a low hanging chandelier, a murderer in a railway train, a mustard plaster, an officer in a red cap, Orvieto wine, a piano that needs tuning, pulling a woman from behind a bed, the shape of a table, sleigh bells, strawberries, 3 theater tickets, 2 black trunks, 2 sisters, and an uncle smoking a cigarette.

1916X 16/481
Introductory lectures on psycho-analysis (1916-17). Index of symbols.

An index of 139 symbols is presented. They include: apples, balloons, beheading, blossoms, books, bottles, boxes, breaking, bushes, cases, castle, cavities, chapels, chests, churches, citadel, city, climbing, cloaks, clothes, crafts, cupboards, daggers, dancing, departure, doors, emperor and empress, falling, fishes, flame, flowers, flying, foot, fortress, fountains, gardens, gates, gliding, hammers, hand, hats, head, hearth, hills, hollows, horseshoe, house, instruments, jewels, keys, knives, ladders, landscape, limbs, linen, materials, mouth, mushroom, mussels, neckties, ovens, overcoats, paper, peaches, pencils, piano playing, pig, pillow, pistols, pits, playing, plough, pockets, posts, receptacles, reptiles, revolvers, riding, rifles, rocks, rooms, sabres, ships, shoes, sliding, staircases, steps, sticks, sweets, tables, three, tools, train journey, treasure, trees, trunks, umbrellas, underclothing, uniforms, vermin, water, windows, wood, and zeppelins.

VOL. XVII An Infantile Neurosis and Other Works (1917-1919)

1918B 17/3
From the history of an infantile neurosis (1918). Editor's note. (1955).

From the History of an Infantile Neurosis is the most elaborate and the most important of all Freud's case histories. It was in February, 1910, that the wealthy young Russian who is its subject came to Freud for analysis. His first course of treatment, which is the one reported, lasted from then until July, 1914. The primary significance of the case history at the time of its publication was clearly the support it provided for his criticisms of Adler and more especially of Jung. Here was conclusive evidence to refute any denial of infantile sexuality. The analysis sheds light on the earlier, oral, organization of the libido. Perhaps the chief clinical finding was the evidence revealed of the determining part played in the patient's neurosis by his primary feminine impulses. The marked degree of bisexuality of the patient is discussed.

1918B 17/7
From the history of an infantile neurosis (1918). Part I. Introductory remarks about the "Wolfman."

The case which Freud reports is characterized by a number of peculiarities which require emphasis. It is concerned with a young man whose health had broken down in his eighteenth year after a gonorrhoeal infection, and who was entirely incapacitated and completely dependent upon other people when he began his psychoanalytic treatment several years later. His early years were dominated by a severe neurotic disturbance, which began immediately before his fourth birthday as an anxiety hysteria (in the shape of an animal phobia), then changed into an obsessional neurosis with a religious content, and lasted as far as into his tenth year. Freud's description and analysis of the case are restricted to the aspect of infantile neurosis, 15 years after its termination. The first years of the treatment produced scarcely any change. The patient remained for a long time unassailably entrenched behind an attitude of obliging apathy. His shrinking from a self-sufficient existence was a great problem. Freud waited until the patient became strongly enough attached to him to counterbalance this shrinking. Freud told the patient that the treatment had to come to an end at a fixed date; and under the pressure of this limit his resistance and his fixation to the illness gave way. It is concluded that the length of analysis and the quantity of material which must be mastered are of no importance in comparison with the resistance which is met within the course of the work, and are only of importance insofar as they are necessarily proportional to the resistance.

1918B   17/13

From the history of an infantile neurosis (1918). Part II. General survey of the patient's environment and of the history of the case.

A general survey is made of the patient's environment and of the history of the case. His mother suffered from abdominal disorders, and his father from attacks of depression, which led to his absence from home. As a consequence of her weak health, the patient's mother had little to do with her children. As far back as he could remember he was looked after by a nurse, an uneducated old woman of peasant birth, with an untiring affection for him. He seems at first to have been a very good natured, tractable, and even quiet child, so that they used to say of him that he ought to have been the girl and his elder sister the boy. But once, when his parents came back from their summer holiday, they found him transformed. He had become discontented, irritable and violent, took offense on every possible occasion, and then flew into a rage and screamed like a savage. This happened during the summer while the English governess was with them. The patient's sister tormented him by always displaying a picture of a wolf which frightened him. During the years of his childhood he went through an easily recognizable attack of obsessional neurosis. He related that during a long period he was very pious. The patient's more mature years were marked by a very unsatisfactory relation to his father, who, after repeated attacks of depression, was no longer

able to conceal the pathological features of his character. All of the phenomena which the patient associated with the phase of his life that began with his naughtiness disappeared in about his eighth year.

1918B   17/19

From the history of an infantile neurosis (1918). Part III. The seduction and its immediate consequences.

A case history of seduction and its immediate consequences are discussed. When Freud's patient was very small, his sister seduced him into sexual practices. His sister took hold of his penis and played with it. The phantasies that the patient had were meant to efface the memory of an event which later on seemed offensive to his masculine self-esteem. According to these phantasies it was not he who had played the passive part towards his sister, but he had been aggressive, had tried to see his sister undressed, had been rejected and punished, and had for that reason got into the rage which the family tradition talked of. The boy's age at the time at which his sister began her seductions was 3¼ years. He held aloof from her and her solicitations soon ceased. The patient envied her the respect which his father showed for her mental capacity and intellectual achievements, while he, intellectually inhibited since his neurosis, had to be content with a lower estimation. But he tried to win, instead of her, his nurse, Nanya. He began to play with his penis in Nanya's presence but Nanya disillusioned him and threatened castration. His sexual life which was beginning to come under the sway of the genital zone, gave way before an external obstacle, and was thrown back by its influence into an earlier phase of pregenital organization. At the suppression of his masturbation, the boy's sexual life took on a sadistic anal character. There was an intense and constant ambivalence in the patient, shown in the development of both members of the pairs of contrary component instincts. After the refusal by his Nanya, his libidinal expectation detached itself from her and began to contemplate his father as a sexual object. By bringing his naughtiness forward he was trying to force punishments and beatings out of his father, and in that way to obtain from him the masochistic sexual satisfaction that he desired. The signs of alteration in the patient's character were not accompanied by any symptoms of anxiety until after the occurrence of a particular event (wolf dream).

1918B   17/29

From the history of an infantile neurosis (1918). Part IV. The dream and the primal scene.

The dream of Freud's patient in relation to the primal scene is discussed. The patient dreamed that the bedroom window opened and he saw 6 or 7 white wolves in the walnut tree outside the window. In great terror, evidently of being eaten up, he screamed and woke up. Interpretation of this dream was a task which lasted several years. The only piece of action in the dream was the opening of the window. The wolves sat quite still and without making any movement on the branches of the tree. He had always connected this dream with the recollection that during these years of his childhood he was most tremendously afraid of the picture of a wolf in a book of fairy tales. What sprang into activity that night out of the chaos of the dreamer's unconscious memory traces was the picture of copulation between his parents, copulation in circumstances which were not entirely usual and were especially favorable for observation. The child's age at the date of the observation was established as being about 1½ years. The postures which he saw his parents adopt had the man upright, and the woman bent down like an animal. He thought that the posture of the wolf in the fairy tale *The Wolf and the Seven Little Goats*, might have reminded him of that of his father during the constructed primal scene. At all events, the picture became the point of departure for further manifestations of anxiety. His anxiety was a repudiation of the wish for sexual satisfaction from his father, the trend which had put the dream into his head. The form taken by the anxiety, the fear of him being eaten by the wolf, was only the transposition of the wish to be copulated with by his father, that is, to be given sexual satisfaction in the same way as his mother. His last sexual aim, the passive attitude towards his father, succumbed to repression, and a fear of his father appeared in its place in the shape of the wolf phobia. His mother took the part of the castrated wolf, which let the others climb upon it; his father took the part of the wolf that climbed. He had identified with his castrated mother (no penis) during the dream and was fighting against the fact. His masculinity protested against being castrated (like Mother) in order to be sexually satisfied by Father. It was not only a single sexual current that started from the primal scene but a whole set of them.

1918B 17/48

From the history of an infantile neurosis (1918). Part V. A few discussions.

Scenes from early infancy, such as those brought up by an exhaustive analysis of neuroses, are not reproductions of real occurrences. They are products of the imagination, which are intended to serve as some kind of symbolic representation of real wishes and interests, and which owe their origin to a regressive tendency, to a turning away from the tasks of the present. The influence of childhood makes itself felt at the beginning of the formation of a neurosis, since it plays a decisive part in determining whether and at what point the individual shall fail to master the real problems of life. The occurrence of a neurotic disorder in the fourth and fifth years of childhood proves, that infantile experiences are in a position to produce a neurosis. In the case of Freud's patient, the content of the primal scene is a picture of sexual intercourse between the boy's parents in a posture especially favorable for certain observations. Shortly before his dream, the boy was taken to visit flocks of sheep, and there he saw large white dogs and probably also observed them copulating. What probably supervened during the expectant excitement of the night of his dream was the transference on to his parents of his recently acquired memory picture, with all its details, and it was only thus that the powerful emotional effects which followed were made possible. The transference from the copulating dogs on to his parents was accomplished not by means of his making an inference accompanied by words but by his searching out in his memory a real scene in which his parents had been together and which could be coalesced with the situation of the copulation.

1918B 17/61

From the history of an infantile neurosis (1918). Part VI. The obsessional neurosis.

Obsessional child neurosis is discussed. When the patient was 4½ years old, and as his state or irritability and apprehensiveness had not improved, his mother determined to make him acquainted with the Bible story in the hope of distracting and elevating him. His initiation into religion brought the previous phase to an end, but at the same time it led to the anxiety symptoms being replaced by obsessional symptoms. Up to then he had not been able to get to sleep easily because he had been afraid of having bad dreams; now he was obliged before he went to bed to kiss all the holy pictures in the room, to recite prayers, and to make innumerable signs of the cross upon himself and upon his bed. His childhood falls into the following epochs: 1) the earliest period up to the seduction when he was 3¼ years old, during which the primal scene took place; 2) the period of the alteration in his character up to the anxiety dream (4 years old); 3) the period of the animal phobia up to his initiation into religion (4½ years old); and 4) the period of the obsessional neurosis up to a time later than his tenth year. After the rebuff from his Nanya and the consequent suppression of the beginnings of genital activity, his sexual life developed in the direction of sadism and masochism. His knowledge of the sacred story gave him a chance of sublimating his predominant masochistic attitude towards his father.

1918B 17/72

From the history of an infantile neurosis (1918). Part VII. Anal erotism and the castration complex.

Anal erotism in relation to the castration complex is discussed. The obsessional neurosis grew up on the basis of a sadistic anal constitution. For a long time before the analysis, feces had the significance of money for the patient. During his later illness he suffered from disturbances of his intestinal function. He found a great deal of enjoyment in anal jokes and exhibitions, and this enjoyment had been retained by him until after the beginning of his later illness. Under the influence of the primal scene he came to the conclusion that his mother had been made ill by what his father had done to her (intercourse); and his dread of having blood in his stool, of being as ill as his mother, was his repudiation of being identified with her in this sexual scene. But the dread was also a proof that in his later elaboration of the primal scene he had put himself in his mother's place and had envied her this relation with his father. The organ by which his identification with women, his passive homosexual attitude to men, was able to express itself was the anal one. The disorders in the function of this zone had acquired the significance of feminine impulses of tenderness, and they retained it during the later illness as well. He rejected castration, and held to his theory of intercourse by the anus. His identification of his father with the castrator became important as being the source of an intense unconscious hostility towards him and of a sense of guilt which reacted against it.

1918B 17/89

From the history of an infantile neurosis (1918). Part VIII. Fresh material from the primal period—Solution.

It happens in many analyses that as one approaches their end new recollections emerge which have hitherto been kept carefully concealed. Early in the analysis, the patient told Freud of a memory of the period in which his naughtiness had been in the habit of suddenly turning into anxiety. He was chasing a beautiful big butterfly but suddenly, when the butterfly had settled on a flower, he was seized with a dreadful fear of the creature, and ran away screaming. In this anxiety scene, a recollection of some female person had been aroused. Behind the screen memory of the hunted butterfly, the memory of the nursery maid lay concealed. When the patient saw this girl scrubbing the floor, he had micturated in the room, and she had rejoined with a threat of castration. When he saw the girl on the floor engaged in scrubbing it, and kneeling down, with her buttocks projecting and her back horizontal, he was faced once again with the posture which his mother had assumed in the copulation scene. She became his mother to him; he was seized with sexual excitement; and, like his father, he behaved in a masculine way towards her. The disturbance of appetite, the wolf phobia, and the obsessional piety constituted the complete series of infantile disorders which laid down the predisposition for his neurotic breakdown after he had passed the age

of puberty. Every neurosis in an adult is built upon a neurosis which has occurred in his childhood. The phase used by the patient to sum up the troubles of which he complained was that the world was hidden from him by a veil. The veil was torn in 1 situation only: at the moment when, as a result of an enema, he passed a motion through his anus, at which time he felt well again, and briefly saw the world clearly. He remembered that he had been born with a caul, thus the caul was the "veil" (birth veil) which hid him from the world. The phantasy of re-birth is discussed in relation to the birth veil.

1918B 17/104

From the history of an infantile neurosis (1918). Part IX. Recapitulations and problems.

The advantage of having a wealth of information about the patient's childhood was purchased at the expense of disjointed analysis. The first sign of the patient's sexual development is in the disturbance of his appetite. This earliest recognizable sexual organization is called the cannibalistic or oral phase, during which the original attachment of sexual excitation to the nutritional instinct still dominates the scene. The sadistic anal organization is regarded as a continuation and development of the oral one. The boy's anal erotism was not particularly noticeable. His seduction continued to make its influence felt, by maintaining the passivity of his sexual aim and it transformed his sadism into the masochism which was its passive counterpart. The sadistic anal organization continued to exist during the phase of the animal phobia which set in, only it suffered an admixture of anxiety phenomena. The phobia came into existence on the level of the genital organization, and showed the relatively simple mechanism of an anxiety hysteria. The ego, by developing anxiety, was protecting itself against homosexual satisfaction but the process of repression left behind a trace. What became conscious was fear not of the father but of the wolf and the anxiety that was concerned in the formation of these phobias was a fear of castration. Religion achieved all the aims for the sake of which it is included in the education of the individual: It put a restraint on his sexual education, and lowered the importance of his family relationships.

1917C 17/125

On transformations of instinct as exemplified in anal erotism (1917).

Observations made during psychoanalysis led Freud to suspect that the constant coexistence in any one of the 3 character traits of orderliness, parsimony, and obstinancy indicated an intensification of the anal erotic components in a subject's sexual constitution, and that these modes of reaction, which were favored by his ego, had been established during the course of his development through the assimilation of his anal erotism. In the development of the libido in man, the phase of genital primacy must be preceded by a pregential organization in which sadism and anal erotism play the leading parts. It appears that, in products of the unconscious such as spontaneous ideas, phantasies, and symptoms, the concepts of feces (money, gift), baby, and penis are ill distinguished from one another and are easily interchangeable. If we penetrate deeply enough into the neurosis of a woman, we meet the repressed wish to possess a penis like a man. The female's wish for a penis and the wish for a baby are fundamentally identical. The ultimate outcome of the infantile wish for a penis, in women in whom the determinants of a neurosis in later life are absent, is that it changes into the wish for a man, and thus puts up with the man as an appendage to the penis. This transformation, therefore, turns an impulse which is hostile to the female sexual function into one which is favorable to it. Anal erotism finds a narcissistic application in the production of defiance, which constitutes an important reaction on the part of the ego against demands made by other people. A baby is regarded as feces ("lumf"), as something which becomes detached from the body by passing through the bowel. Interest in feces is carried over first to interest in gifts, and then to interest in money.

1917A 17/135
A difficulty in the path of psycho-analysis (1917).

A difficulty in the path of psychoanalysis is discussed. The difficulty consists of the reaction of man to the psychological blow to his narcissism, due to an awareness of the limitations of the ego. When we try to understand neurotic disorders, by far the greater significance attaches to the sexual instincts. Neuroses are, in fact, the specific disorders of the sexual function. In general, whether or not a person develops a neurosis depends on the quantity of his libido, and on the possibility of satisfying it and of discharging it through satisfaction. The form taken by the disease is determined by the way in which the individual passes through the course of development of his sexual function, or as it is put, by the fixations his libido has undergone in the course of its development. Therapeutic efforts have their greatest success with a certain class of neuroses which proceed from a conflict between the ego instincts and the sexual instincts. The psychoanalytic method of treatment is able to subject the process of repression to revision and to bring about a solution of the conflict, one that is compatible with health. During the work of treatment, we have to consider the distribution of the patient's libido; we look for the object presentations to which the libido is bound and free it from them, so as to

place it at the disposal of the ego. The condition in which the ego retains the libido is called narcissism. The individual advances from narcissism to object love. Psychoanalysis has sought to educate the ego, which is not master in its own house.

1917B 17/145
A childhood recollection from 'Dichtung und Wahrheit' (1917).

A childhood recollection from Goethe's *Dichtung und Wahrheit* is discussed in relation to cases of psychoanalysis. If we try to recollect what happened to us in the earliest years of childhood, we often find that we confuse what we have heard from others with what is really a possession of our own derived from what we ourselves have witnessed. In every psychoanalytic investigation of a life history, it is usually possible to explain the meaning of the earliest childhood memories along the line of screen memories. Screen memories are unimportant or indifferent memories of childhood that owe their preservation not to their own content but to an associative relation between their content and another which is repressed. Goethe wrote about having thrown all his dishes, pots, and pans out of the window. The opinion might be formed that the throwing of crockery out of the window is a symbolic action, or, a magic action by which a child gives violent expression to his wish to get rid of a disturbing intruder. The bitterness children feel about the expected or actual appearance of a rival finds expression in throwing objects out of the window and in other acts of naughtiness or destructiveness.

1919A 17/157
Lines of advance in psycho-analytic therapy (1919).

The task of physicians is to bring to the patient's knowledge the unconscious, repressed impulses existing in him, and, for that purpose, to uncover the resistances that oppose this extension of his knowledge about himself. The work by which we bring the repressed mental material into the patient's consciousness is called psychoanalysis. The neurotic patient presents us with a torn mind, divided by resistances. As we analyze it and remove the resistances, it grows together; the great unity which we call his ego fits into itself all the instinctual impulses which before had been split off and held apart from it. The psychosynthesis is thus achieved during analytic treatment without intervention, automatically and inevitably. Analytic treatment should be carried through, as far as is possible, under privation, in a state of abstinence. It is frustration that made the patient ill, and his symptoms serve him as substitutive satisfactions. Activity on the part of the physician must take the form of energetic opposition to premature substitutive satisfactions. The patient looks for his substitutive satisfaction in the treatment itself, in his transference relationship with the physician; and he may even strive to compensate himself by this means for all the other privations laid upon him. It is necessary to deny the patient precisely those satisfactions which he desires most intensely and expresses most importunately. If everything is made pleasant for the patient he is not given the necessary strength for facing life.

1919J 17/169
On the teaching of psycho-analysis in universities (1919).

The teaching of psychoanalysis in the Universities is discussed. The inclusion of psychoanalysis in the University curriculum would be regarded with satisfaction by every psychoanalyst. At the same time, it is clear that the psychoanalyst can dispense entirely with the University without any loss to himself. So far as the Universities are concerned, the question depends on their deciding whether they are willing to attribute any value at all to psychoanalysis in the training of physicians and scientists. The training has been criticized during the last few decades for the one-sided way in which it directs the student into the field of anatomy, physics and chemistry, while failing, to make plain to him the significance of mental factors in the different vital functions as well as in illnesses and their treatment. This obvious deficiency led to the inclusion in the University curriculum of courses of lectures on medical psychology. Psychoanalysis, more than any other system, is fitted for teaching psychology to the medical student. The teaching of psychoanalysis would have to proceed in 2 stages: an elementary course, designed for all medical students, and a course of specialized lectures for psychiatrists. In the investigation of mental processes and intellectual functions, psychoanalysis pursues a specific method of its own. The application of this method extends to the solution of problems in art, philosophy and religion. A University stands only to gain by the inclusion in its curriculum of the teaching of psychoanalysis.

1919E 17/175
'A child is being beaten': A contribution to the study of the origin of sexual perversions (1919): Editor's note. (1955).

The greater part of the paper called *A Child is Being Beaten, a Contribution to the Study of the Origin of Sexual Perversions*, consists of a very detailed clinical enquiry into a particular kind of perversion. Freud's findings throw a special light on the problem of masochism; and, as the subtitle implies, the paper was also designed to extend our knowledge of the perversions in general. The mechanism of repression is exhaustively discussed in 2 of Freud's metapsychological papers; but the question of the motives leading to repression is nowhere examined more fully than in the present paper. The problem was one which had interested and also puzzled Freud from very early days.

1919E 17/179
'A child is being beaten': A contribution to the study of the origin of sexual perversions (1919). Parts I, II, & III.

People who seek analytic treatment for hysteria or an obsessional neurosis often confess to having indulged in the phantasy: A child is being beaten. The phantasy has feelings of pleasure attached to it, and on their account the patient has reproduced it on innumerable occasions in the past or may even still be doing so. At the climax of the imaginary situation there is almost invariably a masturbatory satisfaction. At first this takes place voluntarily, but later on it does so in spite of the patient's efforts, and with the characteristics of an obsession. The first phantasies of the kind are entertained very early in life: before school age, and not later than in the fifth or sixth year. This phantasy is cathected with a high degree of pleasure and has its issue in an act of pleasurable autoerotic satisfaction. A phantasy of this kind, arising in early childhood and retained for the purpose of autoerotic satisfaction, can be regarded as a primary trait of perversion. One of the components of the sexual function has developed in advance of the rest, has made itself prematurely independent, has undergone fixation and in consequence been withdrawn from the later processes of development, and has in this way given evidence of a peculiar and abnormal constitution in the individual. If the sexual component which has broken loose prematurely is the sadistic one, then we may expect that its subsequent repression will result in a disposition to an obsessional neurosis. Between the ages of 2 and 4 or 5, the congenital libidinal factors are first awakened. The beating phantasies appear toward the end of this period or after its termination. Analysis shows that these beating phantasies have a hysterical development that involves many transformations (as regards the phantasies' relation to the author of the phantasy and as regards their object, content and significance). In the first phase of beating phantasies among girls the child beaten is never the one producing the phantasy but is most often a brother or sister. It is always an adult that is beating the child in all these phantasies. The first phase is completely represented in the phrase 'My father is beating the child.' The second (and most important) phase can be stated as 'I am being beaten by my father.' The third involves a phantasy with strong and unambiguous sexual excitement attached to it, thus providing a means for masturbatory satisfaction.

1919E   17/186

'A child is being beaten': A contribution to the study of the origin of sexual perversions (1919). Parts IV & V.

If analysis is carried through the early period to which the beating phantasies are referred and from which they are recollected, it shows us that the child is involved in the agitations of its parental complex. The affections of the girl are fixed on her father. The first phase (sadism) of the beating phantasy in which another disliked sibling is beaten by the father gratifies the child's jealousy and is dependent upon the erotic side of the child's life, but is also powerfully reinforced by the child's egoistic interest. The phantasy of the second phase, being beaten by the father is a direct expression of the girl's sense of guilt: the phantasy therefore has become masochistic. A sense of guilt is invariably the main factor that transforms sadism into masochism; another factor is the love impulse. This phantasy is not only the punishment for the forbidden genital relation, but also the regressive substitute for that relation, and from this latter source, it derives the libidinal excitation which is attached to it, and which finds its source, it derives the libidinal excitation which is attached to it, and which finds its outlet in masturbatory acts. The third phase of the beating phantasy is again sadistic. A perversion in childhood may become the basis for the construction of a perversion having a similar sense and persisting throughout life, one which consumes the subject's whole sexual life. Masochism is not the manifestation of a primary instinct, but originates from sadism which has been turned round upon the self, by means of regression from an object to the ego. People who harbor phantasies of this kind develop a special sensitiveness and irritability towards anyone whom they can include in the class of fathers. They are easily offended by a person of this kind, and in that way bring about the realization of the imagined situation of being beaten by their father.

1919E   17/195

'A child is being beaten': A contribution to the study of the origin of sexual perversions (1919). Part VI.

The little girl's beating phantasy passes through 3 phases, of which the first and third are consciously remembered. The 2 conscious phases appear to be sadistic; the middle and unconscious one is masochistic in nature; it consists in the child's being beaten by her father, and it carries with it libidinal charge and a sense of guilt. In the first and third phantasies, the child who is being beaten is someone other than the subject; in the middle phase it is the child herself; in the third phase it is usually boys who are being beaten. The person who does the beating is the father, replaced later on by a substitute taken from the class of fathers. The uncon-

scious phantasy of the middle phase has a genital significance and develops by means of repression and regression out of an incestuous wish to be loved by the father. There are only a few male cases with an infantile beating phantasy that do not have some other gross injury to their sexual activities. They include persons who can be described as masochists, in the sense of being sexual perverts. These men invariably transfer themselves into the part of a woman, while their masochistic attitude coincides with a feminine one. In the male phantasy, being beaten stands for being loved (in a genital sense). The boy's beating phantasy is passive and is derived from a feminine attitude towards his father. Adler proposes, in his theory of the masculine protest, that every individual makes efforts not to remain on the inferior feminine line of development, and struggles towards the masculine line, from which satisfaction alone can be derived. The theory of psychoanalysis holds firmly to the view that the motive forces of repression must not be sexualized. No great change is effected by the repression of the original unconscious phantasy. Infantile sexuality, which is held under repression, acts as the chief motive force in the formation of symptoms; and the essential part of its content, the Oedipus complex, is the nuclear complex of neuroses.

1919D   17/205

Introduction to 'psycho-analysis and the war neuroses' (1919).

The war neuroses, in so far as they are distinguished from the ordinary neuroses of peacetime by special characteristics, are to be regarded as traumatic neuroses whose occurrence has been made possible or has been promoted by a conflict in the ego. The conflict is between the soldier's old peaceful ego and his new war-like one, and it becomes acute as soon as the peace ego realizes what danger it runs of losing its life owing to the rashness of its newly formed, parasitic double. The precondition of the war neuroses would seem to be a national army; there would be no possibility of their arising in an army of professional soldiers or mercenaries. The war neuroses are only traumatic neuroses. The traumatic neuroses and war neuroses may proclaim too loudly the effects of mortal danger and may be silent or speak only in muffled tones of the effects of frustration in love. In traumatic and war neuroses the human ego is defending itself from a danger which threatens it from without or which is embodied in a shape assumed by the ego itself. In the transference neuroses of peace, the enemy from which the ego is defending itself is actually the libido, whose demands seem to it to be menacing. In both cases the ego is afraid of being damaged.

Introduction to 'Psychoanalysis and the war neuroses' (1919). Appendix: Memorandum on the electrical treatment of war neurotics (1955) (1920).

A memorandum on the electrical treatment of war neurotics is presented. Although the war neuroses manifested themselves for the most part as motor disturbances, tremors and paralyses, and although it was plausible to suppose that such a gross impact as that produced by the concussion due to the explosion of a shell nearby or to being buried by a fall of earth would lead to gross mechanical effects, observations were nevertheless made which left no doubt as to the psychical nature of the causation of these so-called war neuroses. It was inferred that the immediate cause of all war neuroses was an unconscious inclination in the soldier to withdraw from the demands, dangerous or outrageous to his feelings, made upon him by active service. It seemed expedient to treat the neurotic as a malingerer and to disregard the psychological distinction between conscious and unconscious intentions. Just as he had fled from the war into illness, means were adopted which compelled him to flee back from illness into health. For this purpose painful electrical treatment was employed. This treatment, however, was not effective. In 1918, Dr. Ernst Simmel, head of a hospital for war neuroses at Posen, published a pamphlet in which he reported the extraordinarily favorable results achieved in severe cases of war neurosis by the psychotherapeutic method introduced by Freud. With the end of the war, the war neurotics disappeared.

1919H 17/219

The 'uncanny' (1919). Part I. Linguistic approach to the uncanny.

The uncanny is discussed. The uncanny is related to what is frightening, to what arouses dread and horror. As good as nothing is to be found upon this subject in comprehensive treatises on esthetics. In his study of the uncanny, Jentsch lays stress on the obstacle presented by the fact that people vary greatly in their sensitivity to this quality of feeling. Not everything that is new and unfamiliar is frightening. The German word *unheimlich* is the opposite of *heimlich* (homelike), *heimisch* (native); the opposite of what is familiar. Among its different shades of meaning the word *heimlich* exhibits one which is identical with its opposite, *unheimlich*. The word *heimlich* is not unambiguous, but belongs to 2 sets of ideas, which without being contradictory, are yet very different (homelike and secretly). Thus *heimlich* is a word, the meaning of which develops in the direction of ambivalence, until it finally coincides with its opposite, *unheimlich*. *Unheimlich* is in some way or other a subspecies of *heimlich*.

1919H 17/226

The 'uncanny' (1919). Part II. Phenomenology of uncanny affects.

Jentsch has taken, as a very good instance of the uncanny, doubts whether an apparently animate being is really alive; or conversely, whether a lifeless object might not be in fact animate. To these he adds the uncanny effect of epileptic fits, and of manifestations of insanity. These doubts of alive versus inanimate are thoroughly discussed in the story of The Sand-Man in E. T. A. Hoffmann's *Nachtstucken*. The feeling of something uncanny is directly attached to the figure of the Sand-Man, that is, to the idea of being robbed of one's eyes. The fear of damaging or losing one's eyes is a terrible threat to children. This fear of blindness is seen as part of a castration complex. If psychoanalytic theory is correct in maintaining that every effect belonging to an emotional impulse, whatever its kind, is transformed, if it is repressed, into anxiety, then among instances of frightening things there must be one class in which the frightening element can be shown to be something repressed which recurs. This class of frightening things would then constitute the uncanny. Many people experience the feeling in the highest degree in relation to death and dead bodies, to the return of the dead, and to spirits and ghosts. The uncanny effect of epilepsy and of madness has the same origin. The layman sees in them the working of forces hitherto unsuspected in his fellow men, but at the same time he is dimly aware of them in remote corners of his own being. An uncanny effect is often easily produced when the distinction between imagination and reality is effaced, as when something that we have hitherto regarded as imaginary appears before us in reality, or when a symbol takes over the full functions of the thing it symbolizes.

1919H 17/245

The 'uncanny' (1919). Part III. Relation of imagination to reality.

It may be true that the uncanny, *unheimlich*, is something which is secretly familiar, *heimlich–heimisch*, which has undergone repression and then returned from it and that everything that is uncanny fulfills this condition. But the selection of material on this basis does not enable us to solve the problem of the uncanny. Apparent death and the reanimation of the dead have been represented as most uncanny themes. As soon as something actually happens in our lives which seems to confirm the old discarded beliefs, we get a feeling of the uncanny. When the uncanny comes from infantile complexes, the question of material reality does not arise; its place is taken by psychical reality. What is involved is an actual repression of some content of thought and a return of this repressed content, not a cessation of belief in the reality of such a content. An uncanny experience occurs either when infantile complexes which have been repressed are once more revived by some impression, or when primitive beliefs which have been surmounted seem once more to be confirmed. A great deal that is not uncanny in fiction would be so if it happened in real life. There are many more means of creating uncanny effects in fiction than there are in real life. The factors of silence, solitude, and darkness are actually elements in the production of the infantile anxiety from which the majority of human beings have never become quite free.

1919H 17/253
The 'uncanny' (1919). Appendix: Extract from Daniel Sander's 'Worterbuch der Deutschen Sprache.

Although the German title of Freud's paper has been translated as "The Uncanny," an appended extract from an authoritative dictionary of the German language suggests some of the difficulties involved in choosing an appropriate equivalent for the original title. Discussed at some length are the denotations, connotations, and implications of the German word "heimlich" (or "die Heimlichkeit") and its oppositive. The latter is said to be essentially equivalent to the German "unbehaglich" (cf. Freud's "das Unbehagen in der Kultur"), but also suggests unreasoning discomfort or a reaction of frightened aversion, as from some ill defined evil or the discovery of some unsuspected secret which should have been kept hidden away, but which has nonetheless become manifest. Although "heimlich" is substantially identified with the concept represented by the Latin "familiarities" or the original implications of the English word "homely," it is also, and perhaps equally, identified with the idea of something hidden away, or something of which only a severely limited group has any cognizance or any right to either cognizance or contact. "Unheimlich," in turn, suggests a breach of that condition and privilege, which is associated inevitably with both a considerable degree of existential guilt and potential threat, punishment, or vengeance.

1919G 17/257
Preface to Reik's 'Ritual: Psycho-analytic studies' (1919).

The preface to Reik's *Ritual: Psychoanalytic Studies* is presented. Psychoanalysis sprang from the need for bringing help to neurotic patients, who had found no relief through rest cures, through the arts of hydropathy, or through electricity. In 1913, Otto Rank and Hanns Sachs, brought together the results which had been achieved up to that time in the application of psycho-analysis to the mental sciences. The overcoming of the Oedipus complex conicides with the most efficient way of mastering the archaic, animal heritage of humanity. What is today the heritage of the individual was once a

new acquisition and has been handed on from one to another of a long series of generations. The Oedipus complex too may have had stages of development. Investigation suggests that life in the human family took a quite different form in those remote days from that with which we are now familiar. If the prehistoric and ethnological material on this subject is worked over psychoanalytically, the result is that God the Father once walked upon earth in bodily form and exercised His sovereignty as chieftain of the primal human horde until his sons united to slay Him. This crime of liberation and the reactions to it had as their result the appearance of the first social ties, the basic moral restrictions and the oldest form of religion, totemism. This hypothesis has been taken by Theodor Reik as the basis of his studies on the problems of the psychology of religion.

1919C 17/267
A note on psycho-analytic publications and prizes (1919).

In the autumn of 1918, a member of the Budapest Psychoanalytical Society informed Freud that a fund had been set aside for cultural purposes from the profits made by industrial undertakings during the war. The fund was placed at Freud's disposal, was given his name, and was allotted by him to the foundation of an international psychoanalytic publishing business (the Internationaler Psychoanalytischer Verlag). The 2 periodical publications (*Internationale Zeitschrift fur arztliche Psychoanalyse* and *Imago*) survived the war. The new publishing house, supported by the funds of the Budapest endowment, assumed the task of ensuring the regular appearance and reliable distribution of the 2 journals. Simultaneously with the establishment of the psychoanalytic publishing house it was decided to award annual prizes out of the interest on the Budapest endowment, to 2 outstanding peices of work, one each in the field of medical and of applied psychoanalysis. It was intended that these prizes should be awarded every year and that the choice should fall within the whole field of the psychoanalytically important literature published during that period, irrespective of whether or not the author of the work in question was a Member of the International Psychoanalytic Association.

1919B 17/271
James J. Putnam (1919).

Among the first pieces of news that reached Freud after the raising of the barrier separating him from the Anglo-Saxon countries was the report of the death of Putnam, President of the Pan-American psychoanalytic group. Putnam lived to be over 72 years old, remained intellectually active to the end, and died peacefully of heart failure in his sleep in November 1918. Putnam was the great support of psychoanalysis in America. J. J.

Putnam's personal appearance was made familiar to European analysts through the part he took in the Weimar Congress of 1911.

1919F   17/273
Victor Tausk (1919).

Shortly before the outbreak of the first World War, Dr. Victor Tausk, (previously a lawyer, then a journalist) had obtained his second doctor's degree and set up in Vienna as a nerve specialist. He was called up for active service and was soon promoted to senior rank. The stresses of many years' service in the field could exercise a severely damaging psychological effect on this intensely conscientious man. At the last Psycho-analytical Congress, held in Budapest in September 1918, Dr. Tausk showed signs of unusual nervous irritability. Soon afterwards he came to the end of his military service, returned to Vienna, and was faced for the third time, in his state of mental exhaustion, with the hard task of building up a new existence. On the morning of July 3, 1919 (at the age of 42) he put an end to his life. Dr. Tausk had been a member of the Vienna Psycho-Analytical Society since autumn of 1909. His writings exhibit the philosophical training which he was able to combine with the exact methods of science. Tausk also possessed an exceptional medico-psychological capacity. Psychoanalysis was particularly indebted to Dr. Tausk, who was a brilliant speaker, for the courses of lectures which he gave over a period of many years to large audiences of both sexes and in which he introduced them to the principles and problems of psychoanalysis.

VOL. XVIII   Beyond the Pleasure Principle, Group Psychology and Other Works (1920-1922)

1920G   18/3
Beyond the pleasure principle (1920). Editor's note. (1955).

Freud began working on a first draft of *Beyond the Pleasure Principle* in March, 1919, and he reported the draft as finished in the following May. The work was finally completed by the middle of July, 1920. In the series of Freud's metapsychological writings, *Beyond the Pleasure Principle* may be regarded as introducing the final phase of his views. He had already drawn attention to the compulsion to repeat as a clinical phenomenon, but here he attributes to it the characteristics of an instinct; here too for the first time he brings forward the new dichotomy between Eros and the death instincts. The problem of destructiveness, which played an ever more prominent part in his theoretical works, makes its first explicit appearance.

1920G   18/7
Beyond the pleasure principle (1920). Part I. Review of the pleasure principle. Part II. Traumatic neurosis and children's play are repetitions.

In the theory of psychoanalysis it is assumed that mental events are automatically regulated by the pleasure principle. The course of those events is invariably set in motion by an unpleasurable tension. The final outcome coincides with a lowering of that tension. The mental apparatus endeavors to keep the quantity of excitation present in it as low as possible. Under the influence of the ego's instincts of self-preservation, the pleasure principle is replaced by the reality principle. Another occasion of the release of unpleasure is to be found in the conflicts and dissensions that take place in the mental apparatus while the ego is passing through its development into more highly composite organizations. Most of the unpleasure that we experience is perceptual unpleasure. The study of dreams may be considered the most trustworthy method of investigating deep mental processes. Dreams occurring in traumatic neuroses have the characteristic of repeatedly bringing the patient back into the situation of his accident, a situation from which he wakes up in another fright. A game that a 1½-year-old child invented was related to the child's great cultural achievement; the instinctual renunciation which he made in allowing his mother to go away without protesting. At the outset, he was in a passive situation; but, by repeating it, unpleasurable though it was, as a game, he took on an active part. There is no need to assume the existence of a special imitative instinct in order to provide a motive for play. It is concluded that even under the dominance of the pleasure principle, there are ways and means enough of making what is in itself unpleasurable into a subject to be recollected and worked over in the mind.

1920G   18/18
Beyond the pleasure principle (1919). Part III. Transference neurosis is a repetition.

Psychoanalysis is first and foremost an art of interpreting. A further aim comes in view: to oblige the patient to confirm the analyst's construction from his own memory. The chief emphasis lies upon the patient's resistances: the art consists in uncovering these as quickly as possible, in pointing them out to the patient, and in inducing him to abandon his resistances. However, the patient cannot remember the whole of what is repressed in him, and what he cannot remember may be precisely the essential part of it. He is obliged to repeat the repressed material instead of remembering it as something belonging to the past. These reproductions always concern some portion of infantile sexual life. When things have reached this stage, it is said that the earlier neurosis has been replaced by a transference neurosis. The physician must get the patient to reexperience some portion of his forgotten life but he must see to it that the patient retains some degree of aloofness. The resistance of the conscious and unconscious ego operates under the sway of the pleasure principle: it seeks to avoid the unpleasure which would be produced by the liberation of the repressed. The early efflorescence of infantile sexual life is doomed to extinction because its wishes are incompatible with reality and with the inadequate stage of development which the child has reached. Patients repeat all of the unwanted situations and painful emotions in the transference and revive them with the greatest ingenuity. What psychoanalysis reveals in the transference phenomena of neurotics can also be observed in the lives of some normal people: those whose human relationships have the same outcome.

1920G   18/24
Beyond the pleasure principle (1920). Part IV. Speculations on the death instinct.

Psychoanalytic speculation takes as its point of departure the impression that consciousness may be not the most universal attribute of mental processes, but only a particular function of them. What consciousness yields consists essentially of perceptions of excitations coming from the external world and of feelings of pleasure and unpleasure which arise from within the mental apparatus. The conscious system is characterized by the peculiarity that in it, excitatory processes do not leave behind any permanent change in its elements but expire in the phenomenon of becoming conscious. The living vesicle is provided with a shield against stimuli from the external world. The cortical layer next to that shield must be differentiated as an organ for receiving stimuli from without. This sensitivity cortex which later becomes the conscious system, also receives excitations from within. The unpleasure of physical pain is probably the result of the protective shield having been broken through. There is then a continuous stream of excitations from the part of the periphery concerned to the central apparatus of the mind, such as could normally arise only from within the apparatus. Cathectic energy is summoned from all sides to provide sufficiently high cathexes of energy in the environs of the breach. An anticathexis on a grand scale is set up and the other phychical systems are impoverished so that the remaining psychical functions are extensively paralyzed or reduced. The common traumatic neurosis is regarded as a consequence of an extensive breach being made in the protective shield against stimuli. Preparedness for anxiety and the hypercathexis of the receptive systems constitute the last line of defense of the shield against stimuli. Dreams endeavor to master the stimulus

retrospectively, by developing the anxiety whose omission was the cause of the traumatic neurosis. An exception to the proposition that dreams are wish fulfillments is dreams occurring in traumatic neuroses; these arise in obedience to the compulsion to repeat. Thus it would seem that the function of dreams, which consists in setting aside any motives that might interrupt sleep, by fulfilling the wishes of disturbing impulses, is not their original function. If there is a 'beyond the pleasure principle,' then there was also a time before the purpose of dreams was the fulfillment of wishes.

1920G   18/34
Beyond the pleasure principle (1920). Part V. Revision of the theory of instincts.

The fact that the cortical layer which receives stimuli is without any protective shield against excitations from within must have as its result that these latter transmissions of stimulus have a preponderance in economic importance and often occasion economic disturbances comparable with traumatic neuroses. The impulses arising from the instincts do not belong to the type of bound nervous processes but of freely mobile processes which press towards discharge. The manifestations of a compulsion to repeat (which is described as occurring in the early activities of infantile mental life as well as among the events of psychoanalytic treatment) exhibit to a high degree an instinctual character and, when they act in opposition to the pleasure principle, give the appearance of some demonic force at work. It seems that an instinct is an urge inherent in organic life to restore an earlier state of things which the living entity has been obliged to abandon under the pressure of external disturbing forces. The instincts which watch over the destinies of the elementary organisms that survive the whole individual which provide them with a safe shelter while they are defenseless against the stimuli of the external world, which bring about their meeting with other germ cells, etc., constitute the group of the sexual instincts. These instincts are peculiarly conservative in their resistance to external influences and that they preserve life itself. Apart from the sexual instincts, there are no instincts that do not seek to restore an earlier state of things. Both higher development and involution might be the consequences of adaption to the pressure of external forces; and in both cases, the part played by instincts might be limited to the retention of an obligatory modification. What appears in a majority of individuals as an untiring impulsion towards perfection can be understood as a result of the instinctual repression upon which is based all that is most precious in human civilization. The repressed instinct never ceases to strive for complete satisfaction. It is concluded that there is no instinct towards perfection at work in human beings. The difference in the amount between the pleasure of satisfaction which is demanded and that which is actually achieved is what provides the driving factor.

1920G 18/44

Beyond the pleasure principle (1920). Part VI. Biological arguments for death instincts. Part VII. Summary.

The ego instincts exercise pressure towards death while the sexual instincts exercise pressure towards prolongation of life. It is hypothesized that the ego instincts arise from the coming to life of inanimate matter and seek to restore the inanimate while sexual instincts aim at conjugation of the germ cell. Without this union the cell dies. The assumption that death is internal (natural) is discussed. Biological experiments dealing with organisms such as ciliate infusorian give the following 2 facts: if 2 of the animalculae, at the moment before they show signs of senescene, are able to conjugate, they are saved from growing old and become rejuvenated. It is also probable that infusoria die a natural death as a result of their own vital processes. It is concluded that biology does not contradict the recognition of the death instincts. Psychoanalysis observed the regularity with which libido is withdrawn from the object and directed to the ego. By studying the libidinal development of children it was concluded that the ego is the true and original reservoir of libido, and that it is only from that reservoir that libido is extended onto objects. A portion of the ego instincts was seen to be libidinal and sexual instincts operated in the ego. Thus the distinction between these 2 instincts has changed from qualitative to topographical. We cannot ascribe to the sexual instinct the characteristic of a compulsion to repeat. The dominating tendency of mental life (and perhaps of nervous life) is the effort to reduce, keep constant, or remove internal tension due to stimuli, a tendency which finds expression in the pleasure principle; our recognition of this fact is a major reason for believing in the existence of death instincts. One of the earliest and most important functions of the mental apparatus is to bind the instinctual impulses which impinge it, to replace the primary process prevailing in them by the secondary process and convert their freely mobile cathectic energy into a mainly quiescent cathexis. The pleasure principle is a tendency operating in the service of a function to free the mental apparatus from excitation or to keep the amount of excitation in it constant or as low as possible. At the beginning of mental life the struggle for pleasure was far more intense than later but not so unrestricted.

1921C 18/67

Group psychology and the analysis of the ego (1921). Editor's note. (1955).

Freud's letter showed that the first idea of an explanation of group psychology occurred to him during the spring of 1919. In February, 1920, he was working at the subject and he had written a first draft in August of the same year. It was not until February, 1921, however, that he began giving it its final form. There is little direct connection between this work and *Beyond the Pleasure Principle*. The trains of thought which Freud takes up in *Group Psychology and the Analysis of the Ego* are more especially derived from the fourth essay in *Totem and Taboo* and his papers on narcissism and *Mourning and Melancholia*. The work is important in 2 different directions. On the one hand it explains the psychology of groups on the basis of changes in the psychology of the individual mind. On the other hand it carries a stage further Freud's investigation of the anatomical structure of the mind.

1921C 18/69

Group psychology and analysis of the ego (1921). Part I: Introduction.

Individual psychology is concerned with the individual man and explores the paths by which he seeks to find satisfaction for his instinctual impulses. In the individual's mental life someone else is invariably involved, as a model, as an object, as a helper, or as an opponent. The contrast between social and narcissistic mental acts falls wholly within the domain of individual psychology, and is not well calculated to differentiate it from a social or group psychology. The individual in the relations to his parents and to his brothers and sisters, to the person he is in love with, to his friend, and to his physician, comes under the influence of only a single person, or of a very small number of persons, each one of whom has become enormously important to him. Group psychology is concerned with the individual man as a member of a race, of a nation, of a caste, of a profession, or an institution, or as a component part of a crowd of people who have been organized into a group at some particular time for some definite purpose. Group psychology embraces an immense number of separate issues and offers to investigators countless problems which have hitherto not even been properly distinguished from one another.

1921C 18/72

Group psychology and the analysis of the ego (1921). Part II: Le Bon's description of the group mind.

Le Bon's description of the group mind is discussed. If the individuals in a group are combined into a unity, there must be something to unite them, and this bond might be precisely the thing that is characteristic of a group. Le Bon thinks that the particular acquirements of individuals become obliterated in a group, and that in this way their distinctiveness vanishes. The racial unconscious emerges; what is heterogenous is submerged in what is homogeneous. The mental superstructure, the development of which in individuals shows such dissimilarities, is removed, and the unconscious foundations, which are similar in everyone, stand exposed to view. In a group, the individual is brought under conditions which allow him to throw off the repressions of his unconscious instinctual impulses. The apparently new characteristics which he then displays are in fact the manifestations of this unconscious. Le Bon believes that the individuals in a group display new characteristics which they have not previously possessed. Three factors are put forth as reasons for this: 1) the individual forming part of a group acquires a sentiment of invincible power which allows him to yield to instincts which, had he been alone, he would perforce have kept under restraint; 2) contagion; and 3) suggestibility. A group is impulsive, changeable, and irritable. It is led almost exclusively by the unconscious. A group is credulous and open to influence, it has no critical faculty, and the improbable does not exist for it. A group is subject to the magical power of words. Groups have never thirsted after truth.

1921C   18/82

Group psychology and the analysis of the ego (1921). Part III: Other accounts of collective mental life.

The 2 theses which comprise the most important of Le Bon's opinions, those touching upon the collective inhibition of intellectual functioning and the heightening of affectivity in groups, had been formulated shortly before by Sighele. However, the group mind is capable of creative genius in the field of intelligence, as is shown above all by language itself, as well as by folksong, folklore and the like. The most remarkable and also the most important result of the formation of a group is the exaltation or intensification of emotion produced in every member of it. In McDougall's opinion, men's emotions are stirred in a group to a pitch that they seldom or never attain under other conditions. The manner in which individuals are carried away by a common impulse is by means of emotional contagion. A group impresses the individual as being an unlimited power and an insurmountable peril. Five principal conditions for raising collective mental life to a higher level are enumerated by McDougall. 1) There should be some degree of continuity of existence in the group. 2) In the individual member of the group, some definite idea should be formed of the nature, composition, functions and capacities of the group. 3) The group

should be brought into interaction with other groups. 4) The group should possess traditions, customs and habits. 5) The group should have a definite structure.

1921C   18/88

Group psychology and the analysis of the ego (1921). Part IV: Suggestion and libido.

Suggestion and libido are investigated. An individual in a group is subject, through its influence, to what is often a profound alteration in his mental activity. Rational factors do not cover the observable phenomena. What is usually offered as an explanation is suggestion. Suggestion is actually an irreducible, primitive phenomenon, a fundamental fact in the mental life of man. An attempt at using the concept of libido is presented for the purpose of throwing light upon group psychology. Libido is an expression taken from the theory of the emotions. We call by that name the energy, regarded as a quantitative magnitude, of those instincts which have to do with all that may be comprised under the word love. Psychoanalysis gives these love instincts the name of sexual instincts. It is supposed that love relationships also constitute the essence of the group mind. A group is clearly held together by a power of some kind: to what power could this feat be better ascribed than to Eros? If an individual gives up his distinctiveness in a group and lets its other members influence him by suggestion, it gives one the impression that he does it because he feels the need of being in harmony with them rather than in opposition to them.

1921C   18/93

Group psychology and the analysis of the ego (1921). Part V: Two artificial groups. The church and the army.

Two artificial groups, the Church and the army, are examined. In a Church as well as in an army, however different the 2 may be in other respects, the same illusion holds good of there being a head who loves all the individuals in the group with an equal love. Everything depends upon this illusion. In these 2 artificial groups, each individual is bound by libidinal ties on the one hand to the leader (Christ, the Commander in Chief) and on the other hand to the other members of the group. The essence of a group lies in the libidinal ties existing in it. Panic arises if a group becomes disintegrated; the mutual ties have ceased to exist, and a gigantic and senseless fear is set free. Panic fear presupposes a relaxation in the libidinal structure of the group and reacts to that relaxation in a justifiable manner.

1921C 18/100

Group psychology and the analysis of the ego (1921). Part VI: Further problems and lines of work.

A mere collection of people is not a group. In any collection of people the tendency to form a psychological group may very easily come to the fore. The evidence of psychoanalysis shows that almost every intimate emotional relation between 2 people which lasts for some time contains a sediment of feelings of aversion and hostility, which only escapes perception as a result of repression. This is less disguised in the common wrangles between buisness partners or in the grumbles of a subordinate at his superior. In the undisguised antipathies and the aversions which people feel towards strangers, we may recognize the expression of self-love, of narcissism. This self-love works for the preservation of the individual. But when a group is formed, the whole of this intolerance vanishes, temporarily or permanently, within the group. The same thing occurs in men's social relations as has become familiar to psychoanalytic research in the course of the development of the individual libido. The libido attaches itself to the satisfaction of the great vital needs, and chooses as its first objects the people who have a share in that process. If therefore in groups, narcissistic self-love is subject to limitations which do not operate outside them, that is cogent evidence that the essence of a group formation consists in new kinds of libidinal ties among the members of the group.

1921C 18/105

Group psychology and the analysis of the ego (1921). Part VII: Identification.

Identification is known to psychoanalysis as the earliest expression of an emotional tie with another person. It plays a part in the early history of the Oedipus complex. There are 3 sources of identification. First, identification is the original form of emotional ties with an object; secondly, in a regressive way it becomes a substitue for a libidinal object tie, as it were by means of introjection of the object into the ego, and thirdly, it may arise with any new perception of a common quality shared with some other person who is not an object of the sexual instinct. The mutual tie between members of a group is in the nature of an identification based upon an important emotional common quality.

1921C 18/111

Group psychology and the analysis of the ego (1921). Part VIII: Being in love and hypnosis.

Being in love is an object cathexis on the part of the sexual instincts with a view to sexual satisfaction, a cathexis which expires when this aim has been reached. The loved object enjoys a certain amount of freedom from criticism; all its characteristics are valued more highly than those of people who are not loved, or than its own were at a time when it itself was not loved. The tendency which falsifies judgment in this respect is that of idealization. Traits of humility, of the limitation of narcissism and of self-injury occur in every case of being in love. This happens especially easily with love that is unhappy and cannot be satisfied; for in spite of everything each sexual satisfaction always involves a reduction in sexual overvaluation. Contemporaneously with this devotion of the ego to the object, the functions allotted to the ego ideal cease to operate. The object has been put in the place of an ego ideal. From being in love to hypnosis is only a short step. This is the same humble subjection, the same compliance, the same absence of criticism, towards the hypnotist as towards the love object. The hypnotic relation is a group formation with 2 members. A formula for the libidinal constitution of groups is presented: a primary group is a number of individuals who have put the same object in the place of their ego ideal and have consequently identified themselves with one another in their ego.

1921C 18/117

Group psychology and the analysis of the ego (1921). Part IX: The herd instinct.

The herd instinct is discussed. Trotter derives the mental phenomena that are described as occurring in groups from a herd instinct (gregariousness), which is innate in human beings just as in other species of animals. Biologically, he says, this gregariousness is an analogy to multicellularity and a continuation of it. In terms of the libido theory, it is a further manifestation of the tendency which proceeds from the libido and which is felt by all living beings of the same kind, to combine in more and more comprehensive units. Trotter gives, as the list of instincts which he considers as primary, those of self-preservation, of nutrition, of sex, and of the herd. Social feeling is based upon the reversal of what was first a hostile feeling into a positively toned tie in the nature of an identification. The demand for equality in a group applies only to its members and not to the leader. All the members must be equal to one another, but they all want to be ruled by one person. Freud concludes that man is not a herd animal, but rather, he is a horde animal, an individual creature in a horde led by a chief.

1921C 18/122

Group psychology and the analysis of the ego (1921). Part X: The group and the primal horde

Human groups exhibit the picture of an individual of superior strength among a troop of equal companions, a picture which is also contained in the idea of the primal horde. The psychology of such a group, the dwindling of the conscious individual personality, the focusing of thoughts and feelings into a common direction, the predominance of the affective side of the mind and of unconscious psychical life, the tendency to the immediate carrying out of intentions as they emerge, corresponds to a state of regression to a primitive mental activity, of just such a sort as is ascribed to the primal horde. The primal father prevented his sons from satisfying their directly sexual impulses; he forced them into abstinence and consequently into the emotional ties with him and with one another. Whoever became his successor was given the possibility of sexual satisfaction. The fixation of the libido to woman and the possibility of satisfaction without any need for delay or accumulation made an end of the importance of those of his sexual impulses that were inhibited in their aim, and allowed his narcissism always to rise to its full height. The uncanny and coercive characteristics of group formations, which are shown in the phenomena of suggestion that accompany them, may be traced back to the fact of their origin from the primal horde. The leader of the group is still the dreaded primal father; the group still wishes to be governed by unrestricted force; it has an extreme passion for authority.

1921C 18/129

Group psychology and the analysis of the ego (1921). Part XI: A differentiating grade in the ego.

Each individual is a component part of numerous groups; he is bound by ties of identification in many directions, and he has built up his ego ideal upon the most various models. Each individual therefore has a share in numerous group minds and he can also raise himself above them to the extent of having a scrap of independence and originality. In many individuals, the separation between the ego and the ego ideal is not very far advanced; the 2 still coincide readily; the ego has often preserved its earlier narcissistic self-complacency. There are people, the general color of whose mood oscillates periodically from an excessive depression through some kind of intermediate state to an exalted sense of well-being. The foundation of these spontaneous oscillations of mood is unknown. In cases of mania, the ego and the ego ideal have fused together, so that the person, in a mood of triumph and self-satisfaction, disturbed by no self-criticism, can enjoy the abolition of his inhibitions, his feelings of consideration for others, and his self-reproaches.

1921C 18/134

Group psychology and the analysis of the ego (1921). Part XII: Postscript.

The distinction between identification of the ego with an object and replacement of the ego ideal by an object finds an illustration in 2 artificial groups, the army and the Christian Church. A soldier takes his superior as his ideal, while he identifies himself with his equals. The Church requires that the position of the libido, which is given by group formation, should be supplemented. The development of the libido in children has made us acquainted with the first example of sexual instincts which are inhibited in their aims. The first configuration of the child's love, which in typical cases takes the shape of the Oedipus complex, succumbs from the beginning of the period of latency onwards to a wave of repression. Sexual impulses that are inhibited in their aims arise out of the directly sexual ones when internal or external obstacles make the sexual aims unattainable. In the history of the development of the family there have been group relations of sexual love; but the more important sexual love became for the ego, and the more it developed the characteristics of being in love, the more it required to be limited to 2 people. Being in love is based on the simultaneous presence of directly sexual impulses and of sexual impulses that are inhibited in their aims, while the object draws a part of the subject's narcissistic ego libido to itself. Hypnosis resembles being in love in being limited to 2 persons. The group multiples this process. Neurosis stands outside this series.

1920A 18/146

The psychogenesis of a case of homosexuality in a woman (1920). Part I.

Homosexuality in women has not only been ignored by the law, but has also been neglected by psychoanalytic research. A single case is presented and discussed. A beautiful and clever girl of 18, belonging to a family of good standing, had aroused displeasure and concern in her parents by the devoted adoration with which she pursued a certain society lady who was about 10 years older than herself. It was well known that this lady lived with a friend, a married woman, and had intimate relations with her, while at the same time she carried on promiscuous affairs with a number of men. The girl appeared in the most frequented streets in the company of her undesirable friend, being thus quite neglectful of her own reputation. However, she disdained no means of deception, no excuses and no lies that would make meetings with her possible and cover them. About 6 months after she attempted to commit suicide, her parents sought medical advice. There was something about the daughter's homosexuality that aroused the deepest bitterness in the father, and he was determined to combat it with all the means in his power. The mother did not take her daughter's infatuation so tragically as did the father, nor was she so incensed at it. The girl was not in any way ill. The patient had not enjoyed anything beyond a few kisses and embraces with the object of her adoration; her genital chasity had remained intact. There was no obvious deviation from the feminine physical type, nor any menstrual disturbance.

1920A 18/155

The psychogenesis of a case of homosexuality in a woman (1920). Part II.

A case of homosexuality in a woman is presented. In childhood the girl had passed through the normal attitude characteristic of the feminine, she did not remember any sexual traumas in early life, nor were any discovered by the analysis. During the prepubertal years at school she gradually became acquainted with the facts of sex, and she received this knowledge with mixed feelings of lasciviousness and frightened aversion, in a way which may be normal. At the age of 13 and 14 she displayed a tender and, according to general opinion, exaggerated affection for a small boy, not quite 3 years old, whom she used to see regularly in a children's playground. After a short time she grew indifferent to the boy, and began to take an interest in mature, but still youthful, women. The manifestations of this interest soon brought upon her a severe chastisement at the hands of her father. The birth of a third brother when she was about 16 was a significant event. Just when the girl was experiencing the revival of her infantile Oedipus complex at puberty she became conscious of the wish to have a male child (unconscious was the wish for her father's child, in his image). Because she did not bear the child, and her unconsciously hated rival, her mother, did bear a child, the patient became resentful and embittered and turned away from her father and from men altogether. Before it happened her libido was concentrated on a maternal attitude, while afterwards she became a homosexual attracted to mature women, and remained so ever since. This libidinal position of the girl's was greatly reinforced as soon as she perceived how much it displeased her father. The girl's inversion received its final reinforcement when she found in her lady an object which promised to satisfy not only her homosexual trends, but also that part of her heterosexual libido which was still attached to her brother.

1920A 18/160

The psychogenesis of a case of homosexuality in a woman (1920). Part III.

A case of homosexuality in a woman is presented. In her behavior to her adored lady, the girl adopted the characteristic masculine type of love. When the girl learned later that her adored lady lived simply by giving her bodily favors, her reaction took the form of great compassion and of phantasies and plans for rescuing her

beloved from these ignoble circumstances. She attempted suicide after her father saw them together and her beloved wanted to end the affair. The attempted suicide was the fulfillment of a punishment, and the fulfillment of a wish. She transferred to Freud the sweeping repudiation of men which had dominated her ever since the disappointment she had suffered from her father. The affective factor of revenge against her father made her cool reserve possible. The 2 intentions, to betray and to please her father, originated in the same complex, the former resulted from the repression of the latter, and the latter one was brought back by the dream work to the earlier one.

1920A 18/167

The psychogenesis of a case of homosexuality in a woman (1920). Part IV.

Freud does not maintain that every girl who experiences a disappointment such as that of the longing for love that springs from the Oedipus attitude at puberty will, necessarily on that account, fall a victim to homosexuality. Even in a normal person it takes a certain time before the decision in regard to the sex of the love object is finally made. Homosexual enthusiasms, exaggerated strong friendships tinged with sensuality, are common enough in both sexes during the first years after puberty. The analysis showed that the girl had brought along with her from her childhood a strongly masked masculinity complex. It is concluded that this is a case of congenital homosexuality which became fixed and unmistakably manifest only in the period following puberty. Mental sexual character and object choice do not necessarily coincide. The mystery of homosexuality is a question of 3 sets of characteristics: physical sexual characters (physical hermaphroditism), mental sexual characters (masculine or feminine attitude), and kind of object choice.

1941D 18/175

Psycho-analysis and telepathy (1941; 1921). Editor's note (1955) and introduction.

Psychoanalysis and Telepathy is the first of Freud's papers on telepathy, but was never published in his lifetime, though the greater part of the material in it was included in various forms in his later published papers on the subject. It does not follow that an intensified interest in occultism must involve a danger to psychoanalysis. The immense majority of occultists are not driven by a desire for knowledge or by a sense of shame that science has so long refused to take cognizance of what are indisputable problems or by a desire to conquer this new sphere of phenomena. They are convinced believers who are looking for confirmation and for something that will justify them in openly confessing their faith. There is little doubt that if attention is directed to occult phenomena the outcome will very soon be that the occurrence of a number of them will be confirmed; and it will probably be a very long time before an acceptable theory covering these new facts can be arrived at. At the very first confirmation, the occultists will proclaim the triumph of their views.

1941D 18/181

Psychoanalysis and telepathy (1941; 1921). Parts I & II.

Three examples of telepathy are presented and discussed. A young man going through analysis told Freud that a fortune teller told him that his borther-in-law would die of crayfish or oyster poisoning in July or August. His brother-in-law did not die but was very seriously ill at that time from crayfish poisoning. This is interpreted as the communication (thought transference) of an unconscious, repressed death wish against his brother-in-law to the fortune teller. The second case concerns the eldest girl of a family of 5 who married well but had no children. Because of the lack of children due to her husband's inability to produce them, she became depressed and was hospitalized. After 10 years of illness, she was treated by Freud at which time she related that at the age of 27, she removed her wedding ring, placed her hand down in a plate of sand, and had a fortune teller announce that she would be married and have 2 children by the age of 32. She was now 40 years old and had no children. The patient's mother had not married till she was 30 and, in her thirty-second year, she gave birth to 2 children. The third episode discussed a graphologist, Rafael Schermann. The phenomenon of thought transference occurred between the graphologist and one of Freud's patients who eventually broke off an affair he was having and married a girl of whom Schermann approved.

1922A 18/196

Dreams and telepathy (1922). Editor's note (1955) and introduction.

The relation of the telepathic occurrences to dreams, or more exactly, to the theory of dreams, is presented. Freud maintains that the 2 have little to do with each other, and that if the existence of telepathic dreams were to be established there would be no need to alter the conception of dreams in any way. The material on which the communication is based is very slight. During some 27 years as an analyst, Freud had never been in a position to observe a truly telepathic dream of any of his patients.

1922A 18/200

Dreams and telepathy (1922). Part I.

Dreams and telepathy are discussed. One of Freud's patients dreamed that his wife had twins. His daughter was pregnant but she was not expecting her confinement for 4 weeks. The next day, he received a telegram from his son-in-law that his daughter had had twins. The dream goes into great detail of the likeness of the children to the parents, discusses the color of their hair and the probable change of color at a later age. In the dream the dreamer's second wife had twins. The occurrence, however, was that his daughter had given birth to twins in the distant home. If we consult the associative material to this dream, it shows, in spite of its sparseness, that an intimate bond of feeling existed between the father and daughter, a bond of feeling which is so usual and so natural that we ought to cease to be ashamed of it, one that in daily life merely finds expression as a tender interest and is only pushed to its logical conclusion in dreams. Two conceptions of the dream are presented. According to the first, the dream is a reaction to a telepathic message: 'your daughter has just brought twins into the world.' According to the second an unconscious process of thought underlies the dream, which may be reproduced somewhat as follows: 'Today is the day the confinement should take place if the young people in Berlin are really out in their reckoning by a month, as I suspect. And if my first wife were still alive, she certainly would not be content with 1 grandchild. To please her there would have to be at least twins. All dreams come from within, are products of our mental life, whereas the very conception of the purely 'telepathic dream' lies in its being a perception of something external, in relation to which the mind remains passive and receptive.

1922A 18/208

Dreams and telepathy (1922). Part II.

The second case concerning the relationship between dreams and telepathy is not a telepathic dream, but a dream that has recurred from childhood onwards, in a person who has had many telepathic experiences. In the recurrent dreams, the dreamer saw a tongue of land surrounded by water. The waves were being driven forward and then back by the breakers. On this piece of land stood a palm tree, bent somewhat towards the water. A woman had her arm wound round the stem of the palm and was bending low towards the water, where a man was trying to reach the shore. At last she lay down on the ground, held tightly to the palm tree with her left hand and stretched out her right hand as far as she could towards the man in the water, but without reaching him. The dream is a rescuing from water, a typical birth dream. The tree trunk is a phallic symbol.

The man's face remained hidden. It must have been her father. The instances of telepathic messages belonged to the sphere of the Oedipus complex. Telepathy has no relation to the essential nature of dreams. It is an incontestable fact that sleep creates favorable conditions for telepathy. Just as sleep is not indispensable to the occurrence of telepathic messages, dream formation does not necessarily wait for the onset of sleep before it begins. If the phenomenon of telepathy is only an activity of the unconscious mind, the laws of unconscious mental life may then apply to this telepathy.

1922B 18/221

Some neurotic mechanisms in jealousy, paranoia and homosexuality (1922).

Jealousy is an affective state, like grief, that may be described as normal. There are 3 layers or grades of jealousy: competitive or normal, projected, and delusional jealousy. Normal jealousy is compounded of grief, the pain caused by the thought of losing the loved object, and of the narcissistic wound, in so far as this is distinguishable from the other wound. Projected jealousy is derived in both men and women either from their own actual unfaithfulness in real life or from impulses towards it which have succumbed to repression. Delusional jealousy has its origin in repressed impulses towards unfaithfulness; but the object in these cases is of the same sex as the subject. Cases of paranoia are not usually amenable to analytic investigation. A case of paranoia was presented that was of a youngish man with a fully developed paranoia of jealousy, the object of which was his impeccably faithful wife. After he broke up an affair he had been having, his projected jealousy broke out. Since in paranoia it is precisely the most loved person of the same sex that becomes the persecutor, this reversal of affect takes its origin from the ambivalence of feeling while the nonfulfillment of this claim for love strengthens it. This ambivalence thus serves the same purpose for the persecuted paranoiac as jealousy in the patient, that of a defense against homosexuality. The whole of the patient's youth was governed by a strong attachment to his mother of whom he was her favorite son. Another case of persecutory paranoia was presented in which the patient was both a rebel and a submissive son. After his father's death he denied himself enjoyment of woman out of guilt. His actual relations with other men were clearly dominated by suspiciousness. The qualitative factor, the presence of certain neurotic formations, has less practical significance than the quantitative factor, the degree of attention or, the amount of cathexis that these structures are able to attract to themselves. The typical process of homosexuality is that a few years after the termination of puberty a young man, who has hitherto

been strongly fixated to his mother, changes his attitude; identifies with his mother and looks for love objects in whom he can rediscover himself, and whom he might love as his mother loved him. The choice is towards a narcissistic object which is readier to hand and easier to put into effect than movement towards the opposite sex. Another mechanism of homosexual object choice, its origin in male sibling rivalry, is discussed.

1923A 18/234

Two encyclopedia articles (1923). (A). Psycho-analysis.

The following 29 topics pertaining to psychoanalysis are summarized: history of psychoanalysis; catharsis; the transition to psychoanalysis (from belief in hypnoid states to repression and defense); abandonment of hypnosis; free association; the 'Fundamental Technical Rule' (in which the patient is required to put himself in the position of an attentive and dispassionate self-observed, to read off the surface of his consciousness, and to make a duty of complete honesty while not holding back any idea from communication); psychoanalysis as an interpretative art; the interpretation of parapraxes and haphazard acts; the interpretation of dreams; the dynamic theory of dream formation (involving wish fulfillment); symbolism; the etiological significance of sexual life; infantile sexuality; the development of the libido; the process of finding an object, and the Oedipus Complex; the diphasic onset of sexual development; the theory of repression; transference; the cornerstones of psychoanalytic theory; later history of psychoanalysis; more recent advances in psychoanalysis; narcissism; development of technique; psychoanalysis as the therapeutic procedure; comparison between psychoanalysis and hypnotic and suggestive methods; the relation of psychoanalysis to psychiatry; criticisms and misunderstandings of psychoanalysis; the nonmedical applications and correlations of psychoanalysis; and psychoanalysis as an empirical science.

1923A 18/255

Two encyclopedia articles (1923). (B). The libido theory.

Libido is a term used in the theory of the instincts for describing the dynamic manifestation of sexuality. The first sphere of phenomena to be studied by psychoanalysis comprised what are known as the transference neuroses. It was found that their symptoms came about by sexual instinctual impulses being rejected by the subject's personality (his ego) and then finding expression by circuitous paths through the unconscious. What is described as the sexual instinct turns out to be of a highly composite nature and is liable to disintegrate once more into its component instincts. Each component instinct is unalterably characterized by its source, that is, by the region or zone of the body from which its excitation is derived. The pathogenic process in schizophrenia (dementia praecox) is the withdrawal of the libido from objects and its introduction into the ego, while the clamorous symptoms of the disease arise from the vain struggles of the libido to find a pathway back to objects. Instincts are characterized as tendencies inherent in living substance towards restoring an earlier state of things. Both classes of instincts, Eros as well as the death of instinct, have been in operation and working against each other from the first origin of life.

1920B 18/263
A note on the prehistory of the technique of analysis (1920).

A book by Havelock Ellis which bears the title of *The Philosophy of Conflict* includes an essay on "Psychoanalysis in Relation to Sex." The aim of this essay is to show that the writings of the creator of analysis should be judged not as a piece of scientific work but as an artistic production. Havelock Ellis's wide reading enabled him to bring forward an author who practiced and recommended free association as a technique, though for purposes other than Freud's, and thus has a claim to be regarded as a forerunner of psychoanalysis. In 1857, Dr. J. J. Garth Wilkinson published a volume of mystic doggerel verse written by what he considered a new method, the method of impression. A theme was chosen and everything that thereafter impressed the mind was written down. In Schiller's correspondence with Korner, the great poet and thinker recommended anyone who desires to be productive to adopt the method of free association. Dr. Hugo Dubowitz drew Dr. Ferenczi's attention to a short essay covering only 4½ pages by Ludwig Borne. The essay advises to take a few sheets of paper and for 3 days, write down, without fabrication or hypocrisy, everything that comes into your head. When 3 days have passed you will be quite out of your senses with atonishment at the new and unheard of thoughts you have had. Freud had been greatly influenced by Borne's work from the age of 14 on.

1920D 18/266
Associations of a four-year-old child (1920).

The associations of a 4-year-old child are presented. The child said that if Emily gets married, she'll have a baby. She knows that when anyone gets married, a baby always comes. The girl said that she knows a lot besides. She knows that trees grow in the ground and that God made the world. What the girl was trying to say was that babies grow inside their mother. She symbolically replaced the mother to Mother Earth. In her last remark she replaced the direct thought that it's all the work of the father by the appropriate sublimation, that God makes the world.

1920C 18/267
Dr. Anton von Freund (1920).

Dr. Anton von Freund, who was General Secretary of the International Psychoanalytical Association since the Budapest Congress in September 1918, died on January 20, 1920, in a Vienna sanatorium, a few days after completing his fortieth year. He used his material powers to assist others and to soften the hardness of their destiny as well as to sharpen in all directions the sense of social justice. When, during his last years, he came to know psychoanalysis, it seemed to him to promise the fulfillment of his 2 great wishes. He set himself the task of helping the masses by psychoanalysis and of making use of the therapeutic effects of that medical technique in order to mitigate the neurotic suffering of the poor. With the concurrence of Dr. Stephan von Barczy, the then Burgomaster, he assigned a sum of money for the foundation of a psychoanalytic institute in Budapest, in which analysis was to be practiced, taught, and made accessible to the people. It was intended to train a considerable number of physicians in this Institute who would receive an honorarium from it for the treatment of poor neurotics in an outpatient clinic. The Institute, furthermore, was to be a center for further scientific research in analysis. Von Freund's premature death has put an end to these philantropic schemes, with all their scientific hopes.

1921A 18/269
Preface to J. J. Putnam's 'Addresses on psycho-analysis' (1921).

The preface to J. J. Putnam's *Addresses on Psychoanalysis* is presented. Professor Putnam, who died in 1918 at the age of 72, was not only the first American to interest himself in psychoanalysis, but soon became its most decided supporter and its most influential representative in America. The papers that are collected into a single volume were written by Putnam between 1909 and the end of his life. They give a good picture of his relations to psychoanalysis. They show how he was at first occupied in correcting a provisional judgment which was based on insufficient knowledge; how he then accepted the essence of analysis, recognized its capacity for throwing a clear light upon the origin of human imperfections and failings, and how he was struck by the prospect of contributing towards the improvement of humanity along analytical lines.

1921B 18/271

Introduction to J. Varendonck's 'The psychology of day-dreams' (1921).

The Introduction to J. Varendonck's *The Psychology of Day Dreams* is presented. Varendonck has succeeded in getting hold of the mode of thought activity to which one abandons oneself during the state of distraction into which we readily pass before sleep or upon incomplete awakening. The author includes the sort of thought activity which he has observed in Bleuler's autistic thinking, but calls it, as a rule fore - conscious thinking. However, the autistic thinking of Bleuler does not, by any means, correspond with the extension and the contents of the fore - conscious. Daydreaming does not owe its peculiarities to the circumstances that it proceeds mostly fore - consciously. Even strictly directed reflection may be achieved without the cooperation of consciousness. The daydream, as well as the chains of thought studied by Varendonck, should be designated as freely wandering or phantastic thinking, in opposition to intentionally directed reflection.

1940C 18/273

Medusa's Head (1940; 1922).

An interpretation of the decapitated head of Medusa is presented. To decapitate is synonymous with to castrate. The terror of Medusa is thus a terror of castration that is linked to the sight of something. The hair upon Medusa's head is frequently represented in works of art in the form of snakes, and these are derived from the castration complex. However frightening they may be in themselves, they serve as a mitigation of the horror, for they replace the penis, the absence of which is the cause of the horror. If Medusa's head takes the place of a representation of the female genitals, or rather if it isolates their horrifying effects from their pleasure-giving ones, it may be recalled that displaying the genitals is familiar in other connections as an apotropaic act. The erect male organ also has an apotropaic effect.

VOL. XIX The Ego and the Id and Other Works (1923–1925)

1923B 19/3

The ego and the id (1923). Editor's introduction. (1961).

The Ego and the Id appeared in the third week of April, 1923, though it had been in Freud's mind since at least the previous July. *The Ego and the Id* is the last of Freud's major theoretical works. It offers a description of the mind and its workings which is at first sight new and even revolutionary; and indeed all psychoanalytic writings that date from after its publication bear the unmistakable imprint of its effects, at least in regard to their terminology. The forerunners of the present general picture of the mind had been successively the 'Project' of 1895, the seventh chapter of the *Interpretation of Dreams* and the metapsychological papers of 1915. A simple scheme underlay all of Freud's earlier theoretical ideas: functionally, a repressed force endeavoring to make its way into activity but held in check by a repressing force, and structurally, an unconscious opposed by an ego. In the structural picture of the mind, what had from the first been most clearly differentiated from the unconscious had been the ego. It now began to appear that the ego itself ought partly to be described as unconscious. Being conscious was hence forward to be regarded simply as a quality which might or might not be attached to a mental state. In *The Ego and the Id*, the 2 main ideas consist of 1) the thesis of the threefold division of the mind and 2) the genesis of the superego.

1923B 19/12

The Ego and the id (1923). Preface and Part I: Consciousness and what is unconscious.

The division of the psychical into what is conscious and what is unconscious is the fundamental premise of psychoanalysis; and it alone makes it possible for psychoanalysis to understand the pathological processes in mental life, which are as common as they are important, and to find a place for them in the framework of science. Being conscious is in the first place a purely descriptive term, resting on perception of the most immediate and certain character. A psychical element is not as a rule conscious for a protracted length of time. Very powerful mental processes or ideas exist which can produce all the effects in mental life that ordinary ideas do, though they themselves do not become conscious. The reason why such ideas cannot become conscious is that a certain force opposes them, that otherwise they could become conscious, and that it would then be apparent how little they differ from other elements which are admittedly psychical. The state in which the ideas existed before being made conscious is called repression, and we assert that the force which instituted the repression and maintains it is perceived as resistance during the work of analysis. We obtain our concept of the unconscious from the theory of repression. The latent, which is unconscious only descriptively, not in the dynamic sense we call preconscious; we restrict the term unconscious to the dynamically unconscious repressed. In each individual there is a coherent organization of mental processes called ego; consciousness is attached to this ego. The ego controls the approaches to motility and from this ego proceeds the repressions by means of which it is sought to exclude certain trends in the mind not merely from consciousness but also from other forms of effectiveness and activity. Resistance, which is also found in the ego, is unconscious, and behaves like the repressed. A part of the ego may be unconscious, and this unconsciousness belonging to the ego is not latent like the preconscious.

1923B 19/19
The ego and the id (1923). Part II: The ego and the id.

All our knowledge is invariably bound up with consciousness. We can come to know even the unconscious (Ucs) only by making it conscious. Consciousness is the surface of the mental apparatus. All perceptions which are received from without and from within are conscious (Cs). The real difference between a Ucs and a preconscious (Pcs) idea (thought) consists in that the former is carried out on some material which remains unknown, whereas the latter (the Pcs) is in addition brought into connection with word presentations. These word presentations are residues of memories; they were- at one time perceptions, and like all mnemonic residues they can become conscious again. We think of the mnemonic residues as being contained in systems which are directly adjacent to the perceptual conscious (Pcpt Cs) system, so that the cathexes of those residues can readily extend from within on to the elements of the latter system. The distinction between Cs and Pcs has no meaning where feelings are concerned; the Pcs drops out and feelings are either Cs or Ucs. We can look upon an individual as a psychical id, unknown and unconscious, upon whose surface rests the ego, developed from its nucleus the Pcpt system. Pictorially, the ego does not completely envelop the id, but only does so to the extent to which the system Pcpt forms its surface. The ego is not sharply separated from the id but part merges into it. The repressed ego merges into the id as well, and is merely a part of it. The ego is that part of the id which has been modified by the direct influence of the external world through the medium of the Pcpt Cs; in a sense it is an extension of the surface differentiation. The ego is first and foremost a body ego. Not only what is lowest but also what is highest in the ego can be unconscious.

1923B 19/28
The ego and the id (1923). Part III: The ego and the super-ego (ego ideal).

The ego ideal or superego is not firmly connected with consciousness. The transformation of an erotic object choice into an alteration of the ego is a method by which the ego can obtain control over the id. The transformation of object libido into narcissistic libido implies an abandonment of sexual aims. Behind the ego ideal there lies hidden an individual's first and most important identification, his identification with the father in his own personal prehistory. In both sexes, the

relative strength of the masculine and feminine sexual dispositions is what determines whether the outcome of the Oedipus situation shall be an identification with the father or with the mother. The broad general outcome of the sexual phase dominated by the Oedipus complex may be taken to be the forming of a precipitate in the ego, consisting of the 2 identifications of father identification and mother identification in some way united with each other. The modification of the ego retains its special position; it confronts the other contents of the ego as an ego ideal or superego. The superego is not simply a residue of the earliest object choices of the id; it also represents an energetic reaction formation against those choices. The ego ideal is the heir of the Oedipus complex. It is easy to show that the ego ideal answers to everything that is expected of the higher nature of man.

1923B 19/40
The ego and the id (1923). Part IV: The two classes of instincts.

Two classes of instincts are distinguished, one of which, the sexual instincts or Eros, is by far the more conspicuous and accessible to study. It comprises not merely the uninhibited sexual instinct proper and the instinctual impulses of an aim inhibited or sublimated nature derived from it, but also the self-preservative instinct. The second class of instincts is called the death instinct. It appears that, as a result of the combination of unicellular organisms into multicellular forms of life, the death instinct of the single cell can successfully be neutralized and the destructive impulses be diverted on to the external world through the instrumentality of a special organ. The sadistic component of the sexual instinct would be a classical example of a serviceable instinctual fusion and the sadism which has made itself independent as a perversion would be typical of a defusion. Love is regularly accompanied by hate (ambivalence); in human relationships, hate is frequently a forerunner of love. It seems a plausible view that the displaceable and neutral energy, which is no doubt active both in the ego and in the id, proceeds from the narcissistic store of libido, that is desexualized Eros. This displaceable libido is employed in the service of the pleasure principle to obviate blockages and to facilitate discharge. This displaceable energy may also be described as sublimated energy. The transformation of erotic libido into ego libido involves an abandonment of sexual aims, a desexualization.

1923B 19/48
The ego and the id (1923). Part V: the dependent relationships of the ego.

The ego is formed out of identifications which take the place of abandoned cathexes by the id. The first of these identifications, the superego, owes its special position in relation to the ego, to 2 factors 1) it was the first identification and one which took place while the ego was still feeble, and 2) it is the heir to the Oedipus complex. The superego is always close to the id and can act as its representative towards the ego. Part of the sense of guilt normally remains unconscious, because the origin of conscience is intimately connected with the Oedipus complex, which belongs to the unconscious. A sense of guilt expresses itself differently under different conditions. The normal, conscious sense of guilt is based on the tension between the ego and the ego ideal. The sense of guilt is excessively strongly conscious in obsessional neurosis and melancholia but remains unconscious in hysteria. The obsessional neurotic, in contrast to the melancholic, never performs self-destruction. The id is totally nonmoral; the ego strives to be moral, and the superego can be super-moral and then become as cruel as only the id can be. The ego owes service to 3 masters and consequently, is menaced by 3 dangers: from the external world, from the libido of the id, and from the severity of the superego. The great significance which the sense of guilt has in the neuroses makes it conceivable that common neurotic anxiety is reinforced in severe cases by the generating of anxiety between the ego and the superego (fear of castration, of conscience, of death). The id has no means of showing the ego either love or hate.

1923B 19/60

The ego and the id (1923). Appendix A: the descriptive and the dynamic unconscious. Appendix B: The great reservoir of libido.

In the descriptive sense there are 2 kinds of unconscious: the latent unconscious and the repressed unconscious. Unconscious, in its dynamic sense, covers only one thing, the repressed unconscious. The fact that the latent unconscious is only descriptively unconscious does not imply that it is the only thing that is descriptively unconscious. In this book Freud speaks of the id as "the great reservoir of libido". This appears to contradict his reference to the ego as such a reservoir in a number of other writings both before and after this. The contradiction is diminished if we consider other passages where he indicates that it is the undifferentiated ego-id that is the original "great reservoir" and that after differentiation the ego becomes a storage tank for narcissistic libido.

1923D 19/69

A seventeenth-century demonological neurosis (1923). Editor's note (1961) and introduction.

A Seventeen-Century Demonological Neurosis was written in the last months of 1922. Freud's interest in witchcraft, possession and allied phenomena was of long

standing. Freud passes beyond the discussion of an individual case and of the limited demonological problem to a consideration of some of the wider questions involved in the adoption by males of a feminine attitude towards the father. The neuroses of childhood have taught us that a number of things can easily be seen in them with the naked eye which at a later age are only to be discovered after a thorough investigation. We may expect that the same will turn out to be true of neurotic illnesses in earlier centuries, provided that we are prepared to recognize them under names other than those of our present day neuroses. The demonological theory of those dark times has won against all the somatic views of the period of exact science. The states of possession correspond to our neuroses, for the explanation of which we once more have recourse to psychical powers. In our eyes, the demons are bad and reprehensible wishes, derivatives of instinctual impulses that have been repudiated and repressed.

1923D 19/73

A seventeenth-century demonological neurosis (1923). Part I: The story of Christoph Haizmann the painter.

The story of Christoph Haizmann the painter, who presented with a demonological neurosis, is discussed. On August 29, 1677 in a church in Pottenbrunn, he was seized with convulsions and later admitted these were due to a previous pact with the Devil in which he agreed in writing to belong to him in body and soul after 9 years. This period would expire September 29, 1677. After the painter had undergone a prolonged period of penance and prayer at Mariazell, the Devil appeared to him in the sacred Chapel at midnight September 8, the Nativity of the Virgin, in the form of a winged dragon, and gave him back the pact, which was written in blood. After a short time the painter left Mariazell in the best of health and went to Vienna, where he lived with a married sister. On October 11, fresh attacks began, some of them very severe. They consisted in visions and absences, in which he saw and experienced every kind of thing, in convulsive seizures accompanied by the most painful sensations. This time, however, it was not the Devil who tormented him; it was by sacred figures that he was vexed. In May, 1678, he returned to Mariazell and told the reverent Fathers that his reason for returning was that he had to require the Devil to give him back another earlier bond, which had been written in ink. This time once more the Blessed Virgin and the pious Fathers helped him to obtain the fulfillment of his request. He entered the Order of the Brothers Hospitallers and was again repeatedly tempted by the Evil Spirit, who tried to make a fresh pact. These attempts were repelled and Brother Chrysostomus died of a hectic fever peacefully and of good comfort in 1700.

1923D 19/79

A seventeenth-century demonological neurosis (1923).
Part II: The motive for the pact with the devil.

The motive for Christoph Haizmann's pact with the Devil is discussed. He signed to a bond with the Devil in order to be freed from a state of depression, which had been brought on by the death of his father. The bonds mention no undertaking given by the Devil in return for whose fulfillment the painter pledges his eternal bliss, but only a demand made by the Devil which the painter must satisfy. The painter was to be bound to the Devil, as his son, for 9 years. At the end of that time, the painter was to become the property, body and soul, of the Devil. The train of thought which motivated the painter in making the pact seems to have been this: his father's death had made him lose his spirits and his capacity to work; if he could only obtain a father substitute he might hope to regain what he had lost; in return for the painter's soul the Devil was to become his father for 9 years.

1923D 19/83

A seventeenth century demonological neurosis (1923).
Part III: The devil as father-substitute.

The Devil is discussed as a father substitute. The Devil first appeared to Christoph Haizmann as an honest elderly citizen with a brown beard, dressed in a red cloak and leaning with his right hand on a stick, with a black dog beside him. Later on, his appearance became more and more terrifying: he was equipped with horns, eagle's claws, and bat's wings, and finally he appeared in the chapel as a flying dragon. We know that God is a father substitute. The evil demon is regarded as the antithesis of God and yet is very close to him in nature. God and the Devil were originally identical. The pact that Haizmann made with the Devil was for 9 years. The number 9 is of great significance for neurotic phantasies. It is the number of months of pregnancy. Although the 9 appears as years, it could be interpreted as months. The female sexual character of the Devil is stressed by introducing large pendulous breasts. It is concluded that what the painter is rebelling against is his feminine attitude to his father which culminates in a phantasy of bearing him a child.

1923D 19/93

A seventeenth century demonological neurosis (1923).
Part IV: The two bonds.

A remarkable detail in the story of Christoph Haizmann is the statement that he signed 2 different bonds with the Devil. It is unusual for anyone to sign a bond with the Devil twice, in such a way that the first document is replaced by the second, but without losing its own validity. Freud's view is that when the painter first came to Mariazell he spoke only of one bond, written in the regular way in blood, which was about to fall due. In Mariazell, too, he presented this bond in blood as the one which the demon had given back to him under compulsion from the Holy Mother. The painter left the shrine soon afterwards and went to Vienna, where he felt free till the middle of October. Then, however, he began once more to be subjected to sufferings and apparitions, in which he saw the work of the evil spirit. He again felt in need of redemption, but was faced with the difficulty of explaining why the exorcism in the Holy Chapel had not brought him a lasting deliverance. He invented an earlier, first bond, which was to be written in ink, so that its supersession in favor of a later bond, written in blood should seem more plausible. He could not avoid the awkward result that he had redeemed one, the blood bond, too soon (in the eighth year), and the other, the black bond, too late (in the tenth year).

1923D 19/100

A seventeenth-century demonological neurosis (1923).
Part V: The further course of the neurosis.

The further course of the neurosis of Christoph Haizmann is presented. Examination of the painter's diary affords deep insight into the motivation or exploitation of his neurosis. Until October 11, he felt very well in Vienna, where he lived with a married sister; but after that he had fresh attacks which fell into 3 phases: First, temptation appeared in the form of a finely dressed cavalier, who tried to persuade him to throw away the document attesting his admission to the Brotherhood of the Holy Rosary. An ascetic reaction appeared. On October 20, a great light appeared, and a voice came from it, making itself known as Christ, and commanded him to forswear this wicked world and serve God in the wilderness for 6 years. The painter's phantasies of temptation were succeeded by ascetic ones and finally by phantasies of punishment. The painter signed a bond with the Devil because, after his father's death, feeling depressed and unable to work, he was worried about making a livelihood. This pact still did not help him. Finally, with his entrance into a Holy Order, both his internal struggle and his material needs came to an end. In his neurosis, his seizures and visions were brought to an end by the return of an alleged first bond. It was concluded that all he wanted was to make his life secure. He followed a path which led from his father, by way of the Devil as a father substitute, to the pious Fathers of the Church. The painter's wretched situation in life would not have provoked a demonological neurosis if his material need had not intensified his longing for his father.

1923C 19/108
Remarks on the theory and practice of dream-interpretation (1923). Parts I-VI.

In interpreting a dream there are several choices concerning technical procedures: 1) a chronological procedure in which the dreamer brings up his associations to the elements of the dream in the order in which those elements occurred; 2) starting from one particular element of the dream, for example, the most striking piece of it or the piece with the most sensory intensity; 3) asking the dreamer what events of the previous day are associated in his mind with the dream he has just described; and 4) leaving it to the dreamer to decide with which associations to the dream he shall begin. When the pressure of resistance is high, one may succeed in discovering what the things are with which the dream is concerned, but not what they mean. When the resistance is kept within moderate limits, the familiar picture of the work of interpretation comes into view: the dreamer's associations begin by diverging widely from the manifest elements, so that a great number of subjects and ranges of ideas are touched on, after which, a second series of associations converge from these on to the dream thoughts that are being sought. Dreams from below are provoked by the strength of an unconscious (repressed) wish. Dreams from above correspond to thoughts or intentions of the day before which have contrived during the night to obtain reinforcement from repressed material that is debarred from the ego. The interpretation of a dream falls into 2 phases: the phase in which it is translated and the phase in which it is judged or has its value assessed. One should not let the second phase influence the work of the first phase. Deciding on the value of a correctly translated dream is difficult and all other indications, including those of waking life, must be taken into account.

1923C 19/113
Remarks on the theory and practice of dream-interpretation (1923). Parts VII & VIII.

The question of the value to be assigned to dreams is intimately related to the other question of their susceptibility to influence from suggestion by the physician. The fact that the manifest content of dreams is influenced by the analytic treatment stands in no need of proof. Latent dream thoughts have to be arrived at by interpretation and can be influenced or suggested by the analyst. A portion of these latent dream thoughts correspond to preconscious thought formations, thought formations with which the dreamer might well have reacted to the physician's remarks. They are perfectly capable of being conscious. One never exercises any influence on the mechanism of dream formation itself, on the dream work in the strict sense of the word. Every

true dream contains indications of the repressed wishful impulses to which it owes the possibility of its formation. With these and with material which refers to scenes from the dreamer's past, it is often difficult to prove that they are not the result of suggestion; but the way in which fragments fit together like a complicated jigsaw puzzle finally convinces us that this is not so. It may well be that dreams during psychoanalysis succeed in bringing to light what is repressed to a greater extent than dreams outside that situation. But it cannot be proved, since the 2 situations are not comparable: the employment of dreams in analysis is something very remote from their original purpose. Positive transference gives assistance to the compulsion to repeat.

1923C 19/118
Remarks on the theory and practice of dream-interpretation (1923). Part IX.

Dreams that occur in a traumatic neurosis are the only genuine exceptions and punishment dreams are the only apparent exceptions to the rule that dreams are directed towards wish fulfillment. In the latter class of dreams we are met by the remarkable fact that actually nothing belonging to the latent dream thoughts is taken up into the manifest content of the dream. Something quite different appears instead, which must be described as a reaction formation against the dream thoughts, a rejection and complete contradiction of them. This must be ascribed to the critical agency of the ego which has been temporarily reestablished even during sleep, and which replaces the objectionable dream wish with a punishment dream. Astonishment is sometimes expressed at the fact that the dreamer's ego can appear 2 or more times in the manifest dream, once as himself and again disguised behind the figures of other people. During the course of the construction of the dream, the secondary revision has evidently sought to obliterate this multiplicity of the ego, which cannot fit in with any possible scenic situation but it is reestablished by the work of interpretation. Separation of the ego from an observing, critical, punishing agency (an ego ideal) must be taken into account in the interpretation of dreams, and often accounts for the multiple appearances of the ego in the same dream.

1925I 19/125
Some additional notes on dream-interpretation as a whole (1925). Editor's note (1961). (A). The limits to the possibility of interpretation.

The limits to the possibility of interpretation of dreams are discussed. Dreaming is an activity of play or phantasy. When a dream deals with a problem of actual life, it solves it in the manner of an irrational wish and not in the manner of a reasonable reflection. There is only one useful task, only one function, that can be ascribed to a dream, and that is the guarding of sleep from interruption. A dream may be described as a piece of phantasy working on behalf of the maintenance of sleep. It is on the whole a matter of indifference to the sleeping ego what may be dreamt during the night so long as the dream performs its task, and that those dreams best fulfill their function about which one knows nothing after waking. No one can practice the interpretation of dreams as an isolated activity: it remains a part of the work of analysis. If one practices dream interpretation according to the sole justifiable technical procedure, one soon notices that success depends entirely upon the tension of resistance between the awakened ego and the repressed unconscious. Because resistance is often strong, only a certain portion of a patient's dream products can be translated and often only incompletely. Since many incomprehensible dreams become understood in the light of knowledge obtained later in the analysis it is justifiable to assert that dreams are quite generally mental structures that are capable of interpretation, though the situation may not always allow an interpretation being reached. When the interpretation of a dream has been discovered it is not always easy to decide whether it is a complete one. In that case, we must consider the meaning proved which is based on the dreamer's association and our estimate of the situation, without feeling bound to reject the other meaning.

1925I 19/131
Some additional notes on dream-interpretation as a whole (1925). (B). Moral responsibility for the content of dreams.

Moral responsibility for the content of dreams is discussed. The manifest content is a deception, a facade. When the content of the dream is spoken of, what must be referred to can only be the content of the preconscious thoughts and of the repressed wishful impulse which are revealed behind the facade of the dream by the work of interpretation. Our interest in the genesis of manifestly immoral dreams is greatly reduced when we find from analysis that the majority of dreams are revealed as the fulfillments of immoral, egoistic, sadistic, perverse or incestuous, wishful impulses. Dreams do not always offer immoral wish fulfillments, but often energetic reactions against them in the form of punishment dreams. In other words, the dream censorship can not only express itself in distortions and the generation of anxiety, but can go so far as to blot out the immoral subject matter completely and replace it by something else that serves as an atonement, though it allows one to see what lies behind. One must hold oneself responsible for the evil impulses of one's dreams. The ethical narcissism of humanity should rest content with the knowledge that the fact of distortion in dreams, as well as the

existence of anxiety dreams and punishment dreams, afford just as clear evidence of his moral nature as dream interpretation gives of the existence and strength of his evil nature.

1925I 19/135
Some additional notes on dream-interpretation as a whole (1925). (C). The occult significance of dreams

The occult significance of dreams is discussed. There would seem to be 2 categories of dreams with a claim to being reckoned as occult phenomena: prophetic dreams and telepathic dreams. In Freud's opinion, there is no validity to prophetic dreams. Telepathy is not a dream problem: our judgment upon whether it exists or not need not be based on a study of telepathic dreams. Freud believes that there may be some truth to the phenomenon of telepathy. He mentions a class of material which is exempt from doubts which are otherwise justified: unfulfilled prophecies by professional fortune tellers. An example is given in which a fortune teller predicted that a woman would give birth to 2 children by age 32. The woman remained childless but in analysis at age 43 it became evident that her dominant unconscious wish at the time of the prophecy had been to have 2 children before age 32 as her mother had done and thus to satisfy her wish for her own father by putting herself in her mother's place. Freud concluded that the strongest unconscious wish had made itself manifest to the fortune teller by being directly transferred to him while his attention was being distracted by the performances he was going through. If there are such things as telepathic messages, the possibility cannot be dismissed of their reaching someone during sleep and coming to his knowledge in a dream.

1923E 19/41
The infantile genital organization: An interpolation into the theory of sexuality (1923).

The infantile genital organization is discussed. The main characteristic of the infantile genital organization is its difference from the final genital organization of the adult. This consists in the fact that, for both sexes, only one genital, namely the male one, comes into account. What is present, therefore, is not a primacy of the genitals, but a primacy of the phallus. The small boy perceives the distinction between men and women, but to begin with he has no occasion to connect it with a difference in their genitals. The driving force which the male portion of the body will develop later at puberty expresses itself at this period of life mainly as an urge to investigate, as sexual curiosity. Many of the acts of exhibitionism and aggression which children commit, and which in later years would be judged without hesitation to be expressions of lust, prove in analysis to be experiments undertaken in the service of sexual research. In the course of these researches the child arrives at the discovery that the penis is not a possession which is common to all creatures that are like himself, and concludes that the lack is due to castration. The significance of the castration complex can only be rightly appreciated if its origin in the phase of phallic primacy is also taken into account. The child believes that it is only unworthy female persons that have lost their genitals. Women whom he respects, like his mother, retain a penis for a long time. The sexual polarity of male-female finally seen at puberty appears in different transformations in childhood sexual development. The earliest antithesis is subject-object; later in the sadistic anal stage it is active-passive; and in the stage of infantile genital organization it is male-genital-castrated.

1924B 19/149
Neurosis and psychosis (1924).

Neurosis and psychosis are discussed. Neurosis is the result of a conflict between the ego and its id, whereas psychosis is the analogous outcome of a similar disturbance in the relations between the ego and the external world. All the analyses show that the transference neuroses originate from the ego's refusing to accept a powerful instinctual impulse in the id or to help it to find a motor outlet, or from the ego's forbidding that impulse the object at which it is aiming. In such a case the ego defends itself against the instinctual impulse by the mechanism of repression. The repressed material struggles against this fate and creates a substitute representation, the symptom. The ego finds its unity threatened and impaired by this intruder, and it continues to struggle against the symptom, just as it fended off the original instinctual impulse. The etiology common to the onset of psychoneurosis and of a psychosis always remains the same. It consists in a frustration, a nonfulfillment, of one of those childhood wishes which are forever undefeated and which are so deeply rooted in our phylogenetically determined organization. The pathogenic effect depends on whether the ego remains true to its dependence on the external world and attempts to silence the id, as in the transference neuroses, or whether it lets itself be overcome by the id and thus torn away from reality, as in the psychoses. A third group of illnesses, the narcissistic neuroses, are characterized by a conflict between the ego and the superego. The thesis that neuroses and psychoses originate in the ego's conflicts with its various ruling agencies needs to be supplemented in one further point. One would like to know in what circumstances and by what means the ego can succeed in merging from such conflicts, which are certainly always present, without falling ill. This is a new field of research, in which economic considerations and the ego's capacity to avoid a rupture by deforming itself will be 2 important factors.

1924C 19/157
The economic problem of masochism (1924).

The economic problem of masochism is discussed. Masochism comes under observation in 3 forms: as a condition imposed on sexual excitation, as an expression of the feminine nature, and as a norm of behavior. We may, accordingly, distinguish an erotogenic, a feminine, and a moral masochism. The first, the erotogenic masochism, pleasure in pain, lies at the bottom of the other 2 forms as well. Its basis must be sought along biological and constitutional lines. The third form has been recognized as a sense of guilt which is mostly unconscious; but it can already be completely explained and fitted into the rest of our knowledge. Analysis of cases shows the subjects in a characteristically female situation; they signify, being castrated, or copulated with or giving birth to a baby. The clinical description of feminine masochism is discussed along with a theoretical explanation of erotogenic masochism. Feminine masochism is based on the primary, erotogenic masochism, on pleasure in pain. Erotogenic masochism accompanies the libido through all its developmental phases and derives from them its changing psychical coatings. The fear of being eaten by the totem animal (father) originates from the primitive oral organization; the wish to be beaten by the father comes from the sadistic anal phase which follows it; castration enters into the content of masochistic phantasies as a precipitate of the phallic stage or organization; and from the final genital organization there arise the situations of being copulated with and of giving birth. The third form of masochism, moral masochism, is chiefly remarkable for having loosened its connection with what we recognize as sexuality, and does not need a loved one as one of its conditions. Individuals with this type of masochism give an impression of being excessively morally inhibited although not being conscious of this ultramorality. Moral masochism is unconscious. The expression "unconscious sense of guilt" means a need for punishment at the hands of a parental power. The wish to be beaten by the father is very close to the wish to have a passive (feminine) sexual relation with him and is only a regressive distortion of it. The sadism of the superego and the masochism of the ego supplement each other and unite to produce the same effects.

1924D 19/173
The dissolution of the Oedipus complex (1924).

The dissolution of the Oedipus complex is discussed. The Oedipus complex reveals its importance as the central phenomenon of the sexual period of early childhood. After that, its dissolution takes place; it succumbs to repression and is followed by the latency period. In one view, the Oedipus complex goes to its destruction from its lack of success. Another view is that the Oedipus complex must collapse because the time has come for its disintegration. Both of these views are compatible. Freud believes that what brings about the destruction of the child's phallic genital organization is the threat of castration. To begin with, the boy does not believe in the threat or obey it in the least. It is not until the child observes the female genitals that his unbelief is broken down. The child's ego turns away from the Oedipus complex and the object cathexes are given up and replaced by identifications. The authority of the father or the parents is introjected into the ego, and there it forms the nucleus of the superego, which takes over the severity of the father and perpetuates his prohibition against incest, and so secures the ego from the return of the libidinal object cathexis. The libidinal trends belonging to the Oedipus complex are in part desexualized and sublimated and in part inhibited in their aim and changed into impulses of affection. The whole process has preserved the genital organ (averted its loss) and has paralyzed it (removed its function). This starts the latency period. The ego's turning away from the Oedipus complex can be called repression. This process is equivalent to a destruction and an abolition of the complex. Here is the borderline between normal and pathological; if the ego has not achieved much more than a repression of the complex, the latter persists in an unconscious state in the id and will later manifest its pathological effects. The connections between the phallic organization, the Oedipus complex, the threat of castration, superego formation and latency period justify the statement that the destruction of the Oedipus complex is brought about by the threat of castration. In female children the Oedipus complex is gradually given up because the wish for a child (formerly a wish for a penis) is never fulfilled.

1924E 19/183
The loss of reality in neurosis and psychosis (1924).

The loss of reality in neurosis and psychosis is discussed. In a neurosis, the ego, in its dependence on reality, supresses a piece of the id, whereas in a psychosis, this same ego, in the service of the id, withdraws from a piece of reality. For a neurosis, the decisive factor would be the predominance of the influence of reality, whereas for a psychosis it would be the predominance of the id. In a psychosis, a loss of reality would necessarily be present, whereas in a neurosis, it would seem, this loss would be avoided. Every neurosis disturbs the patient's relation to reality in some way and serves him as a means of withdrawing from reality. The neurosis consists in the processes which provide a compensation for the portion of the id that has been damaged. Neurosis is characterized as the result of a repression that has failed. When a psychosis comes into being, something analogous to the process in a neurosis occurs, though, of course, between different agencies of

the mind. In neurosis, a piece of reality is avoided by a sort of flight, whereas in psychosis it is remodeled. In psychosis, the initial flight is succeeded by an active phase of remodeling; in neurosis, the initial obedience is succeeded by a deferred attempt at flight. Neurosis does not disavow reality, it only ignores it; psychosis disavows it and tries to replace it. In psychosis the transforming of reality is carried out upon the memory traces and ideas and judgments previously derived from reality and is continually being enriched with fresh perceptions. This task of procuring perceptions to correspond to the new reality is effected by means of hallucination. It is probable that in psychosis the rejected piece of reality constantly forces itself upon the mind as the repressed instinct does in neurosis. Distinctions between neurosis and psychosis are a result of the topographical difference in the initial situation for the pathogenic conflict, namely whether in it the ego yielded to its allegiance to the real world or to its dependence on the id.

1924F 19/191
A short account of psycho-analysis (1924).

A brief history of psychoanalysis is presented. Psychoanalysis initially had only the single aim of understanding something of the nature of the functional nervous diseases. The importance of hypnosis (later to be replaced by the method of free association plus interpretation) in the origin of psychoanalysis and in the study of the neuroses is discussed. Contributions of Breuer and Freud to the development of psychotherapy through introduction of the cathartic method are outlined and the mechanisms of repression and resistance are presented. A theory which accounts for the origin, meaning, and purpose of neurotic symptoms includes emphasis on instinctual life, on mental dynamics, on the fact that even the apparently most obscure and arbitrary mental phenomena invariably have a meaning and a causation, the theory of psychical conflict and of the pathogenic nature of repression, the view that symptoms are substitutive satisfactions, the recognition of the etiological importance of sexual life, and the beginnings of infantile sexuality. The significance and meaning of dreams in psychotherapy and methods of interpretation are discussed. Psychoanalytic theory began to grow (with the development of many journals) and attracted followers. A list of concepts which enable the physician to deal with analytical material includes: libido, object libido, narcissistic or ego libido, and Oedipus complex. The importance of psychoanalysis for psychiatry drew attention from the intellectual world through its relation to normal behavior. Study of the psychical functions of groups of peoples (group therapy) allowed psychoanalysis to be proclaimed as 'depth psychology'. The stresses imposed on our mental faculties by civilization are discussed and it is concluded that it is predominately the sexual instinctual impulses that have succumbed to cultural suppression. If the mental apparatus can be divided into an ego, (turned towards the external world and equipped with consciousness) and an unconscious id (dominated by its instinctual needs), then psycho-analysis is to be described as a psychology of the id.

1925E   19/213
The resistances to psycho-analysis (1925).

The resistances to psychoanalysis are discussed. Psychoanalysis derives nothing but disadvantages from its middle position between medicine and philosophy. Doctors regard it as a speculative system and refuse to believe that, like every other natural science, it is based on a patient and tireless elaboration of facts from the world of perception; philosophers, measuring it by the standard of their own artificially constructed systems, find that it starts from impossible premises such as the existence of unconscious mental activity, and reproach it because its most general concepts lack clarity and pre-cision. Psychoanalysis proposes that there should be a reduction in the strictness with which instincts are re-pressed and that correspondingly more play be given to truthfulness. By its theory of the instincts, psycho-analysis offended the feelings of individuals in so far as they regarded themselves as members of the social community. Psychoanalysis disposed of the fairytale of an asexual childhood. It demonstrated that sexual interest and activities occur in small children from the beginning of their lives. The idea is, in general, unaccept-able to adults who have energetically repressed their own memories of this period. The strongest resistances to psychoanalysis were not of an intellectual kind but arose from emotional sources.

19/223
The resistances to psychoanalysis (1925). Appendix: Extract from Schopenhauer's 'The world as will and idea'.

An extract from Schopenhauer's *The World as Will and Idea* is presented. In his later works, Freud made several references to the emphasis which Schopenhauer laid on the importance of sexuality. Schopenhauer wrote that the relation of the sexes is really the invisible central point of all action and conduct. It is the cause of war and the end of peace, the basis of what is serious, and the aim of the jest, the inexhaustible source of wit, the key to all allusions, and the meaning of all myste-rious hints, or all spoken offers and all stolen glances, the daily meditation of the young, and often also of the old, the hourly thought of the unchaste, and even against their will the constantly recurring imagination of the chaste, the ever-ready material of a joke, just because

the profoundest seriousness lies at its foundation. Sexual passion is the most perfect manifestation of the will to live, its most distinctly expressed type; and the origin of the individual in it, and its primacy over all other desires of the natural man, are both in complete agreement with this.

1925A   19/227
A note upon the 'Mystic writing-pad' (1925).

The Mystic Writing Pad is a slab of dark brown resin or wax over which is laid a thin transparent sheet, the top end of which is firmly secured to the slab. The transparent sheet contains 2 layers, which can be detached from each other except at the top end. The upper layer is a transparent piece of celluloid. One writes with a pointed stylus upon the celluloid portion of the covering sheet which rests on the wax slab. If one wishes to destroy what has been written, all that is necessary is to raise the double covering sheet from the wax slab by a light pull. If, while the Mystic Pad has writing on it, the celluloid is cautiously raised from the waxed paper, the writing can be seen on the surface of the latter. The Pad provides not only a receptive surface that can be used over and over again, but also permanent traces of what has been written. The 'Mystic writing pad' is used as a concrete representation of Freud's views on the func-tioning of the perceptual apparatus of the mind. The unusual capacity of the mental apparatus to contain an unlimited receptive capacity for new perceptions and nevertheless lay down permanent memory traces is divided between 2 different systems: A perceptual conscious system (Pcpt. Cs.) which receives perceptions but retains no permanent trace of them, while the per-manent traces of the excitations which have been received are preserved in 'mnemonic systems' lying behind the perceptual system. The perceptual apparatus consists of 2 layers, an external protective shield against stimuli whose task it is to diminish the strength of exci-tations coming in, and a surface behind it which receives the stimuli, namely the Pcpt Cs. The Pad solves the problem of combining the 2 functions (permanent and temporary memory) by dividing them between 2 separate but interrelated component parts or systems. The layer which receives the stimuli (Pcpt Cs.) forms no permanent traces; the foundations of memory come about in other adjoining systems.

1925H   19/235
Negation (1925).

Negation is discussed. The content of a repressed image or idea can make its way into consciousness on condition that it is negated. Negation is a way of taking cognizance of what is repressed. To affirm or negate the content of thoughts is the task of the function of intellectual judgment. The function of judgment is concerned in the main with 2 sorts of decisions. It affirms or disaffirms the possession by a thing of a particular attribute; and it asserts or disputes that a presentation has an existence in reality. Judging is the intellectual action which decides the choice of motor action, which puts an end to the postponement due to thought and which leads over from thinking to acting. Judging is a continuation, along the lines of expediency, of the original process by which the ego took things into itself or expelled them from itself, according to the pleasure principle.

1925J 19/243
Some psychical consequences of the anatomical distinction between the sexes (1925). Editor's note. (1961).

From early days Freud made complaints of the obscurity enveloping the sexual life of women. One result of this obscurity was to lead Freud to assume very often that the psychology of women could be taken simply as analogous to that of men. But in fact over a long period, Freud's interest had not been directed to psychology. A number of previous papers make passing reference to different aspects of feminine sexual development, but Freud's new thesis is fully stated for the first time in this paper. It is the synthesis of the various pieces of knowledge, derived from widely separated historical strata of Freud's work, which gives its importance to the present paper.

1925J 19/248
Some psychical consequences of the anatomical distinction between the sexes (1925).

Some psychical consequences of the anatomical distinction between the sexes are studied. The analyses of neurotics should deal thoroughly with the remotest period of their childhood, the time of the early efflorescence of sexual life. In boys, the situation of the Oedipus complex is the first stage that can be recognized with certainty. At that stage a child retains the same object which he previously cathected with his libido during the preceding period while he was being nursed. He regards his father as a disturbing rival and would like to get rid of him and take his place. The Oedipus attitude in boys belongs to the phallic phase; its destruction is brought about by the fear of castration. The prehistory of the Oedipus complex in boys includes an identification of an affectionate sort with the father and masturbatory activity. The masturbatory activity makes its first appearance spontaneously as an activity of a body organ and is brought into relation with the Oedipus complex at some later date. Observation of the primal scene at this stage and its impact is discussed. In little girls the Oedipus complex raises one problem more than

in boys. In both cases the mother is the original object, but girls abandon it and instead take their father as an object. The first step in the phallic phase for little girls is the discovery of the penis and immediate envy of what she considers a superior organ. After a woman has become aware of the wound to her narcissism she develops a sense of inferiority. Even after penis envy has abandoned its true object, it continues to exist: bv an easy displacement, it persists in the character trait of jealousy. In boys, the Oedipus complex is destroyed by the castration complex; in girls, it is made possible and led up to by the castration complex. Other consequences of penis envy are a loosening of the girl's relation with her mother as a love object and discovery of the inferiority of the clitoris. The intense current of feeling against masturbation appearing in girls is discussed in relation to her narcissistic sense of humiliation which is bound up with penis envy—that she cannot compete with boys and should give up. Thus her recognition of the anatomical distinction between the sexes forces her away from masculinity to the development of femininity. Further views are presented on the difference in the Oedipus complex of boys and girls.

1923F 19/261
Josef Popper-Lynkeus and the theory of dreams (1923).

The essential part of Freud's theory of dreams, the dream censorship, was discovered independently by Josef Popper-Lynkeus. Freud started out from the strange, confused, and senseless character of so many dreams, and hit upon the notion that dreams were bound to become like that because something was struggling for expression in them which was opposed by a resistance from other mental forces. In dreams hidden impulses were stirring which stood in contradiction to what might be called the dreamer's official ethical and esthetic creed. To the mental force in human beings which keeps watch on the internal contradictions and distorts the dream's primitive instinctual impulses in favor of conventional or of higher moral standards, Freud gave the name of dream censorship. What enabled Freud to discover the cause of dream distortion was his moral courage. In the case of Popper, it was the purity, love of truth and moral serenity of his nature.

1923I 19/267
Dr. Sandor Ferenczi (on his 50th birthday) (1923).

Dr. Sandor Ferenczi was discussed on his fiftieth birthday. Ferenczi has repeatedly played a part in the affairs of psychoanalysis. He was born in 1873 and has been the leader of the Budapest Psychoanalytical Society for 10 years. Ferenczi, as a middle child in a large family, had to struggle with a powerful brother complex and under the influence of analysis, became an irreproachable elder brother, a kindly teacher and pro-moter of young talent. Ferenczi's analytic writings have become universally known and appreciated. Ferenczi's scientific achievement is impressive above all from its many-sidedness. Besides well-chosen case histories and acutely observed clinical communications, we find exemplary critical writings, as well as effective polemical writings. But besides all these, there are the papers upon which Ferenczi's fame principally rests, in which his originality, his wealth of ideas and his command over a well-directed scientific imagination find such happy expression, and with which he has enlarged the discovery of fundamental situations in mental life: 'Introjection and Transference', including a discussion of the theory of hypnosis; 'Stages in the Development of the Sense of Reality'; and his discussion of symbolism.

1925F   19/273
Preface to Aichhorn's 'Wayward Youth' (1925).

The preface to Aichhorn's *Wayward Youth* is pre-sented. None of the applications of psychoanalysis has excited so much interest and aroused so many hopes, and none, consequently, has attracted so many capable workers, as its use in the theory and practice of educa-tion. The volume by August Aichhorn is concerned with one department of the great problem, with the educa-tional influencing of juvenile delinquents. The author had worked for many years in an official capacity as a director of municipal institutions for delinquents before he became acquainted with psychoanalysis. Two lessons may be derived from the experience and the success of August Aichhorn. One is that every such person should receive a psychoanalytic training, since without it, child-ren must remain an inaccessible problem. The second lesson is that the work of education is not to be con-fused with psychoanalytic influence and cannot be re-placed by it.

1925G   19/279
Josef Breuer (1925).

On June 20, 1925, Josef Breuer died in Vienna in his eighty-fourth year. He was the creator of the cathartic method, and his name is for that reason indissolubly linked with the beginnings of psychoanalysis. Breuer was a physician. It was in 1880 that chance brought into his hands an unusual patient, a girl of more than ordinary intelligence who had fallen ill of severe hysteria while she was nursing her sick father. It was only 14 years later, in the joint publication of *Studies on Hysteria* that the world learned the nature of the treatment of this celebrated first case. Freud's share in the *Studies* lay chiefly in reviving in Breuer an interest which seemed to have become extinct, and in then urging him on to publi-cation. A kind of reserve which was characteristic of him, an inner modesty, surprising in a man of such a

brilliant personality, had led him to keep his astonishing discovery secret for so long. A purely emotional factor had given him an aversion to further work on the eluci-dation of the neuroses. He had come up against some-thing that is never absent, his patient's transference on to her physician, and he had not grasped the impersonal nature of the process. Besides the case history of his first patient Breuer contributed a theoretical paper in the *Studies* which is far from being out of date.

1922E   19/283
Preface to Raymond De Saussure's 'the psycho-analytic method' (1922).

The preface to Raymond de Saussure's *The Psycho-analytic Method* is presented. Dr. de Saussure has con-scientiously studied Freud's writings and in addition he has made the sacrifice of coming to Freud to undergo an analysis lasting several months. This has put him in a position to form his own judgment on the majority of those questions in psychoanalysis which are still unde-cided, and to avoid the many distortions and errors which one is accustomed to finding in French as well as in German expositions of psychoanalysis. The excellent dream which Dr. Odier has put at the author's disposal may give even the uninitiated an idea of the wealth of dream associations and of the relation between the mani-fest dream image and the latent thoughts concealed behind it. Today psychoanalysis is beginning to arouse in a larger measure the interest of professional men and of the lay public in France as well.

1923G   19/285
Preface to Max Eitingon's 'report on the Berlin psycho-analytical policlinic' (1923).

The preface to Max Eitingon's *Report on the Berlin Psychoanalytical Policlinic* is presented. If psychoanaly-sis has a value as a therapeutic procedure, if it is capable of giving help to sufferers in their struggle to fulfill the demands of civilization, this help should be accessible to the great multitude who are too poor themselves to pay an analyst for his laborious work. This seems to be a social necessity particularly in our times, when the intel-lectual strata of the population, which are especially prone to neurosis, are sinking irresistibly into poverty. Institutes such as the Berlin Policlinic make possible the education of a considerable number of trained analysts, whose activity must be regarded as the sole possible protection against injury to patients by ignorant and unqualified persons, whether they are laymen or doc-tors.

1924G 19/286
Letter to Fritz Wittels (1924).

A letter to Fritz Wittels, who had written a biography of Freud, is presented. Freud neither expected nor desired the publication of a biography of himself. In some respects, Freud thinks there are positive distortions in the work, and he believes that these are the outcome of a preconceived notion on the part of the author. Wittels inferred that Freud has often been compelled to make detours when following his own path. Freud acknowledged this. Freud also has no use for other people's ideas when they are presented to him in an inopportune moment. A list of suggested emendations is enclosed by Freud. These are based on trustworthy data, and are quite independent of his own prepossessions. Some of them relate to matters of trifling importance, but some of them may cause the author to modify certain inferences.

1923H 19/289
Letter, to Senor Luis Lopez-Ballesteros y de Torres (1923).

A letter to Senor Luis Lopez-Ballesteros y de Torres, the Spanish translator of Freud's work, is presented. Freud is able to read in Spanish because of his youthful desire to read *Don Quixote* in the original of Cervantes. Because of his ability to read Spanish, he is able to test the accuracy of the Spanish version of his works, the reading of which invariably provokes a lively appreciation of the correct interpretation of his thoughts.

1924A 19/290
Letter to 'Le Disque Vert' (1924).

In a letter to *Le Disque Vert*, a French periodical, Freud states that 2 of Charcot's lessons left him with a deep impression. One was that a person should never tire of considering the same phenomena again and again (or of submitting to their effects). The other was that a person should not mind meeting with contradiction on every side provided one has worked sincerely.

1925B 19/291
Letter to the editor of the 'Jewish press centre in Zurich' (1925).

In a letter to the editor of the *Jewish Press Center in Zurich*, Freud states that he stands apart from the Jewish religion, as from all other religions. They are of great significance as a subject of scientific interest, but he has no part in them emotionally. On the other hand, he has always had a strong feeling of solidarity with his fellow people, and has always encouraged it in his children as well. He has always regretted that his education in Hebrew was lacking.

1925C 19/292
On the occasion of the opening of the Hebrew university (1925).

Although Freud was unable to attend the opening of the Hebrew University, he wrote a message concerning this occasion. He states that a University is a place in which knowledge is taught above all differences of religions and of nations, where investigation is carried on, which is to show mankind how far they understand the world around them and how far they can control it. The opening of this university is a noble witness to the development of the Jewish people who have endured 2,000 years of persecution.

1924H 19/293
Editorial changes in the 'Zeitschrift' (1924).

Editorial changes in the *Zeitschrift* are discussed. Dr. Otto Rank has acted as editor of this journal ever since its foundation in 1913. Dr. Rank's place will be taken by Dr. S. Rado of Berlin. Dr. Rado will be supported by Dr. M. Eitingon and Dr. S. Ferenczi as advisors and collaborators. At Easter, 1924, Dr. Rank accepted an invitation which took him to New York. On his return home he announced that he had decided to transfer his activity as a teaching and practicing analyst to America, at least for a part of the year. This was the reason for the change in editor.

VOL. XX An Autobiographical Study, Inhibitions, Symptoms and Anxiety, Lay Analysis and Other Works (1925-1926)

1925D 20/3
An autobiographical study (1925). Editor's note. (1959).

The English translation of the *Autobiographical Study*, when it was first published in America in 1927, was included in the same volume as Freud's discussion of lay analysis. This work is commonly, and quite misleadingly, referred to as Freud's 'Autobiography'. The aim of its editors was to present an account of the recent history of medical science from the pens of those who had played a chief part in making it. Freud's study is essentially an account of his personal share in the development of psychoanalysis. Those who wish for the story of his personal life must be referred to the 3 volumes of Ernest Jones's biography.

1925D 20/7
An autobiographical study (1925). Part I. Pre-analytic period.

Freud was born on May 6, 1856, at Freiberg in Moravia, Czechoslovakia. His parents were Jews, and he remained a Jew. He came to Vienna at the age of 4 and went through his education there. Freud went to the University. His turning point came in 1882, when his teacher advised him to abandon his theoretical career. Freud left the physiological laboratory and entered the General Hospital as a Clinical Assistant. He became an active worker in the Institute of Cerebral Anatomy. He began to study nervous diseases. In the spring of 1885, he was appointed Lecturer in Neuropathology on the ground of his histological and clinical publications. He became a student at the Salpetriere. What impressed Freud most of all while he was with Charcot were his latest investigations upon hysteria. He had proved the genuineness of hysterical phenomena and their conformity to laws, the frequent occurrence of hysteria in men, and the production of hysterical paralyses and contractures by hypnotic suggestion. His therapeutic arsenal contained only 2 weapons, electrotherapy and hypnotism. During the period from 1886 to 1891, Freud did little scientific work.

1925D 20/19

An autobiographical study (1925). Part II. Hypnosis, hysteria, actual neuroses.

Freud used hypnosis for questioning the patient upon the origin of his symptom, which in his waking state he could often describe only very imperfectly or not at all. While Freud was working in Brucke's laboratory, he made the acquaintance of Dr. Josef Breuer. Breuer told Freud about a case of hysteria which, between 1880 and 1882, he had treated in a manner which enabled him to penetrate into the causation and significance of hysterical symptoms. Breuer spoke of the method as cathartic; its therapeutic aim was explained as being to provide that the quota of affect used for maintaining the symptom, which had got on to the wrong lines and had, as it were, become strangulated there, should be directed on to the normal path along which it could obtain discharge (or abreaction). The stage of development which followed was the transition from catharsis to psychoanalysis proper. Freud regarded the neuroses as being, without exception, disturbances of the sexual function, the so-called actual neuroses being the direct toxic expression of such disturbances, and the psychoneuroses, their mental expression. Freud altered the technique of catharsis. He abandoned hypnotism and sought to replace it by some other method after grasping the mysterious element that was at work behind hypnotism when a patient, with whom he obtained excellent results, threw her arms around his neck after awaking from a trance. However, he retained the practice of requiring the patient to lie upon a sofa while Freud sat behind him, seeing the patient but not being seen.

1925D 20/29

An autobiographical study (1925). Part III. Basic theories of psychoanalysis.

When Freud was set free from hypnotism, the work of catharsis took on a new complexion. Everything that had been forgotten had in some way or other been distressing. In order to make it conscious again, it was necessary to make efforts on one's own part so as to urge and compel him to remember. The expenditure of force on the part of the physician was the measure of a resistance on the part of the patient. The ego drew back on its first collision with the objectionable instinctual impulse; it debarred the impulse from access to consciousness and to direct motor discharge, but at the same time the impulse retained its full cathexis of energy. This process is called repression. The theory of repression became the cornerstone of the understanding of the neuroses. Psychoanalysis separates the unconscious into a preconscious and an unconscious proper. The investigation of the precipitating and underlying causes of the neuroses led Freud to conflicts between the subject's sexual impulses and his resistances to sexuality. He was carried further and further back into the patient's life and ended by reaching the first years of his childhood. Freud discovered that the seduction scenes reported by his patients so regularly as having happened in childhood were really wishful fantasies. He was thereby led to the conclusion that neurotic symptoms (compromise formations between the regressed impulse striving for satisfaction and the resistance of the ego opposed to it) were not related to actual events but to wishful fantasies. The sexual function is in existence from the very beginning of the individual's life, though at first it is attached to the other vital functions and does not become independent of them until later. Sexual energy is called libido. It does not pass through its prescribed course of development smoothly and can become fixated at various points as a result. The various stages of object relationship are chronologically described (autoerotic, oedipal) and the diphasic nature of sexual growth is discussed.

1925D 20/40

An autobiographical study (1925). Part IV. Technique of psychoanalysis.

The theories of resistance and of repression, of the unconscious, of the etiological significance of sexual life and of the importance of infantile experiences form the principal constituents of the theoretical structure of psychoanalysis. Freud asked his patient to abandon himself to a process of free association. The factor of transference was discovered. An intense emotional relationship develops between the patient and the analyst which cannot be accounted for by the actual situation. It can be positive (to the extreme of unbridled love) or negative (to the extreme of hatred). Transference is the mainspring of the joint work of analysis. It can become a major resistance. Analysis without transference is an impossibility. With the help of the method of free association and of the related art of interpretation, psychoanalysis succeeded in proving that dreams have a meaning. The latent dream thoughts contain the meaning of the dream, while its manifest content is simply a make believe, which can serve as a starting point for the associations but not for the interpretation. The unconscious impulse makes use of the nocturnal relaxation of repression in order to push its way into consciousness with the dream. But the repressive resistance of the ego is not abolished in sleep but merely reduced. Some of it remains in the shape of a censorship of dreams and forbids the unconscious impulse to express itself as the fulfillment of a repressed wish. Dreams have access to the forgotten material of childhood, and so it happens that infantile amnesia is for the most part overcome in connection with the interpretation of dreams. In the same way that psychoanalysis makes use of dream interpretation, it also profits by the study of the numerous little slips and mistakes which people make, symptomatic actions, as they are called.

1925D 20/48

An autobiographical study (1925). Part V. Collaborators, defectors and new instinct theory.

For more than 10 years after his separation from Breuer, Freud had no followers. The main obstacle to agreement lay in the fact that Freud's opponents regarded psychoanalysis as a product of his speculative imagination and were unwilling to believe in the long, patient and unbiased work which had gone to its making. The result of the official anathema against psychoanalysis was that the analysts began to come closer together. Official disapproval could not hinder the spread of psychoanalysis either in Germany or in other countries. If the preliminary cathartic period is left on one side, the history of psychoanalysis falls, from Freud's point of view, into 2 phases. In the first of these, he stood alone and had to do all the work himself: this was from 1895 until 1906 or 1907. In the second phase, the contributions of his pupils and collaborators were growing more and more in importance. Increasing experience showed more and more plainly that the Oedipus complex was the nucleus of the neurosis. In the Oedipus complex, the libido was seen to be attached to the image of the parental figures. The picture which life presents to us is the result of the concurrent and mutually opposing action of Eros and the death of instinct. The neuroses were the first subject of analysis. However, Freud was able, very early (1896) to establish in a case of paranoid dementia the presence of the same etiological factors and the same emotional complexes as

in the neuroses. Freud also discussed the concept of narcissism. This was a state where the subject's libido filled his own ego and had that for its object. Narcissism developed at an earlier period than the Oedipus complex. Narcissistic libido was part of the ego instincts (those of self-preservation) as opposed to the libidinal instincts. This was later replaced by the contract between narcissistic libido and object libido. He also postulated a death instinct as opposed to Eros (self-preservative instincts). In his latest speculative work (The Ego and The Id) Freud outlined the structural aspect of the mental apparatus by describing the id, ego and superego.

1925D 20/62

An autobiographical study (1925). Part VI. History of applied analysis.

From the time of the writing of *The Interpretation of Dreams*, psychoanalysis ceased to be a purely medical subject. Between its appearance in Germany and in France, lies the history of its numerous applications to departments of literature and of esthetics, to the history of religions and to prehistory, to mythology, to folklore, to education, and so on. A number of suggestions came to Freud out of the Oedipus complex, the ubiquity of which gradually dawned on him. From understanding the Oedipus tragedy of destiny, it was only a step further to understanding a tragedy of character, *Hamlet*. It could scarcely be a chance that this neurotic creation of the poet should have come to grief, like his numberless fellows in the real world, over the Oedipus complex. Freud set a high value on his contributions to the psychology of religion, which began with the establishment of a remarkable similarity between obsessive actions and religious practices or ritual. The obsessional neurosis is described as a distorted private religion and religion as a kind of universal obsessional neurosis. It is only a step from the phantasies of individual neurotics to the imaginative creations of groups and peoples as we find them in myths, legends, and fairy tales.

1935A 20/71

An autobiographical study (1925). Postscript. (1935).

An Autobiographical Study first appeared in America in 1927. Two themes run through these pages: the story of Freud's life and the history of psychoanalysis. They are intimately interwoven. *An Autobiographical Study* shows how psychoanalysis came to be the whole content of Freud's life and assumes that no personal experiences of his are of any interest in comparison to his relations with that science. At the end of his life Freud returned to the investigation of interests that held his attention as a youth, that of culture. There can no longer be any doubt that psychoanalysis will continue; it has proved its capacity to survive and to develop both as a branch of knowledge and as a therapeutic method. The number of its supporters has considerably increased. Some supporters lay most stress upon clarifying and deepening our knowledge of psychology, while others are concerned with keeping in contact with medicine and psychiatry. From the practical point of view, some analysts have set themselves the task of bringing about the recognition of psychoanalysis at the universities and its inclusion in the medical curriculum, whereas others are content to remain outside these institutions and will not allow that psychoanalysis is less important in the field of education than in that of medicine.

1926D 20/77

Inhibitions, symptoms and anxiety (1926). Editor's introduction. (1959).

Inhibitions, Symptoms and Anxiety was written in July, 1925, was revised in December of the same year, and published in the third week of the following February. The topics with which it deals range over a wide field, and there are signs that Freud found an unusual difficulty in unifying the work. In spite of such important side issues as the different classes of resistance, the distinction between repression and defense, and the relations between anxiety, pain and mourning, the problem of anxiety is its main theme. The problem of anxiety includes the following aspects: anxiety as transformed libido; realistic and neurotic anxiety; the traumatic situation and situations of danger; anxiety as a signal; and anxiety and birth. The book by Rank, *Trauma of Birth*, prescribed ideas which focussed on the trauma of birth giving it the central role in all neuroses, and giving it greater importance than the Oedipus complex. It was the primal anxiety from which all later anxiety sprang. Freud repudiated this idea. However, his consideration of Rank's notions of anxiety led him to reconsider his own and *Inhibitions, Symptoms and Anxiety* was the result.

1926D 20/87

Inhibitions, symptoms and anxiety (1926). Part I. Inhibitions reflect restrictions of ego functions.

The 2 concepts of inhibitions and symptoms are not upon the same plane. Inhibition does not necessarily have a pathological implication. A symptom actually denotes the presence of some pathological process. The sexual function is liable to a great number of disturbances which can be classed as simple inhibitions. Disturbances of the sexual function are brought about by a great variety of means: 1) the libido may simply be turned away; 2) the function may be less well carried out; 3) it may be hampered by having conditions attached to it, or modified by being diverted to other

aims; 4) it may be prevented by security measures; 5) if it cannot be prevented from starting, it may be immediately interrupted by the appearance of anxiety; and 6) if it is nevertheless carried out, there may be a subsequent reaction of protest against it and an attempt to undo what has been done. The function of nutrition is most frequently disturbed by a disinclination to eat, brought about by a withdrawal of libido. In some neurotic conditions, locomotion is inhibited by a disinclination to walk or a weakness in walking. In inhibition in work, the subject feels a decrease in his pleasure in it or becomes less able to do it well. Inhibitions are described as resistances of the functions of the ego which have been either imposed as a measure of precaution or brought about as a result of an impoverishment of energy. Inhibitions are undertaken by the ego in order to avoid coming into conflict with the id or with the superego.

1926D 20/91

Inhibitions, symptoms and anxiety (1926). Part II. Symptoms reflect intersystemic conflicts.

A symptom is a sign of, and a substitute for, an instinctual satisfaction which has remained in abeyance; it is a consequence of the process of repression. Repression proceeds from the ego when the latter refuses to associate itself with an instinctual cathexis which has been aroused in the id. The ego is able, by means of repression, to keep the idea which is the vehicle of the reprehensible impulse from becoming conscious. The ego is the seat of anxiety. In order for the ego to oppose an instinctual process in the id it has only to give a signal of unpleasure in order to enlist the aid of the pleasure principle in overpowering the id. The ego also obtains its influence in virtue of its intimate connections with the phenomenon of consciousness. The ego wards off internal and external dangers alike along identical lines. Just as the ego controls the path to action in regard to the external world, so it controls access to consciousness. In repression, it exercises its power in both directions, acting in the one manner upon the instinctual impulse itself and in the other upon the psychical representative of that impulse. Most regressions dealt with in therapeutic work are cases of after-pressure. A symptom arises from an instinctual impulse detrimentally affected by regression. The impulse finds expression through a substitute which is seduced, displaced, and inhibited. Freud showed that the ego can exert control over the id as well as be dependent on it. The same applied to the superego. He warned against making a "Weltanschauung" out of any one statement since conceptions in analysis are always open to revision.

1926D 20/97

Inhibitions, symptoms and anxiety (1926). Part III. Relation of ego to the id and to symptoms.

The ego is the organized portion of the id. As a rule, the instinctual impulse which is to be repressed remains isolated. The initial act of repression is followed by a tedious or interminable sequel in which the struggle against the instinctual impulse is prolonged into a struggle against the symptom. In this secondary defensive struggle the ego presents 2 faces with contradictory expressions. One line of behavior, it adopts, springs from the fact that its very nature obliges it to make what must be regarded as an attempt at restoration or reconciliation. The presence of a symptom may entail a certain impairment of capacity, and this can be exploited to appease some demand on the part of the superego or to refuse some claim from the external world. In this way the symptom gradually comes to be the representative of important interests. In obsessional neurosis and paranoia the forms which the symptoms assume become very valuable to the ego because they obtain for it, not certain advantages, but a narcissistic satisfaction which it would otherwise be without. All of this results in the secondary gain from illness which follows a neurosis. The second line of behavior adopted by the ego is less friendly in character, since it continues in the direction of repression.

1926D 20/101

Inhibitions, symptoms and anxiety (1926). Part IV. Anxiety produces repression.

An infantile hysterical phobia of animals, Little Hans's phobia of horses, is presented. Little Hans refused to go out into the street because he was afraid that a horse would bite him. He was in the jealous and hostile Oedipus attitude towards his father, whom nevertheless he dearly loved. Here is a conflict due to ambivalence: a well-grounded love and a no less justifiable hatred directed towards one and the same person. Little Hans's phobia must have been an attempt to solve this conflict. The instinctual impulse which underwent repression in Little Hans was a hostile one against his father. Little Hans alleged that what he was afraid of was that a horse would bite him. The idea of being devoured by the father is typical age-old childhood material. It has the familiar parallels in mythology and in the animal kingdom. Two instinctual impulses have been overtaken by repression, sadistic aggressiveness towards the father and a tender passive attitude to him. The formation of his phobia had had the effect of abolishing his affectionate object cathexis of his mother as well. The motive force of the repression was the fear of impending castration. His fear that a horse would bite him can be given the full sense of a fear that a horse would bite off

his genitals, would castrate him. A comparison of the phobias presented by Wolf Man and that of Little Hans showed that, although there were marked differences in their histories, the outcome was the same. This was explained by examining the anxiety of the 2 patients. Anxiety was seen as response to fear of castration either seen as real or impending. It was this anxiety, occurring in the ego, which set the process of regression into motion which ultimately led to the phobia formation. Anxiety now had 2 sources: one from the id (disturbed libido), and the other from the ego.

1926D 20/111

Inhibitions, symptoms and anxiety (1926). Part V. Defences other than repression.

Conversion hysteria exhibits no anxiety whatever. The formation of symptoms in conversion hysteria is obscure. It presents a manifold and varied picture with no uniform explanation available. The more common symptoms of conversion hysteria are motor paralyses, contractures, involuntary actions or discharges, pains, and hallucinations. They are cathectic processes which are either permanently maintained or intermittent. The symptoms belonging to the obsessional neuroses fall into 2 groups, each having an opposite trend. They are either prohibitions, precautions, and expiations or they are substitutive satisfactions which often appear in symbolic disguise. In enforcing regression, the ego scores its first success in its defensive struggle against the demands of the libido. It is perhaps in obsessional cases more than in normal or hysterical ones that the motive force of defense is the castration complex and that what is being fended off are the trends of the Oedipus complex. The reaction formations in the ego of the obsessional neurotic should be regarded as yet another mechanism of defense. Other defense mechanisms alluded to in this condition are: undoing, regression, isolation. Ambivalence is also described as contributing greatly to the formation of obsessional neurosis for some unknown reason. The chief task during the latency period seems to be the fending off of the temptation to masturbate. This struggle produces a series of symptoms which appear in a typical fashion in the most different individuals and which in general have the character of a ceremonial. The advent of puberty opens a decisive chapter in the history of an obsessional neurosis. The overstrict superego insists on the suppression of sexuality. In obsessional neurosis, the conflict is aggravated in 2 directions: the defensive forces become more intolerant and the forces that are to be fended off become more intolerable. Both effects are due to regression of the libido. Obsessional states which have no guilt attached are mentioned. These seem more closely related to the satisfaction of masochistic impulses.

1926D   20/119

Inhibitions, symptoms and anxiety (1926). Part VI. Undoing and isolation.

There are 2 activities of the ego which form symptoms and which deserve special attention because they are surrogates of repression. The 2 activities are undoing what has been done and isolating. The first of these has a wide range of application. It is, as it were, negative magic, and endeavors, by means of motor symbolism, to blow away not merely the consequences of some event but the event itself. In obsessional neurosis the technique of undoing what has been done is first met within the diphasic symptoms in which one action is cancelled out by a second, so that it is as though neither action had taken place. This aim of undoing is the second underlying motive of obsessional ceremonials, the first being to take the rational precautions in order to prevent the occurrence or recurrence of some particular event. The second technique, isolating, is peculiar to obsessional neurosis. When something unpleasant has happened to the subject, or when he himself has done something which has a significance for his neurosis, he interpolates an interval during which nothing further must happen. It is especially difficult for an obsessional neurotic to carry out the fundamental rule of psychoanalysis. His ego is more watchful and makes sharper isolations, probably because of the high degree of tension due to conflict that exists between his superego and his id. In endeavoring to prevent associations and connections of thought, the ego is obeying one of the oldest and most fundamental commands of obsessional neurosis, the taboo on touching. The avoidance of touching is of paramount importance in this illness because it is the immediate aim of the aggressive as well as the loving object cathexes.

1926D   20/124

Inhibitions, symptoms and anxiety (1926). Part VII. Anxiety is a signal of dangerous separation.

In animal phobias, the ego has to oppose a libidinal object cathexis coming from the id, a cathexis that belongs either to the positive or negative Oedipus complex, because it believes that to give way to it would entail the danger of castration. The aggressive impulse flows mainly from the destructive instinct. As soon as the ego recognizes the danger of castration, it gives the signal of anxiety and inhibits, through the pleasure-unpleasure agency, the impending cathectic process in the id. At the same time the phobia is formed. Now the castration anxiety is directed to a different object and expressed in a distorted form, so that the patient is afraid, not of being castrated by his father, but of being bitten by a horse or devoured by a wolf. Phobias have the character of a projection in that they replace an internal, instinctual danger by an external, perceptual

one. The anxiety felt in animal phobias is an affective reaction on the part of the ego to danger; and the danger which is being signalled in this way is the danger of castration. A phobia generally sets in after a first anxiety attack has been experienced in specific circumstances, such as in the street or in a train or in solitude. Anxiety is a reaction to a situation of danger. It is obviated by the ego's doing something to avoid that situation or to withdraw from it. Symptoms are then viewed as created so as to avoid a danger situation whose presence was signalled by the generation of anxiety. The narcissistic neuroses are explained in terms of a sexual factor being present, namely narcissism, which emphasizes the libidinal nature of the instinct of self-preservation. Since the unconscious can not conceive of its annihilation, and since the unconscious must contribute something to the formation of the narcissistic neuroses, then the fear of death must be analogous to the fear of castration. The ego responds to being abandoned by the protecting superego, the powers of destiny. Also, the protective shield against excessive amounts of external excitation is broken.

1926D   20/132

Inhibitions, symptoms and anxiety (1926). Part VII. Anxiety reproduces feelings of helplessness.

Anxiety is an affective state. Analysis of anxiety states reveals the existence of: 1) a specific character of unpleasure, 2) acts of discharge, and 3) perceptions of those acts. Anxiety states are regarded as a reproduction of the trauma of birth. Anxiety arose originally as a reaction to a state of danger. It is reproduced whenever the danger stage recurs. Only a few of the manifestations of anxiety in children are comprehensible to us. They occur, for instance, when a child is alone, or in the dark or when it finds itself with an unknown person instead of one to whom it is used. These 3 instances can be reduced to a single condition, namely, that of missing someone who is loved and longed for. The child's mnemonic image of the person longed for is no doubt intensely cathected, probably in a hallucinatory way at first. But this has no effect; and now it seems as though the longing turns into anxiety. Economic disturbance caused by an accumulation of amounts of stimulation which need disposal is the real essence of the "danger". The nonsatisfaction of a growing tension due to need against which the infant wants to be safeguarded repeats the danger situation of being born. From this point anxiety undergoes various transformations parallel to the various stages of libidinal development. The significance of the loss of object as a determinant of anxiety extends for a long period of time. The castration anxiety, belonging to the phallic phase, is also a fear of separation and is thus attached to the same determinant. In this case the danger is of being separated from one's genitals.

The next transformation is caused by the power of the superego. Castration anxiety develops into moral anxiety. Loss of love plays much the same part in hysteria as the threat of castration does in phobias and fear of the superego in obsessional neurosis. The present conception of anxiety is that of a signal given by the ego in order to affect the pleasure-unpleasure agency. There is no anxiety of the superego or id. The id only can be the site of processes which cause the ego to produce anxiety.

1926D 20/144

Inhibitions, symptoms and anxiety (1926). Part IX. Relation between symptom formation and anxiety.

The relationship between the formation of symptoms and the generating of anxiety is considered. There are 2 very widely held opinions on this subject. One is that anxiety is itself a symptom of neurosis. The other is that there is a much more intimate relation between the 2. According to the second opinion, symptoms are only formed in order to avoid anxiety. Symptoms are created in order to remove the ego from a situation of danger. If the symptoms are prevented from being formed, the danger does in fact materialize. Symptom formation puts an end to the danger situation. The defensive process is analogous to the flight by means of which the ego removes itself from a danger that threatens it from outside. The defensive process is an attempt at flight from an instinctual danger. The study of the determinants of anxiety shows the defensive behavior of the ego transfigured in a rational light. Each danger situation corresponds to a particular period of life or developmental phase of the mental apparatus and is justifiable for it. A great many people remain infantile in their behavior in regard to danger and do not overcome determinants of anxiety which have grown out of date. Signs of childhood neuroses can be detected in all adult neurotics; however, all children who show those signs do not become neurotic in later life. It must be, therefore, that certain determinants of anxiety are relinquished and certain danger situations lose their significance as the individual becomes more mature. Moreover, some of these danger situations manage to survive into later times by modifying their determinants of anxiety so as to bring them up to date. Other determinants of anxiety, such as fear of the superego, are destined not to disappear at all.

1926D 20/150

Inhibitions, symptoms and anxiety (1926). Part X. Repetition is the consequence of repression.

Anxiety is the reaction to danger. If the ego succeeds in protecting itself from a dangerous instinctual impulse through the process of repression, it has inhibited and damaged the particular part of the id concerned; but it has at the same time given it some independence and has

renounced some of its own sovereignty. Among the factors that play a part in the causation of neuroses and that have created the conditions under which the forces of the mind are pitted against one another, 3 emerge into prominence: a biological, a phylogenetic, and a purely psychological factor. The biological factor is the long period of time during which the young of the human species is in a condition of helplessness and dependence. The existence of the phylogenetic factor is based only upon inference. We have been led to assume its existence by a remarkable feature in the development of the libido. The sexual life of man does not make a steady advance from birth to maturity, but after an early efflorescence up to the fifth year, it undergoes a very decided interruption; and it then starts on its course once more at puberty taking up again the beginnings broken off in early childhood. The third, psychological, factor resides in a defect of our mental apparatus which has to do precisely with its differentiation into an id and an ego, and which is therefore also attributable ultimately to the influence of the external world. The ego cannot protect itself from internal instinctual dangers as well as it can from reality. It acquiesces in the formation of symptoms in exchange for impairing the instinct.

1926D 20/157

Inhibitions, symptoms and anxiety (1926). Part XI. Addenda: A. Modification of earlier views.

An important element in the theory of repression is the view that repression is not an event that occurs once but that it requires a permanent expenditure of energy. If this expenditure were to cease, the repressed impulse, which is being fed all the time from its sources, would on the next occasion, flow along the channels from which it had been forced away, and the repression would either fail in its purpose or would have to be repeated an indefinite number of times. It is because instincts are continuous in their nature that the ego has to make its defensive action secure by a permanent expenditure. This action undertaken to protect repression is observable in analytic treatment as resistance. Resistance presupposes what is called anticathexis. The resistance that has to be overcome in analysis proceeds from the ego, which clings to its anticathexes. Five types of resistance were noted: the ego resistances subdivided into regression resistance, transference resistance, and gain from illness; the id resistance *i.e.*, the compulsion to repeat; the superego resistance, the sense of guilt or the need for punishment. The ego is the source of anxiety. Anxiety is the general reaction to situations of danger. The term defense is employed explicitly as a general designation for all the techniques which the ego makes use of in conflicts which may lead to a neurosis. Repression is retained for a special method of defense. The concept of defense covers all the processes that have the same purpose, the protection of the ego against instinctual demands. Repression is subsumed under it as a special case.

1926D 20/164
Inhibitions, symptoms and anxiety (1926). Part XI. Addenda: B. Supplementary remarks on anxiety.

Anxiety has an unmistakable relation to expectation: it is anxiety about something. It has a quality of indefiniteness and lack of object. In precise words we use the word fear rather than anxiety if it has found an object. There are 2 reactions to real danger. One is an affective reaction, an outbreak of anxiety. The other is a protective action. A danger situation is a recognized, remembered, expected situation of helplessness. Anxiety is the original reaction to helplessness in the trauma and is reproduced later on in the danger situation as a signal for help. The ego, which experienced the trauma passively, now repeats it actively in a weakened version, in the hope of being able itself to direct its course. There seems to be a close connection between anxiety and neurosis because the ego defends itself against an instinctual danger with the help of the anxiety reaction just as it does against an external real danger; however, this line of defensive activity eventuates in a neurosis owing to an imperfection of the mental apparatus.

1926D 20/169
Inhibitions, symptoms and anxiety (1926). Part XI. Addenda. C. Anxiety, pain and mourning.

The situation of the infant's missing its mother is not a danger situation but a traumatic one. It is a traumatic situation if the infant happens to be feeling a need which its mother should be the one to satisfy. It turns into a danger situation if this need is not present at the moment. The first determinant of anxiety, which the ego itself introduces, is loss of perception of the object. Later on, experiences teaches the child that the object can be present but angry with it; and then loss of love from the object becomes a new and much more enduring danger and determinant of anxiety. Pain is the actual reaction to loss of an object while anxiety is the reaction to the danger which the loss entails. Pain occurs in the first instance and as a regular thing whenever a stimulus which impinges on the periphery breaks through the devices of the protective shield against stimuli and proceeds to act like a continuous instinctual stimulus, against which muscular action, which is as a rule effective because it withdraws the place that is being stimulated from the stimulus, is powerless. When there is physical pain, a high degree of what may be termed narcissistic cathexis of the painful place occurs. This cathexis continues to increase and tends to empty the ego. The transition from physical to mental pain corresponds to a change from narcissistic cathexis to

object cathexis. Mourning occurs under the influence of reality testing; for the latter function demands categorically from the bereaved person that he should separate himself from the object, since it no longer exists. Mourning is entrusted with the task of carrying out this retreat from the object in all those situations in which it was the recipient of a high degree of cathexis.

1926D 20/173
Inhibitions, symptoms and anxiety (1926). Appendix A: 'Repression' and 'defence'.

Repression and defense are discussed. Both repression and defense occurred very freely during Freud's Breuer period. The first appearance of repression was in the *Preliminary Communication*, and of defense in the first paper on *The Neuropsychoses of Defence*. In the *Studies on Hysteria*, repression appeared about a dozen times and defense somewhat more often than that. After the Breuer period, there was a falling off in the frequency of the use of defense. It was not dropped entirely, however. But repression was already beginning to predominate and was almost exclusively used in the Dora case history and the *Three Essays*. Soon after this, attention was explicitly drawn to the change, in a paper on sexuality in the neuroses, dated June, 1905. After 1905, the predominance of repression increased still more. But it was not long before the usefulness of defense as a more inclusive term than repression began unobtrusively to make its appearance, particularly in the metapsychological papers. Thus, the vicissitudes of the instincts, only one of which is repression, were regarded as modes of defense against them and projection was spoken of as a mechanism or means of defense.

1926E 20/179
The question of lay analysis (1926). Conversations with an impartial person. Editor's note. (1959).

In the late spring of 1926 proceedings were begun in Vienna against Theodor Reik, a prominent nonmedical member of the Vienna Psychoanalytic Society. He was charged, on information laid by someone whom he had been treating analytically, with a breach of an old Austrian law against quackery, a law which made it illegal for a person without a medical degree to treat patients. Freud intervened energetically. He argued the position privately with an official of high standing, and went on to compose the pamphlet, *The Question of Lay Analysis*, for immediate publication. The publication of Freud's booklet brought into the foreground the strong differences of opinion on the permissibility of nonmedical psychoanalysis which existed within the psychoanalytic societies themselves. From early times, Freud held the opinion that psychoanalysis was not to be regarded as purely a concern of the medical profession.

1926E 20/183
The question of lay analysis (1926). Introduction & Part I.

The question of lay analysis is discussed. Layman is equivalent to nondoctor. In Germany and America, every patient can have himself treated how and by whom he chooses, and anyone who chooses can handle any patients. The law does not intervene until it is called in to expiate some injury done to the patient. But in Austria, there is a preventive law, which forbids non-doctors from undertaking the treatment of patients, without waiting for its outcome. A patient recognizes that he is ill and goes to doctors, by whom people expect nervous disorders to be removed. The doctors lay down the categories into which these complaints are divided. They diagnose them under different names: neurasthenia, psychasthenia, phobias, obsessional neurosis, hysteria. They examine the organs which produce the symptoms and find them healthy. They recommend interruptions in the patient's accustomed mode of life and these means bring about temporary improvements, or no results at all. Eventually the patients hear that there are people who are concerned quite specially with the treatment of such complaints and start an analysis with them. The analyst and the patient talk to each other. We call on the patient to be completely straightforward with his analyst, to keep nothing back intentionally that comes into his head, and then to put aside every reservation that might prevent his reporting certain thoughts or memories.

1926E 20/191
The question of lay analysis (1926). Part II.

The question of lay analysis is discussed. We picture the unknown apparatus which serves the activities of the mind as being really like an instrument constructed of several parts, agencies, each of which performs a particular function and which have a fixed spatial relation to one another. We recognize in human beings a mental organization which is interpolated between their sensory stimuli and the perception of their somatic needs on the one hand and their motor acts on the other, and which meditates between them for a particular purpose. This organization is called their ego. There is another mental region, more extensive, more imposing and more obscure than the ego: this is called the id. We suppose that the ego is the layer of the mental apparatus (of the id) which has been modified by the influence of the external world. The ego and the id differ greatly from each other in several respects. The rules governing the course of mental acts are different in the ego and the id; the ego pursues different purposes and by other methods. Everything that happens in the id is, and remains, unconscious; processes in the ego can become

conscious. But not all of them are, nor always, nor necessarily; and large portions of the ego can remain permanently unconscious. The ego is the external, peripheral layer of the id. We require that everyone who wants to practice analysis on other people shall first himself submit to an analysis.

1926E 20/200
The question of lay analysis (1926). Part III.

The question of lay analysis is discussed. The bodily needs, in so far as they represent an instigation to mental activity, are given the name of instincts. These instincts fill the id: all the energy in the id originates from them. The forces in the ego are derived from those in the id. These instincts want satisfaction. If the id's instinctual demands meet with no satisfaction, intolerable conditions arise. The instincts in the id press for immediate satisfaction at all costs, and in that way they achieve nothing or even bring about appreciable damage. It is the task of the ego to guard against such mishaps, to mediate between the claims of the id and the objections of the external world. There is no natural opposition between ego and id. If the ego experiences an instinctual demand from the id which it would like to resist but which it cannot control, the ego treats the instinctual danger as if it were an external one; it makes an attempt at flight. The ego institutes a repression of the instinctual impulses. The ego has made an attempt to suppress certain portions of the id in an inappropriate manner, this attempt has failed and the id has taken its revenge in the neurosis. A neurosis is the result of a conflict between the ego and the id. The therapeutic aim is to restore the ego and give it back command over the id. The ego is urged to correct the repressions. This involves analyzing back to childhood through the patient's symptoms, dreams and free associations.

1926E 20/206
The question of lay analysis (1926). Part IV.

The question of lay analysis is discussed. Analysis is founded on complete candor. This obligation to candor puts a grave moral responsibility on the analyst as well as on the patient. Factors from sexual life play an extremely important, a dominating, perhaps even a specific part among the causes and precipitating factors of neurotic illness. The recognition of sexuality has become the strongest motive for people's hostility to analysis. Sexual life is not simply something spicy; it is also a serious scientific problem. Analysis has to go back into the early years of the patient's childhood, because the decisive repressions have taken place then, while his ego was feeble. Sexual instinctual impulses accompany life from birth onwards, and it is precisely in order to fend off those instincts that the infantile ego institutes repressions. The sexual function undergoes a complicated process of development. If obstacles arise later on to the exercise of the sexual function, the sexual urge, the libido, is apt to hark back to the earlier point of fixation. The diphasic onset of sexual life has a great deal to do with the genesis of neurotic illnesses. It seems to occur only in human beings, and it is perhaps one of the determinants of the human privilege of becoming neurotic. The children's 2 excretory needs are cathected with sexual interest. It takes quite a long time for children to develop feelings of disgust. Children regularly direct their sexual wishes towards their nearest relatives. It is the sexual wishes towards the parent of the opposite sex with concomitant hostility felt toward the other parent which constitutes the basis for the Oedipus complex. The revival of this complex in puberty may have serious consequences. The child's first choice of the object therefore is an incestuous one. The evidence for this is supported through the study of history, mythology, and anthropology.

1926E   20/218
The question of lay analysis (1926). Part V.

The question of lay analysis is discussed. The analyst infers, from what the patient says, the kind of impressions, experiences and wishes which he has repressed because he came across them at a time when his ego was still feeble and was afraid of them instead of dealing with them. When the patient has learned this, he puts himself back in the old situations and manages better. The limitations to which his ego was tied then disappear, and he is cured. The material has to be interpreted at the right moment which is when the patient has come so near the repressed material that only a few more stages are needed to get to it. It can be shown that patients profess a desire to get well, but on the other hand do not want to get well. This results from the "gain from illness." This represents one of the resistances to psychoanalysis. There are 3 other resistances: the sense of guilt and need for punishment stemming from the superego; the need for the instinctual impulse to find satisfaction along a path it has always known, an id resistance; repression resistance coming from the ego. The emotional relation which the patient adopts towards the analysis is of a quite peculiar nature. This emotional relation is in the nature of falling in love. This love is of a positively compulsive kind. It has taken the place of the neurosis. The patient is repeating, in the form of falling in love with the analyst, mental experiences which he has already been through once before; he has transferred on to the analyst mental attitudes that were lying ready in him and were intimately connected with his neurosis. This transference love, because of its being really a pathological love, acts as a resistance to analysis (and is thus the fifth major resistance in analysis). He is

also repeating his old defensive actions. The whole skill in handling the transference is devoted to bringing it about. There are 2 Institutes at which instruction in psychoanalysis is given. Anyone who has passed through a course of instruction, who has been analyzed himself, who has learned the delicate technique of psychoanalysis (the art of interpretation, fighting resistances, handling the transference), is no longer a layman in the field of psychoanalysis.

1926E   20/229
The question of lay analysis (1926). Part VI.

The question of lay analysis is discussed. It seems as if the neuroses are a particular kind of illness and analysis is a particular method of treating them, a specialized branch of medicine. However, doctors have no historical claim to the sole possession of analysis. In his medical school, a doctor receives a training which is more or less the opposite of what he would need as a preparation for psychoanalysis, particularly since medical education gives a false and detrimental attitude towards the neuroses. The activity of an untrained analyst does less harm to his patients than that of an unskilled surgeon. Freud maintains that no one should practice analysis who has not acquired the right to do so by a particular training. It is said that the authorities, at the instigation of the medical profession, want to forbid the practice of analysis by laymen altogether. Such a prohibition would also affect the nonmedical members of the Psychoanalytic Society, who have enjoyed an excellent training and have perfected themselves greatly by practice. According to Austrian law, a quack (layman) is anyone who treats patients without possessing a state diploma to prove he is a doctor. Freud proposes another definition: a quack is anyone who undertakes a treatment without possessing the knowledge and capacities necessary for it.

1926E   20/239
The question of lay analysis (1926). Part VII.

The question of lay analysis is discussed. A medical doctor has a decided advantage over a layman in analytic practice regarding the question of diagnosis. The patient may exhibit the external picture of a neurosis, and yet it may be something else: the beginning of an incurable mental disease or the preliminary of brain destruction. If a later physical illness can bring about an enfeeblement of the ego then that illness can also produce a neurosis. If an analyst, medical or otherwise, suspects organic illness, Freud maintains that the analyst should call in the help of a medical doctor. He lists 3 reasons for it: 1) it is not a good plan for a combination of organic and psychical treatments to be carried out by the same person; 2) the relation in the transference may make it inadvisable for the analyst to examine the patient physically; and 3) the analyst has every reason for doubting whether he is unprejudiced, since his interests are directed so intensely to the psychical factors. For the patient, it is a matter of indifference whether the analyst is a doctor or not, provided only that the danger of his condition being misunderstood is excluded by the necessary medical report before the treatment begins and on some possible occasions during the course of it. Analytic training cuts across the field of medical education, but neither includes the other. Freud did not believe that a medical education was necessary for an analyst. He did not consider it desirable for an analyst. He did not consider it desirable for psychoanalysis to be swallowed up by medicine and be subsumed as a subordinate area of psychiatry. The training of social workers analytically to help combat neuroses was envisioned. He thought that the internal development of psychoanalysis could never be affected by regulation or prohibition.

1927A 20/251
The question of lay analysis (1926). Postscript. (1927).

The charge against Dr. Theodor Reik, in the Vienna Courts, was dropped. The prosecution's case was too weak, and the person who brought the charge as an aggrieved party proved an untrustworthy witness. Freud's main thesis in *The Question of Lay Analysis* was that the important question is not whether an analyst possesses a medical diploma but whether he has had the special training necessary for the practice of analysis. A scheme of training for analysts has still to be created. It must include elements from the mental sciences, from psychology, the history of civilization and sociology, as well as from anatomy, biology, and the study of evolution. Psychoanalysis is a part of psychology; not of medical psychology, not of the psychology of morbid processes, but simply of psychology. He enjoins his American colleagues not to exclude lay analysts from receiving training since this might interest them in raising their own ethical and intellectual level while gaining influence over them so as to try and prevent their unscrupulous practices.

1926F 20/261
Psycho-analysis (1926). Editors note. (1959) and article.

The Eleventh Edition of the *Encyclopedia Britannica* appeared in 1910 and 1911. It contained no reference to psychoanalysis. An article on psychoanalysis appeared in the Thirteenth Edition, written by Freud himself. This article included the prehistory, subject matter, and external history of psychoanalysis. The prehistory includes the contribution made by Josef Breuer who, in 1880 discovered a procedure by means of which he relieved a girl, who was suffering from severe hysteria, of her many and various symptoms. His cathartic treatment gave excellent therapeutic results. Psychoanalysis finds a constantly increasing amount of support as a therapeutic procedure, owing to the fact that it can do more for its patients than any other method of treatment. The principal field of its application is in the milder neuroses: hysterias, phobias, and obsessional states. The therapeutic influence of psychoanalysis depends on the replacement of unconscious mental acts by conscious ones and is effective within the limits of that factor. The analytic theory of the neuroses is based on 3 cornerstones: the recognition 1) of repression, 2) of the importance of the sexual instinct, and 3) of transference. Psychoanalysis in its character of depth psychology considers mental life from 3 points of view: dynamic, economic, and topographical. The dynamic considers the interplay of forces which assist, inhibit, combine, or compromise with one another. The forces originate in the instincts of which there are 2 types: ego instincts and object instincts. The economic considers the quantum of psychic energy with its charge (cathexis). The course of mental processes is regulated by the pleasure-unpleasure principle. The pleasure principle is modified by the reality principle during the course of development. The topographic considers the mental apparatus is composed of the id, ego, superego. The ego and superego develop out of the id. The id is wholly unconscious while parts of the ego and superego are conscious. The beginnings of psychoanalysis may be marked by 2 dates: 1895, which saw the publication of Breuer and Freud's *Studies on Hysteria*, and 1900, which saw that of Freud's *Interpretation of Dreams*.

1941E 20/271
Address to the Society of B'nai B'rith (1941, 1926).

An address to the Society of B'nai B'rith was read on Freud's behalf at a meeting held on May 6, 1926, in honor of his seventieth birthday. In the years from 1895 onwards, Freud was subjected to 2 powerful impressions which combined to produce the same effect on him. On the one hand, he had gained his first insight into the depths of the life of the human instincts. On the other hand, the announcement of his unpleasing discoveries had, as its result, the severance of the greater part of his human contacts. In his loneliness he was seized with a longing to find a circle of picked men of high character who would receive him in a friendly spirit in spite of his temerity. The B'nai B'rith was pointed out to him. His attraction to Jewry consisted of powerful emotional forces that could not be expressed in words. Being a Jew prepared him to join the opposition and not need the agreement of the "compact majority'. Because he was a Jew, he found himself free from many prejudices which restricted others in the use of their intellect. For some two-thirds of the long period that elapsed since Freud's entry, he persisted with the B'nai B'rith conscientiously, and found refreshment and stimulation in his relations with it. The B'nai B'rith was kind enough not to hold it against him that during his last third of the time, he kept away. He was overwhelmed with work, and the demands connected with his work forced themselves on him. The day ceased to be long enough for him to attend the meetings. Finally came the years of his illness. Freud concluded that the B'nai B'rith meant a great deal to him.

1926B 20/277
Karl Abraham (1926).

Dr. Karl Abraham, President of the Berlin group, of which he was the founder, and President at the time of the International Psychoanalytical Association, died in Berlin on December 25, 1925. He had not reached the age of 50. Among all those who followed Freud along the dark paths of psychoanalytic research, Abraham won so preeminent a place that only one other name could be set beside his, Ferenczi. It is likely that the boundless trust of his colleagues and pupils would have called him to the leadership; and he would, without doubt, have been a model leader in the pursuit of truth, led astray neither by the praise or blame of the many nor by the seductive illusion of his own phantasies.

1926A 20/279
To Romain Rolland (1926).

A letter to Romain Rolland on the occasion of his sixtieth birthday, is presented. Freud honored him as an artist and as an apostle of the love of mankind. When Freud came to know Romain Rolland personally, Freud was surprised to find that he valued strength and energy so highly and that he embodied such force of will.

1926C 20/280
Prefatory note to a paper by E. Pickworth Farrow (1926).

A prefatory note to a paper by E. Pickworth Farrow is presented. Farrow is a man of strong and independent intelligence. He failed to get on to good terms with 2 analysts with whom he made the attempt. He thereupon proceeded to make a systematic application of the procedure of self-analysis which Freud himself employed in the past for the analysis of his own dreams. His work deserves attention because of the peculiar character of his personality and his technique.

VOL. XXI The Future of an Illusion, Civilization and its Discontents and Other Works (1927–1931)

1927C 21/3
The future of an illusion (1927). Editor's note (1961) and Part I. Civilization rests upon renunciation of instinctual wishes.

The Future of an Illusion began a series of studies which were to be Freud's major concern for the rest of his life. Human civilization presents 2 aspects to the observer. It includes all the knowledge and capacity that men have acquired in order to control the forces of nature and extract its wealth for the satisfaction of human needs, and, all the regulations necessary in order to adjust the relations of men to one another and especially the distribution of the available wealth. One gets an impression that civilization is something which was imposed on a resisting majority by a minority which understood how to obtain possession of the means to power and coercion. It is only through the influence of individuals who can set an example and whom masses recognize as their leaders that they can be induced to perform the work and undergo the renunciations on which the existence of civilization depends. All is well if these leaders are persons who possess superior insight into the necessities of life and who have risen to the height of mastering their own instinctual wishes. But there is a danger that in order not to lose their influence they may give way to the mass more than it gives way to them, and it therefore seems necessary that they will be independent of the mass by having means to power at their disposal.

1927C 21/10
The future of an illusion (1927). Part II. Consequences of instinctual renunciation. Part III. In what does the peculiar value of religious ideas lie.

Every civilization rests on a compulsion to work and a renunciation of instinct and therefore inevitably provokes opposition from those affected by these demands. The fact that an instinct cannot be satisfied is a frustration. The regulation by which this frustration is established is called a prohibition, and the condition which is produced by this prohibition is called a privation. The privations which affect everyone include the instinctual wishes of incest, cannibalism, and lust for killing. People will be only too readily inclined to include among the psychical assets of a culture its ideals. The narcissistic satisfaction provided by the cultural ideal rests upon pride in what has already been successfully achieved and is also among the forces which are successful in combating the hostility to culture within the cultural unit. A different kind of satisfaction is afforded by art to the

participants in a cultural unit; it offers substitutive satisfaction for the oldest and still most deeply felt cultural
renunciations. A store of religious ideas was created,
born from man's need to make his helplessness tolerable
and built up from the material of memories of the helplessness of his own childhood and the childhood of the
human race. The possession of these ideas protects him
in 2 directions, against the dangers of nature and Fate,
and against the injuries that threaten him from human
society itself.

1927C 21/21

**The future of an illusion (1927). Part IV. Origins of
religions.**

Freud tried to show that religious ideas have arisen
from the same need as have all the other achievements of
civilization: from the necessity of defending oneself
against the crushingly superior force of nature. To this, a
second motive was added: the urge to rectify the shortcomings of civilization which made themselves painfully
felt. When the growing individual finds that he is destined to remain a child forever, that he can never do
without protection against strange superior powers, he
lends those powers the features belonging to the figure
of his father; he creates for himself the gods whom he
dreads, whom he seeks to propitiate, and whom he
nevertheless entrusts with his own protection. Thus his
longing for a father is a motive identical with his need
for protection against the consequences of his human
weakness. The defense against childish helplessness is
what lends its characteristic features to the adult's reaction to the helplessness which he has to acknowledge, a
reaction which is precisely the formation of religion.

1927C 21/25

**The future of an illusion (1927). Part V. The psycho-
logical significance of religious ideas. Part VI. Religious
ideas are illusions.**

Religious ideas are teachings and assertions about
facts and conditions of external or internal reality which
tell one something one has not discovered for oneself
and which lay claim to one's belief. Since they give us
information about what is most important and interesting to us in life, they are particularly highly prized.
Religious teachings base their claim to belief firstly
because they were already believed by our primal ancestors; secondly, we possess proofs which have been
handed down to us from these same primeval times; and
thirdly, it is forbidden to raise the question of their
authentication at all. Illusions are derived from human
wishes. Freud maintains that religious doctrines are
psychological illusions and are therefore insusceptible of
proof.

1927C 21/34

**The future of an illusion (1927). Part VII. Relations
between civilization and religion.**

Religion has performed great services for human
civilization. It has contributed much, but not enough,
towards the taming of the asocial instincts. It has ruled
human society for many thousands of years and has had
time to show what it can achieve. If it had succeeded in
making the majority of mankind happy, in comforting
them, in reconciling them to life and in making them
into vehicles of civilization, no one would dream of
attempting to alter the existing conditions. However,
there is an appalling large number of people who are
dissatisfied with civilization and unhappy with it. Civilization has little to fear from educated people and brain
workers. In them, the replacement of religious motives
for civilized behavior by other, secular motives would
proceed unobtrusively; moreover, such people are to a
large extent themselves vehicles of civilization. But it is
another matter with the great mass of the uneducated
and oppressed, who have every reason for being enemies
of civilization. Either these dangerous masses must be
held down most severely and kept most carefully away
from any chance of intellectual awakening, or else the
relationship between civilization and religion must
undergo a fundamental revision.

1927C 21/40

**The future of an illusion (1927). Part VIII. Religion is a
substitute for rationality.**

When civilization laid down the commandment that a
man shall not kill the neighbor whom he hates or who is
in his way or whose property he covets, this was clearly
done in the interest of man's communal existence, which
would not otherwise be practicable. The primal father
was the original image of God, the model on which later
generations have shaped the figure of God. God actually
played a part in the genesis of that prohibition; it was
His influence, not any insight into social necessity,
which created it. Men knew that they had disposed of
their father by violence, and in their reaction to that
impious deed, they determined to respect his will thence
forward. The store of religious ideas includes not only
wish fulfillments but important historical recollections.
The analogy between religion and obsessional neurosis
has been repeatedly demonstrated. Many of the peculiarities and vicissitudes in the formation of religion can
be understood in that light. It is proposed that certain
religious doctrines should cease to be put forward as the
reasons for the precepts of civilization. The religious
teachings are viewed as neurotic relics and Freud states
that the time has come for replacing the effects of repression by the results of the rational operation of the
intellect.

1927C 21/46

The future of an illusion (1927). Part IX. Is rationality possible. Part X. Relation of religion to science.

A believer is bound to the teachings of religion by certain ties of affection. It is certainly senseless to begin by trying to do away with religion by force and at a single blow. Religion is comparable to a childhood neurosis, and just as so many children grow out of their similar neurosis, so mankind will surmount this neurotic phase. The primacy of the intellect lies in a distant future, but probably not in an infinitely distant one. It will presumably set for itself the same aims as those whose realization you expect from your God, namely, the love of man and the decrease of suffering. Our mental apparatus has been developed precisely in the attempt to explore the external world, and it must therefore have realized in its structure some degree of expediency. It is itself a constituent part of the world which we set to investigate, and it readily admits of such an investigation. The task of science is fully covered if we limit it to showing how the world must appear to us in consequence of the particular character of our organization. The ultimate findings of science, precisely because of the way in which they are acquired, are determined not only by our organization but by the things which have affected that organization. The problem of the nature of the world without regard to our percipient mental apparatus is an empty abstraction, devoid of practical interest. Science is no illusion. But it would be an illusion to suppose that what science cannot give us we can get elsewhere.

1930A 21/59

Civilization and its discontents (1930). Editor's introduction. (1961).

The main theme of *Civilization and Its Discontents,* the irremediable antagonism between the demands of instinct and the restrictions of civilization may be traced back to some of Freud's very earliest psychological writings. The construction of dams against the sexual instinct during the latency period of childhood is organically determined and fixed by heredity, rather than being solely a product of education. The history of Freud's views on the aggressive or destructive instinct is a complicated one. Throughout his earlier writings, the context in which he viewed it predominantly was that of sadism. Later on, the original independence of the aggressive impulses was recognized. The independent sources indicated, were to be traced to the self-preservative instincts. Impulses of aggressiveness, and of hatred too, had from the first seemed to belong to the self-preservative instinct, and since this was subsumed under the libido, no independent aggressive instinct was called for. This was so in spite of the bipolarity of object relations, of the frequent admixtures of love and hate,

and of the complex origin of hate itself. It was not until Freud's hypothesis of a death instinct that a truly independent aggressive instinct came into view in *Beyond the Pleasure Principle.* In Freud's later writings, the aggressive instinct was still something secondary, derived from the primary self-destructive death instinct, although in the present work the stress is much more upon the death instinct's manifestations outwards.

1930A 21/64

Civilization and its discontents (1930). Part I. Man's need for religion arises from feelings of helplessness.

It is impossible to escape the impression that people commonly use false standards of measurement, that they seek power, success and wealth for themselves and admire them in others, and that they underestimate what is of true value in life. However, we are in danger of forgetting how variegated the human world and its mental life are. One objection to Freud's treatment of religion as an illusion was that he had not properly appreciated the true source of religious sentiments, which were in an oceanic feeling of something limitless, of being one with the external world as a whole. The genetic explanation of such a feeling concludes that originally the ego includes everything and later it separates an external world from itself. Our present ego feeling is only a shrunken residue of a much more inclusive, all embracing feeling which corresponded to a more intimate bond between the ego and the world about it. Thus, although we are willing to acknowledge that the "oceanic" feeling exists in many people, it is not the origin of the religious attitude, which can be traced back to the feeling of infantile helplessness.

1930A 21/74

Civilization and its discontents (1930). Part II. Man copes with unhappiness through diversion, substitution and intoxication.

The question of the purpose of human life has been raised countless times; it has never yet received a satisfactory answer. Men strive after happiness. This endeavor has two sides: it aims at an absence of pain and unpleasure, and at the experiencing of strong feelings of pleasure. One of the methods of averting suffering is the chemical one, intoxication. Another technique is the employment of displacements of libido which our mental apparatus permits of and through which its function gains so much in flexibility. In another procedure, satisfaction is obtained from illusions, which are recognized as such without the discrepancy between them and reality being allowed to interfere with enjoyment. Another procedure regards reality as the sole enemy and as the source of all suffering, with which it is impossible to live, so that one must break off all relations with it if one is to be happy in any way. Happiness in life can be predominantly sought in the enjoyment of beauty. The man who is predominantly erotic will give first perference to his emotional relationships to other people; the narcissistic man, who inclines to be self-sufficient, will seek his main satisfactions in his internal mental processes; the man of action will never give up the external world on which he can try out his strength. Religion restricts the play of choice and adaption, since it imposes equally on everyone its own path to the acquisition of happiness and protection from suffering.

1930A   21/86
Civilization and its discontents (1930). Part III. Man's conflict with civilization: Liberty versus equality.

Suffering comes from three sources: the superior power of nature, the feebleness of our own bodies, and the inadequacy of the regulations which adjust the mutual relationships of human beings in the family, the state and society. Civilization describes the whole sum of the achievement and the regulations which distinguish our lives from those of our animal ancestors and which serve two purposes: to protect men against nature and to adjust their mutual relations. We recognize as cultural all activities and resources which are useful to men for making the earth serviceable to them and for protecting them against the violence of the forces of nature. The first acts of civilization were the use of tools, the gaining of control over fire and the construction of dwellings. Psychoanalytic experience regularly testifies to the connection between ambition, fire, and urethal eroticism. We recognize that countries have attained a high level of civilization if we find that in them everything which can assist in the exploitation of the earth by man and in his protection against the forces is attended to and effectively carried out. Beauty, cleanliness, and order occupy a special position among the requirements of civilization. No feature seems better to characterize civilization than its esteem and encouragement of man's higher mental activities, his intellectual, scientific, and artistic achievements, and the leading role that it assigns to ideas in human life. Foremost among those ideas are the religious systems; next come the speculations of philosophy; and finally what might be called man's ideals—his ideas of a possible perfection of individuals, or of peoples, or of the whole of humanity and the demands he sets up on the basis of such ideas.

1930A   21/99
Civilization and its discontents (1930). Part IV. Two pillars of civilization: Eros and Ananke.

After primal man had discovered that it lay in his own hands, literally, to improve his lot on earth by working, it cannot have been a matter of indifference to him whether another man worked with or against him.

The other man acquired the value for him of a fellow worker. Man's discovery that sexual love afforded him the strongest experiences of satisfaction, and in fact provided him with the prototype of all happiness, must have suggested to him that he should continue to seek the satisfaction of happiness in his life along the path of sexual relations and that he should make genital eroticism the central point of his life. With the assumption of an erect posture by man and with the depreciation of his sense of smell, it was not only his anal eroticism which threatened to fall victim to organic repression, but the whole of his sexuality, leading since then to a repugnance which prevents its complete satisfaction and forces it away from the sexual aim into sublimations and libidinal displacements. The love which founded the family continues to operate in civilization both in its original form, in which it does not renounce direct sexual satisfaction, and in its modified form as aim-inhibited affection. In each, it continues to carry on its function of binding together considerable numbers of people, and it does so in a more intensive fashion than can be effected through the interest of work in common. The tendency on the part of civilization to restrict sexual life is no less clear than its other tendency to expand the cultural unit.

1930A   21/108
Civilization and its discontents (1930). Part V. Security at the cost of restricting sexuality and aggression.

Psychoanalytic work has shown us that it is precisely the frustrations of sexual life which people known as neurotics, cannot tolerate. The neurotic creates substitutive satisfactions for himself in his symptoms, and these either cause him suffering in themselves or become sources of suffering for him by raising difficulties in his relations with his environment and the society he belongs to. Men are not gentle creatures who want to be loved, and who at the most can defend themselves if they are attacked; they are, on the contrary, creatures whose instinctual endowments include a powerful share of aggressiveness. The existence of this inclination to aggression is the factor which disturbs our relations with our neighbor and which forces civilization into such a high expenditure of energy. In consequence of this primary mutual hostility of human beings, civilized society is perpetually threatened with disintegration. The communist system is based on an untenable psychological illusion, for in abolishing private property, we have in no way altered the differences in power and influence which are misused by aggression, nor have we altered anything in its nature. Because of civilization's imposition of such great sacrifices on man's sexuality and aggression, civilized man has exchanged a portion of his possibilities of happiness for a portion of security.

1930A   21/117
Civilization and its discontents (1930). Part VI. Arguments for an instinct of aggression and destruction.

The theory of the instincts is the one part of analytic theory that has felt its way the most painfully forward. At first the ego instincts (hunger) and the object instincts (love) confronted each other. The introduction of the concept of narcissism convinced Freud that the instincts could not all be of the same kind. Besides the instinct to preserve living substance and to join it into ever larger units, there must exist another, contrary instinct seeking to dissolve those units. Thus, as well as Eros, there was an instinct of death, the activities of which were not easy to demonstrate. A portion of the instinct is diverted towards the external world and comes to light as an instinct of aggressiveness and destructiveness. Sadism and masochism are examples of Eros and the death instinct appearing as allies with each other. Even where it emerges without any sexual purpose, the satisfaction of the instinct through destructiveness is accompanied by an extraordinarily high degree of narcissistic enjoyment. The inclination to aggression is an original, self-subsisting instinctual disposition. It constitutes the greatest impediment to civilization. Civilization is a process in the service of Eros, whose purpose is to combine single human individuals, and after that families, then places, peoples, and nations, into one great unity, the unity of mankind. The work of Eros is precisely this. The aggressive instinct is the derivative and the main representative of the death instinct which we have found alongside of Eros and which shares world dominion with it. The evolution of civilization must present the struggle between Eros and Death, between the instinct of life and the instinct of destruction, as it works itself out in the human species.

1930A   21/123
Civilization and its discontents (1930). Part VII. Development of the superego and its severity.

Civilization obtains mastery over the individual's dangerous desire for aggression by weakening and disarming it and by setting up an agency within him to watch over it, like a garrison in a conquered city. There are 2 origins of the sense of guilt: one arising from fear of an authority, and the other, later on, arising from fear of the superego. The first insists upon a renunciation of instinctual satisfactions; the second, as well as doing this, presses for punishment, since the continuance of the forbidden wishes cannot be concealed from the superego. The severity of the superego is simply a continuation of the severity of the external authority, to which it has succeeded and which it has in part replaced. Since civilization obeys an internal erotic impulse which causes human beings to unite in a closely knit group, it can only achieve this aim through an ever increasing reinforcement of the sense of guilt. If civilization is a necessary course of development from the family to humanity as a whole, then there is inextricably bound up with it an increase of the sense of guilt, which will perhaps reach heights that the individual finds hard to tolerate.

1930A   21/134
Civilization and its discontents (1930). Part VIII. Conclusions about effects of civilization upon psyche.

The superego is an agency which has been inferred by Freud; conscience is a function which Freud ascribes, among other functions, to that agency. This function consists in keeping a watch over the actions and intentions of the ego and judging them, in exercising a censorship. The sense of guilt, the harshness of the superego, is thus the same thing as the severity of the conscience. In the developmental process of the individual, the program of the pleasure principle, which consists in finding the satisfaction of happiness, is retained as the main aim. Integration in, or adaptation to, a human community appears as a scarcely avoidable condition which must be fulfilled before this aim of happiness can be achieved. The development of the individual seems to be a product of the interaction between two urges, the urge towards happiness, which is usually called egoistic, and the urge towards union with others in the community, which is called altruistic. It can be asserted that the community evolves a superego under whose influence cultural development proceeds. The cultural superego has set up its ideals and set up its demands. Among the latter, those which deal with the relations of human beings to one another are comprised under the heading of ethics. The fateful question for the human species seems to be whether and to what extent their cultural development will succeed in mastering the disturbance of their communal life by the human instinct of aggression and self-destruction.

1927E   21/149
Fetishism (1927). Editor's note. (1961).

Fetishism was finished at the end of the first week of August, 1927 and was published in the autumn of 1927. The paper is of importance as a bringing together and enlarging on Freud's earlier views on fetishism. Its major interest lies in a fresh metapsychological development which it introduces. For several years past Freud had been using the concept of disavowal especially in relation to children's reactions to the observation of the anatomical distinction between the sexes. In the present paper, basing himself on fresh clinical observations, he puts forward reasons for supposing that this disavowal necessarily implies a split in the subject's ego.

1927E   21/152
Fetishism (1927)

Freud had an opportunity of studying analytically a number of men whose object choice was dominated by a fetish. The most extraordinary case seemed to be one in which a young man had exalted a certain sort of shine on the nose into a fetishistic precondition. The fetish, which originated from his earliest childhood, had to be understood in his native English, not German. The shine on the nose was in reality a glance at the nose. The nose was thus the fetish. In every instance, the meaning and the purpose of the fetish turned out, in analysis, to be the same. The fetish is a substitute for the penis: the woman's (the mother's) penis that the little boy once believed in and does not want to give up. The fetish achieves a token of triumph over the threat of castration and serves as a protection against it. It also saves the fetishist from becoming a homosexual, by endowing women with the characteristic which makes them tolerable as sexual objects. Because the fetish is easily accessible, the fetishist can readily obtain the sexual satisfaction attached to it. The choice of the fetish object seems determined by the last impression before the uncanny and traumatic one. In very subtle instances both the disavowal and the affirmation of the castration have found their way into the construction of the fetish itself. In conclusion, Freud says that the normal prototype of fetishes is a man's penis, just as the normal prototype of interior organ is a woman's real small penis, the clitoris.

1927D   21/160
Humour (1927).

Humor is discussed. There are two ways in which the humorous process can take place. It may take place in regard to a single person, who himself adopts the humorous attitude, while a second person plays the part of the spectator who derives enjoyment from it; or it may take place between two persons, of whom one takes no part at all in the humorous process, but is made the object of humorous contemplation by the other. Like jokes and the comic, humor has something liberating about it; but it also has something of grandeur and elevation, which is lacking in the other two ways of obtaining pleasure from intellectual activity. The grandeur in it clearly lies in the trumph of narcissism, the victorious assertion of the ego's invulnerability. The rejection of the claims of reality and the putting through of the pleasure principle bring humor near to the regressive or reactionary processes which engage our attention so extensively in psychopathology. In a particular situation the subject suddenly hypercathects his superego and then, proceeding from it, alters the reactions of the ego. A joke is the contribution to the comic by the unconscious. In just the same way, humor would be the contribution made to the comic through the agency of the superego. If the superego tries, by means of humor, to console the ego and protect it from suffering, this does not contradict its origin in the parental agency.

1928A   21/167
A religious experience (1928).

In the autumn of 1927, G. S. Viereck, a journalist, published an account of a conversation with Freud, in the course of which he mentioned Freud's lack of religious faith and his indifference on the subject of survival after death. This interview was widely read and brought many letters. One was from an American physician who wrote to tell Freud of his religious experience. The physician described a woman who was in the dissecting room and he thought that God would not allow such a thing to happen. For the next several days, he meditated and then received the proof that he needed that there is a God. Freud thinks that the doctor is swayed by the emotion roused in him by the sight of a woman's dead body which reminded him of his mother. It roused in him a longing for his mother which sprang from his Oedipus complex; this was immediately completed by a feeling of indignation against his father. His ideas of father and God had not yet become widely separated; his desire to destroy his father could become conscious as doubt in the existence of God and could seek to justify itself in the eyes of reason as indignation about the ill-treatment of a mother object. The outcome of the struggle was displayed in the sphere of religion and it was of a kind predetermined by the fate of the Oedipus complex: complete submission to the will of God the Father. He had had a religious experience and had undergone conversion. This case may throw some light on the psychology of conversion in general.

1928B   21/175
Dostoevsky and parricide (1928). Editor's note. (1961).

The essay on *Dostoevsky and Parricide* falls into two distinct parts. The first deals with Dostoevsky's character in general, with his masochism, his sense of guilt, his epileptoid attacks and his double attitude in the Oedipus complex. The second discusses the special point of his passion for gambling and leads to an account of a short story by Stefan Zweig which throws light on the genesis of that addiction. The essay contains Freud's first discussion of hysterical attacks since his early paper on the subject written 20 years before, a restatement of his later views on the Oedipus complex and the sense of guilt, and a sidelight on the problem of masturbation. Above all, Freud had an opportunity here for expressing his views on a writer whom he placed in the very front rank of all.

1928B 21/177
Dostoevsky and parricide (1928).

Four facets may be distinguished in the rich personality of Dostoevsky: the creative artist, the neurotic, the moralist, and the sinner. Dostoevsky called himself an epileptic, and was regarded as such by other people. It is highly probable that this so-called epilepsy was only a symptom of his neurosis and must be classified as hysteroepilepsy. Dostoevsky's attacks did not assume epileptic form until after his eighteenth year, when his father was murdered. Prior to that, however, he suffered in his early years from lethargic, somnolent states, signifying an identification with someone whom he wished dead. Parricide, according to a well-known view, is the principal and primal crime of humanity as well as of the individual. It is the main source of the sense of guilt. It comes from the Oedipus complex. What makes hatred of the father unacceptable is fear of the father; castration is terrible, whether as a punishment or as the price of love. The addition of a second factor to the fear of punishment, the fear of the feminine attitude, a strong innate bisexual disposition, becomes the reinforcement of the neurosis. The publication of Dostoevsky's posthumous papers and of his wife's diaries has thrown a glaring light on the period in Germany when he was obsessed with a mania for gambling, which no one could regard as anything but an unmistakable fit of pathological passion. If the addiction to gambling, with the unsuccessful struggles to break the habit and the opportunities it affords for self-punishment, is a repetition of the compulsion to masturbate, we shall not be surprised to find that it occupied such a large space in Dostoevsky's life. In all cases of severe neurosis, the efforts to supress autoerotic satisfaction and their relation to fear of the father are well known.

1928B 21/195
Dostoevsky and parricide (1928). Appendix: A letter from Freud to Theodor Reik.

A few months after the publication of Freud's essay on Dostoevsky, a discussion of it by Theodor Reik appeared in *Imago*. Freud wrote to Dr. Reik in reply. Reik argued that Freud's judgment on Dostoevsky's morals was unjustifiably severe and disagreed with what Freud wrote about morality. Freud acknowledged that all the objections deserve consideration and must be recognized as, in a sense, apt. We may expect, wrote Freud, that in the history of a neurosis accompanied by such a severe sense of guilt, a special part will be played by the struggle against masturbation, as evidenced by Dostoevsky's pathological addiction to gambling. Freud wrote that he holds firmly to a scientifically objective social assessment of ethics. He included Dostoevsky the psychologist under the creative artist, as Reik suggests. Freud wrote that, in spite of all his admiration for Dostoevsky's intensity and preeminence, he does not really like him because having become exhausted with pathological natures in analysis, he finds himself intolerant of them in art and life.

1929B 21/199
Some dreams of Descartes: A letter to Maxime Leroy. (1929).

While Maxime Leroy was preparing his book on Descartes, he submitted a series of the philosopher's dreams to Freud for his comments. Descartes' original account and interpretation of the dreams seem to have occupied the opening pages of a manuscript known as the 'Olympica'. It was seen by the seventeenth century abbe, Adrien Baillet, who published a paraphrased translation, containing some quotations from the original Latin. Freud states that the philosopher's dreams are what are known as dreams from above. That is to say, they are formulations of ideas which could have been created just as well in a waking state as during the state of sleep, and which have derived their content only in certain parts from mental states at a comparatively deep level. That is why these dreams offer, for the most part, a content which has an abstract, poetic, or symbolic form. Analysis of dreams of this kind usually leads to the position that the analyst cannot understand the dream but the dreamer can translate it immediately because its content is very close to his conscious thoughts. It is those parts of the dream about which the dreamer does not know what to say that belong to the unconscious.

1930E 21/207
The Goethe Prize (1930).

In a letter to Dr. Alfons Paquet, Freud asserts that the award of the Goethe Prize of the City of Frankfurt has given him great pleasure. The address delivered in the Goethe house at Frankfurt is presented. Freud's life work has been directed to a single aim. He has observed the more subtle disturbances of mental function in healthy and sick people and has sought to infer from signs of this kind how the apparatus which serves those functions is constructed and what concurrent and mutually opposing forces are at work in it. Goethe can be compared in versatility to Leonardo da Vinci, who like him was both artist and scientific investigator. Goethe approached psychoanalysis at a number of points, recognized much through his own insight that has since been confirmed, and some views, which have brought criticism and mockery down upon us, were expounded by him as self-evident. Thus he was familiar with the incomparable strength of the first affective ties of human creatures. Goethe always rated Eros high, never tried to belittle its power, followed its primitive and even wanton expressions with no less attentiveness than its highly sublimated ones and has expounded its essential unity throughout all its manifestations no less decisively than Plato did in the remote past.

1931A   21/215
Libidinal types (1931).

Libidinal types are discussed. As the libido is predominatly allocated to the provinces of the mental apparatus, we can distinguish three main libidinal types: erotic, narcissistic, and obsessional types. Erotics are those whose main interest is turned towards love. The obsessional type is distinguished by the predominance of the superego. In the narcissistic type, there is no tension between ego and superego and there is no preponderance of erotic needs. The subject's main interest is directed to self-preservation; he is independent and not open to intimidation. There are mixed types too: the erotic obsessional, the erotic narcissistic, and the narcissistic obsessional. These seem to afford a good classification of the individual psychical structures. In the erotic obsessional type, it appears that the preponderance of instinctual life is restricted by the influence of the superego. The erotic narcissistic type is perhaps the one we must regard as the commonest of all. It unites opposites, which are able to moderate one another in it. The narcissistic obsessional type produces the variation which is most valuable from a cultural standpoint; for it adds to independence of the external world and a regard for the demands of conscience, a capacity for vigorous actions, and it strengthens the ego against the superego. When people of the erotic type fall ill, they will develop hysteria, just as those of the obsessional type will develop obsessional neurosis. People of the narcissistic type are peculiarly disposed to psychosis.

1931B   21/223
Female sexuality (1931). Editor's note (1961) and Part I. Female Oedipus complex differs from male.

Female Sexuality is a restatement of the findings first announced by Freud 6 years earlier in his paper on "Some Psychical Consequences of the Anatomical Distinction between the Sexes". This paper, however, lays further emphasis on the intensity and long duration of the little girl's pre-Oedipus attachment to her mother. During the phase of the normal Oedipus complex, we find the child tenderly attached to the parent of the opposite sex, while its relation to the parent of its own sex is predominantly hostile. The development of female sexuality is complicated by the fact that the girl has the task of giving up what was originally her leading genital zone, the clitoris, in favor of a new zone, the vagina. There are many women who have a strong attachment to their father. Where the woman's attachment to her father was particularly intense, analysis showed that it

has been preceded by a phase of exclusive attachment to her mother which had been equally intense and passionate. Except for the change of her love object, the second phase had scarcely added any new feature to her erotic life. The duration of this attachment had been greatly underestimated. In several cases it lasted until well into the fourth year, so that it covered by far the longer part of the period of early sexual efflorescence.

1931B   21/227
Female sexuality (1931). Part II. Girl's pre-Oedipal motives for turning away from mother.

A woman's strong dependence on her father takes over the heritage of an equally strong attachment to her mother. A female's first love object must be her mother. But at the end of her development, her father should have become her new love object. One thing that is left over in men from the influence of the Oedipus complex is a certain amount of disparagement in their attitude towards women, whom they regard as being castrated. The female acknowledges the fact of her castration, and with it, too, the superiority of the male and her own inferiority; but she rebels against this unwelcome state of affairs. From this divided attitude three lines of development open up. The first leads to a general revulsion from sexuality. The second leads her to cling with defiant self-assertiveness to her threatened masculinity. Only if her development follows the third, very circuitous path does she reach the final normal female attitude, in which she takes her father as her object and so finds her way to the feminine form of the Oedipus complex. The range of motives for turning away from the mother include: failure to provide the girl with the only proper genital, failure to feed her sufficiently, compelling her to share her mother's love with others, failure to fulfill all the girl's expectations of love, and an arousal of her sexual activity and then a forbidding of it.

1931B   21/235
Female sexuality (1931). Part III. Girl's pre-Oedipal sexual aims toward mother.

The girl's sexual aims in regard to her mother are active as well as passive and are determined by the libidinal phases through which the child passes. The first sexual and sexually-colored experiences which a child has in relation to its mother are of a passive character. It is suckled, fed, cleaned, and dressed by her, and taught to perform all its functions. A part of its libido goes on clinging to those experiences and enjoys the satisfactions bound up with them; but another part strives to turn them into activity. The sexual activity of little girls in relation to their mother is manifested chronologically in oral, sadistic, and finally even in phallic trends directed towards her. Girls regularly accuse their mother of seducing them. The turning away from her mother is an extremely important step in the course of a little girl's development.

1931B   21/240

Female sexuality (1931). Part IV. Critique of analytic literature on female sexuality.

Female sexuality is discussed. Arbraham's description of the manifestations of the castration complex in the female is still unsurpassed; but Freud would have been glad if it had included the factor of the girl's original exclusive attachment to her mother. Freud is in agreement with the principal points in Jeanne Lampl-de Groot's important paper. In this the complete identity of the pre-Oedipus phase in boys and girls is recognized, and the girl's sexual (phallic) activity towards her mother is affirmed and substantiated by observations. In Helene Deutsch's paper on feminine masochism and its relation to frigidity, the girl's phallic activity and the intensity of her attachment to her mother are recognized. Helene Deutsch states further that the girl's turning towards her father takes place via her passive trends. Fenichel rightly emphasizes the difficulty of recognizing in the material produced in analysis what parts of it represent the unchanged content of the pre-Oedipus phase and what parts have been distorted by regression. Some writers are inclined to reduce the importance of the child's first and most original libidinal impulses in favor of later developmental processes so that the only role left to the former is merely to indicate certain paths, while the psychical intensities which flow along those paths are supplied by later regressions and reaction formations.

1926I   21/247

Dr. Reik and the problem of quackery. A letter to the 'Neue Freie Presse' (1926).

A letter to the *Neue Freie Presse* concerning Dr. Reik and the problem of quackery is presented. Freud acknowledged that he availed himself of Reik's skill in particularly difficult cases, but only where the symptoms lay in a sphere far removed from the physical one. Freud never failed to inform a patient that Reik was not a physician but a psychologist. His daughter Anna has devoted herself to the pedagogic analysis of children and adolescents. Freud never referred a case of severe neurotic illness in an adult to her. In *The Question of Lay Analysis*, Freud tried to show what psychoanalysis is and what demands it makes on the analyst. The conclusion was drawn that any mechanical application to trained analysts of the section against quackery in the criminal code is open to grave doubts.

1929A   21/249

Dr. Ernest Jones (on his 50th birthday) (1929).

Dr. Ernest Jones, on his fiftieth birthday, is discussed and praised. Among the men who met at Salzburg in the spring of 1908 for the first psychoanalytical congress, Dr. Jones delivered a short paper on "Rationalization in Everyday Life." The contents of this paper hold good to this day: psychoanalysis was enriched by an important concept and an indispensable term. In his various responsibilities (such as professor in Toronto, physician in London, founder and teacher of a Branch Society, director of a Press, editor of a journal, head of a training institute) he has worked tirelessly for psychoanalysis, making its findings known and defending them. He wrote, among others, "Papers on Psycho-Analysis" and "Essays in Applied Psycho-Analysis." Presently he is not only indisputably the leading figure among English-speaking analysts, but is also recognized as one of the foremost representatives of psychoanalysis as a whole, a mainstay for his friends and a hope for the future of psychoanalysis.

1931D   21/251

The expert opinion in the Halsmann case (1931).

The expert opinion in the Halsmann Case is discussed. If it had been objectively demonstrated that Philipp Halsmann murdered his father, there would be some grounds for introducing the Oedipus complex to provide a motive for an otherwise unexplained deed. Since no such proof has been adduced, mention of the Oedipus complex has a misleading effect. The Opinion of the Innsbruck Faculty of Medicine seems inclined to attribute an effective Oedipus complex to Philipp Halsmann, but refrains from defining the measure of this effectiveness, since under the pressure of the accusation the necessary conditions for an unreserved disclosure on Philipp Halsmann's part were not fulfilled. The possible influence of emotional shock on the disturbance of memory with regard to impressions before and during the critical time is minimized to the extreme, in Freud's opinion unjustly. The assumptions of an exceptional state of mind or of mental illness are decisively rejected, but the explanation of a repression having taken place in Philipp Halsmann after the deed is readily allowed, in the opinion of the Innsbruck Faculty of Medicine. A repression of this kind, occurring out of the blue in an adult who gives no indication of a severe neurosis, the repression of an action which would certainly be more important than any debatable details of distance and the passage of time and which takes place in a normal state or one altered only by physical fatigue, would be a rarity of the first order.

1930C 21/254

Introduction to the special psychopathology number of 'the medical review of reviews' (1930).

An introduction to the special psychopathology of the *Medical Review of Reviews* is presented. The popularity of the name of psychoanalysis in America signifies neither a friendly attitude to the thing itself nor any specially wide or deep knowledge of it. Although America possesses several excellent analysts and at least one authority, the contributions to our science from that vast country are exiguous and provide little that is new. Psychiatrists and neurologists make frequent use of psychoanalysis as a therapeutic method, but as a rule they show little interest in its scientific problems and its cultural significance. There is a general tendency in America to shorten study and preparation and to proceed as fast as possible to practical application. There is a preference, too, for studying a subject like psychoanalysis not from the original sources but from second-hand and often inferior accounts.

1931C 21/256

Introduction to Edoardo Weiss's 'Elements of Psychoanalysis' (1931).

An introduction to Edoardo Weiss's *Elements of Psychoanalysis* in presented. All who know how to appreciate the seriousness of a scientific endeavor, how to value the honesty of an investigator who does not seek to belittle or deny the difficulties, and how to take pleasure in the skill of a teacher who brings light into darkness and order into chaos by his exposition, must form a high estimate of this book and share Freud's hope that it will awaken among cultivated and learned circles in Italy a lasting interest in the young science of psychoanalysis.

1930B 21/257

Preface to 'ten years of the Berlin psycho-analytic institute' (1930).

The preface to *Ten Years of the Berlin Psychoanalytic Institute* is presented. The Berlin Psychoanalytic Institute has three functions within the psychoanalytic movement. First, it endeavors to make psychoanalytic therapy accessible to the great multitude who suffer under their neuroses no less than the wealthy, but who are not in a position to meet the cost of their treatment. Secondly, it seeks to provide a center at which analysis can be taught theoretically and at which the experience of older analysts can be handed on to pupils who are anxious to learn. Third, it aims at perfecting psychoanalytic knowledge of neurotic illnesses and therapeutic technique by applying them and testing them under fresh conditions. Ten years ago, Dr. Max Eitingon created this institute from his own resources, and has since then maintained and directed it by his own efforts.

1932B 21/258

Preface to Hermann Nunberg's 'General theory of the neuroses on a psycho-analytic basis' (1932).

The preface to Hermann Nunberg's *General Theory of the Neuroses on a Psychoanalytic Basis* is presented. This volume by Nunberg contains the most complete and conscientious presentation of a psychoanalytic therapy of neurotic processes at this time. Those who expect to have the relevant problems simplified and smoothed over will not find satisfaction in this work but those who prefer scientific thinking and can appreciate it or who can enjoy the beautiful diversity of mental happenings will value this work and study it assiduously.

1931E 21/259

Letter to the burgomaster of Pribor (1931).

A letter to the mayor of Pribor (formerly Freiberg, Austria) is presented, in which he thanks the city for the celebration and the commemoration of the house of his birth with a plaque in his honor. Freud left Freiberg at the age of 3 and visited it when he was 16, during his school holidays, and never returned to it again. At 75, it is not easy for him to put himself back into those early times. But of one thing, Freud feels sure: deeply buried within him there still lives the happy child of Freiberg, the first-born son of a youthful mother, who received his first indelible impressions from this air, from this soil.

VOL. XXII   New Introductory Lectures on Psycho-Analysis and Other Works (1932–1936)

1933A 22/3

New introductory lectures on psycho-analysis (1933). Editor's note (1964) and Preface.

The *New Introductory Lectures on Psychoanalysis* was published on December 6, 1932. The first lecture, on dreams, is a recapitulation of the dream section in the earlier series. The third, fourth, and fifth lectures (on the structure of the mind, on anxiety and the theory of the instincts and on female psychology) introduce entirely new material and theories and, at all events in the case of the third and fourth lectures, plunge into metapsychological and theoretical discussions of a difficulty which had been studiously avoided 15 years earlier. The remaining three lectures deal with a number of miscellaneous topics only indirectly related to psychoanalysis and deal with them in what might almost be described as a popular manner. The *Introductory Lectures on Psychoanalysis* were delivered during the two Winter

Terms of 1915 to 1916 and 1916 to 1917 in a lecture room of the Vienna Psychiatric Clinic before an audience gathered from all the Faculties of the University. The new lectures were never delivered. They are continuations and supplements. These lectures are addressed to the nonprofessional multitude of educated people to whom a benevolent, even though cautious interest in the characteristics and discoveries of psychoanalysis, is attributed.

1933A   22/7

New introductory lectures on psycho-analysis (1933). Lecture XXIX: Revision of the theory of dreams.

A revision of the theory of dreams is presented. What has been called the dream is described as the text of the dream or the manifest dream and what we are looking for, is described as the latent dream thoughts. We have to transform the manifest dream into the latent one, and to explain how, in the dreamer's mind, the latter has become the former. The patient makes associations to the separate portions of the manifest dream. The longer and more roundabout the chain of associations, the stronger the resistance. The dream is a compromise structure. It has a double function; on the one hand it is egosyntonic, since, by getting rid of the stimuli which are interfering with sleep, it serves the wish to sleep; on the other hand it allows a repressed instinctual impulse to obtain the satisfaction that is possible in these circumstances, in the form of the hallucinated fulfillment of a wish. The whole process of forming a dream which is permitted by the sleeping ego is, however, subject to the condition of the censorship, which is exercised by the residue of the repression still in operation. Under the influence of the censorship the processes of condensation and displacement subject the dream thoughts to distortion after which secondary revision provides the dream with a smooth facade. Dreams are divided into wishful dreams, anxiety dreams, and punishment dreams. Punishment dreams are fulfillment of wishes, though not of wishes of the instinctual impulses but of those of the critical, censoring, and punishing agency in the mind.

1933A   22/31

New introductory lectures on psycho-analysis (1933). Lecture XXX: Dreams and occultism.

Dreams and occultism are discussed. Dreams have often been regarded as the gateway into the world of mysticism, and even today are themselves looked on by many people as an occult phenomenon. Psychoanalysis may throw a little light on events described as occult. Freud gained the impression from his patients that fortunetellers merely bring to expression the thoughts, and more especially the secret wishes, of those who are questioning the tellers. He concludes that we are

therefore justified in analyzing these prophecies as though they were subjective products, phantasies or dreams of the people concerned. If there is such a thing as telepathy as a real process, we may suspect that, in spite of its being so hard to demonstrate, it is quite a common phenomenon. We are reminded of the frequent anxiety felt by children over the idea that their parents know all their thoughts without having to be told them, an exact counterpart and perhaps the source of the belief of adults in the omniscience of God.

1933A   22/57

New introductory lectures on psycho-analysis (1933). Lecture XXXI: The dissection of the psychical personality.

The dissection of the psychical personality is presented. Symptoms are derived from the repressed; they are, as it were, its representatives before the ego. The ego can take itself as an object, can treat itself like other objects, can observe itself, criticize itself, and be split. The superego, which takes over the power, function, and even the methods of the parental agency, is not merely its successor but actually the legitimate heir of its body. The basis of the process is called identification and follows from the Oedipus complex. The superego, the ego, and the id are the three realms, regions, provinces, into which we divide an individual's mental apparatus, and we shall be concerned with the relations between them. In addition to the id being unconscious, portions of the ego and superego are unconscious as well. The id is the dark, inaccessible part of our personality. The id knows no judgments of value: no good and evil, no morality. Instinctual cathexes seeking discharge is all there is in the id. The ego is that part of the id which is adapted for the reception of stimuli from the external world, for remembering these, for testing reality, for controlling motility, and for synthesizing and organizing its mental processes. The superego merges into the id; indeed, as heir to the Oedipus complex it has intimate relations with the id; it is more remote than the ego from the perceptual system. The id has intercourse with the external world only through the ego. The intention of psychoanalysis is to strengthen the ego, to make it more independent of the superego, to widen its field of perception and enlarge its organization, so that it can appropriate fresh portions of the id. Where id was, there ego shall be.

1933A   22/81

New introductory lectures on psycho-analysis (1933). Lecture XXXII: Anxiety and instinctual life.

The earlier lecture (XXV) on anxiety is recapitulated. The ego produces anxiety as a signal announcing a situation of danger. The typical danger situations in life are loss of mother, loss of love, castration and superego reproach. The signal anxiety is called forth when an emerging impulse is felt that would result in a danger situation. The signal anxiety results in repression and subsequently either symptom formation or reaction formation. Probably all of the danger situations are reminders of an earlier traumatic situation which consisted of a state of high excitation felt as unpleasure which could not be discharged. Earlier instinct theory is recapitulated preparatory to mentioning new discoveries in libido theory. There is a preambivalent oral incorporative stage followed by an ambivalent oral sadistic stage. After these come the anal sadistic and anal retentive stage. The instinctual transformations in anal erotism are described: the feces-money-baby-penis equation modeled on the anal birth fantasy; the character traits of orderliness, parsimoniousness and obstinacy arise from anal erotism. There are 2 major classes of instincts, sexual and aggressive, and every impulse consists of a fusion of the 2. Masochism is derived from an unconscious sense of guilt which in turn comes from the aggressiveness towards one's parents which is found in the formation of the superego.

1933A   22/112
New introductory lectures on psycho-analysis (1933). Lecture XXXIII: Femininity.

Femininity is discussed. We approach the investigation of the sexual development of women with two expectations. The first is that the constitution will not adapt itself to its function without a struggle. The second is that the decisive turning points will already have been prepared for or completed before puberty. In the phallic phases of girls, the clitoris is the leading erotogenic zone. With the change of femininity the clitoris should wholly or in part hand over its sensitivity, and at the same time its importance, to the vagina. For a girl, her first object must be her mother. But in the Oedipus situation the girl's father has become her love object, and we expect that in the normal course of development she will find her way from this paternal object to her final choice of an object, both of which a boy retains. The girl turns away from her mother because of her realization that she does not possess a penis: the discovery that she is castrated can lead to neurosis, a masculinity complex, or normal femininity. Along with the abandonment of clitoral masturbation a certain amount of activity is renounced. Passivity now has the upper hand, and the girl's turning to her father is accomplished principally with the help of passive instinctual impulses. With the transference of the wish for a penis baby on to her father, the girl has entered the situation of the Oedipus complex. A women's identification with her mother allows us to distinguish two strata: the pre-Oedipus one which rests on her affectionate attachment to her mother and takes her as a model, and the later one from the Oedipus complex which seeks to get rid of her mother and take the mother's place with her father.

1933A   22/136
New Introductory lectures on psychoanalysis (1933). Lecture XXXIV: Explanations, applications and orientations.

Explanations and applications of psychoanalysis are presented. Whether a man is a homosexual or a necrophiliac, a hysteric suffering from anxiety, an obsessional neurotic cut off from society, or a raving lunatic, the Individual Psychologist of the Adlerian school will declare that the impelling motive of his condition is that he wishes to assert himself, to overcompensate for his inferiority, to remain on top, to pass from the feminine to the masculine line. One of the first applications of psychoanalysis was to understand the opposition offered by the contemporaries because of the practice of psychoanalysis. The first purpose was to understand the disorders of the human mind. The application of psychoanalysis to education is discussed. The first task of education is to teach the child to control his instincts; but we have learned from analysis that suppression of instincts involves the risk of neurotic illness. Therefore education must find its way between gratification and frustration. Freud suggests that teachers would be helped to find this way through psychoanalytic training. Parallel with the efforts of analysts to influence education, other investigations are being made into the origin and prevention of delinquency and crime. The therapeutic effectiveness of psychoanalysis remains cramped by a number of factors. In the case of children, the difficulties are the external ones connected with their relation to their parents. In the case of adults the difficulties arise in the first instance from two factors: the amount of psychical rigidity present and the form of the illness. Psychoanalysis began as a method of treatment. If it were without therapeutic value it would not have been discovered in connection with sick people and would not have gone on developing for more than 30 years.

1933A   22/158
New introductory lectures on psychoanalysis (1933). Lecture XXXV: The question of a 'Weltanschauung'.

The question of a *Weltanschauung* is discussed. A *Weltanschauung* is an intellectual construction which solves all the problems of our existence uniformly on the basis of one overriding hypothesis, which, accordingly, leaves no question unanswered and in which everything that interests us finds its fixed place. The religious *Weltanschauung* is determined by the situation of our childhood. The scientific spirit has begun to treat religion as a human affair and to submit it to a critical examination. While the different religions wrangle with one another as to which of them is in possession of the truth, our view is that the question of the truth of religious beliefs may be left altogether on one side. Religion is an attempt to master the sensory world in which we are situated by means of the wishful world which we have developed within us as a result of biological and psychological necessities. Psychoanalysis is incapable of creating a *Weltanschauung* of its own. It does not need one; it is a part of science and can adhere to the scientific *Weltanschauung*. Scientific thought is still very young among human beings; there are too many of the great problems which it has not yet been able to solve. A *Weltanschauung* erected upon science has, apart from its emphasis on the real external world, mainly passive traits, such as submission to the truth and rejection of illusions.

1932A   22/185
The acquisition and control of fire (1932).

The connection between fire and micturition, which is the central feature of this discussion of the myth of Prometheus, has long been familiar to Freud. The myth tells us that Prometheus, a culture hero who was still a god and who was perhaps originally himself a demiurge and a creator of men, brought fire to men, hidden in a hollow stick, after stealing it from the gods. Such an object is regarded as a penis symbol. As punishment, Prometheus was chained to a rock, and every day a vulture fed on his liver. In ancient times the liver was regarded as the seat of all passions and desires; hence a punishment like that of Prometheus was the right one for a criminal driven by instinct, who had committed an offense at the prompting of evil desires. The sexual organ of the male has two functions; and there are those to whom this association is an annoyance. When the penis is erect, urination is impossible; and conversely, when the organ is serving to evacuate urine (the water of the body) all its connections with the genital function seem to be quenched. The antithesis between the two functions might lead us to say that man quenches his own fire with his own water.

1933B   22/197
Why war? (1933). Editor's note (1964).

The letters on war between Freud and Einstein were written in 1932. The two men were never at all intimate with each other and only met once, at the beginning of 1927, in the house of Freud's youngest son in Berlin. Freud had written on the subject of war before: in the first section of his paper "Thoughts for the Times on War and Death" produced soon after the beginning of

the first World War. Although some of the considerations discussed in the present paper appear in the earlier one, they are more closely related to the thoughts expressed in his recent writings on sociological subjects.

1933B   22/199
Why war? Letter from Einstein (1933).

Einstein wrote a letter to Freud, dated July 20, 1932. With the advance of modern science, the issue of war has come to mean a matter of life or death for civilization as we know it; nevertheless, for all the zeal displayed, every attempt at its solution has ended in a lamentable breakdown. As one immune from nationalist bias, Einstein sees a simple way of dealing with the superficial, (*i.e.*, administrative) aspect of the problem: the setting up, by international consent, of a legislative and judicial body to settle every conflict arising between nations. Each nation would invoke this body's decision in every dispute, accept its judgments unreservedly and carry out every measure the tribunal deems necessary for the execution of its decrees. However, a tribunal is a human institution which, when the power at its disposal is inadequate to enforce its verdicts, is all the more prone to suffer these to be deflected by extrajudicial pressure. The quest of international security involves the unconditional surrender by every nation, in a certain measure, of its liberty of action or its sovereignty. It is clear beyond all doubt that no other road can lead to such security.

1933B   22/203
Letter from Freud (1933).

Freud wrote a letter to Einstein, dated September, 1932. It is a general principle that conflicts of interest between men are settled by the use of violence. Right is the might of a community. A violent solution of conflicts of interest is not avoided even inside a community. Wars will only be prevented with certainty if mankind unites in setting up a central authority to which the right of giving judgment upon all conflicts of interest shall be handed over. There is no use in trying to get rid of men's aggressive inclinations. For incalculable ages, mankind has been passing through a process of evolution of culture. The psychical modifications that go along with the process of civilization are striking and unambiguous. They consist in a progressive displacement of instinctual aims and a restriction of instinctual impulses. War is in the crassest opposition to the psychical attitude imposed on us by the process of civilization, and for that reason we are bound to rebel against it; we simply cannot any longer put up with it. Whatever fosters the growth of civilization works at the same time against war.

1932C   22/219

My contact with Josef Popper-Lynkeus (1932).

Freud's contact with Josef Popper-Lynkeus is presented. Freud's explanation of dream distortion seemed new to him. He had nowhere found anything like it. Years later, he came across Josef Popper-Lynkeus' book *Phantasies of a Realist,* a collection of stories first published, like the *Interpretation of Dreams,* in 1899. One of the stories contained in it bore the title of "Dreaming like Waking", and it aroused Freud's deepest interest. There was a description in it of a man who could boast that he had never dreamt anything nonsensical. In the case of this man, no dream distortion occurred. Popper allowed the man complete insight into the reasons for his peculiarity. Distortion was a compromise, something in its very nature disingenuous, the product of a conflict between thought and feeling. Where a conflict of this kind was not present and repression was unnecessary, dreams could not be strange or senseless. The man who dreamed in a way no different from that in which he thought while awake was granted by Popper the very condition of internal harmony which, as a social reformer, he aimed at producing in the body politic.

1933C   22/227

Sandor Ferenczi (1933).

Sandor Ferenczi was born on July 16, 1873, and died on May 22, 1933. Since the days when he was led to Freud by his interest in psychoanalysis, still in its youth, they shared many things with each other. Ten years earlier, when the *Internationale Zeitschrift* dedicated a special number to Ferenczi on his fiftieth birthday, he had already published most of the works which have made all analysts into his pupils. But he was holding back his most brilliant and most fertile achievement. In 1924, his *Versuch einer Genitaltheorie* appeared. This little book is a biological rather than a psychoanalytic study; it is an application of the attitudes and insights associated with psychoanalysis to the biology of the sexual processes and, beyond them, to organic life in general. As its governing thought it lays stress on the conservative nature of the instincts, which seek to reestablish every state of things that has been abandoned owing to an external interference. Symbols are recognized as evidence of ancient connections. Later, the need to cure and to help had become paramount in him. From unexhausted springs of emotion the conviction was held that one could effect far more with one's patients if one gave them enough of the love which they had longed for as children.

1935B   22/233

The subtleties of a faulty action (1935).

The subtleties of a faulty action are discussed. Freud was preparing a birthday present for a woman friend, a small engraved gem for insertion into a ring. It was fixed in the center of a piece of stout cardboard and on this, Freud wrote the following words: "Voucher for the supply by Messrs. L., jewelers, of a gold ring. . . .for the attached stone bearing an engraved ship with sail and oars." But at the point where there is a gap, between "ring" and "for," there stood a word which Freud was obliged to cross out since it was entirely irrelevant. It was the little German word "bis," meaning "until"—and meaning "twice" or "for a second time" in Latin. At first, Freud was pacified with the explanation that he objected—unconsciously—to using "for" twice in the same sentence, until his daughter reminded him that he had given his friend a similar stone for a ring on a previous occasion. The objection, therefore, was to a repetition of the same present, the ring, not of the same word, "for." There had been a displacement on to something trivial with the object of diverting attention from something more important: an esthetic difficulty, perhaps, in place of an instinctual conflict.

1936A   22/239

A disturbance of memory on the Acropolis (1936).

An open letter to Romain Rolland on the occasion of his seventieth birthday is presented. When Freud stood on the Acropolis and cast his eyes around upon the landscape, a surprising thought entered his mind: "So all this really does exist, just as we learned at school!" The whole psychical situation, which seemed so confused and is so difficult to describe, can be satisfactorily cleared up by assuming that at the time Freud had a momentary feeling: "What I see here is not real." Such a feeling is known as a feeling of derealization. These derealizations are remarkable phenomena which are still little understood. They are spoken of as sensations, but they are obviously complicated processes, attached to particular mental contents and bound up with decisions made about those contents. There are two general characteristics of the phenomena of derealization. The first is that they all serve the purpose of defense; they aim at keeping something away from the ego, at disavowing it. The second is their dependence upon the past, upon the ego's store of memories and upon earlier distressing experiences which have since, perhaps, fallen victim to repression.

1931F   22/251

Letter to Georg Fuchs (1931).

In reply to a request by Georg Fuchs, asking Freud to indorse his book *Wir Zuchthausler* (We Convicts), Freud stated that he could not subscribe to the assertion that the treatment of convicted prisoners is a disgrace to our civilization. On the contrary, it seems to be in perfect harmony with our civilization, a necessary expression of the brutality and lack of understanding which dominate contemporary civilized humanity.

1936B   22/253

Preface to Richard Sterba's 'Dictionary of psychoanalysis' (1936).

Freud wrote a preface to Richard Sterba's *Dictionary of Psychoanalysis*. The *Dictionary* gives the impression of being a valuable aid to learners and of being a fine achievement on its own account. The precision and correctness of the individual entries is in fact of commendable excellence. English and French translations of the headings are not indispensable but would add further to the value of the work.

1933D   22/254

Preface to Marie Bonaparte's 'The life and works of Edgar Allan Poe: A psycho-analytic interpretation' (1933).

Freud wrote a preface to Marie Bonaparte's *The Life and Works of Edgar Allan Poe: A Psychoanalytic Interpretation*. Thanks to her interpretative efforts, we can now understand how much of the characteristics of Poe's work were determined by their author's special nature; but we also learn that this was itself the precipitate of powerful emotional ties and painful experiences in his early youth.

1935C   22/255

To Thomas Mann on his sixtieth birthday (1935).

In Freud's letter to Thomas Mann on his sixtieth birthday he wrote that wishing is cheap and strikes him as a relapse to the days when people believed in the magical omnipotence of thoughts. In the name of a countless number of Mann's contemporaries, Freud expressed their confidence that Mann will never do or say anything that is cowardly or base, for an author's words are deeds.

VOL. XXIII   Moses and Monotheism,
An Outline of Psycho-Analysis and
Other Works (1937–1939)

1939A   23/3

Moses and monotheism: Three essays (1939). Editor's note (1964) and a note on the transcription of proper names.

Moses and Monotheism consists of three essays of greatly differing length, two prefaces, both situated at the begin-

ning of the third essay, and a third preface situated halfway through that same essay. The book took 4 or more years for completion, during which it was being constantly revised. There were acute external difficulties in the final phase which consisted of a succession of political disorders in Austria culminating in the Nazi occupation of Vienna and Freud's enforced migration to England. The whole work is to be regarded as a continuation of Freud's earlier studies of the origins of human social organization in *Totem and Taboo* and *Group Psychology*.

1939A   23/7

Moses and monotheism: Three essays (1939). Essay I. Moses an Egyptian.

The man Moses, who set the Jewish people free, who gave them their laws and founded their religion, dates from such remote times (thirteenth or fourteenth century B.C.) that we cannot evade a preliminary enquiry as to whether he was a historical personage or a creature of legend. The name, Moses, was Egyptian, coming from the Egyptian word "mose" meaning "child." The recognition that the name of Moses is Egyptian has not been considered decisive evidence of his origin, and no further conclusions have been drawn from it. In 1909 Otto Rank published the book *The Myth of the Birth of the Hero* which points out that almost all the prominent civilized nations began at an early stage to glorify their heros and invest the birth of these heroes with phantastic features. An average legend brings into prominence the following essential features: the hero is the child of the most aristocratic parents; his conception is preceded by difficulties; the newborn child is condemned to death or to exposure, usually by the orders of his father or of someone representing him; as a rule he is given over to the water in a casket; he is afterwards rescued; after he has grown up, he rediscovers his aristocratic parents and takes his revenge on his father. The two families in the myth of Moses (the aristocratic and the humble family) are both reflections of the child's own family as they appeared to him in successive periods of his life. In every instance which it has been possible to test, the first family, the one from which the child was exposed, was the invented one, and the second one, in which he was received and grew up, was the real one. Thus it is concluded that Moses was an Egyptian, probably an aristocrat, whom the legend turned into a Jew. The deviation of the legend of Moses from all the others of its kind can be traced back to a special feature of his history. Whereas normally a hero rises above his humble beginnings, the heroic life of the man Moses began with his stepping down from his exalted position and descending to the level of the Children of Israel.

1939A   23/17

Moses and monotheism: Three essays (1939). Eassay II. If Moses was an Egyptian: Part I. If Moses was an Egyptian. Part 2. Moses introduced an exclusive religion.

The idea of Moses as an Egyptian is discussed. It was Freud's hope that the hypothesis that Moses was an Egyptian would turn out to be fruitful and illuminating; however, the first conclusion to be drawn from that hypothesis, that the new religion which he gave to the Jews was his own Egyptian one, has been invalidated by the realization of the different and contradictory character of the two religions. It remains possible that the religion which Moses gave to his Jewish people was nevertheless his own, that it was an Egyptian religion, Aten, though not the Egyptian religion. The Aten religion excludes everything to do with myths, magic and sorcery. The sun god was no longer represented by a small pyramid and a falcon, but by a round disk with rays proceeding from it, which end in human hands. In spite of all the exuberant art of the Amarna period, no other representation of the sun god has been found. There was complete silence about the god of the dead, Osiris, and the kingdom of the dead.

1939A   23/24

Moses and monotheism: Three essays (1939). Essay II. If Moses was an Egyptian. Part 3. Comparison of Jewish and Aten religions.

If Moses were an Egyptian and if he communicated his own religion to the Jews, it must have been Akhenaten's, the Aten religion. The similarities as well as the differences between the two religions are easily discernible. Both of them were forms of a strict monotheism. Jewish monotheism was in some respects even more harsh than the Egyptian. The most essential difference is that the Jewish religion was entirely without sun worship. Moses did not only give the Jews a new religion; he also introduced the custom of circumcision. Freud concludes that if Moses gave the Jews not only a new religion but also the commandment for circumcision, he was not a Jew but an Egyptian, and in that case the Mosaic religion was probably an Egyptian one and, in view of its contrast to the popular religion, the religion of the Aten, with which the later Jewish religion agrees in some remarkable respects. According to Freud's construction, the Exodus from Egypt occurred during the period between 1358 and 1350 B.C., after Akhenaten's death and before Haremhab's reestablishment of state authority. If it were admitted that circumcision was an Egyptian custom introduced by Moses, that would be almost admitting that the religion delivered to them by Moses was an Egyptian one too. There were good reasons for denying that fact, so the truth about circumcision must also be contradicted.

1939A   23/30

Moses and monotheism: Three essays (1939). Essay II. If Moses was an Egyptian. Part 4. Two gods and two Moses.

The Jews possess a copious literature apart from the Bible, including the legends and myths which grew up in the course of centuries round the imposing figure of their first leader and the founder of their religion. Scattered in this material there may be fragments of trustworthy tradition for which no room was found in the Pentateuch. A legend of this sort gives an engaging account of how the ambition of the man Moses found expression even in his childhood. Moses is said to have been slow of speech. This may suggest that Moses spoke another language and could not communicate with his Semitic neo-Egyptians without an interpreter. Modern historians agree that the Jewish tribes, which later developed into the people of Israel, took on a new religion at a certain point of time. But in their view this did not take place in Egypt or at the foot of a mountain in the Sinai Peninsula, but in a certain locality known as Meribah-Kadesh, an oasis distinguished by its wealth of springs and wells in the stretch of country south of Palestine, between the eastern exit from the Sinai Peninsula and the western border of Arabia. There they took over the worship of a god Yahweh, a volcano god. According to Meyer, the mediator between God and the people in the founding of this religion was named Moses. He was the son-in-law of the Midianite priest Jethro, and was keeping his flocks when he received the summons from God.

1939A   23/36

Moses and monotheism: Three essays (1939). Essay II. If Moses was an Egyptian. Part 5.

Efforts to see in Moses a figure that goes beyond the priest of Kadesh, and to confirm the grandeur with which tradition glorifies him, have not ceased ever since Eduard Meyer. In 1922, Ernst Sellin found in the Prophet Hosea unmistakable signs of a tradition that Moses, the founder of their religion, met with a violent end in a rising of his refractory and stiff-necked people, and that at the same time the religion he had introduced was thrown off. One of the greatest enigmas of Jewish prehistory is that of the origin of the Levites. They are traced back to 1 of the 12 tribes of Israel, that of Levi, but no tradition has ventured to say where that tribe was originally located to what portion of the conquered land of Canaan was allotted to it. It is incredible that a great lord, like Moses the Egyptian, should have joined this alien people unaccompanied. He certainly must have brought a retinue with him. This is who the Levites originally were. The Levites were the followers of Moses. It is hypothesized that 2 generations or even a century elapsed between the fall of Moses and the establishment of the new religion at Kadesh. The retention of circumcision is evidence that the founding of the religion at Kadesh involved a compromise. Moses was transferred to Kadesh or to Sinai-Horeb and put in the place of the Midianite priests. Yahweh, who lived on a mountain in Midian, was allowed to extend over into Egypt, and in exchange for this, the existence and activity of Moses were extended to Kadesh and as far as the country east of the Jordan. Thus he was fused with the figure of the later religious founder (the son-in-law of the Midianite Jethro) and lent him his name of Moses. Of this second Moses we can give no personal account except to pick out the contradictions in the Biblical description of the character of Moses. Freud concludes that the Egyptian Moses was never at Kadesh and had never heard the name of Yahweh, and the Midianite Moses had never been in Egypt and knew nothing of Aten. In order to fuse the two figures together, tradition or legend had the task of bringing the Egyptian Moses to Midian.

1939A   23/41

Moses and monotheism: Three essays (1939). Essay II. If Moses was an Egyptian. Part 6. One hundred years of history suppressed.

With the setting up of the new god, Yahweh, at Kadesh, it became necessary to do something to glorify him. It became necessary to fit him in, to make room for him, to wipe out the traces of earlier religions. The man Moses was dealt with by shifting him to Midian and Kadesh, and by fusing him with the priest of Yahweh who founded the religion. Circumcision, the most suspicious indication of dependence on Egypt, was retained but no attempts were spared to detach the custom from Egypt. The patriots were brought into the Biblical stories for two reasons: 1) to acknowledge that Yahweh was worshipped by Abraham, Isaac, and Jacob, although not under that name; and 2) to link their memory with particular localities in Canaan. Freud concluded that between the Exodus from Egypt and the fixing of the text of the Bible under Ezra and Nehemiah some 800 years elapsed. The form of the Yahweh religion changed to conform with the original religion of Moses.

1939A   23/47

Moses and monotheism: Three essays (1939). Essay II. If Moses was an Egyptian. Part 7. The murder of Moses.

The murder of Moses, discovered by Sellin from hints in the writings of the Prophets, is discussed. Moses commanded and forced his faith upon the people, thus forcing the Semites to rid themselves of him. The

account of "wandering in the wilderness" described in the Bible depicts a succession of serious revolts against his authority. The people began to regret and sought to forget the murder of Moses. When the Exodus and the foundation of the religion at the oasis of Kadesh were brought closer together, and Moses was represented as being concerned in the latter instead of the other man (the Midianite priest), not only were the demands of the followers of Moses satisfied but his violent end was successfully disavowed. The chronological relations of these events are discussed. Freud concludes that Jewish history is familiar for its dualities: two groups of people who came together to form the nation, two kingdoms into which this nation fell apart, two gods' names in the documentary source of the Bible. To these, Freud adds two fresh ones: the foundation of two religions, the first repressed by the second but nevertheless emerging victoriously behind it, and two religious founders, who are both called by the same name of Moses and whose personalities we have to distinguish from each other. All of these dualities are the necessary consequences of the first one: one portion of the people had an experience which must be regarded as traumatic and which the other portion escaped.

1939A   23/54

Moses and monotheism: Three essays(1939). Essay III. Moses, his people and monotheist religion: Part I. Prefatory Notes I (Vienna) & II (London).

Two prefatory notes to *Moses, His People and Monotheist Religion*, are presented. Freud proposes to add a final portion to his two essays on Moses in *Imago*. Psychoanalytic research such as this is viewed with suspicious attention by Catholicism. If psychoanalytic work leads to a conclusion which reduces religion to a neurosis of humanity and explains its enormous power in the same way as a neurotic compulsion, we may be sure of drawing the resentment of our ruling powers down upon us. Freud does not intend these essays for public display or to cause sensationalism. He predicts that sometime in the future they may be read and evaluated without bias. The first prefatory note was written in Vienna, the second in London. When Germany invaded Austria, Freud escaped to London where he felt relatively free to publish his views on Moses. Since Freud wrote *Totem and Taboo* he never doubted that religious phenomena are only to be understood on the pattern of the individual neurotic symptoms familiar to him. Freud concludes that if he could not find support in an analytic interpretation of the exposure myth and could not pass from there to Sellin's suspicion about the end of Moses, the whole thing would have had to remain unwritten.

1939A   23/59

Moses and monotheism: Three essays (1939). Essay III. Moses, his people and monotheist religion. Part II. Summary and recapitulation.

The historical premise concerning Moses and the Jewish religion is presented. The idea arose of a universal god Aten who is no longer restricted to a single country and a single people. Amenophis the Fourth, a Pharaoh, promoted the religion of Aten into a state religion. Under Akhenaten's feeble successors, all that he had created collapsed. Among those in Akhenaten's entourage there was a man who was called perhaps Tuthmosis. He was in a high position and a convinced adherent of the Aten religion, but in contrast to the meditative king, he was energetic and passionate. He turned to a Semitic tribe, foreigners, and with them sought compensation for his losses. He chose them as his people and tried to realize his ideals in them. After he had left Egypt with them, accompanied by his followers, he made them holy by the mark of circumcision, gave them laws and introduced them into the doctrines of the Aten religion. The union and founding of the religion at Kadesh were accompanied by a compromise in which the two sides are distinguishable. The one partner was only concerned to disavow the novelty and foreign character of the god Yahweh and to increase his claim to the people's devotion; the other partner was anxious not to sacrifice to him precious memories of the liberation from Egypt and of the grand figure of the leader, Moses.

1939A   23/66

Moses and monotheism: Three essays (1939). Essay III. Moses, his people and monotheist religion. Part I. B. The latency period and tradition.

The idea of a single god, as well as the rejection of magically effective ceremonial and the stress upon ethical demands made in his name were in fact Mosaic doctrines, to which no attention was paid to begin with, but which, after a long interval had elapsed, came into operation and became permanently established. The two portions of what was later to be the Jewish people came together at Kadesh to receive a new religion. In those who had been in Egypt, the memories of the Exodus and of the figure of Moses were still so strong and vivid that they demanded their inclusion in an account of early times. The determining purpose of the other portion of the people was to glorify the new god and to dispute his being foreign. The phenomenon of latency in the history of the Jewish religion may be explained by the circumstance that the facts and ideas which were intentionally disavowed by the official historians were in fact never lost. Information about them persisted in traditions which survived among the people. These traditions, instead of becoming weaker with time, became more and

more powerful in the course of centuries, forced their way into the later revisions of the official accounts, and finally showed themselves strong enough to have a decisive influence on the thoughts and actions of the people. The Jewish people had abandoned the Aten religion brought to them by Moses and had turned to the worship of another god who differed little from the Baalim of the neighboring peoples. The formation of epics pertaining to the Jewish culture is discussed.

1939A   23/72

Moses and monotheism: Three essays (1939). Essay III. Moses, his people and monotheist religion. Part I. C. The analogy.

The only satisfying analogy to the remarkable course of events that we have found in the history of the Jewish religion lies in the genesis of human neuroses. We give the name of traumas to those impressions, experienced early and later forgotten, to which we attach such great importance in the etiology of the neuroses. Researches have shown that the phenomena (symptoms) of a neurosis are the result of certain experiences and impressions which for that very reason are regarded as etiological traumas. All these traumas occur in early childhood up to about the fifth year. The experiences in question are as a rule totally forgotten. They relate to impressions of a sexual and aggressive nature. The effects of traumas are of two kinds, positive and negative. All these phenomena, the symptoms as well as the restrictions on the ego and the stable character changes, have a compulsive quality: that is to say that they have great psychical intensity and at the same time exhibit a far reaching independence of the organization of the other mental processes, which are adjusted to the demands of the real external world and obey the laws of logical thinking. A trauma in childhood may be followed immediately by a neurotic outbreak, an infantile neurosis, with an abundance of efforts at defense, and accompanied by the formation of symptoms. The phenomenon of a latency of the neurosis between the first reactions to the trauma and the later outbreak of the illness must be regarded as typical.

1939A   23/80

Moses and monotheism: Three essays (1939). Essay III. Moses, his people and monotheist religion. Part I. D. Application.

Freud's construction of early history asserts that in primeval times, primitive man lived in small groups, each under the domination of a powerful male. The lot of his sons was a hard one: if they roused their father's jealousy they were killed, castrated, or driven out. Their only resource was to collect together in small communities, to get themselves wives by robbery, and, when one or other of them could succeed in it, to raise themselves into a position similar to their father's in the primal group. Totemism is regarded as the first form in which religion was manifested in human history. The first step away from totemism was the humanizing of the being who was worshipped. The reestablishment of the primal father in his historic rights was a great step forward but it could not be the end. The killing of Moses by his Jewish people, recognized by Sellin from the trace of it in tradition becomes an indispensable part of Freud's construction, an important link between the forgotten event of primeval times and its later emergence in the form of the monotheist religions. It is plausible to conjecture that remorse for the murder of Moses provided the stimulus for the wishful phantasy of the Messiah who was to return and lead his people to redemption and the promised world dominion. Some deep motives for hatred of the Jews are analysed and include: jealousy of those people who declare themselves the firstborn, favorite children of God and their practice of circumcision which recalls castration.

1939A   23/92

Moses and monotheism: Three essays (1939). Essay III. Moses, his people and monotheist religion. Part I. E. Difficulties.

In the transference from individual to group psychology, two difficulties arise, differing in their nature and importance. The first of these is that we have dealt with only a single instance from the copious phenomenology of religions and have thrown no light on any others. The second difficulty raises the question in what form the operative tradition in the life of peoples is present. The compromise at Kadesh has been attributed to the survival of a powerful tradition among those who had returned from Egypt. In the group an impression of the past is retained in unconscious memory traces. If we assume the survival of memory traces in the archaic heritage, we have bridged the gulf between individual and group psychology: we can deal with peoples as we do with an individual neurotic. A tradition that was based only on communication could not lead to the compulsive character that attaches to religious phenomena. It would be listened to, judged, and perhaps dismissed, like any other piece of information from outside; it would never attain the privilege of being liberated from the constraint of logical thought.

1939A   23/103

Moses and monotheism: Three essays (1939). Essay III. Moses, his people and monotheist religion. Part II. Summary and recapitulation.

A summary and recapitulation of *Moses and Monotheism* is presented. Two pieces were published in *Imago*: the psychoanalytic starting point of the whole thing "Moses an Egyptian", and the historical construc-

tion erected on this "If Moses was an Egyptian". The remainder, which included what was really open to objection and dangerous, the application of the findings to the genesis of monotheism and the view of religion in general, Freud held back. In March 1938, came the unexpected German invasion of Vienna, which forced him to leave his home but also freed him from his anxiety lest his publication might conjure up a prohibition of psychoanalysis in a place where it was still tolerated.

1939A   23/105

Moses and monotheism: Three essays (1939). Essay III. Moses, his people and monotheist religion. Part II. A. The people of Israel.

Of all the peoples who lived round the basin of the Mediterranean in antiquity, the Jewish people is almost the only one which still exists in name and also in substance. It has met misfortunes and ill treatment with an unexampled capacity for resistance; it has developed special character traits and has earned the hearty dislike of every other people. We may start from a character trait of the Jews which dominates their relation to others. There is no doubt that they have a particularly high opinion of themselves, that they regard themselves as more distinguished, of higher standing, as superior to other people. At the same time they are inspired by a peculiar confidence in life, such as is derived from the secret ownership of some precious possession, a kind of optimism: pious people would call it trust in God. They really regard themselves as God's chosen people, they believe that they stand especially close to him; and this makes them proud and confident. If one is the declared favorite of the dreaded father, one need not be surprised at the jealousy of one's brothers and sisters. The course of world history seemed to justify the presumption of the Jews, since, when later on it pleased God to send mankind a Messiah and redeemer, he once again chose him from the Jewish people. It was the man Moses who imprinted this trait upon the Jewish people. He raised their self-esteem by assuring them that they were God's chosen people, he enjoined them to holiness and pledged them to be apart from others.

1939A   23/107

Moses and monotheism: Three essays (1939). Essay III. Moses, his people and monotheist religion. Part II. B. The great man.

If the investigation of a particular case demonstrates to us the transcendent influence of a single personality, our conscience need not reproach us with having, by this hypothesis, flown in the face of the doctrine of the importance of general and impersonal factors. The development of monotheism was linked with the establishment of closer relations between different nations and with the building up of a great empire. A great man influences his fellow men in two ways: by his personality and by the idea which he puts forward. In the mass of mankind there is a powerful need for an authority who can be admired, before whom one bows down, by whom one is ruled and perhaps even ill treated. The origin of this is a longing for the father felt by everyone from his childhood onwards, for the same father whom the hero of legend boasts he has overcome. There is no doubt that it was a mighty prototype of a father which, in the person of Moses, stooped to the poor Jewish bondsmen to assure them that they were his dear children. And no less overwhelming must have been the effect upon them of the idea of a single, eternal, almighty God, who made a covenant with them and who promised to care for them if they remained loyal to his worship. The great religious idea for which the man Moses stood out was not his own property: he had taken it over from King Akhenaten.

1939A   23/111

Moses and monotheism: Three essays (1939). Essay III. Moses, his people and monotheist religion. Part II. C. The advance in intellectuality.

In order to bring about lasting psychical results in a people, it is clearly not enough to assure them that they have been chosen by the diety. The fact must also be proved to them in some way if they are to believe it and to draw consequences from the belief. In the religion of Moses, the Exodus from Egypt served as the proof; God, or Moses in his name, was never tired of appealing to this evidence of favor. The feat of the Passover was introduced in order to maintain the memory of that event. The religion of Moses brought the Jews a grand conception of God. Anyone who belived in this God had some kind of share in his greatness, might feel exalted himself. Among the precepts of the Mosaic religion there is one that is of the greatest importance. This is the prohibition against making an image of God, the compulsion to worship a God whom one cannot see. The Mosaic prohibition elevated God to a higher degree of intellectuality. All advances in intellectuality have as their consequence that the individual's self-esteem is increased, that he is made proud, so that he feels superior to other people who have remained under the spell of sensuality. Moses conveyed to the Jews an exalted sense of being a chosen people. The dematerialization of God brought a fresh and valuable contribution to their secret treasure. The Jews retained their inclination to intellectual interests.

1939A   23/116

Moses and monotheism: Three essays (1939). Essay III. Moses, his people and monotheist religion. Part II. D. Renunciation of instinct.

It is not obvious and not immediately understandable why an advance in intellectuality, a setback to sensuality, should raise the self-regard both of an individual and of a people. It seems to presuppose the existence of a definite standard of value and of some other person or agency which maintains it. If the id in a human being gives rise to an instinctual demand of an erotic or aggressive nature, the simplest and most natural thing is that the ego, which has the apparatus of thought and the muscular apparatus at its disposal, should satisfy the demand by an action. This satisfaction of the instinct is felt by the ego as pleasure. Instinctual renunciation can be imposed for both internal and external reasons. The religion which began with the prohibition against making an image of god develops more and more in the course of centuries into a religion of instinctual renunciations; it is content with a marked restriction of sexual freedom. God, however, becomes entirely removed from sexuality and elevated into the ideal of ethical perfection. Moses made his people holy by introducing the custom of circumcision. Circumcision is the symbolic substitute for the castration which the primal father once inflicted upon his sons in the plenitude of his absolute power, and whoever accepted that symbol was showing by it that he was prepared to submit to the father's will, even if it imposed the most painful sacrifice on him. A part of the precepts of ethics is justified rationally by the necessity for delimiting the rights of the individual with respect to society and those of individuals with respect to one another.

1939A   23/122

Moses and monotheism: Three essays (1939). Essay III. Moses, his people, and monotheist religion. Part II. E. What is true in religion.

The man Moses impressed the special character of the Jewish people on them by giving them a religion which increased their self-esteem so much that they thought themselves superior to all other peoples. Thereafter they survived by keeping apart from others. Mixtures of blood interfered little with this, since what held them together was an ideal factor, the possession in common of certain intellectual and emotional wealth. The religion of Moses led to this result because: (1) it allowed the people to take a share in the grandeur of a new idea of God; (2) it asserted that this people had been chosen by this great God and were destined to receive evidences of his special favor; and (3) it forced upon the people an advance in intellectuality which, important enough in itself, opened the way, in addition, to the appreciation of intellectual work and to further renunciations of instinct. The religion of Moses did not disappear without leaving a trace. A kind of memory of it had survived, obscured and distorted, supported, perhaps, among individual members of the priestly caste by ancient records. It was this tradition of a great past which continued to work in the background, as it were, which gradually gained more and more power over men's minds, and which finally succeeded in transforming the god Yahweh into the god of Moses and in calling back to life the religion of Moses which had been established and then abandoned long centuries earlier.

1939A 23/124

Moses and monotheism: Three essays (1939). Essay III. Moses, his people and monotheist religion. Part II. F. The return of the repressed.

The experiences of a person's first 5 years exercise a determining effect on his life, which nothing later can withstand. What children have experienced at the age of 2 and have not understood, need never be remembered by them except in dreams. But at some later time it will break into their life with obsessional impulses, it will govern their actions, it will decide their sympathies and antipathies and will quite often determine their choice of a love object. It is not easy to introduce the idea of the unconscious into group psychology. Regular contributions are made to these phenomena by the mechanisms which lead to the formation of neuroses. Here again the determining events occur in early childhood, but here the stress is not upon the time but upon the process by which the event is met, the reaction to it. It is described schematically: as a result of the experience, an instinctual demand arises which calls for satisfaction. The ego refuses that satisfaction, either because it is paralyzed by the magnitude of the demand or because it recognizes it as a danger. The ego fends off the danger by the process of repression. The instinctual impulse is in some way inhibited and its precipitating cause, with its attendant perceptions and ideas, is forgotten. The formation of symptoms may be described as the return of the repressed. Their distinguishing characteristic is the greater distortion to which the returning material has been subjected as compared with the original.

1939A 23/127

Moses and monotheism: three essays (1939). Essay III. Moses, his people and monotheist religion. Part II. G. Historical truth.

The religion of Moses only carried through its effect on the Jewish people as a tradition. A primitive man is in need of a god as creator of the universe, as chief of his clan, as personal protector. This god takes his position behind the dead fathers about whom tradition still has something to say. The idea of a single god means in itself an advance in intellectuality. When Moses brought the

people the idea of a single god, it was not a novelty but signified the revival of an experience in the primeval ages of the human family which had long vanished from men's conscious memory. We have learned from the psychoanalyses of individuals that their earliest impressions, received at a time when the child was scarcely yet capable of speaking, produce at some time or another effects of a compulsive character without themselves being consciously remembered. The same assumption is made about the earliest experiences of the whole of humanity. One of these effects would be the emergence of the idea of a single great god, an idea which must be recognized as a completely justified memory, though, it is true, one that has been distorted. An idea such as this has a compulsive character: it must be believed. Since it is distorted, it may be described as a delusion; insofar as it brings a return of the past, it must be called the truth.

1939A 23/132

Moses and monotheism: three essays (1939). Essay III. Moses, his people and monotheist religion. Part II. H. The historical development.

After the institution of the combination of brother clan, matriarchy, exogamy, and totemism, a development began which must be described as a slow return of the repressed. The return of the repressed took place under the influence of all the changes in conditions of life which fill the history of human civilization. The first effect of meeting the being who had so long been missed and longed for was overwhelming and was like the traditional description of the law giving from Mount Sinai. Admiration, awe and thankfulness for having found grace in his eyes, were part of the positive feelings towards the father god. A rapture of devotion to God was the first reaction to the return of the great father. There was no place in the framework of the religion of Moses for a direct expression of the murderous hatred of the father. All that could come to light was a mighty reaction against it, a sense of guilt on account of that hostility, a bad conscience for having sinned against God and for not ceasing to sin. Further development of this point takes us beyond Judaism. Original sin and redemption by the sacrifice of a victim became the foundation stones of the new religion founded by Paul. Christianity, having arisen out of a father religion, became a son religion but has not escaped the fate of having to get rid of the father. Only a portion of the Jewish people accepted the new doctrine. Those who refused to are still called Jews today.

1940A 23/141

An outline of psychoanalysis (1940). Editor's note (1964) and Preface.

An *Outline of Psychoanalysis* was first published both in German and English. The *Outline* must be described as unfinished, but it is difficult to regard it as incomplete. The last chapter is shorter than the rest and might have gone on to a discussion of such things as the sense of guilt, though this had already been touched on in Chapter 6. In general, however, the question of how far and in what direction Freud would have proceeded with the book is an intriguing one, for the program laid down by the author in his preface seems already to be reasonably well carried out. In the long succession of Freud's expository works the *Outline* exhibits a unique character. The others are, without exception, aimed at explaining psychoanalysis to an outside public, a public with varying degrees and types of general approach to Freud's subject, but always a relatively ignorant public. This cannot be said of the *Outline*..This is not a book for beginners; it is something much more like a refresher course for advanced students.

1940A   23/144

An outline of psychoanalysis (1940). Part I. The mind and its workings. Chapter I: The psychical apparatus.

The id, the oldest of the psychic agencies, contains everything that is inherited, that is present at birth, that is laid down in the constitution, therefore, instincts. Under the influence of the real external world, one portion of the id has undergone a special development: from what was originally a cortical layer, a special organization (called the ego) has arisen which acts as an intermediary between the id and the external world. The principal characteristics of the ego are discussed. It has the task of self-preservation. As regards external events, it becomes aware of stimuli, sorts experiences about them, avoids excessively strong stimuli, deals with moderate stimuli, and learns to bring about expedient changes in the external world to its own advantage. As regards internal events, in relation to the id, the ego performs that task by gaining control over the demands of the instincts, by deciding whether they are to be allowed satisfaction, by postponing that satisfaction to times and circumstances favorable in the external world, or by suppressing their excitations entirely. The long period of childhood, during which the growing human being lives in dependence on his parents, leaves behind it a special agency, the superego, in which this parental influence is prolonged. An action by the ego should satisfy simultaneously the demands of the id, of the superego and of reality. The id and superego have 1 thing in common: both represent the influences of the past, the id the influence of heredity, the superego the influence of what is taken over from other people. The ego is principally determined by the individual's own experience.

1940A   23/148

An outline of psychoanalysis (1940). Part I. The mind and its workings. Chapter II: The theory of the instincts.

The theory of the instincts is presented. The power of the id expresses the true purpose of the individual organism's life. The ego has the task of self-preservation. The main function of the superego is the limitation of satisfactions. The forces which exist behind the tensions caused by the needs of the id are called instincts. The existence of only two basic instincts is assumed: Eros and the destructive instinct. The aim of the first of these basic instincts is to establish ever greater unities and to preserve them; the aim of the second is to undo connections and so to destroy them. So long as the second instinct operates internally, as a death instinct, it remains silent; it only comes to our notice when it is diverted outwards as an instinct of destruction. The whole aviailable quota of libido is stored up in the ego. This state is called absolute, primary narcissism. It lasts till the ego begins to cathect the ideas of objects with libido, to transform narcissistic libido into object libido. Throughout the whole of life the ego remains the great reservoir from which libidinal cathexes are sent out to objects and into which they are also once more withdrawn. The most prominent of the parts of the body from which the libido arises are known by the name of erotogenic zones.

1940A   23/152

An outline of psychoanalysis (1940). Part I. The mind and its workings. Chapter III: The development of the sexual function.

The development of the sexual function is presented. The principal findings of psychoanalysis are: (1) sexual life does not begin at puberty, but is clearly manifested soon after birth; (2) it is necessary to distinguish sharply between the concepts of sexual and genital; (3) sexual life includes the function of obtaining pleasure from zones of the body, a function which is subsequently brought into the service of reproduction. The first organ to emerge as an erotogenic zone and to make libidinal demands on the mind is the mouth. During this oral phase, sadistic impulses already occur sporadically along with the appearance of the teeth. Their extent is far greater in the second phase, which is described as the sadistic anal one, because satisfaction is then sought in aggression and in the excretory function. The third phase is that known as the phallic one, which is, as it were, a forerunner of the final form taken by sexual life and already much resembles it. With the phallic phase and in the course of it, the sexuality of early childhood reaches its height and approaches its dissolution. Thereafter boys and girls have different histories. The boy enters the Oedipus phase. The girl, after vainly attempting to do the same as the boy, comes to recognize her lack of a penis or rather the inferiority of her clitoris, with permanent effects on the development of her character. The complete sexual organization is only achieved at puberty, in a fourth, genital phase. A state of things is then established in which (1) some earlier libidinal cathexes are retained (2) others are taken into the sexual function as preparatory, auxiliary acts, the satisfaction of which produces what is known as forepleasure, and (3) other urges are excluded from the organization, and are either suppressed altogether or employed in the ego in another way, forming character traits or undergoing sublimation with a displacement of their aims. When this process malfunctions, disturbances of sexual life result. An example of a developmental inhibition would be homosexuality. The normal and abnormal manifestations observed by us need to be described from the point of view of their dynamics and economics. The etiology of neurotic disorders is to be looked for in the individual's developmental history.

1940A   23/157

An outline of psychoanalysis (1940). Part I. The mind and its workings. Chapter IV: Psychical qualities.

Psychical qualities are discussed. Psychoanalysis explains the supposedly somatic concommitant phenomena as being what is truly psychical, and thus in the first instance disregards the quality of consciousness. What Freud calls conscious is the same as the consciousness of philosophers and of everyday opinions. Everything else psychical is the unconscious. However. some processes become conscious easily; they may then cease to be conscious, but can become conscious once more without any trouble: as people say, they can be reproduced or remembered. In general, consciousness is a highly fugitive state. Everything unconscious that is capable of becoming conscious is called preconscious. Three qualities are attributed to psychical processes: they are either conscious, preconscious, or unconscious. What is preconscious becomes conscious, and in the process we may have a feeling that we are often overcoming very strong resistances. The process of something becoming conscious is linked with the perceptions which our sense organs receive from the external world. This process takes place in the outermost cortex of the ego. The inside of the ego, which comprises all the thought processes, has the quality of being preconscious. The sole prevailing quality in the id is that of being unconscious. The processes in the unconscious or in the id obey different laws from those in the preconscious ego. We name these laws in their totality the primary process, in contrast to the secondary process which governs the course of events in the preconscious, in the ego.

1940A   23/165

An outline of psychoanalysis (1940). Part I. The mind and its workings. Chapter V: Dream-interpretation as an illustration.

We find our way to the understanding of a dream by assuming that what we recollect as the dream after we have woken up is not the true dream process but only a facade behind which the process lies concealed. The process which produces the manifest dream content out of the latent dream thoughts is described as the dream work. The study of the dream work teaches us the way in which unconscious material from the id forces its way into the ego, becomes preconscious and, as a result of the ego's opposition, undergoes the changes known as dream distortion. Dream formation can be provoked if (1) an ordinarily suppressed instinctual impulse finds sufficient strength during sleep to make itself felt by the ego or (2) an urge left over from waking life finds reinforcement during sleep from an unconscious element. Thus dreams arise from either the id or the ego. Evidence for the share taken by the unconscious id in the dream formation is discussed. Dream work is essentially an instance of the unconscious working over of preconscious thought processes. Two peculiarities of dream work (condensation and displacement) are discussed. With the help of the unconscious, every dream that is in the process of formation makes a demand upon the ego, for the satisfaction of an instinct, if the dream originates from the id; for the solution of a conflict, the removal of a doubt or the forming of an intention, if the dream originates from a residue of preconscious activity in waking life. The sleeping ego, however, is focused on the wish to maintain sleep; it feels this demand as a disturbance and seeks to get rid of the disturbance. The ego succeeds in doing this by what appears to be an act of compliance: it meets the demand with a harmless fulfillment of a wish and so gets rid of it. This replacement of the demand by the fulfillment of a wish remains the essential function of the dream work.

1940A   23/172

An outline of psychoanalysis (1940). Part II. The practical task. Chapter VI: The technique of psychoanalysis.

The technique of psychoanalysis is presented. It is the ego's task to meet the demands raised by its three dependent relations: to reality, to the id, and to the superego; and nevertheless at the same time to preserve its own organization and maintain its own autonomy. If the patient's ego is to be a useful ally, it must have retained a certain amount of coherence and some fragment of understanding for the demands of reality, however hard it may be pressed by the hostile powers. The method is only useful with neurotics, not psychotics. The fundamental rule of analysis pledges the patient to tell everything that his self-observation yields including the irrelevant, nonsensual or disagreeable. The patient is not satisfied with regarding the analyst as a helper and adviser but sees in him some important figure out of his childhood and consequently transfers on to him feelings and reactions which applied to this prototype. This fact of transference soon proves to be a factor of importance. If the patient puts the analyst in the palce of his father, he is also giving him the power which his superego exercises over his ego. The new superego now has an opportunity for a sort of after-education of the neurotic. The ego protects itself against the invasion of the undesired elements from the unconscious and repressed id by means of anticathexes, which must remain intact if it is to function normally. The overcoming of resistances is the part of the work that requires the most time and the greatest trouble.Two new factors, as sources of resistance, are: (1) the sense of guilt or consciousness of built, and (2) those cases in which the instinct of self-preservation has actually been reversed and the patient aims at nothing other than self-injury and self-destruction. Standing in the way of successful psychoanalysis are the negative transference, the ego's resistance due to repression, the sense of guilt arising from its relation to the superego and the need to be ill due to profound changes in the economics of the patient's instincts.

1940A 23/183

An outline of psychoanalysis (1940). Part II. The practical task. Chapter VII: An example of psychoanalytic work.

The neuroses and psychoses are the states in which disturbances in the functioning of the psychical apparatus come to expression. Neuroses have been chosen as the subjects of study because they alone seem accessible to the psychological methods of intervention. The neuroses have no specific determinants. Quantitative disharmonies are what must be held responsible for the inadequacy and sufferings of neurotics. It seems that neuroses are acquired only in early childhood (up to the age of 6), even though their symptoms may not make their appearance till much later. The neuroses are disorders of the ego. The ego, when it is feeble, immature and incapable of resistance, fails to deal with tasks which it could cope with later on with utmost ease. Instinctual demands from within, no less than excitations from the external world, operate as traumas, particularly if they are met halfway by certain innate dispositions. The helpless ego fends them off by means of attempts at flight (repressions), which later turn out to be inefficient and which involve permanent restrictions on further development. The symptoms of neurosis are either a substitutive satisfaction of some sexual urge or measures to prevent such a satisfaction or compro-

mises between the two. The relation of the child to his mother is analyzed with regard to her as a love object and her threats to punish his masturbation with castration. The mother usually delegates the act of castration to the boy's father. The Oedipus complex is a major event in the lives of both boys and girls. The difference between the Oedipus complex and the castration complex in females and males is discussed at length. In males, the threat of castration brings the Oedipus complex to an end; in females, it is their lack of a penis that forces them into their Oedipus complex.

1940A 23/195

An outline of psychoanalysis (1940). Part III. The theoretical yield. Chapter VIII: The psychical apparatus and the external world.

The core of our being is formed by the obscure id, which has no direct communication with the external world and is accessible to knowledge only through the medium of another agency. Within this id the organic instincts operate, which are themselves compounded of fusions of two primal forces (Eros and destructiveness) in varying proportions and are differentiated from one another by their relation to organs or systems of organs. The id, cut off from the external world, has a world of perception of its own. The ego has been developed out of the id's cortical layer, which, through being adapted to the reception and exclusion of stimuli, is in direct contact with the external world (reality). Starting from conscious perception it has subjected to its influence ever larger regions and deeper strata of the id and, in the persistence with which it maintains its dependence on the external world, it bears the indelible stamp of its origin. Its psychological function consists in raising the passage of events in the id to a higher dynamic level; its constructive function consists in interpolating the activity of thought which endeavours by means of experimental actions to calculate the consequences of the course of action proposed. Thus the ego decides whether the attempt to obtain satisfaction is to be carried out or postponed or if it is not necessary for the demand by the instinct to be suppressed altogether as being dangerous. This is the reality principle. Since memory traces can become conscious just as perceptions do, the possibility arises of a confusion which would lead to a mistaking of reality; the ego guards itself against this by the institution of reality testing. In the period of childhood the weak and immature ego is permanently damaged by the stresses put upon it in its efforts to fend off the dangers peculiar to that period of life. Children are protected against dangers from the external world by the solicitude of their parents; they pay for this security by fear of loss of love. The ego pathological states are founded on a cessation or slackening of its relation to the external world. The view postulating that in all psychoses there is a splitting of the ego (two different attitudes) is discussed with fetishism used as an example.

1940A   23/205

An outline of psychoanalysis (1940). Part III. The theoretical yield. Chapter IX. The internal world.

The internal world is discussed. Until the end of the first period of childhood (about age 5), the ego mediates between the id and the external world, takes over the instinctual demands of the former in order to lead them to satisfaction, derives perceptions from the latter and uses them as memories. Intent on its self-preservation, the ego puts itself in defense against excessively strong claims from both sides and at the same time, is guided in all its decisions by the injunctions of a modified pleasure principle. At this age, a portion of the external world becomes abandoned as an object and is instead taken into the ego and thus becomes an integral part of the internal world. This new psychical agency continues to carry on the functions which have hitherto been performed by the people in the external world: it observes the ego, gives its orders, judges it and threatens it with punishments. This agency is called the superego and functions as the conscience. The superego is the heir to the Oedipus complex and is established only after that complex has been disposed of. So long as the ego works in full harmony with the superego it is not easy to distinguish between their manifestations; but tensions and estrangements between them make themselves very plainly visible. The superego takes up a kind of intermediate position between the id and the external world, it unites in itself the influences of the present and the past.

1937C   23/209

Analysis terminable and interminable (1937). Editor's note (1964).

Analysis Terminable and Interminable was written early in 1937 and published in June. The paper as a whole is pessimistic about the therapeutic efficacy of psychoanalysis. Its limitations are constantly stressed, the difficulties of the procedure and the obstacles standing in its way are insisted upon. The factors to which Freud draws attention are of a physiological and biological nature: they are thus generally unsusceptible to psychological influences. There is one respect in which the views expressed by Freud in this paper do seem to differ from, or even to contradict, his earlier ones; namely, in the scepticism expressed by him in regard to the prophylactic power of psychoanalysis. His doubts extend to the prospects of preventing not merely the occurrence of a fresh and different neurosis but even a return of a neurosis that has already been treated. The

basis of this increased scepticism of Freud's seems to be a conviction of the impossibility of dealing with a conflict that is not current and of the grave objections to converting a latent conflict into a current one. It is of interest to note that at the very beginning of his practice Freud was worried by very much the same problems as these, which may thus be said to have extended over the entire length of his analytic studies.

1937C   23/216

Analysis terminable and interminable (1937). Part I. Setting a time limit for termination. Part II. Factors which may make analysis interminable.

From the very first, attempts have been made to shorten the duration of psychoanalyses. Otto Rank, following his book, *The Trauma of Birth*, supposed that the true source of neurosis was the act of birth. He hoped that if this primal trauma were dealt with by a subsequent analysis, the whole neurosis would be got rid of. To speed up an analytic treatment Freud used the fixing of a time limit for analysis. The only verdict about the value of this device is that it is effective provided that one hits the right time for it. But it cannot guarantee to accomplish the task completely. The end of analysis can mean different things. From a practical standpoint, it means that the patient and the analyst have ceased to meet each other for the analytic session. The other meaning is that the analyst has had such a far-reaching influence on the patient that no further change could be expected to take place in him if his analysis were continued. A constitutional strength of instinct and an unfavorable alteration of the ego acquired in its defensive struggle in the sense of its being dislocated and restricted are the factors which are prejudicial to the effectiveness of analysis and which may make its duration interminable. Two examples are given illustrating that even a successful analytic treatment does not prevent the patient from falling ill later on from another neurosis, or, of a neurosis derived from the same instinctual root recurrence of the same old trouble. The exacting demands upon analytic therapy hardly call for a shortening of its duration.

1937C   23/224

Analysis terminable and interminable (1937). Part III. The strength of the instincts vis-a-vis the other psychical agencies.

There are three factors which are decisive for the success or failure of analytic treatment: the influence of traumas, the constitutional strength of the instincts, and the laterations of the ego. The constitutional factor is of decisive importance from the very beginning; however, a reinforcement of instinct coming later in life might produce the same effects. Twice in the course of individual development certain instincts are considerably reinforced: at puberty and, in women, at the menopause. We are not in the least surprised if a person who was not neurotic before becomes so at these times. In endeavoring to replace insecure repressions by reliable ego syntonic controls, we do not always achieve our aim to its full extent, that is, do not achieve it thoroughly enough. The transformation is achieved, but often only partially. Analysis does not always succeed in ensuring to a sufficient degree the foundations on which a control of instinct is based. The cause of such a partial failure is easily discovered. In the past, the quantitative factor of instinctual strength opposed the ego's defensive efforts; for that reason we called in the work of analysis to help; and now that same factor sets a limit to the efficacy of this new effort. If the strength of the instinct is excessive, the mature ego, supported by analysis, fails in its task, just as the helpless ego failed formerly.

1937C   23/230
Analysis terminable and interminable (1937). Part IV. Protecting against future conflicts.

Two problems are considered: whether we can protect a patient from future conflicts while we are treating one instinctual conflict, and wehther it is feasible and expedient, for prophylactic purposes, to stir up a conflict which is not at the time manifest. The first task can only be carried out in so far as the second one is; that is, in so far as a possible future conflict is turned into an actual present one upon which influence is then brought to bear. If an instinctual conflict is not a currently active one, is not manifesting itself, we cannot influence it even by analysis. In analytic prophylaxis against instinctual conflicts, the only methods which come into consideration are: (1) the artificial production of new conflicts in the transference (conflicts which lack the character of reality), and (2) the arousing of such conflicts in the patient's imagination by talking to him about them and making him familiar with their possibility. By telling the patient about the possibilities of other instinctual conflicts, we arouse his expectation that such conflicts may occur in him. What we hope is that this information and this warning will have the effect of activating in him one of the conflicts in a modest degree and yet sufficiently for treatment. The expected result does not come about; all we have done is increased his knowledge but altered nothing else in him. An analogous experience in which children are given sexual enlightenment is discussed.

1937C   23/234
Analysis terminable and interminable (1937). Part V. Alterations of the ego affect prognosis.

The factors which are decisive for the success of the therapeutic efforts are the influence of traumatic etiol-

ogy, the relative strength of the instincts which have to be controlled, and an alteration of the ego. The analytic situation consists in our allying ourselves with the ego of the person under treatment, in order to subdue portions of his id which are uncontrolled. The ego has to try to fulfill its task of mediating between its id and the external world in the service of the pleasure principle, and to protect the id from the dangers of the external world. Under the influence of education the ego grows accustomed to removing the scene of the fight from outside to within and to mastering the internal danger of before it has become an external one. During this fight on two fronts, the ego makes use of various procedures for fulfilling its task, which is to avoid danger, anxiety, and unpleasure. These procedures are called mechanisms of defense. In psychoanalysis the defensive mechanisms directed against former danger recur in the treatment procedure as resistances against recovery. Thus the ego treats recovery as a new danger. The therapeutic effect depends on making conscious what is repressed in the id. The effect brought about in the ego by the defenses can rightly be described as an alteration of the ego if by that we understand a deviation from the normal ego which would guarantee unshakable loyalty to the work of analysis. The outcome of an analytic treatment depends essentially on the strength and on the depth of these resistances that bring about an alteration of the ego.

1937C   23/240
Analysis terminable and interminable (1937). Part VI. Constitutional variables in ego, libido and free aggressiveness.

Each ego is endowed with individual dispositions and trends. The properties of the ego which we meet with in the form of resistances can be determined by heredity or can be acquired in defensive struggles. There are various kinds of resistance. There are people to whom is attributed a special adhesiveness of the libido. Another group of patients has an attitude which can only be put down to a depletion of plasticity, the capacity for change and further development. In yet another group of cases the distinguishing characteristics of the ego, which are to be held responsible as sources of resistance against analytic treatment and as impediments to the therapeutic success, may spring from different and deeper roots. Here we are dealing with the ultimate things which psychological research can learn about: the behavior of the two primal instincts, their distribution, mingling, and defusion. In studying the phenomena which testify to the activity of the destructive instinct, we are not confined to observations on pathological material. There have always been, as there still are, people who can take as their sexual objects members of their own sex as well as of the opposite one, without the one trend interfering with the other. The two fundamental principles of Empedocles are the same as Eros and destructiveness: the first endeavors to combine what exists into ever greater unities, while the second endeavors to dissolve those combinations and to destroy the structures to which they have given rise.

1937C   23/247

Analysis terminable and interminable (1937). Part VII. Factors in the analyst affect prognosis.

In 1927, Ferenczi read an instructive paper on the problem of terminating analyses. It ends with a comforting assurance that analysis is not an endless process, but one which can be brought to a natural end with sufficient skill and patience on the analyst's part. Ferenczi makes the further important point that success depends very largely on the analyst's having learnt sufficiently from his own errors and mistakes and having got the better of the weak points in his personality. It cannot be disputed that analysts in their own personalities have not invariably come up to the standard of psychical normality to which they wish to educate their patients. Opponents of analysis often point to this fact with scorn and use it as an argument to show the uselessness of analytic exertions. The special conditions of analytic work do actually cause the analyst's own defects to interfere with his making a correct assessment of the state of things in his patient and reacting to them in a useful way. The termination of an analysis is a practical matter. Every experienced analyst will be able to recall a number of cases in which he has bidden his patient a permanent farewell. The purpose of the analysis is to secure the best possible psychological conditions for the functions of the ego; with that it has discharged its task.

1937C   23/250

Analysis terminable and interminable (1937). Part VIII. Bisexuality is the strongest resistance to analysis.

Both in therapeutic and in character analyses, two themes come into prominence and give the analyst an unusual amount of trouble. The two themes are an envy for the penis, a positive striving to possess a male genital in the female and, in the male, a struggle against his passive or feminine attitude to another male. What is common to the two themes was singled out at an early date by psychoanalytic nomenclature as an attitude towards the castration complex. In both cases, it is the attitude to the opposite sex which has succumbed to repression. The paramount importance of these two themes did not escape Ferenczi's notice. In the paper read by him in 1927, he made it a requirement that in every successful analysis these two complexes must be mastered. At no other point in one's analytic work does one suffer more from an oppressive feeling that all one's repeated efforts have been in vain than when one is

trying to persuade a woman to abandon her wish for a penis since it is unrealizable. or when one is seeking to convince a man that a passive attitude to men does not always signify castration and that it is indispensable in many relationships in life. The rebellious overcompensation of the male produces one of the strongest transference resistances. The resistance prevents any change from taking place.

1937D   23/255

Constructions in analysis (1937). Part I. The analyst's task requires constructions in analysis.

Constructions in Analysis was published in December, 1937. Three examples of constructions in Freud's writings: the Rat Man, the Wolf Man, and the case history of a homosexual girl. It is familiar ground that the work of analysis aims at inducing the patient to give up the repressions belonging to his early development and to replace them by reactions of a sort that would correspond to a psychically mature condition. With this purpose in view, he must be brought to recollect certain experiences and the affective impulses called up by them which he has for the time being forgotten. His present symptoms and inhibitions are the consequences of repressions of this kind: thus they are a substitute for these things that he has forgotten. What we are in search of is a picture of the patient's forgotten years that shall be both trustworthy and, in all essential respects, complete. The analyst's work of construction, or of reconstruction, resembles to a great extent an archaeologist's excavation of some dwelling place or of some ancient edifice that has been destroyed and buried. Only by analytic technique can we succeed in bringing what is concealed completely to light.

1937D   23/260

Constructions in analysis (1937). Part II. Evaluating the patient's reactions to a construction.

Every analyst knows that two kinds of work are carried on side by side. The analyst finishes a piece of construction and communicates it to the subject so that it may work upon him; the analyst then constructs a further piece out of the fresh material pouring in upon him, deals with it in the same way and proceeds in this alternating fashion until the end. We cannot neglect the indications that can be inferred from the patient's reaction upon offering him one of our constructions, nevertheless a straight Yes or No answer is not to be taken at face value. These Yes and No answers are both considered ambiguous. The direct utterances of the patient after he has been offered a construction afford very little evidence about whether we have been right or wrong. The indirect forms of confirmation are used. One of these is a form of words that is used with very little variation by the most different people: "I didn't ever think." This can be translated into: "Yes, you're right this time, about my unconscious." Indirect confirmation from associations that fit in with the content of a construction is likely to be confirmed in the course of the analysis. It is particularly striking when, by means of a parapraxis, a confirmation of this kind insinuates itself into a direct denial. There is no justification for the reproach that we neglect or underestimate the importance of the attitude taken up by those under analysis towards our constructions. We pay attention to them and often derive valuable information from them. But these reactions are rarely unambiguous and give no opportunity for a final judgment. Only the further course of the analysis enables us to decide whether our constructions are correct or unserviceable.

1937D   23/265
Constructions in analysis (1937). Part III. The distinction between historical and material truth.

The path that starts from the analyst's construction ought to end in the patient's recollection; but it does not always lead so far. Quite often we do not succeed in bringing the patient to recollect what has been repressed. Instead of that, if the analysis is carried out correctly, we produce in him an assured conviction of the truth of the construction which achieves the same therapeutic result as a recaptured memory. Freud is struck by the manner in which the communication of an apt construction has evoked a surprising phenomenon in the patients. They have had lively recollections called up in them, but what they have recollected has not been the event that was the subject of the construction, but details relating to that subject. The upward drive of the repressed, stirred into activity by the putting forward of the construction, has striven to carry the important memory traces into consciousness; but a resistance has succeeded, not in stopping that movement, but in displacing it on to adjacent objects of minor significance. These recollections might have been described as hallucinations if a belief in their actual presence had been added to their clearness. Freud hypothesizes that in delusions, the dynamic process is that the turning away from reality is exploited by the upward drive of the repressed in order to force its content into consciousness, while the resistances stirred up by this process and the trend to wish fulfillment are responsible for the distortion and displacement of what is recollected.

1940E   23/271
Splitting of the ego in the process of defence (1940).

The Splitting of the Ego in the Process of Defence, published posthumously, was dated January 2, 1938. The ego of a person whom we know as a patient in analysis must, dozens of years earlier, when it was young, have behaved in a remarkable manner in certain particular situations of pressure. The conditions under which this happens can be called the influence of a psychical trauma. Let us suppose that a child's ego is under the sway of a powerful instinctual demand which it is accustomed to satisfy and that it is suddenly frightened by an experience which teaches it that the continuance of this satisfaction will result in an almost intolerable real danger. It must now decide either to recognize the real danger, give way to it and renounce the instinctual satisfaction, or to disavow reality and make itself believe that there is no reason for fear, so that it may be able to retain the satisfaction. The child replies to the conflict with two contrary reactions. On the one hand, with the help of certain mechanisms he rejects reality and refuses to accept any prohibition; on the other hand, in the same breath he recognizes the danger of reality, takes over the fear of that danger as a pathological symptom, and tries subsequently to divest himself of the fear. The two contrary reactions to the conflict persist as the center point of a splitting of the ego. An individual case history is discussed concerning this point. A small boy created a substitute (fetish) for the penis which he missed in females. So long as he was not obliged to acknowledge that females have lost their penis, there was no need for him to believe the threat of castration in punishment for his masturbation. The boy did not simply contradict his perceptions and hallucinate a penis. He effected no more than a displacement of value: he transferred the importance of the penis to another part of the body through the assistance of regression. He had a great fear of his father.

1940B   23/279
Some elementary lessons in psycho-analysis (1940). The nature of the psychical.

Some Elementary Lessons in Psycho-analysis, written in London, is dated October 20, 1938. Psychoanalysis has little prospect of becoming liked or popular. Being conscious is only a quality of what is psychical; the psychical is in itself unconscious and probably similar in kind to all the other natural processes. Psychoanalysis bases this assertion on a number of facts, of which Freud proceeded to give a selection. (1) We know what is meant by ideas occurring to one, thoughts that suddenly come into consciousness without one's being aware of the steps that led up to them, though they, too, must have been psychical acts. (2) The second class of phenomena includes the parapraxes, the slips of the tongues. (3) As a third example, Freud states that it is possible in the case of persons in a state of hypnosis to prove experimentally that there are such things as unconscious psychical acts and that consciousness is not an indispensable condition of psychical activity. Freud concludes that consciousness is only a quality or attribute of what is psychical, and moreover an inconstant one.

1938A   23/287
A comment on anti-Semitism (1938).

A Comment on Anti-Semitism consists almost wholly of a quotation from a source which Freud declares that he can no longer trace. It has been suggested that the quotation is in fact by Freud himself, who chose an indirect manner of expressing some rather uncongenial views. The views were written by an author who claimed that he was not Jewish. Many derogatory, as well as the following favorable remarks are made about Jews. For long centuries the Jewish people have been treated unjustly and are continuing to be judged unjustly. The Jews do not need alcohol to make life tolerable; crimes of brutality, murder, robbery, and sexual violence are great rarities among them; they have always set a high value on intellectual achievement and interests; their family life is intimate; they take care of the poor; and charity is a sacred duty to them.

1937A   23/297
Lou Andreas-Salome (1937).

On February 5, 1937, Frau Lou Andreas-Salome died at the age of 76 years. For the last 25 years of her life she was attached to psychoanalysis, to which she contributed valuable writings and which she practiced as well. It was known that as a girl she had kept up an intense friendship with Friedrich Nietzsche, founded upon her deep understanding of the philosopher's bold ideas. Many years later she had acted as Muse and protecting mother to Rainer Maria Rilke, the great poet, who was somewhat helpless in facing life. In 1912 she returned to Vienna in order to be initiated into psychoanalysis. Anna Freud, who was her close friend, once heard her regret that she had not known psychoanalysis in her youth, but in those days it had not been defined.

1941F   23/299
Findings, ideas, problems (1941).

A series of short disconnected paragraphs (in order by date) were printed at the end of the volume of posthumous works published in 1941 under the heading of *Findings, Ideas, Problems*: London, June, 1938. One dated June 16 points out that in connection with early experiences, as contrasted with later experiences, all the various reactions to them survive, of course including contradictory ones. July 12: As a substitute for penis envy, identification with the clitoris is proposed: neatest expression of inferiority, source of all inhibitions. At the same time, there is a disavowal of the discovery that other women too are without a penis. July 12: With neurotics, it is as though we were in a prehistoric landscape. July 20: The individual perishes from his internal conflicts, the species perishes in its struggle with the external world to which it is no longer adapted. August 3: A sense of guilt originates from unsatisfied love as well as from hate. The ultimate ground of all intellectual inhibition and all inhibitions of work seems to be the inhibition of masturbation in childhood. August 22: Space may be the projection of the extension of the psychical apparatus. Mysticism is the obscure self-perception of the realm outside the ego, of the id.

1938D   23/301
Anti-semitism in England (1938).

Anti-Semitism is discussed in a letter to the editor of London's *Time and Tide*. After 68 years of work in Vienna, Freud had to leave his home, saw the scientific society he had founded dissolved, his institutions destroyed, his printing press taken over by the invaders, the books he had published confiscated or reduced to pulp, and his children expelled from their professions. Freud suggested that the column should be reserved for the opinions of non-Jewish people less involved than himself. Freud was deeply affected by the acknowledgement of a certain growth of anti-Semitism even in England. Freud felt that the persecution ought to give rise to a wave of sympathy.

Appendix to the Abstracts of the Standard Edition

This cross-reference list relates the Tyson-Strachey "Chronological Hand-List of Freud's Works" to the volume and page number of the *Standard Edition* and is arranged by Tyson-Strachey number. Page numbers may vary by one or two from the number assigned in the abstract section due to allowances for Editor's notes and introductions in the *Standard Edition* or the combining of two or more short subjects into one abstract.

Subject Index to the Abstracts of the Standard Edition

The subject index is machine generated. Keywords in the titles of abstracts appear alphabetically in the left hand margin; under each keyword is a list of titles in which the keyword appears. The spelling of words in the titles of abstracts has not been changed; hence, two spellings of the same word may appear in this index--for example, BEHAVIOR and BEHAVIOUR.

ABBREVIATIONS

PROJECT FOR A SCIENTIFIC PSYCHOLOGY: EDITOR'S INTRODUCTION AND KEY TO ABBREVIATIONS IN THE PROJECT. — 1950A 1/283

ABERRATIONS

THREE ESSAYS ON THE THEORY OF SEXUALITY. THE SEXUAL ABERRATIONS. DEVIATIONS IN RESPECT OF THE SEXUAL OBJECT. INVERSION. SEXUALLY IMMATURE PERSONS AND ANIMALS AS SEXUAL OBJECTS. — 1905D 7/136

THREE ESSAYS ON THE THEORY OF SEXUALITY. THE SEXUAL ABERRATIONS. DEVIATIONS IN RESPECT OF THE SEXUAL AIM. ANATOMICAL EXTENSIONS. FIXATION OF PRELIMINARY SEXUAL AIMS. — 1905D 7/149

THREE ESSAYS ON THE THEORY OF SEXUALITY. THE SEXUAL ABERRATIONS. THE PERVERSIONS IN GENERAL. — 1905D 7/160

THREE ESSAYS ON THE THEORY OF SEXUALITY. THE SEXUAL ABERRATIONS. THE SEXUAL INSTINCT IN NEUROTICS. — 1905D 7/163

THREE ESSAYS ON THE THEORY OF SEXUALITY. THE SEXUAL ABERRATIONS. COMPONENT INSTINCTS AND EROTOGENIC ZONES. — 1905D 7/167

THREE ESSAYS ON THE THEORY OF SEXUALITY. THE SEXUAL ABERRATIONS. REASONS FOR THE APPARENT PREPONDERANCE OF PERVERSE SEXUALITY IN THE PSYCHONEUROSES. INTIMATION OF THE INFANTILE CHARACTER OF SEXUALITY. — 1905D 7/170

ABRAHAM

KARL ABRAHAM. — 1926B20/277

ABSTRACTS

ABSTRACTS OF THE SCIENTIFIC WRITINGS OF DR. SIGM. FREUD 1877-1897. — 1897B 3/225

ABSURD

THE INTERPRETATION OF DREAMS. THE DREAM-WORK. ABSURD DREAMS - INTELLECTUAL ACTIVITY IN DREAMS. — 1900A 5/426

ABSURDITY

JOKES AND THEIR RELATION TO THE UNCONSCIOUS. ANALYTIC PART. THE TECHNIQUE OF JOKES. PUNS; ABSURDITY AS A JOKE TECHNIQUE. — 1905C 8/ 47

ACCOUNTS

GROUP PSYCHOLOGY AND THE ANALYSIS OF THE EGO. OTHER ACCOUNTS OF COLLECTIVE MENTAL LIFE. — 1921C18/ 82

ACQUISITION

THE ACQUISITION AND CONTROL OF FIRE. — 1932A22/185

ACROPOLIS

A DISTURBANCE OF MEMORY ON THE ACROPOLIS. — 1936A22/239

ACTION

THE SUBTLETIES OF A FAULTY ACTION. — 1935B22/233

ACTIONS

THE PSYCHOPATHOLOGY OF EVERYDAY LIFE. BUNGLED ACTIONS. — 1901B 6/162

THE PSYCHOPATHOLOGY OF EVERYDAY LIFE. SYMPTOMATIC AND CHANCE ACTIONS. — 1901B 6/191

OBSESSIVE ACTIONS AND RELIGIOUS PRACTICES. — 1907B 9/115

ACTIVITY

THE INTERPRETATION OF DREAMS. THE DREAM-WORK. ABSURD DREAMS - INTELLECTUAL ACTIVITY IN DREAMS. — 1900A 5/426

ACUTE

TWO SHORT REVIEWS. AVERBECK'S ACUTE NEURASTHENIA AND WEIR MITCHELL'S NEURASTHENIA AND HYSTERIA. — 1887B 1/ 35

ADDENDUM

NOTES UPON A CASE OF OBSESSIONAL NEUROSIS. ADDENDUM: ORIGINAL RECORD OF THE CASE. (RAT-MAN). — 1955A10/251

ADDICTION

LETTER 79. (MASTURBATION, ADDICTION AND OBSESSIONAL NEUROSIS.). — 1950A 1/272

ADDRESS

ADDRESS TO THE SOCIETY OF B'NAI-B'RITH. — 1941E20/271

ADLER

ON THE HISTORY OF THE PSYCHOANALYTIC MOVEMENT. DEPARTURES OF JUNG AND ADLER. — 1914D14/ 42

ADVANCE

LINES OF ADVANCE IN PSYCHOANALYTIC THERAPY. — 1919A17/157

MOSES AND MONOTHEISM: THREE ESSAYS. MOSES, HIS PEOPLE AND MONOTHEIST RELIGION. THE ADVANCE IN INTELLECTUALITY. — 1939A23/111

AETIOLOGICAL

LETTER 14. (COITUS-INTERRUPTUS AS AN AETIOLOGICAL FACTOR.). — 1950A 1/184

AETIOLOGY

OBSESSIONS AND PHOBIAS: THEIR PSYCHICAL MECHANISM AND THEIR AETIOLOGY. APPENDIX: FREUD S VIEWS ON PHOBIAS. — 3/ 83

ON THE GROUNDS FOR DETACHING A PARTICULAR SYNDROME FROM NEURASTHENIA UNDER THE DESCRIPTION ANXIETY NEUROSIS. INCIDENCE AND AETIOLOGY OF ANXIETY NEUROSIS. — 1895B 3/ 99

OBSESSIONS AND PHOBIAS: THEIR PSYCHICAL MECHANISM AND THEIR AETIOLOGY. — 1895C 3/ 71

HEREDITY AND THE AETIOLOGY OF THE NEUROSES. — 1896A 3/141

FURTHER REMARKS ON THE NEUROPSYCHOSES OF DEFENCE. THE SPECIFIC AETIOLOGY OF HYSTERIA. — 1896B 3/162

THE AETIOLOGY OF HYSTERIA. — 1896C 3/189

SEXUALITY IN THE AETIOLOGY OF THE NEUROSES. — 1898A 3/261

MY VIEWS ON THE PART PLAYED BY SEXUALITY IN THE AETIOLOGY OF THE NEUROSES. — 1906A 7/271

INTRODUCTORY LECTURES ON PSYCHOANALYSIS. GENERAL THEORY OF THE NEUROSIS. SOME THOUGHTS ON DEVELOPMENT AND REGRESSION - AETIOLOGY. — 1916X16/339

DRAFT A. (AETIOLOGY OF ACTUAL NEUROSES.). — 1950A 1/177

DRAFT B. THE AETIOLOGY OF THE NEUROSES. — 1950A 1/179

DRAFT D. ON THE AETIOLOGY AND THEORY OF THE MAJOR NEUROSES. — 1950A 1/186

LETTER 46. (FOUR PERIODS OF LIFE AND AETIOLOGY.). — 1950A 1/229

AGE

LETTER 59. (AGE OF HYSTERICAL FANTASIES.). — 1950A 1/244

AGENCIES

ANALYSIS TERMINABLE AND INTERMINABLE. THE STRENGTH OF THE INSTINCTS VIS-A-VIS THE OTHER PSYCHICAL AGENCIES. — 1937C23/224

AGGRESSION

CIVILIZATION AND ITS DISCONTENTS. SECURITY AT THE COST OF RESTRICTING SEXUALITY AND AGGRESSION. — 1930A21/108

CIVILIZATION AND ITS DISCONTENTS. ARGUMENTS FOR AN INSTINCT OF AGGRESSION AND DESTRUCTION. — 1930A21/117

AGGRESSIVENESS

ANALYSIS TERMINABLE AND INTERMINABLE. CONSTITUTIONAL VARIABLES IN EGO, LIBIDO AND FREE AGGRESSIVENESS. — 1937C23/240

AICHHORN'S

PREFACE TO AICHHORN'S WAYWARD YOUTH. — 1925F19/273

AIM

THREE ESSAYS ON THE THEORY OF SEXUALITY. THE SEXUAL ABERRATIONS. DEVIATIONS IN RESPECT OF THE SEXUAL AIM. ANATOMICAL EXTENSIONS. FIXATION OF PRELIMINARY SEXUAL AIMS. — 1905D 7/149

THREE ESSAYS ON THE THEORY OF SEXUALITY. INFANTILE SEXUALITY. THE SEXUAL AIM OF INFANTILE SEXUALITY. — 1905D 7/183

AIMS

THREE ESSAYS ON THE THEORY OF SEXUALITY. THE SEXUAL ABERRATIONS. DEVIATIONS IN RESPECT OF THE SEXUAL AIM. ANATOMICAL EXTENSIONS. FIXATION OF PRELIMINARY SEXUAL AIMS. — 1905D 7/149

FEMALE SEXUALITY. GIRL'S PRE-OEDIPAL SEXUAL AIMS TOWARD MOTHER. — 1931B21/235

ALTERATIONS

ANALYSIS TERMINABLE AND INTERMINABLE. ALTERATIONS OF THE EGO AFFECT PROGNOSIS. — 1937C23/234

AMBIVALENCE

TOTEM AND TABOO. TABOO AND EMOTIONAL AMBIVALENCE (1). — 1912X13/ 18

TOTEM AND TABOO. TABOO AND EMOTIONAL AMBIVALENCE. PARALLEL BETWEEN TABOO AND OBSESSIONAL NEUROSIS. — 1912X13/ 26

TOTEM AND TABOO. TABOO AND EMOTIONAL AMBIVALENCE. THE TREATMENT OF ENEMIES. — 1912X13/ 35

TOTEM AND TABOO. TABOO AND EMOTIONAL AMBIVALENCE. THE TABOO UPON RULERS. — 1912X13/ 41

TOTEM AND TABOO. TABOO AND EMOTIONAL AMBIVALENCE. THE TABOO UPON THE DEAD. TABOO AND CONSCIENCE. — 1912X13/ 51

ANAL

CHARACTER AND ANAL EROTISM. — 1908B 9/167

ANATOMICAL

THREE ESSAYS ON THE THEORY OF SEXUALITY. THE SEXUAL
ABERRATIONS. DEVIATIONS IN RESPECT OF THE SEXUAL AIM.
ANATOMICAL EXTENSIONS. FIXATION OF PRELIMINARY SEXUAL
AIMS.   1905D 7/149

SOME PSYCHICAL CONSEQUENCES OF THE ANATOMICAL
DISTINCTION BETWEEN THE SEXES.   1925J19/243

SOME PSYCHICAL CONSEQUENCES OF THE ANATOMICAL
DISTINCTION BETWEEN THE SEXES.   1925J19/248

ANDREAS-SALOME

LOU ANDREAS-SALOME.   1937A23/297

ANGEWANDTEN

PROSPECTUS FOR SCHRIFTEN ZUR ANGEWANDTEN SEELENKUNDE.   1907E 9/248

ANGST

ON THE GROUNDS FOR DETACHING A PARTICULAR SYNDROME FROM
NEURASTHENIA UNDER THE DESCRIPTION ANXIETY NEUROSIS.
THE TERM ANGST AND ITS ENGLISH TRANSLATION.   3/116

ANIMAL

TOTEM AND TABOO. THE RETURN OF TOTEMISM IN CHILDHOOD.
ANIMAL PHOBIAS. SACRIFICIAL FEASTS.   1912X13/126

ANIMALS

THREE ESSAYS ON THE THEORY OF SEXUALITY. THE SEXUAL
ABERRATIONS. DEVIATIONS IN RESPECT OF THE SEXUAL
OBJECT. INVERSION. SEXUALLY IMMATURE PERSONS AND
ANIMALS AS SEXUAL OBJECTS.   1905D 7/136

ANIMISIM

TOTEM AND TABOO. ANIMISIM, MAGIC, OMNIPOTENCE OF
THOUGHTS. OMNIPOTENCE OF THOUGHTS. TOTEMISM IS A
SYSTEM.   1912X13/ 85

ANIMISM

TOTEM AND TABOO. ANIMISM, MAGIC AND THE OMNIPOTENCE OF
THOUGHTS. ANIMISM. MAGIC.   1912X13/ 75

ANNA-O

STUDIES ON HYSTERIA. CASE HISTORIES: FRAULEIN ANNA-O.   1895D 2/ 21

ANTI-SEMITISM

A COMMENT ON ANTI-SEMITISM.   1938A23/287

ANTI-SEMITISM IN ENGLAND.   1938D23/301

ANTITHETICAL

THE ANTITHETICAL MEANING OF PRIMAL WORDS.   1910E11/153

ANXIETY

ON THE GROUNDS FOR DETACHING A PARTICULAR SYNDROME FROM
NEURASTHENIA UNDER THE DESCRIPTION ANXIETY NEUROSIS.
THE TERM ANGST AND ITS ENGLISH TRANSLATION.   3/116

ON THE GROUNDS FOR DETACHING A PARTICULAR SYNDROME FROM
NEURASTHENIA UNDER THE DESCRIPTION ANXIETY NEUROSIS.
THE CLINICAL SYMPTOMATOLOGY OF ANXIETY NEUROSIS.   1895B 3/ 90

ON THE GROUNDS FOR DETACHING A PARTICULAR SYNDROME FROM
NEURASTHENIA UNDER THE DESCRIPTION ANXIETY NEUROSIS.
INCIDENCE AND AETIOLOGY OF ANXIETY NEUROSIS.   1895B 3/ 99

ON THE GROUNDS FOR DETACHING A PARTICULAR SYNDROME FROM
NEURASTHENIA UNDER THE DESCRIPTION ANXIETY NEUROSIS.
FIRST STEPS TOWARDS A THEORY OF ANXIETY NEUROSIS.   1895B 3/106

ON THE GROUNDS FOR DETACHING A PARTICULAR SYNDROME FROM
NEURASTHENIA UNDER THE DESCRIPTION ANXIETY NEUROSIS.
RELATION TO OTHER NEUROSES.   1895B 3/112

A REPLY TO CRITICISMS OF MY PAPER ON ANXIETY NEUROSIS.   1895F 3/121

THE INTERPRETATION OF DREAMS. THE PSYCHOLOGY OF THE
DREAM PROCESSES. AROUSAL BY DREAMS - THE FUNCTION OF
DREAMS - ANXIETY DREAMS.   1900A 5/573

PREFACE TO WILHELM STEKEL'S NERVOUS ANXIETY STATES AND
THEIR TREATMENT.   1908F 9/250

INTRODUCTORY LECTURES ON PSYCHOANALYSIS. GENERAL THEORY
OF THE NEUROSES. ANXIETY.   1916X16/392

INHIBITIONS, SYMPTOMS AND ANXIETY.   1926D20/ 77

INHIBITIONS, SYMPTOMS AND ANXIETY. INHIBITIONS REFLECT
RESTRICTIONS OF EGO FUNCTIONS.   1926D20/ 87

INHIBITIONS, SYMPTOMS AND ANXIETY. SYMPTOMS REFLECT
INTERSYSTEMIC CONFLICTS.   1926D20/ 91

INHIBITIONS, SYMPTOMS AND ANXIETY. RELATION OF EGO TO
THE ID AND TO SYMPTOMS.   1926D20/ 97

INHIBITIONS, SYMPTOMS AND ANXIETY. ANXIETY PRODUCES
REPRESSION.   1926D20/101

INHIBITIONS, SYMPTOMS AND ANXIETY. DEFENSES OTHER THAN

ANXIETY   CONTINUATIO

REPRESSION.   1926D20/111

INHIBITIONS, SYMPTOMS AND ANXIETY. UNDOING AND
ISOLATION.   1926D20/119

INHIBITIONS, SYMPTOMS AND ANXIETY. ANXIETY IS A SIGNAL
OF DANGEROUS SEPARATION.   1926D20/124

INHIBITIONS, SYMPTOMS AND ANXIETY. ANXIETY REPRODUCES
FEELINGS OF HELPLESSNESS.   1926D20/132

INHIBITIONS, SYMPTOMS AND ANXIETY. RELATION BETWEEN
SYMPTOM FORMATION AND ANXIETY.   1926D20/144

INHIBITIONS, SYMPTOMS AND ANXIETY. REPETITION IS THE
CONSEQUENCE OF REPRESSION.   1926D20/150

INHIBITIONS, SYMPTOMS AND ANXIETY. MODIFICATION OF
EARLIER VIEWS.   1926D20/157

INHIBITIONS, SYMPTOMS AND ANXIETY. SUPPLEMENTARY
REMARKS ON ANXIETY.   1926D20/164

INHIBITIONS, SYMPTOMS AND ANXIETY. ANXIETY, PAIN AND
MOURNING.   1926D20/169

INHIBITIONS, SYMPTOMS AND ANXIETY. REPRESSION AND
DEFENCE.   1926D20/173

NEW INTRODUCTORY LECTURES ON PSYCHOANALYSIS. ANXIETY
AND INSTINCTUAL LIFE.   1933A22/ 81

DRAFT E. HOW ANXIETY ORIGINATES.   1950A 1/189

APPARATUS

AN OUTLINE OF PSYCHOANALYSIS. THE MIND AND ITS
WORKINGS. THE PSYCHICAL APPARATUS.   1940A23/144

AN OUTLINE OF PSYCHOANALYSIS. THE THEORETICAL YIELD.
THE PSYCHICAL APPARATUS AND THE EXTERNAL WORLD.   1940A23/195

THE FUNCTIONING OF THE APPARATUS; THE PATHS OF
CONDUCTION; THE EXPERIENCE OF SATISFACTION; THE
EXPERIENCE OF PAIN; AFFECTS AND WISHFUL STATES.   1950A 1/312

APPLICATIONS

NEW INTRODUCTORY LECTURES ON PSYCHOANALYSIS.
EXPLANATIONS, APPLICATIONS AND ORIENTATIONS.   1933A22/136

APPROACH

THE UNCANNY. LINGUISTIC APPROACH TO THE UNCANNY.   1919H17/219

APPROACHES

INTRODUCTORY LECTURES ON PSYCHOANALYSIS. DREAMS.
DIFFICULTIES AND FIRST APPROACHES.   1916X15/ 83

ARCHAIC

INTRODUCTORY LECTURES ON PSYCHOANALYSIS. DREAMS. THE
ARCHAIC FEATURES AND INFANTILISM OF DREAMS.   1916X15/199

ARCHITECTURE

DRAFT L. (ARCHITECTURE OF HYSTERIA.).   1950A 1/248

ARGUMENTS

BEYOND THE PLEASURE PRINCIPLE. BIOLOGICAL ARGUMENTS FOR
DEATH INSTINCTS. SUMMARY.   1920G18/ 44

CIVILIZATION AND ITS DISCONTENTS. ARGUMENTS FOR AN
INSTINCT OF AGGRESSION AND DESTRUCTION.   1930A21/117

ARMY

GROUP PSYCHOLOGY AND THE ANALYSIS OF THE EGO. TWO
ARTIFICIAL GROUPS: THE CHURCH AND THE ARMY.   1921C18/ 93

AROUSAL

THE INTERPRETATION OF DREAMS. THE PSYCHOLOGY OF THE
DREAM PROCESSES. AROUSAL BY DREAMS - THE FUNCTION OF
DREAMS - ANXIETY DREAMS.   1900A 5/573

ARTIFICIAL

GROUP PSYCHOLOGY AND THE ANALYSIS OF THE EGO. TWO
ARTIFICIAL GROUPS: THE CHURCH AND THE ARMY.   1921C18/ 93

ASSESSMENT

PAPERS ON METAPSYCHOLOGY. THE UNCONSCIOUS. ASSESSMENT
OF THE UNCONSCIOUS.   1915E14/196

ASSOCIATIONS

ASSOCIATIONS OF A FOUR-YEAR-OLD CHILD.   1920D18/266

ATEN

MOSES AND MONOTHEISM: THREE ESSAYS. IF MOSES WAS AN
EGYPTIAN. COMPARISON OF JEWISH AND ATEN RELIGIONS.   1939A23/ 24

ATTACKS

SOME GENERAL REMARKS ON HYSTERICAL ATTACKS.   1909A 9/227

CHILDHOOD

LETTER 97. (CHILDHOOD ENURESIS.). — 1950A 1/275

CHILDREN

THE SEXUAL ENLIGHTENMENT OF CHILDREN. — 1907C 9/129

ON THE SEXUAL THEORIES OF CHILDREN. — 1908C 9/205

TABOO AND TOTEM. THE RETURN OF TOTEMISM IN CHILDREN. THE ORIGIN OF TOTEMISM; THE ORIGIN OF EXOGAMY AND ITS RELATION TO TOTEMISM. — 1912X13/108

TWO LIES TOLD BY CHILDREN. — 1913G12/303

INTRODUCTORY LECTURES ON PSYCHOANALYSIS. DREAMS. CHILDREN S DREAMS. — 1916X15/126

BEYOND THE PLEASURE PRINCIPLE. REVIEW OF THE PLEASURE PRINCIPLE. TRAUMATIC NEUROSIS AND CHILDREN S PLAY ARE REPETITIONS. — 1920G18/ 7

LETTER 73. (CHILDREN S SPEECH DURING SLEEP.). — 1950A 1/267

CHOICE

A SPECIAL TYPE OF CHOICE OF OBJECT MADE BY MEN. (CONTRIBUTIONS TO THE PSYCHOLOGY OF LOVE). — 1910H11/163

THE DISPOSITION TO OBSESSIONAL NEUROSIS. A CONTRIBUTION TO THE PROBLEM OF CHOICE OF NEUROSIS. — 1913I12/311

LETTER 125. (CHOICE OF NEUROSIS.). — 1950A 1/279

CHRISTMAS

DRAFT K. THE NEUROSES OF DEFENCE. (A CHRISTMAS FAIRY TALE.). — 1950A 1/220

CHRONIC

FURTHER REMARKS ON THE NEUROPSYCHOSIS OF DEFENSE. ANALYSIS OF A CASE OF CHRONIC PARANOIA. — 1896B 3/174

CHRONOLOGY

STUDIES ON HYSTERIA. APPENDIX A: THE CHRONOLOGY OF THE CASE OF FRAU EMMY-VON-N. APPENDIX B: LIST OF WRITINGS BY FREUD DEALING PRINCIPALLY WITH CONVERSION HYSTERIA. — 1895D 2/307

CHURCH

GROUP PSYCHOLOGY AND THE ANALYSIS OF THE EGO. TWO ARTIFICIAL GROUPS: THE CHURCH AND THE ARMY. — 1921C18/ 93

CIVILIZATION

THE FUTURE OF AN ILLUSION. CIVILIZATION RESTS UPON RENUNCIATION OF INSTINCTUAL WISHES. — 1927C21/ 3

THE FUTURE OF AN ILLUSION. RELATIONS BETWEEN CIVILIZATION AND RELIGION. — 1927C21/ 34

CIVILIZATION AND ITS DISCONTENTS. — 1930A21/ 59

CIVILIZATION AND ITS DISCONTENTS. MAN'S NEED FOR RELIGION ARISES FROM FEELINGS OF HELPLESSNESS. — 1930A21/ 64

CIVILIZATION AND ITS DISCONTENTS. MAN COPES WITH UNHAPPINESS THROUGH DIVERSION, SUBSTITUTION AND INTOXICATION. — 1930A21/ 74

CIVILIZATION AND ITS DISCONTENTS. MAN S CONFLICT WITH CIVILIZATION: LIBERTY VERSUS EQUALITY. — 1930A21/ 86

CIVILIZATION AND ITS DISCONTENTS. TWO PILLARS OF CIVILIZATION: EROS AND ANANKE. — 1930A21/ 99

CIVILIZATION AND ITS DISCONTENTS. SECURITY AT THE COST OF RESTRICTING SEXUALITY AND AGGRESSION. — 1930A21/108

CIVILIZATION AND ITS DISCONTENTS. ARGUMENTS FOR AN INSTINCT OF AGGRESSION AND DESTRUCTION. — 1930A21/117

CIVILIZATION AND ITS DISCONTENTS. DEVELOPMENT OF THE SUPEREGO AND ITS SEVERITY. — 1930A21/123

CIVILIZATION AND ITS DISCONTENTS. CONCLUSIONS ABOUT EFFECTS OF CIVILIZATION UPON PSYCHE. — 1930A21/134

CIVILIZED

CIVILIZED SEXUAL MORALITY AND MODERN NERVOUS ILLNESS. — 1908D 9/177

CLAIMS

THE CLAIMS OF PSYCHOANALYSIS TO SCIENTIFIC INTEREST. THE PSYCHOLOGICAL INTEREST OF PSYCHOANALYSIS. — 1913J13/165

THE CLAIMS OF PSYCHOANALYSIS TO SCIENTIFIC INTEREST. THE CLAIMS OF PSYCHOANALYSIS TO THE INTEREST OF THE NON-PSYCHOLOGICAL SCIENCES. THE PHILOLOGICAL, PHILOSOPHICAL AND BIOLOGICAL INTEREST OF PSYCHOANALYSIS. — 1913J13/176

THE CLAIMS OF PSYCHOANALYSIS TO SCIENTIFIC INTEREST. THE CLAIMS OF PSYCHOANALYSIS TO THE INTEREST OF THE NON-PSYCHOLOGICAL SCIENCES. THE INTEREST OF PSYCHOANALYSIS FROM A DEVELOPMENTAL POINT OF VIEW. — 1913J13/182

CLASSES

THE EGO AND THE ID . THE TWO CLASSES OF INSTINCTS. — 1923B19/ 40

CLINICAL

ON THE GROUNDS FOR DETACHING A PARTICULAR SYNDROME FROM NEURASTHENIA UNDER THE DESCRIPTION ANXIETY NEUROSIS. THE CLINICAL SYMPTOMATOLOGY OF ANXIETY NEUROSIS. — 1895B 3/ 90

FRAGMENT OF AN ANALYSIS OF A CASE OF HYSTERIA. THE CLINICAL PICTURE. — 1905E 7/ 15

COGNITION

INTRODUCTION OF THE EGO PRIMARY AND SECONDARY PROCESS IN PSI; COGNITION AND REPRODUCTIVE THOUGHT; REMEMBERING AND JUDGING; THOUGHT AND REALITY. — 1950A 1/322

COITUS-INTERRUPTUS

LETTER 14. (COITUS-INTERRUPTUS AS AN AETIOLOGICAL FACTOR.). — 1950A 1/184

COLLABORATORS

AN AUTOBIOGRAPHICAL STUDY. COLLABORATORS, DEFECTORS AND NEW INSTINCT THEORY. — 1925D20/ 48

COLLECTION

DRAFT F. COLLECTION III. (TWO CASE HISTORIES.). — 1950A 1/195

COLLECTIVE

GROUP PSYCHOLOGY AND THE ANALYSIS OF THE EGO. OTHER ACCOUNTS OF COLLECTIVE MENTAL LIFE. — 1921C18/ 82

COMBINED

THE PSYCHOPATHOLOGY OF EVERYDAY LIFE. COMBINED PARAPRAXES. — 1901B 6/230

COMIC

JOKES AND THEIR RELATION TO THE UNCONSCIOUS. ANALYTIC PART. THE TECHNIQUE OF JOKES. RELATION OF JOKES TO THE COMIC; UNIFICATION AS A JOKE TECHNIQUE. — 1905C 8/ 60

JOKES AND THEIR RELATION TO THE UNCONSCIOUS. THEORETIC PART. JOKES AND THE SPECIES OF THE COMIC. — 1905C 8/181

JOKES AND THEIR RELATION TO THE UNCONSCIOUS. THEORETIC PART. JOKES AND THE SPECIES OF THE COMIC. PSYCHICAL LOCATION DISTINGUISHES JOKES FROM THE COMIC. — 1905C 8/199

JOKES AND THEIR RELATION TO THE UNCONSCIOUS. THEORETIC PART. JOKES AND THE SPECIES OF THE COMIC. DIFFERENCES BETWEEN JOKES AND COMIC. — 1905C 8/208

JOKES AND THEIR RELATION TO THE UNCONSCIOUS. THEORETIC PART. JOKES AND THE SPECIES OF THE COMIC. COMIC THINGS ARE NOT PROPER IN JOKES; RELATION OF HUMOUR TO JOKES. — 1905C 8/221

COMMUNICATION

STUDIES ON HYSTERIA. ON THE PSYCHICAL MECHANISM OF HYSTERICAL PHENOMENA: PRELIMINARY COMMUNICATION. — 1893A 2/ 1

PAPERS ON METAPSYCHOLOGY. THE UNCONSCIOUS. COMMUNICATION BETWEEN THE TWO SYSTEMS. — 1915E14/190

SKETCHES FOR THE PRELIMINARY COMMUNICATION OF 1893. ON THE THEORY OF HYSTERICAL ATTACKS. — 1941A 1/147

COMPARISON

MOSES AND MONOTHEISM: THREE ESSAYS. IF MOSES WAS AN EGYPTIAN. COMPARISON OF JEWISH AND ATEN RELIGIONS. — 1939A23/ 24

COMPLEX

NOTES UPON A CASE OF OBSESSIONAL NEUROSIS. EXTRACTS FROM THE CASE HISTORY. THE FATHER COMPLEX AND THE SOLUTION OF THE RAT IDEA. — 1909D10/200

TOTEM AND TABOO. RETURN OF TOTEMISM IN CHILDHOOD. OEDIPUS COMPLEX AND SOCIETY. — 1912X13/155

FROM THE HISTORY OF AN INFANTILE NEUROSIS. ANAL EROTISM AND THE CASTRATION COMPLEX. (WOLFMAN). — 1918B17/ 72

THE DISSOLUTION OF THE OEDIPUS COMPLEX. — 1924D19/173

FEMALE SEXUALITY. FEMALE OEDIPUS COMPLEX DIFFERS FROM MALE. — 1931B21/223

LETTER 71. (UNIVERSALITY OF OEDIPUS COMPLEX.). — 1950A 1/263

COMPULSION

NOTES UPON A CASE OF OBSESSIONAL NEUROSIS. INSTINCTUAL LIFE OF OBSESSIONAL NEUROTICS, AND THE ORIGINS OF COMPULSION AND DOUBT. — 1909D10/237

PSYCHOPATHOLOGY OF HYSTERIA: HYSTERICAL COMPULSION; THE GENESIS OF HYSTERICAL COMPULSION. — 1950A 1/347

CONCEPT

PAPERS ON METAPSYCHOLOGY. THE UNCONSCIOUS. JUSTIFICATION FOR THE CONCEPT OF THE UNCONSCIOUS. — 1915E14/166

EGO

ANALYSIS TERMINABLE AND INTERMINABLE. ALTERATIONS OF
THE EGO AFFECT PROGNOSIS.   1937C23/234

ANALYSIS TERMINABLE AND INTERMINABLE. CONSTITUTIONAL
VARIABLES IN EGO, LIBIDO AND FREE AGGRESSIVENESS.   1937C23/240

SPLITTING OF THE EGO IN THE PROCESS OF DEFENCE.   1940E23/271

INTRODUCTION OF THE EGO PRIMARY AND SECONDARY PROCESS
IN PSI: COGNITION AND REPRODUCTIVE THOUGHT: REMEMBERING
AND JUDGING: THOUGHT AND REALITY.   1950A 1/322

EGO-IDEAL

ON NARCISSISM. EGO-IDEAL, INHERITOR OF NARCISSISM.   1914C14/ 92

THE EGO AND THE ID . THE EGO AND THE SUPEREGO
(EGO-IDEAL).   1923B19/ 28

EGYPTIAN

MOSES AND MONOTHEISM: THREE ESSAYS. MOSES AN EGYPTIAN.   1939A23/ 7

MOSES AND MONOTHEISM: THREE ESSAYS. IF MOSES WAS AN
EGYPTIAN: IF MOSES WAS AN EGYPTIAN. MOSES INTRODUCED AN
EXCLUSIVE RELIGION.   1939A23/ 17

MOSES AND MONOTHEISM: THREE ESSAYS. IF MOSES WAS AN
EGYPTIAN. COMPARISON OF JEWISH AND ATEN RELIGIONS.   1939A23/ 24

MOSES AND MONOTHEISM: THREE ESSAYS. IF MOSES WAS AN
EGYPTIAN. TWO GODS AND TWO MOSES.   1939A23/ 30

MOSES AND MONOTHEISM: THREE ESSAYS. IF MOSES WAS AN
EGYPTIAN.   1939A23/ 36

MOSES AND MONOTHEISM: THREE ESSAYS. IF MOSES WAS AN
EGYPTIAN. ONE HUNDRED YEARS OF HISTORY SUPPRESSED.   1939A23/ 41

MOSES AND MONOTHEISM: THREE ESSAYS. IF MOSES WAS AN
EGYPTIAN. THE MURDER OF MOSES.   1939A23/ 47

EINSTEIN

WHY WAR?: LETTER FROM EINSTEIN.   1933B22/199

EITINGON'S

PREFACE TO MAX EITINGON'S REPORT ON THE BERLIN
PSYCHOANALYTICAL POLICLINIC.   1923G19/285

ELECTRICAL

INTRODUCTION TO PSYCHOANALYSIS AND THE WAR NEUROSES.
MEMORANDUM ON THE ELECTRICAL TREATMENT OF WAR
NEUROTICS.   1955C17/211

ELISABETH-VON-R

STUDIES ON HYSTERIA. CASE HISTORIES: FRAULEIN
ELISABETH-VON-R.   1895D 2/135

EMBARASSING

THE INTERPRETATION OF DREAMS. THE MATERIAL AND SOURCES
OF DREAMS. TYPICAL DREAMS: EMBARASSING DREAMS OF BEING
NAKED.   1900A 4/242

EMMY-VON-N

STUDIES ON HYSTERIA. CASE HISTORIES: FRAU EMMY-VON-N.   1895D 2/ 48

STUDIES ON HYSTERIA. APPENDIX A: THE CHRONOLOGY OF THE
CASE OF FRAU EMMY-VON-N. APPENDIX B: LIST OF WRITINGS
BY FREUD DEALING PRINCIPALLY WITH CONVERSION HYSTERIA.   1895D 2/307

EMOTIONAL

TOTEM AND TABOO. TABOO AND EMOTIONAL AMBIVALENCE (1).   1912X13/ 18

TOTEM AND TABOO. TABOO AND EMOTIONAL AMBIVALENCE.
PARALLEL BETWEEN TABOO AND OBSESSIONAL NEUROSIS.   1912X13/ 26

TOTEM AND TABOO. TABOO AND EMOTIONAL AMBIVALENCE. THE
TREATMENT OF ENEMIES.   1912X13/ 35

TOTEM AND TABOO. TABOO AND EMOTIONAL AMBIVALENCE. THE
TABOO UPON RULERS.   1912X13/ 41

TOTEM AND TABOO. TABOO AND EMOTIONAL AMBIVALENCE. THE
TABOO UPON THE DEAD. TABOO AND CONSCIENCE.   1912X13/ 51

EMOTIONS

PAPERS ON METAPSYCHOLOGY. THE UNCONSCIOUS. UNCONSCIOUS
EMOTIONS.   1915E14/177

ENCYCLOPEDIA

TWO ENCYCLOPEDIA ARTICLES. PSYCHOANALYSIS.   1923A18/234

TWO ENCYCLOPEDIA ARTICLES. THE LIBIDO THEORY.   1923A18/255

ENEMIES

TOTEM AND TABOO. TABOO AND EMOTIONAL AMBIVALENCE. THE
TREATMENT OF ENEMIES.   1912X13/ 35

ENGLAND

ANTI-SEMITISM IN ENGLAND.   1938D23/301

CONTINUATIO ENGLISH

ON THE GROUNDS FOR DETACHING A PARTICULAR SYNDROME FROM
NEURASTHENIA UNDER THE DESCRIPTION ANXIETY NEUROSIS.
THE TERM ANGST AND ITS ENGLISH TRANSLATION.   3/116

THE INTERPRETATION OF DREAMS. PREFACE TO THE FIRST,
SECOND, THIRD, FOURTH, FIFTH, SIXTH, EIGHTH EDITIONS
AND THIRD (REVISED) ENGLISH EDITION.   1900A 4/XXI

ENLIGHTENMENT

THE SEXUAL ENLIGHTENMENT OF CHILDREN.   1907C 9/129

ENURESIS

LETTER 97. (CHILDHOOD ENURESIS.).   1950A 1/275

ENVIRONMENT

FROM THE HISTORY OF AN INFANTILE NEUROSIS. GENERAL
SURVEY OF THE PATIENT'S ENVIRONMENT AND OF THE HISTORY
OF THE CASE. (WOLFMAN).   1918B17/ 13

EPHESIANS

GREAT IS DIANA OF THE EPHESIANS.   1911F12/342

EQUALITY

CIVILIZATION AND ITS DISCONTENTS. MAN S CONFLICT WITH
CIVILIZATION: LIBERTY VERSUS EQUALITY.   1930A21/ 86

EROS

CIVILIZATION AND ITS DISCONTENTS. TWO PILLARS OF
CIVILIZATION: EROS AND ANANKE.   1930A21/ 99

EROTIC

ON NARCISSISM. NARCISSISM IN ORGANIC DISEASE,
HYPOCHONDRIA, AND EROTIC LIFE.   1914C14/ 82

EROTISM

CHARACTER AND ANAL EROTISM.   1908B 9/167

ON TRANSFORMATIONS OF INSTINCT AS EXEMPLIFIED IN ANAL
EROTISM.   1917C17/125

FROM THE HISTORY OF AN INFANTILE NEUROSIS. ANAL EROTISM
AND THE CASTRATION COMPLEX. (WOLFMAN).   1918B17/ 72

EROTOGENIC

THREE ESSAYS ON THE THEORY OF SEXUALITY. THE SEXUAL
ABERRATIONS. COMPONENT INSTINCTS AND EROTOGENIC ZONES.   1905D 7/167

LETTER 75. (EROTOGENIC ZONES.).   1950A 1/268

ERRORS

THE PSYCHOPATHOLOGY OF EVERYDAY LIFE. ERRORS.   1901B 6/217

ESSAYS

THREE ESSAYS ON THE THEORY OF SEXUALITY. APPENDIX: LIST
OF WRITINGS BY FREUD DEALING PREDOMINANTLY OR LARGELY
WITH SEXUALITY.   7/244

THREE ESSAYS ON THE THEORY OF SEXUALITY.   1905D 7/125

THREE ESSAYS ON THE THEORY OF SEXUALITY. THE SEXUAL
ABERRATIONS. DEVIATIONS IN RESPECT OF THE SEXUAL
OBJECT. INVERSION. SEXUALLY IMMATURE PERSONS AND
ANIMALS AS SEXUAL OBJECTS.   1905D 7/136

THREE ESSAYS ON THE THEORY OF SEXUALITY. THE SEXUAL
ABERRATIONS. DEVIATIONS IN RESPECT OF THE SEXUAL AIM.
ANATOMICAL EXTENSIONS. FIXATION OF PRELIMINARY SEXUAL
AIMS.   1905D 7/149

THREE ESSAYS ON THE THEORY OF SEXUALITY. THE SEXUAL
ABERRATIONS. THE PERVERSIONS-IN GENERAL.   1905D 7/160

THREE ESSAYS ON THE THEORY OF SEXUALITY. THE SEXUAL
ABERRATIONS. THE SEXUAL INSTINCT IN NEUROTICS.   1905D 7/163

THREE ESSAYS ON THE THEORY OF SEXUALITY. THE SEXUAL
ABERRATIONS. COMPONENT INSTINCTS AND EROTOGENIC ZONES.   1905D 7/167

THREE ESSAYS ON THE THEORY OF SEXUALITY. THE SEXUAL
ABERRATIONS. REASONS FOR THE APPARENT PREPONDERANCE OF
PERVERSE SEXUALITY IN THE PSYCHONEUROSES. INTIMATION OF
THE INFANTILE CHARACTER OF SEXUALITY.   1905D 7/170

THREE ESSAYS ON THE THEORY OF SEXUALITY. INFANTILE
SEXUALITY: THE PERIOD OF SEXUAL LATENCY IN CHILDHOOD
AND ITS INTERRUPTIONS.   1905D 7/173

THREE ESSAYS ON THE THEORY OF SEXUALITY. INFANTILE
SEXUALITY. THE MANIFESTATIONS OF INFANTILE SEXUALITY.   1905D 7/179

THREE ESSAYS ON THE THEORY OF SEXUALITY. INFANTILE
SEXUALITY. THE SEXUAL AIM OF INFANTILE SEXUALITY.   1905D 7/183

THREE ESSAYS ON THE THEORY OF SEXUALITY. INFANTILE
SEXUALITY. MASTURBATORY SEXUAL MANIFESTATIONS.   1905D 7/185

THREE ESSAYS ON THE THEORY OF SEXUALITY. INFANTILE
SEXUALITY. THE SEXUAL RESEARCHES OF CHILDHOOD.   1905D 7/194

THREE ESSAYS ON THE THEORY OF SEXUALITY. INFANTILE

MAN

CIVILIZATION AND ITS DISCONTENTS. MAN COPES WITH
UNHAPPINESS THROUGH DIVERSION, SUBSTITUTION AND
INTOXICATION.   1930A21/ 74

CIVILIZATION AND ITS DISCONTENTS. MAN S CONFLICT WITH
CIVILIZATION: LIBERTY VERSUS EQUALITY.   1930A21/ 86

MOSES AND MONOTHEISM: THREE ESSAYS. MOSES, HIS PEOPLE
AND MONOTHEIST RELIGION. THE GREAT MAN.   1939A23/107

MAN'S

CIVILIZATION AND ITS DISCONTENTS. MAN'S NEED FOR
RELIGION ARISES FROM FEELINGS OF HELPLESSNESS.   1930A21/ 64

MANIFESTATIONS

THREE ESSAYS ON THE THEORY OF SEXUALITY. INFANTILE
SEXUALITY. THE MANIFESTATIONS OF INFANTILE SEXUALITY.   1905D 7/179

THREE ESSAYS ON THE THEORY OF SEXUALITY. INFANTILE
SEXUALITY. MASTURBATORY SEXUAL MANIFESTATIONS.   1905D 7/185

MANN

TO THOMAS MANN ON HIS SIXTIETH BIRTHDAY.   1935C22/255

MASOCHISM

THE ECONOMIC PROBLEM OF MASOCHISM.   1924C19/157

MASTURBATION

CONTRIBUTIONS TO A DISCUSSION ON MASTURBATION.   1912F12/239

LETTER 79. (MASTURBATION, ADDICTION AND OBSESSIONAL
NEUROSIS.).   1950A 1/272

MASTURBATORY

THREE ESSAYS ON THE THEORY OF SEXUALITY. INFANTILE
SEXUALITY. MASTURBATORY SEXUAL MANIFESTATIONS.   1905D 7/185

MEALS

TOTEM AND TABOO. THE RETURN OF TOTEMISM IN CHILDHOOD.
RELATION OF TOTEM MEALS TO FATHER AND GOD.   1912X13/140

MEANING

FIVE LECTURES ON PSYCHOANALYSIS. FIRST LECTURE.
SYMPTOMS HAVE PSYCHOLOGICAL MEANING.   1910A11/ 9

THE ANTITHETICAL MEANING OF PRIMAL WORDS.   1910E11/153

MEANINGS

PAPERS ON METAPSYCHOLOGY. THE UNCONSCIOUS. VARIOUS
MEANINGS OF THE UNCONSCIOUS - THE TOPOGRAPHICAL POINT
OF VIEW.   1915E14/172

MECHANISM

OBSESSIONS AND PHOBIAS: THEIR PSYCHICAL MECHANISM AND
THEIR AETIOLOGY. APPENDIX: FREUD S VIEWS ON PHOBIAS.   3/ 83

STUDIES ON HYSTERIA. ON THE PSYCHICAL MECHANISM OF
HYSTERICAL PHENOMENA: PRELIMINARY COMMUNICATION.   1893A 2/ 1

ON THE PSYCHICAL MECHANISM OF HYSTERICAL PHENOMENA.   1893H 3/ 25

OBSESSIONS AND PHOBIAS: THEIR PSYCHICAL MECHANISM AND
THEIR AETIOLOGY.   1895C 3/ 71

FURTHER REMARKS ON THE NEUROPSYCHOSIS OF DEFENCE. THE
NATURE AND MECHANISM OF OBSESSIONAL NEUROSIS.   1896B 3/168

THE PSYCHICAL MECHANISM OF FORGETFULNESS.   1898B 3/287

JOKES AND THEIR RELATION TO THE UNCONSCIOUS. SYNTHETIC
PART. THE MECHANISM OF PLEASURE AND THE PSYCHOGENESIS
OF JOKES.   1905C 8/117

JOKES AND THEIR RELATION TO THE UNCONSCIOUS. SYNTHETIC
PART. THE MECHANISM OF PLEASURE AND THE PSYCHOGENESIS
OF JOKES. THE PURPOSE AND FUNCTIONS OF JOKES.   1905C 8/128

PSYCHOANALYTIC NOTES ON AN AUTOBIOGRAPHICAL ACCOUNT OF
A CASE OF PARANOIA (DEMENTIA PARANOIDES). ON THE
MECHANISM OF PARANOIA.   1911C12/ 59

MECHANISMS

SOME NEUROTIC MECHANISMS IN JEALOUSY, PARANOIA AND
HOMOSEXUALITY.   1922B18/221

MEDICAL

INTRODUCTION TO THE SPECIAL PSYCHOPATHOLOGY NUMBER OF
THE MEDICAL REVIEW OF REVIEWS.   1930C21/254

MEDUSA'S

MEDUSA'S HEAD.   1940C18/273

MELANCHOLIA

PAPERS ON METAPSYCHOLOGY. MOURNING AND MELANCHOLIA.   1917E14/237

PAPERS ON METAPSYCHOLOGY. MOURNING AND MELANCHOLIA.   1917E14/243

MELANCHOLIA   CONTINUATIO

DRAFT G. MELANCHOLIA.   1950A 1/200

MEMORIES

SCREEN MEMORIES.   1899A 3/301

THE PSYCHOPATHOLOGY OF EVERYDAY LIFE. CHILDHOOD
MEMORIES AND SCREEN MEMORIES.   1901B 6/ 43

LETTER 66. (DEFENSE AGAINST MEMORIES.).   1950A 1/257

LETTER 70. (FREUD S EARLY MEMORIES FROM
SELF-ANALYSIS.).   1950A 1/261

MEMORY

THE INTERPRETATION OF DREAMS. THE SCIENTIFIC LITERATURE
DEALING WITH THE PROBLEMS OF DREAMS. THE MATERIAL OF
DREAMS - MEMORY IN DREAMS.   1900A 4/ 11

LEONARDO-DA-VINCI AND A MEMORY OF HIS CHILDHOOD.   1910C11/ 59

LEONARDO-DA-VINCI AND A MEMORY OF HIS CHILDHOOD.
BIOGRAPHICAL MATERIAL.   1910C11/ 63

LEONARDO-DA-VINCI AND A MEMORY OF HIS CHILDHOOD.
LEONARDO'S CHILDHOOD MEMORY.   1910C11/ 82

LEONARDO-DA-VINCI AND A MEMORY OF HIS CHILDHOOD. SEXUAL
INTERPRETATION OF LEONARDO'S CHILDHOOD MEMORY.   1910C11/ 93

LEONARDO-DA-VINCI AND A MEMORY OF HIS CHILDHOOD. THE
BLISSFUL SMILES IN LEONARDO'S PAINTINGS.   1910C11/107

LEONARDO-DA-VINCI AND A MEMORY OF HIS CHILDHOOD.
EFFECTS OF FATHER-LOSS ON LEONARDO.   1910C11/119

LEONARDO-DA-VINCI AND A MEMORY OF HIS CHILDHOOD.
JUSTIFICATION OF PATHOBIOGRAPHY.   1910C11/130

A DISTURBANCE OF MEMORY ON THE ACROPOLIS.   1936A22/239

LETTER 52. (STRATIFICATION OF MEMORY TRACES.).   1950A 1/234

MEN

THREE ESSAYS ON THE THEORY OF SEXUALITY. THE
TRANSFORMATIONS OF PUBERTY. THE DIFFERENTIATION BETWEEN
MEN AND WOMEN.   1905D 7/219

A SPECIAL TYPE OF CHOICE OF OBJECT MADE BY MEN.
(CONTRIBUTIONS TO THE PSYCHOLOGY OF LOVE).   1910H11/163

MENTAL

THE INTERPRETATION OF DREAMS. THE SCIENTIFIC LITERATURE
DEALING WITH THE PROBLEMS OF DREAMS. THE RELATIONS
BETWEEN DREAMS AND MENTAL DISEASES.   1900A 4/ 88

PSYCHICAL (OR MENTAL) TREATMENT.   1905B 7/283

FORMULATIONS ON THE TWO PRINCIPLES OF MENTAL
FUNCTIONING.   1911B12/213

GROUP PSYCHOLOGY AND THE ANALYSIS OF THE EGO. OTHER
ACCOUNTS OF COLLECTIVE MENTAL LIFE.   1921C18/ 82

METAPSYCHOLOGICAL

PAPERS ON METAPSYCHOLOGY. A METAPSYCHOLOGICAL
SUPPLEMENT TO THE THEORY OF DREAMS.   1917D14/219

METAPSYCHOLOGY

PAPERS ON METAPSYCHOLOGY.   14/105

PAPERS ON METAPSYCHOLOGY. THE UNCONSCIOUS. APPENDIX A:
FREUD AND EWALD HERING. APPENDIX B: PSYCHO-PHYSICAL
PARALLELISM. APPENDIX C: WORDS AND THINGS.   1891B14/205

PAPERS ON METAPSYCHOLOGY. INSTINCTS AND THEIR
VICISSITUDES.   1915C14/111

PAPERS ON METAPSYCHOLOGY. INSTINCTS AND THEIR
VICISSITUDES.   1915C14/117

PAPERS ON METAPSYCHOLOGY. REPRESSION.   1915D14/141

PAPERS ON METAPSYCHOLOGY. REPRESSION.   1915D14/146

PAPERS ON METAPSYCHOLOGY. THE UNCONSCIOUS.   1915E14/159

PAPERS ON METAPSYCHOLOGY. THE UNCONSCIOUS.
JUSTIFICATION FOR THE CONCEPT OF THE UNCONSCIOUS.   1915E14/166

PAPERS ON METAPSYCHOLOGY. THE UNCONSCIOUS. VARIOUS
MEANINGS OF THE UNCONSCIOUS - THE TOPOGRAPHICAL POINT
OF VIEW.   1915E14/172

PAPERS ON METAPSYCHOLOGY. THE UNCONSCIOUS. UNCONSCIOUS
EMOTIONS.   1915E14/177

PAPERS ON METAPSYCHOLOGY. THE UNCONSCIOUS. TOPOGRAPHY
AND DYNAMICS OF REPRESSION.   1915E14/180

PAPERS ON METAPSYCHOLOGY. THE UNCONSCIOUS. THE SPECIAL
CHARACTERISTICS OF THE SYSTEM UCS.   1915E14/186

PAPERS ON METAPSYCHOLOGY. THE UNCONSCIOUS.
COMMUNICATION BETWEEN THE TWO SYSTEMS.   1915E14/190

NEUROSIS

FROM THE HISTORY OF AN INFANTILE NEUROSIS.
RECAPITULATIONS AND PROBLEMS. (WOLFMAN).   1918B17/104

BEYOND THE PLEASURE PRINCIPLE. REVIEW OF THE PLEASURE
PRINCIPLE. TRAUMATIC NEUROSIS AND CHILDREN S PLAY ARE
REPETITIONS.   1920G18/ 7

BEYOND THE PLEASURE PRINCIPLE. TRANSFERENCE NEUROSIS IS
A REPETITION.   1920G18/ 18

A SEVENTEENTH-CENTURY DEMONOLOGICAL NEUROSIS.   1923D19/ 69

A SEVENTEENTH-CENTURY DEMONOLOGICAL NEUROSIS. THE STORY
OF CHRISTOPH HAIZMANN THE PAINTER.   1923D19/ 73

A SEVENTEENTH-CENTURY DEMONOLOGICAL NEUROSIS. THE
MOTIVE FOR THE PACT WITH THE DEVIL.   1923D19/ 79

A SEVENTEENTH-CENTURY DEMONOLOGICAL NEUROSIS. THE DEVIL
AS FATHER-SUBSTITUTE.   1923D19/ 83

A SEVENTEENTH-CENTURY DEMONOLOGICAL NEUROSIS. THE TWO
BONDS.   1923D19/ 93

A SEVENTEENTH-CENTURY DEMONOLOGICAL NEUROSIS. THE
FURTHER COURSE OF THE NEUROSIS.   1923D19/100

NEUROSIS AND PSYCHOSIS.   1924B19/149

THE LOSS OF REALITY IN NEUROSIS AND PSYCHOSIS.   1924E19/183

LETTER 79. (MASTURBATION, ADDICTION AND OBSESSIONAL
NEUROSIS.).   1950A 1/272

LETTER 125. (CHOICE OF NEUROSIS.).   1950A 1/279

NOTES UPON A CASE OF OBSESSIONAL NEUROSIS. ADDENDUM:
ORIGINAL RECORD OF THE CASE. (RAT-MAN).   1955A10/251

NOTES UPON A CASE OF OBSESSIONAL NEUROSIS. ORIGINAL
RECORD OF THE CASE. (RAT-MAN).   1955A10/259

NEUROTIC

REVIEW OF WILHELM NEUTRA'S LETTERS TO NEUROTIC WOMEN.   1910M11/238

INTRODUCTORY LECTURES ON PSYCHOANALYSIS. GENERAL THEORY
OF THE NEUROSES. THE COMMON NEUROTIC STATE.   1916X16/378

SOME NEUROTIC MECHANISMS IN JEALOUSY, PARANOIA AND
HOMOSEXUALITY.   1922B18/221

NEUROTICS

THREE ESSAYS ON THE THEORY OF SEXUALITY. THE SEXUAL
ABERRATIONS. THE SEXUAL INSTINCT IN NEUROTICS.   1905D 7/163

NOTES UPON A CASE OF OBSESSIONAL NEUROSIS. SOME
PSYCHOLOGICAL PECULIARITIES OF OBSESSIONAL NEUROTICS:
THEIR ATTITUDE TOWARDS REALITY, SUPERSTITION AND DEATH.   1909D10/229

NOTES UPON A CASE OF OBSESSIONAL NEUROSIS. INSTINCTUAL
LIFE OF OBSESSIONAL NEUROTICS, AND THE ORIGINS OF
COMPULSION AND DOUBT.   1909D10/237

INTRODUCTION TO PSYCHOANALYSIS AND THE WAR NEUROSES.
MEMORANDUM ON THE ELECTRICAL TREATMENT OF WAR
NEUROTICS.   1955C17/211

NEUTRA'S

REVIEW OF WILHELM NEUTRA'S LETTERS TO NEUROTIC WOMEN.   1910M11/238

NON-PSYCHOLOGICAL

THE CLAIMS OF PSYCHOANALYSIS TO SCIENTIFIC INTEREST.
THE CLAIMS OF PSYCHOANALYSIS TO THE INTEREST OF THE
NON-PSYCHOLOGICAL SCIENCES. THE PHILOLOGICAL,
PHILOSOPHICAL AND BIOLOGICAL INTEREST OF
PSYCHOANALYSIS.   1913J13/176

THE CLAIMS OF PSYCHOANALYSIS TO SCIENTIFIC INTEREST.
THE CLAIMS OF PSYCHOANALYSIS TO THE INTEREST OF THE
NON-PSYCHOLOGICAL SCIENCES. THE INTEREST OF
PSYCHOANALYSIS FROM A DEVELOPMENTAL POINT OF VIEW.   1913J13/182

NORMAL

ATTEMPT TO REPRESENT NORMAL PSI PROCESSES   1950A 1/360

NOXAE

LETTER 18. (EFFECT OF SEXUAL NOXAE.).   1950A 1/188

NUNBERG'S

PREFACE TO HERMANN NUNBERG'S GENERAL THEORY OF THE
NEUROSES ON A PSYCHOANALYTIC BASIS.   1932B21/258

OBJECT

THREE ESSAYS ON THE THEORY OF SEXUALITY. THE SEXUAL
ABERRATIONS. DEVIATIONS IN RESPECT OF THE SEXUAL
OBJECT. INVERSION. SEXUALLY IMMATURE PERSONS AND
ANIMALS AS SEXUAL OBJECTS.   1905D 7/136

THREE ESSAYS ON THE THEORY OF SEXUALITY. THE
TRANSFORMATIONS OF PUBERTY. THE FINDING OF AN OBJECT.   1905D 7/222

A SPECIAL TYPE OF CHOICE OF OBJECT MADE BY MEN.
(CONTRIBUTIONS TO THE PSYCHOLOGY OF LOVE).   1910H11/163

CONTINUATION OBJECTS

THREE ESSAYS ON THE THEORY OF SEXUALITY. THE SEXUAL
ABERRATIONS. DEVIATIONS IN RESPECT OF THE SEXUAL
OBJECT. INVERSION. SEXUALLY IMMATURE PERSONS AND
ANIMALS AS SEXUAL OBJECTS.   1905D 7/136

OBSERVATION

OBSERVATION OF A SEVERE CASE OF HEMI-ANAESTHESIA IN A
HYSTERICAL MALE.   1886D 1/ 23

OBSERVATIONS

OBSERVATIONS AND EXAMPLES FROM ANALYTIC PRACTICE.   1913H13/193

PAPERS ON TECHNIQUE. OBSERVATIONS ON TRANSFERENCE LOVE.
(FURTHER RECOMMENDATIONS ON THE TECHNIQUE OF
PSYCHOANALYSIS).   1915A12/157

OBSESSION

A MYTHOLOGICAL PARALLEL TO A VISUAL OBSESSION.   1916B14/337

OBSESSIONAL

FURTHER REMARKS ON THE NEUROPSYCHOSIS OF DEFENCE. THE
NATURE AND MECHANISM OF OBSESSIONAL NEUROSIS.   1896B 3/168

NOTES UPON A CASE OF OBSESSIONAL NEUROSIS.   1909D10/153

NOTES UPON A CASE OF OBSESSIONAL NEUROSIS. EXTRACTS
FROM THE CASE HISTORY: THE BEGINNING OF THE TREATMENT.
INFANTILE SEXUALITY. (RAT-MAN).   1909D10/158

NOTES UPON A CASE OF OBSESSIONAL NEUROSIS. EXTRACTS
FROM THE CASE HISTORY. THE GREAT OBSESSIVE FEAR.
(RAT-MAN).   1909D10/165

NOTES UPON A CASE OF OBSESSIONAL NEUROSIS. EXTRACTS
FROM THE CASE HISTORY. INITIATION INTO THE NATURE OF
THE TREATMENT. (RAT-MAN).   1909D10/173

NOTES UPON A CASE OF OBSESSIONAL NEUROSIS. EXTRACTS
FROM THE CASE HISTORY. SOME OBSESSIONAL IDEAS AND THEIR
EXPLANATION. (RAT-MAN).   1909D10/186

NOTES UPON A CASE OF OBSESSIONAL NEUROSIS. EXTRACTS
FROM THE CASE HISTORY. THE PRECIPITATING CAUSE OF THE
ILLNESS. (RAT-MAN).   1909D10/195

NOTES UPON A CASE OF OBSESSIONAL NEUROSIS. EXTRACTS
FROM THE CASE HISTORY. THE FATHER COMPLEX AND THE
SOLUTION OF THE RAT IDEA.   1909D10/200

NOTES UPON A CASE OF OBSESSIONAL NEUROSIS. THEORETICAL
SECTION. SOME GENERAL CHARACTERISTICS OF OBSESSIONAL
STRUCTURES.   1909D10/221

NOTES UPON A CASE OF OBSESSIONAL NEUROSIS. SOME
PSYCHOLOGICAL PECULIARITIES OF OBSESSIONAL NEUROTICS:
THEIR ATTITUDE TOWARDS REALITY, SUPERSTITION AND DEATH.   1909D10/229

NOTES UPON A CASE OF OBSESSIONAL NEUROSIS. INSTINCTUAL
LIFE OF OBSESSIONAL NEUROTICS, AND THE ORIGINS OF
COMPULSION AND DOUBT.   1909D10/237

TOTEM AND TABOO. TABOO AND EMOTIONAL AMBIVALENCE.
PARALLEL BETWEEN TABOO AND OBSESSIONAL NEUROSIS.   1912X13/ 26

THE DISPOSITION TO OBSESSIONAL NEUROSIS. A CONTRIBUTION
TO THE PROBLEM OF CHOICE OF NEUROSIS.   1913I12/311

FROM THE HISTORY OF AN INFANTILE NEUROSIS. THE
OBSESSIONAL NEUROSIS. (WOLFMAN).   1918B17/ 61

LETTER 79. (MASTURBATION, ADDICTION AND OBSESSIONAL
NEUROSIS.).   1950A 1/272

NOTES UPON A CASE OF OBSESSIONAL NEUROSIS. ADDENDUM:
ORIGINAL RECORD OF THE CASE. (RAT-MAN).   1955A10/251

NOTES UPON A CASE OF OBSESSIONAL NEUROSIS. ORIGINAL
RECORD OF THE CASE. (RAT-MAN).   1955A10/259

OBSESSIONS

OBSESSIONS AND PHOBIAS: THEIR PSYCHICAL MECHANISM AND
THEIR AETIOLOGY. APPENDIX: FREUD S VIEWS ON PHOBIAS.   3/ 83

OBSESSIONS AND PHOBIAS: THEIR PSYCHICAL MECHANISM AND
THEIR AETIOLOGY.   1895C 3/ 71

OBSESSIVE

OBSESSIVE ACTIONS AND RELIGIOUS PRACTICES.   1907B 9/115

NOTES UPON A CASE OF OBSESSIONAL NEUROSIS. EXTRACTS
FROM THE CASE HISTORY. THE GREAT OBSESSIVE FEAR.
(RAT-MAN).   1909D10/165

OCCULT

SOME ADDITIONAL NOTES ON DREAM INTERPRETATION AS A
WHOLE. THE OCCULT SIGNIFICANCE OF DREAMS.   1925I19/135

OCCULTISM

NEW INTRODUCTORY LECTURES ON PSYCHOANALYSIS. DREAMS AND
OCCULTISM.   1933A22/ 31

REPETITION

INHIBITIONS, SYMPTOMS AND ANXIETY. REPETITION IS THE
CONSEQUENCE OF REPRESSION.   1926D20/150

REPETITIONS

BEYOND THE PLEASURE PRINCIPLE. REVIEW OF THE PLEASURE
PRINCIPLE. TRAUMATIC NEUROSIS AND CHILDREN S PLAY ARE
REPETITIONS.   1920G18/ 7

REPRESENT

ATTEMPT TO REPRESENT NORMAL PSI PROCESSES   1950A 1/360

REPRESENTABILITY

THE INTERPRETATION OF DREAMS. THE DREAM-WORK.
CONSIDERATIONS OF REPRESENTABILITY.   1900A 5/339

REPRESENTATION

THE INTERPRETATION OF DREAMS. THE DREAM-WORK. THE MEANS
OF REPRESENTATION IN DREAMS.   1900A 4/310

THE INTERPRETATION OF DREAMS. THE DREAM-WORK.
REPRESENTATION BY SYMBOLS IN DREAMS - SOME FURTHER
TYPICAL DREAMS.   1900A 5/350

JOKES AND THEIR RELATION TO THE UNCONSCIOUS. ANALYTIC
PART. THE TECHNIQUE OF JOKES. REPRESENTATION BY
OPPOSITE; CONCEPTUAL JOKES.   1905C 8/ 70

REPRESSED

MOSES AND MONOTHEISM: THREE ESSAYS. MOSES, HIS PEOPLE
AND MONOTHEIST RELIGION. THE RETURN OF THE REPRESSED.   1939A23/124

REPRESSION

THE INTERPRETATION OF DREAMS. THE PSYCHOLOGY OF THE
DREAM PROCESSES. THE PRIMARY AND SECONDARY PROCESSES -
REPRESSION.   1900A 5/588

FIVE LECTURES ON PSYCHOANALYSIS. SECOND LECTURE.
REPRESSION AND SYMPTOM FORMATION.   1910A11/ 21

PAPERS ON METAPSYCHOLOGY. REPRESSION.   1915D14/141

PAPERS ON METAPSYCHOLOGY. REPRESSION.   1915D14/146

PAPERS ON METAPSYCHOLOGY. THE UNCONSCIOUS. TOPOGRAPHY
AND DYNAMICS OF REPRESSION.   1915E14/180

INTRODUCTORY LECTURES ON PSYCHOANALYSIS. GENERAL THEORY
OF THE NEUROSES. RESISTANCE AND REPRESSION.   1916X16/286

INHIBITIONS, SYMPTOMS AND ANXIETY. ANXIETY PRODUCES
REPRESSION.   1926D20/101

INHIBITIONS, SYMPTOMS AND ANXIETY. DEFENSES OTHER THAN
REPRESSION.   1926D20/111

INHIBITIONS, SYMPTOMS AND ANXIETY. REPETITION IS THE
CONSEQUENCE OF REPRESSION.   1926D20/150

INHIBITIONS, SYMPTOMS AND ANXIETY. REPRESSION AND
DEFENCE.   1926D20/173

DRAFT M. (REPRESSION IN HYSTERIA.).   1950A 1/250

REPRODUCES

INHIBITIONS, SYMPTOMS AND ANXIETY. ANXIETY REPRODUCES
FEELINGS OF HELPLESSNESS.   1926D20/132

REPRODUCTIVE

INTRODUCTION OF THE EGO PRIMARY AND SECONDARY PROCESS
IN PSI; COGNITION AND REPRODUCTIVE THOUGHT; REMEMBERING
AND JUDGING; THOUGHT AND REALITY.   1950A 1/322

REQUIRES

CONSTRUCTIONS IN ANALYSIS. THE ANALYST S TASK REQUIRES
CONSTRUCTIONS IN ANALYSIS.   1937D23/255

RESEARCHES

THREE ESSAYS ON THE THEORY OF SEXUALITY. INFANTILE
SEXUALITY. THE SEXUAL RESEARCHES OF CHILDHOOD.   1905D 7/194

RESERVOIR

THE EGO AND THE ID . THE DESCRIPTIVE AND THE DYNAMIC
UNCONSCIOUS. THE GREAT RESERVOIR OF LIBIDO.   1923B19/ 60

RESISTANCE

FIVE LECTURES ON PSYCHOANALYSIS. FIFTH LECTURE.
TRANSFERENCE AND RESISTANCE.   1910A11/ 49

INTRODUCTORY LECTURES ON PSYCHOANALYSIS. GENERAL THEORY
OF THE NEUROSES. RESISTANCE AND REPRESSION.   1916X16/286

ANALYSIS TERMINABLE AND INTERMINABLE. BISEXUALITY IS
THE STRONGEST RESISTANCE TO ANALYSIS.   1937C23/250

RESISTANCES

THE RESISTANCES TO PSYCHOANALYSIS. APPENDIX: EXTRACT
FROM SCHOPENHAUER'S THE WORLD AS WILL AND IDEA.   19/223

CONTINUATIO RESISTANCES   CONTINUATIO

THE RESISTANCES TO PSYCHOANALYSIS.   1925E19/213

LETTER 72. (RESISTANCES REFLECT CHILDHOOD.).   1950A 1/266

RESPONSIBILITY

SOME ADDITIONAL NOTES ON DREAM INTERPRETATION AS A
WHOLE. MORAL RESPONSIBILITY FOR THE CONTENT OF DREAMS.   1925I19/131

RESTRICTING

CIVILIZATION AND ITS DISCONTENTS. SECURITY AT THE COST
OF RESTRICTING SEXUALITY AND AGGRESSION.   1930A21/108

RESTRICTIONS

INHIBITIONS, SYMPTOMS AND ANXIETY. INHIBITIONS REFLECT
RESTRICTIONS OF EGO FUNCTIONS.   1926D20/ 87

RETROSPECTIVE

LETTER 101. (RETROSPECTIVE FANTASIES.).   1950A 1/276

REVIEW

REVIEW OF AUGUST FOREL'S HYPNOTISM.   1889A 1/ 89

REVIEW OF WILHELM NEUTRA'S LETTERS TO NEUROTIC WOMEN.   1910M11/238

BEYOND THE PLEASURE PRINCIPLE. REVIEW OF THE PLEASURE
PRINCIPLE. TRAUMATIC NEUROSIS AND CHILDREN S PLAY ARE
REPETITIONS.   1920G18/ 7

INTRODUCTION TO THE SPECIAL PSYCHOPATHOLOGY NUMBER OF
THE MEDICAL REVIEW OF REVIEWS.   1930C21/254

REVISION

THE INTERPRETATION OF DREAMS. THE DREAM-WORK. SECONDARY
REVISION.   1900A 5/488

BEYOND THE PLEASURE PRINCIPLE. REVISION OF THE THEORY
OF INSTINCTS.   1920G18/ 34

NEW INTRODUCTORY LECTURES ON PSYCHOANALYSIS. REVISION
OF THE THEORY OF DREAMS.   1933A22/ 7

RIDDLES

JOKES AND THEIR RELATION TO THE UNCONSCIOUS. APPENDIX:
FRANZ BRENTANO'S RIDDLES.   1905C 8/237

RITES

PREFACE TO BOURKE'S SCATALOGIC RITES OF ALL NATIONS.   1913K12/333

RITUAL

PREFACE TO REIK S RITUAL: PSYCHOANALYTIC STUDIES.   1919G17/257

ROLLAND

TO ROMAIN ROLLAND.   1926A20/279

ROMANCES

FAMILY ROMANCES.   1909C 9/235

RULERS

TOTEM AND TABOO. TABOO AND EMOTIONAL AMBIVALENCE. THE
TABOO UPON RULERS.   1912X13/ 41

SACRIFICIAL

TOTEM AND TABOO. THE RETURN OF TOTEMISM IN CHILDHOOD.
ANIMAL PHOBIAS. SACRIFICIAL FEASTS.   1912X13/126

SAMPLE

INTRODUCTORY LECTURES ON PSYCHOANALYSIS. DREAMS. SOME
ANALYSES OF SAMPLE DREAMS.   1916X15/184

SANDER'S

THE UNCANNY. APPENDIX: EXTRACT FROM DANIEL SANDER'S
WORTERBUCH DER DEUTSCHEN SPRACHE.   1919H17/253

SATISFACTION

THE FUNCTIONING OF THE APPARATUS; THE PATHS OF
CONDUCTION; THE EXPERIENCE OF SATISFACTION; THE
EXPERIENCE OF PAIN; AFFECTS AND WISHFUL STATES.   1950A 1/312

SAUSSURE'S

PREFACE TO RAYMOND DE SAUSSURE'S THE PSYCHOANALYTIC
METHOD.   1922E19/283

SCATALOGIC

PREFACE TO BOURKE'S SCATALOGIC RITES OF ALL NATIONS.   1913K12/333

SCENE

FROM THE HISTORY OF AN INFANTILE NEUROSIS. THE DREAM
AND THE PRIMAL SCENE. (WOLFMAN).   1918B17/ 29

SCHOOLBOY

SOME REFLECTIONS ON SCHOOLBOY PSYCHOLOGY.   1914F13/241

CONTINUATIO   CONTINUATIC

UNCONSCIOUS

JOKES AND THEIR RELATION TO THE UNCONSCIOUS. ANALYTIC
PART. THE TECHNIQUE OF JOKES. RELATION OF JOKES TO THE
COMIC: UNIFICATION AS A JOKE TECHNIQUE.   1905C 8/ 60

JOKES AND THEIR RELATION TO THE UNCONSCIOUS. ANALYTIC
PART. THE TECHNIQUE OF JOKES. REPRESENTATION BY
OPPOSITE: CONCEPTUAL JOKES.   1905C 8/ 70

JOKES AND THEIR RELATION TO THE UNCONSCIOUS. ANALYTIC
PART. THE TECHNIQUE OF JOKES. ANALOGY AS A JOKE
TECHNIQUE.   1905C 8/ 81

JOKES AND THEIR RELATION TO THE UNCONSCIOUS. ANALYTIC
PART. THE PURPOSES OF JOKES. INNOCENT JOKES; SMUT AND
THE PURPOSE OF JOKES.   1905C 8/ 91

JOKES AND THEIR RELATION TO THE UNCONSCIOUS. A ANALYTIC
PART. THE PURPOSE OF JOKES. HOSTILE, CYNICAL AND
SKEPTICAL JOKES.   1905C 8/102

JOKES AND THEIR RELATION TO THE UNCONSCIOUS. SYNTHETIC
PART. THE MECHANISM OF PLEASURE AND THE PSYCHOGENESIS
OF JOKES.   1905C 8/117

JOKES AND THEIR RELATION TO THE UNCONSCIOUS. SYNTHETIC
PART. THE MECHANISM OF PLEASURE AND THE PSYCHOGENESIS
OF JOKES. THE PURPOSE AND FUNCTIONS OF JOKES.   1905C 8/128

JOKES AND THEIR RELATION TO THE UNCONSCIOUS. SYNTHETIC
PART. THE MOTIVES OF JOKES - JOKES AS A SOCIAL
PROCESS.   1905C 8/140

JOKES AND THEIR RELATION TO THE UNCONSCIOUS. THEORETIC
PART. THE RELATION OF JOKES TO DREAMS AND TO THE
UNCONSCIOUS.   1905C 8/159

JOKES AND THEIR RELATION TO THE UNCONSCIOUS. THEORETIC
PART. JOKES AND THE SPECIES OF THE COMIC.   1905C 8/181

JOKES AND THEIR RELATION TO THE UNCONSCIOUS. THEORETIC
PART. JOKES AND THE SPECIES OF THE COMIC. PSYCHICAL
LOCATION DISTINGUISHES JOKES FROM THE COMIC.   1905C 8/199

JOKES AND THEIR RELATION TO THE UNCONSCIOUS. THEORETIC
PART. JOKES AND THE SPECIES OF THE COMIC. DIFFERENCES
BETWEEN JOKES AND COMIC.   1905C 8/208

JOKES AND THEIR RELATION TO THE UNCONSCIOUS. THEORETIC
PART. JOKES AND THE SPECIES OF THE COMIC. COMIC THINGS
ARE NOT PROPER IN JOKES; RELATION OF HUMOUR TO JOKES.   1905C 8/221

JOKES AND THEIR RELATION TO THE UNCONSCIOUS. APPENDIX:
FRANZ BRENTANO'S RIDDLES.   1905C 8/237

DELUSIONS AND DREAMS IN JENSEN'S GRADIVA. GRADIVA AND
THE PSYCHOLOGY OF THE UNCONSCIOUS.   1907A 9/ 41

A NOTE ON THE UNCONSCIOUS IN PSYCHOANALYSIS.   1912G12/255

PAPERS ON METAPSYCHOLOGY. THE UNCONSCIOUS.   1915E14/159

PAPERS ON METAPSYCHOLOGY. THE UNCONSCIOUS.
JUSTIFICATION FOR THE CONCEPT OF THE UNCONSCIOUS.   1915E14/166

PAPERS ON METAPSYCHOLOGY. THE UNCONSCIOUS. VARIOUS
MEANINGS OF THE UNCONSCIOUS - THE TOPOGRAPHICAL POINT
OF VIEW.   1915E14/172

PAPERS ON METAPSYCHOLOGY. THE UNCONSCIOUS. UNCONSCIOUS
EMOTIONS.   1915E14/177

PAPERS ON METAPSYCHOLOGY. THE UNCONSCIOUS. TOPOGRAPHY
AND DYNAMICS OF REPRESSION.   1915E14/180

PAPERS ON METAPSYCHOLOGY. THE UNCONSCIOUS. THE SPECIAL
CHARACTERISTICS OF THE SYSTEM UCS.   1915E14/186

PAPERS ON METAPSYCHOLOGY. THE UNCONSCIOUS.
COMMUNICATION BETWEEN THE TWO SYSTEMS.   1915E14/190

PAPERS ON METAPSYCHOLOGY. THE UNCONSCIOUS. ASSESSMENT
OF THE UNCONSCIOUS.   1915E14/196

INTRODUCTORY LECTURES ON PSYCHOANALYSIS. GENERAL THEORY
OF THE NEUROSES. FIXATION TO TRAUMAS - THE UNCONSCIOUS.   1916X16/273

THE EGO AND THE ID . CONSCIOUSNESS AND WHAT IS
UNCONSCIOUS.   1923B19/ 12

THE EGO AND THE ID . THE DESCRIPTIVE AND THE DYNAMIC
UNCONSCIOUS. THE GREAT RESERVOIR OF LIBIDO.   1923B19/ 60

UNDOING

INHIBITIONS, SYMPTOMS AND ANXIETY. UNDOING AND
ISOLATION.   1926D20/119

UNHAPPINESS

CIVILIZATION AND ITS DISCONTENTS. MAN COPES WITH
UNHAPPINESS THROUGH DIVERSION, SUBSTITUTION AND
INTOXICATION.   1930A21/ 74

UNIFICATION

JOKES AND THEIR RELATION TO THE UNCONSCIOUS. ANALYTIC
PART. THE TECHNIQUE OF JOKES. RELATION OF JOKES TO THE
COMIC: UNIFICATION AS A JOKE TECHNIQUE.   1905C 8/ 60

UNIVERSAL

ON THE UNIVERSAL TENDENCY TO DEBASEMENT IN THE SPHERE
OF LOVE. (CONTRIBUTIONS TO THE PSYCHOLOGY OF LOVE).   1912D11/177

UNIVERSALITY

LETTER 71. (UNIVERSALITY OF OEDIPUS COMPLEX.).   1950A 1/263

UNIVERSITIES

ON THE TEACHING OF PSYCHOANALYSIS IN UNIVERSITIES.   1919J17/169

UNIVERSITY

ON THE OCCASION OF THE OPENING OF THE HEBREW
UNIVERSITY.   1925C19/292

VALUE

THE FUTURE OF AN ILLUSION. CONSEQUENCES OF INSTINCTUAL
RENUNCIATION. IN WHAT DOES THE PECULIAR VALUE OF
RELIGIOUS IDEAS LIE.   1927C21/ 10

VANEEDEN

THOUGHTS FOR THE TIMES ON WAR AND DEATH. OUR ATTITUDE
TOWARDS DEATH. APPENDIX: LETTER TO DR. FREDERIK
VANEEDEN.   1915B14/289

VARENDONCK'S

INTRODUCTION TO J. VARENDONCK'S THE PSYCHOLOGY OF
DAY-DREAMS.   1921B18/271

VARIABLES

ANALYSIS TERMINABLE AND INTERMINABLE. CONSTITUTIONAL
VARIABLES IN EGO, LIBIDO AND FREE AGGRESSIVENESS.   1937C23/240

VICISSITUDES

PAPERS ON METAPSYCHOLOGY. INSTINCTS AND THEIR
VICISSITUDES.   1915C14/111

PAPERS ON METAPSYCHOLOGY. INSTINCTS AND THEIR
VICISSITUDES.   1915C14/117

VIENNA

MOSES AND MONOTHEISM: THREE ESSAYS. MOSES, HIS PEOPLE
AND MONOTHEIST RELIGION: PREFATORY NOTES I (VIENNA) &
II (LONDON).   1939A23/ 54

VIRGINITY

THE TABOO OF VIRGINITY. (CONTRIBUTIONS TO THE
PSYCHOLOGY OF LOVE).   1918A11/191

VISION

THE PSYCHOANALYTIC VIEW OF PSYCHOGENIC DISTURBANCE OF
VISION.   1910I11/209

VISUAL

A MYTHOLOGICAL PARALLEL TO A VISUAL OBSESSION.   1916B14/337

VON-FREUND

DR. ANTON VON-FREUND.   1920C18/267

VON-HUG-HELLMUTH

LETTER TO DR. HERMINE VON-HUG-HELLMUTH.   1919I14/341

VOWELS

THE SIGNIFICANCE OF SEQUENCES OF VOWELS.   1911D12/341

WAHRHEIT

A CHILDHOOD RECOLLECTION FROM DICHTUNG UND WAHRHEIT.   1917B17/145

WAKING

THE INTERPRETATION OF DREAMS. THE SCIENTIFIC LITERATURE
DEALING WITH THE PROBLEMS OF DREAMS. THE RELATION OF
DREAMS TO WAKING LIFE.   1900A 4/ 1

THE INTERPRETATION OF DREAMS. THE SCIENTIFIC LITERATURE
DEALING WITH THE PROBLEMS OF DREAMS. WHY DREAMS ARE
FORGOTTEN AFTER WAKING.   1900A 4/ 43

WAR

THOUGHTS FOR THE TIMES ON WAR AND DEATH. THE
DISILLUSIONMENT OF THE WAR.   1915B14/275

THOUGHTS FOR THE TIMES ON WAR AND DEATH. OUR ATTITUDE
TOWARDS DEATH. APPENDIX: LETTER TO DR. FREDERIK
VANEEDEN.   1915B14/289

INTRODUCTION TO PSYCHOANALYSIS AND THE WAR NEUROSES.   1919D17/205

WHY WAR?   1933B22/197

WHY WAR?: LETTER FROM EINSTEIN.   1933B22/199

INTRODUCTION TO PSYCHOANALYSIS AND THE WAR NEUROSES.
MEMORANDUM ON THE ELECTRICAL TREATMENT OF WAR
NEUROTICS.   1955C17/211